Acknowledgments

I wish to thank all those who have assisted me in the preparation of this book: Mary Boblitz and Jan Greene for the typing and graphics for the first edition; my son, Steven, for an editorial review of the final draft; and my daughter, Katherine, for her patient and invaluable assistance during the compilation of the second edition.

Forecasting On Your Microcomputer

Second Edition

Daniel B. Nickell

TAB BOOKS Inc.
Blue Ridge Summit, PA

SECOND EDITION
FIRST PRINTING

Copyright © 1988 by TAB BOOKS Inc.
First edition copyright © 1983 by TAB BOOKS Inc.
Printed in the United States of America

Library of Congress Cataloging in Publication Data

Nickell, Daniel B.
Forecasting on your microcomputer / by Daniel B. Nickell.
— 2nd ed.
p. cm.
Includes index.
ISBN 0-8306-2907-6 (pbk.)
1. Forecasting—Data processing. I. Title.
CB 158.N5 1988   87-26713
303.4′9′0285416—dc 19   CIP

Questions regarding the content of this book
should be addressed to:

Reader Inquiry Branch
Editorial Department
TAB BOOKS Inc.
Blue Ridge Summit, PA 17294-0214

Contents

Preface to the Second Edition

The first edition of this book was written during the summer of 1982. All the programs, and much of the first draft, were written on my first computer—a Tandy TRS-80 Model I, Level II, with 16K memory. That was just four years after Tandy introduced one of the first viable main-line consumer computers, and three years after I took the plunge into personal computing.

This edition is to be delivered to the publisher on the same date as the first—just four years after the first edition. This isn't because I enjoy writing that much, but out of necessity. In these last four years, incredible advances have been made in personal computers. This edition is being written on a 16-bit, 640K memory, 10Mb hard disk, IBM-compatible computer with a color monitor that boasts 16 colors on a 640×400 pixel matrix—features that were not even thought of during the early days of Tandy's computers. Back then, a screen resolution of 256×96 would have been considered high resolution.

This time, I do not have to call on my next-door neighbor to check my frequently horrible spelling. Instead, the word processor has its own 100,000 + word dictionary built in, supplemented by a personal dictionary of my devising of some 2-3,000 words. The operational speed of this computer is about ten times that of my Model I.

Since 1982 several versions of BASIC have been developed and introduced (GW-BASIC and BASICA), becoming industry standards for the now dominant IBM and IBM-compatible computers. In the process, Tandy's version of BASIC fell into disuse, giving way to the more powerful versions. Tandy systems now seek to be compatible with the competition. Although the programs in the first edition at first glance resemble a version of BASIC that would run on the IBM systems (and most of them will, with some minor modification), the type and number of modifications required grew to be too tedious for most readers. The software on floppy disk, in Multi-DOS format, is totally unreadable by IBMs and compatibles without the help of translation software. So, it is timely to offer a version of this work in a form usable by one of the dominant manufacturers in the industry. We were concerned about the other major force in the marketplace, Apple computers, but, happily, technology has provided disk drives and interface software that let Apple systems read and use IBM-format software. The primary limitation on Apple computers will be in the area of graphic displays, unless the interface software translates those commands as well. For all but two or three programs in this book, graphics are a complement to the programs, not their heart. Absence of the graphic output will not preclude use of the mathematical processes and alphanumeric output.

The first task of this edition is to provide versions of the programs that can be typed into systems running GW-BASIC or BASICA that will run the first time. I accomplished this by running a translation program on a TRS-80 Model III and transferring the programs verbatim to an IBM-format disk. Then, on the IBM-compatible, another translation program converted the transformed programs into GW-BASIC/BASICA format. The final step in the process was to rewrite fragments of some of the programs to take advantage of improved graphics or processing capabilities.

It fascinates me that the last time anyone typed in the text (about 95 percent of the programs now in IBM format) was four years ago on a Model I. They were then CSAVEd to cassette tape. The tape was later read into a Model III and SAVEd to floppy disk. The same disks were read back into a Model III for translation to the IBM format. The converted and refined programs were then copied from the master disk to the retail disks. But, in spite of all the computer-assisted transfers, the original work actually took place in 1982! Some were written even earlier, in 1979.

My next task was to review the software for utility and application. In this process I dropped a couple of programs that didn't seem to support the central objectives of this book, and added some routines that seemed more appropriate.

My last task was to address the application of available database management and integrated software packages to forecasting. For the most part, the utility of the database management programs (e.g., *dBASE III PLUS*) is to create data files that may be used by the BASIC routines for processing. The macro instructions included with better database management programs are often sufficient to perform most, if not all, of the programs in this book. However, the instructions and details required to properly illuminate and describe database analogs of the BASIC programs are beyond the scope of this book. If you have appropriate data sets in database files, you can use file translation routines (creating "delimited" files) to produce files readable by these programs.

Spreadsheets are more direct applications of the concepts offered herein. Appendix C contains a number of listings in a fairly standard spreadsheet format based on the routines in the main body of the text.

Finally, I must reiterate a point made in the original edition of this work: this is meant to be a source book of routines and concepts showing how to use a personal computer to evaluate data from a broad range of subjects and academic disciplines, and to prepare forecasts based on that data. Therefore, few of the programs are optimized for commercial application. The user is frequently requested to input system configuration information that more expensive commercial programs would input without user intervention. Likewise, some of the programs presume your data to be in a particular form, size, and format. Feel free to modify the programs to suit your data format and system configuration.

I hope and trust you will find this book to be useful and helpful to you in your work. Best wishes for successful forecasting.

Introduction

A famous mentalist used to open his program by saying: "We are all interested in the future because that is where we are going to spend the rest of our lives." The function of scientific forecasting is to provide a rational and acceptable basis for what we believe the future holds for us.

The purpose of this book is to help a wide range of readers use a microcomputer in the process of formulating forecasts over a fairly broad range of human interests. The definition of the average reader of this book is rather difficult to state meaningfully. I purposefully did not write it specifically for stock brokers, math teachers, child prodigies, business planners, or any other group likely to have a vested interest in forecasting. Rather, I wrote it as a resource book for each of the foregoing, as well as for others that might have an interest in some aspect of the subject. There is a section of particular interest to one tracking the stock market or similar data sets. For the amateur astronomer, there is a section that provides some useful routines for computing planetary positions and related information.

The gambler in us will find some satisfaction in the section on random events in which an effort is made to put some order into chaos.

In the book are some 90 programs (all in BASIC) that illustrate or support one aspect of forecasting or another. Although some of them are obviously demonstration routines, many of them are intended mainly as utilities to be embedded in programs of your own making. Finally, there are several long programs that present some rather useful analysis of variance (ANOVA), multiple correlation, and tabular computation routines that stand on their own merits.

While this book doesn't presume to address the interests of the youngest or the most sophisticated of computer programmers, I hope it will reach and be of use to the general population of computer users.

A LITTLE ABOUT THE BOOK

The material in this book is grouped into four main divisions: fundamentals, techniques, applications, and dispositions. Each division consists of two or more chapters. Each chapter contains a main body of information, including related programs and examples, several exercises or questions on the chapter's material, and suggested reading.

Fundamentals

In this section I attempt to cover the numerical and mathematical foundations for modern forecasting and to describe its nature, applications, and limitations. This division attempts to convey the notion that forecasts vary considerably in their reliability, depending on a number of factors, including the quality of the database. Reliable forecasting requires rationally chosen, accurate data that are appropriately quantified. The types of data, scales, and measures that are used to quantify data are examined. Also presented are the dichotomous concepts of absolute and relative scales, parametric and nonparametric data, and continuous and discrete distributions. It is in this section that I provide you with the tools with which to do a descriptive analysis of a set of data and to compute the probabilities of a variety of conditions. The division also includes a primer on database management, with an emphasis on databases suitable for microcomputers. I conclude with a few words on the prudent choice of techniques with which to do accurate forecasting.

Techniques

This book presents four basic families of forecasting techniques: correlation and regression analysis, time-series analysis, modeling and simulations, and numerical techniques. Correlation and regression analysis attempts to fit a smoothed curve through available data, assuming the future data will continue to follow the smoothed curve. Time-series analysis assumes that the data found are functions of the passage of time. Curve-fitting routines, in time-functional data, often lead to rather bizarre unnecessary shapes and equations. Time-series equations, on the other hand, concentrate on the state of the data at given instants. Modeling a problem is frequently the easiest way to forecast the state of a complex system after a number of operations

or periods of time. Closely related to modeling is creating simulations. The distinctions between the terms are so vague that I am likely to use them interchangeably. Conceptually, a model is thought of as a representation of a real or proposed thing or system (such as an oil factory), whereas a simulation may be used to reflect a less specifically organized set of objects (such as a simulation of water flow through a swampland) in which arbitrary starting values are assigned. Numerical analysis is sort of a coverall for all the other miscellaneous techniques that can be used in attempts to fit some sort of conceptual model against the real world. For example, we are given the problem of a lost person in the Arctic. We know where he started and that he appears to be moving clockwise in a circular fashion (it is snowing and drifts often block out the trail) except that the radius of revolutions is increasing. None of the first three techniques will lead quickly to a satisfactory solution. However, by simply fitting one of the spirals of Archimedes noted in Chapter 8, the appropriate search pattern can be developed and the current, most likely location forecast.

Applications

Examples from seven basic areas of human interest in which forecasting techniques can be applied are presented. In addition, there is a brief chapter on miscellaneous techniques that were not otherwise classifiable. It was with a great deal of humility that I undertook these chapters and with an even greater sense of humility that I presumed to finish them. While they each come from some area of my personal and professional experiences, the requisite research to prepare the text led me back into broad domains of human knowledge, the vastness of which I had forgotten in my haste to keep pace with the present. Behind each chapter stands several thousands of years of specialized scientific inquiry, which has been cataloged, analyzed, digested and disseminated by hundreds of thousands of scholars—better than 80 percent of them alive since the year A.D. 1800. In translating their concepts into microcomputer BASIC, I hope I have been faithful to the true and underlying concepts.

Dispositions

Many forecasts fail to be implemented due to a misconception, often on the part of the forecaster, as to what to do with the "bottom line" data. In this division the different ways scientific data can be displayed effectively to non-scientific people are illustrated. I also offer some techniques, using the microcomputer, or using results from forecasting efforts to reach meaningful decisions.

The Programs

Listings always include the complete program written in BASIC. There are short routines that you can simply type in to see what it is I am talking about. There are long programs that perform a number of functions. The intent of these longer program listings is to provide complete programs, which you can use intact or from which you can borrow subroutines for other applications. In some instances I use a technique used by a major retail outlet: I offer a good routine, a better routine, and a best routine. With the longer, more complex programs I also include flowcharts of the program and, if needed, additional documentation showing line references and variable names.

Most of the chapters also include exercises.

These are intended to be used either to check your programming skills and understanding of the material just presented or to check student progress in a computer applications course in which this book is used as a text or reference source.

The language used in the book is Microsoft's GW-BASIC version. I use the DEF FN command to define a subroutine used frequently. If your computer does not support this command, you can replace it at each occurrence, for example, X = FNM, with a GO-SUB command in which the subroutine performs the same function.

While the major thrust of this work is an exploration of forecasting by using microcomputers and BASIC, a number of the routines lend themselves well to translation to spreadsheet processing. Accordingly, Appendix C contains spreadsheet listings of some of the programs found in the text.

In brief, this book attempts to define what the forecast process is and what the underlying mathematical principles are, to illustrate ways forecasting has been accomplished in the past, and to suggest what to do with a forecast once it's made. By definition, analogy, example, and actual data resources, I attempt to equip the conscientious reader with a basic forecasting toolkit.

NOTE: Most of the programs in this book are written to be used with a printer. If you do not want to print the output of any of these programs, delete all LPRINT statements from them. If there is no printer connected and you do not delete these statements, the programs will not function and no error message will appear.

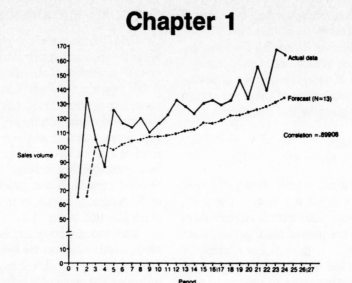

## Chapter 1

Forecasting Philosophies

Forecasting is an art that exploits science in an effort to identify future events or conditions. Later in this book we will stress the necessity for obtaining as much precise data as possible and emphasize the role of mathematics in forecasting. Nonetheless, forecasting remains an art. For virtually every project, the data available for the solution of the problem exceeds both the memory capacity of our computers and the time allotted to reach a forecast; we must artfully select a sample from the data and forecast from that.

SELECTING DATA SETS

While there are techniques, which will be described herein, that help in the process of selecting the more appropriate data sets, there is no practical way of knowing that the best data and only the best data have been chosen for processing. The quality of the forecast is directly related to the quality of the input data we elect to use. It is very much like the the the computing maxim: "garbage in—garbage out." If we select relevant data sets and use ap-

propriate processing techniques, our forecasts will be as responsible as anyone could expect. In preparing a weather forecast, for example, we would probably want to consult historic weather records for the area of coverage, current temperatures, humidity, and wind direction. According to some weather forecasting techniques, we may even want to determine the current sunspot condition. On the other hand, we have no reason to believe any of these databases would have any utility in the forecasting of future gold prices. The dividing line between the merely good and the truly great forecaster is drawn according to the skill of the forecaster in selecting databases that will lead consistently to accurate predictions.

Why can't we just crank in all the databases and pick out the best predictors? In the first place, the volume of data available in the world at any given moment, even in the available, processable form, is tremendous. For one person to attempt to enter even a fraction of some of these databases into a microcomputer would be an undertaking of several lifetimes. Secondly, assuming we had some sort of device which could handle all of these data for us, the processing needed to determine the most appropriate sets to use quickly becomes unmanageable. Given N sets of data, the number of unique combinations or *permutations* of these sets taken R sets at a time is given by the equation:

$$P = \frac{N!}{R! \ (N-R)!}$$

N! is an expression which means "N factorial" and is computed by N! $\times 1 \times 2 \times 3 \times 4 \ldots \times N-1$, and (N − R)! progresses downward in increments of 1 each, the results are then added together, [i.e., $(10-6) + (9-5) + \ldots (5-1)$]. For example, if we have 10 people and 6 chairs, we compute the number of unique permutations of seating 10 people, 6 at a time, as:

$$P = \frac{3628800}{6!(10-6)!} = \frac{3628800}{720 \times 24} = 210.$$

There are 210 ways to seat 10 people 6 at a time without repeating any possible combination. If we have 10 databases, there are 252 unique ways we can test the utility of them, taking them 4 at a time. But, to check out the utility of the databases properly, we first need to check them one at a time. This requires 10 evaluations, one at a time, then 45 evaluations doing 2 at a time, 120 evaluations with 3 at a time, and so forth. To check all possible permutations, from 1 to N sets at a time, requires $2^N - 1$ evaluations. In the case of 10 data sets, there must be at least 1023 evaluations. Adding just one data set, making the total N, 11, doubles the number of evaluations required: $2^{11} - 1 = 2047$. The 1975 *Statistical Abstract of the United States* offers well over 1400 tables of data. To evaluate just these tables, even with very fast microcomputers using optimum programs, would require many years of processing. The working forecaster, of course, rejects such an approach and, by some intuitive process, selects perhaps two or three tables from which to compute a prediction. It is for this reason that forecasting is as much an art as a science.

THE QUALIFICATIONS OF A FORECASTER

The difficulties and complexities just alluded to notwithstanding, it appears that forecasting is a skill or craft a number of so-called laymen can master. A few years ago a study was conducted to determine, among other things, the impact of training and experience on the accuracy of forecasts. The initial hypothesis was that as the experience or training level of a given forecaster increased, there would be a corresponding increase in the accuracy of his or her forecasts. It was anticipated that the graph of the accuracy/experience table would appear very much like that in Fig. 1-1.

Interestingly, however, the data obtained in the study failed to support the hypothesis. Instead, the data suggested that almost anyone with average intelligence and reasonable judgement can become an effective forecaster. The actual relationship between accuracy and training are illustrated in Fig. 1-2.

The implications are clear. You don't necessarily need to have a Ph.D in economics to do financial forecasting, nor do you need advanced degrees in political science to make useful contributions in voter preference studies.

One explanation of the unusual outcome of the study is that the future is really the composite outcome of such a multitude of factors that, beyond a certain level, the precise computations of the highly trained and expensively equipped add little over common sense and a more generalized approach to a problem. With reasonable technical preparation and modest computing gear (such as microcomputers), you can become a very credible forecaster.

The point here is to encourage you to tackle forecasting seriously and not to be intimidated by a shortfall in formal training or professional credentials. The forecaster's best credential is a demonstrated forecasting accuracy.

PRECISION IN FORECASTING

It is best to avoid the lure of the double-precision mathematics capabilities of most of the current microcomputers. There is no point in computing to 16 decimal places data that are meaningful to

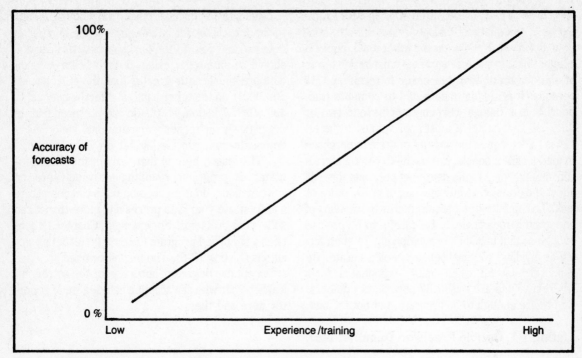

Fig. 1-1. Hypothetical relationship between training and accuracy of forecasts.

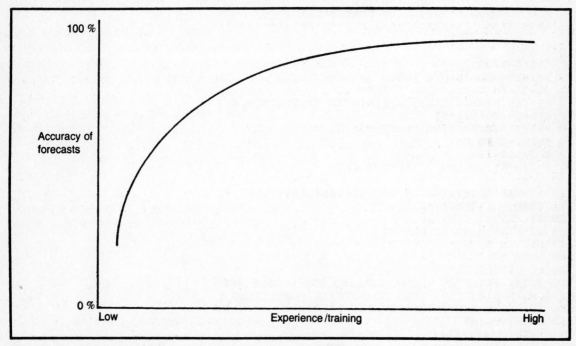

Fig. 1-2. Actual relationship between training and accuracy of forecasts.

only three or four. Curve-fitting routines, for example, lead to equations that generate smooth, continuous curves. People, on the other hand, come in integer units. In the real world we must deal in terms of one person or two, but never in terms of 1.34 persons. It is seldom meaningful to compute fractional human beings, certainly not beyond two or three decimal points in most applications. If the effort is to determine the amount of grain to purchase to feed a million people, it is useful to compute grain consumption only to the degree of precision that will affect the decision to buy one bag of grain, more or less. To compute grain requirements to fractions of one grain is meaningless. Be careful to be precise enough so that in adding or multiplying (or subtracting or dividing) the final result is still accurate. Be especially careful when using exponential tools wherein values are raised by powers of numbers. Be precise enough to be accurate, but not tedious.

A candidate for political office, for example, looks to the forecaster for an estimate of the number of vote pro and con. In the final analysis, this can and should be an integer value. 501 votes for a candidate are significantly greater than the 499 against: 500.0001, on the other hand, is effectively equal to 499.9999. Additionally, the double-precision feature dramatically increases computational time. As a demonstration, run Listing 1-1 on your system.

The lesson here is that, except for short programs or programs requiring extremely precise computations, double-precision math can complicate and frustrate your data processing more than it can solve your problems. For example, Chapter 12 contains a simplified program to compute planetary positions (Listing 12-6). The technique used provides an acceptable degree of accuracy for the astronomical hobbyist who can accept a half-degree of arc error here and there.

Listing 1-1. Double Precision Demonstrator.

```
1 '*********************************************
2 '*              Listing 1-1               *
3 '*       Double-Precision Demonstrator     *
4 '*********************************************
5 '
10 FLAG=0
20 CLS:N=1000
30 PRINT"WHEN READY, TOUCH ANY KEY ....."
40 Q$=""+INKEY$:IF Q$="" THEN 40
50 S1=VAL(RIGHT$(TIME$,2)):M1=VAL(MID$(TIME$,4,2
)):START=(60*M1)+S1
60 PRINT"SYSTEM WILL COUNT TO";N
70 FOR I=2 TO N
80 X=3/LOG(I)
90 Y=SIN(X):LOCATE 8,1:PRINT I;Y,
100 NEXT I
110 S2=VAL(RIGHT$(TIME$,2)):M2=VAL(MID$(TIME$,4,
2)):STAP = (60*M2)+S2
120 IF FLAG=1 THEN 160
130 T1=STAP - START:FLAG=1
140 DEFDBL X,Y
150 GOTO 30
160 T2=STAP-START
170 PRINT:PRINT"BY SIMPLY CALLING FOR DOUBLE PRE
CISION IN LINE 110, YOUR COMPUTER'S PROCESSING T
IME IS INCREASED";100*((T2/T1)-1);" %"
180 PRINT:PRINT
190 PRINT "(A)nother        (M)ain menu ";
200 Q$=""+INKEY$:IF Q$="" THEN 200
210 IF Q$="A" OR Q$="a" THEN RUN 10 ELSE RUN "A:
MENU"
```

THE DECISION-MAKING PROCESS

Forecasting involves two philosophies: an internal philosophy that enables the forecaster to remain calm and serene when it appears that the available databases are either incomplete or inappropriately formatted—thus creating the need for original research before the project can continue—or when it appears the decision-maker is not inclined to be rational this month; and an external philosophy that is skeptical and inquiring at its foundation, but includes a reasonable faith in properly collected and processed data as potentially rational indicators of future events or conditions.

Perhaps the dichotomy between the analyst and the decision-maker is created by otherwise useful personality differences. By nature the analyst proceeds in an orderly and frequently plodding manner, working through the various steps of a problem very methodically and conscientiously. By the time the final analysis is done and conclusions are reached, it is often too much of a temptation to lead the decision-maker through the same process one step at a time. The decision-maker, on the other hand, frequently cares about neither the process nor the standard errors and deviations surrounding the bottom line conclusions. Will the widget sell? Yes or no? Will sufficient units be sold to offset all production and sales costs so an acceptable net profit can be realized? Yes or no? All too often, the decision-maker expects the forecaster to simply enter the office, and announce: "Sell (or Don't Sell) the Widget!" and promptly leave. If the original instructions included words and guidance that facilitated such decision-making on the part of the forecaster, the expectation above is valid; otherwise, it is not. The decision could be made if, for example, the Widget marketing task was accompanied by these instructions:

A. If the marketing data can be applied to 95% (or better) of the total marketplace, with a standard error of plus or minus three,

and

B. if the forecast is for a minimum of 1,000 sales in the first year, 1250 the second year, and, in the third and subsequent years, growth at a rate of 50% per year.

then

C. recommend we sell the Widget; otherwise, recommend we do not sell the Widget.

The point is that the rational way to handle scientific data is through some orderly process. While Chapter 18 goes into some detail concerning decision-making techniques, this concept is introduced now in hope that the forecaster in you will be mindful that at the end of all of the analysis, someone has to make a decision about what to do based on the information. Sometimes it can be precisely expressed, as above. These kind of criterion can often be developed independent of any market research. A good plan designer, knowing the function each division and machine will have to perform, and in what sequence, can compute the cost of equipment and operators based on information concerning a nominal number of items under production at that particular time. It is the market analyst who must forecast what the most likely product demand volume will be.

EXERCISES

1. Identify conditions or circumstances that affect the reliability of forecasts.
2. Give examples of areas in which precise forecasts can be made. Give an example of an area in which forecasting is probably a waste of time.
3. Identify an area in your personal life for which you could develop a useful forecasting tool.
4. Select a published forecasting effort (economic, business, or weather, for example) and keep a record of the forecasts and actual performance for a month or two. How well do the forecasters do? Can you explain their successes or failures?
5. Develop a convincing case for conducting and publishing political surveys. Develop a convincing case for not doing political surveys.

SUGGESTED READING

Ayers, R. U., 1969. *Technological Forecasting and Long Range Planning*. New York: McGraw-Hill.

Makridakis, S. and S. C. Wheelwright, 1976. *Forecasting Methods & Applications*. New York: John Wiley & Sons.

Reichard, R.S., 1966. *Practical Techniques of Sales Forecasting*. New York: McGraw-Hill.

## Chapter 2

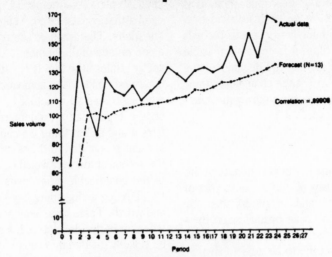

Underlying Mathematical Principles

Related to practically any subject selected for forecasting are all manner of data that may range from the purely subjective ("Yeller was a good ole' dog . . .") to the precise and absolute ("Water freezes at 273° Kelvin (K) and boils at 373° K.) I am hard pressed, in this book, to help anyone to do forecasting from the subjective or anecodotal end of the data spectrum. At the same time the data need not all be from absolute scales of measurement. We can frequently (and more often than not, in fact do) make sense and produce effective forecasts from a variety of data types as long as we can count, measure, or by some other means, quantify the data. The key is quantification. If by some rational means or process you can assign some numerical value to an element under investigation, the data are quantifiable and, more than likely, forecastable to some degree. All that follows, then, deals with numerical or quantified data.

SCALES

Scalar data (those data that describe things in terms of hot to cold, good to bad, little to much, and so forth) can be categorized into four types of measurement scales: *nominal, ordinal, interval,* and *ratio*. These scales are listed in this order for a purpose. There are a certain number of mathematical operations one may do with nominal data, but only relatively few. With ordinal data, however, one may perform all of those operations, plus a number more. This rule continues through interval and ratio scale data as well. It is important to be sure to use mathematical operations appropriate to the data. Failure to do so results in meaningless forecasts.

Nominal Scales

A nominal scale consists of two or more categories or classifications into which the subjects of the study can be divided. One example of the use of a nominal scale is a census of a population described by nationality. At a particular university there are 3256 Americans, 245 British, 178 French, 89 Italians, 78 Gambians, and 2 Swiss. These categories can be totaled; percentages can be computed, and other similar simple numerical relationships can be established. Assignment to a category is not a value judgment, nor are the numbers that are generated meaningful beyond a limited application. It is entirely proper, however, to use such scales in forecasting. Given a series of university census records taken over a period of time, it is certainly feasible to compute the overall growth (or decline) of the university population and the changing ethnic makeup of the student body, and to draw meaningful conclusions from these data.

Ordinal Scales

An ordinal scale is one in which elements of the population under study are placed in some sort of relative order. Different brands of laundry soap, for example, may be placed on an ordinal scale by a panel of judges. The key feature of the scale is that the ratings or measures tend to be adjectival; that is, the items are rated as good or bad or satisfactory or unsatisfactory according to some criterion (smell, shape, apparent utility). The researcher may even attempt to define a certain precision in all this subjectivity by having the item rated numerically, as "on a scale of 1 to 10, how do you rate the President's foreign policy?" The essential element to remember, though, is that the interval between these scale increments is not constant; rather, it is elastic. In reality, the scale for the responses to the foreign policy question are distributed along a scale that is not measured evenly like this:

```
1   2   3   4   5   6   7   8   9
Poor        Average         Good
```

but one much like this:

```
1 2 3     4      5 6 7           8 9
Poor        Average         Good
```

For this reason, the complexity of the scale will serve to confound rather than aid the analyst, and the recommendation is to reduce the number of increments to three or five. It is even more important to avoid any computations that assume even intervals. It would be irresponsible to imply that a rating of four is just one notch below five, or that a rating of two is to four as four is to six. Such relationships will exist only coincidentally. A very common misuse of ordinal scales occurs in schoolrooms

across the nation. Students are frequently given spelling tests, mathematics quizzes, and history exams that consist of a certain number of items or questions. The grade or score is then computed as a percentage of the number of items answered correctly. Unless the test is constructed with extraordinary care and skill, it is most unlikely that a student who scores an 89 is actually 2 percent "smarter" on the topic than a student receiving an 87. The fairest and safest thing we can say is that the first student responded to the test items "better" than the second student. It would be wrong to make much of the quantifiable differences between them.

Testing and grading have demonstrable utility and worth. Tests have been constructed such that, when properly administered, a group of subjects can be reliably divided into those who are likely to succeed at some future effort from those who are likely to fail. One who cannot carry a fifty-pound weight ten paces in a test cannot reliably be expected to carry a hundred and fifty-pound weight from a real burning building. Likewise, one who completes examinations in analytic geometry and algebra well above a responsibly established cutoff score can be expected to do well in calculus. To infer anything of consequence from the fine gradations between scores, however, is quite risky.

Interval Scales

Interval scales are those upon which two or more items can be compared in units of constant measure. An example often given is that of temperature as measured on the centigrade scale. Zero is established as the freezing point of water and one hundred degrees as the boiling point of water. All other aspects of the scale are derived from this interval. To say that something 20°C is twice as cold as something 10°C is incorrect. At the same time, using ratios of differences is acceptable. It is correct to say there is twice as much change in a score that moves from 3 to 7 as in a score that moves from 3 to 5. The essential element of an interval scale is that it has no absolute zero base or starting point. Only with such a point can we say that twenty of something is twice ten of that thing. Twenty people is twice ten people because there is a condition of absolutely zero people. 10°C is not half 20°C because 0°C is not really the bottom of the scale, but only an arbitrary point on it selected for convenience. (Degrees on the Kelvin scale, however, are measureds of absolute temperature because the starting or zero point of the scale is at the point of absolute cold, the point at which nothing, theoretically, can be any colder.)

Ratio Scales

The main distinction between interval and ratio scales is that the ratio scale always has a zero point. Units of weight, time, length, area, volume, angular measure, and the cardinal numbers used to count people, eggs, and money are examples of ratio scales.

All of the mathematical operations that can be applied to the foregoing scales can be used with ratio scales, as well as all the remaining statistical tests and measures, especially those requiring ratio differences from an absolute base.

SUMMATION RULES

Numerical tables are very frequently used in statistical studies and projections. Equally as common is the symbol: ΣX. This means to sum up the values of X, given a set or listing of X values. If there is a set of numbers [1,4,8,2,4,8,3,7], then $\Sigma X = 1 + 4 + 8 + 2 + 4 + 8 + 3 + 7 = 37$.

There are three principles in summation that make the task a little easier and less error-prone:

1. Always work from right to left. When two or more summation symbols are given, follow the direction of the symbol on the right first and then move to the left.
2. Complete all work within parentheses first.

$$\sum_{i=1}^{3} X_i^2 = X_1^2 + X_2^2 + X_3^2$$

$$\left(\sum_{i=1}^{3} X_1\right)^2 = (X_1 + X_2 + X_3)^2$$

3. $\sum_{i=1}^{N} KX_1 = K \sum_{i=1}^{N} X_1$ where K is some constant; e.g.:

$$KX_1 + KX_2 + KX_3 = K(X_1 + X_2 + X_3)$$

The following are examples of the summation principles:

$$\sum_{i=1}^{N} (X + Y_i) = \sum_{i=1}^{N} X_i + \sum_{i=1}^{N} Y_i$$

$$\sum_{i=1}^{N} (X_i + 2) = \sum_{i=1}^{N} X_i + 2N$$

$$\sum_{i=1}^{N} (Y - a)^2 = \sum_{i=1}^{N} (Y^2 - 2aY + a^2)$$

$$\sum_{i=1}^{N} \bar{Y}^2 - 2a \sum^{N} Y + Na^2$$

STATISTICS

Statistics are numbers that give us information on a given subject. Related to any subject are usually a set of numbers: quantity, size, speed, time values, scale values of attitudes, and whatever else the human imagination can devise to count or measure. Those statistics that *describe* the available data are referred to as *descriptive statistics*. These normally include such things as the frequency, mean, median, mode, range, and skew of a distribution of numbers or values, and the percentages and percentiles derived from them.

Distribution of Data

Data collected on a subject may be described in a number of different types of distributions, but the two we are most concerned with in this book are those describing the magnitude of a characteristic at a given moment (such as voter attitudes, city population, etc.), and those describing the time of the occurrence of an event or a set of related events. The first type is referred to as a frequency distribu-

9

tion, while the second is known as a time-series distribution.

Frequency Distribution. Table 2-1 represents the results of a survey of the number of registered voters in a political region of a state.

These data are evaluated to determine the range; the largest precinct contains 2757 registered voters, while the smallest contains 430. The range then is 2327. We then divide these data into a number (normally, six to twenty) of subsets called *class intervals*, making an effort to ensure the interval is broad enough to include at least five data elements in each division. Initial estimates of the size of the class interval can be obtained from the equation:

$$C = \frac{\text{range}}{1 + (3.322 \; \text{L}n\text{N})}$$

Where C = class interval

N = number of elements or observations

Applying the equation to the data in Table 2-1, we compute C to be:

$$C = \frac{2327}{1 + (3.322 \; \text{Log} \; 128)} = \frac{2327}{17.1184} = 135.936$$

The number of class intervals, then, is computed by dividing the largest value (2757) by the interval: 2757/135.936 = 20.2816, or about 21 subsets. The class interval is adjusted by the user so as to specify a size of class interval that:

a. Ensures that each interval includes a sample of at least five elements.

Table 2-1. Number of Registered Voters by Precinct.

PCT	# Voters	PCT	# Voters	PCT	# Voters	PCT	# Voters
1	1607	2	1554	3	846	4	969
5	1408	6	682	7	1739	8	1494
9	2068	10	784	11	2048	12	1905
13	1210	14	2063	15	1832	16	1162
17	2757	18	1419	19	1486	20	1201
21	1586	22	1794	23	1832	24	1417
25	1651	26	1332	27	1434	28	1899
29	1784	30	1093	31	1287	32	1780
33	1616	34	1908	35	1995	36	1576
37	1387	38	1590	39	1948	40	1086
41	1272	42	2203	43	1397	44	1563
45	1480	46	1068	47	1226	48	1346
49	1592	50	1923	51	1578	52	2069
53	1333	54	1584	55	1174	56	1788
57	1369	58	2396	59	1734	60	1952
61	1727	62	1595	63	1404	64	1523
65	1356	66	1484	67	1497	68	430
69	2038	70	1109	71	1271	72	1914
73	1137	74	2022	75	1693	76	2115
77	1832	78	1317	79	1842	80	2372
81	1081	82	1315	83	1327	84	1697
85	1697	86	1532	87	1647	88	768
89	1533	90	868	91	2013	92	1498
93	1323	94	895	95	2167	96	1308
97	2402	98	1856	99	758	100	1166
101	1641	102	1940	103	1884	104	1363
105	1604	106	1651	107	1363	108	1676
109	1658	110	1971	111	1494	112	1515
113	1726	114	1847	115	1346	116	1615
117	1648	118	1730	119	807	120	1842
121	1153	122	1421	123	1452	124	1454
125	1363	126	1972	127	1871	128	1918

b. The interval range is an easily computed or comfortable unit of measure. For example, it is easier to handle the interval if it is 5 instead of 3.456: 5-9.9, 10-14.9, and 15-19.9. . . instead of 3.456-6.911, 6.912-10.367, and 10.368-13.823. . . .

c. The class intervals do not overlap. If the intervals are stated as 0-5, 5-10, and 10-15, definite ambiguities are created at the point of overlap.

d. All efforts should be taken to ensure a constant interval size.

The data then are tallied according to class interval. Figure 2-1 illustrates our data in the tally format. Each class interval is scored. This tally process develops the group frequency data to be used in the subsequent analysis and provides a visual impression of the nature of the data distribution.

Listing 2-1 is a brief routine to input and tally raw data according to the user-defined class intervals. It was used to generate the results in Fig. 2-1, but I would recommend the reader proceed to the program in Listing 2-2 for a more comprehensive evaluation.

The second phase of this analysis is to compute a variety of statistics which better describe the data.

These include the mean, median, mode, skew, kurtosis, and several other related measures.

Mean. This is the preferred term for what we commonly call the average of a set of values. Unless specified as a geometric mean or a harmonic mean or described by some other qualifier, we understand the *mean* of a set of numbers to be the sum of those numbers divided by the number of data elements:

$$X = \frac{A_1 + A_2 + A_3 + \ldots + A_n}{n}$$

In the evaluation of a set of data, the mean is the most frequently used value due to the ease with which it can be computed and to its long-standing use. The drawback to the mean is that it is greatly affected by extreme values. Consider the following list of per capita incomes for 6 countries:

Country	Per Capita Income
1	50
2	67
3	78
4	12545
5	17893
6	21378

Class interval	Tally	Total frequency
0 - 249		0
250 - 499		1
500 - 749		1
750 - 999		8
1000 - 1249		13
1250 - 1499		34
1500 - 1749		32
1750 - 1999		25
2000 - 2249		10
2250 - 2499		3
2500 - 2749		0
2750 - 2999		1
Total		128

Fig. 2-1. Data shown in tally format.

Listing 2-1. Routine to Tally Raw Data.

```
1 '*********************************************
2 '*                  Listing 2-1               *
3 '*          Routine to Tally Raw Data         *
4 '*********************************************
5 '
10 T=0:LG=0
20 CLS
30 PRINT"Raw Data Tally"
40 PRINT
50 INPUT"NUMBER OF ITEMS";N
60 DIM DI(N)
70 FOR I=1 TO N
80    PRINT"ENTER VALUE OF ITEM #";I,: INPUT DI(I
): T=T+DI(I)
90    IF DI(I)<=LG THEN 110
100   LG=DI(I)
110 NEXT
120 PRINT"Compute by (C)lass Interval or (N)umbe
r of classes ";
130 Q$=""+INKEY$:IF Q$="" THEN 130
140 IF Q$="C" OR Q$="c" THEN 160
150 PRINT: INPUT "Number of classes";NC: CI=INT(
LG/NC)+1:PRINT"The Class Interval will be: ";CI:
GOTO 170
160 PRINT: INPUT "Class Interval";CI: NC=INT(LG/
CI)+1:PRINT"The Number of Classes will be: ";NC
170 DIM B(NC)
180 FOR I=1 TO N
190   A=INT(DI(I)/CI): B(A)=B(A)+1
200 NEXT
210 CLS
220 PRINT"CLASS","","","TOTAL": PRINT"INTERVAL",
"  TALLY","","FREQUENCY"
230 LPRINT"": LPRINT"CLASS","","","","","","TOTA
L": LPRINT"INTERVAL","","","",""       TALLY       FREQ
UENCY": LPRINT""
240 FOR I=1 TO NC
250 S=0: PRINT ((I-1)*CI);"-";(I*CI)-.001,: LPRI
NT ((I-1)*CI);"-";(I*CI)-.001,: IF B(I)=0 THEN 3
00
260 FOR J=1 TO B(I)
270 PRINT"/";: LPRINT"/";: S=S+1: IF S<5 THEN 29
0
280 PRINT" ";: LPRINT" ";: S=0
290 NEXT J
300 ZOG%=120+(I*64): GOSUB 350: PRINT B(I): LPRI
NT STRING$(72-B(I)+INT(B(I)/5)," ");B(I)
310 NEXT I
320 LPRINT STRING$(96," ");N
330 PRINT"":PRINT"":GOTO 360
350 ZAG%=INT(ZOG%/64):ZOG%=ZOG%-64*ZAG%+1:ZAG%=Z
AG%+1:                            LOCATE ZAG%,
ZOG%:RETURN
360 PRINT"(A)nother      (M)ain menu ";
370 Q$=""+INKEY$:IF Q$="" THEN 370
380 IF Q$="A" OR Q$="a" THEN RUN 10 ELSE RUN "A:
MENU"
```

The mean of this set is 8668.500. Unfortunately, there is no value on the table that is meaningfully close to the mean. We need some other measures.

Geometric Mean. This mean is technically defined as the nth root of the product of the n items or values. It is computed according to the expression:

$$G_m = \sqrt[n]{A_1 \bullet A_2 \bullet A_3 \bullet A_n}$$

The following eight numbers were randomly generated from a set zero to one thousand:

N	Value
1	510
2	452
3	631
4	755
5	102
6	452
7	268
8	106

Total 3276   Product 1.438348708238136 $\times 10^{20}$

Mean 409.500 Geometric Mean 330.928

The geometric mean has the advantage of not being unduly influenced by extreme values in a distribution and is more typically representative of the distribution than the arithmetic mean. On the other hand, it is more difficult to compute, and if any value in the distribution is zero, the geometric mean becomes zero. In addition, it is not a widely known or understood statistic.

Median. The median value of a distribution is the actual midway point at which one-half of the values lie below it and the other half lie above it. Where there is an odd number of items in a list, the median value is the centermost item in the list. With an even number of items in the list, it is the sum of the two central items divided by two. This value is easily computed and is not adversely affected by extreme values. Negatively, it is not as widely understood as the mean, and it requires that the data be sorted by magnitude before it can be identified. Also, it cannot be manipulated algebraically. The data below illustrate the notion of the median:

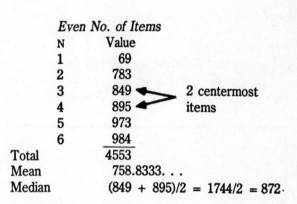

Odd No. of Items

N	Value
1	609
2	748
3	770
4	859 ← centermost item
5	958
6	960
7	994

Total 5898
Mean 842.5714
Median 859

Even No. of Items

N	Value
1	69
2	783
3	849
4	895
5	973
6	984

2 centermost items

Total 4553
Mean 758.8333. . .
Median (849 + 895)/2 = 1744/2 = 872

Mode. The mode of a set of numbers is the number that occurs most frequently, provided the data set is large enough. Identification of the mode is not especially difficult, particularly if the data have been sorted into an ordered list to find the median. Simply scan the list and find the value that reappears most often. In the event this is too much of a bother, the mode can be estimated from the expression

mode = mean − 3(mean − median)

If the median has not been identified, there are a couple of other ways to compute an estimate of the mode, although they are based on values we have yet to introduce. From the *skew* of the distribution:

mode = mean − (skew •standard deviation)

From the *theory of moments*:

mode = $M_1 - [(M_3/\sqrt{M_2^3})$ standard deviation]

The relationship between these three values, mean, median, and mode, is illustrated in Fig. 2-2.

Skew. You will notice in Fig. 2-2 that the curve is not centered about the mean, but lopsided. The degree of lopsidedness is referred to as *skew*. Unfortunately, generations of mathematicians have established a convention to be used when talking about skew that can be confusing. When the peak of the curve is pushed over to the righthand side of the graph, it is said to be "skewed to the left," and when the peak is closer to the left of the graph, it is "skewed to the right." The equation to determine the degree of skew is:

$$S = \frac{3(\text{mean} - \text{median})}{\text{standard deviation}}$$

(The standard deviation is described below.)

If the value for S is less than zero, the curve is said to be skewed to the left. If it is greater than

zero it is skewed to the right. When $S = 0$, the curve is said to be *normal* or symmetrical.

Kurtosis. The pointedness of the curve is defined by the value of its kurtosis. Where the value is a positive figure, the curve is fairly peaked. When it is a negative figure, it is a flat-topped curve. When kurtosis is zero, then it is normally peaked. Theoretically, zero values for both skew and kurtosis should be related to a distribution of data which is normal. Kurtosis is computed from the various *moments* of the curve, which are discussed below, and is described in the equation:

$$K = (M_4/M_2^2) - 3$$

Standard Deviation. An underlying concept in statistics is the principle of *central tendency*. That is, if we collect *parametric data* about something (height, weight, grades, ages, etc.), we find the data group around the mean, in a hill-shaped curve, in

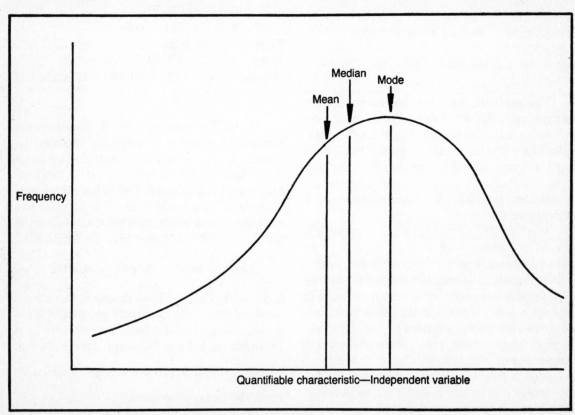

Fig. 2-2. Generalized distribution with mean, mode, and median.

14

skew and kurtosis. Few
, lie exactly on the mean.
w by some degree. The
. The first step is to sum
mean:

N	Value
1	123
2	96
3	146
4	45
5	142
6	93
7	66
8	95
9	121
10	93
Sum	102

(Mean = 1020/10 = 102.00

The next step is to subtract the mean from each of the input values and sum these. For reasons that will be made clear, you must also square each deviation and sum these:

N	Value	Deviation	Deviation Squared
1	123	21	441
2	96	− 6	36
3	146	44	1936
4	45	− 57	3249
5	142	40	1600
6	93	− 9	81
7	66	− 36	1296
8	95	− 7	49
9	121	19	361
10		− 9	81
Sum	1020	0	9130
Mean	102.00	0	913.00

The mean deviation will always be zero. Since you still need some measure or estimate of the general or normal deviation from the mean, you must use the next available value, the squared deviations. The computed value is called the *standard deviation* and is derived from the equation:

$$\varrho = \sqrt{\frac{\sum(x^2)}{N}}$$

where x^2 is the square of each deviation. From our data:

$$\varrho = \sqrt{\frac{9130}{10}} = \frac{30}{2159}$$

This value is quite handy. If, from the other values computed from the data, we know the data to be in a fairly normal distribution (skew close to zero), we can reasonably assume that about 68 percent of the data are within one standard deviation, plus or minus, from the mean; 95 percent are within two standard deviations, plus or minus, from the mean; and all but a very small fraction of the remainder are within three standard deviations. These relationships are illustrated in Fig. 2-3. From the value of the standard deviation, σ, in a normal or even moderately skewed distribution, we can compute the mean deviation as being approximately $.7979\sigma$. Additionally, in a normal distribution, the standard deviation is roughly one-sixth of the range.

The values computed above are based on the assumption that in the entire universe, there are only ten of the items that were measured. Normally, we are not so fortunate to be able to measure each of a given item. Frequently, it is not economical to do so. For example, if we wanted to start a new shoe factory, but needed to know what sizes to make, it would not be practical to go out and measure everyone's feet. Rather, we would measure the feet of a sample of only a few thousand people. If we have properly selected our sample, we can reasonably assume that the mean size and standard deviations computed from the sample are applicable to the whole population. When we sample from a population, however, we must make a minor adjustment in the computations so that the results are more applicable to the whole population. The standard deviation of a sample is computed from:

$$s = \sqrt{\frac{\sum(x^2)}{N-1}}$$

Applying this equation to the data given above:

$$s = \sqrt{\frac{9130}{9}} = 31.8504$$

15

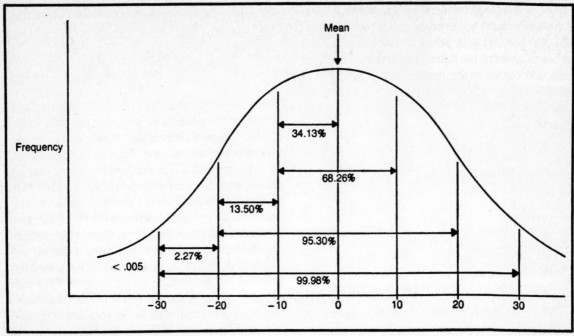

Fig. 2-3. Proportions under normal curve.

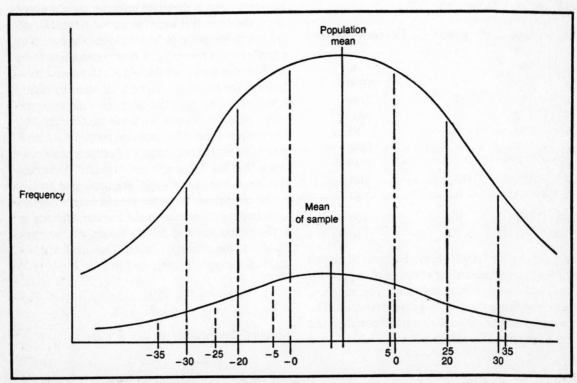

Fig. 2-4. Comparison between sample and population deviations.

The relationship between the distribution of a whole population and the data from a sample is illustrated in Fig. 2-4.

In order to find the standard deviation using a BASIC program, the mean must be computed prior to the computation of the standard deviations. During the collection of the data phase, the program line would read:

XY10 INPUT"ENTER VALUE";V(I):T=T+V(I)

and the processing lines would be:

```
YZ10   M=T/N
YZ20   FOR I=I TO N
YZ30   D=V(I)-M:D2+D]2
YZ40   NEXT
YZ50   S=SQR(D2/(N-1))
```

A shorter approach is to use this equation:

$$s = \sqrt{\dfrac{\sum\left(x - \dfrac{X}{N}\right)^1}{N}}$$

This permits a much shorter routine and no repetitions of the data:

```
XY10   INPUT"ENTER VALUE";
       V(I):T=T+V(I):X2=X2+2X]2

. . . .

YZ10   M=T/N:S=SQR((X2-((T]2))/(N-I))
```

Moments. The *moments* of a distribution are constants that are computed to facilitate analysis of a curve of the distribution. Space does not permit the development of the equations, nor is a more comprehensive explanation necessary for the use of moments in forecasting. We will leave the subject with a listing of the equations used to compute them.

In general: $M_r = \dfrac{1}{N} \sum\limits_{i=1}^{N} (X_i - \overline{X})^r$

Then: $M_1 = 0$

$$M_2 = \dfrac{1}{N} \sum\limits_{i=1}^{N} (X_i - \overline{X})^2$$

$$M_3 = \dfrac{1}{N} \sum\limits_{i=1}^{N} (X_i - \overline{X})^3$$

$$M_4 = \dfrac{1}{N} \sum\limits_{i=1}^{N} (X_i - \overline{X})^4$$

Skew can be computed: $S_k = \dfrac{M_3}{\sqrt{2M_2^{\,3}}}$

Kurtosis, then, is: $K = \dfrac{M_4}{M_2^{\,2}}$

Happily, the microcomputer makes fairly short work of all these computations and tedious summations. Listing 2-2 is a program which implements all of the foregoing data collection and processing routines to compute the descriptive values relative to a distribution. While it is not necessary to key in and run the program as written, it does provide a working example of the ways to implement the different equations.

To describe the data is often only the first of two steps in the statistical process. Frequently, the data are measures of a sample taken from a larger population. We use statistics as a tool to learn useful information about large populations or universes by sampling small portions of the whole. To aid us in the inductive process of generalizing from the data related to the sample to conclusions about the whole, we use *inferential statistics*.

For example, a biologist wants to determine whether the water contained in a larger wooden barrel is suitable for use in a series of experiments. The water within the barrel constitutes the universe understudy. The one-quart ladle of water drawn is the sample. The convention is that the water in the ladle is reliably representative of all of the water. (Whether the one-quart sample is statistically adequate to support the subsequent conclusions is the subject of a later section on sampling theory.) Having drawn the water, the biologist examines the sample microscopically and chemically. It is understood that virtually all samples of water will contain some contaminants; the question is whether the level of contamination exceeds some prescribed level or percentage. One procedure the biologist might use is

Listing 2-2. Data Distribution Analysis.

```
1 '************************************************
2 '*                 Listing 2-2                  *
3 '*          Data Distribution Analysis          *
4 '************************************************
5 '
10 CLS: SM=1E+10: LG=1E-10: XG=1
20 PRINT"INITIAL DISTRIBUTION ANALYSIS": PRINT:
PRINT
30 INPUT"ENTER NUMBER OF DATA ITEMS TO BE ENTERE
D";N: DIM V(N)
40 FOR I=1 TO N: PRINT"ENTER DATA FOR ITEM #";I,
: INPUT V(I): T=T+V(I): X2=X2+V(I)^2: NEXT I
50 A=1: PRINT: IF N>48 THEN B=48 ELSE B=N
60 PRINT: FOR I=A TO B: PRINT I;V(I),: NEXT
70 'CORRECTION SUBROUTINE
80 PRINT: PRINT"ARE ALL THESE ITEMS CORRECT?  (Y
/N)";
90 Q$=""+INKEY$: IF Q$="" THEN 90 ELSE IF Q$="Y"
 OR Q$="y" THEN 120
100 PRINT: INPUT"ENTER ITEM NUMBER AND CORRECT V
ALUE";X,V(X)
110 GOTO 60
120 IF B=N THEN 160
130 A=A+48: B=B+48: IF B>N THEN B=N
140 GOTO 60
150 'COMPUTATION OF SMALLEST AND LARGEST VALUES
160 PRINT: PRINT"DOING INITIAL COMPUTATIONS": PR
INT
170 FOR I=1 TO N
180 IF SM<V(I) THEN 200
190 SM=V(I): GOTO 220
200 IF V(I)<LG THEN 220
210 LG=V(I)
220 NEXT
230 'COMPUTATION OF RANGE, CLASS INTERVAL, # CLA
SSES
240 RG=LG-SM: C=RG/(1+(3.322*LOG(N))): NC=INT(RG
/C)+1
250 PRINT: PRINT"THE COMPUTED CLASS INTERVAL IS
";C: PRINT"THIS IMPLIES";NC;"CLASSES.  DO YOU CO
NCUR?  (Y/N)": SF=127/NC
260 Q$=""+INKEY$: IF Q$="" THEN 260
270 IF Q$="Y" OR Q$="y" THEN 330
280 PRINT: PRINT"      A  --  NUMBER OF CLASSES
                              B  --  CLAS
S INTERVAL": PRINT: INPUT"ENTER TYPE VALUE AND V
ALUE";V$,V
290 IF V$="A" THEN 310
300 C=V: NC=INT(RG/C)+1: GOTO 320
310 NC=V: C=RG/NC
320 GOTO 250
330 DIM F(NC+1),U(N),E(N)
340 CLS: PRINT"COMPUTING AGAIN";: SF=0
350 'SET UP SORTING LIST (U(I)), CHECK EACH INPU
T VALUE FOR CLASS INTERVAL
360 FOR I=1 TO N
```

```
370 U(I)=V(I): E(I)=1
380 LOCATE 1,31: PRINT I;
390 NEXT I
400 'HEAPSORT SORTING ROUTINE TO PUT INPUT LIST
IN ORDER
410 LOCATE 1,1: PRINT"SORTING                    ";:
 K=N: L=INT(N/2)+1
420 IF L=1 THEN 530
430 L=L-1: A=U(L)
440 J=L
450 I=J: J=2*J
460 IF J=K THEN 500
470 IF J>K THEN 520
480 IF U(J)>=U(J+1) THEN 500
490 J=J+1
500 IF A>U(J) THEN 520
510 U(I)=U(J): GOTO 450
520 U(I)=A: LOCATE 1,51: PRINT K;: GOTO 420
530 A=U(K): U(K)=U(1)
540 K=K-1
550 IF K<>1 THEN 440
560 U(1)=A
570 'PRINT SORTED LIST
580 PRINT: FOR I=1 TO N: PRINT U(I),: NEXT I
590 'COMPLETE COMPUTATIONS OF MEAN, MEDIAN, MODE
, SKEW, AND KURTOSIS
600 AV=T/N: SD=SQR((X2-((T^2)/N))/(N-1))
610 IF INT(N/2)=N/2 THEN 630
620 ME=U(((N-1)/2)+1): GOTO 640
630 ME=(U(N/2)+U((N/2)+1))/2
640 GM=EXP(XG/N)
650 LOCATE 1,1: PRINT"COMPUTING MOMENTS";: FOR I
=2 TO 4: FOR J=1 TO N: LOCATE 1,41: PRINT I;J;:
M(I)=M(I)+(V(J)-AV)^I: NEXT J: M(I)=M(I)/N: NEXT
 I
660 SK=M(3)/SQR(2*(M(2)^3)): K=(M(4)/(M(2)^2))-3
670 MC=AV-(SK*SD)
680 CLS
690 PRINT: PRINT: PRINT"NUMBER OF ITEMS = ";N
700 PRINT"SMALLEST = ";SM:PRINT"LARGEST = ";LG:P
RINT"RANGE =";LG-SM:PRINT"TOTAL = ";T,"MEAN = ";
AV:PRINT"STANDARD DEVIATION = ";SD:PRINT"MEDIAN
= ";ME:PRINT"COMPUTED MODE = ";MC:PRINT"    (DO Y
OU WANT TO KNOW THE ACTUAL MODE?  (Y/N)";
710 Q$=""+INKEY$: IF Q$="" THEN 710 ELSE IF Q$="
N" OR Q$="n" THEN 850
720 PRINT: PRINT"        PLEASE BE PATIENT.   THIS W
ILL TAKE A MOMENT..."
730 'LOCATE ACTUAL MODE
740 FOR I=1 TO N-1
750 FOR J=I+1 TO N
760 IF V(I)<>V(J) THEN 780
770 E(I)=E(I)+1
780 NEXT J
790 NEXT I
800 FOR I=1 TO N
810 IF E(I)<=MA THEN 830
820 MA=E(I): AM=I
```

Listing 2-2. Data Distribution Analysis. (Continued From Page 19.)

```
830 NEXT
840 PRINT: PRINT"THE ACTUAL MODE IS ";V(AM);"WIT
H";MA;"REPETITIONS"
850 PRINT: PRINT"SKEW = ";SK
860 IF SK<0 THEN PRINT"   (LEFT, PEAK TO THE RIGH
T)" ELSE IF SK=0 THEN PRINT"   (NORMAL CURVE)" E
LSE PRINT"   (RIGHT, PEAK TO THE LEFT)"
870 IF K<0 THEN K$="Flat-Topped" ELSE IF K=0 THE
N K$="Normal" ELSE IF K>0 THEN K$="Pointed"
880 PRINT"KURTOSIS = ";K,K$: PRINT"GEOMETRIC MEA
N = ";GM: PRINT"MOMENTS  -- M1 = ";M(1);"   M2
= ";M(2);"M3 = ";M(3);"   M4 = ";M(4): PRINT
890 LOCATE 24,1: PRINT"(P)RINT STATISTICS   (T)AB
LE OF DATA   (G)RAPH OF DATA   (M)ain Menu   (N)
EW";
900 Q$=""+INKEY$: IF Q$="" THEN 900
910 IF Q$="P" OR Q$="p" THEN 930 ELSE IF Q$="T"
OR Q$="t" THEN 690 ELSE IF Q$="M" OR Q$="m" THEN
 980 ELSE IF Q$="G" OR Q$="g" THEN 990 ELSE IF Q
$="N" OR Q$="n" THEN RUN 10 ELSE 900
920 RUN 10
930 LPRINT"SORTED INPUT DATA   (READ: ITEM NUMBER
, VALUE)": LPRINT""
940 FOR I=1 TO N: LPRINT I;U(I),: NEXT: LPRINT""
950 LPRINT"NUMBER OF ITEMS =";N,"SMALLEST = ";SM
,"LARGEST = ";LG,"RANGE = ";R,"SUM OF ALL ITEMS
= ";T,"MEAN = ";AV,"GEOMETRIC MEAN = ";GM,"STAND
ARD DEVIATION = ";SD,"MEDIAN = ";ME,"MODE(S) =";
MC;V(AM),"SKEW = ";SK,"KURTOSIS = ";K,
960 LPRINT"MOMENTS: M1 = ";M(1),"M2 = ";M(2),"M3
 = ";M(3),"M4 = ";M(4)
970 GOTO 890
980 RUN"A:MENU"
990 'DATA DISPLAY
1000 KEY OFF
1010 DIM Y(N),X(N)
1020 FOR I=1 TO N:Y(I)=V(I):X(I)=I:NEXT:SX=1:LX=
N
1030 FOR I=1 TO N
1040   IF Y(I)=>SY THEN 1060
1050   SY=Y(I):GOTO 1080
1060   IF Y(I)<=LY THEN 1080
1070   LY=Y(I)
1080 NEXT I
1090 GOSUB 1270:SCREEN SC
1100 CLS
1110 D=INT(LOG(LX)/2.302585)+1       ' DETERMINE L
ENGTH OF NUMBER
1120 XA=INT(.1328*XX):YA=INT(.7875*YY):XB=XX-XA
        ' SET LEFT AND BOTTOM BOUNDARIES
1130 RX=LX-SX:RY=LY-SY             ' COMPUTE RANG
E
1140 LINE(XA,1)-(XA,YA):LINE(XA,YA)-(XX,YA)
' DRAW BOUNDARY
1150 ' COMPUTE AND DRAW INTERVAL MARKERS
1160 FOR I=1 TO 9:LINE(XA-2,(I*(YA/10))-1)-(XA,(
```

```
I*(YA/10))-1):NEXT
1170 FOR I=1 TO 9:LINE(XA+(I*((XX-XA)/10)-1),YA+
2)-(XA+(I*((XX-XA)/10)-1),YA):NEXT
1180 ' PRINT SCALE VALUES
1190 LOCATE 1,(XA/8)-4:PRINT LY;:LOCATE 20,(XA/8
)-4:PRINT SY;:LOCATE 21,(XA/8)-1:PRINT SX;:LOCAT
E 21,(XX/8)-(D+2):PRINT INT(LX);
1200 ' DISPLAY LOCATION OF ACTUAL DATA ON SCALE
1210 FOR I=1 TO N
1220    X1=XA+INT(XB*((I-SX)/RX))+1
1230    Y1=INT(YA-(YA*((V(I)-SY)/RY)))
1240    PSET(X1,Y1)
1250 NEXT I
1260 LOCATE 24,1:INPUT"Use PrtScrn to save Graph
, <CR> to Continue";XX:GOTO 890
1270 CLS
1280 PRINT"1  --   320 X 200    2  --   640 X 200
    3  --   640 X 400 "
1290 PRINT:PRINT"Indicate screen dimensions ";
1300 Q$=""+INKEY$:IF Q$="" THEN 1300
1310 IF Q$<"1" OR Q$>"3" THEN 1300
1320 ON VAL(Q$) GOTO 1330, 1340, 1350
1330 XX=320:YY=200:SC=1:XL=39:ZY=8:ZX=4:RETURN
1340 XX=640:YY=200:XL=39:SC=2:ZY=8:ZX=8:RETURN
1350 XX=640:YY=400:SC=100:XL=79:ZY=16:ZX=8:RETUR
N
```

to place a sample (from the sample) under the microscope to count larger microbes. In the viewing area, the plane is optically divided into a matrix of smaller cells. Each cell is surveyed to determine the number of microbes in it. These are summed to obtain the total population of the sample. This process is repeated a number of times. Since we know the volume of water in each sample drop, as well as the number of drops and the number of microbes in each drop, we can compute the mean number of microbes in each drop. We can also determine the mode and median values, the standard deviations from these norms, the skew of the distribution, and finally, an estimate of the total number of microbes in the barrel itself. This last step and the subsequent test undertaken to make the inductive leap are the inferential portions of the effort.

PROBABILITY

As a science, the study of probability is often considered a major subset of statistics. As a practical effort, probability and statistical studies had separate origins. The accepted origin of modern probability study is the French mathematician, Pascal, who was employed by a gambler, the Chevalier de Mere, to develop some rational basis for a better gaming strategy in a dice game popular at the time. The broader statistical practices of counting inventories; determining average (mean) crop yield; rainfall, or production rates for hand labor; and using other industrial or agricultural measures, which became systematically organized into statistical science, have their origins much further back, perhaps several thousand years ago. Today, probability theory contributes several powerful tools to inferential statistics, and the systematic procedures of descriptive statistics enhance the preliminary probabilistic analysis.

Set Operations

Any well-defined collection of objects is considered to be a set. A well-defined collection of sets is considered to be a universe. For example, a local high school can be considered a universe containing several sets. These sets can be variously described as: all students, all students who are male, all students who are female, all teachers, all visitors, all administrators, all janitorial staff, everyone within the facility over (or under) a certain age, and on and on.

We normally denote a set with a capital letter (A) and elements of sets with small letters (a). The symbol ϵ is used as a shorthand way to relate an element to a set. Thus, the notation a ϵ A signifies that a is an element of the set A. "John is a member of the band" could be noted as: jϵB. The second symbol often used is the vertical bar: |, and is taken to mean "such that" or "given." Hence, the expression [a | a < 12] is understood to mean that a is a member or element of a set of numbers such that it is less than 12. The symbol $\subset$ means inclusion in the sense of a subset; that is, B$\subset$A is taken to mean "B is a subset of A." The observation that "flutes are among the normal range of band instruments" could be noted: F$\subset$B.

Venn diagrams (named after a leading proponent) are useful tools for graphically describing sets and working out appropriate logical relationships. Figure 2-5 illustrates a standard Venn diagram.

The box around the sets is understood to represent the universe relevant to the sets. It can represent Ohio State University. Set A represents all males present there. Set B represents all graduate students. Given this setting, the following operations can be described: union, intersection, complements, and subtraction.

Figure 2-5 shows a *union* of two sets. The notation used is: A$\cup$B. Any element that is contained in either set A or set B or both is included in the expression A$\cup$B.

Figure 2-6 is the same as Fig. 2-5, except that a portion of it is shaded to highlight that area of overlap or mutual inclusion. This area is the *intersection* of sets and is noted: A$\cap$B.

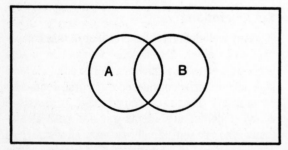

Fig. 2-5. Generalized Venn diagram.

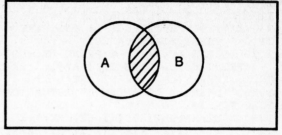

Fig. 2-6. Venn diagram with intersection.

If A is a set containing the number 1, 3, 7, and B is another set containing the numbers, 2, 4, 7 then A$\cap$B = 7 and A$\cup$B = 1, 2, 3, 4, 7.

The *complement* of a set includes all those things which are not elements of that set, and is noted by an overscore, $\overline{A}$. If all graduate students are represented by the notation, G, $\overline{G}$ represents everyone who is not a graduate student.

Subtraction of sets uses the complement of a set for its description: [A] − [B] = A$\cap\overline{B}$. The effect or meaning of the subtraction of set B from set A is described as the intersection of set A with all those elements of the specified universe that are not elements of set B.

Given this notation, we can now summarize the various possible associations, called *distributive rules*:

1. A$\cup$B = B$\cup$A
2. A$\cap$B = B$\cap$A
3. (A$\cup$B)$\cup$C = A$\cup$(B$\cup$C)
4. (A$\cap$B)$\cap$C = A$\cap$(B$\cap$C)
5. A$\cup$(B$\cap$C) = (A$\cup$B)$\cap$(A$\cup$C)
6. A$\cap$(B$\cup$C) = (A$\cap$B)$\cup$(A$\cap$C)

Application of Set Operations Probability

The number of graduate students will be described with the expression n(a), and the total number of people, regardless of sex, occupation, or function, normally found at the university by the value N. The probability, then, of anyone we might encounter being a graduate student is defined by this relationship: p(a) = n(a)/N. If there are 6000 students and 1000 graduate students, the probability of running into a graduate student is 1000/6000 or .166666666 . . . . Yes, that is the same probability given one six-sided die. The die's universe consists of six sides, one of which at rest, will normally be up.

The complement rule lets us also define the probability as: $p(a) = 1 - p(\bar{a})$. That is, the probability of "a" is one minus the probability of all other related events. At our mythical university, there are 5000 nongraduate students. The value $p(\bar{a})$ is $5000/6000 = .833333. \ldots$ Therefore, $p(a) = 1 - .833333 \ldots = .166666 \ldots$ Elsewhere in probability texts the probability of an event may be noted as P or P_a. Concurrently, the complement of P is given as ': ' $= 1 - P$. The following relationships are also true:

1. $P(a) = n(a)/N$
2. $p(a) = 1 - p(a)$
3. $p(A - B) = p(A) - p(B)$
4. $p(A \cup B) = p(A) + p(B) - p(A \cap B)$
5. $p(A \cup B \cup C) = p(A) + p(C) - p(A \cap B) - p(B \cap C) - p(A \cap C) + p(A \cap B \cap C)$

Two or more events are said to be *independent* of each other if the happening of one does not depend on the happening or nonhappening of the other. A fair die is one which can be relied upon to deliver truly random results when rolled. The outcome of the second roll, therefore, is independent of the outcome of the first roll. This permits the following relationships:

6. $p(a \mid b) = p(a)$ (probability of "a" given "b" happens)
7. $p(b \mid a) = p(b)$
8. $p(A \cap B) = p(A) \times p(B)$

The last relationship asks a slightly different question than rules 6 and 7. Rule 6 says, in effect, the probability of a 5 on the roll of a die, given that a 4 has just been rolled is still simply equal to the normal probability of rolling a 5. Rolling a 4 does not make a 5 any more or less likely to happen. Rule 8, on the other hand, defines the probability of rolling a 4 and then rolling a 5. Such a relationship is called a *conditional probability*. It is useful in computing the probability of flipping four heads in a row ($P_{4\,heads} = .0625$), dealing four aces in a row ($P_{4\,aces}$

$= 4/52 \times 3/51 \times 2/50 \times 1/49 = .076923 \times .058824 \times .040000 \times .020408 = .00000369379$); or figuring the probability of more serious but equally independent matters. What about those relationships that are not so independent? Time for rule number 9.

9. $(B \mid A) = \dfrac{p(A \cap B)}{p(A)}$

For purpose of illustration, let us assume the following relationships are true:

a. Females (F) are 51% of the population (M = 49%).
b. 11% of the population is left-handed (L).
c. Only 5% of females are left-handed ($p(F \mid L) = .05$).
d. 20% of the males are left-handed ($p(M \mid L) = .20$).

Therefore,

$$p(L \mid M) = \frac{p(M \cap L)}{p(M)} = \frac{.20}{.49} = .408163$$

The probability of being left-handed, provided one is male, is .408163 according to the data.
Likewise,

$$p(L \mid F) = \frac{p(F \cap L)}{p(F)} = \frac{.05}{.51} = .0980392$$

In reality, left-handedness is not nearly so sexist, but the illustration above accurately portrays the hypothetical data.

If the foregoing is true (and it is), rule 10 must be true:

10. $p(A \cap B) = p(A) \times p(B \mid A) = p(B) \times p(A \mid B)$
    $= p(B)/p(a) = p(B \mid A)/p(A \mid B)$

At this point we are ready for a more serious and useful application of some of these rules and their combinations. Such an application is found in Baye's Theorem, the algebraic expression of which is:

$$p(A \mid B) = \frac{p(B \mid A)p(A)}{p(B \mid A)p(A) + p(B \mid \overline{A})p(\overline{A})}$$

Let us assume these variables represent these relationships:

A $=$ Took poison tablets $= p(A) = .333$

$\overline{A}$ = Took aspirin = p(A) = .667

B = Experiencing stomach/intestinal distress after taking poison = p(B | A) = .8000

$\overline{B}$ = Feeling good after taking aspirin = p($\overline{B}$ | $\overline{A}$) = .95. Experiencing stomach/intestinal distress after taking aspirin = p(B | $\overline{A}$) = .05

The question, then, is: presented with a person complaining of stomach pains, after taking a tablet from one of three unmarked bottles, what is the probability that the person has taken poison? The computed answer is:

$$
\begin{aligned}
p(A \mid B) &= \frac{.80 \times .333}{(.80 \times .333) + (.05 \times .667)} \\
&= \frac{.2664}{.2664 + .03335} \\
&= .888741
\end{aligned}
$$

Listing 2-3 is a short routine which implements and facilitates Baye's Theorem in the form we have just presented above.

Very often, however, there are a number of variables related to a given phenomenon. For ex-

ample, related to winter in northern regions are wind, rain, and snow—among others. There is a modification of Baye's Theorem which will facilitate the computation of the appropriate probability. It is:

$$
p(B_K \mid A) = \frac{p(B_K) \times p(A \mid B_K)}{\sum_{i=1}^{N} p(B_i) \times p(A \mid B_i)}
$$

To illustrate:

p(Wind) = .33333 p(Winter | Wind) = .75
p(Rain) = .15000 p(Winter | Rain) = .05
p(Snow) = .25000 p(Winter | Snow) = .90

Using the equation above, the probability of one of those variables happening, given the condition of winter, can be computed to be:

p(Wind | Winter) = .5181320
p(Rain | Winter) = .0155441
p(Snow | Winter) = .4663240

Listing 2-4 is a short program which implements the more complex version of Baye's Theorem.

Counting Rules

The following principles help define many use-

Listing 2-3. Simple Baye's Theorem.

```
1 '**********************************************
2 '*                 Listing 2-3                *
3 '*              Bayes' Theorem                *
4 '**********************************************
5 '
10 CLS:KEY OFF:PRINT"Simple Bayes' Theorem":PRIN
T
20 INPUT"NAME OF EVENT # 1";N1$
30 PRINT"PROBABILITY OF ";N1$," (5%=5)",:INPUT A
:PA=A/100:QA=1-PA
40 INPUT"NAME OF RELATED EVENT # 2";N2$
50 PRINT"PROBABILITY OF ";N2$;" GIVEN ";N1$,"(5%
=5)",:INPUT B:PB=B/100
60 PRINT"PROBABILITY OF ";N2$;" GIVEN NOT ";N1$,
"(5%=5)",:INPUT C:QB=C/100
70 AB=(PB*PA)/((PB*PA)+(QB*QA)):PRINT
80 PRINT"THE PROBABILITY OF ";N2$;" GIVEN ";N1$;
" IS = ";AB
90 PRINT:PRINT"(A)nother Set          (M)ain M
enu "
100 Q$=""+INKEY$:IF Q$="" THEN 100
110 IF Q$="A" OR Q$= "a" THEN RUN 10
120 RUN "A:MENU"
```

Listing 2-4. Complex Baye's Theorem.

```
1 '**********************************************
2 '*                 Listing 2-4                *
3 '*           Complex Bayes' Theorem           *
4 '**********************************************
5 '
10 CLS
20 INPUT"NAME OF PRIMARY EVENT";A$
30 PRINT"NUMBER OF EVENTS/CONDITIONS RELATED TO
";A$,:INPUT N
40 DIM E$(N),E(N),AE(N):PE=0
50 FOR I=1 TO N
60    PRINT"NAME OF EVENT/CONDITION #";I,:INPUT E
$(I)
70    PRINT"PROBABILITY OF ";E$(I),"(5%=5)",:INPU
T E:E(I)=E/100
80    PRINT"PROBABILITY OF ";A$;" GIVEN ";E$(I),"
(5%=5)",:INPUT P
90    AE(I)=P/100:PE=PE+(E(I)*AE(I))
100 NEXT I
110 CLS
120 PRINT"B = ";A$
130 PRINT"ITEM","NAME   (A)","P(A)","P(A GIVEN B)
"
140 FOR I=1 TO N:PRINT I,E$(I),E(I),(E(I)*AE(I))
/PE:NEXT:PRINT
150 PRINT"(A)nother set     (M)ain menu "
160 Q$=""+INKEY$:IF Q$="" THEN 160
170 IF Q$="A" OR Q$="a" THEN 10
180 RUN "A:MENU"
```

ful probabilistic characteristics:

K = number of possible outcomes in a single trial (in a normal cube die, K = 6)

N = number of trials

K^N = total possible sequences of outcomes

A coin toss has two outcomes: heads or tails. If we are to toss a coin five times (N = 5), there are 2^5 or 32 possible sequences. Even with just three flips there are 2^3 or 8 possible outcomes. HHH, HHT, HTH, THH, HTT, THT, TTH, TTT. This concept leads us into the notions of *combination and permutations*.

If you have three objects, it can be shown there are six ways, or permutations, that these objects can be arranged in a line: ABC, BAC, BCA, CAB, CBA. The general formula to determine the number of permutations given N objects is:

C = N! (read "N factorial")

$$N! = 1 \times 2 \times 3 \times 4 \ldots \times N-1$$

This gives us the number of different ways N number of objects can be arranged using all N objects. Frequently, however, we are faced with situations in which we want to know the number of combinations possible using only R number of the N objects at a time. For example, a car dealer has ten cars in stock, but only room for three of the cars to be displayed in the showroom. How many different combinations does the salesman have to consider? The notation used to solve this sort of problem is:

$$P\left(\frac{N}{R}\right) = \frac{N!}{(N-R)!}$$

Therefore:

$$P\left(\frac{10}{3}\right) = \frac{10!}{(10-3)!} = \frac{10!}{7!} = \frac{3628800}{5040} = 720$$

The only problem with this computation is that it includes reflections of combinations. That is, it counts the combination of ABC as different from BAC. In trying to determine the number of arrangements of three cars this is not a meaningful count, unless the dealer is also trying to determine the number of ways each combination could be arranged. There is one more equation to help sort out the combinations:

$$C\left(\frac{N}{R}\right) = \frac{N!}{R!(N-R)!}$$

Using this equation:

$$C\left(\frac{10}{3}\right) = \frac{10!}{3!(10-3)!} = \frac{3628800}{6 \times 5040} = \frac{3628800}{30240} = 120$$

That makes the selection process a lot easier—only 120 different combinations have to be evaluated for sales effect. Having made the selection of what three cars to use, there only remains the task of picking which of the six (N!) lineups are the most effective.

From time to time it might be useful or interesting to know what the total number of combinations of objects is possible taking one at a time, two at a time, three at a time, and so on, to N at a time. For example:

| | N = 4 | | | N = 5 | |
R	P	C	R	P	C
1	4	4	1	5	5
2	12	6	2	20	10
3	24	4	3	60	10
4	24	1	4	120	5
			5	120	1
Total	64	15		325	31

On examination we find that the sum of all possible permutations (P), given N, is $\quad P = \sum\limits_{R=1}^{N}$

$C\left(\frac{N}{R}\right)$; and the sum of all possible combinations is $\sum C = 2^{N-1}$. Therefore, the car salesman has 1023

unique ways to display the ten cars ($2^{10} - 1 = 1024 - 1 = 1023$).

Listing 2-5 is a short routine used to do the various computations to determine the permutations and combinations of numbers less than 34. A number equal to or greater than 34 will cause most 8-bit systems to overflow. If normal use of such a program would involve numbers of N larger than 33, the basic factorial lines can be amended to use logarithms. For example:

N < 34
```
100 N!=1
110 FOR I=1 TO N
120 N!=N!*I
130 NEXT
140 R!=1
150 FOR I=1 TO(N-R)
160 R!R=R!*I
170 NEXT
180 P=N!/R!
190 PRINT"PERMUTATIONS=";P
200 END
```
33 > N
```
100 N!=0
110 FOR I=1 TO N
120 N!=N!+LOG(I)
130 NEXT
140 R!=0
150 FOR I=1 TO (N-R)
160 R!=R!+LOG(I)
170 NEXT
180 P=N!-R!
190 IF P 87.3366 THEN 210
200 PRINT"LOG OF
    PERMUTATIONS=";P:END
210 PRINT"PERMUTATIONS=";ESP(P);
    END
```

Probabilities and Permutations

By combining the various principles just presented, a very useful relationship can be demonstrated. Remember, not too many pages ago we defined the probability of something happening with P and its complement Q where: Q = 1 − P. As an illustration consider this information:

26

Listing 2-5. Combinations and Permutations.

```
1 '************************************************
2 '*                   Listing 2-5                *
3 '*          Combinations and Permutations       *
4 '************************************************
5 '
10 CLS
20 INPUT"ENTER NUMBER OF OBJECTS";N
30 IF N=>34 THEN 250
40 PRINT N;"OBJECTS CAN BE ARRANGED INTO";(2^N)-
1;"UNIQUE AND DIFFERENT SETS"
50 P!=1
60 FOR I=1 TO N
70 P!=P!*I
80 NEXT
90 PRINT:INPUT"HOW MANY OBJECTS ARE TO BE TAKEN
AT A TIME";R
100 P1=1
110 FOR I=1 TO (N-R)
120 P1=P1*I
130 NEXT I
140 PR=1
150 FOR I=1 TO R
160 PR=PR*I
170 NEXT I
180 C1=INT(P!/P1):C2=INT(P!/(PR*P1))
190 PRINT:PRINT"THE NUMBER OF COMBINATIONS WITH
REFLECTIONS =";C1
200 PRINT"THE NUMBER OF UNIQUE COMBINATIONS =";C
2
210 PRINT:PRINT"(A)nother set          (M)ain m
enu   "
220 Q$=""+INKEY$:IF Q$="" THEN 220
230 IF Q$="A" OR Q$="a" THEN 20
240 RUN "A:MENU"
250 PRINT"Sorry, 'N' must be less than 34":PRINT
:GOTO 20
```

P = Probability of a defective item coming off an assembly line = .1 $Q = 1 - .1 = .9$

The supervisor of the assembly line has indicated that a run with forty percent or more defective items will result in a complete shutdown and start-up. We need to compute the probability that we would find two defective items out of five. The general equation to solve this problem is:

$$P_{R,N} = \frac{N!}{R!(N-R)!}(P^R Q^{(n-R)})$$

Solving:

$$P_{2,5} = \frac{5!}{2!(5-2)!}(.1^2 \times .9^{(5-2)})$$

$$= \frac{120}{2 \times 6}(.1^2 \times .9^3)$$

$$= \frac{120}{12}(.01 \times .729 = 10 \times .0729$$

$$= .72900$$

Based on the foregoing, there is a good likelihood that the line will shut down frequently. The recommendation would be to retool the line or otherwise improve their production technique.

The equation above computes the probability of exactly R defective items appearing in N objects. There are two other equations that are also useful:

1. $\displaystyle\sum_{i=R}^{i=N} \frac{N!}{i!(N-i)!}\,(p^i \times Q^{n-i})$

2. $\displaystyle\sum_{i=0}^{=R} \frac{N!}{i!(N-i)!}\,(p^i \times Q^{n-i})$

Probability of at most R defective items out of N. Listing 2-6 is a modification of the program in

Probability of at least R defective items out of N.

Listing 2-6. Combinations and Permutations Modified.

```
1  '**********************************************
2  '*                 Listing 2-6                *
3  '*   Expanded Combinations and Permutations   *
4  '**********************************************
5  '
10 CLS
20 INPUT"ENTER NUMBER OF OBJECTS";N
30 PRINT N;"OBJECTS CAN BE ARRANGED INTO";(2^N)-
1;"UNIQUE AND DIFFERENT SETS"
40 R=0:PRINT:INPUT"HOW MANY OBJECTS ARE TO BE TA
KEN AT A TIME";R
50 IF R>N THEN 40
60 INPUT"WHAT IS THE PROBABILITY OF 'SUCCESS'  (
5%=.05)";P
70 IF P>1 THEN 60 ELSE Q=1-P
80 IF N>33 THEN 250
90 NF=1:FOR I=1 TO N:NF=NF*I:NEXT
100 FOR I=0 TO N
110 X=I:Y=N-I:XF=1:YF=1
120 FOR J=1 TO X:XF=XF*J:NEXT J
130 FOR J=1 TO Y:YF=YF*J:NEXT J
140 PI=(P^I)*(Q^(N-I))
150 PX=(NF/(XF*YF))*PI:IF I>R THEN 180
160 P1=P1+PX:IF I<R THEN 190
170 P2=PX
180 P3=P3+PX
190 NEXT
200 PRINT:PRINT"THE PROBABILITY OF....":PRINT
210 PRINT"     EXACTLY   ";R;"SUCCESSES IN";N;"TR
IALS IS";P2
220 PRINT"     AT LEAST ";R;"SUCCESSES IN";N;"TR
IALS IS";P3
230 PRINT"     AT MOST  ";R;"SUCCESSES IN";N;"TR
IALS IS";P1
240 PRINT:PRINT:RUN 20
250 NF=0:FOR I=1 TO N:NF=NF+LOG(I):NEXT
260 FOR I=0 TO N
270 X=I:Y=N-I:XF=0:YF=0
280 FOR J=1 TO X:XF=XF+LOG(J):NEXT J
290 FOR J=1 TO Y:YF=YF+LOG(J):NEXT J
300 PI=(P^I)*(Q^(N-I))
310 PX=EXP(NF-(XF+YF))*PI:IF I>R THEN 340
320 P1=P1+PX:IF I<R THEN 350
330 P2=PX
340 P3=P3+PX
350 NEXT
360 GOTO 200
```

Listing 2-5 that includes these computations. It includes a check for numbers larger than 33, which sends the computations into a logarithmic process if N is greater than 33.

Probability and Forecasting

A forecast is an estimate of some future condition. A probability is an estimate of the likelihood of that forecast being true. As we have just observed, however, there are several ways to view that forecast and probability. Given a forecast, we should ask whether the estimate is "at least," "at most," or "exactly." It is incumbent upon a responsible forecaster to make these aspects clear to the consumer of the information.

EXERCISES

1. Give two examples each of nominal, ordinal, interval, and ratio scales.
2. Given the following data, $x_1 = 23, x_2 = 45, x_3 = 32, x_4 = 123, x_5 = 43, x_6 = 56, x_7 = 98, x_8 = 67, x_9 = 78$, compute the correct value of $\sum x \sum x^2$.
3. Collect the ages of thirty to fifty friends or classmates. Tally these data and identify appropriate class intervals.
4. Using the data collected for exercise 3, compute the mean and standard deviation of the data. Using the third standard deviation as the limit, define significantly "younger," and "older" ages.
5. Discuss kurtosis and skew and their utility in describing distributions.

SUGGESTED READING

Arkin, H., and R. R., Colton, 1970. *Statistical Methods.* New York: Barnes & Noble, Inc.

Bruning, J. L. and B. L., Kintz, 1968. *Computational Handbook of Statistics.* Glenview, IL: Scott, Foresman Company.

Byrkit, D. R., 1972. *Elements of Statistics.* New York: Van Nostrand Reinhold Company.

Minium, E. W., 1970. *Statistical Reasoning in Psychology and Education.* New York: John Wiley & Sons, Inc.

Chapter 3

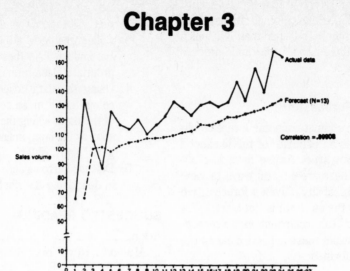

Database Management

This chapter has two objectives or levels of interest: how to manage data in the development of a program and how to manage data in the operation of a program. The nature of higher-language operation, especially interpretative languages such as BASIC, make it very easy to program directly on the computer as opposed to the older procedure of coding the program on paper and then keying the program into the computer for compiling and subsequent operation. During this period of program building and debugging, we are more interested in getting the program to work than we are in processing large amounts of data. Accordingly, we only need to enter a minimal amount to get all of the subroutines checked out. Only when the program is completed do we really need to approach the large database. At the same time, we must develop a clear notion of the types of data processing we are going to require as these will influence the structure of the database and aspects of the program. The conceptual processing is done in the stages shown in Fig. 3-1.

The task begins when the programmer perceives a need to write or create a program. The first step is to conceptually describe the output of the program and decide what kind of data are required to be input to the program to generate the desired output. Are these the types of data that remain static and well-defined, or do they vary with each use of the program? For example, in Chapter 12, we have an extensive program to compute the positions of the planets in the solar system for any given date. We depend upon a number of numerical constants that can be placed in a database, as well as the desired data which is user-supplied. Therefore, we create a database of the unchanging data and supply an input routine for the rest of the data. If we decide the nature of the program is such that no database is required, we go directly to the building, debugging, and operating of the program. During the building process, however, we may want to create a small database to help in the debugging. This application is discussed in the section on program building.

To users of personal or microcomputers, the term "database management" (DBM) has taken on a new and radically different meaning in the last five

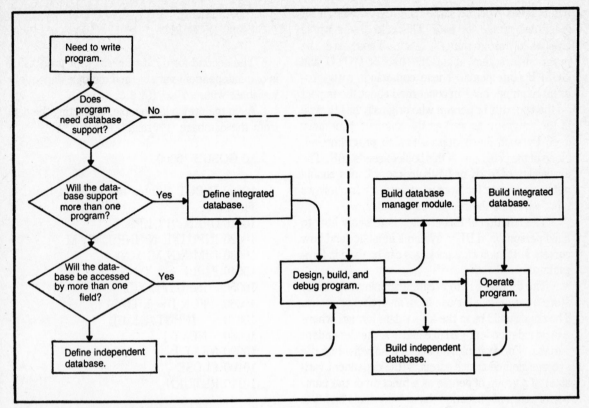

Fig. 3-1. Program development flowchart.

years. Originally, DBM meant either an approach to storing and processing data in terms meaningful only to large mainframe system users, or a totally different approach, in which the microcomputer stored data for retrieval and processing in basic programs. Indeed, an earlier edition of this text dealt with this very problem. Comprehensive texts on DBM offered routines and solutions significant to systems beginning with "IBM" (at the time, a non-player in microcomputers) or "VAX." Users of 16K systems, apparently (judging from the literature available), had little need for DBM. Our position then and now is quite the opposite. The smaller the available memory, the greater the need for DBM. If all relevant data cannot be held in active memory, it must be stored off-line, in a database.

Several hundred programs are currently available for microcomputers that fall under the heading "Database Management." *Lotus 1-2-3* © and Ashton-Tate's *dBase III PLUS* © are notable ex-

amples. These programs are extraordinarily powerful in the execution of their primary tasks and functions, but have limited utility within the context and limits of this text. Although better DBM programs can be programmed using macro instructions, it is often more efficient to write a DBM routine in BASIC then to prepare a similar routine within *dBase III PLUS*, for example.

In this text I presume the user is faced with a set of data consisting of *n* items of independent data point values and *n* items of M different dependent variables. The task is to select one of the techniques discussed in this book and process the data within the protocol of the selected technique. First write a short DBM routine in which to tuck these data away. Then write a processing routine to call up the stored data for processing. This will be much easier than writing a processing routine and typing in the data each time the program is run.

The foregoing highlights a basic rule of programming: never type the same thing twice, whether it is a command-set or data. This rule drives whole families of programmers crazy. These are the programmers that abhor the use of GOTO and GOSUB statements. These commands slow program run time, but I'm concerned about the impact on the operator or person who originally has to type in the program, as well as the amount of memory used by such linear approaches to programming. None of the programs in this book exceeds 16K. The availability of 512K or 640K memory banks should not be an excuse for large programs. "Form follows function," not the resources available.

The function of this chapter is to show how to build personalized DBM systems in BASIC, and how current DBM software packages can be used in forecasting.

The first task is to create a simple program to store a set of data for use in an analytical program. The data should be in the X – Y data format, where X is an independent variable and Y is the dependent variable. For example, a table of data reflecting the average lifetime annual earnings (the dependent variable) of a group of people as a function of the number of years of education those individuals had (the independent variable). Having written the program (see Listing 3-1), the process is fairly straightforward:

1. Collect the data to be filed.
2. Enter the data as called for in the program.

Getting the data out of the database is even easier. Into whatever program you are using to process the data, place these lines:

```
10 GOSUB 10000
. . . .
10000 INPUT "Enter the name of the data
file";F$
10010 OPEN "I",1,F$
10020 INPUT#1, N
10030 DIM X(N),Y(N)
10040 FOR I = 1 TO N
10050    INPUT#1, X(I):INPUT#1, Y(I)
10060 NEXT I
```

```
10070 CLOSE
10080 RETURN
```

The second form data can take for processing is one independent variable and multiple dependent variables where $Y' = f(A,B,C, \ldots n)$.

As in the previous example, extracting the data from the database is straightforward:

```
10 GOSUB 10000
. . . .
10000 INPUT "Enter the name of the data
file"F$
10010 OPEN "I",1,F$
10020 INPUT#1, N: INPUT#1, M
10030 DIM X(N,M),Y(N)
10040 FOR I = 1 TO N
10050    INPUT#1, Y(I)
10060    FOR J = 1 TO M
10070       INPUT#1,X(I,J)
10080    NEXT J
10090 NEXT I
10100 CLOSE
10110 RETURN
```

If we decide a database is desirable for the regular operation of the program, we should ask whether we have or will have other programs that can use the same kind of data. We may have only one application for astronomical data, but several applications for stock market data. Even if the decision is that there is only one program in which the database will be used, we still should ask whether or not the program subroutines would call upon different aspects of the data. If the database can support two or more programs or if the database can be accessed by more than one subroutine, each one calling for different aspects of the data, an integrated database should be defined; otherwise a file-type database is sufficient. In either event, the database should be defined adequately so that the program will call the same type of variables (integer, string, double precision, etc.), that are in the database, and so that the database will be ready to deliver the types of data required. Definition of the database at this stage is also useful in determining whether or not to em-

Listing 3-1. Data File Manager (Build).

```
1 '**********************************************
2 '*                 Listing 3-1                *
3 '*          Data File Manager (Build)         *
4 '**********************************************
5 '
10 CLS:CLEAR 500:PRINT"DATA FILE MANAGER   (CONST
RUCT)":PRINT:PRINT
20 INPUT"WHAT WILL BE THE FILE NAME";N$
30 INPUT"ENTER BEGINNING YEAR";Y1:INPUT"ENDING Y
EAR";Y2
40 PRINT:PRINT"A  --   ANNUAL":PRINT"B  --   SEMI-
ANNUAL":PRINT"C  --   QUARTERLY":PRINT"D  --   MON
THLY":PRINT"E  --   WEEKLY":PRINT"F  --   DAILY":P
RINT"SELECT PERIOD   ";
50 GOSUB 380:P$=Q$
60 PRINT:INPUT"NUMBER OF COLUMNS FOR EACH ENTRY"
;C:DIM F$(C)
70 FOR I=1 TO C
80 PRINT"WHAT IS THE HEADING FOR COLUMN #";I,:IN
PUT F$(I)
90 NEXT
100 IF P$="A" THEN P=1 ELSE IF P$="B" THEN P=2 E
LSE IF P$="C" THEN P=4 ELSE IF P$="D" THEN P=12
ELSE IF P$="E" THEN P=52 ELSE IF P$="F" THEN P=3
65
110 M=C*(P*((Y2-Y1)+1))
120 DIM M(M)
130 FOR I=1 TO M STEP C
140 FOR J=1 TO C
150 PRINT F$(J)
160 PRINT"ENTER VALUE, PERIOD";INT(I/C)+1;", COL
UMN ";J,:INPUT M(I+J-1)
170 NEXT J
180 NEXT I
190 CLS:FOR I=1 TO M:PRINT I;M(I),:NEXT
200 PRINT:PRINT"ALL DATA CORRECT?   (Y/N)   ";:GOS
UB 380
210 IF Q$="Y" THEN 230
220 INPUT"ENTER ITEM NUMBER AND CORRECT VALUE";I
,M(I):GOTO 190
230 OPEN "O",1,N$
240 PRINT#1,N$
250 PRINT#1,Y1,Y2,C
260 FOR I=1 TO C
270 PRINT#1,F$(I)
280 NEXT I
290 PRINT#1,M
300 FOR I=1 TO M STEP C
310 FOR J=1 TO C
320 PRINT#1,M(I+J-1)
330 NEXT:NEXT
340 CLOSE #1
350 PRINT:PRINT"(A)nother          (M)ain Menu ";:GO
SUB 380
360 IF Q$="A" OR Q$="a" THEN RUN 10
```

·Listing 3-1. Data File Manager (Build). (Continued From Page 33.)

```
370 RUN "A:MENU"
380 Q$=""+INKEY$:IF Q$="" THEN 380
390 IF ASC(Q$)>96 THEN Q$=CHR$(ASC(Q$)-32)
400 PRINT Q$:RETURN
```

bed the database in the program itself as data statements or to use external data storage. The number of string variables in the database will influence the need to use the clear in command in the program.

The next step is to build the program and debug it. Later in this chapter you will find a short section on program building and debugging, which includes several approaches to interim databases.

Once the program is constructed, the master database, if required, is built. In the case of a multiple-program, integrated database, you will also need to build the database manager module. Each of these aspects will be covered in greater detail.

DATABASE TYPES

For our purposes, we will divide databases into two basic types: *independent* and *integrated*. These two forms are illustrated in Fig. 3-2.

Using the astronomical example, independent database #1 could hold all of the ephemeral data related to each planet's motion around the sun, while independent database #2 could hold all of the data related to each planet's physical constitution, such as mass, mean temperature, atmospheric chemistry, and so forth, as well as the number of satellites and the physical aspects of them. Given the task of preparing a report on the physical aspects of each

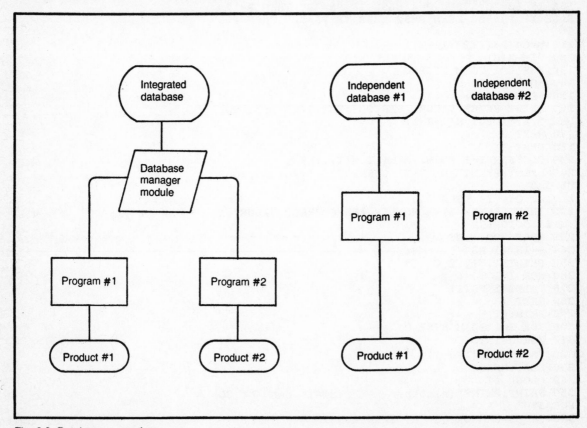

Fig. 3-2. Database comparison.

planetary system, you would have to go to program #2 for the physical data and then to program #1 for orbital computations. Conversely, given the task of doing a very precise computation of a planet's orbit, you must include the influence of the planet's satellites, obtained from database #2 and reentered into program #1. Alternatively, the data concerning the satellites would have to be held in both databases. A simpler solution might be to create an integrated database containing all the relevant data. While larger than either of the independent databases, it would be smaller than the sum of the two.

Management Module

In larger computing systems, the database management module is a separate program or computing system that our own terminal would address for assistance in obtaining the required information.

In microcomputer systems, we refer to this manager as a module, meaning that it is a subroutine normally built into each program using the common database. Listing 3-1 is an example of such a module. It standardizes the format in which the data is read from the database and the procedures used to modify the database. Every program using the master data file uses this module as written. Knowing this, the user can use a separate database management program to update the file by adding to, subtracting or deleting from, or changing the entries without having to load and use one of the operating programs. Listing 3-2 is an example of the external database manager/housecleaning program. In programs in which the data are contained within data statements, the external maintenance routine is inappropriate and would have to be built into the main program.

Listing 3-2. Data File Manager (Examine).

```
1  '***********************************************
2  '*                Listing 3-2                  *
3  '*          Data File Manager (Examine)        *
4  '***********************************************
5  '
10 CLS:CLEAR:PRINT "DATA FILE MANAGER  (EXAMINE)
":PRINT:PRINT
20 INPUT"WHAT WILL BE THE FILE NAME";B$
30 OPEN "I",1,B$
40 INPUT#1,N$
50 INPUT#1,Y1,Y2,C:DIM F$(C)
60 FOR I=1 TO C
70 INPUT#1,F$(I)
80 NEXT I
90 INPUT#1,M:DIM M(M)
100 FOR I=1 TO M STEP C
110 FOR J=1 TO C
120 INPUT#1,M(I+J-1)
130 NEXT:NEXT
140 CLOSE #1
150 PRINT
160 PRINT"PERIOD",
170 FOR I=1 TO C
180 PRINT F$(I),
190 NEXT I
200 PRINT
210 FOR I=1 TO M STEP C
220 PRINT INT(I/C)+1,
230 FOR J=1 TO C
240 PRINT M(I+J-1),
250 NEXT J
260 PRINT
```

Listing 3-2. Data File Manager (Examine). (Continued From Page 35.)

```
270 NEXT I
280 PRINT:PRINT"DATA OK?   (Y/N)   ";:GOSUB 470
290 IF Q$="Y" THEN 320
300 CLS:FOR I=1 TO M:PRINT I;M(I),:NEXT:PRINT
310 PRINT:INPUT"ENTER ITEM NUMBER AND CORRECT VA
LUE";X,M(X):GOTO 280
320 OPEN "O",1,B$
330 PRINT#1,N$
340 PRINT#1,Y1,Y2,C
350 FOR I=1 TO C
360 PRINT#1,F$(I)
370 NEXT I
380 PRINT#1,M
390 FOR I=1 TO M STEP C
400 FOR J=1 TO C
410 PRINT#1,M(I+J-1)
420 NEXT:NEXT
430 CLOSE #1
440 PRINT:PRINT"(A)nother            (M)ain Menu ";
:GOSUB 470
450 IF Q$="A" THEN RUN 10
460 RUN "A:MENU"
470 Q$=""+INKEY$:IF Q$="" THEN 470
480 IF ASC(Q$)>96 THEN Q$=CHR$(ASC(Q$)-32)
490 PRINT Q$:RETURN
```

Data Arrays

Data may be entered into the file in a free form tied to a primary key only by sequence or may be coded to show a relationship to the primary or secondary keys. For example, we may enter the planetary data in a specified sequence: name, motion 1, motion 2, size, distance, and so on. If we make a mistake or want to process another portion of the data, we have to reenter the data in the same sequence until we find what we are looking for. On the other hand, we can create arrays that are called up by key numbers. We can create a set of single dimension arrays, one for each planet. For example, $N\$(I)$ is the planet's name, $M1(I)$ is the planet's motion 1, $M2(I)$ is motion 2, $S(I)$ is the planet's size, and $D(I)$ is the planet's distance. By arbitrarily numbering each planet 1 through 9 in any sequence—largest to smallest, nearest to the sun to the farthest from the sun, or whatever—we can call up any of the desired elements. Alternatively, we can create a two-dimensional array, $V\$(I,J)$, in which I is the planet's number, as above, and J is the variable identifier. As we obtain knowledge of other planetary systems around other stars, we could create a three-dimensional array, $V\$(I,J,K)$, in which K identifies the particular stellar system. The numerical values would be read first as strings and then converted to mathematical properties by using the $V = VAL$ $(V\$(I,J,K))$ command structure.

PROGRAM BUILDING

This book really doesn't presume to be a text on the finer points of computer programming techniques, but a few words on how the programs in this book were developed may be of some use to the less-experienced programmer. The principles noted here were arrived at pragmatically and are recommended on that basis; that is, we recommend them because they work.

Top Down Programming

Programs are solutions to computational or data manipulation problems or tasks. In the old days of computer programming, the first several periods of activity were consumed by conceptual and graphic analysis and flowcharting of the problem and the program. Sections of the program were written to solve subsets of the problem and were painstakingly hand-encoded and toggle-switched number by number into the computer. The operation of the computer itself was very fast, once the program was written and installed. The time to complete the program, on the other hand, was so time-consuming that it was undertaken only for the most serious of purposes.

BASIC, and a number of other higher languages, however, have made light work of many programming tasks. The penalty we pay for the ease of programming is loss of speed of operation. Using interpretive languages forces the computer to take precious computing time to translate each instruction into a form it really understands. Unfortunately, we are easily lulled into inefficient programming habits by the friendliness of the language. The nature of BASIC encourages us to use a technique known as *top down* programming. This technique works pretty much like it sounds. We start at the top of the program (line 10) with the beginning of the solution to the problem. As we go from the top of the program down to the end we can trace the flow of the solution to the problem. Some programmers place data statements in the program at the point in the processing where the data is required. To the extent the problem and its solution are straightforward and noniterative, this is as acceptable an approach as any. When we begin to move into complex programs calling for subroutines (using GOSUB commands) and other complex operations, top down programming loses some of its utility. Computers operating in BASIC begin at the first line number and work their way through the program listing as you would read a book: from the top left, to bottom right. Whenever you use a GOTO statement, the computer goes to the first line number and then counts down until it finds the indicated line number. If we are at line 2350 and use GOTO 2380, the computer will not jump ahead three lines, but will go to line 10 and then read 238 lines until it reaches line 2380. Even though it doesn't execute the instructions, the computer must take time to recognize the line number and check it to see if the destination has been reached. The same process

is undertaken with even worse consequences when a GOSUB command is used. Not only does the computer go to the top of the program to start hunting for the indicated line, but it has to remember where it came from. When it completes the subroutine, it has to go to the top of the program and start hunting for the instruction immediately following the GOSUB instruction. To demonstrate this effect, take the longest program you have and load it into your computer. Assuming your program begins at line number 10 and ends before line number 60000, add this routine to your program:

```
1   GOTO 60000
2   PRINT"SUBROUTINE TIME TEST".
3   RETURN
. . . . .
60000 GOSUB 2
60010 I=I+1
60020 IF I=1000 THEN 60000
60030 STOP
```

Run your new program! It is doing the six instructions you've just added. Time the execution of the 1000 iterations. Now, delete all the lines of the program except for the six lines above. Run the program and time the execution. Subtract the time of the second run from the time of the first run. Divide the difference by the number of lines in the original program plus one. The result is the time each line of a program adds when the computer is told to go on a GOSUB search. The way to speed up the operation of your computer, then, is to put the subroutine(s) at the head of the program. The first line of the program is a GOTO instruction pointing to the first line of the operational program, bypassing the block of subroutines at the head. If you have a number of complex subroutines, try to determine the one most frequently used and sequence the subroutines according to the frequency with which they are used. Having said all that, I must confess that a number of the programs in this book place subroutines where they logically appear in the process. This is not because I don't believe what I say, but because I have balanced the cost of the time lost in the operation of the program against the desire to present a readable program. The time consumed by GOSUBs becomes most critical in executing graphics-intensive programs in which you want to create or manipulate an image rapidly. It can be very frustrating to watch a program compute a point, search through 200 lines, set the point, search back through 250 lines, compute the next point, and so forth. In this instance, optimum placement of both the computation and the setting components is very desirable.

Whether you use top down or some other approach to programming, I recommend that you decide early on what your data requirements are going to be (Fig. 3-1). Even if your program will ultimately not use database information, you may want to create a line or two of data statements containing the type of data (and in the proper format) that the program will ask the user for when operational. In the example, you will need to know the user's day, month, and year of birth. You may also want to use the exact time of birth. It is a lot easier to debug the program and tidy up the displays if you don't have to take the time to reenter these data each time you run the program. The way to do this is shown below:

```
 9  RESTORE
10  PRINT"BIORHYTHM PROGRAM"
11  READ M,D,Y: PRINT"DATE =",
    M,D,Y
12  GOTO 30
20  INPUT"ENTER  MONTH,  DAY,
    AND YEAR OF BIRTH"M,D,Y
30  . . . . (Compute and display biorhythms
. . . )
. . . .
10000  DATA 5,29,1942
```

When the program is complete and the displays look just the way you want, delete lines 9, 11, 12, and 10000. In a similar fashion, if the program you are writing involves extensive and time-consuming computations followed by a complicated graphic display, you may want to develop the computational part of the program first and then use the computed data as above, skipping the computations, but reading data statements for the input to the graphics section. Alternatively, it may be expedient to let your computer generate a temporary database. For example, let's say you've written a program to analyze several year's worth of temperature data. Rather than constructing an extensive table of data, let the computer build the table for you. At the very beginning and end of the program, add these lines:

```
 9  RANDOM: DIM T(60)
20000  FOR I = 1 TO 60
20010  M = 6.28 * (I/12 − INT(I/12))
20020  T(I) = (40 * SIN(M)) + RND(15) +
       20
20030  NEXT
20040  RETURN
```

This routine generates a series of numbers that range from −35 to +75 along a twelve-month sine wave for a five-year period. You can change the values of the data in line 20030 so that the range more resembles the locality in which you are interested. You can change the period by altering the value in lines 9 and 20010. At the point in the program where you would normally enter the actual data or read the data from data statements, use: XXXX GOSUB 20000. These data will be sufficient to develop and debug the operation of the program and the graphic displays. In the process, it may occur to you that you need data of a different sort or that you can successfully use fewer data elements, etc. In the end, you will have a good idea of the volume and type of data you need to properly run the program without having wasted the time typing in actual data at the beginning.

Program Development

In closing this all-too-brief section on programming techniques, we offer several guidelines that may make the task simpler and the program more enjoyable:

1. Define in words and illustrations exactly what it is that you want as an output.
2. Consider the number of times you need to perform this task (generate the output), and

decide whether or not computer processing or assistance is the quickest, easiest way to go. If not, cease and desist. Do it the easy way.

3. If the computerized way is the optimum way, examine the output required to determine what process and what sort of equations are required to generate that output.

4. As a function of the processing required, determine what sort of input data items are required. Refer to Fig. 3-1. Do you need to build a database? Can you access someone else's database? Follow the program development recommended in the figure.

DATABASES FOR MICROCOMPUTERS

Having decided that your program requires database support, you have two options: build your own database or tap existing databases.

Existing Databases

Massive databases are available on-line that, just five years ago, required mainframe computing systems to access and process. Through services such as DIALOG, CompuServe, The Source, Western Union's "EasyLink," and GE's "GEnie," the user can access a wide variety of data and download desired portions directly into local memory or disk storage for processing at a later time. Users of the DIALOG service are able to format the output of numerical databases into forms directly readable by the popular spreadsheets and database programs such as Lotus 1-2-3 or dBase III PLUS.

Database Construction

Entering data by keyboard is the course of last resort. If there is any way for you to enter data from an electronic source (disk, tape, remote database), do so. If there is a way to enter the data via light pen or bar code reader, use it. Keyboard entry of data has at least two strikes against it: it is tediously time consuming, and it is prone to human error. In the event that it must be done, as will often be the case, I highly recommend you devise a way to avoid doing the task twice. Develop a fairly standardized format and enter the data in such a way that it can be saved on either disk or tape for subsequent use in other programs. When developing the database, be sure to allow for expansion and correction of entries.

DATA FILE ORGANIZATION

The computer industry has developed three basic ways to arrange data files for processing: sequential access method (SAM), indexed sequential access method (ISAM), and direct access method (DAM). The file organizations are pretty well suggested by their names.

The microcomputer industry has adopted this approach to file structure and management, but simplifies the technique a little by retaining the sequential access method but combining the indexed and direct access methods into "random access."

Sequential Access Method

Sequential access data files consist of subfiles or records of variable length. These data are entered and extracted as one long string of data. Random access files are quite structured and each component of a file is structurally identical from record to record. That is, if an address file contains a subcomponent for NAME, the sequential access file space allocated for NAME varies from record to record as the length of each name input requires. In a random access file, each record allows only one specified character length in every file. To extract a specific record from a file, the entire file must be read into the computer—at least until the desired record is located.

Random Access Files

By contrast, the rigid file structure of random access files permits rapid and efficient extraction of desired data without having to sort through the undesired portions of the file. The penalty for this ease of access is disk space and attention to programming detail. To build the file, the user must think carefully about the file structure so just the right amount of space is allocated.

Menu-Based Database Systems

Sometimes the easiest approach to accessing the databases is to offer the user a menu of each portion of the database that can be accessed. The commercial databases, such as the Source, Dow-Jones News Service, or CompuServe, are examples of systems that use a menu to access the subsections. In such systems it is frequently useful to have one or more layers of menus and sub-menus. Figure 3-3 illustrates the concept of a tree of menus.

It is not until the lowest level in a menu branch is reached that the actual database is defined and loaded into the system for reading or processing.

dBASE III PLUS
and Similar Database Programs

Commercially available database management programs, such as dBASE III PLUS, support the use of macro instructions. These are a form of a programming language that gives the programs greater flexibility and utility than exists in the vanilla version of the program present at initial load and start. dBASE III PLUS macros include most, if not all, of the mathematical functions used in the programs in this book, though not all of the graphic display options. Theoretically, it is possible to process data existing in dBASE III PLUS files using macros based on these BASIC programs. As a practical matter, the user might wish to consider whether it is easier to translate the data file into a from usable by the BASIC version of the programs than to prepare the macros necessary to process the data within the database program. The process required is:

1. While in the desired database, create a new data file using the command:

   COPY TO <new filename.DLM> [scope] [FIELDS <field list>] [WHILE <condition>][FOR<condition>] [TYPE DELIMITED]

Example 1:   COPY TO NEWFILE.DLM TYPE DELIMITED

Example 2:   COPY TO NEWFILE.DLM FIELDS STU_NAME, AGE, SEX, TEST1, TEST2, TEST3, FINAL_EXAM TYPE DELIMITED

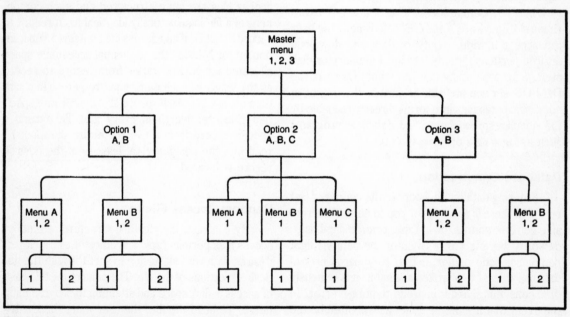

Fig. 3-3. Menu-based database.

Listing 3-3. Delimited Data File Build.

```
1 '*********************************************
2 '*              Listing 3-3              *
3 '*         Delimited Data File Build     *
4 '*********************************************
5 '
10 CLS:CLEAR 500:PRINT"Delimited Data File Build
":PRINT:PRINT
20 INPUT"WHAT WILL BE THE FILE NAME";N$
30 INPUT"ENTER BEGINNING YEAR";Y1:INPUT"ENDING Y
EAR";Y2
40 PRINT:PRINT"A  --   ANNUAL":PRINT"B  --   SEMI-
ANNUAL":PRINT"C  --   QUARTERLY":PRINT"D  --   MON
THLY":PRINT"E  --   WEEKLY":PRINT"F  --   DAILY":P
RINT"SELECT PERIOD   ";
50 GOSUB 330:P$=Q$
60 PRINT:INPUT"NUMBER OF COLUMNS FOR EACH ENTRY"
;C:DIM F$(C)
70 FOR I=1 TO C
80 PRINT"WHAT IS THE HEADING FOR COLUMN #";I,:IN
PUT F$(I)
90 NEXT
100 IF P$="A" THEN P=1 ELSE IF P$="B" THEN P=2 E
LSE IF P$="C" THEN P=4 ELSE IF P$="D" THEN P=12
ELSE IF P$="E" THEN P=52 ELSE IF P$="F" THEN P=3
65
110 M=C*(P*((Y2-Y1)+1))
120 DIM M(M)
130 FOR I=1 TO M STEP C
140 FOR J=1 TO C
150 PRINT F$(J)
160 PRINT"ENTER VALUE, PERIOD";INT(I/C)+1;", COL
UMN ";J,:INPUT M(I+J-1)
170 NEXT J
180 NEXT I
190 CLS:FOR I=1 TO M:PRINT I;M(I),:NEXT
200 PRINT:PRINT"ALL DATA CORRECT?  (Y/N)   ";:GOS
UB 330
210 IF Q$="Y" THEN 230
220 INPUT"ENTER ITEM NUMBER AND CORRECT VALUE";I
,M(I):GOTO 190
230 OPEN "O",1,N$
240 FOR I=1 TO M STEP C
250 FOR J=1 TO C
260    PRINT#1,"#"
270 PRINT#1,M(I+J-1)
280 NEXT:PRINT#1,"#":NEXT
290 CLOSE #1
300 PRINT:PRINT"(A)nother           (M)ain Menu ";:GO
SUB 330
310 IF Q$="A" OR Q$="a" THEN RUN 10
320 RUN "A:MENU"
330 Q$=""+INKEY$:IF Q$="" THEN 330
340 IF ASC(Q$)>96 THEN Q$=CHR$(ASC(Q$)-32)
350 PRINT Q$:RETURN
```

Listing 3-4. Delimited Data File Extract.

```
1 '*************************************************
2 '*                Listing 3-4                    *
3 '*          Delimited Data File Extract          *
4 '*************************************************
5 '
10 CLS:CLEAR 500:PRINT"Delimited Data File Extra
ct":PRINT:PRINT
20 INPUT"WHAT WILL IS THE FILE NAME";N$
30 INPUT"ENTER BEGINNING YEAR";Y1:INPUT"ENDING Y
EAR";Y2
40 PRINT:PRINT"A -- ANNUAL":PRINT"B --  SEMI-
ANNUAL":PRINT"C --  QUARTERLY":PRINT"D --  MON
THLY":PRINT"E --  WEEKLY":PRINT"F --  DAILY":P
RINT"SELECT PERIOD   ";
50 GOSUB 330:P$=Q$
60 PRINT:INPUT"NUMBER OF COLUMNS FOR EACH ENTRY"
;C:DIM F$(C)
70 FOR I=1 TO C
80 PRINT"WHAT IS THE HEADING FOR COLUMN #";I,:IN
PUT F$(I)
90 NEXT
100 IF P$="A" THEN P=1 ELSE IF P$="B" THEN P=2 E
LSE IF P$="C" THEN P=4 ELSE IF P$="D" THEN P=12
ELSE IF P$="E" THEN P=52 ELSE IF P$="F" THEN P=3
65
110 M=C*(P*((Y2-Y1)+1))
120 INPUT "How many items to be entered from the
 file?";N
130 DIM M(M)
140 GOSUB 250
150 FOR I=1 TO M STEP C
160 FOR J=1 TO C
170 PRINT F$(J)
180 PRINT M(I+J-1),
190 NEXT J
200 PRINT""
210 NEXT I
220 PRINT:PRINT"ALL DATA CORRECT?  (Y/N)  ";:GOS
UB 330
230 IF Q$="Y" THEN 360
240 INPUT"ENTER ITEM NUMBER AND CORRECT VALUE";I
,M(I):GOTO 220
250 OPEN "I",1,N$
260 FOR I=1 TO M STEP C
270 FOR J=1 TO C
280    INPUT#1,X$
290    INPUT#1,M(I+J-1)
300 NEXT:INPUT#1,X$:NEXT
310 CLOSE
320 RETURN
330 Q$=""+INKEY$:IF Q$="" THEN 330
340 IF ASC(Q$)>96 THEN Q$=CHR$(ASC(Q$)-32)
350 PRINT Q$:RETURN
360 'use this portion of the program to process
your data.
```

2. Use the program in Listing 3-3 to translate the "delimited" file into the format created in Listing 3-1.
3. Run the applicable processing program.

It is beyond the scope of this text (and, frankly, the skill of this writer) to offer translations of all the programs into all the macro versions currently available in the leading database management systems.

Listing 3-4 enables a reversal of the process; that is, it translates data files created by Listing 3-1 into DELIMITED format files readable by database programs.

Spreadsheets: *Symphony,* and Similar Integrated Programs

A number of the programs in this text can and have been translated into a format that may be used by spreadsheet programs.

Listings of the translated versions follow the BASIC version and are designated as the spreadsheet version. The version used in this text is for *Symphony,* version 1.0. While only *Symphony* users will be able to read the software directly, the logic and syntax is generally consistent with other spreadsheet protocols. Each of the *Symphony* programs has been translated to the DIF format. Other spreadsheet programs offer import or translation routines for this format.

EXERCISES

1. Give three examples of data processing tasks in which independent databases are appropriate.
2. Give three examples of data processing tasks in which integrated databases are appropriate.
3. Develop a program to manage a mailing list using a sequential access method.
4. Develop a menu-based program to manage a database consisting of at least five levels of refinement with at least two alternative options at each level for each superior option (see Fig. 3-3).

SUGGESTED READING

Katzan, H., 1975. *Computer Data Management and Data Base Technology.* New York: Van Nostrand Reinhold Company.
Martin, J., 1975. *Computer Data-Base Organizations.* Englewood Cliffs, NJ: Prentice-Hall.
Sprowles, R.C., 1976. *Management Data Bases.* New York: Wiley/Hamilton.
The National Technical Information Service (NTIS), a division of the U.S. Department of Commerce, 5285 Port Royal Road, Springfield, VA 22161, offers listings of databases.

Chapter 4

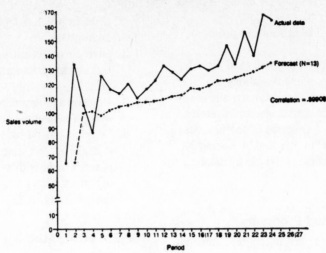

Technique Selections

The basic approach of this book assumes there are four main families of techniques available for use in forecasting efforts: correlation and regression analysis, time-series analysis, modeling and simulations, and numerical techniques. While there are certainly other techniques that have been contrived by mankind over the last several thousand years for looking ahead, some more practical than others, they are not generally suitable for immediate application using microcomputers. Selecting the most appropriate technique for a forecasting effort is at once a simple, straightforward task, and a complex, deceptive effort. Consider Fig. 4-1. This illustrates some hypothetical data generated to cover an extended period of time, say, ten to twenty years.

How do we handle this complex curve from a forecasting perspective? The answer, in this instance, depends on how much of the curve you need to handle at one time. The curve section shown in Fig. 4-2 is taken directly from a segment of Fig. 4-1. If this is all we have to work with, however, we might be induced to assume we could do a forecast from a simple linear regression analysis.

This might work if it were the basis for the data. In reality, the data were generated as the sum of the three curves and one linear trend shown in Fig. 4-3.

In the final analysis, the solution to the problem requires a time-series decomposition approach —not readily evident from the initial data curve. The first task in technique selection, then, is to determine, as best you can, just what the available data represent. The second task is to determine the different components that influence a given data point magnitude. In the data just illustrated, do the points represent sales data? For how many profit centers? What is the product line? How many different customer types constitute the market? Is it a youth fad item or a staple product? Is the region going through any significant population change? What is the prevailing economic environment? The answers to questions such as these are most useful in establishing the analytic parameters of the forecast.

In general, the selection of techniques can be based on the following guidelines. When the data appear to be functionally related to, or a function of,

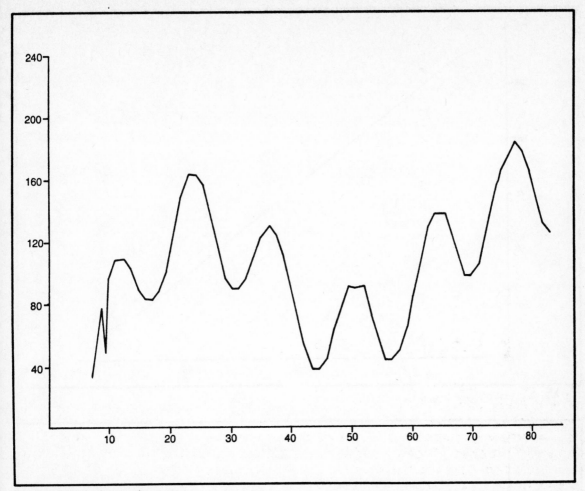

Fig. 4-1. Complex/composite curves.

the passage of time, the forecaster will be inclined to pursue one or another of the time-series routines. When the data are not clearly time-related, the correlation and regression analysis area, often depending upon multivariate regression analysis, should be considered. When the data are too obscure and are derived as the output of a complex process, you may, instead, choose to model or simulate the process itself in an effort to forecast future states by accelerating the flow of information through the model. Alternatively, it might be time and cost effective to exploit standard numerical techniques to build a mathematical model of a process which yields the desired output without duplication of the actual internal process or structure.

The final test of a forecaster's skill is the correlation between the forecast and the outcome, regardless of the method used to produce the forecast. From a scientific point of view, it is most desirable to build a forecast based on a rational basis. That is, if the data are largely a function of time, the technique used should be a time-series approach. If correlation and regression analysis can be used to demonstrate a cause and effect relationship, we probably ought to use one of those techniques.

EXERCISES

1. Give two examples of applications for each of the four basic techniques used in forecasting.

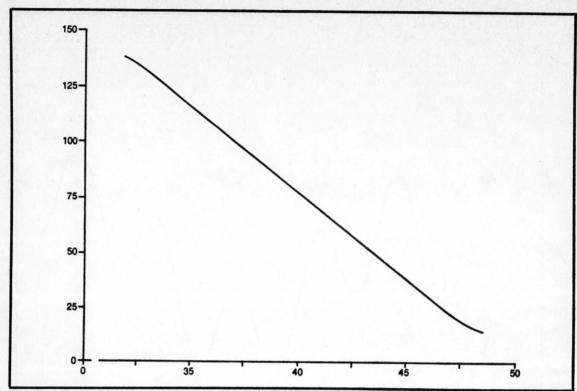

Fig. 4-2. Segment of curve (Fig. 4-1).

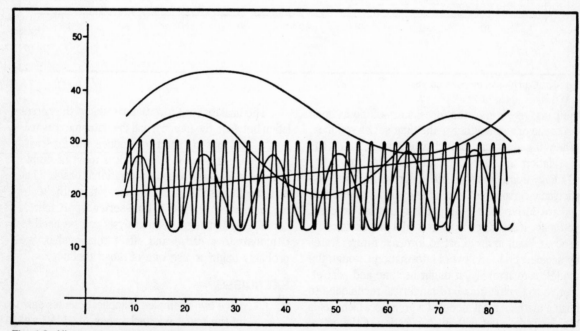

Fig. 4-3. All components of curve (Fig. 4-1).

46

2. Identify the optimum technique for predicting the outcome of a football game.
3. Identify the optimum technique to forecast the outcome of the second half of a season of football games among a league of six or more teams.
4. Define the primary distinction between correlation/regression analysis and time-series forecasting.
5. Research and develop a fifth family or technique for forecasting on a microcomputer.

SUGGESTED READING

Ayers, R. U., 1969, *Technological Forecasting and Long Range Planning*. New York: McGraw-Hill.

Bruning, J. L., and B. L. Kintz, 1968. *Computational Handbook of Statistics*. Glenview, IL: Scott, Foresman Company.

Edwards, A. L., 1976. *An Introduction to Linear Regression and Correlation*. San Francisco: W. H. Freeman and Company.

Makridakis, S., and S. C., Wheelwright, 1976. *Forecasting Methods & Applications*. New York: John Wiley & Sons.

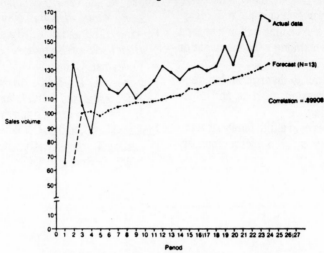

## Chapter 5

Correlation and Regression Analysis

Forecasting is frequently accomplished with the assistance of two statistical operations: correlation and regression analysis. For example, after some research the administrators of a school system have determined that there is a reliable relationship, or correlation, between the current population of the city and the number of students enrolled. Since the operating costs of the school (salaries, supplies, utilities) are all functions of the number of students, a forecast of the number of students will provide the data necessary for proper funding projections. If the board can project an accurate forecast of the city population far enough in advance, useful budget forecasts are possible. The relationship between total population and the number of students is a correlation. The estimate of the city population as a function of time is derived (in this example) from regression analysis. Correlations can be computed between two variables (normally an independent and a dependent variable). This procedure leads to a simple correlation. A correlation between a dependent variable and two or more independent variables is called a multiple correlation.

Regression analysis normally leads to the development of an equation that predicts the value of the dependent variable as a function of the independent variable(s). The basic form is $Y = A + BX$. That is, the dependent variable, Y, is the function of a constant, A, and the magnitude of the independent variable, X, multiplied by some coefficient, B. While B can take a fairly complex form, the basic principle remains the same. In very broad terms, regression equations, when plotted, can be said to take either linear or curvilinear form. The linear form is simply a straight line, as illustrated in Fig. 5-1.

Curvilinear regression equations can produce, on the other hand, a wide variety of curves and shapes. Which form to use is determined by the correlation function. The regression equation gives estimates of the dependent variable as a function of the independent. The regression equation that produces the highest correlation between the known or real data and the estimate is the preferred equation.

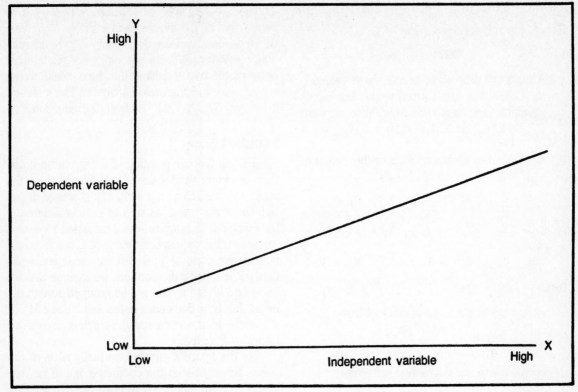

Fig. 5-1. Linear trend form.

This chapter outlines the procedures to compute both simple and multiple correlations and linear and curvilinear equations.

SIMPLE CORRELATION

Table 5-1 lists data in the form of a dependent variable, Y, as a function of the independent variable, X.

The task is to determine the relationship, if any, between the two. An algebraic solution yields the following relationships:

$$Y = A + BX$$

$$B = \frac{\sum (X - \bar{X})(Y - \bar{Y})}{\sum (X - \bar{X})^2} \quad \text{or} \quad B = \frac{XY - NXY}{\sum X^2 - N\bar{X}^2}$$

$$A = \bar{Y} - B\bar{X}$$

where $\bar{X}$ and $\bar{Y}$ are the arithmetic means of X and Y.

The simple computation uses the sum of the product of X and Y, XY. Therefore:

$$B = \frac{\sum XY - N\overline{XY}}{\sum X^2 - N\bar{X}^2} = \frac{1295 - 10 \cdot 5.5 \cdot 19.1}{385 - 10 - 3.25}$$

$$= \frac{244.50}{82.5} = 2.96364$$

Table 5-1. Sample Data.

X	Y
1	6
2	10
3	10
4	13
5	19
6	22
7	23
8	26
9	29
10	33
Sum 55	191
Mean 5.5	19.1

$$A = \overline{Y} - \overline{BX} = 19.1 - 5.5 \cdot 2.96364 \times 2.79998$$

Hence, for any specified value of X:

$$Y = 2.79998 + 2.96364 \text{ X}$$

The formal process to derive these values is:

1. Collect the data related to the dependent and independent variables. These pairs are identified as: X_1,Y_1 ; X_2,Y_2 ; X_3,Y_3 ; . . .; X_N,Y_N.

2. Table the data according to this scheme:

m	X_i	X_i^2	Y_i	Y_i^2	X_iY_i
1	X_1	X_1^2	Y_1	Y_1^2	$X_1 \times Y_1$
2	X_2	X_2^2	Y_2	Y_2^2	$X_2 \times Y_2$
3	X_3	X_3^2	Y_3	Y_3^2	$X_3 \times Y_3$
. . .					
N	X_N	X_N^2	Y_N	Y_N^2	$X_N \times Y_N$
Totals	ΣX_i	ΣX_i^2	ΣY_i	ΣY_i^2	ΣX_iY_i

3. Compute the Beta coefficient from:

$$B = \frac{XY_i - NX_iY_i}{X_i^2 - NX_i^2}$$

4. Compute the Alpha residual from:

$$A = Y_i/N - B\,X_i/N$$

5. Compute the coefficient of correlation (r). The last value computed, r, is formally known as the Pearson product-moment correlation, and is one of the most widely known and used coefficients of correlation. Without subscripts the equation looks a little tidier:

$$r = \frac{X_iY_i - (\Sigma X_i)(\Sigma Y_i)}{\sqrt{[N \Sigma X_i^2 - (\Sigma X_i)^2][N \Sigma Y^2 - (\Sigma Y)^2]}}$$

$$\frac{N\Sigma XY - (\Sigma X)(\Sigma Y)}{\sqrt{[N\Sigma X^2 - (\Sigma X)^2][N\Sigma Y^2 - (\Sigma Y)^2]}}$$

and works just as well.

The coefficient of correlation, properly computed, will fall in the range $-1 < = r < = +1$. A correlation of either -1 or $+1$ means that the regression equation perfectly predicts the dependent variable from the independent. A positive correlation, $0 < r < = +1$, means that as the independent variable increases, the dependent will also increase. A negative correlation, $-1 < = r\,0$, means that as the independent variable increases, the dependent variable decreases. A zero correlation, $r = 0$, means there is no apparent relationship between the two variables. But, how confident can we be about the regression analysis? The standard error and the "t-Test" answer the question.

Standard Error

During the computation of a regression equation we obtain several useful variables such as the mean and median of the data, the standard deviation about the mean, as well as the coefficients of the equation. In practice, the expression $Y' = A + BX$ means that for a specific value of X, we will compute an estimate of Y. Given the mean and standard deviation of a distribution, we assume that we know how all of the data will be grouped around the mean, but how does each estimated value of Y, or Y', relate to the corresponding points in reality? Consider Fig. 5-2.

As the figure illustrates, virtually none of the points actually lie on the computed line of regression. On closer examination, however, we see that they do group about the line of regression in a manner very similar to data grouping about a mean. What we want to compute is a value very similar to the standard deviation that will give us some measure of the accuracy of the estimates. Such a value can be computed and is the "standard error of the estimate." It gives us the capability not only to forecast an estimate, but to specify with some reliability the range within which the estimate will fall. For regression equations, the standard error is computed from the equation:

$$S_{yx} = \sqrt{\sum (Y - Y')^2/N}$$

in which there is an estimate, Y', for each of N points for which there is a known value, Y. This is algebraically equal to the expression: $S_y = S_y \sqrt{1 - R_{xy}^2}$ in which S_y is the standard deviation of Y and R_{xy} is the coefficient correlation between X and Y, a factor easily derived from the computation of the regression equation data. The basic regression program developed in this chapter contains a section to compute the standard error of the estimate.

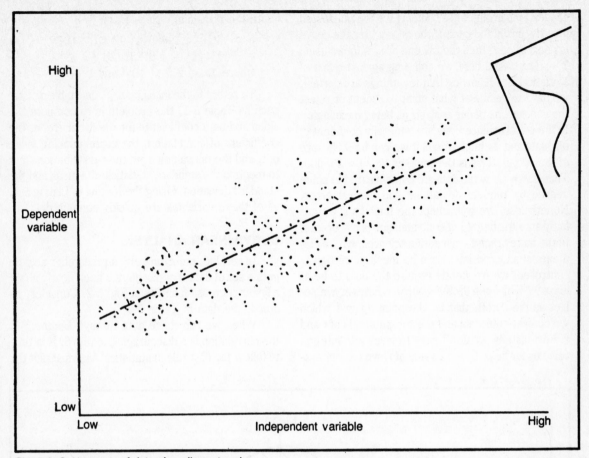

Fig. 5-2. Scattergram of data along linear trend.

t-TEST FOR SIGNIFICANCE

Two sets of data can be found to have the same coefficient of correlation, yet one is more meaningful than the other. How can this be? The difference is a function of sample size. The theory is that a coefficient computed from a sample of a thousand items is more meaningful than that computed from a sample of twenty. The *t-Test* is a measure of the confidence level of a correlation. The value of t is computed from:

$$t = \frac{r \sqrt{N - 2}}{\sqrt{1 - r^2}}$$

where N is the number of items in the sample.

The value of t can be any real number from nearly negative infinity to positive infinity. As r ap-proaches zero, t approaches zero. As r approaches unity, plus or minus, the N grows larger, t approaches infinity, plus or minus. The value thus computed, however, has little immediate meaning, but is used to compute the probability that the coefficient of correlation is significantly free from chance error. Using calculus, the value of t is computed from the integral:

$$I(x,v) = \int_{-x}^{x} \frac{\frac{v + 1}{2} \left(1 + \frac{y^2}{v}\right)^{- \frac{v + 1}{2}}}{\sqrt{\pi v} \frac{v}{2}} \, dy$$

where $x > 0$
and v is the degrees of freedom.

The integral, I(x,v) is represented by the

shaded area in Fig. 5-3. The part we are interested in is the unshaded part. If the area under the curve is equal to one, then the tail end area is found using $1 - I(x,v)$. And here we come up against a fact of statistical life. Knowing that few things are certain, we have to decide at what point to accept or reject the conclusions of our analysis as being meaningful. In the social sciences, we are generally confident of our data and its implications if we can be 95% sure of the output. This is the same as $I(x,v) = .95000$. That is, we know the data are contaminated to some degree by random deviations and clerical error. Nonetheless, we will accept the findings if we are fairly sure the degree of contamination is 5% or less. In the more precise engineering sciences, where elements of an experiment can be much more tightly controlled, we frequently require the data to be at least 99% or even 99.99% pure. Whatever we select as the cutoff, that is, the point against which we compare our data and the computations of r and t. Fortunately, we don't have to wade into integral calculus for help. Given a value of t, we can approx-imate the remaining values from:

$$p = .5(1 + .196854x + .115194x^2 + .000344x^3 + 1.019527x^4)^{-4} + \Sigma$$

where $\Sigma < 2.5 \times 10^{-4}$ and $D = v$.

To return to the initial task: given a table of data, such as Table 5-1, the problem is to compute the alpha and beta coefficients for the linear trend, the coefficient of correlation, the corresponding value of t, and the tail values from the t-distribution—not to mention the standard statistics: the mean and the standard deviation. Using the routine in Listing 5-1, all of these variables are quickly computed.

CURVILINEAR ANALYSIS

In real life, unfortunately, a researcher seldom gets a set of data that distributes itself neatly about a linear regression line as in Fig. 5-2. Consider, instead, the data in Table 5-2.

When we run these data through Listing 5-1, the correlation is a discouraging .648776. It is time to follow the first rule in statistical analysis: plot the

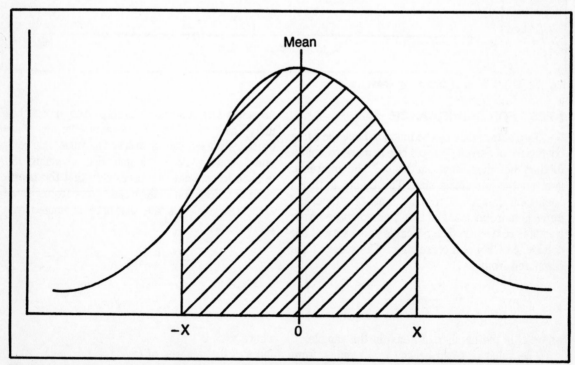

Fig. 5-3. Area under normal curve between +/-x standard deviations.

Listing 5-1. Linear Trend.

```
1 '**********************************************
2 '*                 Listing 5-1                 *
3 '*                Linear Trend                 *
4 '**********************************************
5 '
10 KEY OFF:GOSUB 770
20 PRINT"":PRINT"":INPUT"HOW MANY DATA PAIRS ARE
  THERE";N
30 DIM X(N),Y(N)
40 FOR I=1 TO N
50 PRINT"ENTER PAIR #";I,:INPUT X(I),Y(I)
60 TX=TX+X(I):TY=TY+Y(I):X2=X2+(X(I)^2):Y2=Y2+(Y
(I)^2):XY=XY+(X(I)*Y(I))
70 NEXT
80 MX=TX/N:MY=TY/N
90 SX=SQR((X2-((TX/N)^2))/(N-1)):SY=SQR((Y2-((TY
/N)^2))/(N-1))
100 R=((N*XY)-(TX*TY))/SQR(((N*X2)-(TX^2))*((N*Y
2)-(TY^2)))
110 XE=SX/SQR(N):YE=SY/SQR(N):RE=SY*SQR(1-(R^2))
120 B=(XY-(N*MX*MY))/(X2-(N*(MX^2))):A=MY-(B*MX)
130 PRINT:PRINT"ITEM      SUM          MEAN          S.
D.        S.E."
140 A$=" \  \   #####.##  #####.##  #####.##  ####
#.##"
150 PRINT USING A$;"X";TX;MX;SX;XE:PRINT USING A
$;"Y";TY;MY;SY;YE
160 PRINT"COEFFICIENT OF CORRELATION = ";R
170 PRINT"REGRESSION EQUATION:  Y' = ";
180 IF A<0 THEN 220
190 PRINT A;:IF B<0 THEN 210
200 PRINT"+";
210 PRINT B;"X":GOTO 230
220 PRINT B;"X";A
230 T=(R*SQR(N-2))/SQR(1-(R^2))
240 PRINT"STANDARD ERROR OF REGRESSION = ";RE
250 PRINT"STUDENT'S T OF THIS DISTRIBUTION = ";T
260 V=N-1:X=1:Y=1:T=T^2:D=V:IF T<1 THEN 280
270 S=Y:R=D:Z=T:GOTO 290
280 S=D:R=Y:Z=1/T
290 J=S*.22222:K=R*.22222:L=ABS((1-K)*Z^(1/3)-1+
J)/SQR(K*Z^(2/3)+J):IF R<4 THEN 310
300 X=.5/(1+L*(.196854+L*(.115194+L*(.000344+L*.
019527))))^4:GOTO 320
310 L=L*(1+.08*L^4/R^3):GOTO 300
320 IF T>=1 THEN 340
330 X=1-X
340 PRINT"TAIL VALUE = ";X
350 PRINT"PERCENT WITHIN CURVE =";100*(1-X);" %"
360 PRINT
370 GOTO 860
380 'Data Display
390 SX=0:SY=0:LY=0:LX=0
400 'DETERMINE LARGEST AND SMALLEST VALUES
410 FOR I=1 TO N
420   IF X(I)=>SX THEN 440
```

Listing 5-1. Linear Trend. (Continued From Page 53.)

```
430   SX=X(I):GOTO 460
440   IF X(I)<=LX THEN 460
450   LX=X(I)
460   IF Y(I)=>SY THEN 480
470   SY=Y(I):GOTO 500
480   IF Y(I)<=LY THEN 500
490   LY=Y(I)
500 NEXT I
510 SCREEN SC
520 CLS
530 D=INT(LOG(LX)/2.302585)+1      ' DETERMINE LE
NGTH OF NUMBER
540 XA=INT(.1328*XX):YA=INT(.7875*YY):XB=XX-XA
      ' SET LEFT AND BOTTOM BOUNDARIES
550 RX=LX-SX:RY=LY-SY              ' COMPUTE RANGE
560 LINE(XA,1)-(XA,YA):LINE(XA,YA)-(XX,YA)      '
 DRAW BOUNDARY
570 ' COMPUTE AND DRAW INTERVAL MARKERS
580 FOR I=1 TO 9:LINE(XA-2,(I*(YA/10))-1)-(XA,(I
*(YA/10))-1):NEXT
590 FOR I=1 TO 9:LINE(XA+(I*((XX-XA)/10)-1),YA+2
)-(XA+(I*((XX-XA)/10)-1),YA):NEXT
600 ' COMPUTE AND DRAW ZERO AXIS LINES
610 IF LX=<0 THEN X0=XX ELSE X0=XX-(INT((XX-XA)*
(LX/RX)))
620 IF LY=<0 THEN Y0=1 ELSE Y0=INT(YA*(LY/RY))
630 X1=X0:X2=X1:Y1=1:Y2=YA:LINE (X1,Y1)-(X2,Y2)
640 X1=XA:X2=XX:Y1=Y0:Y2=Y1:LINE (X1,Y1)-(X2,Y2)
650 ' PRINT SCALE VALUES
660 LOCATE 1,(XA/8)-4:PRINT LY;:LOCATE 20,(XA/8)
-4:PRINT SY;:LOCATE 21,(XA/8)-1:PRINT SX;:LOCATE
 21,(XX/8)-(D+2):PRINT INT(LX);:LOCATE (Y0/ZY)+1
,(XA/8)-3):PRINT 0;:LOCATE (YA/ZY)+1,X0/8:PRINT
0;
670 ' DISPLAY LOCATION OF ACTUAL DATA ON SCALE
680 FOR I=1 TO N:X1=XA+INT(XB*((X(I)-SX)/RX))+1:
Y1=INT(YA-(YA*((Y(I)-SY)/RY))):PSET(X1,Y1):NEXT
I
690 'PLOT PROJECTED DATA
700 FOR I=1 TO LX
710   X1=XA+INT(XB*((I-SX)/RX))+1
720   X=I:Y=(B*X)+A
730   Y1=INT(YA-(YA*((Y-SY)/RY)))
740   PSET(X1,Y1)
750 NEXT I
760 LOCATE 24,1:INPUT"Use PrtScrn to save Graph,
 <CR> to Continue";ZZ:GOTO 860
770 CLS
780 PRINT"1  --  320 X 200    2  --  640 X 200
  3  --  640 X 400 "
790 PRINT:PRINT"Indicate screen dimensions ";
800 Q$=""+INKEY$:IF Q$="" THEN 800
810 IF Q$<"1" OR Q$>"3" THEN 800
820 ON VAL(Q$) GOTO 830, 840, 850
830 XX=320:YY=200:SC=1:XL=39:ZY=8:ZX=4:RETURN
840 XX=640:YY=200:XL=39:SC=2:ZY=8:ZX=8:RETURN
```

```
850 XX=640:YY=400:SC=100:XL=79:ZY=16:ZX=8:RETURN
860 PRINT"(A)nother      (G)raph      (M)ain menu
   ";
870 Q$=""+INKEY$:IF Q$="" THEN 870
880 IF Q$="A" OR Q$="a" THEN RUN 10 ELSE IF Q$="
G" OR Q$="g" THEN GOTO 380 ELSE IF Q$="M" OR Q$=
"m" THEN RUN "A:MENU" ELSE GOTO 870
```

data—draw a picture. Figure 5-4 is a picture of the data from Table 5-2.

How can such a neat little line have such a horrible coefficient of correlation? Easy—we used the wrong process. We need a nonlinear process.

Simple, Nonlinear Regression Analysis

Figure 5-5 illustrates standard nonlinear curve functions that can be computed from the routine to compute a linear equation, with only a few additions.

The equations of the curves in the figure are listed below. To the right of each equation is the linear form of the same equation.

Power $Y = A X^B$
Exponential $Y = A e^{BX}$
Logarithmic $Y = A + B \log X$
$\log Y = B \log X + \log A$

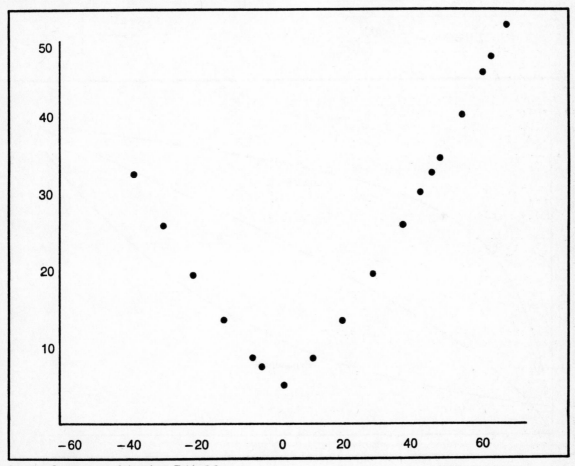

Fig. 5-4. Scattergram of data from Table 5-2.

Table 5-2. Sample Data.

X	Y	X	Y	X	Y	X	Y
− 40	32.980	− 32	26.035	− 24	29.560	− 16	13.669
− 8	8.572	0	5.000	8	8.572	16	12.669
24	19.560	32	26.035	40	32.983	48	40.331
56	48.031	60	52.000	42	34.784	− 6	7.473
54	46.075	37	30.327				

$$\text{Log}_e\, Y = B\,X + \text{Log}_e A$$
same

The regression equations for each of these are:

Power:

$$B = \frac{\Sigma\,(\text{Log}X)\,(\text{Log}\,Y) - \dfrac{(\Sigma\,\text{Log}X)\,(\Sigma\,\text{Log}Y)}{N}}{\Sigma\,(\text{Log}X)^2 - \dfrac{(\Sigma\,\text{Log}X)^2}{N}}$$

$$A = \exp\left[\frac{\Sigma\,\text{Log}Y}{N} - B\,\frac{\Sigma\,\text{Log}X}{N}\right]$$

$$r^2 = \frac{\left[\Sigma(\text{Log}X)\,(\text{Log}Y) - \dfrac{(\Sigma\,\text{Log}X)\,(\Sigma\,\text{Log}Y)}{N}\right]^2}{\left[\Sigma\,(\text{Log }x)^2 - \dfrac{\Sigma\,\text{Log}X)^2}{N}\right]\left[\Sigma\,(\text{Log }Y)^2 - \dfrac{(\Sigma\,\text{Log }Y)^2}{N}\right]}$$

$$r = \sqrt{r^2}$$

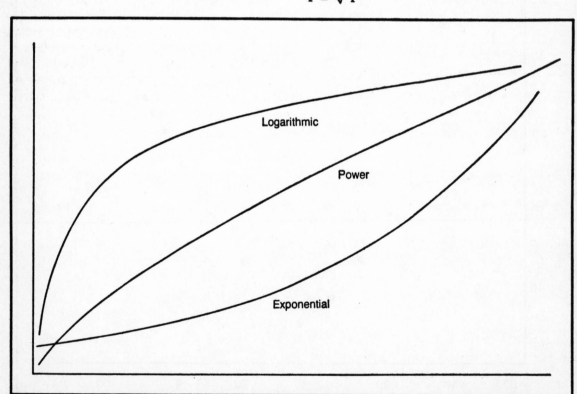

Fig. 5-5. Standard curve forms.

Exponential:

$$B = \frac{\Sigma \, X \, \text{Log} \, Y - \dfrac{1}{N} (\Sigma X)(\Sigma \text{Log} \, Y)}{\Sigma \, X^2 - \dfrac{1}{N}(\Sigma X)^2}$$

$$A = \exp\left[\frac{\Sigma \, \text{Log} \, Y}{N} - B \, \frac{\Sigma X}{N}\right]$$

$$r^2 = \frac{\left[\Sigma \, X \, \text{Log} \, Y - \dfrac{1}{N} \Sigma X \Sigma \text{Log} \, Y\right]^2}{\left[\Sigma X^2 = \dfrac{(X)^2}{N}\right]\left[\Sigma (\text{Log} \, Y)^2 - \dfrac{(\Sigma \text{Log} \, Y)^2}{N}\right]}$$

Logarithmic:

$$B = \frac{\Sigma Y \, \text{Log} \, X = \dfrac{1}{N} \, \text{Log} \, X \, \Sigma \, Y}{\Sigma (\text{Log} \, X)^2 - \dfrac{1}{N} (\Sigma \text{Log} X)^2}$$

$$A = \frac{1}{N}(\Sigma \, Y - B \, \Sigma \, \text{Log} \, X)$$

$$r^2 = \frac{\left[\Sigma \, Y \, \text{Log} \, X - \dfrac{1}{N} \, \Sigma \, \text{Log} \, X \, \Sigma \, Y^2\right]}{\left[\Sigma (\text{Log} \, X)^2 - \dfrac{1}{N} (\Sigma \, \text{Log} \, X)^2\right]\left[\Sigma \, Y^2 - \dfrac{1}{N} (\Sigma Y)^2\right]}$$

Listing 5-2 provides a combination of routines to compute all of the functions in this chapter to this point. After an input routine, the data are verified for accuracy. The program then computes the coefficients for each of the three curvilinear forms above, as well as the coefficients for a standard linear regression. For each equation a coefficient of correlation is computed. The program displays each of the resulting equations and then selects the one for which the correlation is the best. At this point the user is offered the option of computing interpolated points or proceeding to the graphic display of the input data. The graphic display can be directed to a printer if desired.

Although the lines generated by the power, exponential, and logarithmic equations are frequently anything but straight and linear, they are referred to as linear because they are computed from the basic form of the least-squares linear regression equation. They are referred to as simple regressions, in that the dependent variable is a function (we assume) of one independent variable. While the data in Table 5-2, which is graphed in Fig. 5-4, were derived from a single independent variable generating the dependent variable, the computation of the trend line is not based on the foregoing linear regression, but on a form called a *parabolic regression*. The basic equation for this type is:

$$Y = A + BX + CX^2$$

Listing 5-2. Linear Curve Fitting.

```
1 '********************************************
2 '*              Listing 5-2                 *
3 '*          Linear Curve Fitting            *
4 '********************************************
5 '
10 CLEAR 500:CLS:KEY OFF
20 PRINT"******   LINEAR CURVE FITTING   ******"
30 PRINT:PRINT:PRINT"WILL THE LINE PRINTER BE US
ED?  (Y/N)"
40 GOSUB 1630
50 IF Q$="Y" OR Q$="y" THEN LP=1 ELSE LP=0:Q$=""
:PRINT
60 PRINT:PRINT"THIS ROUTINE ACCEPTS THE DATA IN
PAIRED X,Y FORMAT AND ATTEMPTS TO IDENTIFY THE B
EST LINEAR OR CURVE FIT."
70 PRINT:PRINT:INPUT"ENTER NUMBER OF PAIRS:";P:D
IM XY(30),XX(P),YY(P),X(I),Y(I):PRINT
```

Listing 5-2. Linear Curve Fitting. (Continued From Page 57.)

```
80 FOR I=1 TO P:INPUT"ENTER NEW X & Y VALUES:";X
X(I),YY(I):NEXT I
90 CLS:PRINT"# ";"X ";"Y ","# ";"X ";"Y ","# ";"
X ";"Y ","# ";"X ";"Y":FOR I=1 TO P:PRINT I;XX(I
);YY(I),:NEXT I:PRINT
100 PRINT:PRINT"ARE THESE VALUES CORRECT?   (Y/N)
"
110 GOSUB 1630
120 IF Q$="Y" THEN 140
130 INPUT"ENTER ITEM NUMBER, NEW X VALUE, NEW Y
VALUE:";I,XX(I),YY(I):GOTO 100
140 CLS:LOCATE 9,1:PRINT"PLEASE BE PATIENT, COMP
UTING"
150 FOR I=1 TO P
160 ON ERROR GOTO 860
170 X=XX(I):Y=(YY(I)):E(1)=E(1)+(X*Y):E(2)=E(2)+
(X*LOG(Y))
180 IF XX(I)>LX THEN LX=XX(I)
190 E(3)=E(3)+(Y*LOG(X)):E(4)=E(4)+(LOG(X)*LOG(Y
))
200 IF XX(I)<SX THEN SX=XX(I)
210 F(1)=F(1)+X:F(2)=F(1):F(3)=F(3)+LOG(X):F(4)=
F(3)
220 IF YY(I)>LY THEN LY=YY(I)
230 G(1)=G(1)+Y:G(3)=G(1):G(2)=G(2)+LOG(Y):G(4)=
G(2)
240 IF YY(I)<SY THEN SY=YY(I)
250 H(1)=H(1)+X^2:H(2)=H(1):H(3)=H(3)+LOG(X)^2:H
(4)=H(3)
260 I(1)=F(1)^2:I(2)=I(1):I(3)=F(3)^2:I(4)=I(3)
270 J(1)=J(1)+Y^2:J(3)=J(1):J(2)=J(2)+LOG(Y)^2:J
(4)=J(2)
280 K(1)=G(1)^2:K(3)=K(1):K(2)=G(2)^2:K(4)=K(2)
290 LOCATE 11,1:PRINT"I =";I;
300 NEXT I
310 FOR M=1 TO 4
320 B(M)=(E(M)-(F(M)*G(M))/P)/(H(M)-I(M)/P)
330 A(M)=(G(M)-B(M)*F(M))/P
340 R(M)=SQR((E(M)-F(M)*G(M)/P)^2/((H(M)-I(M)/P)
*(J(M)-K(M)/P)))
350 LOCATE 12,1:PRINT"M =";M;
360 NEXT M
370 CLS:PRINT"","A","B","R":PRINT"LINEAR:",A(1),
B(1),R(1):PRINT"EXPONENTIAL:",EXP(A(2)),B(2),R(2
):PRINT"LOGARITHMIC:",A(3),B(3),R(3):PRINT"POWER
:",EXP(A(4)),B(4),R(4):A(4)=EXP(A(4)):A(2)=EXP(A
(2))
380 FOR I=1 TO 6:R(I)=ABS(R(I)):NEXT I
390 IF R(1)>R(2) THEN 430
400 IF R(2)>R(3) THEN 450
410 IF R(3)>R(4) THEN 480
420 M=4:GOTO 490
430 IF R(1)<R(3) THEN 410
440 IF R(1)>R(4) THEN 460 ELSE 420
450 IF R(2)>R(4) THEN 470 ELSE 420
```

```
460 M=1:GOTO 490
470 M=2:GOTO 490
480 M=3
490 PRINT
500 F$(1)="LINEAR":F$(2)="EXPONENTIAL":F$(3)="LO
GARITHMIC":F$(4)="POWER":E$(1)="Y = A + BX":E$(2
)="Y = EXP(LOG A + BX)":E$(3)="Y = A + B LOG X":
E$(4)="Y = EXP(LOG A + B LOG X)"
510 PRINT"THE BEST CURVE FIT IS ";F$(M):PRINT"TH
E EQUATION IS: ";E$(M):PRINT"A =";A(M);"     B =";
B(M);"    R =";R(M):PRINT""
520 IF SX=>0 AND SY=>0 THEN 540
530 ZZ=1:PRINT:PRINT"(DATA INCLUDES NEGATIVE VAL
UES, ONLY THE LINEAR EQUATION ISVALID.   IF ANOTH
ER FORM IS RECOMMENDED, PROGRAM WILL DISREGARD


AND COMPUTE LINEAR.)"
540 PRINT"DO YOU WANT TO COMPUTE A TERM?   (Y/N)
";
550 GOSUB 1630
560 IF Q$="N" THEN GOTO 1100
570 LOCATE 16,1:PRINT"ENTER '@' TO STOP:";
580 LOCATE 9,1:PRINT"WHICH VALUE (X OR Y) WILL B
E ENTERED?";:LOCATE 10,1:PRINT"
  ";
590 GOSUB 1630
600 IF Q$="Y" THEN 650
610 IF Q$="@" THEN 840
620 PRINT:INPUT"ENTER X-VALUE";X
630 ON M GOSUB 680,720,760,800
640 GOTO 670
650 PRINT:INPUT"ENTER Y-VALUE";Y
660 ON M GOSUB 700,740,780,820
670 CLS:LOCATE 7,1:PRINT"X =";X;"      Y =";Y:PRI
NT:GOTO 560
680 Y=A(1)+B(1)*X
690 RETURN
700 X=(Y-(A(1))/B(1)
710 RETURN
720 Y=EXP(LOG(A(2))+B(2)*X)
730 RETURN
740 X=(LOG(Y)-LOG(A(2)))/B(2)
750 RETURN
760 Y=A(3)+B(3)*LOG(X)
770 RETURN
780 X=EXP((Y-A(3))/B(3)
790 RETURN
800 Y=A(4)*(X^B(4))
810 RETURN
820 X=(Y/A(4))^(1/B(4))
830 RETURN
840 GOSUB 1100
850 GOTO 910
860 RESUME NEXT
870 P=N:GOSUB 1070
880 GOTO 910
```

Listing 5-2. Linear Curve Fitting. (Continued From Page 59.)

```
890 END
900 PRINT:PRINT"THANKS FOR USING CURVE FITTING!!
"
910 IF LP<>1 RUN 10
920 LPRINT STRING$(2,10)
930 LPRINT" ":LPRINT"TABLE OF INPUT/OUTPUT VALUE
S":LPRINT" "
940 LPRINT"INPUT":LPRINT"X","Y","X","Y","X","Y",
"X","Y"
950 FOR I=1 TO P:LPRINT XX(I),YY(I),:NEXT I
960 IF RR=2 THEN 1050
970 LPRINT" ":LPRINT"INTERMEDIATE VALUES":LPRINT
"I","E(I)","F(I)","G(I)","H(I)","I(I)","J(I)","K
(I)"
980 FOR I=1 TO 4:LPRINT I,E(I),F(I),G(I),H(I),I(
I),J(I),K(I):TT(I)=(R(I)*SQR(P-2))/SQR(1-(R(I)^2
)):NEXT I
990 LPRINT" ":LPRINT"OUTPUT":LPRINT" ","A","B","
R","t-TEST","EQUATIONS"
1000 LPRINT"LINEAR",A(1),B(1),R(1),TT(1),E$(1)
1010 LPRINT"EXPONENTIAL",A(2),B(2),R(2),TT(2),E$
(2)
1020 LPRINT"LOGARITHMIC",A(3),B(3),R(3),TT(3),E$
(3)
1030 LPRINT"POWER",A(4),B(4),R(4),TT(4),E$(4)
1040 LPRINT STRING$(5,10):CLS:RUN 10
1050 LPRINT STRING$(3,10)
1060 END
1070 GOSUB 1100
1080 END
1090 RESUME NEXT
1100 'DATA DISPLAY
1110 GOSUB 1540:SCREEN SC
1120 SX=0:SY=0:LX=0:LY=0
1130 FOR I=1 TO P
1140    IF XX(I)=>SX THEN 1160
1150    SX=XX(I):GOTO 1180
1160    IF XX(I)<=LX THEN 1180
1170    LX=XX(I)
1180    IF YY(I)=>SY THEN 1200
1190    SY=YY(I):GOTO 1220
1200    IF YY(I)<=LY THEN 1220
1210    LY=YY(I)
1220 NEXT I
1230 CLS
1240 D=INT(LOG(LX)/2.302585)+1         ' DETERMINE L
ENGTH OF NUMBER
1250 XA=INT(.1328*XX):YA=INT(.7875*YY):XB=XX-XA
        ' SET LEFT AND BOTTOM BOUNDARIES
1260 RX=LX-SX:RY=LY-SY                  ' COMPUTE RANG
E
1270 LINE(XA,1)-(XA,YA):LINE(XA,YA)-(XX,YA)
' DRAW BOUNDARY
1280 ' COMPUTE AND DRAW INTERVAL MARKERS
1290 FOR I=1 TO 9:LINE(XA-2,(I*(YA/10))-1)-(XA,((
```

```
I*(YA/10))-1):NEXT
1300 FOR I=1 TO 9:LINE(XA+(I*((XX-XA)/10)-1),YA+
2)-(XA+(I*((XX-XA)/10)-1),YA):NEXT
1310 ' COMPUTE AND DRAW ZERO AXIS LINES
1320 IF LX=<0 THEN X0=XX ELSE X0=XX-(INT((XX-XA)
*(LX/RX)))
1330 IF LY=<0 THEN Y0=1 ELSE Y0=INT(YA*(LY/RY))
1340 X1=X0:X2=X1:Y1=1:Y2=YA:LINE (X1,Y1)-(X2,Y2)
1350 X1=XA:X2=XX:Y1=Y0:Y2=Y1:LINE (X1,Y1)-(X2,Y2
)
1360 ' PRINT SCALE VALUES
1370 LOCATE 1,(XA/8)-4:PRINT LY;:LOCATE 20,(XA/8
)-4:PRINT SY;:LOCATE 21,(XA/8)-1:PRINT SX;:LOCAT
E 21,(XX/8)-(D+2):PRINT INT(LX);:LOCATE (Y0/ZY)+
1,(XA/8)-3):PRINT 0;:LOCATE (YA/ZY)+1,X0/8:PRINT
 0;
1380 ' DISPLAY LOCATION OF ACTUAL DATA ON SCALE
1390 FOR I=1 TO P:X1=XA+INT(XB*((XX(I)-SX)/RX))+
1:Y1=INT(YA-(YA*((YY(I)-SY)/RY))):PSET(X1,Y1):NE
XT I
1400 'PLOT PROJECTED DATA
1410 IF M=1 THEN 1440
1420 IF SX=>0 AND SY=>0 THEN 1440
1430 LOCATE 24,1:PRINT"Sorry, data sets containi
ng negative values cannot be plotted.";:GOTO 166
0
1440 FOR I=1 TO LX
1450    X1=XA+INT(XB*((I-SX)/RX))+1
1460    X=I:ON M GOSUB 680,720,760,800
1470    Y1=INT(YA-(YA*((Y-SY)/RY)))
1480    PSET(X1,Y1)
1490    IF I=1 THEN 1510
1500    LINE (XZ,YZ)-(X1,Y1)
1510    XZ=X1:YZ=Y1
1520 NEXT I
1530 LOCATE 24,1:INPUT"Use PrtScrn to save Graph
, <CR> to Continue";XX:GOTO 1660
1540 CLS
1550 PRINT"1  --  320 X 200    2  --  640 X 200
    3  --  640 X 400 "
1560 PRINT:PRINT"Indicate screen dimensions ";
1570 Q$=""+INKEY$:IF Q$="" THEN 1570
1580 IF Q$<"1" OR Q$>"4" THEN 1570
1590 ON VAL(Q$) GOTO 1600, 1610, 1620
1600 XX=320:YY=200:SC=1:XL=39:ZY=8:ZX=4:RETURN
1610 XX=640:YY=200:XL=39:SC=2:ZY=8:ZX=8:RETURN
1620 XX=640:YY=400:SC=100:XL=79:ZY=16:ZX=8:RETUR
N
1630 Q$=""+INKEY$:IF Q$="" THEN 1630
1640 IF Q$="y" THEN Q$="Y" ELSE IF Q$="n" THEN Q
$="N" ELSE Q$=Q$
1650 PRINT Q$:RETURN
1660 '
1670 PRINT"(A)nother        (M)ain menu ";
1680 GOSUB 1640
1690 IF Q$="A" OR Q$="a" THEN RUN 10 ELSE RUN "A
:MENU"
```

Using the routine shown in Listing 5-3, the coefficient of correlation becomes a healthy .984398, and the specific equation reads:

$$Y' = 10.0401 - .0194275X + .0121101X^2$$

This program collects a number of variables not used in Listing 5-2, so the programs have not been merged. Depending on the available memory in your system, this routine could be incorporated, at some loss of processing speed, into the previous program.

An interesting variation on the foregoing regression form is a more generalized approach called an *nth order regression*. This regression takes the generic form:

$$Y = A + BX + CX^2 + DX^3 + \ldots + NX^n$$

Listing 5-3. Least Squares Parabolic Fit.

```
1 '*********************************************
2 '*              Listing 5-3                  *
3 '*         Least Squares Parabolic Fit       *
4 '*********************************************
5 '
10 CLS:KEY OFF:INPUT"NUMBER OF DATA POINTS";N
20 IF N<3 THEN 10
30 DIM X(N),Y(N),YY(N)
40 PRINT
50 FOR I=1 TO N:PRINT I,"X, Y DATA";:INPUT X(I),
Y(I):NEXT I
60 FOR I=1 TO N:PRINT I;X(I);Y(I),:NEXT I:PRINT
70 PRINT"ARE ALL DATA CORRECT  (Y/N)";
80 Q$=""+INKEY$:IF Q$="" THEN 80
90 IF Q$="Y" OR Q$="y" THEN 110
100 PRINT:INPUT"ENTER ITEM NUMBER AND CORRECT VA
LUES";I,X(I),Y(I):GOTO 60
110 PRINT:PRINT"COMPUTING ...":PRINT
120 FOR I=1 TO N
130 A1=A1+X(I):A2=A2+(X(I)^2):A3=A3+(X(I)^3):A4=
A4+(X(I)^4):B0=B0+Y(I):B1=B1+(Y(I)*X(I)):B2=B2+(
Y(I)*(X(I)^2))
140 NEXT I
150 A1=A1/N:A2=A2/N:A3=A3/N:A4=A4/N:B0=B0/N:B1=B
1/N:B2=B2/N
160 D=(A2*A4-A3^2)-A1*(A1*A4-A3*A2)+A2*(A1*A3-A2
^2)
170 U=(B0*(A2*A4-A3^2)+B1*(A3*A2-A1*A4)+B2*(A1*A
3-A2^2))/D
180 V=(B0*(A3*A2-A1*A4)+B1*(A4-A2^2)+B2*(A2*A1-A
3))/D
190 W=(B0*(A1*A3-A2*A2)+B1*(A1*A2-A3)+B2*(1*A2-A
1*A1))/D
200 PRINT:PRINT"   Y' = ";U;:IF V<0 THEN 220
210 PRINT"+";
220 PRINT V;"X ";:IF W<0 THEN 240
230 PRINT"+";
240 PRINT W;"X^2 ":PRINT
250 PRINT"COMPUTING .... AGAIN ..."
260 FOR I=1 TO N
270 TX=TX+Y(I):Y=U+(V*X(I))+(W*(X(I)^2)):YY(I)=Y
:TY=TY+Y
280 X2=X2+(Y(I)^2):Y2=Y2+(Y^2):XY=XY+(Y(I)*Y)
290 IF X(I)<=LX THEN 310
300 LX=X(I)
```

```
310 IF Y>Y(I) THEN 340
320 IF Y(I)<=LY THEN 360
330 LY=Y(I):GOTO 360
340 IF Y<=LY THEN 360
350 LY=Y
360 IF X(I)>SX THEN 380
370 SX=X(I)
380 IF Y<Y(I) THEN 410
390 IF Y(I)>SY THEN 430
400 SY=Y(I):GOTO 430
410 IF Y>SY THEN 430
420 SY=Y
430 NEXT I
440 R=((N*XY)-(TX*TY))/SQR(((N*X2)-(TX^2))*((N*Y
2)-(TY^2)))
450 PRINT"COEFFICIENT OF CORRELATION = ";R:PRINT
460 PRINT"(N)EW DATA    (G)RAPH    (I)NTERPOLATION
    (E)ND";
470 Q$=""+INKEY$:IF Q$="" THEN 470 ELSE IF Q$="G
" OR Q$="g" THEN 510 ELSE IF Q$="I" OR Q$="i" TH
EN 490 ELSE IF Q$="E" OR Q$="e" THEN RUN "A:MENU
" ELSE IF Q$<>"N" AND Q$=<>"n" THEN 470
480 CLS
490 INPUT "Enter X coordinate";X
500 Y=U+(V*X)+(W*(X^2)):PRINT"Y = ";Y:GOTO 460
510 'DATA DISPLAY
520 GOSUB 780:SCREEN SC
530 CLS
540 D=INT(LOG(LX)/2.302585)+1        ' DETERMINE LE
NGTH OF NUMBER
550 XA=INT(.1328*XX):YA=INT(.7875*YY):XB=XX-XA
      ' SET LEFT AND BOTTOM BOUNDARIES
560 RX=LX-SX:RY=LY-SY               ' COMPUTE RANGE
570 LINE(XA,1)-(XA,YA):LINE(XA,YA)-(XX,YA)        '
 DRAW BOUNDARY
580 ' COMPUTE AND DRAW INTERVAL MARKERS
590 FOR I=1 TO 9:LINE(XA-2,(I*(YA/10))-1)-(XA,(I
*(YA/10))-1):NEXT
600 FOR I=1 TO 9:LINE(XA+(I*((XX-XA)/10)-1),YA+2
)-(XA+(I*((XX-XA)/10)-1),YA):NEXT
610 ' COMPUTE AND DRAW ZERO AXIS LINES
620 IF LX=<0 THEN X0=XX ELSE X0=XX-(INT((XX-XA)*
(LX/RX)))
630 IF LY=<0 THEN Y0=1 ELSE Y0=INT(YA*(LY/RY))
640 X1=X0:X2=X1:Y1=1:Y2=YA:LINE (X1,Y1)-(X2,Y2)
650 X1=XA:X2=XX:Y1=Y0:Y2=Y1:LINE (X1,Y1)-(X2,Y2)
660 ' PRINT SCALE VALUES
670 LOCATE 1,(XA/8)-4:PRINT LY;:LOCATE 20,(XA/8)
-4:PRINT SY;:LOCATE 21,(XA/8)-1:PRINT SX;:LOCATE
 21,(XX/8)-(D+2):PRINT INT(LX);:LOCATE (Y0/ZY)+1
,(XA/8)-3):PRINT 0;:LOCATE (YA/ZY)+1,X0/8:PRINT
0;
680 ' DISPLAY LOCATION OF ACTUAL DATA ON SCALE
690 FOR I=1 TO N:X1=XA+INT(XB*((X(I)-SX)/RX))+1:
Y1=INT(YA-(YA*((Y(I)-SY)/RY))):PSET(X1,Y1):NEXT
I
700 'PLOT PROJECTED DATA
710 FOR I=SX TO LX
```

Listing 5-3. Least Squares Parabolic Fit. (Continued From Page 63.)

```
720    X1=XA+INT(XB*((I-SX)/RX))+1
730    Y=U+(V*I)+(W*(I^2))
740    Y1=INT(YA-(YA*((Y-SY)/RY)))
750    PSET(X1,Y1):LINE (OLDX,OLDY)-(X1,Y1):OLDX=
X1:OLDY=Y1
760 NEXT I
770 LOCATE 24,1:INPUT"Use PrtScrn to save Graph,
 <CR> to Continue";XX:GOTO 870
780 CLS
790 PRINT"1  --  320 X 200    2  --  640 X 200
   3  --  640 X 400 "
800 PRINT:PRINT"Indicate screen dimensions ";
810 Q$=""+INKEY$:IF Q$="" THEN 810
820 ON VAL(Q$) GOTO 830, 840, 850
830 XX=320:YY=200:SC=1:XL=39:ZY=8:ZX=4:RETURN
840 XX=640:YY=200:XL=39:SC=2:ZY=8:ZX=8:RETURN
850 XX=640:YY=400:SC=100:XL=79:ZY=16:ZX=8:RETURN
860 ZAG%=INT(ZOG%/64):ZOG%=ZOG%-64*ZAG%+1:ZAG%=Z
AG%+1:LOCATE ZAG%,ZOG%:RETURN
870 PRINT"(A)nother        (M)ain menu ";
880 GOSUB 900
890 IF Q$="A" OR Q$="a" THEN RUN 10 ELSE RUN "A:
MENU"
900 Q$=""+INKEY$:IF Q$="" THEN 900
910 RETURN
```

The coefficient of correlation will vary according to the degree of the equation specified by the user, which will depend on the input and the number of items. The program in Listing 5-4 computes the various coefficients and related statistics, depending only on the degree of the equation specified by the user. The only real limitation, other than the memory capacity of the computer, is that the number of data points must be at least two more than the degree of the equation. After the first pass, the program gives the user the option of a step-wise check to verify which degree provides the best correlation. Again, as with the program in Listing 5-3, the variables collected are in a different format from those in Listing 5-2, making inclusion in that program cumbersome. Nonetheless, provided that memory capacity is not strained, it would be useful to embed this program in one similar to the one in Listing 5-2.

To this point we have presented some routines to process data in a basic two-variable (independent and dependent variables) format. To the extent the dependent variable is a direct function of the independent variable, we should usually be able to predict the dependent variable by using one of the equations below:

$$Y = A + BX \qquad \text{normal}$$
$$Y = AX^B \qquad \text{power}$$
$$Y = Ae^{BX} \qquad \text{exponential}$$
$$Y = A + B \log X \qquad \text{logarithmic}$$
$$Y = A + BX + CX^2 +$$
$$\cdots + NX^N \qquad \text{Nth Order}$$
$$Y = A + BX + CX^2 \qquad \text{parabolic (special case of Nth Order)}$$

Seldom, however, are things quite so neat and tidy. Dependent variables have a disagreeable habit of being related to two or more otherwise independent variables. How tall are you? Is that a function of age, sex, family genetics, or diet? Probably a little bit of each of those and others. To compute height as a function of just one variable would produce results of only limited value. Never fear, however, we have techniques to handle multiple variables, and we refer to these as multiple regression techniques.

Listing 5-4. Nth Order Regression.

```
1  '***********************************************
2  '*              Listing 5-4                    *
3  '*           N-th Order Regression             *
4  '***********************************************
5  '
10 CLS:INPUT"DEGREE OF EQUATION";D
20 INPUT"NUMBER OF KNOWN POINTS";N
30 IF N>(D+1) THEN 50
40 PRINT"SORRY--WE NEED AT LEAST";D+2;"POINTS":G
OTO 20
50 DIM XX(N),YY(N),A((2*(N))+1),R(N,N),T(N):A(1)
=N
60 FOR I=1 TO N:PRINT"X, Y OF POINT #";I;:INPUT
XX(I),YY(I):NEXT
70 FOR I=1 TO N:PRINT I;XX(I);YY(I),:NEXT I
80 PRINT:PRINT"ARE THESE CORRECT?  (Y/N)"
90 Q$=""+INKEY$:IF Q$="" THEN 90 ELSE IF Q$="Y"
OR Q$="y" THEN 110
100 PRINT:INPUT"ITEM #, X, Y";I,XX(I),YY(I):GOTO
 70
110 CLS:PRINT"COMPUTING...":PRINT
120 FOR I=1 TO N
130 X=XX(I):Y=YY(I)
140 FOR J=2 TO ((2*D)+1):A(J)=A(J)+(X^(J-1)):NEX
T
150 FOR K=1 TO D+1:R(K,D+2)=T(K)+(Y*(X^(K-1))):T
(K)=T(K)+(Y*(X^(K-1))):NEXT K
160 T(D+2)=T(D+2)+(Y^2)
170 NEXT I
180 FOR J=1 TO D+1:FOR K=1 TO D+1:R(J,K)=A(J+K-1
):NEXT K:NEXT J
190 FOR J=1 TO D+1
200 FOR K=J TO D+1
210 IF R(K,J)<>0 THEN 240
220 NEXT K
230 PRINT"NO UNIQUE SOLUTION":GOTO 510
240 FOR I=1 TO D+2:S=R(J,I):R(J,I)=R(K,I):R(K,I)
=S:NEXT I
250 Z=1/R(J,J):FOR I=1 TO D+2:R(J,I)=Z*R(J,I):NE
XT I
260 FOR K=1 TO D+1
270 IF K=J THEN 300
280 Z=-R(K,J)
290 FOR I=1 TO D+2:R(K,I)=R(K,I)+(Z*R(J,I)):NEXT
 I
300 NEXT K
310 NEXT J
320 IF Q$="C" THEN 350
330 PRINT"                CONSTANT = ";R(1,D+2)
340 FOR J=1 TO D:PRINT J;"DEGREE COEFFICIENT = "
;R(J+1,D+2):NEXT J:PRINT
350 P=0
360 FOR J=2 TO D+1:P=P+(R(J,D+2)*(T(J)-(A(J)*(T(
1)/N)))):NEXT J
370 Q=T(D+2)-((T(1)^2)/N):Z=Q-P:I=N-D-1:J=P/Q:PR
INT
```

Listing 5-4. Nth Order Regression. (Continued From Page 65.)

```
380 IF Q$="C" THEN 400
390 PRINT"COEFFICIENT OF DETERMINATION (R^2) = "
;J
400 IF J=>0 THEN 420
410 PRINT"COEFFICIENT OF CORRELATION        = "
;-1*SQR(ABS(J)):GOTO 430
420 PRINT"COEFFICIENT OF CORRELATION        = "
;SQR(J)
430 IF Q$="C" THEN 580 ELSE IF Z=>0 THEN 450
440 PRINT"STANDARD ERROR OF ESTIMATE        =";
-1*SQR(ABS(Z/I)):GOTO 460
450 PRINT"STANDARD ERROR OF ESTIMATE        = "
;SQR(Z/I)
460 PRINT:PRINT"(I)NTERPOLATION    (C)ORRELATION
ANALYSIS    (N)EW        (E)ND"
470 Q$=""+INKEY$:IF Q$="" THEN 470 ELSE IF Q$="N
" OR Q$="n" THEN 510 ELSE IF Q$="C" OR Q$="c" TH
EN 530 ELSE IF Q$="E" OR Q$="e" THEN 600 ELSE IF
 Q$<>"I" THEN 470
480 PRINT:P=R(1,D+2):INPUT"ENTER X VALUE";X
490 FOR J=1 TO D:P=P+(R(J+1,D+2)*(X^J)):NEXT J
500 PRINT"Y = ";P:GOTO 460
510 RUN 10
520 END
530 PRINT:PRINT"COMPUTING";N-2;"REGRESSION CORRE
LATION COMPARISONS"
540 FOR D=1 TO N-2
550 FOR I=2 TO ((2*N)+1):A(I)=0:NEXT I
560 FOR I=1 TO N:FOR J=1 TO N:R(I,J)=0:NEXT J:T(
I)=0:NEXT I
570 PRINT"D =";D,:GOTO 120
580 NEXT D
590 PRINT:INPUT"COMPLETE STATISTICS FOR WHAT DEG
REE";D:Q$="":GOTO 120
600 PRINT"(A)nother        (M)ain menu ";
610 GOSUB 630
620 IF Q$="A" OR Q$="a" THEN RUN 10 ELSE RUN "A:
MENU"
630 Q$=""+INKEY$:IF Q$="" THEN 630
640 RETURN
```

MULTIPLE REGRESSION

The generalized form of a multiple regression equation is:

$$Y = A + BX_1 + CX_2 + \ldots + nX_N$$

where X_k are different variables, such as X_1 = age, X_2 = weight, X_3 = reading level, X_4 = number of sisters, ... X_n = number of pets (or any other kinds of variables).

Listing 5-5 provides a technique for evaluation of the effect of a set of multiple variables upon a de-pendent. Provided you have the patience and your computer has the memory capacity, any number of variables can be entered into this program and processed against some specified dependent variable. The program outputs the appropriate coefficients for each variable and the residual for the equation. In addition, it computes the coefficient of correlation. At the end of the first run, the program offers the options of using a trial value (an interpolation subroutine), entering new data, or computing a *best fit*. This last subroutine redefines the parameters of the task and recomputes the various coefficients and

Listing 5-5. Multiple Linear Regression.

```
1 '*********************************************
2 '*              Listing 5-5                  *
3 '*        Multiple Linear Regression         *
4 '*********************************************
5 '
10 DEFDBL A,P
20 CLS:INPUT"NUMBER OF KNOWN POINTS";N
30 DIM X(N+1),S(N+1),T(N+1),A(N+1,N+2)
40 INPUT"NUMBER OF INDEPENDENT VARIABLES";V:DIM
Y(N,V+1),YY(N,V+1)
50 FOR I=1 TO N:PRINT"POINT #";I:FOR J=1 TO V:PR
INT"      INDEPENDENT VARIABLE #";J,:INPUT YY(I,J
):NEXT J:INPUT"            DEPENDENT VARIABLE";YY(
I,J):NEXT I:VV=V
60 LPRINT"":LPRINT"INPUT VARIABLES"
70 FOR I=1 TO N
80 PRINT"POINT ";I:FOR J=1 TO V:PRINT"",J,YY(I,J
):Y(I,J)=YY(I,J):NEXT J:PRINT"",J;"DEPENDENT = "
;YY(I,J):Y(I,J)=YY(I,J)
90 PRINT"ARE THESE DATA CORRECT?   (Y/N)";
100 Q$=""+INKEY$:IF Q$="" THEN 100 ELSE IF Q$="Y
" OR Q$="y" THEN 120
110 PRINT:INPUT"ENTER VARIABLE NUMBER AND CORREC
T VALUE";J,YY(I,J):GOTO 80
120 PRINT:LPRINT"POINT ";I:FOR J=1 TO V:LPRINT"
  VARIABLE",J,YY(I,J):NEXT J:LPRINT"","DEPENDENT
 = ";YY(I,J)
130 NEXT I
140 X(1)=1:PRINT:PRINT"COMPUTING..."
150 FOR I=1 TO N
160 FOR J=1 TO V:X(J+1)=Y(I,J):NEXT J:X(V+2)=Y(I
,J)
170 FOR K=1 TO V+1:FOR L=1 TO V+2:A(K,L)=A(K,L)+
(X(K)*X(L)):S(K)=A(K,V+2):NEXT L:NEXT K
180 S(V+2)=S(V+2)+(X(V+2)^2)
190 NEXT I
200 FOR I=2 TO V+1:T(I)=A(1,I):NEXT I
210 FOR I=1 TO V+1
220 J=I
230 IF A(J,I)<>0 THEN 260
240 J=J+1:IF J<=(V+1) THEN 230
250 PRINT"NO UNIQUE SOLUTION":GOTO 450
260 FOR K=1 TO V+2:B=A(I,K):A(I,K)=A(J,K):A(J,K)
=B:NEXT K
270 Z=1/A(I,I)
280 FOR K=1 TO V+2:A(I,K)=Z*A(I,K):NEXT K
290 FOR J=1 TO V+2
300 IF J=I THEN 330
310 Z=-A(J,I)
320 FOR K=1 TO V+2:A(J,K)=A(J,K)+(Z*A(I,K)):NEXT
 K
330 NEXT J
340 NEXT I
350 LPRINT"":LPRINT"EQUATION COEFFICIENTS:"
360 PRINT:PRINT"EQUATION COEFFICIENTS:":PRINT"
  CONSTANT: ";A(1,V+2):LPRINT"       CONSTANT = "
```

Listing 5-5. Multiple Linear Regression. (Con ^{tinued} From Page 67.)

```
;A(1,V+2)
370 FOR I=2 TO V+1:PRINT"  VARIABLE #";I-1,A(I,V
+2):LPRINT"  VARIABLE #";I-1,"=";A(I,V+2):NEXT I
380 P=0
390 FOR I=2 TO V+1:P=P+(A(I,V+2)*(S(I)-(T(I)*S(1
)/N))):NEXT I
400 R=S(V+2)-((S(1)^2)/N):Z=R-P:L=N-V-1:I=P/R:PR
INT
410 PRINT"COEFFICIENT OF DETERMINATION = ";I:LPR
INT"COEFFICIENT OF DETERMINATION = ";I,:IF I<0 T
HEN 430
420 PRINT"COEFFICIENT OF MULTIPLE CORRELATION =
";SQR(I):LPRINT"COEFFICIENT OF MULTIPLE CORRELAT
ION = ";SQR(I):GOTO 440
430 PRINT"COEFFICIENT OF MULTIPLE CORRELATION =
";-1*SQR(ABS(I))
440 IF L<>0 THEN PRINT"STANDARD ERROR OF ESTIMAT
E = ";SQR(ABS(Z/L)):LPRINT"STANDAR ERROR OF ESTI
MATE = ";SQR(ABS(Z/L))
450 IF Q$="B" THEN 630
460 PRINT:PRINT"(T)RIAL VALUE   (N)EW DATA RUN
 (B)EST FIT";
470 Q$=""+INKEY$:IF Q$="" THEN 470 ELSE IF Q$="N
" OR Q$="n" THEN 510 ELSE IF Q$="B" OR Q$="b" TH
EN 530 ELSE Q$="E" OR Q$="e" THEN RUN "A:MENU" E
LSE IF Q$<>"T" THEN 470
480 PRINT:P=A(1,V+2)
490 FOR J=1 TO V:PRINT"INDEPENDANT VARIABLE #";J
;:INPUT X:P=P+(A(J+1,V+2)*X):NEXT J
500 PRINT:PRINT"  DEPENDANT VARIABLE = ";P:GOTO
 460
510 PRINT:RUN 20
520 END
530 ZZ=(2^V)-1:PRINT" ",Q$
540 FOR II=1 TO ZZ
550 A=II:PRINT"USING VARIABLE(S) #";:LPRINT"":LP
RINT"USING VARIABLE(S) #",
560 FOR J=1 TO N+1:X(J)=0:S(J)=0:T(J)=0:FOR K=1
TO N+2:A(J,K)=0:NEXT K:NEXT J:K=0
570 FOR J=VV TO 1 STEP -1
580 IF (2^(J-1))>A THEN 610
590 A=A-(2^(J-1)):PRINT J;:LPRINT J,
600 K=K+1:FOR L=1 TO N:Y(L,K)=YY(L,J):NEXT L
610 NEXT J
620 V=K:GOTO 140
630 NEXT II
```

correlations to determine which set of variables, taken singly or in combination, produce the best predictor of the dependent variable. Of course, the program does not concern itself with logical relationships, but simply identifies those variables that seem to relate best to the dependent variable. If the number of goldfish in your tank at home relates best to your SAT score, so be it.

The data in Table 5-3 were processed using the following program and the results are given. Although we began with four variables, it is clear that only three of the variables are of any use in forecasting the magnitude of the dependent variable.

OTHER CORRELATIONS

So far, the coefficient of correlation we have

Table 5-3. Multivariate Sample Input Data.

Item #	Independent Variables 1	2	3	4	Dependent Variable
1	1.9245	2.04412	4.15012	6.43881	1
2	2.54461	5.83935	8.74113	5.59329	4
3	3.60942	7.7939	9.28686	4.99721	6
4	4.31564	9.51458	12.9678	6.70319	8
5	5.24965	11.6141	15.6512	1.465	10
6	6.49682	12.5547	18.2942	1.70637	12
7	7.50094	14.992	21.7468	1.98965	14
8	8.67358	17.6187	26.6055	6.98466	16
9	9.75344	18.5086	29.4656	6.93737	18
10	10.9158	21.9598	30.3651	.638662	20

been referring to has been the Pearson product-moment correlation, or the *rho-correlation*. This is not, however, the only coefficient of correlation available, nor even the most appropriate in some instances. What follows, then, is a brief description of a number of alternative coefficients of correlation and their computation.

Point-Biserial Correlation Coefficient

You often have data of which one variable is continuous and the other is dichotomous. For example, the independent variable may be lifting strength (a continuous variable) and the dependent variable may be the sex of the lifter (a dichotomous variable). Table 5-4 summarizes a hypothetical set of test data. Column A identifies the sex of the lifter 0 = female, 1 = male), and column B gives the maximum weight lifted in four trials.

Two equations for the computation of a biserial correlation are shown following:

$$(1)\ r_b = \frac{N(\Sigma'Y) - \Sigma N_1 Y}{NA\ \sqrt{N\Sigma Y^2 - (\Sigma Y)^2}}$$

Where:
- N = total number of points
- N_1 = number of points where the dichotomous variable is "1"
- $\Sigma'Y$ = sum of all points (y) where the dichotomous is "1"
- ΣY = sum of all continuous variables
- A = height of the ordinate of a normal curve at a distance from the

mean where the area of the tail is equal to:

N_1/N.

An easier equation is:

$$(2)\ r_b = \frac{\bar{Y}_0 - \bar{Y}_1}{\sigma}\ \sqrt{pq}$$

Where:
- σ = is the standard deviation of all the points
- $\bar{Y}_0$ = mean score of those items in category 0
- $\bar{Y}_1$ = mean score in those items in category 1
- P = N_1/N
- q = $1 - p$

From the data given in Table 5-4, we compute the values:

σ = 215.523 Y_0 = 270 Y_1 = 465
p = .444444 q = .555556

solving for r_b:

$$r_b = \frac{270 - 465}{215.523}\ \sqrt{.444444 \times .555556}$$

$$= -.449588$$

Spearman's Rank-Order Correlation

The data in Table 5-5 summarizes the grades one class of students received in two different subjects. The question the teacher has is whether or not there is a relationship between the skills used in the two subjects. That is, if a student is good in one subject, will he or she also be good in the other?

Table 5-4. Test Results.

Lifter #	Sex Code	Weight Lifted
1	0	310 lbs
2	1	280
3	1	560
4	0	30
5	1	250
6	0	240
7	0	480
8	0	290
9	1	770

Table 5-5. Rank-Ordered Grade Data.

Student Number	Math Grade	English Grade	Math Rank	English Rank	Difference D	D²
1	92	86	1	2	1	1
2	47	24	5	8	-3	9
3	48	42	4	5	-1	1
4	61	60	3	4	-1	1
5	7	14	10	10	0	0
6	23	35	7	7	0	0
7	85	38	2	6	-4	16
8	33	23	6	9	-3	9
9	15	92	9	1	8	64
10	20	68	8	3	5	25
					2	126

$n = 10$

The values in columns two and three are simple enough; they are the grades received on a recent test. In columns four and five are the corresponding ranks each score represents. The equation for computing Spearman's correlation is

$$r_s = 1 - \frac{6 \, \Sigma \, D_i^2}{n(n^2 - 1)}$$

where: n = number of data pairs
D_i = rank (x_i) – rank (y_i)

With this coefficient there is a test value to measure the degree of reliability of the correlation. It is computed from $z = r_s \sqrt{n - 1}$. The z-score is roughly equal to the standard deviation of the normal curve that includes the data. That is, if z is greater than ± 1.96, the value of r_s is significant at the 5% level or better. There is also another relationship in interest where:

$$r = 2 \sin\left(\frac{\pi}{6} \, r_s\right)$$ where r is Pearson's rho.

From the basic equation:

$$r_s = 1 \frac{6 \times 126}{10 \times (10^2 - 1)} = 1 - \frac{756}{10 \times 99} = 1 - \frac{756}{990}$$

$$= .236364$$

$$r = 2 \sin\left(\frac{\pi}{6} \, r_s\right) = 2 \sin (.523599 \times .236364)$$

$$= 2 \sin (.12376) = 2 \times .123444 = .246888$$
$$z = r_s \, \sqrt{n - 1} = .236364 \times 9 = 2.12728$$

Partial and Multiple Coefficients of Correlation

After a long evening of computing correlations between pairs of data sets you may be in a position to ask: if I know the relationship between A and B, the relationship between A and C, and the relationship between B and C, and if I know that A is a function of both B and C, what is the relationship between A and B without the benefit of C and, likewise, what is the relationship between A and C without the benefit of B? The answer is found in the equation:

$$r_{ab.c} = \frac{r_{ab} - r_{ac} \, r_{bc}}{\sqrt{(1 - r_{ac}^2)(1 - r_{bc}^2)}}$$

Likewise:

$$r_{ac.b} = \frac{r_{ac} - r_{ab} \, r_{bc}}{\sqrt{(1 - r_{ac}^2)(1 - r_{bc}^2)}}$$

And:

$$r_{bc.a} = \frac{r_{bc} - r_{ab} \, r_{ac}}{\sqrt{(1 - r_{bc}^2)(1 - r_{ab}^2)}}$$

The multiple coefficient of correlation from these data is computed from:

$$r_{ab.c} = \sqrt{\frac{r_{ab}^2 + r_{ac}^2 - 2 \, r_{ab} \, r_{ac} \, r_{bc}}{1 - r_{bc}^2}}$$

Listing 5-6 implements all of the foregoing equations to compute the biserial and rank-order correlations, as well as the partial and multiple correlations.

KENDALL'S COEFFICIENT OF CONCORDANCE

Kendall's coefficient of concordance (W) is a useful tool to evaluate the relationship between the ratings a panel of judges give to individuals in some comparative activity, such as sports events, where part or all of the score is based on a subject evaluation of the event; in the results of a panel of judges rating musicians; or in any other situation in which

Listing 5-6. Miscellaneous Correlations

```
1 '*********************************************
2 '*            Listing 5-6                   *
3 '*      Miscellaneous Correlations          *
4 '*********************************************
5 '
10 CLS:PRINT"CORRELATIONS":PRINT:PRINT:PRINT"1
-- POINT-BISERIAL CORRELATION  2  --  SPEARMAN'
S RANK-ORDER CORRELATION      3  --  PARTIAL/MULT
IPLE CORRELATIONS"
20 PRINT"SELECT ONE";
30 Q$=""+INKEY$:IF Q$="" THEN 30 ELSE ON VAL(Q$)
 GOTO 40,230,340
40 CLS'POINT-BISERIAL CORRELATION
50 INPUT"TOTAL NUMBER OF ITEMS TO BE ENTERED";N
60 FOR I=1 TO N
70 PRINT"ENTER DATA FOR SUBJECT #";I;"
                                        DICHOTO
MOUS CHARACTERISTIC (1 OR 0)    ";
80 Q$=""+INKEY$:IF Q$="" THEN 80
90 IF Q$<"0" OR Q$>"1" THEN 80
100 PRINT Q$:Q=VAL(Q$):INPUT"      ENTER CONTINUO
US VALUE";X
110 IF Q=1 THEN 130
120 N(0)=N(0)+1:S(0)=S(0)+X:GOTO 140
130 N(1)=N(1)+1:S(1)=S(1)+X
140 TX=TX+X:X2=X2+(X^2)
150 NEXT I
160 S=SQR((X2-((TX^2)/N))/(N-1))
170 Y0=S(0)/N(0):Y1=S(1)/N(1):P=N(0)/N:Q=1-P
180 RB=((Y1-Y0)/S)*SQR(P*Q)
190 PRINT:PRINT"SUM OF Y1 = ";S(1);"   MEAN = ";
Y1;"    PERCENT = ";P
200 PRINT"SUM OF Y0 = ";S(0);"   MEAN = ";Y0;"
 PERCENT = ";Q
210 PRINT"STANDARD DEVIATION = ";S
220 PRINT:PRINT"POINT-BISERIAL CORRELATION = ";R
B:PRINT:RUN 510
230 CLS'SPEARMAN'S RANK CORRELATION
240 INPUT"NUMBER OF DATA PAIRS";N
250 FOR I=1 TO N
260 PRINT"PAIR #";I
270 INPUT"ENTER RANK, VARIABLE # 1";R1
280 INPUT"ENTER RANK, VARIABLE # 2";R2
290 DI=DI+((R1-R2)^2)
300 NEXT I
310 RS=1-((6*DI)/(N*((N^2)-1))):Z=RS*SQR(N-1)
320 R=2*SIN(.5235991*RS)
330 PRINT:PRINT"SPEARMAN'S RANK CORRELATION = ";
RS:PRINT"PEARSON'S RHO CORRELATION = ";R:PRINT"Z
-SCORE = ";Z:RUN 510
340 CLS'PARTIAL CORRELATIONS
350 PRINT"A IS THE CRITERION OR DEPENDENT VARIAB
LE"
360 INPUT"ENTER CORRELATION BETWEEN SET A AND SE
T B";R(1)
370 INPUT"ENTER CORRELATION BETWEEN SET A AND SE
```

Listing 5-6. Miscellaneous Correlations. (Continued From Page 71.)

```
T C";R(2)
380 INPUT"ENTER CORRELATION BETWEEN SET B AND SE
T C";R(3)
390 PR(1)=(R(1)-(R(2)*R(3)))/(SQR(1-(R(2)^2))*SQ
R(1-(R(3)^2)))
400 PR(2)=(R(2)-(R(1)*R(3)))/(SQR(1-(R(1)^2))*SQ
R(1-(R(3)^2)))
410 PR(3)=(R(3)-(R(1)*R(2)))/(SQR(1-(R(1)^2))*SQ
R(1-(R(2)^2)))
420 PR(4)=(((R(1)^2)+(R(2)^2))-(2*R(1)*R(2)*R(3)
))/(1-(R(3)^2))
430 IF PR(4)<0 THEN 450
440 PR(4)=SQR(PR(4)):GOTO 460
450 PR(4)=-1*SQR(ABS(PR(4)))
460 PRINT:PRINT"PARTIAL CORRELATIONS:"
470 PRINT"   A WITH B LESS C = ";PR(1)
480 PRINT"   A WITH C LESS B = ";PR(2)
490 PRINT"   B WITH C LESS A = ";PR(3)
500 PRINT:PRINT"MULTIPLE CORRELATION OF THE DEPE
NDENT VARIABLE A AND THE INDEPENDENT VARIABLES B
 AND C = ";PR(4)
510 PRINT:PRINT"(A)nother set          (M)ain m
enu ";
520 Q$=""+INKEY$:IF Q$="" THEN 520
530 PRINT Q$
540 IF Q$="A" OR Q$="a" THEN RUN 10 ELSE IF Q$="
M" OR Q$="m" THEN RUN "A:MENU" ELSE RUN 510
```

N individuals are ranked 1 to N according to some characteristic by K judges. The degree to which these judges agree (or their concordance) is given by the equation:

$$W = \frac{12 \sum\limits_{i=1}^{N} \left(\sum\limits_{j=1}^{K} R_{ij} \right)^2}{K^2 N(N^2 - 1)} - \frac{3(N + 1)}{N - 1}$$

where R_{ij} is the rank given to the ith individual by the jth judge.

Very much like a coefficient of correlation, W ranges from 0 (no agreement between judges) and 1 (total agreement among judges). If the number of judges is greater than seven, the degree of confidence one can place in the coefficient can be estimated from:

$$\chi^2 = K(N - 1) W$$

which has an approximate relationship with the chi-square distribution (see the next section).

Table 5-6 gives the hypothetical outcome of a diving competition as rated by seven judges.

The computation of the coefficient starts by tabulating the row scores, and then squaring each one.

Item	Score	Score Squared
1	27	729
2	42	1764
3	40	1600
4	33	1089

Table 5-6. Diving Scores, Multiple Judges.

Diver i	1	2	3	Judge 4	5	6	7	Total	Score	Final Rank
1	2	2	3	8	3	1	8	27	1	1
2	6	6	7	5	10	3	5	42	5	5
3	4	10	5	2	6	7	6	40	4	4
4	3	9	2	1	5	9	4	33	2	2
5	10	9	1	7	4	10	1	36	3	3
6	9	5	10	3	1	2	10	40	4	4
7	7	7	6	4	9	5	2	40	4	4
8	1	4	8	9	8	4	9	43	6	6
9	5	1	4	10	7	8	7	42	5	5
10	8	8	9	6	2	6	3	42	5	5

Item	Score	Score Squared
5	36	1296
6	40	1600
7	40	1600
8	43	1849
9	42	1764
10	42	1764
	Sum =	15055

Then:

$$W = \frac{12 \times 25055}{7^2 \times 10(10^2 - 1)} - \frac{3(10 + 1)}{10 - 1}$$

$$= \frac{180660}{48510} - \frac{33}{9} = 3.72418 - 3.66666$$

$$= .057513$$

The chi-square statistic is:

$$7 \times (10 - 1) \times W\ 3\ 3.6233.$$

One concludes with a reasonable assurance that there is actually little real agreement among the judges. A protest of the scores would not be out of order. Listing 5-7 implements this process, making the tabulations a little quicker.

CHI-SQUARE DISTRIBUTIONS

By using a number of the techniques given in this book, you can use the microcomputer to develop a mathematical model or algorithm with which future values can be computed as a function of some set of known or estimated values. Later you will be

Listing 5-7. Kendall's Coefficient of Concordance.

```
1 '*********************************************
2 '*              Listing 5-7                  *
3 '*    Kendall's Coefficient of Concordance   *
4 '*********************************************
5 '
10 CLS
20 INPUT"NUMBER OF INDIVIDUALS";N
30 INPUT"NUMBER OF JUDGES";K
40 DIM S(N,K),TS(N):PRINT
50 FOR I=1 TO N
60   PRINT"INDIVIDUAL #";I
70   FOR J=1 TO K
80     PRINT"   RATING BY JUDGE #";J,:INPUT S(I,
J)
90     SR=SR+S(I,J):TS(I)=TS(I)+S(I,J)
100   NEXT J
110   SN=SN+(SR^2):SR=0
120   PRINT
130 NEXT I
140 CLS
150 PRINT"Score Results":PRINT:PRINT"Person","To
tal Score","Average Score"
160 FOR I=1 TO N:PRINT PRINT I,TS(I),TS(I)/K:NEX
T I
170 PRINT:PRINT
180 W=((12*SN)/((K^2)*(N*((N^2)-1))))-((3*(N+1))
/(N-1))
190 PRINT:PRINT"KENDALL'S COEFFICIENT OF CONCORD
ANCE = ";W
200 PRINT"CHI-SQUARE = ";K*(N-1)*W;"WITH";N-1;"D
EGREES OF FREEDOM"
210 PRINT:PRINT"(A)nother set          (M)ain m
enu ";
220 Q$=""+INKEY$:IF Q$="" THEN 220
230 IF Q$="A" OR Q$="a" THEN RUN 10 ELSE IF Q$="
M" OR Q$="m" THEN RUN "A:MENU" ELSE RUN 210
```

able to evaluate the relationship between the model and the actual outcome by a process known as the chi-square distribution. It is beyond the scope of this book to go into the development of the statistic, but Listing 5-8 facilitates the computation of chi-square with:

— Expected values equal
— Expected values unequal
— 2 × K contingency
— 2 × 2 contingency

— Bartlett's chi-square
— Chi-square for difference between correlations
— Distribution and density functions of the chi-square statistic

With these seven routines, virtually all of the common forms of the statistic and an evaluation of the curve can be computed. A brief description of each of the foregoing follows.

Listing 5-8. Chi-Square Computations.

```
1 '**********************************************
2 '*                 Listing 5-8                 *
3 '*          Chi-Square Computations            *
4 '**********************************************
5 '
10 CLS:PI=3.1415929#:E=2.71828:DIM Y(650),YY(650
):KEY OFF
20 PRINT"********* Chi-Square Unlimited *****
*****":PRINT:PRINT
30 PRINT"1 -- Expected Values Equal":PRINT"2
-- Expected Values Unequal":PRINT"3 -- 2 x K
Contingency":PRINT"4 -- 2 x 2 Contingency with
 Yates Correction":PRINT"5 -- Bartlett's Chi-S
quare":PRINT"6 -- Chi-Square for Difference Be
tween Correlations
40 PRINT"7 -- Distribution and Density Functio
ns":PRINT:PRINT"8 -- End":PRINT:PRINT:PRINT"En
ter number of desired function:  ";:GOSUB 1370
50 IF Q$<"1" OR Q$>"8" THEN GOSUB 1370
60 ON VAL(Q$) GOTO 310,350,390,450,600,810,70,13
90
70 ' on error goto 1350
80 PRINT"":PRINT"Chi-Square Distribution and Den
sity Functions":PRINT:PRINT
90 INPUT "Enter 'X' value";X
100 INPUT "Enter degrees of freedom";V:V1=V:GOTO
 120
110 V=DF:V1=DF
120 A=1:FOR I=V TO 2 STEP -2:A=A*I:NEXT I
130 B=X^(INT((V+1)/2))*EXP(-X/2)/A
140 IF B<1E-37 THEN B=1E-37
150 IF INT(V/2)=V/2 THEN 180
160 C=SQR(2/X/PI)
170 GOTO 190
180 C=1
190 D=1:E=1
200 'ON ERROR GOTO 590
210 V=V+2:E=E*X/V:IF E<.0000001 THEN 230
220 D=D+E:GOTO 210
230 CH=INT(X):P=C*B*D:T=1-P:FX=(P/D)/((2*X)/V1)
240 PRINT"Cumulative Distribution = ";P
```

```
250 PRINT"Density Function          = ";FX
260 PRINT"Tail-end value            = ";T
270 PRINT:PRINT"Will these data be printed? (Y/N
) ";:GOSUB 1370
280 IF Q$="y" OR Q$="Y" THEN 1010
290 PRINT:PRINT"Do you want a graphic presentati
on? (Y/N) ";:GOSUB 1370
300 IF Q$="y" OR Q$="Y" THEN 1080 ELSE RUN 10
310 PRINT:PRINT"Expected Values Equal:?"":?""
320 INPUT "How many items";N
330 FOR I=1 TO N:INPUT "Enter Observed Value";O:
O2=O2+(O^2):SO=SO+O:NEXT I
340 X2=((N*O2)/SO)-SO:DF=N-1:GOTO 540
350 PRINT:PRINT"Expect Values Unequal":PRINT"":P
RINT""
360 INPUT "How many item pairs";N
370 FOR I=1 TO N:PRINT:INPUT "Enter Expected Val
ue";E:INPUT "Enter Observed Value";O:X2=X2+(((O-
E)^2)/E):NEXT I:DF=N-1
380 GOTO 540
390 PRINT:PRINT"2 x K Contingency Table":PRINT""
:PRINT""
400 INPUT "What is the value of K";K
410 FOR I=1 TO K:INPUT "Enter 'A' value";A:INPUT
"Enter 'B' value";B:N=N+A+B:NA=NA+A:NB=NB+B:NI=
A+B:SA=SA+((A^2)/NI):SB=SB+((B^2)/NI):NEXT I
420 X2=((N/NA)*SA)+((N/NB)*SB)-N:C=SQR(X2/(N+X2)
)
430 X=X2:DF=K-1
440 PRINT:PRINT"Pearson's Coefficient of Conting
ency = ";C:PRINT:GOTO 540
450 SCREEN 2:PRINT:PRINT"2 x 2 Contingency":PRIN
T"":PRINT""
460 'on error goto 590
470 LOCATE 16,15:PRINT"1                 2":LOCATE 18
,1:PRINT"Group A          A          B":LOCATE 20
,1:PRINT"Group B          C          D":LINE (1,1
32)-(264,132):LINE (1,148)-(264,148):LINE (72,12
0)-(72,160):LINE (176,128)-(176,160)
480 LOCATE 24,1:PRINT"Enter A";:LOCATE 18,13:INP
UT A:LOCATE 18,35:PRINT A;:LOCATE 22,13:PRINT A;
:LOCATE 24,1:PRINT"Enter B";:LOCATE 18,26:INPUT
B:LOCATE 18,35:PRINT A+B;:LOCATE 22,26:PRINT B;
490 LOCATE 24,1:PRINT"Enter C";:LOCATE 20,13:INP
UT C:LOCATE 22,13:PRINT A+C;:LOCATE 20,35:PRINT
C;:LOCATE 24,1:PRINT"Enter D";:LOCATE 20,26:INPU
T D:LOCATE 22,26:PRINT B+D;:LOCATE 20,35:PRINT C
+D:LOCATE 22,50:PRINT"Table Total = ";A+B+C+D;
500 DF=3:X2=((A+B+C+D)*((ABS((A*D)-(B*C))-((A+B+
C+D)/2))^2))/((A+B)*(A+C)*(C+D)*(B+D))
510 N=A+B+C+D
520 C=SQR(X2/(N+X2))
530 GOTO 440
540 PRINT:PRINT"Chi-Square = ";X2;" with ";DF;"
 degrees of freedom."
550 X=X2
560 GOTO 110
570 'if err = 6 then 610
```

Listing 5-8. Chi-Square Computations. (Continued From page 75.)

```
580 GOTO 1390
590 P=.999999:T=1-P:FX=(P/D)/((2*X)/V1):GOTO 240
600 PRINT:PRINT"Bartlett's Chi-Square Statistic"
:PRINT:PRINT
610 INPUT "How many samples in study";K
620 DIMR SI(K),FI(K),X(K,100):F=0:SX=0
630 PRINT:PRINT"Do you already have the sample s
tatistics?  (Y/N) ";:GOSUB 1370
640 IF Q$="Y" OR Q$="y" THEN 730
650 CLS
660 FOR I=1 TO K
670  PRINT"How many items in sample";I;"  (max 1
00)";:INPUT SS
680  FOR J=1 TO SS:PRINT"Enter value for item ";
J;:INPUT X(I,J):SX=SX+X(I,J):XT=XT+(X(I,J)^2):NE
XT J
690  SI(I)=SQR((XT-((SX^2)/SS))/(SS-1)):FI(I)=SS
-1:F=F+FI(I):X1=X1+(FI(I)*SI(I))):NEXT I
700  SX=0:XT=0
710 NEXT I
720 GOTO 740
730 PRINT:PRINT:FOR I=1 TO K:PRINT"Enter varianc
e for sample ";I;" and number of items";:INPUT S
I(I),FI(I):F=F+FI(I):X1=X1+(FI(I)*(SI(I))):NEXT
I
740 S2=X1/F:DF=K-1
750 FOR I=1 TO K
760  A=A+(FI(I)*LOG(SI(I))):B=B+(1/FI(I))
770 NEXT I
780 X=(F*LOG(S2)-A)/(1+((1/(3*(K-1)))*(B-(1/F)))
)
790 PRINT:PRINT"Chi-Square Value = ";X;"  with "
;DF;" degrees of freedom."
800 GOTO 110
810 PRINT:PRINT"Chi-Square for the Difference Be
tween Correlation Coefficients":PRINT:PRINT
820 PRINT"Do you have the necessary statistics c
ollected?  (Y/N) ";
830 GOSUB 1370:IF Q$="Y" OR Q$="y" THEN 950
840 FOR S=1 TO 2
850  PRINT:PRINT"How many pairs in set #";S;" (m
ust be >3)";:INPUT N(S)
860  IF N(S)<4 THEN 850
870  FOR I=1 TO N(S)
880   INPUT "Enter x,y data";X,Y
890   TX=TX+X:TY=TY+Y:X2=X2+(X^2):Y2=Y2+(Y^2):XY
=XY+(X*Y)
900  NEXT I
910 R(S)=((N(S)*XY)-(TX*TY))/SQR(((N(S)*X2)-(TX
^2))*((N(S)*Y2)-(TY^2))):TX=0:TY=0:X2=0:Y2=0:XY=
0
920  PRINT"Correlation, set #";S;" = ";R(S)
930 NEXT S
940 GOTO 960
950 PRINT:PRINT:FOR I=1 TO 2:PRINT"Enter correla
tion and number of pairs in set ";I;:INPUT R(I),
```

```
N(I):NEXT I
960 DF=1
970 FOR I=1 TO 2:Z(I)=.5*(LOG(1+R(I))-LOG(1-R(I)
)):NEXT I
980 X=((N(1)-3)*(Z(1)^2))+((N(2)-3)*(Z(2)^2))-((
((N(1)-3)*Z(1))+((N(2)-3)*Z(2)))^2)/((N(1)-3)+(N
(2)-3)))
990 PRINT:PRINT"Chi-Square = ";X;" with 1 degre
e of freedom."
1000 GOTO 110
1010 LPRINT"":LPRINT"Chi-Square      = ";X;" wit
h ";V1;" degrees of freedom."
1020 LPRINT"Density function         = ";FX
1030 LPRINT"Cumulative distribution = ";P
1040 LPRINT"Tail-end value          = ";T
1050 LPRINT ""
1060 GOTO 290
1070 RUN 10
1080 CLS:SCREEN 2:LINE (1,1)-(1,190):LINE (1,190
)-(640,190)
1090 FOR I=1 TO 640
1100   X=I/10
1110   V=V1
1120   A=1:FOR Z=V TO 2 STEP -2:A=A*Z:NEXT Z
1130   B=X^(INT((V+1)/2))*EXP(-X/2)/A
1140   IF INT(V/2)=V/2 THEN 1170
1150   C=SQR(2/X/PI)
1160   GOTO 1180
1170   C=1
1180   D=1:E=1
1190   V=V+2:E=E*X/V:IF E<.0000001 THEN 1210
1200   D=D+E:GOTO 1190
1210   P=C*B*D:FX=(P/D)/((2*X)/V1):YY(I)=FX
1220   Y=190-(190*FX):IF FX >LG THEN LG=FX
1230   PSET(10*X,Y)
1240   LOCATE 1,50:PRINT X;Y;
1250 NEXT I
1260 CLS:LOCATE 1,1:PRINT LG;:LINE (1,1)-(1,190)
:LINE (1,190)-(640,190)
1270 FOR X=1 TO 640:PSET(X,190-(178*(YY(X)/LG)))
:NEXT X
1280 FOR Y=200-(187*(YY(10*CH)/LG)) TO 200 STEP
2
1290   PSET(10*CH,Y)
1300 NEXT Y
1310 IF CH<12 THEN LOCATE 25,4*CH:PRINT CH;
1320 LOCATE 1,40:PRINT"<CR> to continue";
1330 INPUT ZZ:RUN 10
1340 IF ERR=5 THEN 1360
1350 PRINT:PRINT"Between the two of us an ugly e
rror of some sort has crept into our analysis.
 Let's try again.":GOTO 20
1360 PRINT:PRINT"Sorry, cannot complete the comp
utation with these data.  Try again.":GOTO 20
1370 Q$=""+INKEY$:IF Q$="" THEN 1370
1380 PRINT Q$:RETURN
1390 RUN "A:MENU"
```

Expected Values Equal

In this model the assumption is that a characteristic of each subject will be the same in each sample. For example, one die is tossed N times. If the die is fair, you would expect each number to appear N/6 times, as:

Number	1	2	3	4	5	6
Frequency	44	27	49	46	46	38

N = 250
Expectation = N/6 = 41.6667

Chi-square is computed from:

$$\chi^2 = \frac{N \Sigma 0_i^2}{\Sigma 0_i} - 0_i$$

In this example:

$$\chi^2 = \frac{6 \times 10742}{250} - 250 = 7.80808.$$

Expected Values Unequal

This approach is based on the assumption that the expected value (e) is a function of some variable and will not be constant from sample to sample as the independent variable changes. For example, a market survey suggests that the volume of customers in a store will not be a constant value equal to the average number of weekly customers divided by the number of days the store is open, but will vary according to the day of the week:

Day	Volume
Monday	23
Tuesday	47
Wednesday	49
Thursday	36
Friday	234
Saturday	310

The store owner keeps traffic records for a week, then puts the findings in a table:

	Mon	Tue	Wed	Thu	Fri	Sat
Observed	32	34	56	31	108	452

	Mon	Tue	Wed	Thu	Fri	Sat
Expected	23	47	49	36	234	310
0-E	9	–13	7	–5	–126	142

The equation for this form is:

$$\chi^2 = \sum_{i-1}^{N} \frac{(0_i - E_i)^2}{E_i}$$

Hence,

$$\chi^2 = \frac{9^2}{23} + \frac{-13^2}{47} + \frac{7^2}{49} + \frac{-5^2}{36} + \frac{-126^2}{234} + \frac{142^2}{310}$$
$$= 141.703$$

2 × κ Contingency Table

Contingency tables are used to evaluate the independence of two sets of variable data. The 2 × k implies there are two variables, each producing k items of data. The chi-square equation used to compute the chi-square is:

$$\chi^2 = \frac{N}{N_a} \sum_{i-1}^{k} \frac{A_i^2}{N_i} + \frac{N}{N_b} \sum_{i-1}^{k} \frac{B_i^2}{N_i} - N$$

where N is the total number of items ($N_a + N_b$) and A_i and B_i are data elements from each set.

Mr. Pearson (of Pearson's coefficient of correlation fame) has also developed a coefficient of contingency (C) that gives us an estimate of the degree to which the two variables are associated. It is computed from:

$$C = \sqrt{\frac{\chi^2}{N + \chi_2}}$$

2 × 2 Contingency Table with Yates Correction

This is a delightful little routine used to determine the significance, if any, of the difference between two groups of subjects as measured by some dichotomous variable. For example, let's assume a group of educators and traffic safety experts believe there is a relationship between driver training programs and reduced accident rates. They collect the available data and table as shown on following page.

Casual inspection of the data, in this instance, suggests the hypothesis is true. Indeed, the computed chi-square of these data is $\chi^2 = .840.601$. The probability these data have fallen out this way as the consequence of chance or random error is less

Number of People			
	Accident-Free	Have Had Accidents	Total
Trained	1023	214	1237
Untrained	324	968	1292
Total	1237	1182	2529

than one in a million. The basic equation for this form is:

$$\chi^2 = \Sigma \frac{(0 - E)^2}{N}$$

Unfortunately, the distribution associated with this equation is not quite properly fitted to the chi-square distribution. A statistician named Yates, however, has been kind enough to provide a correction feature which smooths out the curve into a nice and proper form. With the correction, the equation reads:

$$\chi^2 = \Sigma \left[\frac{(| 0 - E | - .5)^2}{N} \right]$$

where the expression $| 0 - E |$ means the absolute difference between 0 and E.

The computational formula for this contingency table is:

$$\chi^2 = \frac{(A = B\ C + D)\ [\ | AD - BC | - .5\ (A\ B + C + D)]^2}{(A + B)\ (A + C)\ (C + D)\ (B + D)}$$

where A, B, C, and D are taken from the form:

	Characteristic	
	1	2
Group A	A	B
Group B	C	D

This formula is numerically equivalent to the basic equation with Yates correction.

Bartlett's Chi-Square

This tool is used by statisticians who have collected data on a variable from a number of different sample groups (such as the computed reading level of junior high school students from several different schools). Having computed the mean and standard deviation from each sample, this routine gives an estimate of whether the students in each of the sample groups came from the same general population or from different educational systems. A major feature of this approach calls for the *variance* of the sample data. The variance, assuming an otherwise normal population distribution, is the square of the standard deviation. If s is the standard deviation of a sample, s^2 is the variance. The equation is:

$$\chi^2 = \frac{F \text{ Log}_e S^2 - \sum_{i=1}^{k} f_i \text{ Log}_e S_i^2}{1 + \frac{1}{3(k - 1)} \left[\left(\sum_{i=1}^{k} \frac{1}{f_i} \right) - \frac{1}{F} \right]}$$

where S_i^2 = sample variance of the ith sample,
f_i = degrees of freedom associated with S_i^2,
k = number of samples,

$$f = \sum_{i=1}^{k} f_i, \text{ and}$$

$$S^2 = \frac{\sum_{i=1}^{k} f_i S_i^2}{F}$$

If we have these data:

	Sample Number				
	1	2	3	4	5
Variance	3.2	4.5	6.7	3.1	7.8
f_i	34	56	87	43	12

the resulting chi-square is: $\chi^2 = 12.77$ with four degrees of freedom.

Chi-Square for the Difference Between Correlation Coefficients

Given coefficients of correlations derived from two samples, the question is whether or not there is a relationship between the two samples: do the findings represent the profile of one homogenous population or two different populations? The equation is:

$$\chi^2 = (N_1 - 3)z_1^2 + (N_2 - 3)z_2^2$$
$$- \frac{[\ (N_1 - 3)z_1 + (N_2 - 3)z_2]^2}{(N_1 - 3) + (N_2 - 3)}$$

where N_1 and N_2 are the sample sizes for each sample. z_1 and z_2 are transformations of the correlation coefficients, and are computed from:

$$z_i = .5\ [Log_e(2 + R_i - Log_e\ (1 - R_i)]$$

Given N_1 = 104 N_2 = 98 and
       R_1 = .98756 R_2 = .87693, then

z_1 = .5 [Log_e (1 + .98756) − Log_e (1 − .98756)] = 2.53687

z_2 = .5 Log_e (1 + .87693) − Log_e (1 − .87693) = 1.36232

χ^2 = 101 × 2.53687² + 95 × 1.36232²

− $\dfrac{[101 \times 2.53687 + 95 \times 1.36232]^2}{101 + 95}$

= 67.5364 with one degree of freedom.

Distribution and Density Functions

Figure 5-6 illustrates the basic range of forms the chi-square distribution can take as a function of the number of degrees of freedom.

Figure 5-7 illustrates a nominal chi-square distribution and shows the portions of the distribution of particular interest to us.

The cumulative distribution under the curve, $P(x)$, is computed from:

$$P(x) = \frac{2x}{v}\ f(x) \left[1 + \sum_{k=1}^{\infty} \frac{x^K}{(v + 2)(v + 4) \ldots (v + 2K)} \right]$$

where $x > 0$, and v is the degrees of freedom. The density function for any value of x is:

$$f(x) = \frac{x^{\frac{v}{2} - 1}}{2^{\frac{v}{2}} \sqrt{\left(\frac{v}{2}\right)}\ e^{\frac{x}{2}}}$$

1. $1 - P(x)$ is the tail value behind x. It is equal to the probability that the data being evaluated result from random or chance error. The smaller this value is, the more likely it is that the experimental findings are the result of the influence of the independent variable.

Listing 5-8 implements all of the foregoing equations and relationships.

ANALYSIS OF VARIANCE

Analysis of Variance (also known as one-way or two-way ANOVA) is a statistical technique frequently used by medical researchers to determine the effect of drugs on humans or animals and by psy-

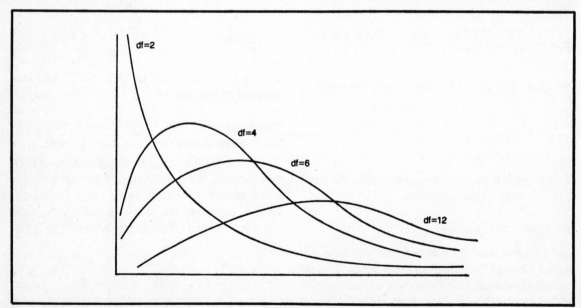

Fig. 5-6. Standard chi-square curves.

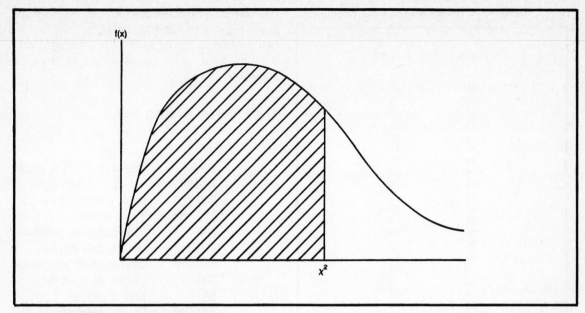

Fig. 5-7. **Area** under chi-square distribution.

chologists to test the effect of different teaching methods on groups of students, to name just a few applications. Whether the ANOVA is called one-way or two-way (or three-way . . .) depends on the number of variables or treatments involved in the experiment. An experiment in which there is only one stimulus affecting the subjects, such as the amount of a drug given or sleep permitted, would constitute an experiment suitable for a one-way ANOVA, while an experiment where there is a combination of stimuli involved, such as both the amount of drug given and the amount of sleep permitted, would be good for a two-way ANOVA. The program offered below gives the user the option of both a two-way and a one-way ANOVA. The program includes provision for the data to be output to a printer as well as the CRT.

It's not necessary for the user of this program to be a trained statistician or researcher. For those interested, the equations and technical considerations are given. There is, however, one feature all users must understand to make proper use of the routines, the *alpha criterion value*. At the beginning of the program, the user will be asked to provide this value. While the computer will accept any number, the answer should be between .00001 and .10000. In virtually all experiments, the collected data are tainted with some degree of random error. The knowledgeable researcher, however, is ready for this and will (must) provide for a certain margin of error. He will say, in effect, that if he can be reasonably sure that the output data are at least XX% pure or free from error, he will accept the theory or hypothesis being tested. The alpha value is the amount of acceptable error, expressed as a decimal; for example, 10% = .10. Researchers normally use either .05 or .01. Research in more exact and controllable sciences often use more rigorous values of .001 or .0001 as cutoff points. Which value you use depends largely on whether you are a chemist or a sociologist.

The second serious consideration for the reader is that this program and the comments about it are concerned solely with the mathematics of the analysis and not with experimental design. Indeed, whole graduate-level courses are taught just on designing experiments. But don't let this deter you. With proper attention paid to detail and cleanly-designed experiments, the output of this program will give reliable indicators.

The final consideration is that the number of subjects in each group or cell should be equal. The

Table 5-7. One-Way ANOVA Input Data.

Group 1	Group 2
7	42
33	25
26	8
27	28
21	30
6	22
14	17
19	32
6	28
11	6
11	1
18	15
14	9
18	15
19	2
14	37
9	13
12	2
6	23
24	18
7	1
10	3
1	4
10	6
343	387

program will compute the necessary statistics regardless of the number of items in a cell, but as the degree of inequality increases, so will the difficulty of producing an accurate analysis. Keep the number of items per cell larger than five and as equal in number as you can. Tables 5-7 and 5-9 are the input data and test results from two different experiments. The numbers could represent the number of correct answers students give after being subjected to different types of teaching methods, or they could be chickens' reaction times, in milliseconds, to a variety of stimuli. The difference between the two sets is that the first involves only one stimulus, applied against two groups, and the second involves two treatments applied against three groups. Tables 5-8 and 5-10 show the data output from the computer.

The Program (Listing 5-9)

Lines		
	10-40	Initial set-up and program selection
	60-660	One-way ANOVA routine
	70-190	Set-up and data input
	200-260	Basic computations
	270-350	Table set-up
	360	Probability computation
	370-440	Output data display
	450-470	Evaluation of probability
	530	Display of input data
	500	End of routine
	550-700	Display subroutine
	670-1550	Two-way ANOVA routine
	670-780	Set-up
	840-870	Basic computations, probability
	880-1020	Table set-up and output data display
	1030-1050	Evaluation of probability
	1100-1230	Data input subroutine
	1430-1550	Display subroutine
	1560-1700	Probability computation subroutine

The tables of output data uses conventional statistical notation: SS = Sum of Squares, DF = Degrees of Freedom, MS = Mean Squares, F = the F-distribution value, and P = the probability function, Q(F).

Table 5-8. One-Way ANOVA Output.

Source	SS	DF	MS	F	P
Total	4801.68	47			
Between	114.09	1	114.09	1.12	.2958
Within	4687.58	46	101.90		

Table 5-9. Two-Way ANOVA Input Data.

	Treatment A			
	Group 1	Group 2	Group 3	
Group 1	7	6	9	
	33	11	12	
	26	11	6	
	27	18	24	
	21	14	7	
	6	18	10	
	14	19	1	
	19	14	10	
	152	111	79	343
	Treatment B			
Group 2	42	28	13	
	25	6	2	
	8	1	18	
	28	15	23	
	30	9	1	
	22	15	3	
	17	2	4	
	32	37	6	
	204	113	70	387
	357	224	149	730

The Equations: One-Way ANOVA

$$\text{Total SS} = \sum_{i=1}^{K} \sum_{j=i}^{Ni} V_{ij}^2 - \frac{\left(\sum_{i=1}^{K} \sum_{j=1}^{Ni} V_{ij}^2\right)}{N_i}$$

$$\text{Treatment SS} = \sum_{i=1}^{K} \frac{\left(\sum_{j=1}^{Ni} V_j\right)^2}{N_i} \left(\frac{\sum_{i=1}^{K} \sum_{j=1}^{Ni} v_{ij}}{N_i}\right)^2$$

Error SS = Total SS – Treatment SS

Treatment DF = K – 1

$$\text{Error DF} = \sum_{i=1}^{K} N_i - K$$

$$\text{Treatment MS} = \frac{\text{Treatment SS}}{\text{Treatment DF}}$$

$$\text{Error MS} = \frac{\text{Error SS}}{\text{Error DF}}$$

$$F = \frac{\text{Treatment MS}}{\text{Error MS}} \text{ with } K-1 \text{ and } \sum_{i=1}^{K} N_i - K \text{ DF.}$$

Two-Way ANOVA

$$\text{Total SS} = \sum_r \sum_c \sum_i V_{irc}^2 - \left(\frac{\sum_r \sum_c \sum_i V_{irc}}{N_t}\right)^2 \quad \text{DF}$$

$$= N - 1$$

Table 5-10. Two-Way ANOVA Output.

Source	SS	DF	MS	F	P
Total	5030.02	47			
Column	1415.38	2	707.69	8.65	.001000
Row	60.77	1	60.77	.74	.601900
Row x Col	115.87	2	57.93	.71	.502800
Error	3438.00	42	81.06		

Listing 5-9. Combined Analysis of Variance.

```
1  '***********************************************
2  '*                 Listing 5-9                 *
3  '*        Combined Analysis of Variance        *
4  '***********************************************
5  '
10 CLS:KEY OFF:PRINT"          ********** ANAL
YSIS OF VARIANCE  **********":PRINT:PRINT:PRINT"
     1 -- ONE-WAY ANOVA                    2 -- T
WO-WAY ANOVA
             3 -- End":PRINT:PRINT
20 PRINT"ENTER LETTER OF FORM DESIRED.";
30 Q$=INKEY$:IF Q$="" THEN 30
40 Q=VAL(Q$):ON Q GOTO 50,670,1710
50 CLS
60 PRINT"          ********  ONE-WAY ANALYSIS OF
 VARIANCE  ********":PRINT:PRINT:PRINT
70 INPUT"WHAT IS THE CRITCAL ALPHA VALUE FOR REJ
ECTING NULL HYPOTHESIS  (0 < X <= 1.00)";CV
80 PRINT:INPUT"HOW MANY GROUPS";G
90 DIM GP(G),GS(G):M=INT(FRE(0)/45):DIM V(G,M)'P
RESERVATION OF VALUE 'V' IS FOR SUMMARY AT END.
 CAN BE CHANGED TO SIMPLY 'V'
100 PRINT:PRINT"THE AVERAGE SIZE OF EACH GROUP S
HOULD BE";INT(M/G);"OR LESS.":PRINT
110 FOR I=1 TO G
120 PRINT"HOW MANY SUBJECTS IN GROUP";I;:INPUT S
:GP(I)=S
130 IF S>LG THEN LG=S
140 FOR J=1 TO S
150 PRINT"ENTER VALUE FOR GROUP";I,"SUBJECT";J;:
INPUT V(I,J)
160 GS(I)=GS(I)+V(I,J):TS=TS+V(I,J)
170 TQ=TQ+(V(I,J)^2):N=N+1
180 NEXT J
190 NEXT I
200 CLS:LOCATE 9,1:PRINT"PLEASE BE PATIENT, COMP
UTING...."
210 SQ=TS^2:QN=SQ/N:SS=TQ-QN
220 FOR I=1 TO G
230 QQ=QQ+((GS(I)^2)/GP(I))
240 NEXT I
250 SB=QQ-QN:SW=SS-SB:FT=N-1:FB=G-1:FW=FT-FB
260 MT=SS/FT:MB=SB/FB:MW=SW/FW:F=MB/MW
270 CLS
280 LPRINT" "
290 LOCATE 6,4:PRINT"SOURCE              SS
DF       MS       F            P";
300 LPRINT"   SOURCE                 SS          DF
 MS        F            P"
310 LPRINT STRING$(70,"*")
320 Z$="  ########.##     ####   ####.## ####.##
    #.######"
330 ZZ$="  ########.##     ####"
340 ZY$="  ########.##     ####   ####.##"
350 DE=FW
360 GOSUB 1560
```

84

```
370 LOCATE 8,1:PRINT"TOTAL      ";:PRINT USING ZZ
$;SS;FT
380 LPRINT"TOTAL      ";:LPRINT USING ZZ$;SS;FT
390 LOCATE 9,1:PRINT"   BETWEEN";:PRINT USING Z$
;SB;FB;MB;F;P
400 LPRINT"   BETWEEN";:LPRINT USING Z$;SB;FB;MB
;F;P
410 LOCATE 10,1:PRINT"    WITHIN";:PRINT USING Z
Y$;SW;FW;MW
420 LPRINT"    WITHIN";:LPRINT USING ZY$;SW;FW;M
W
430 LPRINT" "
440 ' Y=19:FOR X=0 TO 127:SET(X,Y):NEXT X:X=24:F
OR Y=15 TO 31:SET(X,Y):NEXT Y
450 PRINT:IF CV>P THEN 470
460 PRINT"THE DATA IS NOT SUFFICIENT TO REJECT T
HE NULL HYPOTHESIS.";:LPRINT" ":LPRINT"THE DATA
DO NOT SUPPORT REJECTION OF THE NULL HYPOTHESIS"
:GOTO 480
470 PRINT"VARIATIONS NOTED ARE LIKELY TO BE THE
RESULT OF THE TREATMENT.":LPRINT" ":LPRINT"VARIA
TIONS NOTED ARE LIKELY TO BE THE RESULT OF THE T
REATMENT."
480 GOSUB 510
490 PRINT:PRINT:INPUT"'ENTER' WHEN READY";ZZ:RUN
 10
500 END
510 LPRINT" "
520 LPRINT"INPUT VALUES":LPRINT" "
530 FOR I=1 TO G:LPRINT"GROUP";I,:NEXT I
540 LPRINT" "
550 FOR I=1 TO LG
560 FOR J=1 TO G
570 IF GP(J)<I THEN 590
580 LPRINT V(J,I),:GOTO 600
590 LPRINT" ",
600 NEXT J
610 LPRINT" "
620 NEXT I
630 LPRINT" "
640 FOR I=1 TO G:LPRINT GS(I),:NEXT I:LPRINT"
  SUM"
650 LPRINT" ":FOR I=1 TO G:LPRINT GS(I)/GP(I),:N
EXT I:LPRINT"    AVERAGE"
660 RETURN
670 'START
680 CLS
690 CLEAR 100
700 'ANALYSIS OF VARIANCE ROUTINES
710 PRINT"        ******** TWO-WAY ANALYSIS O
F VARIANCE ********":PRINT:PRINT:PRINT
720 INPUT"WHAT IS THE CRITICAL ALPHA VALUE FOR R
EJECTING THE NULL HYPOTHESIS.  (0 < X <=1.0)";CV
730 N=1
740 PRINT:INPUT"TREATMENT 'A' (COLUMNS) CONSISTS
 OF HOW MANY GROUPS";A
750 INPUT"TREATMENT 'B' (ROWS) CONSISTS OF HOW M
ANY GROUPS";B
```

Listing 5-9. Combined Analysis of Variance. (Continued From Page 85.)

```
760 CC=A:RR=B
770 D=90
780 DIM GN(B,A),GT(B,A),GS(B,A),RN(B),RT(B),R2(B
),CN(A),CT(A),C2(A):M=INT(FRE(0)/19):DIM V(M)'PR
ESERVATION OF 'V' IS SIMPLY FOR SUMMARY AT END.
 CAN BE CHANGED TO 'V'
790 PRINT:PRINT"THE AVERAGE CELL SIZE SHOULD NOT
 EXCEED";INT(FRE(0)/(A*B)):PRINT
800 Z$="   ########.##     ####   ####.##   ####.##
   #.######"
810 ZZ$="   ########.##     ####"
820 ZY$="   ########.##     ####   ####.##"
830 GOSUB 1100
840 F=FC:FB=DC:GOSUB 1560
850 PC=P:F=FR:FB=DR:GOSUB 1560
860 PR=P:F=FI:FB=DI:GOSUB 1560
870 PI=P
880 CLS
890 LOCATE 6,4:PRINT"SOURCE              SS
  DF        MS        F         P"
900 LPRINT" ":LPRINT"SOURCE                  SS
         DF         MS         F          P"
910 LPRINT STRING$(70,"*")
920 LOCATE 8,1:PRINT"TOTAL          ";:PRINT USING
 ZZ$;ST;DT
930 LPRINT"TOTAL          ";:LPRINT USING ZZ$;ST;D
T
940 LOCATE 9,1:PRINT"   COLUMN      ";:PRINT USING
 Z$;SC;DC;MC;FC;PC
950 LPRINT"   COLUMN      ";:LPRINT USING Z$;SC;DC
;MC;FC;PC
960 LOCATE 10,1:PRINT"      ROW      ";:PRINT USIN
G Z$;SR;DR;MR;FR;PR
970 LPRINT"      ROW      ";:LPRINT USING Z$;SR;DR
;MR;FR;PR
980 LOCATE 11,1:PRINT" ROW X COL     ";:PRINT USIN
G Z$;SI;DI;MI;FI;PI
990 LPRINT" ROW X COL     ";:LPRINT USING Z$;SI;DI
;MI;FI;PI
1000 LOCATE 12,1:PRINT"      ERROR     ";:PRINT USI
NG ZY$;ES;DE;ME
1010 LPRINT"      ERROR     ";:LPRINT USING ZY$;ES;
DE;ME
1020 PRINT
1030 IF CV>PC THEN PRINT"COLUMN EFFECTS ARE SIGN
IFICANT" ELSE PRINT"COLUMN EFFECTS ARE NOT SIGNI
FICANT"
1040 IF CV>PR THEN PRINT"ROW EFFECTS ARE SIGNIFI
CANT" ELSE PRINT"ROW EFFECTS ARE NOT SIGNIFICANT
"
1050 IF CV>PI THEN PRINT"ROW/COLUMN INTERACTION
IS SIGNIFICANT" ELSE PRINT"ROW/COLUMN EFFECTS AR
E NOT SIGNIFICANT"
1060 GOSUB 1370
1070 LOCATE 1,1:PRINT"'ENTER' WHEN FINISHED";:IN
PUT ZZ
```

```
1080 RUN 10
1090 END
1100 'DATA INPUT AREA
1110 FOR I=1 TO B
1120 FOR J=1 TO A
1130 PRINT"HOW MANY RESPONSES IN CELL";I;"-";J;:
INPUT R:GN(I,J)=R
1140 FOR K=1 TO R
1150 PRINT"ENTER VALUE FOR ITEM";K;:INPUT V(N)
1160 T=T+V(N):TS=TS+V(N)^2:GT(I,J)=GT(I,J)+V(N)
1170 GS(I,J)=GS(I,J)+V(N)^2:N=N+1
1180 NEXT K
1190 CT(J)=CT(J)+GT(I,J):RN(I)=RN(I)+GN(I,J)
1200 CN(J)=CN(J)+GN(I,J):RT(I)=RT(I)+GT(I,J)
1210 NEXT J
1220 R2(I)=RT(I)^2
1230 NEXT I
1240 CLS:LOCATE 9,1:PRINT"PLEASE BE PATIENT, COM
PUTING...."
1250 FOR I=1 TO A:C2(I)=CT(I)^2:NEXT I
1260 N=N-1
1270 T2=(T^2)/N
1280 ST=TS-T2
1290 FOR I=1 TO A:SC=SC+((CT(I)^2)/CN(I)):NEXT I
:SC=SC-T2
1300 FOR I=1 TO B:SR=SR+((RT(I)^2)/RN(I)):NEXT I
:SR=SR-T2
1310 FOR I=1 TO B:FOR J=1 TO A:SI=SI+((GT(I,J)^2
)/GN(I,J)):NEXT J:NEXT I:SI=SI-T2-SC-SR
1320 ES=ST-SC-SR-SI
1330 DT=N-1:DC=A-1:DR=B-1:DI=DC*DR:DE=DT-DC-DR-D
I
1340 MC=SC/DC:MR=SR/DR:MI=SI/DI:ME=ES/DE
1350 FC=MC/ME:FR=MR/ME:FI=MI/ME
1360 RETURN
1370 LPRINT" "
1380 LPRINT"SIGNIFICANT FINDINGS:"
1390 IF CV>PC THEN LPRINT"            COLUMN EFF
ECTS ARE SIGNFICANT"
1400 IF CV>PR THEN LPRINT"            ROW EFFECT
S ARE SIGNIFICANT"
1410 IF CV>PI THEN LPRINT"            ROW/COLUMN
 INTERACTION EFFECTS ARE SIGNIFICANT"
1420 IF PC>CV AND PR>CV AND PI>CV THEN LPRINT"
          NONE"
1430 LPRINT" "
1440 LPRINT"INPUT VARIABLES"
1450 N=1
1460 FOR I=1 TO RR
1470 FOR J=1 TO CC
1480 LPRINT" ":LPRINT"CELL GROUP";I;J;":";
1490 FOR K=1 TO GN(I,J)
1500 LPRINT V(N),:N=N+1
1510 NEXT K
1520 NEXT J
1530 NEXT I
1540 LPRINT" "
1550 RETURN
```

Listing 5-9. Combined Analysis of Variance. (Continued From Page 87.)

```
1560 X=1
1570 IF F<1 THEN 1590
1580 A=FB:B=DE:C=F:GOTO 1600
1590 A=DE:B=FB:C=1/F
1600 D=2/9/A:E=2/9/B:YY=ABS((1-E)*C^(1/3)-1+D)/S
QR(E*C^(2/3)+D)
1610 IF B<4 THEN 1650
1620 XX=.5/(1+YY*(.196854+YY*(.115194+YY*(.00034
4+YY*.019527))))^4
1630 XX=INT(XX*10000+.5)/10000
1640 GOTO 1670
1650 YY=YY*(1+.08*YY^4/B^3)
1660 GOTO 1620
1670 IF F>=1 THEN 1690
1680 P=1-XX:P=1-P:GOTO 1700
1690 P=1-XX
1700 P=1-P:RETURN
1710 RUN "A:MENU"
```

$$\text{Column SS} = \frac{\left(\sum_c \sum_r \sum_i V_{irc}\right)^2}{RN_r} -$$

$$\frac{\left(\sum_r \sum_c \sum_i V_{irc}\right)^2}{N_t} \text{, DF}$$

$$= C - 1$$

$$\text{Row SS} = \frac{\sum_r \left(\sum_c \sum_i V_{irc}\right)^2}{CN_c} \frac{\left(\sum_r \sum_c \sum_i V_{irc}\right)^2}{N_t} \text{, DF}$$

$$= R - 1$$

$$\text{Within SS} = \sum_r \sum_c \sum_i V_{irc}^2 - \frac{\sum_r \sum_c \left(\sum_i V_{irc}\right)^2}{N_w} \text{, DF}$$

$$= RC(N-)$$

$$\text{Between SS} = \frac{\sum_r \sum_c \left(\sum_i V_{irc}^2\right)}{N_{rc}} \frac{\sum_c \left(\sum_r \sum_i V_{irc}^2\right)}{RN_t}$$

$$\frac{\sum_r \left(\sum_c \sum_i V_{irc}\right)^2}{CN_t} + \frac{\left(\sum_r \sum_c \sum_i V_{irc}\right)^2}{N_t}$$

$$DF = (R-1)(C-1)$$

$$F_{row} = \frac{\text{Row SS}^2}{\text{Within SS}^2} \quad F_{column} = \frac{\text{Column SS}^2}{\text{Within SS}^2}$$

$$\text{Between F} = \frac{\text{Between SS}^2}{\text{Within SS}^2}$$

The value P, or A(x) is evaluated as the integral of the F-distribution:

$$Q(F) = \int_F^\infty \frac{\Gamma\left(\frac{D_n + D_m}{2}\right) \frac{D_n}{y^2} - 1\left(\frac{D_n}{D_m}\right) D_n^2}{\Gamma\left(\frac{D_n^-}{2}\right)\Gamma\left(\frac{D_m}{2}\right)\left(1 + \frac{D_n y}{D_m}\right)\left(\frac{D_n + D_m}{2}\right)}$$

dy, D_n = Degrees of freedom, numerator

D_m = Degrees of freedom, denominator

Where:

N = total number of items or responses = N_t
N_r = number of items in a row
N_c = number of items in a column
N_w = number of items within a cell
R = number of rows
C = number of columns
DF = Degrees of Freedom
V_{irc} = Actual value of the item i at the intersection of row r and column c.

ROWS AND COLUMNS

Statistical data are frequently tabulated into a

row and column format. Normally, one or more of the other routines that have just been presented in this chapter are used to evaluate the data against some well-defined hypothesis. The routine defined in Listing 5-10, however, is useful when you have a group of data in tabular form but no real firm notion of what it all means. The data are entered item by item from left to right, starting with row 1, column 1, and going row by row down the table. The program takes over and computes the sum, mean,

Listing 5-10. Rows and Columns.

```
1 '*********************************************
2 '*                 Listing 5.10                *
3 '*               Rows and Columns              *
4 '*********************************************
5 '
6 'This program is written to print out up to 8
columns of input data with the  printer set on 2
0 pitch.  If you have more than 8 columns or if
your printer    won't print at 20 pitch, you wil
l have adjust lines 600-880 accordingly.
7 '
10 CLS:KEY OFF:INPUT "Printer Pitch";PP:LP=8*PP
20 INPUT"HOW MANY ROWS ARE THERE IN THE MATRIX";
R
30 PRINT:INPUT"HOW MANY COLUMNS ARE THERE";C
40 DIM CR(R-1,R),YX(R-1,R),Y(R),Y2(R),RC(C-1,C),
I(R,C),X(C),X2(C),XY(C-1,C)
50 LPRINT" ":LPRINT"NUMBER OF ROWS =";R:LPRINT"N
UMBER OF COLUMNS =";C
60 LPRINT" "
70 CLS
80 FOR J=1 TO R
90 FOR K=1 TO C
100 LOCATE 6,31:PRINT"ROW  COL";
110 LOCATE 8,21:PRINT"ITEM:":LOCATE 8,31:PRINT J
:LOCATE 8,36:PRINT K
120 INPUT I(J,K)
130 NEXT K
140 NEXT J
150 CLS
160 LOCATE 9,1:PRINT"ARE THESE DATA CORRECT?  (Y
/N)"
170 Q$=INKEY$:IF Q$="" THEN 170
180 IF Q$="Y" OR Q$="y" THEN 210 ELSE 190
190 CLS:LOCATE 9,1:PRINT"ENTER ROW AND COLUMN OF
 DATA TO BE CORRECTED":INPUT J,K
200 PRINT:INPUT"ENTER CORRECT DATA";I(J,K):GOTO
150
210 CLS:FOR J=1 TO R
220 LOCATE 9,1:PRINT"J =";J;"          ";
230 FOR K=1 TO C
240 LOCATE 9,1:PRINT"K =";K;"         ";
250 X(K)=X(K)+I(J,K):X2(K)=X2(K)+(I(J,K)^2)
260 Y(J)=Y(J)+I(J,K):Y2(J)=Y2(J)+(I(J,K)^2)
270 NEXT K
280 FOR K=1 TO C-1
290 FOR L=K+1 TO C
300 XY(K,L)=XY(K,L)+(I(J,K)*I(J,L))
310 NEXT L
```

Listing 5-10. Rows and Columns. (Continued From Page 89.)

```
320 NEXT K
330 NEXT J
340 FOR M=1 TO C
350 LOCATE 9,1:PRINT"M=";M;"              ";
360 FOR K=1 TO (R-1)
370 LOCATE 9,1:PRINT"K =";K;"          ";
380 FOR J=K+1 TO R
390 LOCATE 9,1:PRINT"J =";J;"      ";
400 YX(K,J)=YX(K,J)+(I(K,M)*I(J,M))
410 NEXT J
420 NEXT K
430 NEXT M
440 CLS
450 FOR K=1 TO C-1
460 LOCATE 9,1:PRINT"K =";K;"            ";
470 FOR L=K+1 TO C
480 LOCATE 9,1:PRINT"L =";L;"       ";
490 RC(K,L)=((R*XY(K,L))-(X(K)*X(L)))/SQR(((R*X2
(K))-(X(K)^2))*((R*X2(L))-(X(L)^2)))
500 NEXT L
510 NEXT K
520 CLS
530 FOR K=1 TO (R-1)
540 LOCATE 9,1:PRINT"K =";K;"           ";
550 FOR J=K+1 TO R
560 PRINT 512,"J =";J;"         ";
570 CR(K,J)=((C*YX(K,J))-(Y(K)*Y(J)))/SQR(((C*Y2
(K))-(Y(K)^2))*((C*Y2(J))-(Y(J)^2)))
580 NEXT J
590 NEXT K
600 CLS
610 PRINT"":LPRINT"Table of Input Data":LPRINT""
620 LPRINT "                      Columns"
630 LPRINT"Row",:FOR I=1 TO C:LPRINT I,:NEXT:LPR
INT "Sum","Average","Std. Dev."
640 FOR J=1 TO R
650    LPRINT J,
660    FOR K=1 TO C
670       LPRINT I(J,K),
680    NEXT K
690    LPRINT Y(J),Y(J)/C,SQR((Y2(J)-((Y(J)^2)/C)
)/(C-1))
700 NEXT J
710 LPRINT"Sum",:FOR I=1 TO C:LPRINT X(I),:NEXT
I:LPRINT""
720 LPRINT "Average",:FOR I=1 TO C:LPRINT X(I)/R
,:NEXT I:LPRINT""
730 LPRINT "Std. Dev.",:FOR I=1 TO C:LPRINT SQR(
(X2(I)-((X(I)^2)/R))/(R-1)),:NEXT I:LPRINT ""
740 LPRINT"":LPRINT"Table of Column Correlations
":LPRINT""
750 LPRINT "Column A","Column B","Correlation","
t-Test"
760 FOR K=1 TO C-1
770    FOR L=K+1 TO C
780       LPRINT K,L,RC(K,L),((RC(K,L)*SQR(C-2))/
```

```
SQR(1-(RC(K,L)^2))
790    NEXT L
800 NEXT K
810 LPRINT "":LPRINT ""
820 LPRINT "Table of Row Correlations":LPRINT""
830 LPRINT "Row A","Row B","Correlation","t-Test
"
840 FOR M=1 TO R-1
850    FOR N=M+1 TO R
860       LPRINT M,N,CR(M,N),((CR(M,N))*SQR(R-2))/
SQR(1-(CR(M,N)^2))
870    NEXT N
880 NEXT M
890 PRINT"(A)nother        (M)ain menu ";
900 GOSUB 920
910 ' IF Q$="A" OR Q$="a" THEN RUN 10 ELSE RUN "
A:MENU"
920 Q$=""+INKEY$:IF Q$="" THEN 920
930 RETURN
```

and standard deviation of each row and then each column. Following this, the program computes the correlation between each of the rows in a pairwise fashion and then between each of the columns the same way. This routine is not meant to replace the other routines, but to provide a tool for preliminary analysis of a set of raw data. For example, we may want to examine a number of characteristics of a set of students as they enter a course of training to identify those characteristics which seem to be related to success (or failure) later in the course. Before investing a lot of time collecting data that may later prove to be irrelevant, we can use this program to evaluate a smaller set of data from a broad range of characteristics to get a rough notion of relevant characteristics. Having run this program, the more meaningful data items can be collected in depth and processed by one or another of the previous (or subsequent) programs.

EXERCISES

1. Define the phrase *violent crime*. Review the leading local newspaper daily for two or three months. Record the number of violent crimes committed each day and the daily temperature and precipitation. At the end of the test, compute the correlation between crime and weather. If possible, conduct the test during a transitional weather period; that is, from winter into spring or from fall into winter.

2. Select an economic indicator, such as the Dow-Jones stock index. Conduct the experiment in exercise 1 above, using the economic index instead of weather.

3. Attend a sports event, such as a high diving competition, where there are three or more judges giving subjective ratings on the contestants. Keep your own record of each judge's ratings, then compute a Kendall's Coefficient of Concordance.

4. Using sex as the dichotomous variable, and last year's grades for a selected class as the continuous variable, compute a Point-Biserial correlation to determine if there is a sex-related component to the grades.

5. Using the grades identified in exercise 4 above, compute a rank order correlation between last year's grades and the grade of each student for the last test in this course.

SUGGESTED READING

Bruning, J. L. and B. L. Kintz, 1968. *Computational Handbook of Statistics*. Glenview, IL: Scott, Foresman and Company.

Edwards, A. L., 1976. *An Introduction to Linear Regression and Correlation*. San Francisco: W. H. Freeman and Company.

— — — 1979. *Multiple Regression and the Analysis of Variance and Covariance*. San Francisco: W. H. Freeman and Company.

Minium, E. W., 1970. *Statistical Reasoning in Psychology and Education*. New York: John Wiley & Sons.

## Chapter 6

Time-Series Analysis

Perhaps one of the most frequently used techniques in current forecasting are those found under the heading of time-series analysis. The commercial interests in forecasting are very often an effort to determine, as far in advance and as accurately as possible, the future value of a stock, the price of an essential commodity, or the volume of demand for a product—all based on past history, or the preceding time-series. These problems are often complicated by the multitude of factors affecting the magnitude of the desired variable. Other areas suitable for time-series analysis include population studies, weather patterns, sunspot cycles . . . in short, anything the quantity or magnitude of which is, or appears to be, a function of time.

The simplest form of time-series analysis is the computation of the mean of a set of data. Figure 6-1 presents a set of data points and the computed mean, which is shown as a heavy line running from right to left.

To the extent that the data are more or less linear, and the coefficient of correlation is approach-

ing zero, the mean is a reliable predictor of future conditions. As the data becomes less and less linear, more sophisticated methods of analysis are necessary.

The methods we will examine for time-series analysis are: smoothing and decomposition methods, autoregressive/moving averages, multivariate time-series, linear and non-linear curve fitting, seasonal and cyclic trend analysis, and indexing techniques.

SMOOTHING AND DECOMPOSITION METHODS

Underlying this approach is the notion that an observed data point is a function of one or more of the preceding points. Although an average or mean of all of the data points leads to a meaningless result, an average of some of the data points produces useful results.

There are a number of smoothing techniques available. Among them are: single moving averages, single exponential smoothing, linear moving averages, and linear exponential smoothing.

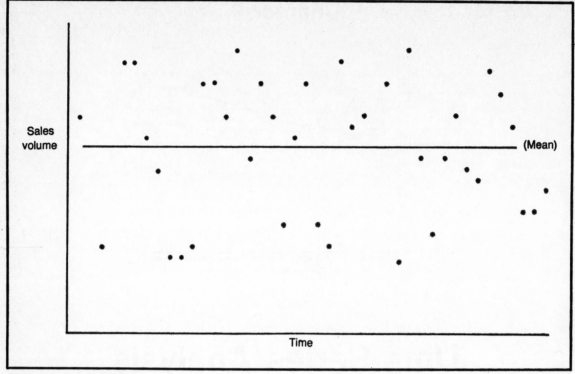

Fig. 6-1. Basic scattergram.

Single Moving Averages

This technique uses the average or mean of N previous periods to compute the next value. An example of this is given in Table 6-1. The resulting graph is shown in Fig. 6-2.

It is possible (and advisable) to evaluate the utility of a given value of N by computing the coefficient of correlation between the actual and predicted values. There is no routine to compute the optimum N, but microcomputers make easy work of selecting this value. Yesterday's statistician had to pick several values of N manually and make the necessary computations, selecting the value that appeared to yield the best results. The microcomputer approach is to compute the moving average for each value of N from two to the number of available data points less one. That is, if there are K data points, the moving average for N = 2 to K − 1 is computed. At the same time, the coefficient of correlation for the predictions for each value of N is computed.

Listing 6-1 is a routine to accept a set of data and evaluate it as just described. The input is simply the value for each data point. The output is the recommended value of N, based on the coefficient of correlation. The user can add features to print the intermediate data and the coefficients of correlation for the other values of N.

Linear Moving Averages

As you will note in Table 6-1, the moving average lags behind (or underestimates) the actual data on a steady trend upward and overstates the estimate on a downward trend. If we compute the moving average of this moving average, however, we find the difference between the two moving averages is equal to the error between the first average and the actual data. We can exploit this fact by using the following procedure:

1. $E' = \dfrac{X_1 + X_2 + X_3 + \ldots + X_n}{N}$

Table 6-1. Input and Output Data from Moving Average Routine.

```
SINGLE MOVING AVERAGE
PERIOD FOR AVERAGING =  0
N    SUM OF X   SUM OF Y   CORREL.    BEST      N    NET ERROR
2    3045.00    2896.00    0.66884    0.66884   2    149.00
3    3045.00    2899.67    0.87197    0.87197   3    179.33
4    3045.00    2873.42    0.85726    0.87197   3    207.92
5    3045.00    2845.33    0.86903    0.87197   3    232.17
6    3045.00    2827.50    0.83758    0.88758   6    255.50
7    3045.00    2809.17    0.88655    0.88758   6    276.00
8    3045.00    2792.07    0.89081    0.89081   8    294.21
9    3045.00    2776.95    0.89334    0.89334   9    311.05
10   3045.00    2761.53    0.89694    0.89694   10   326.69
11   3045.00    2748.24    0.89591    0.89694   10   340.77
12   3045.00    2736.21    0.89319    0.89694   10   353.98
13   3045.00    2725.31    0.89991    0.89991   13   366.70
14   3045.00    2715.01    0.89961    0.89991   13   378.22
15   3045.00    2705.58    0.89465    0.89991   13   388.35
16   3045.00    2698.10    0.89712    0.89991   13   396.90
17   3045.00    2691.39    0.89485    0.89991   13   404.68
18   3045.00    2685.45    0.88976    0.89991   13   411.38
19   3045.00    2680.38    0.88895    0.89991   13   417.28
20   3045.00    2676.27    0.87844    0.89991   13   422.89
21   3045.00    2673.50    0.87976    0.89991   13   426.35
22   3045.00    2672.73    0.87487    0.89991   13   428.79
23   3045.00    2670.83    0.86849    0.89991   13   431.49

PERIOD          ACTUAL          FORECAST     ERROR
1               66              66           0
2               134             66           68
3               107             100          7
4               87              102.333      -15.3333
5               126             98.5         27.5
6               117             104          13
7               114             106.167      7.83334
8               121             107.286      13.7143
9               111             109          2
10              117             109.222      7.77778
11              123             110          13
12              133             111.182      21.8182
13              129             113          16
14              124             114.231      9.76923
15              131             118.692      12.3077
16              133             118.462      14.5385
17              130             120.462      9.53846
18              133             123.769      9.23077
19              147             124.308      22.6923
20              134             126.615      7.38461
21              156             128.154      27.8462
22              140             130.846      9.15384
23              168             133.077      34.9231
24              164             137          27

EACH SET CONTAINS 13 ITEMS, CORRELATION = .899908   NET SUM OF ERROR = 366.695
```

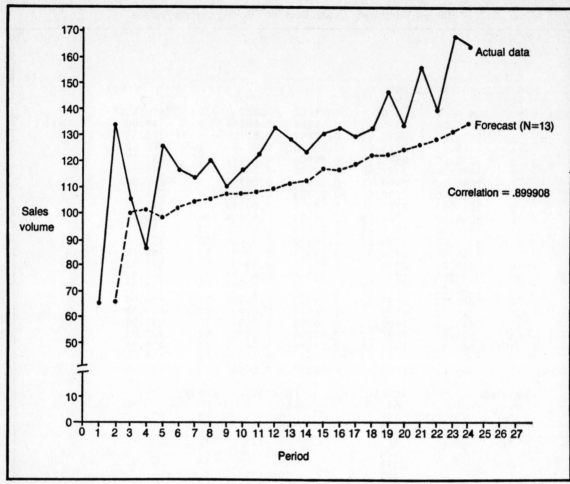

Fig. 6-2. Simple moving averages.

Listing 6-1. Moving Averages.

```
1 '********************************************
2 '*                 Listing 6-1              *
3 '*              Moving Averages             *
4 '********************************************
5 '
10 CLS:KEY OFF
20 INPUT"HOW MANY DATA POINTS";K
30 DIM V(K),R(K),A(K+1,K),ES(K):BR=0
40 FOR I=1 TO K:PRINT"ENTER VALUE FOR POINT #";I
,:INPUT V(I):NEXT
50 FOR I=1 TO K:PRINT I;V(I),:NEXT:PRINT
60 PRINT"ARE THESE ALL OK?  (Y/N)  ";
70 Q$=""+INKEY$:IF Q$="" THEN 70 ELSE PRINT Q$
80 IF Q$="Y" OR Q$="y" THEN 100
90 INPUT"ENTER NUMBER OF ITEM AND CORRECT VALUE"
;J,V(J):GOTO 50
```

```
100 PRINT"PRINTING INPUT DATA":LPRINT"INPUT DATA
":FOR I=1 TO K:LPRINT I;V(I),:NEXT:LPRINT""
110 PRINT"N","SUM OF F'CAST","CORRELATION","NET
ERROR"
120 PRINT:LPRINT"N    SUM OF X    SUM OF Y    CORRE
L.    BEST        N      NET ERROR"
130 N$="##    ####.##    ####.##    #.#####    #.#
####      ##    #####.##"
140 FOR N=2 TO K-1
150 T=0:TX=0:TY=0:X2=0:Y2=0:XY=0:A(1,N)=V(1):ES(
N)=0
160 FOR I=1 TO N-1
170 X=V(I):T=T+X:TX=TX+X:Y=TX/I:TY=TY+Y:X2=X2+(X
^2):Y2=Y2+(Y^2):XY=XY+(X*Y):A(I+1,N)=TX/I:ES(N)=
ES(N)+V(I)-A(I,N)
180 NEXT I
190 FOR I=N TO K
200 A=A(I,N):T=T+V(I):A(I+1,N)=T/N:TX=TX+V(I):TY
=TY+A:X2=X2+(V(I)^2):Y2=Y2+(A^2):XY=XY+(A*V(I)):
T=T-V(I-N+1):ES(N)=ES(N)+V(I)-A(I,N)
210 NEXT
220 R(N)=((K*XY)-(TX*TY))/SQR(((K*X2)-(TX^2))*((
K*Y2)-(TY^2)))
230 IF ABS(R(N))<ABS(BR) THEN 250
240 BR=R(N):RN=N
250 LPRINT USING N$;N;TX;TY;R(N);BR;RN;ES(N)
260 PRINT N,TY,R(N),ES(N)
270 NEXT
280 LPRINT"":ES=0:INPUT"AVERAGE FREQUENCY DESIRE
D";FD
290 LPRINT"PERIOD","ACTUAL","FORECAST","ERROR"
300 FOR I=1 TO K
310 LPRINT I,V(I),A(I,FD),V(I)-A(I,FD)
320 NEXT
330 LPRINT""
340 LPRINT"EACH SET CONTAINS";RN;"ITEMS,   CORREL
ATION = ";R(RN);"   NET SUM OF ERROR = ";ES(RN)
350 PRINT"(A)nother        (M)ain menu ";
360 GOSUB 380
370 IF Q$="A" OR Q$="a" THEN RUN 10 ELSE RUN "A:
MENU"
380 Q$=""+INKEY$:IF Q$="" THEN 380
390 RETURN
```

2. $E' = \dfrac{E_1' + E_2' + E_3' \ldots + E_n'}{N}$

3. $A = 2E' - E''$
4. $B = (2/(N - 1)) \times (E' - E'')$
5. $F = A + BM$

Where M is the number of period ahead to be forecast. Figure 6-3, based on the data in Table 6-2, illustrates the effect of this approach.

Single Exponential Smoothing

The routine used above requires considerable memory space to store each of the input data points. In addition, each point, regardless of position relative to the present, has equal mathematical weight in the computation of the mean. In reality, recent values may be disproportionately more significant than older points. In many firms the sales force is constantly changing, and sales volume is a function

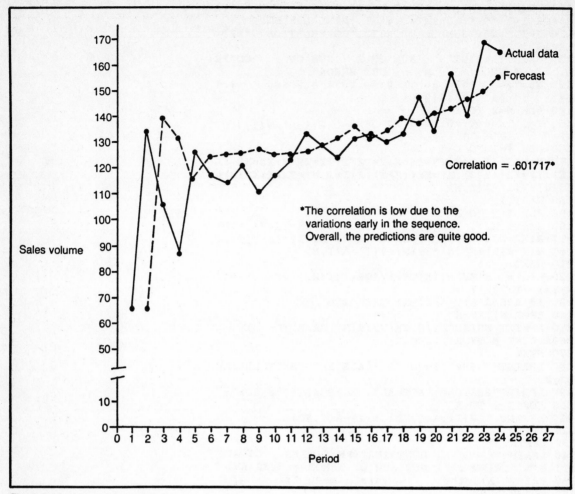

Fig. 6-3. Linear moving averages.

of the skill level of the team and the interaction of personalities, as well as product-related factors.

The basic component for exponential smoothing is the alpha value, A. If X is the most recent actual value, and LF is the last forecast, the current forecast, CF, is computed from:

$$CF = A\ X + (1 - A)\ LF$$

and   LF = CF

The obvious attraction of this approach is that you need only the most recent data for computation. The difficult part of the technique is assigning the proper value to A. The smaller A becomes, the less respon-

sive the forecast will be to current shifts or trends. One approach to this problem is to begin a series of forecasts with A = .3 or so. After a year or so of experience, the value is adjusted to a smaller value, frequently A = .1.

For example, John opens a small ice-cream cone stand in Miami. Since he has to operate on a very narrow margin, he cannot afford to order more ice cream from the supplier than he is likely to use prior to spoilage. At the same time, he cannot afford to buy too little product. It doesn't pay to sell out before the end of the day. Having no prior experience, the first year or so will be a speculative period at best. By using A = .3, his estimates should be fairly

Table 6-2. Linear Moving Average Data.

```
LINEAR MOVING (DOUBLE) AVERAGES
PERIOD FOR AVERAGING = 13

                       MOVING                    DOUBLE
 PERIOD     ACTUAL     AVERAGE      ERROR         AVERAGE       ERROR
    1        66         66           0             66            0
    2       134         66          68             66           68
    3       107        100           7            139.667      -32.6667
    4        87        102.333     -15.3333        131.5       -44.5
    5       126         98.5        27.5           115.903      10.0972
    6       117        104          13             124.339      -7.33889
    7       114        106.167       7.83334       125.644     -11.6435
    8       121        107.286      13.7143        125.286      -4.2857
    9       111        109           2             126.75      -15.75
   10       117        109.222       7.77778       125.259      -8.25926
   11       123        110          13             125.341      -2.34074
   12       133        111.182      21.8182        126.507       6.49329
   13       129        113          16             129.169      -.169052
   14       124        114.231       9.76923       130.592      -6.59193
   15       131        118.692      12.3077        135.93       -4.93022
   16       133        118.462      14.5385        130.701       2.29857
   17       130        120.462       9.53846       133.378      -3.37795
   18       133        123.769       9.23077       138.918      -5.91774
   19       147        124.308      22.6923        137.817       9.18337
   20       134        126.615       7.38461       140.994      -6.99414
   21       156        128.154      27.8462        142.492      13.5077
   22       140        130.846       9.15384       146.453      -6.45291
   23       168        133.077      34.9231        149.326      18.6743
   24       164        137          27             155.685       8.31514
  SUM      3045       3100.58      366.695        1671.45      -24.6491

NEXT FORECAST = 160.095    CORRELATION = .601717
```

responsive to the local demand and shifts in demand. After a year or two, LF should be reliable and A can become .1.

John can maintain the essential forecast data on a small slip of paper: yesterday's forecast and today's sales. Table 6-3 shows the result of using A = .3 for six months and A = .1 for the remainder.

The computational equation is:

1. F″ = F′ + A (X − F′)
2. F′ = F″

when F″ is the current forecast and F′ is the previous forecast.

Linear Exponential Smoothing

Just as we could improve the estimate of the moving average with the linear moving average technique, we can improve the exponential estimate by a similar double averaging of the exponential process. The equations needed for this technique are:

1. CF′ = A X + (1 − A) LF′
2. CF″ = A CF′ + (1 − A) LF″
3. A = 2 CF′ − CF″
4. B = (A/(1 − A)) (CF′ − CF″)
5. F = A + B M

Table 6-3. Single Exponential Moving Average Data.

SINGLE EXPONENTIAL SMOOTHING

EXPONENTIALLY SMOOTHED AVERAGES

PERIOD	ACTUAL	A = .1	A = .2	A = .4	A = .8
1	66	66	66	66	66
2	134	66	66	66	66
3	107	72.8	79.6	93.2	120.4
4	87	76.22	85.08	98.72	109.68
5	126	77.298	85.464	94.032	91.536
6	117	82.1682	93.5712	106.819	119.107
7	114	85.6514	98.257	110.892	117.421
8	121	88.4862	101.406	112.135	114.684
9	111	91.7376	105.324	115.681	119.737
10	117	93.6639	106.46	113.809	112.747
11	123	95.9975	108.568	115.085	116.149
12	133	98.6977	111.454	118.251	121.63
13	129	102.128	115.763	124.151	130.726
14	124	104.815	118.411	126.09	129.345
15	131	106.734	119.529	125.254	125.069
16	133	109.16	121.823	127.553	129.814
17	130	111.544	124.058	129.732	132.363
18	133	113.39	125.247	129.839	130.473
19	147	115.351	126.797	131.103	132.495
20	134	118.516	130.838	137.462	144.099
21	156	120.064	131.47	136.077	136.02
22	140	123.658	136.376	144.046	152.004
23	168	125.292	137.101	142.428	142.401
24	164	129.563	143.281	152.657	162.88
SUM	3045	2374.94	2637.88	2817.02	2922.78

Table 6-4 and Fig. 6-4 illustrate the various estimates derived from the preceding technique. Listing 6-2 is a smoothing program offering all four techniques as options.

Decomposition Methods

Despite its morbid name, decomposition really helps the analyst identify underlying patterns influencing numerical data, frequently those from economic and business efforts. In the previous section, the smoothing techniques were generally based on the notion that the data were the result of two main factors: some basic trend up or down, and random events or noise. The smoothing techniques attempted to isolate or cancel out the random noise and define the basic trend. Decomposition techniques, on the other hand, accept and accommodate the concepts of trend, season, and business cycle and attempt to specify the contribution each factor makes in the computation of a forecast. Decomposition techniques assume that each piece of data representing a given period is the function of the underlying pattern(s) and that:

Data = f(trend, cycle, season) + error.

The basic algorithm for most decomposition methods is:

1. Given a series of data points, X, X, X, X . . . ., compute a moving average making N equal to the length of the season. That is, if the data are given in months, then N = 12 (for quarters, N = 4, for days in a week, N = 7, etc.).
2. Separate the result of the moving average from the data. This leaves data affected by the trend and the cycle.
3. Separate the seasonal factors by averaging them for each of the data points for one season.

4. Examine the plotted shape of the data and determine the appropriate shape: linear trend, ogive curve, non-linear curves, etc.
5. Compute: Data − trend − moving average = cyclic + random error.
6. Compute: Data − trend − moving average − cycle = error.

The simplest solutions to this type of problem can be found in a sine wave and an exponential smoothing technique.

Seasonal Smoothing

If you have reason to believe that your data are

Table 6-4. Linear Exponential Smoothing Data.

```
LINEAR EXPONENTIAL SMOOTHING   ALPHA VALUE =.3         M = 1
PERIOD         ACTUAL          SINGLE EST.  LINEAR EST. FORECAST    ERROR

  1             66               66           66          66          0
  2            134              86.4         72.12       106.8       27.2
  3            107              92.58        78.258      113.04      -6.04
  4             87              90.906       82.0524     103.554    -16.554
  5            126             101.434       87.8669     120.816      5.18399
  6            117             106.104       93.3381     124.341     -7.34097
  7            114             108.473       97.8785     123.608     -9.6075
  8            121             112.231      102.184      126.583     -5.58341
  9            111             111.862      105.087      121.539    -10.5391
 10            117             113.403      107.582      121.719     -4.7189
 11            123             116.282      110.192      124.982     -1.98228
 12            133             121.298      113.524      132.403       .597061
 13            129             123.608      116.549      133.693     -4.6928
 14            124             123.726      118.702      130.902     -6.90248
 15            131             125.908      120.864      133.114     -2.11398
 16            133             128.036      123.015      135.207     -2.20737
 17            130             128.625      124.698      134.234     -4.23448
 18            133             129.937      126.27       135.177     -2.17664
 19            147             135.056      128.906      143.842      3.15759
 20            134             134.739      130.656      140.573     -6.57282
 21            156             141.118      133.794      151.579      4.42085
 22            140             140.782      135.891      147.77      -7.77014
 23            168             148.948      139.808      162.004      5.99559
 24            164             153.463      143.904      167.119     -3.11881
SUM          3045                                       3100.6     -55.6006

CORRELATION = .927893
```

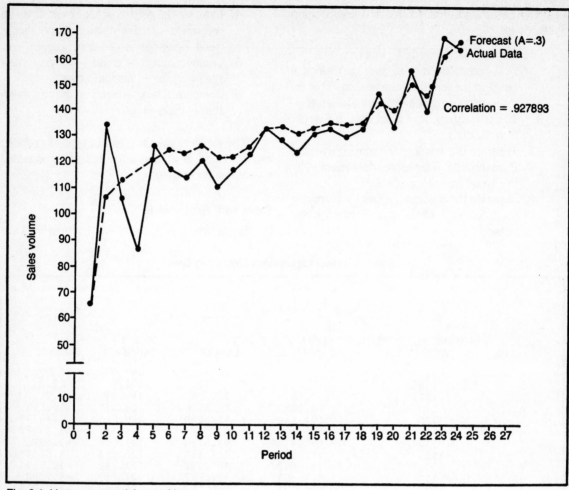

Fig. 6-4. Linear exponential smoothing.

Listing 6-2. Composite Moving Averages.

```
1  '*********************************************
2  '*            Listing 6-2               *
3  '*       Composite Moving Averages      *
4  '*********************************************
5  '
10 CLS:KEY OFF
20 INPUT"HOW MANY DATA POINTS";K
30 DIM V(K),R(K),A(K+1,K),ES(K),F(K+1):BR=0
40 FOR I=1 TO K:PRINT"ENTER VALUE FOR POINT #";I
,:INPUT V(I):NEXT
50 FOR I=1 TO K:PRINT I;V(I),:NEXT:PRINT
60 PRINT"ARE THESE ALL OK?  (Y/N)   ";
70 Q$=""+INKEY$:IF Q$="" THEN 70 ELSE PRINT Q$
80 IF Q$="Y" OR Q$="y" THEN 100
90 INPUT"ENTER NUMBER OF ITEM AND CORRECT VALUE"
;J,V(J):GOTO 50
```

```
100 PRINT"PRINTING INPUT DATA":LPRINT"INPUT DATA
":FOR I=1 TO K:LPRINT I;V(I),:NEXT:LPRINT""
110 PRINT:PRINT"1  --   SINGLE MOVING AVERAGE
               2  --   LINEAR MOVING AVERAGE
3  --   SINGLE EXPONENTIAL SMOOTHING       4 -
-  LINEAR EXPONENTIAL SMOOTHING
                          5  --   END "
120 PRINT:PRINT"Select Routine ";
130 T=0:TX=0:TY=0:X2=0:Y2=0:XY=0
140 Q$=""+INKEY$:IF Q$="" THEN 140 ELSE PRINT Q$
150 ON VAL(Q$) GOTO 170,430,720,1000
160 '          SINGLE MOVING AVERAGES
170 LPRINT"SINGLE MOVING AVERAGE"
180 PRINT"N","SUM OF F'CAST","CORRELATION","NET
ERROR"
190 PRINT:LPRINT"N    SUM OF X    SUM OF Y    CORRE
L.    BEST       N      NET ERROR"
200 N$="##   ####.##    ####.##   #.#####     #.#
####    ##   ######.##"
210 FOR N=2 TO K-1
220 A(1,N)=V(1):ES(N)=0:T=0:TX=0:TY=0:X2=0:Y2=0:
XY=0
230 FOR I=1 TO N-1
240 X=V(I):T=T+X:TX=TX+X:Y=TX/I:TY=TY+Y:X2=X2+(X
^2):Y2=Y2+(Y^2):XY=XY+(X*Y):A(I+1,N)=TX/I:ES(N)=
ES(N)+V(I)-A(I,N)
250 NEXT I
260 FOR I=N TO K
270 A=A(I,N):T=T+V(I):A(I+1,N)=T/N:TX=TX+V(I):TY
=TY+A:X2=X2+(V(I)^2):Y2=Y2+(A^2):XY=XY+(A*V(I)):
T=T-V(I-N+1):ES(N)=ES(N)+V(I)-A(I,N)
280 NEXT
290 R(N)=((K*XY)-(TX*TY))/SQR(((K*X2)-(TX^2))*((
K*Y2)-(TY^2)))
300 IF ABS(R(N))<ABS(BR) THEN 320
310 BR=R(N):RN=N
320 LPRINT USING N$;N;TX;TY;R(N);BR;RN;ES(N)
330 PRINT N,TY,R(N),ES(N)
340 NEXT
350 LPRINT"":ES=0:INPUT"AVERAGE FREQUENCY DESIRE
D";FD
360 LPRINT"PERIOD","ACTUAL","FORECAST","ERROR"
370 FOR I=1 TO K
380 LPRINT I,V(I),A(I,FD),V(I)-A(I,FD)
390 NEXT
400 LPRINT""
410 LPRINT"EACH SET CONTAINS";FD;"ITEMS,  CORREL
ATION = ";R(RN);"   NET SUM OF ERROR = ";ES(RN)
420 GOTO 110
430 '          LINEAR MOVING AVERAGE
440 INPUT"NUMBER OF ITEMS TO BE AVERAGED AT A TI
ME";N:IF N>K THEN 440
450 INPUT"NUMBER OF PERIOD TO BE FORECAST AHEAD"
;M
460 SF=0:E1=0:T=0:ES(N)=0:TX=0:TY=0:X2=0:Y2=0:XY
=0:R(N)=0:A(1,N)=V(1):F(1)=V(1)
470 FOR I=1 TO N-1
480 X=V(I):T=T+X:TX=TX+X:X2=X2+(X^2):A(I+1,N)=TX
```

Listing 6-2. Composite Moving Averages. (Continued From Page 103.)

```
/I
490 T2=0:FOR J=1 TO I:T2=T2+A(J,N):NEXT
500 E2=T2/I:A=(2*A(I+1,N))-E2:B=(2/(N-1))*(A(I+1
,N)-E2):F(I+1)=A+(B*M):Y=F(I):TY=TY+Y:Y2=Y2+(Y^2
):XY=XY+(X*Y):ES(N)=ES(N)+V(I)-F(I):E1=E1+V(I)-A
(I,N):SA=SA+F(I)
510 NEXT I
520 FOR I=N TO K
530 X=V(I):T=T+X:A(I+1,N)=T/N:Y=A(I+1,N):IF I=>(
2*N) THEN 560
540 T2=0:FOR J=I-N+1 TO I:T2=T2+A(J,N):NEXT
550 E2=T2/N:A=(2*A(I+1,N))-E2:B=(2/(N-1))*(A(I+1
,N)-E2):GOTO 580
560 T2=0:FOR J=I-N+1 TO I:T2=T2+A(J,N):NEXT
570 E2=T2/N:A=(2*A(I+1,N))-E2:B=(2/(N-1))*(A(I+1
,N)-E2)
580 F(I+1)=A+(B*M):Y=F(I+1)
590 PRINT I,V(I),F(I),V(I)-F(I)
600 TX=TX+X:TY=TY+Y:X2=X2+(X^2):Y2=Y2+(Y^2):XY=X
Y+(X*Y):ES(N)=ES(N)+V(I)-F(I):T=T-V(I-N+1):E1=E1
+V(I)-A(I,N):SF=SF+F(I)
610 NEXT
620 R=((K*XY)-(TX*TY))/SQR(((K*X2)-(TX^2))*((K*Y
2)-(TY^2)))
630 LPRINT"LINEAR MOVING (DOUBLE) AVERAGES"
640 LPRINT"PERIOD FOR AVERAGING = ";N
650 LPRINT"","","MOVING","","DOUBLE"
660 LPRINT"PERIOD","ACTUAL","AVERAGE","ERROR","A
VERAGE","ERROR
670 FOR I=1 TO K:LPRINT I,V(I),A(I,N),V(I)-A(I,N
),F(I),V(I)-F(I):NEXT
680 LPRINT"SUM",TX,TY,E1,SF,ES(N)
690 LPRINT"NEXT FORECAST = ";F(K+1),"CORRELATION
 = ";R:LPRINT""
700 GOTO 110
710 '          SINGLE EXPONENTIAL SMOOTHING
720 LPRINT"":LPRINT"SINGLE EXPONENTIAL SMOOTHING
"
730 SA=0:FOR I=1 TO 4:F(I)=0:NEXT
740 FOR I=1 TO 4:A(1,I)=V(1):NEXT
750 LPRINT"","","","EXPONENTIALLY SMOOTHED AVERA
GES"
760 LPRINT"PERIOD","ACTUAL","A = .1","A = .2","A
 = .4","A = .8"
770 FOR I=1 TO K
780 FOR J=1 TO 4:A(I+1,J)=A(I,J)+(((2^(J-1))/10)
*(V(I)-A(I,J))):NEXT
790 SA=SA+V(I):FOR J=1 TO 4:F(J)=F(J)+A(I,J):NEX
T
800 LPRINT I,V(I),A(I,1),A(I,2),A(I,3),A(I,4)
810 NEXT
820 LPRINT"SUM",SA,F(1),F(2),F(3),F(4)
830 PRINT:PRINT"ANOTHER ALPHA VALUE?  (Y/N)",
840 Q$=""+INKEY$:IF Q$="" THEN 840 ELSE PRINT Q$
850 IF Q$="N" THEN 980
860 TX=0:TY=0:X2=0:Y2=0:XY=0:SA=0:F(1)=0:E=0
```

```
870 INPUT"DESIRED ALPHA VALUE";A
880 LPRINT"":LPRINT"PERIOD","ACTUAL","FORECAST",
"ERROR","USING A = ";A
890 FOR I=1 TO K
900 X=V(I):A(I+1,1)=A(I,1)+(A*(V(I)-A(I,1))):Y=A
(I,1)
910 TX=TX+X:TY=TY+Y:X2=X2+(X^2):Y2=Y2+(Y^2):XY=X
Y+(X*Y)
920 SA=SA+V(I):F(1)=F(1)+A(I,1):E=E+V(I)-A(I,1)
930 LPRINT I,V(I),A(I,1),V(I)-A(I,1)
940 NEXT
950 LPRINT"SUM",SA,F(1),E
960 R=((K*XY)-(TX*TY))/SQR(((K*X2)-(TX^2))*((K*Y
2)-(TY^2)))
970 LPRINT"CORRELATION = ";R:LPRINT""
980 GOTO 110
990 '          LINEAR EXPONENTIAL SMOOTHING
1000 LPRINT"":LPRINT"LINEAR EXPONENTIAL SMOOTHIN
G",
1010 INPUT"ENTER DESIRED ALPHA VALUE";A
1020 M=1:INPUT"NUMBER OF PERIODS FORECAST AHEAD"
;M
1030 L1=V(1):L2=V(1)
1040 LPRINT"ALPHA VALUE = ";A,"M = ";M:LPRINT"PE
RIOD","ACTUAL","SINGLE EST.","LINEAR EST.","FORE
CAST","ERROR"
1050 FOR I=1 TO K
1060 C1=(A*V(I))+((1-A)*L1)
1070 C2=(A*C1)+((1-A)*L2)
1080 AA=(2*C1)-C2:B=(A/(1-A))*(C1-C2)
1090 F=AA+(B*M):X=V(I):Y=F:ES(1)=ES(1)+V(I)-F
1100 PRINT I;V(I);AA;B;F
1110 LPRINT I,V(I),C1,C2,F,V(I)-F
1120 TX=TX+X:TY=TY+Y:X2=X2+(X^2):Y2=Y2+(Y^2):XY=
XY+(X*Y):L1=C1:L2=C2
1130 NEXT
1140 LPRINT"SUM",TX,"","",TY,ES(1)
1150 R=((K*XY)-(TX*TY))/SQR(((K*X2)-(TX^2))*((K*
Y2)-(TY^2)))
1160 LPRINT"CORRELATION = ";R:LPRINT"":GOTO 110
1170 RUN"A:menu"
```

seasonal, or the forecasts derived from the preceding routines are not satisfying, you may want to consider one of the following procedures.

Sine Wave Smoothing. This approach assumes the seasonal variation is continuously and evenly variable over the range of the year. The distribution of data points fall more or less on a sine wave, as shown in Fig. 6-5.

If the data are more or less horizontal, varying mainly as a function of time of year, the equation to use in this process is:

$$F = ((Sin.9856473321 D) \times (Max - MIN) + MAX$$

$- Min)/2$

where:

D is the number of days since the beginning of the annual cycle. If J1 is the Julian date of the start of the cycle, and J2 is Julian date of the subject day, $D = J3 - J1 + 1$

Max is the normal maximum volume

Min is the normal minimum volume

Where there is an identifiable trend line in which sales volume is both seasonal and, from year to year, either increasing or decreasing, the forecast equa-

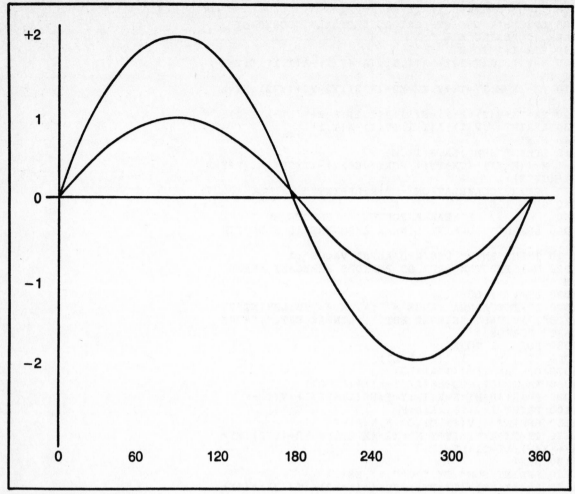

Fig. 6-5. Standard sinewaves.

tion is modified by adding the regression equation describing the long term trend. Computation of this regression equation will provide the mean of the trend line and the coefficients of the line as a function of time. It is possible that the coefficient of correlation will be fairly low as the deviations resulting from the seasonal influences will be considered as random error or random deviation. By combining the regression equation with the sine wave equation, the resulting forecast equation becomes:

$$F = ((Sin.9856473321 \; D(Max - Min) + Max - Min)/2 + A + BD$$

It is equally possible to use any geometric or trigonometric (see Chapter 8) relationships, such as the sine wave, as a predictor protocol. As a matter of fact, many business components don't behave neatly along the sine wave throughout the year. There is no mathematical routine available to identify the optimum waveform in this type of approach. The user should review a chart of standard curve shapes and adapt the one that appears to resemble the pattern of the data best.

Linear and Seasonal Exponential Smoothing (after Winters). Compared to the preceding approach this approach gives the impression of greater objectivity and mathematical precision, but it is really as subjective as the sine wave approach.

The primary advantage is that it automatically accommodates cyclic periods which may not have an annual basis. Rather, whether the period of the cycle is measured in quarters, days, or decades, the routine accepts the period as the user desires. It has the added feature of smoothing out random noise data—true random deviations as opposed to deviations caused by seasonal influence. The equations used in this process are:

1. $S2 = (A(X/I)) + ((1 - A)(S1 + B1))$
2. $B2 = (G(S2 - S1)) + (B1(1 - G))$
3. $I(T) = D(X/S2) + (I(T - L)(1 - D))$
4. $F = I(T - L + M)(S2 + BM)$

where L is the length of seasonality (number of months, quarters, or days in a year), T is the number of units since the beginning of the data, and I(X) is the seasonal adjustment factor.

Listing 6-3 implements these sine wave and exponential smoothing techniques. Listing 6-4 handles a ratio-to-average set.

Classic Decomposition Methods. Both the foregoing and the classic decomposition methods assume a given data point is the sum of the seasonal index value, plus the computed trend, plus the cycle component, plus error:

$$X = I + T + C + E$$

Listing 6-3. Time-Series Smoothing.

```
1 '*************************************************
2 '*                 Listing 6-3                   *
3 '*            Time-Series Smoothing              *
4 '*************************************************
5 '
10 CLS:KEY OFF:GOSUB 710:SCREEN SC
20 INPUT"HOW MANY DATA POINTS";K:DIM V(K),II(K)
30 FOR I=1 TO K:PRINT"ENTER VALUE FOR POINT #";I
,:INPUT V(I):NEXT
40 FOR I=1 TO K:PRINT I;V(I),:NEXT:PRINT
50 PRINT"ARE THESE ALL OK?  (Y/N)  ";
60 Q$=""+INKEY$:IF Q$="" THEN 60 ELSE PRINT Q$
70 IF Q$="Y" OR Q$="y" THEN 100
80 INPUT"ENTER NUMBER OF ITEM AND CORRECT VALUE"
;J,V(J):GOTO 40
90 PRINT"PRINTING INPUT DATA":LPRINT"INPUT DATA"
:FOR I=1 TO K:LPRINT I;V(I),:NEXT:LPRINT""
100 SM=V(1):PRINT:PRINT"(E)XPONENTIAL SMOOTHING
    (S)INEWAVE";
110 Q$=""+INKEY$:IF Q$="" THEN 110 ELSE IF Q$="S
" THEN 270
120 PRINT:INPUT"ALPHA FACTOR";A:INPUT"BETA FACTO
R";B:INPUT"GAMMA FACTOR";G
130 INPUT"LENGTH OF SEASON";L
140 INPUT"LENGTH OF LAG";M
150 S1=.5:B1=.5
160 FOR I=0 TO L:II(I)=1:NEXT
170 S1=V(L-1)
180 LPRINT"","",""           SMOOTHING"
190 LPRINT"PERIOD","ACTUAL","SINGLE","SEASONAL",
"TREND","FORECAST"
200 FOR I=L TO K-1
210 S2=(A*(V(I)/II(I-L)))+((1-A)*(S1+B1)):PRINT
S2,
220 B1=(G*(S2-S1))+((1-G)*B1):S1=S2:PRINT B1,
230 II(I+1)=(B*(V(I)/S2))+((1-B)*II(I-L)):PRINT
II(I+1),
```

Listing 6-3. Time-Series Smoothing. (Continued From Page 107.)

```
240 F=(S2+(B1*I))*II(I-L+M)
250 PRINT F:LPRINT I,V(I),S2,II(I+1),B1,F
260 NEXT
270 FOR I=1 TO K
280 IF V(I)<=LG THEN 300
290 LG=V(I)
300 IF SM<=V(I) THEN 320
310 SM=V(I)
320 T=T+V(I):X2=X2+(V(I)^2)
330 NEXT
340 M=T/K:SD=SQR((X2-((T^2)/K))/(K-1))
350 PRINT"SMALLEST = ";SM,"LARGEST = ";LG:PRINT"
SUM = ",T,"MEAN = ";M,"STAND. DEV. = ";SD
360 GOTO 380
370 LPRINT"SMALLEST = ";SM,"LARGEST = ";LG,"SUM
= ";T,"MEAN = ";M,"STANDARD DEVIATON = ";SD
380 INPUT"DATA REPRESENT HOW MANY YEARS";NY
390 CLS:F=47/LG
400 FOR I=1 TO K
410 X=INT(320*(I/K)):Y=INT(200-(V(I)*F))
420 PSET (X,Y)
430 NEXT
440 Z=NY*6.28318:TX=0:TY=0:X2=0:Y2=0:XY=0
450 FOR I=1 TO K
460 X=INT(320*(I/K)):XX=X+AD
470 Y=((SIN(.9865473321#*((XX*Z)/(NY*320)))*(LG-
SM))+LG-SM)/2
480 PSET(X,200-(Y*F)):X1=X1+X:X3=X3+(X^2):YY=YY+
(X*Y)
490 X=V(I):TX=TX+X:TY=TY+Y:X2=X2+(X^2):Y2=Y2+(Y^
2):XY=XY+(X*Y)
500 NEXT
510 R=((K*XY)-(TX*TY))/SQR(((K*X2)-(TX^2))*((K*Y
2)-(TY^2)))
520 LOCATE 1,1:PRINT"CORRELATION = ";R;
530 B=(YY-(K*((X1/K)*(TY/K))))/(X3-(K*((X1/K)^2)
))
540 A=(TY/K)-(B*(X1/K))
550 FOR I=1 TO K
560 X=INT(320*(I/K)):Y=A+(B*X):PSET(X,200-(Y*F))
570 NEXT
580 LOCATE 16,1:PRINT"(O)K  SHIFT (L)EFT  SHIFT
(R)IGHT";
590 S$=""+INKEY$:IF S$="" THEN 590
600 LOCATE 16,1:PRINT"AMOUNT OF SHIFT";:INPUT V
610 IF S$="R" OR S$="r" THEN AD=AD-V
620 IF S$="L" OR S$="l" THEN AD=AD+V
630 IF S$="O" OR S$="o" THEN 650
640 GOTO 390
650 PRINT"THE EQUATION FOR THIS SEASONAL CYCLE I
S: ((SIN(.9856473321 TIMES ((NUMBER OF DAYS SINC
E JAN 1 TIMES";Z;") DIVIDED BY";NY*320;")) TIMES
";LG-SM;") PLUS";LG-SM;") DIVIDED BY 2"
660 PRINT:PRINT"(A)nother set          (M)ain m
enu ";
670 Q$=""+INKEY$:IF Q$="" THEN 670
```

```
680 IF Q$="A" OR Q$="a" THEN RUN 10
690 IF Q$="M" OR Q$="m" THEN RUN "A:MENU"
700 GOTO 660
710 CLS
720 PRINT"1  --  320 X 200    2  --  640 X 200
  3  --  640 X 400 "
730 PRINT:PRINT"Indicate screen dimensions ";
740 Q$=""+INKEY$:IF Q$="" THEN 740
750 IF Q$<"1" OR Q$>"3" THEN 740
760 ON VAL(Q$) GOTO 770, 780, 790
770 XX=320:YY=200:SC=1:XL=39:ZY=8:ZX=4:RETURN
780 XX=640:YY=200:XL=39:SC=2:ZY=8:ZX=8:RETURN
790 XX=640:YY=400:SC=100:XL=79:ZY=16:ZX=8:RETURN
```

Listing 6-4. Ratio-to-Moving Averages.

```
1 '*******************************************
2 '*               Listing 6-4               *
3 '*          Ratio-to-Moving Averages       *
4 '*******************************************
5 '
10 ON ERROR GOTO 970
20 CLS:GOSUB 980
30 INPUT "Enter printer pitch";PP:LP=PP*8:WIDTH
LPRINT LP
40 INPUT"NUMBER OF ITEMS";V:DIM M(V),Y(12),YY(V)
,D(V),F(V),MA(12),T(V),C(12),A(12),AM(V)
50 B$="YR.   JAN    FEB    MAR    APR    MAY    JUN
JUL    AUG    SEP    OCT    NOV    DEC       TOTAL   AVE
RAGE"
60 A$="### ##.#   ##.#   ##.#   ##.#   ##.#   ##.#   #
#.#   ##.#   ##.#   ##.#   ##.#   ##.#   ######.##   ##
#.##"
70 FA$="###.# ###.# ###.# ###.# ###.# ###.# ###.
# ###.# ###.# ###.# ###.# ###.#    ####.##   ###.
##"
80 GA$="  #.### #.### #.### #.### #.### #.### #.
### #.### #.### #.### #.### #.###    ####.###   ##.
####"
90 FOR I=1 TO V
100   PRINT"Enter data value for point #";I;:INPU
T M(I)
110   X=I+7:Y=100-M(I)
120 NEXT I
130 LPRINT"INPUT DATA":LPRINT B$:J=1
140 FOR I=1 TO V STEP 12
150   YT=0
160   FOR J=0 TO 11
170     IF (I+J)>V THEN 210
180   YT=YT+M(I+J):Y(J+1)=Y(J+1)+M(I+J):TT=TT+M(
I+J):NEXT J
190     LPRINT USING A$;I/12;M(I);M(I+1);M(I+2);M(
I+3);M(I+4);M(I+5);M(I+6);M(I+7);M(I+8);M(I+9);M
(I+10);M(I+11);YT;YT/12
200 NEXT
210 LPRINT"SUM";USING FA$;Y(1);Y(2);Y(3);Y(4);Y(
```

109

Listing 6-4. Ratio-to-Moving Averages. (Continued From Page 109.)

```
5);Y(6);Y(7);Y(8);Y(9);Y(10);Y(11);Y(12);TT;TT/1
2
220 LPRINT"AVE";USING FA$;Y(1)/10;Y(2)/10;Y(3)/1
0;Y(4)/10;Y(5)/10;Y(6)/10;Y(7)/10;Y(8)/10;Y(9)/1
0;Y(10)/10;Y(11)/10;Y(12)/10;TT/10;TT/120
230 LPRINT"":LPRINT"MOVING AVERAGES"
240 LPRINT B$:J=1:YT=0
250 CLS
260 LOCATE 1,1:PRINT"MOVING AVERAGES
    ";
270 FOR I=1 TO V
280 T=T+M(I):IF I<12 THEN 300
290 Y(J)=T/12:YY(I)=M(I)/(T/12):T=T-M(I-11):C(J)
=C(J)+Y(J):A(J)=A(J)+YY(I):GOTO 310
300 Y(J)=T/I:YY(I)=M(I)/(T/I):A(J)=A(J)+YY(I)
310 TX=TX+I:X2=X2+(I^2):TY=TY+M(I):Y2=Y2+(M(I)^2
):XY=XY+(I*M(I)):N=N+1
320 FOR K=1 TO 12:YT=YT+Y(K):NEXT
330 LPRINT USING A$;INT(I/12.001);Y(1);Y(2);Y(3)
;Y(4);Y(5);Y(6);Y(7);Y(8);Y(9);Y(10);Y(11);Y(12)
;YT;YT/12:YT=0:J=1
340 NEXT
350 Z$="SUM"
360 FOR I=1 TO 12:TA=TA+A(I):NEXT
370 IA=12/TA
380 FOR I=1 TO 12:MA(I)=A(I)*IA:NEXT
390 FL=0
400 FOR I=1 TO 12:CC=CC+C(1):NEXT
410 LPRINT Z$;USING FA$;C(1);C(2);C(3);C(4);C(5)
;C(6);C(7);C(8);C(9);C(10);C(11);C(12);CC;CC/12:
CC=0:IF FL=1 THEN 440
420 Z$="AVE"
430 FL=1:FOR I=1 TO 12:C(I)=C(I)/10:NEXT I:GOTO
400
440 LPRINT"":LPRINT"MOVING AVERAGES   (ACTUAL TO
MOVING AVERAGE)"
450 LPRINT B$
460 FOR I=0 TO V-1 STEP 12
470 YR=0:FOR J=1 TO 12:YR=YR+YY(I+J):NEXT
480 LPRINT USING A$;I/12;YY(I+1);YY(I+2);YY(I+3)
;YY(I+4);YY(I+5);YY(I+6);YY(I+7);YY(I+8);YY(I+9)
;YY(I+10);YY(I+11);YY(I+12);YR;YR/12
490 NEXT
500 LPRINT"SUM";USING FA$;A(1);A(2);A(3);A(4);A(
5);A(6);A(7);A(8);A(9);A(10);A(11);A(12);TA;TA/1
2
510 LPRINT"AVE";USING GA$;MA(1);MA(2);MA(3);MA(4
);MA(5);MA(6);MA(7);MA(8);MA(9);MA(10);MA(11);MA
(12);TA/10;TA/120
520 LPRINT CHR$(140)
530 R=((N*XY)-(TX*TY))/SQR(((N*X2)-(TX^2))*((N*Y
2)-(TY^2)))
540 B=(XY-((TX*TY)/N))/(X2-((TX^2)/N))
550 A=(TY/N)-(B*(TX/N))
560 MY=TY/N:SD=SQR((X2-((TX^2)/N))/(N-1))
570 SY=SD/SQR(N)
```

```
580 FOR I=1 TO V
590 Y=100-(A+(B*I)):X=I+7:SET(X,Y)
600 NEXT
610 LOCATE 1,1:PRINT"LINEAR TREND
  "
620 PRINT"LINEAR TREND:  Y = ";A;" + ";B;" X"
630 PRINT"CORRELATION = ";R
640 PRINT"STANDARD ERROR = ";SY
650 PRINT"MEAN = ";MY,"STANDARD DEVIATION = ";SD
660 LPRINT"LINEAR TREND DATA"
670 LPRINT"MON DATA TREND DIFF  MON DATA TREND D
IFF  MON DATA TREND DIFF  MON DATA TREND DIFF"
680 C$="### ### ###.# ###.#  ### ### ###.# ###.#
  ### ### ###.# ###.#  ### ### ###.# ###.#
690 J=1
700 FOR I=1 TO V STEP 4
710 FOR J=I TO I+3
720 T(J)=A+(B*J):D(J)=M(J)-T(J)
730 NEXT
740 J=I+1:K=I+2:L=I+3
750 LPRINT USING C$;I;M(I);T(I);D(I);J;M(J);T(J)
;D(J);K;M(K);T(K);D(K);L;M(L);T(L);D(L)
760 NEXT I
770 LPRINT"LINEAR TREND:   Y = A + B X"
780 LPRINT"A = ";A,"B = ";B;"STANDARD ERROR = ";
SY
790 LPRINT"CORRELATION = ";R,"MEAN = ";MY,"STAND
ARD DEVIATION = ";SD:LPRINT"":LPRINT CHR$(140)
800 D$="### ###   ###.### ###.### ##.### ###.###
###.## ### ###   ###.### ###.### ##.### ###.###
###.##"
810 LPRINT"FORECAST STATISTICS"
820 LPRINT"MON DATA TREND 1  DIFF    CYCLE   TREND
 2 DIFF    MON DATA TREND 1  DIFF    CYCLE TREND
2  DIFF"
830 E$="       ###.###              ###.###
               ###.###              ###.###"
840 GOTO 860
850 CLS:LOCATE 1,1:PRINT"RESIDUAL   (CYCLIC DATA
+ ERROR)";
860 FOR I=0 TO V-12 STEP 12
870 FOR J=1 TO 12 STEP 2
880 T1=A+(B*(I+J)):T2=A+(B*(I+J+1))
890 Y1=T1*MA(J)*(T1/AM(I+J)):Y2=T2*MA(J+1)*(T2/A
M(I+J+1))
900 F(I)=Y1:F(I+1)=Y2:D(1)=D(1)+M(I+J)-T1:D(2)=D
(2)+M(I+J)-Y1:D(3)=D(3)+M(I+J+1)-T2:D(4)=D(4)+M(
I+J+1)-Y2
910 LPRINT USING D$;I+J;M(I+J);T1;M(I+J)-T1;T1/A
M(I+J);Y1;M(I+J)-Y1;I+J+1;M(I+J+1);T2;M(I+J+1)-T
2;T2/AM(I+J+1);Y2;M(I+J+1)-Y2
920 PSET(I+7,100-(M(I+J)-Y1)):PSET(I+8,100-(M(I+
J+1)-Y2))
930 NEXT J
940 NEXT I
950 LPRINT"NET DIFF.";USING E$;D(1);D(2);D(3);D(
4)
960 GOTO 1070
```

Listing 6-4. Ratio-to-Moving Averages. (Continued From Page 111.)

```
970 RESUME NEXT
980 CLS
990 PRINT"1  --   320 X 200    2  --  640 X 200
    3  --   640 X 400 "
1000 PRINT:PRINT"Indicate screen dimensions ";
1010 Q$=""+INKEY$:IF Q$="" THEN 1010
1020 IF Q$<"1" OR Q$>"3" THEN 1010
1030 ON VAL(Q$) GOTO 1040, 1050, 1060
1040 XX=320:YY=200:SC=1:XL=39:ZY=8:ZX=4:RETURN
1050 XX=640:YY=200:XL=39:SC=2:ZY=8:ZX=8:RETURN
1060 XX=640:YY=400:SC=100:XL=79:ZY=16:ZX=8:RETUR
N
1070 PRINT"(A)nother        (M)ain menu ";
1080 GOSUB 1100
1090 IF Q$="A" OR Q$="a" THEN RUN 10 ELSE RUN "A
:MENU"
1100 Q$=""+INKEY$:IF Q$="" THEN 1100
1110 RETURN
```

The following describes how an analysis using the classic decomposition method is performed. Given a set of data, the trend line ($Y = A + BX$) is computed as described in Chapter 4. Whether the trend line is in the linear form noted here or in one of the exponential or logarithmic forms is immaterial; the best version as dictated by the data must be used.

A moving average value for each point is computed and that point is divided by the average. These ratio data are tabled according to season. That is, if the data are in monthly sums, a 12-column matrix is established; if they are quarterly, a 4-column matrix is established; and so forth. For an example, see Table 6-5.

Note that each column is totaled and averaged by the number of season cycles involved. This row of totals is totaled. The indexing (I) is accomplished by dividing the table total by 12 and multiplying the result by each of the column averages.

The computation of the preliminary forecast, then, is:

$$F = I(A + B X)$$

Table 6-5. Seasonal Data Table for Indexing.

Quarterly Sales Data					
Year	Jan-Mar	Apr-Jun	Jul-Sep	Oct-Dec	Total	Mean
1971	240	267	440	538	1485	371.25
1972	276	244	460	525	1505	376.25
1973	262	240	440	567	1509	377.25
1974	278	239	446	576	1539	384.75
1975	264	265	463	561	1553	388.25
Total	1320	1255	2249	2767	7591	1897.75
Mean	264	251	449.8	553.4	1518.2	379.55

Subtracting this forecast from the actual data ordinarily leaves some residual data. It is recommended the analyst examine these residual values for randomness.

AUTOREGRESSION

In Chapter 5 we considered several multivariate regression techniques in which the normal form of the equation was:

$$Y = A + B_1 X_1 + B_2 X_2 + \ldots B_n X_n + e$$

Each value of X represents a different factor: price, temperature, etc., with its own beta weight. In a time-series regression analysis, each value of X is the magnitude of a given variable, but displaced over one or more periods of time. For example, we presume that the current value of the variable Y, using an offset of three periods, becomes:

$$Y_1 = A + B_1 Y_{t-3} + B_2 Y_{t-4} + \ldots B_n Y_{t-n} + e$$

Since the different independent variables are nothing more than time-lagged values of the dependent variable, we can compute a correlation between these values. Such a process is known as an *autoregression* process. It should be evident that different lag factors are likely to produce different autoregressions. It is a fairly simple matter to use the microcomputer to evaluate the data and identify the optimum lag factor. The computation equations used in this process are:

$$r_k = \frac{\displaystyle\sum_{T=1}^{n-k} (Y_T - \overline{Y})(Y_{T+K} - \overline{Y})}{^n(Y_T - \overline{Y})}$$

$$T = \sqrt{\frac{T-1}{\dfrac{\sum (Y - \overline{Y})^2}{n-1}}}$$

From the study of statistics we can derive a principle that states that if a set of numbers is generated randomly, the autoregression of these values must lie within a range defined by the mean of the distribution plus 1.96 times the standard error. If all of the autoregressions are computed to fall within these limits, the data are accepted as randomly ordered. On the other hand, if one or more of the autoregressions fall outside this limit, the data are believed to contain some rational order. Success in forecasting is frequently based on the analyst's ability to distinguish random from rational or patterned data.

Listing 6-5 is a brief routine to determine the optimum lag factor to obtain the maximum correlation between the tabular data and to illustrate degree of randomness in the data.

Having built a predictive model and applied it against known data points, we are left with residual or error data. These are simply the dregs after we have made a prediction. For each data point for which we make a forecast, there is some degree of error. If we table these residuals and then compute an autoregression on these data, we are looking for a high degree of randomness in the error data. The smaller the amount of error and the greater the randomness of the data, the better our forecasting model.

Stationary

When the data are randomly ordered, the distribution of the various regressions will fall within the nominal limits defined above, but in no apparent pattern about the mean. Such data are called *stationary*; that is, there is no growth or decline in the data. Charted, the data would be horizontal along the x-axis.

If the data forms patterns very neatly about the mean and useful forecasts can be computed from the linear or curvilinear trend, then, for practical purposes, we can leave this section of the data analysis. On the other hand, if there are autoregressions that are significant (greater than 1.96 times the standard error), we know the data contain some pattern. The basic procedure we use is:

1. Compute the autoregressions. If they tend to cluster near zero, after one or two time lags the table is said to be stationary. If it is stationary, go to rule 3; otherwise, go to rule 2.
2. Process the data using the principle of *differencing* described below. Return to rule 1.

Listing 6-5. Autoregression.

```
1 '*********************************************
2 '*              Listing 6-5              *
3 '*            Autoregression             *
4 '*********************************************
5 '
10 CLS:KEY OFF:SCREEN 2
20 PRINT"********* Autoregression  **********"
:PRINT:INPUT "Number of items";N
30 DIM X(N),R(N-1)
40 FOR I=1 TO N
50   PRINT"Enter item #";I;:INPUT X(I)
60   TX=TX+X(I)
70 NEXT I
80 MX=TX/N
90 FOR I=1 TO N-J
100   SY=SY+((X(I)-MX)^2)
110 NEXT I
120 FOR K=1 TO N-1
130   PRINT K;
140   FOR I=1 TO N-K
150     SX=SX+((X(I)-MX)*(X(I+K)-MX))
160   NEXT I
170   R(K)=SX/SY:PRINT R(K):SX=0
180 NEXT K
190 CLS
200 PRINT"Time Lag Autocorrelation"
210 FOR I=3 TO N+1
220     LOCATE I,1:PRINT I-2;
230     LOCATE I,40+(15*R(I-2)):PRINT"*";
240     LOCATE I,65:PRINT R(I-2);
250 NEXT I
260 SE=1/SQR(N):ES=1.96*SE:LE=160-(80*ES):RE=160
+(80*ES)
270 LX=LE*2:RX=RE*2
280 LINE (LX,16)-(LX,190):LINE (RX,16)-(RX,190)
290 LINE (65,180)-(560,180)
300 LOCATE 25,(LX/8):PRINT"-1":LOCATE 25,40:PRIN
T"-0-":LOCATE 25,(RX/8):PRINT"+1"
310 LOCATE 1,40:PRINT"(D)ifferencing    (E)nd";:G
OSUB 380
320 IF Q$="E" OR Q$="e" THEN 400
330 J=J+1:TX=0:SX=0:SY=0
340 FOR I=1 TO N-J-1
350     X(I)=X(I+2)-(2*X(I+1)+X(I)):TX=TX+X(I)
360 NEXT I
370 GOTO 80
380 Q$=""+INKEY$:IF Q$="" THEN 380
390 RETURN
400 PRINT"(A)nother      (M)ain menu ";
410 GOSUB 430
420 IF Q$="A" OR Q$="a" THEN RUN 10 ELSE RUN "A:
MENU"
430 Q$=""+INKEY$:IF Q$="" THEN 430
440 RETURN
```

3. If the first three time lags are significant, a nonseasonal pattern in the data is suggested. If these are not significant, but time lags greater than three are significant, we assume a seasonal pattern with a length corresponding to the time lags of the largest autoregression. If none of the autoregressions are significant, then we believe no pattern exists in the data.

Differencing is a process by which the table is rebuilt by subtracting consecutive data points in successive periods. For example,

First Difference $X'_T = X_{T+1} - X_T$
Second Difference $X''_T = X'_{T+1} - X'_T = X_{T+2} - 2X_{T+1} + X_T$

The new table is then run through the autoregression program to recompute the autoregressions. If this process should fail to achieve the desired stationarity, the table is differenced again.

In theory, this process can be continued until you run out of sufficient data or the table becomes stationary. In practice, however, it is rare to have to go beyond the second difference to achieve stationarity.

As you may have concluded, time-series forecasting is, in many respects, a special case of the use of forecasting techniques in general. In place of an independent variable, we use time periods. This is not without some problems, but none that normally outweigh the advantages of the techniques.

S-CURVE OF ADOPTION

Virtually every new innovation goes through a process of adoption consisting of three stages: initial exposure, experimentation, and limited acceptance; wide-spread acceptance and acquisition; and stabilization to a normal level of use. If we introduce a new product to an identified population of consumers and then plot the number of consumers using the product as a percent of the total population, over a period of time the graph will almost always resemble the form in Fig. 6-6.

This relationship is observed in studies of the adoption of new hybrid grains and farming techniques among Iowa farmers, the adoption of skateboards among youngsters throughout the country, the adoption of microcomputers as working aids in small businesses, and in the adoption of any number of similar innovations. The only factor that really varies from innovation to innovation is the scale of the independent variable, time. It may take a decade or two for a new grain or technique to become dominant among a community of farmers, yet only a matter of weeks for skateboards or pet rocks to sweep through the nation. Affecting the rate of acceptance are such factors as the actual cost of the new item, the risk (cost) of adoption as opposed to the known profit of not changing, the perceived profit potential of the innovation, and other social or cultural factors resisting or supporting change. A skateboard is relatively inexpensive. To make the purchase is fairly easy. Not to buy the board is to isolate oneself from a peer activity. It might be fun to use, and there is no great loss if it doesn't work out. At the other end of the spectrum, let's hypothesize an improved farming technique that we want to introduce in India. Unfortunately, a part of the process requires the slaughter and processing of cattle for certain necessary chemicals to be used in the improved technique. Not only will there be a predictable resistance to new ideas, but there will also be the religious or cultural opposition to the use of the sacred cattle in the process. It might require generations before any significant progress is made in adoption of the technique. Interestingly enough, after an initial breakthrough in attitude and acceptance, a bandwagon effect can sometimes be seen, and that which has been resisted for decades will be warmly embraced by almost everyone within the year. During that last period, the adoption rate will resemble the standard ''s'' or ogive curve of acceptance.

The function of this section, however, is not to devise strategies for acceptance of innovations, but to provide a way to use the microcomputer to fit an ogive shape to data available early in the history of an innovation, so that a projected acceptance pattern can be constructed.

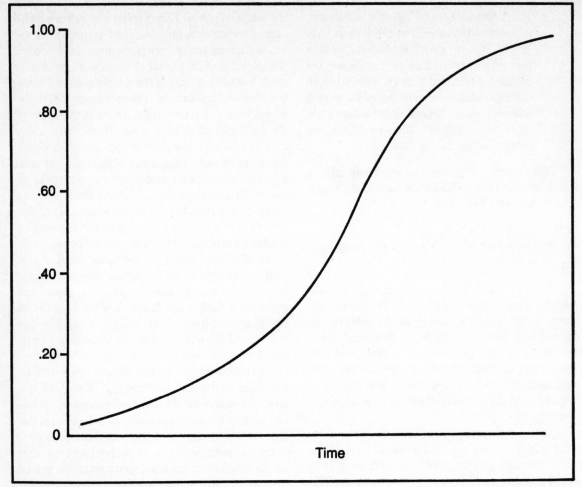

Fig. 6-6. Standard S-curve of adoption.

The ogive curve closely resembles the arctangent family of curves. A program that exploits this information by overlaying a plot of the available acceptance data with an arctangent curve and then adjusting the curve for a best-fit of the data can be devised. The resulting coefficients let us extrapolate the balance of the acceptance pattern.

In addition to the arctangent family of curves, we also have some other equations that can be used in projecting an acceptance pattern. They are:

1. $Y = ae^{bx}$ Exponential

2. $Y = \dfrac{L}{1 + ae^{-bt}}$ Pearl's equation

3. $Y = Le^{-ae^{-bt}}$ Gompertz's equation

4. $Y = (1 - ae^{-bt})^3$ Von Bertalanffy's Curve

where **a** is the intercept of the S-curve; b is the slope; L is the upper limit; and t is the time period.

A little trial and error will produce the coefficients for the first equation. If $L = 1$, the second and third equations can be transformed into a more standard form $(Y = A + B X)$ and the coefficients solved as in the least squares linear trend.

Both of the foregoing approaches are burdened by the same defect: to be of value, the projection must be made so early in the process of acceptance that computation of curves based on available data may be terribly misleading. By the time sufficient data have been collected from which to compute a reliable curve, the utility of the forecast may only be nominal. About the only thing that can be done about this is to run one or the other of the programs you have devised once or twice a week from the beginning of the innovation and revise the long-term forecast accordingly. After a time, the projected data for acceptance by a specified percentage will begin to stabilize. Hopefully, the stabilization will occur prior to the need for the forecast.

Listing 6-6 contains a program that is not very elegant in a mathematical sense, but serves to provide a brute-force estimate of the progress an innovation is making. Instead of fitting the curve to the data, the program fits the data to the curve. Conceptually, the S-curve retains its shape and form while the only thing that changes is the time scale,

Listing 6-6. S-Curve of Adoption.

```
1  '*******************************************
2  '*              Listing 6-6                *
3  '*          S-Curve of Adoption            *
4  '*******************************************
5  '
10 ON ERROR GOTO 610
20 CLS
30 INPUT "How many periods of data are available
?";N
40 DIM D(N):F=40:SHIFT=20
50 FOR I=1 TO N
60     PRINT "Enter per cent (5%=5) completed at p
eriod #";I;:INPUT D(I)
70 NEXT I
80 CLS
90 FOR I=1 TO N:PRINT I;D(I),:NEXT
100 PRINT:PRINT"All data correct?  (Y/N) ";:GOSU
B 520
110 IF Q$="Y" OR Q$="y" THEN 160
120 INPUT "Enter item number and correct value";
X,D(X):GOTO 80
130    IF D(I)<LG THEN 150
140    LG=D(I)
150 NEXT I
160 CLS:SCREEN 2
170 LOCATE 1,1:PRINT"100 %";:LOCATE 23,1:PRINT"0
 %";
180 LINE (24,1)-(24,180):LINE (24,180)-(620,180)
190 FOR X=24 TO 620
200    Y=(X-24)/620:SY=SIN((Y*3.14159)+4.712385)
210    Y=90-(SY*90):PSET (X,Y)
220 NEXT
230 FOR I=1 TO N
240    X=(F*I)+14+SHIFT
250    Y=180-((D(I)/100)*180)
260    PSET (X,Y)
270    LINE (X,181)-(X,185)
280    C=((X+24)/8):LOCATE 25,C-3:PRINT I;
290 NEXT I
300 FOR J=I TO 1000
310    X=(F*J)+14+SHIFT:C=(X+24)/8:LOCATE 25,C-3:I
F (C-3)>78 THEN 350 ELSE PRINT J
320    LAST=J
```

Listing 6-6. S-Curve of Adoption. (Continued From Page 117.)

```
330   LINE (X,181)-(X,185)
340 NEXT J
350 LOCATE 1,5:PRINT"Slant (O)k (D)own (U)p";:GO
SUB 520
360 IF Q$="O" OR Q$="o" THEN 420
370 IF Q$="D" OR Q$="d" THEN 410
380 IF Q$="U" OR Q$="u" THEN 400
390 GOTO 350
400 F=F*.8:GOTO 420
410 F=F*1.2
420 LOCATE 2,5:PRINT"Shift  (O)k  (R)ight  (L)ef
t";:GOSUB 520
430 IF Q$="O" OR Q$="o" THEN 490
440 IF Q$="R" OR Q$="r" THEN 480
450 IF Q$="L" OR Q$="l" THEN 470
460 GOTO 420
470 SHIFT=SHIFT*-1.2:GOTO 160
480 SHIFT=SHIFT*1.2:GOTO 160
490 LOCATE 1,1:PRINT"PrtSc to save   (G)raph   (
P)rint data   (E)nd";
500 GOSUB 520
510 IF Q$="G" OR Q$="g" THEN 160 ELSE IF Q$="P"
OR Q$="p" THEN 540 ELSE IF Q$="E" OR Q$="e" THEN
 620 ELSE 490
520 Q$=""+INKEY$:IF Q$="" THEN 520
530 RETURN
540 LPRINT "Input Data:"
550 INPUT "Printer width in inches";IN:INPUT "Pr
int pitch";PT:WIDTH LPRINT (IN*PT)
560 LPRINT""
570 LPRINT "Period","Data"
580 FOR I=1 TO N:LPRINT I,D(I),:NEXT I
590 LPRINT"":LPRINT "If best fit alignment has b
een reached, then maximum adoption should take
    place about the end of ";LAST;"periods.":LP
RINT""
600 GOTO 350
610 RESUME NEXT
620 PRINT"(A)nother      (M)ain menu ";
630 GOSUB 650
640 IF Q$="A" OR Q$="a" THEN RUN 10 ELSE RUN "A:
MENU"
650 Q$=""+INKEY$:IF Q$="" THEN 650
660 RETURN
```

which is the independent variable along the X-axis. The effect of the program is to adjust the time scale along the X-axis and to position the first data point so that the arbitrary S-curve and the empirical data coincide as closely as can be made to line up.

LINEAR REGRESSION AND TIME-SERIES FORECASTING

In normal regression analysis, two variables

(such as GNP, market prices, weather conditions, etc.), are correlated one to another, one of them being the independent variable and the other being the dependent variable: that is, it is dependent on a value of the independent variable for its magnitude. Such a relationship is known as a *causal model*. Correlations developed using time as the independent variable are known as *time-series models*.

The time-series model has proven to be a

Table 6-6. Five-Year Shoe Sales Record.

JAN	FEB	MAR	APR	MAY	JUN	JUL	AUG	SEP	OCT	NOV	DEC	TOT
362	415	500	422	430	286	223	166	141	89	169	276	3479
423	510	471	427	356	318	173	154	105	149	179	312	3577
361	476	467	423	438	255	165	75	141	126	227	311	3465
426	513	468	497	423	292	168	151	132	120	171	251	3612
401	457	447	431	382	262	220	134	148	142	192	348	3564
1973	2371	2353	2200	2029	1413	949	680	667	626	938	1498	17697

powerful predictor in long range forecasts. Its main shortfall results from the error induced by the rise and fall of seasonal data, such as daily and monthly variations. For this reason, the longer the forecast, in numbers of years, the less likely there will be significant long-term error. Chapter 5 included some useful techniques for this kind of trend analysis. Especially useful are the routines supporting nonlinear curve-fitting.

EXERCISES

1. Contact your local weather station and obtain daily temperature records for the last five years. Compute the seasonal indices, mean daily temperatures and short-term trend, and forecast next month's temperatures. Correlate your forecast with the actual outcome.
2. From the data above, simply smooth the data using a seasonal smoothing technique and forecast next month's temperature from a graph of the smoothed data. Compare this value with the best estimate from exercise 1.
3. Table 6-6 contains the five-year sales records of a shoe store. Prepare an analysis of the sales to include the seasonal indexing, long term trend, and nonseasonal cyclic influence, if any.
4. Census II is a technique developed and used by the federal government to compute populations and population trends using a decomposition method similar to but more complicated than the ones shown in this chapter. Locate a functional description of the technique, and write a routine to implement it.

SUGGESTED READING

Brown, R. G., 1963. *Smoothing Forecasting, and Prediction*. Englewood Cliffs, NJ: Prentice-Hall.

Byrkit, D. R., 1972. *Elements of Statistics*. New York: Van Nostrand Reinhold Company.

McFadden, J. A., 1971. *Physical Concepts of Probability*. New York: Van Nostrand Reinhold Company.

Mendenhall, W. and J. E., Reinmuth, 1971. *Statistics for Management and Economics*. Belmont, CA: Wadsworth Publishing Co.

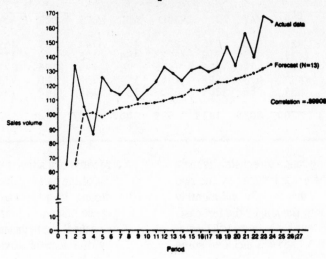

## Chapter 7

Modeling and Simulations

In the preparation of this book, especially the supporting programs, I have come upon problems the solutions to which were not self-evident or easily found in a simple equation. The first exercise item in Chapter 10 grew out of just such a problem. I knew that I could reduce the expression for computing the relative appreciated values to m Log 2(1 + R_1) and m Log (1 + R_2). I was looking for the date at which the two lines would intersect, which would be when:

$$m \text{ Log } 2(1 + R_1) = m \text{ Log } (1 + R_2)$$

I wanted a short algebraic solution to this relationship, but nothing presented itself. The only solution that I was aware of was an iterative approach wherein I used trial values of m to approach the relationship described. The experience taught me several lessons.

First, it illustrated the utility of a model. By constructing a numerical equivalent of the real life situation we can step through the process rapidly to determine conditions that satisfy our objectives. Sec-

ond, we can probably save ourselves a lot of time. Elegant solutions to a variety of problems probably exist throughout a lot of our daily work. Yet, the time required to come to a workable understanding of these solutions may be more than we have available. As a practical matter, the brute-force solution may be the most expedient solution, and we shouldn't be too proud to use it. To the extent that the difference in processing time within the the difference in processing time within the microcomputer is measured only in a few milliseconds, technique selection is determined by the This is not an argument for sloppy science or a cop-out but it is encouragement to the reader who may have a workable solution to a problem but is spending considerable time seeking a more elegant solution. If the enjoyment you receive from microcomputer programming comes from solving such problems in the most elegant fashion, I applaud the effort. On the other hand, if the objective is to get a job done and the program works, leave it alone and get on with the main tasks.

Modeling and simulation frequently offer solutions to problems that would otherwise be too tedious to unravel in the time alloted to the task. The exercise item just mentioned and several of the approaches in a number of the chapters rely upon mathematical models to provide the desired answers. We may not know all of the components of buyer behavior, relevant weather patterns, and other economic elements and interactions, but if we can predict trends in these variables, we can build effective marketing models.

Models allow us to experiment with objects and systems that are otherwise too large or unwieldy to deal with. Models allow system or organizational managers to play the "what if" game. What if we raise salaries 12 percent? What if we raise salaries and increase and achieve production quotas? What if we switch to a new plastic in lieu of the sheet metal we've been using for fifty years? Unfortunately, its Board of Directors would never allow us to tinker with the operational components of General Motors, no matter how honorable our intentions. On the other hand, if we build a model of General Motors in our computer systems, we can tinker to our hearts' delight. Through this process, assuming our computer can handle all of the relevant data, we have the ability to devise winning management strategies.

The problem with models is that they are simply rough representations of the real thing. Seldom do they contain the level of detail and the comprehensive coverage of the "real thing" necessary to assure us that all contingencies can be anticipated. In large corporate settings, the complexity of the total system is such that to develop a program accounting for all aspects would often exceed the capacity of the supporting computer and far exceed the time available for analysis. In using models we make every effort to give adequate consideration to significant factors and trust that what is left unaccounted for will not result in unacceptable consequences.

Beyond this there are few specific rules for model makers to follow. To be useful for microcomputer applications, the model should be quantifiable; that is, the components should be able to be expressed in numerical relationships. Also, given known "settings" or relationships, the model should

yield known and corresponding outputs. For example, if we know that in real life the number of eggs produced by a given number of chickens is partly a function of the quantity of grain consumed in a day, any model we construct of the chicken yard should yield accurate results given known conditions. If, in real life, the normal level of grain consumption will yield 100 eggs, then the computer model, using the normal level of grain as a beginning parameter, should produce the same results. This is especially important within the model. If the state or condition of one component is the function of another, we must fine-tune the corresponding mathematical relationships to yield the same results.

While most of the chapters contain major programs to support the objective of the given chapter, this chapter will not lead to an all-purpose model-making program. Instead, we will use several case studies to illustrate various microcomputer applications of modeling and simulations.

THE "LIFE" SIMULATION

A popular computer programming exercise first inspired by an article in *Scientific American* a number of years ago, Life is an abstraction of the present world in which the prime determinants of existence are overcrowding and isolation. The rules are quite simple:

1. The "world" is represented by a matrix. At any given instant, one or more of the matrix cells will be populated.
2. If that cell has more than three contiguous (touching) neighbors, it will die from overcrowding before the next generation is produced.
3. If that cell has less than two contiguous neighbors, it will die from isolation.
4. If a cell is not populated (not filled) and has exactly three neighbors, a new cell will be created.

The normal process is to establish the matrix, randomly populating the field, and then to check each cell in turn against the rules stated above. Before the next generation is displayed, each overcrowded or isolated cell is removed from the matrix (killed). Each cell with three neighbors generates a new cell occupant.

Figure 7-1 shows a flowchart of the simulation. Life creates such a variety of interesting shapes and forms that only the most esoterically trained mathematician, using little-known techniques, could begin to predict the actual shape of the population distribution at any given moment.

SWAMP MANAGER

Listing 7-1 is a simple simulation of an environ-

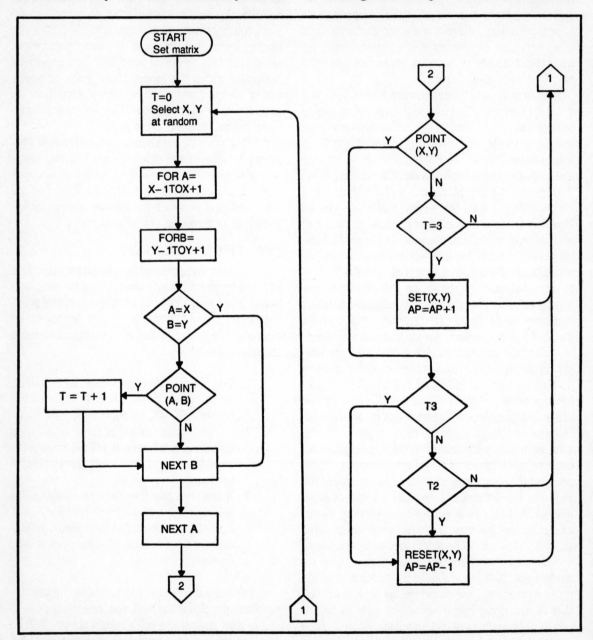

Fig. 7-1. Flowchart for "Life."

Listing 7-1. Swamp Simulation.

```
1 '*******************************************
2 '*              Listing 7-1                *
3 '*            Swamp Simulation             *
4 '*******************************************
5 '
10 CLS:KEY OFF:PRINT"SWAMP SIMULATION":PRINT:PRI
NT
20 INPUT"AVERAGE MOSQUITO POPULATION PER ACRE";M
A
30 INPUT"NUMBER OF ACRES";NA:MP=NA*MA
40 INPUT"MOSQUITO REPRODUCTION RATE (NEW MOSQUIT
OES PER 1000)";RR:R=1+(RR/1000)
50 INPUT"COST TO DESTROY 1000 MOSQUITOES";CD
60 INPUT"COST OF MEDICAL CARE FOR ONE MALARIA VI
CTIM";CM
70 INPUT"NUMBER OF MALARIA VICTIMS PER 1000 MOSQ
UITOES";MV:VM=MV/1000:INPUT"BEGINNING BANK BALAN
CE";BB:B=BB
80 INPUT"COST TO PREPARE AN ACRE FOR LEASING";CP
90 INPUT"NET PROFIT FROM SUBLEASE OF ONE MOSQUIT
O-FREE ACRE";NP:CLS
100 PRINT:PRINT"GENERATION # ";G:B=B+(AD*NP)
110 PRINT"MOSQUITO POPULATION =";MP,:AI=INT(MP/M
A)+1:IF AI>NA THEN AI=NA
120 PRINT"TOTAL ACRES INFESTED =";AI
130 CV=INT(VM*(MP/1000))+1:B=B-(CM*CV)
140 PRINT"CURRENT NUMBER OF MALARIA VICTIMS =";I
NT(VM*(MP/1000))+1:G=G+1
150 PRINT"BANK BALANCE (AFTER MEDICAL EXPENSES)
= $";B
160 PRINT:INPUT"NUMBER OF MOSQUITOES TO BE DESTR
OYED (-1 to end)";N
170 IF N=-1 THEN RUN "A:MENU"
180 C=CD*(N/1000):IF C<=B THEN 220
190 IF B<0 THEN 210
200 PRINT"SORRY, YOU ONLY HAVE THE CASH TO DESTR
OY";1000*(B/CD);"MOSQUITOES":GOTO 160
210 PRINT"SORRY, NO CASH AVAILABLE THIS PERIOD":
GOTO 270
220 B=B-C:MP=INT(MP*R)-N
230 AF=NA-(MP/MA)
240 PRINT AF;"ACRES ARE FREE FOR DEVELOPMENT.  "
;
250 IF AF<0 THEN 100
260 IF B=>0 THEN 280
270 PRINT"NO CASH IS AVAILABLE FOR DEVELOPMENT":
GOTO 100
280 INPUT"NUMBER DESIRED";N:C=CP*N:IF C<=B THEN
300
290 PRINT"SORRY, YOU ONLY HAVE THE CASH TO DEVEL
OP";B/CP;"ACRES":GOTO 280
300 B=B-C+(N*NP):AD=AD+N
310 GOTO 100
```

mental control problem. The premise is this: you own land upon which there is a swamp in which malaria-bearing mosquitoes breed profusely; additionally, the community leaders hold you responsible for the control of the mosquitoes or the compensation for the medical expenses of your neighbors. Your only source of income is through development and leasing of the property. You specify all input values. The objective is to achieve a maximum positive cash flow in minimum time. Of course, you can contrive to reach the objective by manipulation of the input values. So long as the simulation is only a game, that is up to you, but, to the extent that you have a serious interest in the outcome, you must be as realistic as possible about the values input.

ISLAND

There is a remote island that you own. You would like to purchase a certain number of cattle, sheep, or a combination of both, which you would transport to the island for grazing until market time. The objective of the island is to determine the optimum starting population of the herd of livestock so that a maximum herd size will be obtained in minimum time without creating a herd so large that it exceeds the island's capability to generate sufficient vegetation to sustain the herd (Listing 7-2).

Listing 7-2. Island.

```
1 '*************************************************
2 '*                  Listing 7-2                  *
3 '*                    Island                     *
4 '*************************************************
5 '
10 CLS:KEY OFF:PRINT"ISLAND":PRINT:PRINT
20 LOCATE 5,1:PRINT"Default"
30 PRINT AA,:INPUT"WHAT IS THE AREA, IN ACRES, O
F THE ISLAND";AA
40 IA=AA*43560!
50 PRINT NA,:INPUT"NUMBER OF ANIMALS TO BE INTRO
DUCED";NA
60 PRINT SF,:INPUT"SQUARE FOOTAGE COVERED BY EAC
H ANIMAL";SF
70 PRINT BR,:INPUT"NUMBER OF BIRTHS PER 1000 ANI
MALS PER MONTH";BR:R1=1+(BR/1000)
80 PRINT DR,:INPUT"NUMBER NATURAL DEATHS PER 100
0 PER MONTH";DR:R2=1+(DR/1000)
90 PRINT RS,:INPUT"NUMBER OF ANIMALS TO BE REMOV
ED MONTHLY FOR SALE";RS
100 PRINT VC,:INPUT"SQUARE FEET OF VEGETATION CO
NSUMED PER ANIMAL PER MONTH";VC
110 PRINT"TOTAL VEGETATION REQUIRED AT START";VC
*NA
120 PRINT VG,:INPUT"GROWTH RATE OF VEGETATION IN
 SQUARE FEET PER MONTH";VG
130 LS=NA*SF:VS=IA-LS:VV=VS:P=NA:G=0
140 PRINT"AT THE BEGINNING, THE ANIMALS WILL REQ
UIRE ";LS;" SQUARE FEET OF LIVING SPACE.  THIS L
EAVES ";VS;" SQUARE FEET FOR VEGETATION."
150 PRINT:PRINT"ANY KEY TO CONTINUE ";
160 Q$=""+INKEY$:IF Q$="" THEN 160
170 CLS:LOCATE 1,1:PRINT"","NUMBER","SQR FEET":P
RINT"GENERATION","ANIMALS","VEGETATION"
180 VV=VV-(P*VC)+VG:NB=P*R1:ND=P*R2:P=P+NB-ND-RS
190 IF VV>0 THEN 210
200 ND=ABS(VV/VC):P=P-ND
```

```
210 IF P<=0 THEN 250
220 LS=P*SF:VS=IA-LS:G=G+1:IF VV>VS THEN VV=VS
230 LOCATE 3,1:PRINT G,P,VV,
240 GOTO 180
250 LOCATE 24,1:PRINT"Sorry, Herd has died.  Try
 new starting values?"
260 PRINT"(A)nother       (M)ain menu ";
270 GOSUB 290
280 IF Q$="A" OR Q$="a" THEN RUN 10 ELSE RUN "A:
MENU"
290 Q$=""+INKEY$:IF Q$="" THEN 290
300 RETURN
```

QUEUING THEORY

We fully suspect that the first theory related to *queues* (lines of people or items awaiting some sort of processing or service) was developed by a mathematician waiting in line at a bank or supermarket. What began as a trivial exercise to pass the time of day has evolved into a serious science with useful and practical applications. Use of the modern queuing theories has enabled engineers and managers to make optimum use of people and resources so that customers receive prompt service, without using an excessive number of salespeople. Likewise, appliances awaiting repair or goods awaiting a manufacturing process are handled without unnecessary delay or excessive use of capital equipment.

The processing of queuing problems normally begins with the user specifying two values: L, the average number of customers arriving per unit of time (normally per hour) and M, the maximum number of customers the queue can process in one hour, or S, the average time to serve one customer, from which M can be computed. From these values, a number of other values can be computed. These include:

$$EN = \frac{L}{M - L}$$ Mean number of customers in the total system

$$EL = \frac{L^2}{M(M - L)}$$ Mean length of waiting time, not including those being served.

$$EW = \frac{L}{M(M - L)}$$ Mean waiting time in queue.

$$ET = \frac{1}{M - L}$$ Mean total time in system.

In addition, queuing theory includes the value of Q, the *balk point*, which is the number of persons in a queue that will normally cause the next customer who enters the facility and views the queue to balk and leave without waiting for service. As with L and M, this value is normally determined by observation. Alternatively, the analyst may wish to experiment with different values of Q. At any rate, the equations given above can be modified to accommodate Q and are shown below. In the first column is the standard notation. In the second column is the notation used in this book for equations with a balk point.

$U = L/M$ Queue utilization factor.

$S = 60/M$ Average processing time.

$M = 60/S$ Maximum number of customers a queue can process in one unit of time.

$PW = 1 - U$ The probability that a customer will not have to wait.

$PN = U^N (1 - U)$ The probability of N customers in the system at one moment.

$$EN \quad NE = \frac{U}{1 - U} - \frac{U^{Q+1}(1 + Q)}{1 - U^{Q+1}}$$

$$EL \quad LE = NE - 1 + \frac{1}{1 - U^{Q+1}}$$

$$ET \quad TE = \frac{1}{M(1 - U)} - \frac{Q\,U^Q}{M(1 - U^Q)}$$

$$EW \quad WE = TE - \frac{1}{M}$$

125

The other equations remain the same as before.

To this point, the assumption has been that there was only one server and that customers arrived at normal or even intervals. In many instances, however, there are two or more servers and customers tend to arrive in a Poisson distribution instead of a normal distribution. If we designate the number of servers as K, where K is greater than one and KM is greater than L, we can compute the value P_0, which is the probability of zero customers in the system at a given instant, from:

$$P_0 = \frac{1}{\displaystyle\sum_{N=0}^{K-1} \frac{U^N}{N!} + \frac{U^K}{K!} \left(\frac{K M}{K M - L} \right)}$$

Using this value, we can now compute the other basic queue factors from:

$$EN \quad E_1 = \frac{L M U^K}{(K - 1)! \, (K M - L)^2} \, P_0 + U$$

$$EL \quad E_2 = E_1 - U$$

$$ET \quad E_3 = \frac{M U^K}{(K - 1)! \, (K M - L)^2} + P_0 + \frac{1}{M}$$

$$E_4 = E_3 - \frac{1}{M}$$

Listing 7-3 implements the foregoing queuing equations. From the program, the analyst can estimate the various factors in a given system. When the processing time, S, grows relatively large, to the extent there are normally three or more persons in the queue, the likelihood is high that a balk point exists. When the observed data deviate from the predicted data, there is a good possibility that a balk point exists in reality and that it is reached often enough to have an operational impact. In this instance, the analyst should use actual data, such as the actual mean number of customers in the total system at a given time, NE, and solve the equation for Q. The problem with the equations involving Q is that they use exponential forms of Q that are difficult to factor out. The easier solution is to use an iterative solution for the equation:

$$NX = \frac{\dfrac{U}{1 - U} - U^{Q+1} (Q + 1)}{1 - U^{Q+1}}$$

Using trial values of Q until $NX = NE$.

With these basic data, the analyst can design a model of the operation and vary the magnitude of the controllable elements and thereby discover optimum components. For example, knowing the basic variables for a retail operation with two cashiers, the analyst can compute the effect of varying the number of cashiers (K) to determine the optimum

Listing 7-3. Queuing.

```
1 '*******************************************
2 '*            listing 7-3             *
3 '*              Queuing               *
4 '*******************************************
5 '
10 CLS:PRINT"QUEUING":PRINT:PRINT
20 INPUT"AVERAGE NUMBER OF CUSTOMERS ARRIVING PE
R HOUR";L
30 PRINT"EXPECTED INTERVAL BETWEEN CUSTOMERS =";
60/L;"MINUTES"
40 INPUT"AVERAGE NUMBER OF MINUTES TO SERVE ONE
CUSTOMER";S:INPUT"NUMBER OF SERVERS";K
50 M=K*(60/S):PRINT"MAXIMUM NUMBER OF CUSTOMERS
PER HOUR PER SERVER =";M
60 U=L/M:ST=(K*60)-(L*S)
70 PRINT"UTILIZATION FACTOR (U) =";U
80 PRINT"MAXIMUM SLACK TIME (ST) =";ST;"MINUTES
(";ST/60;"SERVER(S) )"
90 PW=1-U:INPUT"TRIAL NUMBER OF CUSTOMERS (N)";N
:PN=PW*(U^N)
100 IF K>1 AND M>L THEN 390
```

```
110 EN=L/(M-L):EL=(L^2)/(M*(M-L)):EW=L/(M*(M-L))
:ET=1/(M-L)
120 PRINT"PROBABILITY OF";N;"CUSTOMERS IS ";PN
130 PRINT"MEAN NUMBER OF CUSTOMERS IN TOTAL SYST
EM =";EN
140 PRINT"MEAN LENGTH OF WAITING TIME =";EL*60;"
MINUTES"
150 PRINT"MEAN WAITING TIME IN QUEUE =";EW*60;"M
INUTES"
160 PRINT"MEAN TOTAL TIME IN SYSTEM =";ET*60;"MI
NUTES"
170 INPUT"VALUE OF BALK POINT (0 IF UNKNOWN)";Q
180 IF Q=0 THEN 330
190 PRINT"COMPUTATIONS USING A BALK POINT OF ";Q
200 NE=(U/(1-U))-((Q+1)*(U^(Q+1))/(1-(U^(Q+1))))
210 LE=NE-1+((1-U)/(1-(U^(Q+1))))
220 TE=(1/(M*(1-U)))-((Q*(U^Q))/(M*(1-(U^Q))))
230 WE=TE-(1/M)
240 PRINT"USING A BALK POINT OF";Q;":"
250 PRINT"MEAN NUMBER OF CUSTOMERS IN SYSTEM =";
NE
260 PRINT"MEAN LENGTH OF WAITING TIME =";LE*60;"
MINUTES"
270 PRINT"MEAN TOTAL TIME IN SYSTEM =";TE*60;"MI
NUTES"
280 PRINT"MEAN WAITING TIME IN QUEUE =";WE*60;"M
INUTES"
290 PRINT:PRINT"(A)nother set                (M)ai
n menu "
300 Q$=""+INKEY$:IF Q$="" THEN 300
310 IF Q$="A" OR "a" THEN 10 ELSE IF Q$="M" OR Q
$="m" THEN RUN "a:menu"
320 END
330 INPUT"OBSERVED MEAN NUMBER OF CUSTOMERS IN S
YSTEM";NE:Q=10:DQ=2
340 NX=(U/(1-U))-((Q+1)*(U^(Q+1))/(1-(U^(Q+1))))
350 IF NX>NE THEN 380
360 IF Q>(NE^3) THEN 200
370 Q=Q+DQ:GOTO 340
380 Q=Q-DQ:DQ=DQ/2:IF DQ>.0001 THEN 370 ELSE 200
390 M=M/K
400 FOR N=0 TO K-1
410 A=U^N
420 B=1
430 FOR F=1 TO N:B=B*F:NEXT
440 B=1/B:C=C+(A*B)
450 NEXT N
460 KF=1
470 FOR F=1 TO K:KF=KF*F:NEXT
480 A=1/KF:B=(K*M)/((K*M)-L):D=A*B
490 P0=1/(C+D)
500 PRINT"Probability of Zero Customers =";P0
510 A=L*M*(U^K)
520 B=1
530 FOR F=1 TO K-1:B=B*F:C=B*(((K*M)-L)^2):NEXT
F
540 E1=((A/C)*P0)+U:E2=E1-U:E3=(((M*(U^K))/(B*((
(K*M)-L)^2)))*P0)+(1/M):E4=E3-(1/M):NE=E1:LE=E2:
TE=E3:WE=E4:GOTO 250
```

number to have on duty at a given time so that the actual number of balks (walk-away business) is minimized. Each walk-away (WA) represents an average sales dollar volume (SD). Each cashier represents a known wage per customer (WC). The objective of the analyst, then, is to compute K where K × WC is equal to or less than SD × WA. The implication of the relationship is fairly clear: an infinite number of cashiers will eliminate the possibility of walk-aways but at an unacceptable wage cost. Too few cashiers could result in an unnecessary profit loss. There may never be a point where K × WC is less than SD × WA, but we should always be able to locate the point where the difference is minimized. This is the value of using the microcomputer for simulations.

FORECASTING USING AN ECONOMIC MODEL

Figure 7-2 illustrates the cash flow of a simple retail operation. At the center of the figure is the retail operation itself. It consists of a proprietor and one or more employees. The proprietor will draw his earnings from the net profit, if any, and will pay personal income tax on that amount. The only source of cash income is from the customers. From this amount must be paid all of the various expenses. Off the top will normally come one or more operating taxes or fees paid to city, county, state, and federal taxing and licensing authorities. These will take two forms. The first will be fixed fees independent of sales volume. The second will be taxes based on the size of the plant facility and the sales volume. The wholesaler, of course, is an essential factor in the successful retail operation. Whether the wholesaler will extend terms (credit) to the retailer, or give discounts for quantity purchases or prompt payment, are central to the success or failure of both new and existing businesses.

The retail process begins with a decision to purchase a certain quantity of goods from the wholesaler. This quantity is a function of the

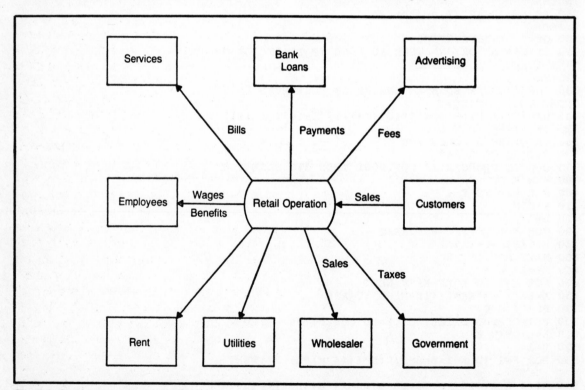

Fig. 7-2. Cash flow model, retail sales.

retailer's anticipation of probable sales volume, capital resources, available lines of credit, and the wholesaler's terms. Subsequent purchases from the wholesaler are a function of actual sales volume experience. Initially, the new retailer's objective is to buy sufficient merchandise from the wholesaler to fill the store well enough to encourage customers to think they are dealing with an established business and to satisfy buyer demand. Yet the retailer must not buy so much that lines of credit are tied up unnecessarily. This is often one of the really tricky problems in retailing.

Utilities include gas and electricity for heat and air conditioning, telephone service, and water. Generally speaking, the amount paid for utilities will be a function of the size of the retail operation, which is a function of sales volume. (This is not quite true. A number of large corporate retail operations mandate a certain square footage regardless of actual market, and then set as a management goal a sales volume to justify the space. In this model we are not concerned with how a national chain establishes a new outlet, but how the sole proprietor of a specialty shop might start up and operate a business.) A large store with tens of thousands of square feet will have to pay proportionately more for utilities than a small shop. Likewise, rent is normally a function of square footage.

The number of employees is a function of the anticipated number of sales and the time required to complete a sale, rather than the total dollar amount of sales. A jewelry store, with a number of big ticket items, needs fewer employees to support a dollar income equal to that of a cookie shop with more employees. If T is the time in minutes required to complete a sale, H is the number of hours the shop is open daily, and A is the average anticipated daily sales volume, the maximum number of sales staff, S, can be computed from: Where INT is the integer value of the equation

$$S = 1 + INT\left[\frac{A \times T}{60 \times H}\right]$$

The smaller the anticipated sales volume, the more demanding personnel management will become. If S is computed to be 1, problems will occur during that person's absence due to vacation or illness. The proprietor will have to either undertake sales duties or hire temporary help. On the other hand, as the value of S increases, the easier it should be to manage absences due to vacation or illness.

In addition to wages, the model must account for employer Social Security contributions, retirement fund payments, medical benefits, and other employee-related expenses.

Although smaller businesses often maintain a working ledger system, it is often prudent or necessary to retain the services of a professional accountant, at least at year's end to handle tax matters. Other services the business may require are legal, catering, and printing services.

It does pay to advertise. Time and time again a clear relationship can be shown between the number of dollars spent for advertising and sales volume. Industry-wide, the relationship is fairly linear; that is, when you plot the amount of sales receipts against the related amount spent for advertising, the general relationship that results is shown in Fig. 7-3.

It would be misleading, however, to suggest that a given store solve its cash flow problems simply by pumping cash into advertising. A number of nonadvertising aspects may be adversely affecting sales volume. These include: market size, competition, location, local employment levels, and so forth. For this reason, we suggest this model use a variation of the linear trend equation ($Y = A + BX$) to limit the utility of advertising to a practical level. The form recommended is: $Y = A + B \log X$, in which X is the dollar amount of the advertising budget and Y is the anticipated sales volume.

Bank loans are frequently used by the retail operation to bridge the time between the purchase of goods and the time these goods are sold at retail prices. This approach is most often encountered in situations where the wholesaler will not grant extension of terms to the retailer but insists on cash payment on or before shipment. Normally, the bank will extend a line of credit to the merchant which requires that the payments, which are computed using the actual amount of the credit used, be paid over 12 to 60 months. The interest rate will vary considerably, depending on the bank's objectives

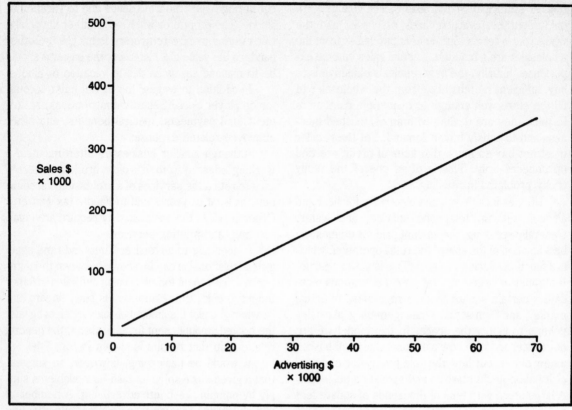

Fig. 7-3. Sales volume as a function of advertising expenditures, nominal form.

Listing 7-4. Economic Model.

```
1 '*********************************************
2 '*              Listing 7-4                  *
3 '*            Economic Model                 *
4 '*********************************************
5 '
10 CLS:KEY OFF:PRINT"ECONOMIC MODEL":PRINT:PRINT
20 PRINT"DEFAULT =";IC,:INPUT"INITIAL CAPITALIZA
TION";IC:I1=IC
30 PRINT"DEFAULT =";MS,:INPUT"ANTICIPATED NUMBER
 OF MONTHLY SALES";MS
40 PRINT"DEFAULT =";AI,:INPUT"AVERAGE INCOME PER
 SALE";AI
50 PRINT"DEFAULT =";RW,:INPUT"RETAIL TO WHOLESAL
E RATIO";RW
60 IP=(MS*AI)/RW:PRINT"INITIAL WHOLESALE PURCHAS
E WILL BE $";IP
70 PRINT"WILL THE WHOLESALER EXTEND TERMS (SHIP
ON CONSIGNMENT)?  (Y/N)";
80 Q1$=""+INKEY$:IF Q1$="" THEN 80
90 PRINT" ";Q1$
100 IF Q1$="N" THEN 120
```

```
110 PRINT"DEFAULT =";WL,:INPUT"CREDIT LIMIT EXTE
NDED BY WHOLESALER";WL
120 PRINT"IS THERE A BANK LINE OF CREDIT AVAILAB
LE  (Y/N)";
130 Q2$=""+INKEY$:IF Q2$="" THEN 130
140 PRINT" ";Q2$
150 IF Q2$="N" THEN 180
160 PRINT"DEFAULT =";CL,:INPUT"AMOUNT OF CREDIT
LINE";CL
170 PRINT"DEFAULT =";TC,:INPUT"TERM OF CREDIT IN
 MONTHS";TC:PRINT"DEFAULT =";MR*1200,:INPUT"ANNU
AL INTEREST RATE (5%=5)";AR:MR=AR/1200
180 PRINT"SQUARE FOOTAGE NECESSARY TO SUPPORT";M
S;"SALES MONTHLY",:PRINT"DEFAULT =";SF,:INPUT SF
190 PRINT"DEFAULT =";MU,:INPUT"MONTHLY UTILITIES
 PAYABLE PER SQUARE FOOT";MU
200 PRINT"DEFAULT =";NR*12,:INPUT"NORMAL ANNUAL
RENTAL PER SQUARE FOOT";NR:NR=NR/12
210 R=SF*NR:U=MU*SF:MP=(MR*((1+MR)^TC))/(((1+MR)
^TC)-1)
220 PRINT"YOUR RENT WILL BE APPROXIMATELY $";R;"
MONTHLY"
230 PRINT"UTILITIES WILL AVERAGE APPROXIMATELY $
";U;"MONTHLY"
240 PRINT"DEFAULT =";T,:INPUT"AVERAGE TIME TO CO
MPLETE ONE SALE";T
250 PRINT"DEFAULT =";D,:INPUT"NUMBER OF DAYS PER
 WEEK STORE IS OPEN";D
260 D=D*4.333:PRINT"DEFAULT =";H,:INPUT"NUMBER O
F HOURS PER DAY STORE IS OPEN";H
270 S=1+INT(((MS/D)*T)/(60*H)):PRINT"ESTIMATED M
AXIMUM STAFF =";S:PRINT"IS THIS ACCEPTABLE  (Y/N
)";
280 Q3$=""+INKEY$:IF Q3$="" THEN 280
290 PRINT" ";Q3$:IF Q3$="Y" THEN 310
300 PRINT"DEFAULT =";S,:INPUT"ENTER ACTUAL STAFF
";S
310 PRINT"DEFAULT =";AW,:INPUT"AVERAGE WAGE PER
STAFF MEMBER";AW
320 PRINT"DEFAULT =";EB,:INPUT"AVERAGE DOLLAR CO
ST PER MONTH OF EMPLOYEE BENEFITS";EB:EC=((AW*S)
*1.17)+EB:PRINT"MONTHLY EMPLOYEE COST = $";EC
330 PRINT"DEFAULT =";CS,:INPUT"MONTHLY COST OF S
ERVICES";CS
340 PRINT"DEFAULT =";Y1,:INPUT"# CUSTOMERS RESUL
TING FROM $20,000 IN ADVERTISING";Y1
350 PRINT"DEFAULT =";Y2,:INPUT"# CUSTOMERS RESUL
TING FROM $40,000 IN ADVERTISING";Y2
360 B=(((Y1*LOG(20000))+(Y2*LOG(40000!)))-(.5*((
LOG(20000)+LOG(40000!))*(Y1+Y2))))/(((LOG(20000)
^2)+(LOG(40000!)^2))-(.5*(LOG(20000)+LOG(40000!)
)^2))
370 A=.5*((Y1+Y2)-(B*(LOG(20000)+LOG(40000!))))
380 IA=EXP((MS-A)/B)
390 PRINT"INITIAL ADVERTISING SHOULD BE = $";IA:
PRINT"ACCEPTABLE  (Y/N) ";
400 Q4$=""+INKEY$:IF Q4$="" THEN 400
410 PRINT Q4$:IF Q4$="Y" THEN 430
```

Listing 7-4. Economic Model. (Continued From Page 131.)

```
420 PRINT"DEFAULT =";X,:INPUT"ADVERTISING DESIRE
D";X:Y=A+(B*LOG(X)):PRINT"ANTICIPATED SALES = $"
;Y*AI,"=";Y;"CUSTOMERS"
430 PRINT"DEFAULT =";(IR-1)*1200,:INPUT"ANNUAL I
NFLATION RATE TO BE APPLIED TO COSTS (5%=5)";IR:
IR=1+(IR/1200):LW=WL:LC=CL:CLS
440 IC=IC-R-U-IA-(S*EC)-CS-MP
450 IF IP>LW THEN 470
460 LW=LW-IP:GOTO 510
470 IF (IP-LW)>CL THEN 490
480 LC=LC+(IP-LW):CL=CL-(IP-LW):GOTO 500
490 LC=LC+CL:CL=0
500 MP=LC*MR:LW=0
510 IC=IC+(MS*AI):I2=IC:LOCATE 1,1:PRINT"CAPITAL
 AVAIL. = $";IC,"NET CHANGE = $ ";I2-I1:IN=I2-I1
:IF IN<0 THEN 540
520 TX=IN/10000:IF TX>.5 THEN TX=.5
530 IC=IC*(1-TX)
540 IC=IC-WL:LW=LW+WL:CL=(CL*(1-MR))+MP
550 I1=I2:R=R*IR:U=U*IR:EC=EC*IR:CS=CS*IR:IP=IP*
IR
560 IF IC>0 THEN 440
570 LOCATE 9,1:PRINT"OPPS.  YOU'VE JUST LOST YOU
R SHIRT.  REPROGRAM STARTING VALUES"
580 PRINT:PRINT"(A)nother try           (M)ain m
enu "
590 Q$=""+INKEY$:IF Q$="" THEN 590
600 IF Q$="A" OR Q$="a" THEN 10 ELSE RUN "a:menu
"
```

(whether it wants to encourage or discourage small business accounts). While rates below commercial levels are possible to negotiate with a friendly banker, a retailer should normally anticipate paying a premium interest rate. Remember, usury laws don't apply to commercial transactions.

We've gone around the model and have returned to the customer. The level of sales is assumed to be a function of the amount spent on advertising. For purposes of simplicity, we include in advertising the money spent to decorate the shop, purchase attractive shopping bags, and to provide other features to attract customers and to make them feel comfortable in the store. In more elaborate models of this retail operation, some of these costs might be placed in other accounting areas.

As with the other models, it is up to the user to specify all of the input variables with the objective to maximizing profits in the minimum amount of time. As a game it is fairly easy to specify a set of no-lose input factors. As a device to aid a would-be entrepreneur, the key element is an honest estimate of the actual components.

EXERCISES

1. Identify a small business in your neighborhood. Interview the owner to determine the general operations routine of his business in sufficient detail to develop a computer model of his business. In this project, remember that many business people, while willing to discuss their business (during slow or quiet periods), are reluctant to discuss specific costs and wholesale prices. In such instances, be willing to settle for approximate cost data or ranges of prices. In exchange for greater candor from the merchant, you may want to offer to share the model and the results of your work with him.

2. Develop a cash flow model of your own finances. Show the source(s) of income and the disposition of it. If you have a savings account or investments, be sure to show the interest paid as a source of income.

3. Write a program to simulate the operation of a roulette wheel. Include in the program a system to keep track of the numbers that appear and the betting options and odds available. Your research should quickly lead you to the fact there are at least two types of wheel layouts, European and American. Determine which one tends to favor the player more.

4. Develop a program to "deal" a complete bridge hand: i.e., 13 cards dealt from a shuffled deck to each of four players (see Chapter 15 for shuffling routines). Display each card by suit and in descending order from right to left in each hand. Show the hands at the top, bottom, and either side of the screen, labeled N, E, W, and S for the compass direction of the hands.

5. If you understand the game well enough, develop a subroutine in the program in exercise 4 so the computer can participate in the bidding of the hands.

SUGGESTED READING

Adler, I., 1957. *Magic House of Numbers*. New York: The John Day Company, Inc.

Dusenberry, J. S., et al., 1965. *The Brookings Quarterly Economic Model of the United States*. Chicago: Rand-McNally.

Epstein, R. A., 1967. *The Theory of Gambling and Statistical Logic*. New York: Academic Press.

Pindyck, R. S. and D. L. Rubenfeld, 1976. *Economic Models and Economic Forecasts*. New York: McGraw-Hill.

Chapter 8

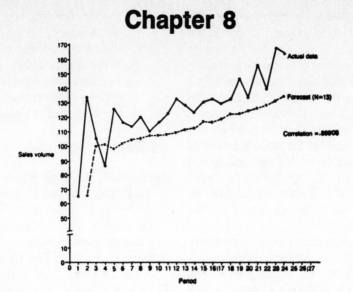

Numerical Analysis

In the real world of higher mathematics, the term *numerical analysis* refers to quite a family of sophisticated equations and complex relationships. Those who have mastered calculus get bogged down in cluster analysis and linear transfer functions. You will find very few such references in this chapter. Instead, what we will present are some practical ways to use fundamental numerical relationships and distributions to assist in a forecasting effort where other techniques fall short of being satisfactory or appear so tedious to implement that it doesn't appear cost or time effective to do it the long way. We offer these techniques from the pragmatic perspective: if it works, use it. The responsible researcher must make every effort to go beyond establishing the means to make a forecast and identify, if at all possible, the casual relationships between the predictor and the dependent variable.

Nonetheless, the techniques that follow often yield useful forecasting tools. We will start with a technique that can deal with rationally related variables and nth order polynomials, and then work towards more abstract approaches, including geometric sections. Along the way we will consider a variety of distributions, trigonometric functions, and fast Fourier Transforms.

NTH ORDER POLYNOMIALS

The underlying assumption with this technique is that the dependent variable, Y, is primarily a function of one independent variable, X. The computation, however, is not simply in the form of the linear trend, $Y = A + BX$, but in the expanded form:

$$Y = A_0 + A_1 X + A_2 X^2 + A_3 X^3 + \ldots + An\, X^n$$

Assuming one chooses to use this approach, the tricky part is to properly identify the appropriate order of the equation. Many values of n will result in a curve form that will fit the sample data points, yet go wandering off in some very esoteric wavy form in-between (see Fig. 8-1). Listing 8-1 offers a routine to evaluate sample data points in the sense and

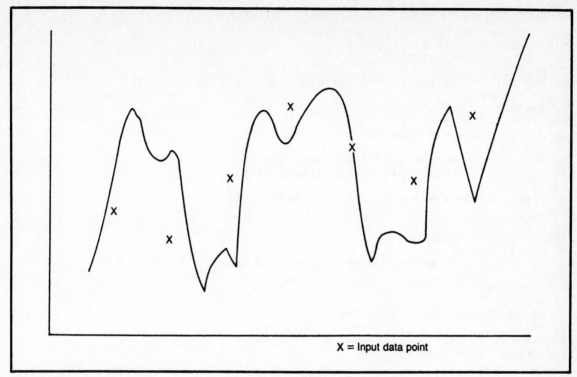

Fig. 8-1. Graph of polynomial.

Listing 8-1. Nth Order Polynomial.

```
1 '***********************************************
2 '*               Listing 8-1                   *
3 '*           N-th Order Polynomial             *
4 '***********************************************
5 '
10 CLS:INPUT "Degree of Equation ";D
20 INPUT "Number of known points ";N
30 IF N>(D+1) THEN 50
40 PRINT"Sorry, we need at least";D+2;"points.":
GOTO 20
50 DIM XX(N),YY(N),A((2*N)+1),R(N,N),T(N):A(1)=N
60 FOR I=1 TO N:PRINT"X, Y of point #";I;:INPUT
XX(I),YY(I):NEXT
70 FOR I=1 TO N:PRINT I;XX(I);YY(I),:NEXT I
80 PRINT:PRINT"Are these all correct?  (Y/N)"
90 Q$=""+INKEY$:IF Q$="" THEN 90 ELSE IF Q$="Y"
OR Q$="y" THEN 110
100 PRINT:INPUT "Item #, correct X, Y";X,XX(X),Y
Y(X):GOTO 70
110 CLS:PRINT"Computing ....":PRINT
120 FOR I=1 TO N
130    X=XX(I):Y=YY(I)
140    FOR J=2 TO ((2*D)+1):A(J)=A(J)+(X^(J-1)):N
EXT J
```

Listing 8-1. Nth Order Polynomial. (Continued From Page 135.)

```
150    FOR K=1 TO D+1:R(K,D+2)=T(K)+(Y*(X^(K-1)))
:T(K)=T(K)+(Y*(X^(K-1))):NEXT K
160    T(D+2)=T(D+2)+(Y^2)
170 NEXT I
180 FOR J=1 TO D+1:FOR K=1 TO D+1:R(J,K)=A(J+K-1
):NEXT K:NEXT J
190 FOR J=1 TO D+1
200    FOR K=J TO D+1
210      IF R(K,J)<>0 THEN 240
220    NEXT K
230    PRINT "No unique solution.":GOTO 450
240    FOR I=1 TO D+2:S=R(J,I):R(J,I)=R(K,I):R(K,
I)=S:NEXT I
250    Z=1/R(J,J):FOR I=1 TO D+2:R(J,I)=Z*R(J,I):
NEXT I
260    FOR K=1 TO D+1
270      IF K=J THEN 300
280      Z=-R(K,J)
290      FOR I=1 TO D+2:R(K,I)=R(K,I)+(Z*R(J,I)):
NEXT I
300    NEXT K
310 NEXT J
320 IF Q$="C" OR Q$="c" THEN 350
330 PRINT"            Constant = ";R(1,D+2)
340 FOR J=1 TO D:PRINT J;"Degree Coefficient = "
;R(J+1,D+2):NEXT J:PRINT
350 P=0
360 FOR J=2 TO D+1:P=P+(R(J,D+2)*(T(J)-(A(J)*(T(
1)/N)))):NEXT J
370 Q=T(D+2)-((T(1)^2)/N):Z=Q-P:I=N-D-1:J=P/Q:PR
INT ""
380 PRINT"Coefficient of Determination (r^2) = "
;J
390 IF J=>0 THEN 410
400 PRINT"Coefficient of Correlation       = "
;-1*SQR(ABS(J)):GOTO 420
410 PRINT"Coefficient of Correlation       = "
;SQR(J)
420 IF Z =>0 THEN 440
430 PRINT"Standard Error of Estimate       = "
;-1*SQR(ABS(Z/I)):GOTO 450
440 PRINT"Standard Error of Estimate       = "
;SQR(Z/I)
450 PRINT:PRINT"(I)nterpolation      (A)nother s
et       (M)ain menu "
460 Q$=""+INKEY$:IF Q$="" THEN 460 ELSE IF Q$="I
" OR Q$="i" THEN 470 ELSE IF Q$="A" OR Q$="a" TH
EN 10 ELSE IF Q$="M" OR Q$="m" THEN RUN "A:MENU"
 ELSE 460
470 PRINT:P=R(1,D+2):INPUT "Enter X value";X
480 FOR J=1 TO D:P=P+(R(J+1,D+2)*(X^J)):NEXT J
490 PRINT"Y = ";P:GOTO 450
```

form of the nth order polynomial. It will begin by asking for the order of the equation, N, and then insist that the user enter at least N + 2 sample data points. The first action, then, is the evaluation of the polynomial as described above. The program outputs the constant, or *residual*, and then specifies the various coefficients. These are followed by the computed coefficient of determination and the coefficient of correlation. Having completed the assigned task, the program goes on to compute all of the possible orders of the equation from n = 1 to n = N − 1. In each instance, the program computes the coefficients of determination and correlation. It is up to the user to choose which form is optimum for the present task.

DISTRIBUTIONS

Data, especially large amounts of data, frequently fall into one of several easily described distribution forms. If we know the basic form, we can forecast or interpolate the unknown points. Types of distributions include, but are not limited to, the normal, binomial, Poisson, and random.

The Normal Distribution

Otherwise known as the *bell curve*, the normal distribution is the most commonly used form of data distribution (see Fig. 2-3). For many statistical functions we assume the data to be normally distributed, even through we know the distribution is not precisely so distributed. The equation of the normal distribution is:

$$Y = f(x) = \frac{1}{\sqrt{2\pi}} \, e^{-\frac{1}{2}x^2}$$

The value of x is expressed in standard deviations from the mean and the magnitude of Y is expressed as a fraction of the total data set. That is, when x = 1.18, Y = .2. If we have reason to believe our data are normally distributed, we can interpolate a point from the equation above.

Binomial Distribution

In this form, the data conform to the shape defined by the probability of a given variable, P. The basic form of the equation is:

$$Y = p(x) = \left(\frac{n}{x} \right) p^x (1 - p)^{n - x} \quad x = 0, 1, 2 \ldots n$$

For example, a card is drawn from a standard deck of 52 playing cards. If it is a heart, a success, S, is recorded; if not, a failure is recorded. After n trials, we have a sum, S, representing the number of successes. This is a binomial variable because the probability of success is constant (p = ¼). The mean and the variance of such a distribution is:

$$m = n p$$
$$s^2 = n p (1 - p)$$

The key element in this distribution is the probability (p) of a given happening. If the other features of the distribution are given, the value of p is all that is necessary to compute the probability of any value of n events. The computation gives the probability of exactly n events happening. If n is the maximum number of possibilities and k is some intermediate value, then by computing all of the values of p(x) for x = 0 to k and summing the result, the computation yields the probability of at least k events happening. By computing the value of p(x) for x = k to n, the probability of having at most k events is calculated.

Poisson Distribution

This distribution is far less known and understood than the binomial distribution, but it is at least as useful. When graphed, the distribution resembles the normal distribution with a skew, normally to the right. The key element in this distribution is the mean, normally designated by the Greek letter lambda, λ. An interesting feature is that the variance is the same as the mean. Its utility comes from the fact that a lot of behavioral data tends to be distributed more according to the Poisson than the normal distribution. People tend to arrive for work or other formal gatherings according to the Poisson distribution. That is, if the designated starting time for work is 8:00 A.M., a tally of actual arrivals at or near that time would look like that in Fig. 8-2. Most of the people arrive shortly before the cutoff time, with the balance arriving at extended times beyond the mean.

The basic equation for the Poisson distribution is:

$$Y = f(x) = \frac{L^x e^{-L}}{x! x} \text{ where } X = 1, 2, 3 \ldots (X-1).X$$

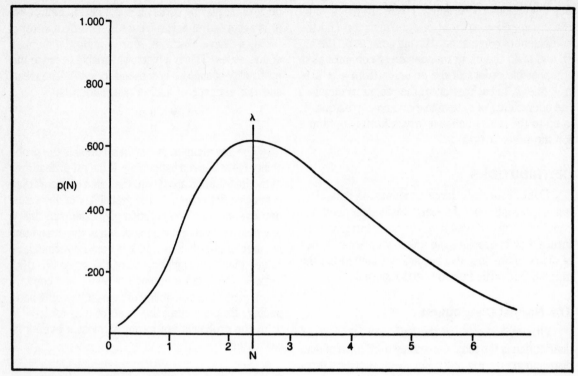

Fig. 8-2. Poisson distribution form.

Listing 8-2 is a useful routine to compute and display various elements of the Poisson distribution. The screen display is shown in Fig. 8-3.

Chi-Square Distribution

Figure 8-4 illustrates the general form of the chi-square distributions. In these, the key variable is the degrees of freedom, v, in each distribution. For example, if there are ten items in a table for which we compute a mean value of 1345.6678, any nine of those values can be any value we want, but those nine values define the tenth value such that the mean remains 1345.6678. Accordingly, we have nine degrees of freedom; $v = 9$. The equation for the general form of these equations is:

$$\chi^2 = \Sigma \frac{(O_i - E_i)^2}{E_i}$$

$$f(x) = \frac{x^{\frac{v}{2} - 1}}{2^{\frac{v}{2}} \Gamma\left(\frac{v}{2}\right) e^{\frac{x}{2}}}$$

Where O_i is the observed value at trial i, and E_i is the expected value.

The Gamma value is fairly easy to compute from the relationship:

$$\Gamma\left(\frac{v}{2}\right) = \left(\frac{v}{2} - 1\right)! \text{ when v is even}$$

or

$$\Gamma\left(\frac{v}{2}\right) = \left(\frac{v}{2} - 1\right)\left(\frac{v}{2} - 2\right)\ldots .8862269$$

when v is odd.

The area under the chi-square up to the value of chi-square is given by the equation:

$$P(x) = \frac{2x}{v} f(x) \left[1 + \sum_{k=1}^{\infty} \frac{x^k}{(v+2)(v+4)\ldots(v+2k)}\right]$$

Listing 8-3 is an extensive program enabling the user to evaluate data according to the foregoing dis-

Listing 8-2. Poisson Distribution.

```
1 '*********************************************
2 '*              Listing 8-2               *
3 '*          Poisson Distributions         *
4 '*********************************************
5 '
10 CLS:CLEAR 1000
20 INPUT"ENTER NUMBER OF TERMS";T
30 DIM M(T),N(T),TX(50),FX(50)
40 FOR I=1 TO T
50 LOCATE 3,1:PRINT"ENTER TERM NUMBER";I;"    ":I
NPUT N(I)
60 S=S+N(I):Q=Q+(N(I)^2)
70 NEXT I
80 L=S/T
90 IF L>20 THEN 100 ELSE 120
100 L=L/10:F=F+1
110 GOTO 90
120 E=2.71828
130 PRINT:PRINT"THE FOLLOWING COMPUTATION WILL TA
KE 2 MINUTES OR LESS:":PRINT:PRINT"X","J","X!","
P(X-1)";:PRINT
140 ON ERROR GOTO 240
150 FOR X=1 TO 50
160 XX=1
170 FOR J=1 TO X
180 XX=XX*J
190 LOCATE 9,1:PRINT X,J,XX,TX(X-1);
200 NEXT J
210 TX(X)=((L^X)*(1/(E^L)))/XX:FX(X)=INT(TX(X)*1
00)
220 IF TX(X)<.000001 AND X>10 THEN 240 ELSE 230
230 NEXT X
240 CLS
250 SCREEN 1
260 KEY OFF
270 FOR X=50 TO 52
280 FOR Y=20 TO 150 STEP 20
290 PSET(X,Y)
300 NEXT Y
310 NEXT X
320 X=55
330 FOR Y=18 TO 170
340 PSET(X,Y)
350 NEXT Y
360 Y=170
370 FOR X=56 TO 292
380 PSET(X,Y)
390 NEXT X
400 PSET(X,Y)
410 LOCATE 6,4:PRINT".30";:LOCATE 13,4:PRINT".15
";:LOCATE 22,4:PRINT".00";:LOCATE 10,1:PRINT"P(x
);
420    LOCATE 23,15::PRINT "5       10      15      20"
430 LOCATE 24,20:PRINT"X *";10^F;
440 FOR I=1 TO 20
450 PSET((I*10)+58,170-INT((TX(I)/.45)*160))
```

Listing 8-2. Poisson Distribution. (Continued From Page 139.)

```
460 NEXT I
470 LOCATE 1,12:PRINT"MEAN =";L;"X";10^F;
480 LOCATE 24,1:PRINT"'C' TO CONTINUE";
490 Q$=INKEY$:IF Q$="" THEN 490
500 IF Q$="C" OR Q$="c" THEN 510 ELSE 490
510 CLS
520 LOCATE 4,29:PRINT"OPTIONS"
530 PRINT:PRINT"1 -- LINE PRINTER       2 -- VIDE
O PLOT     3 -- PROBABILITY COMPUTATION
4 -- END"
540 PRINT:PRINT"ENTER NUMERICAL CHOICE"
550 N$=INKEY$:IF N$="" THEN 550
560 NC=VAL(N$)
570 ON NC GOTO 800,240,580,1080
580 CLS
590 LOCATE 9,1:PRINT"ENTER INTERGER VALUE FOR WH
ICH PROBABILITY IS DESIRED:"
600 INPUT IV:IV=INT(IV)
610 IV=IV/(10^F)
620 IF IV>30 THEN 700
630 FOR I=1 TO 30
640 IF IV=I THEN 650 ELSE 690
650 PRINT:PRINT"THE PROBABILTY OF";IV*(10^F);" E
VENTS IS =";TX(I)
660 PRINT:PRINT"ANOTHER VALUE?   (Y/N)"
670 Q$=INKEY$:IF Q$="" THEN 670
680 IF Q$="Y" THEN 580 ELSE 510
690 NEXT I
700 XX=1
710 ON ERROR GOTO 780
720 FOR J=1 TO IV
730 XX=XX*J
740 NEXT J
750 TT=((L^IV)*(1/(E^L)))/XX
760 PRINT:PRINT"THE PROBABILITY OF";IV*(10^F);"
EVENTS IS =";TT
770 GOTO 660
780 PRINT:PRINT"THE COMPUTATIONS INVOLVED WITH T
HE SOLUTION OF P(";IV;") CAUSE THE COMPUTER TO '
OVERFLOW.'   SORRY.?"
790 GOTO 660
800 LPRINT STRING$(2,10)
810 LPRINT"POISSON DISTRIBUTION ANALYSIS"
820 LPRINT" "
830 LPRINT"MEAN OF DISTRIBUTION OF";T;" ITEMS IS
 =";L*(10^F)
840 LPRINT" "
850 LPRINT TAB(61)"P(X)"
860 LPRINT STRING$(19,32);:LPRINT"0.0
     .1               .2              .3
               .4"
870 LPRINT STRING$(19,32);:LPRINT" I
     I               I               I
               I"
880 LPRINT STRING$(18,32);:LPRINT"---------------
```

```
----------------------------------------------------
------------------""
890 FOR X=1 TO 25
900 LPRINT " I";:LPRINT STRING$(INT(100*(TX(X)*2
)),32);X
910 LPRINT " I"
920 IF TX(X)<.0045 AND X>10 THEN 940 ELSE 930
930 NEXT X
940 LPRINT" ":LPRINT STRING$(25,32);"PROBABILITY
 OF LAST VALUE IS =";TX(X)
950 LPRINT STRING$(3,10)
960 LPRINT"TABLE OF INPUT VALUES AND PROBABILITI
ES"
970 LPRINT" "
980 LPRINT"INPUT VALUE, X","P(X)=","INPUT VALUE,
 X","P(X)=","INPUT VALUE, X","P(X)=","INPUT VALU
E, X","p(X)="
990 FOR I=1 TO T
1000 LPRINT N(I),TX(I),
1010 NEXT I
1020 LPRINT" "
1030 LPRINT"MEAN OF DISTRIBUTION =";L*(10^F)
1040 LPRINT"POISSON STANDARD DEVIATION =";SQR(L*
(10^F))
1050 LPRINT"'NORMAL' STANDARD DEVIATION =";SQR((
Q-((S/T)^2))/(T-1))
1060 LPRINT STRING$(10,10)
1070 GOTO 240
1080 PRINT"(A)nother set      (M)ain menu   "
1090 Q$=""+INKEY$:IF Q$="" THEN 1090
1100 IF Q$="A" OR Q$="a" THEN 10 ELSE RUN "A:
U"
```

cussions, as well as to perform a fundamental analysis of a set of data in an effort to determine underlying distribution forms.

TRIGONOMETRIC FUNCTIONS

Figure 8-5 illustrates a number of curves that are generated by functions of various algebraic and trigonometric relationships. Numerous reference works in mathematics continue this series with countless fascinating shapes and curves. Our purpose here is not to present an encyclopedic catalog of the various possibilities, but simply to alert the reader to the option of using such forms.

Many of the equations can be modified to better fit your data by the simple addition of various coefficients. For example, the normal equation for the coordinates of a sine curve are: $X = \cos A$ and $Y = \sin A$, where A is the angle of revolution (see Fig. 8-6).

We can modify the position of the curve on the chart by adding a constant, K, as in: $X = \cos A$ and $Y = K + \sin A$. This has the effect of raising the whole curve upward K units. We can also multiply the function by a constant: $X = \cos A$ and $Y = K \sin A$. The center line of the curve remains at zero, but the absolute magnitude of the vertical component is increased as a function of K (see Fig. 8-7).

FAST FOURIER TRANSFORMS

Scientists have known for a long time that many complex wave forms in acoustics and electronics are really the result of combining two or more simple sine or cosine wave forms. They say that in general, the complex wave should be able to be represented by the equation:

$$Y = K_1 \cos A_1 + L_1 \sin A_1 + K_2 \cos A_2 + L_2 \sin A_2 \ldots$$

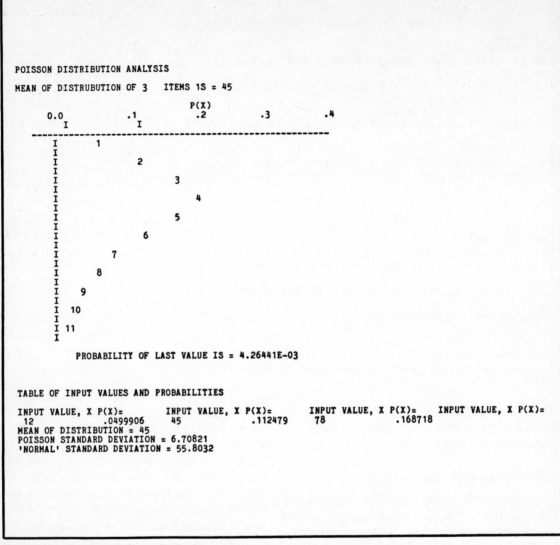

```
POISSON DISTRIBUTION ANALYSIS

MEAN OF DISTRUBUTION OF 3    ITEMS 1S = 45

                              P(X)
       0.0            .1       .2           .3           .4
        I              I
        -------------------------------------------------------
        I        1
        I
        I              2
        I
        I                 3
        I
        I                   4
        I
        I              5
        I
        I          6
        I
        I       7
        I
        I      8
        I
        I    9
        I
        I   10
        I
        I 11
        I
              PROBABILITY OF LAST VALUE IS = 4.26441E-03


TABLE OF INPUT VALUES AND PROBABILITIES

INPUT VALUE, X P(X)=      INPUT VALUE, X P(X)=      INPUT VALUE, X P(X)=      INPUT VALUE, X P(X)=
 12         .0499906       45          .112479      78         .168718
MEAN OF DISTRIBUTION = 45
POISSON STANDARD DEVIATION = 6.70821
'NORMAL' STANDARD DEVIATION = 55.8032
```

Fig. 8-3. Results of the Poisson distribution program.

Figure 8-8 illustrates this combination.

The problem with this concept is that a trial and error approach to defining the coefficients is very frustrating and time-consuming. The classic approaches to the solution of the problem using calculus are beyond the skills of many of us and remain quite tedious even for those who can handle the mathematics. The Fast Fourier Transform (FFT) is a working alternative to both the trial and error method and the use of calculus.

Named after the famous French mathematician, the process is faster than the other techniques. Economists have used the technique in various efforts to analyze the stock market as a complex wave constituted of a number of identifiable and simple cyclic waves. As with all other efforts to determine

142

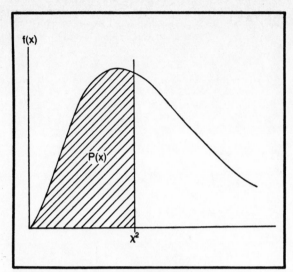

f(x)

P(x)

x^2

Fig. 8-4. Area under chi-square curve.

a predictive key to the market, though, we seldom hear of the successes. Those finding such a key are unlikely to share it openly.

EXERCISES

1. The catenary curve, which describes the natural shape of a rope or chain hanging suspended between two posts or supports, is useful in determining the shape and dimensions of the suspension cables on a bridge. Describe two other applications of the catenary form and equations.
2. Write a program, based on one of the various forms of the spiral to help make search operations for lost persons more efficient.
3. Maintain a record of the stock market average or the price of one stock for a month

Listing 8-3. Distributions.

```
1 '*********************************************.
2 '*              Listing 8-3                  *
3 '*              Distributions                *
4 '*********************************************
5 '
10 CLS:PRINT"       ****  DISTRIBUTIONS  ****
20 DIM U(100),X(100),AA(20),RR(30),M(3)
30 PRINT:PRINT"THESE ROUTINES ALLOW THE USER TO
INPUT VARIABLES TO SEVERAL COMMON DISTRIBUTIONSA
ND FIND THE RESULTING Y-COMPONENT."
40 PRINT
50 PRINT"              1 -- BINOMIAL"
60 PRINT"              2 -- POISSON"
70 PRINT"              3 -- NORMAL"
80 PRINT"              4 -- CHI-SQUARE"
90 PRINT"              5 -- RAW DATA INPUT"
100 PRINT"             6 -- END ROUTINE (RETURN TO
  MENU)"
110 PRINT:PRINT"ENTER NUMBER OF THE DESIRED DIST
RIBUTION:"
120 X$=INKEY$:IF X$="" THEN 120
130 X=VAL(X$):IF X>5 THEN GOTO 10
140 ON X GOTO 150,450,680,1030,1350,2480
150 CLS:PRINT"   ***  BINOMIAL  ***"
160 PRINT:PRINT"ROUTINE COMPUTES THE PROBABILITY
 OF OBTAINING A GIVEN NUMBER OF SUCCESSES IN A G
IVEN NUMBER OF BERNOULLI TRIALS."
170 PRINT
180 ZA=1
190 PRINT"(TO END PROGRAM TYPE @)"
200 PRINT"NUMBER OF TRIALS?"
210 INPUT N$:IF N$="@" THEN 2480
220 N=VAL(N$)
```

143

Listing 8-3. Distributions. (Continued From Page 143.)

```
230 PRINT"EXACT NUMBER OF SUCCESSES";
240 INPUT X
250 PRINT"PROBABILITY OF SUCCESS";
260 INPUT P
270 M(1)=N
280 M(2)=X
290 M(3)=N-X
300 FOR I=1 TO 3
310 IF M(I)>33 THEN 320 ELSE 340
320 PRINT"INPUT VALUE,";M(I);", IS TOO BIG.  TRY
 ANOTHER."
330 GOTO 200
340 IF M(I)=0 THEN 400
350 A=1
360 FOR J=1 TO M(I)
370 A=A*J
380 NEXT J
390 M(I)=LOG(A)
400 NEXT I
410 R=EXP(M(1)-M(2)-M(3)+X*LOG(P)+(N-X)*LOG(1-P)
)
420 PRINT"PROBABILITY OF ";X;" SUCCESSES IN ";N;
" TRIALS = ";R
430 LOCATE 10,1:PRINT""
440 GOTO 200
450 CLS
460 PRINT"           **** POISSON  ****"
470 PRINT:PRINT"THIS ROUTINE COMPUTES THE PROBAB
ILITY OF AN EVENT OCCURRING A GIVEN NUMBER OF TI
MES."
480 ZA=2
490 PRINT:PRINT
500 PRINT"CALCULATED MEAN ('@' to end)"
510 INPUT L$:L=VAL(L$):IF L$="@" THEN 2480
520 IF L=0 THEN 640
530 GOSUB 1350
540 PRINT"TEST FREQUENCY?   ('@' TO END)"
550 INPUT X$
560 IF X$="@" THEN 2480
570 X=VAL(X$):IF X=>34 THEN 580 ELSE 590
580 PRINT"INPUT VALUE,";X;" IS TOO LARGE.  MUST
BE LESS THAN 34.":GOTO 540
590 A=1
600 FOR I=1 TO X
610 A=A*I
620 NEXT I
630 A=LOG(A)
640 A=EXP(-L+X*LOG(L)-A)
650 PRINT"PROBABILITY OF ";X;"OCCURRENCES = ";A
660 PRINT
670 GOTO 500
680 CLS:PRINT"           ****  NORMAL  ****"
690 ZA=3
700 PRINT:PRINT"ROUTINE COMPUTES THE PROBABILTY
AND FREQUENCY OF GIVEN VALUES ON A STANDARD
NORMAL DISTRIBUTION CURVE."
```

```
710 PRINT
720 PRINT"(S=STANDARD, N=NON-STANDARD (IF YOU KN
OW THE MEAN AND SD)  @-ROUTINE END"
730 PRINT"WHICH TYPE OF VARIABLE?"
740 S$=INKEY$:IF S$="" THEN 740
750 IF S$="@" THEN 2480
760 IF S$="S" THEN 820
770 PRINT"MEAN?"
780 INPUT M
790 PRINT"STANDARD DEVIATION?"
800 INPUT S
810 GOTO 860
820 S=1
830 INPUT"ENTER 'Z' SCORE VALUE";Y$
840 Y=VAL(Y$):IF Y$="@" THEN 2480
850 GOTO 930
860 PRINT
870 PRINT"TO END PROGRAM ENTER '@'"
880 PRINT"ENTER TRIAL VALUE";
890 INPUT Y$:IF Y$="@" THEN 2480
900 IF Y$="L" THEN 1390
910 Y=VAL(Y$)
920 Y=(Y-M)/S:PRINT"THE 'Z' SCORE IS =";Y
930 R=EXP(-Y^2/2)/2.5066232746#
940 PRINT"FREQUENCY  F(X) = ";R
950 R1=.2316419:B1=.31938153#:B2=-.356563782#:B3
=1.781477937#:B4=-1.821255978#:B5=1.330274429#
960 T=1/(1+(R*Y))
970 QX=R*((B1*T)+(B2*(T^2))+(B3*(T^3))+(B4*(T^4)
)+(B5*(T^5)))
980 PRINT"PROBABILITY  Q(X) = ";QX;"    ( 1 - Q
=";1-QX;")"
990 PRINT
1000 IF S$="S" THEN 830
1010 GOTO 880
1020 END
1030 CLS:PRINT"           **** CHI-SQUARE  ****"
1040 ZA=4
1050 PRINT:PRINT"THIS ROUTINE COMPUTES THE TAIL-
END VALUE FOR POINTS ON A CHI-SQUARE DISTRIBUTIO
N."
1060 PRINT
1070 PRINT"(TO END TYPE '@')"
1080 PRINT"DEGREES OF FREEDOM?"
1090 INPUT V$:V=VAL(V$)
1100 IF V$="@" THEN 2480
1110 IF V=0 THEN 1340
1120 PRINT"CHI-SQUARE VALUE?"
1130 INPUT W$
1140 W=VAL(W$):WW=W:WV=W
1150 R=1
1160 FOR I=V TO 2 STEP -2
1170 R=R*I
1180 NEXT I
1190 K=W^(INT((V+1)/2))*EXP(-W/2)/R
1200 IF INT(V/2)=V/2 THEN 1230
1210 J=SQR(2/W/3.141592653599#)
1220 GOTO 1240
```

Listing 8-3. Distributions. (Continued From Page 145.)

```
1230 J=1
1240 L=1
1250 M=1
1260 V=V+2
1270 M=M*W/V
1280 IF M<.0000001 THEN 1310
1290 L=L+M
1300 GOTO 1260
1310 PRINT"TAIL-END VALUE = ";1-J*K*L
1320 PRINT"PERCENTILE VALUE = ";J*K*L:WP=J*K*L
1330 PRINT
1340 GOTO 1080
1350 'RAW DATA INPUT
1360 CLS
1370 INPUT"HOW MANY DATA ELEMENTS ARE TO BE ENTE
RED (0 TO END)";N
1380 IF N=0 THEN 2480
1390 IF N>100 THEN 1400 ELSE 1410
1400 PRINT"PLEASE LIMIT INPUT TO 100 ITEMS OR LE
SS.":GOTO 1370
1410 FOR I=1 TO N
1420 PRINT"ENTER DATA ELEMENT #";I;:INPUT X(I)
1430 NEXT I
1440 FOR I=1 TO N
1450 IF X(I)=0 THEN 1460 ELSE 1470
1460 LL=LL+1
1470 NEXT I
1480 IF LL<>0 THEN 1490 ELSE 1500
1490 SM=0:GOTO 1510
1500 SM=X(1)
1510 FOR I=1 TO N
1520 SX=SX+X(I)
1530 QX=QX+X(I)^2
1540 IF X(I)<=SM THEN 1550 ELSE 1560
1550 SM=X(I)
1560 IF X(I)>=LG THEN 1570 ELSE 1580
1570 LG=X(I)
1580 NEXT I
1590 AV=SX/N:SD=SQR((QX-(SX^2)/N)/N-1)
1600 PA=SQR(AV)
1610 CLS
1620 GOSUB 1880
1630 PRINT
1640 PRINT"THERE WERE";N;" ELEMENTS ENTERED.":PR
INT"THE SMALLEST WAS:                    ";S
M:PRINT"THE LARGET WAS:
";LG:PRINT"THE SUM WAS =";SX;" AND THE AVERAGE
WAS = ";AV"
1650 PRINT"THE MEDIAN WAS =
    ";ME:PRINT"THE MODE WAS =
        ";MD:PRINT"THE SKEW WAS =
            ";SK
1660 PRINT:PRINT"IN A NORMAL DISTRIBUTION, THE S
TANDARD DEVIATION IS =";SD:PRINT"THE DISTRIBUTIO
N IS SKEWED TO THE ";SK$:PRINT"IN A POISSON DIST
RIBUTION, THE STANDARD DEVIATION IS =";PA
```

```
1670 PRINT
1680 A$="":B$=""
1690 PRINT"DO YOU WANT TO USE THESE VALUES IN TH
E BASIC ROUTINE? (Y/N)"
1700 A$=INKEY$:IF A$="" THEN 1700
1710 IF A$="Y" THEN 1720 ELSE 1810
1720 PRINT"CHOOSE:  (N)ORMAL OR (P)OISSON DISTRI
BUTIONS"
1730 B$=INKEY$:IF B$="" THEN 1730
1740 IF B$="N" THEN 1780
1750 L=AV
1760 ZA=2
1770 GOTO 540
1780 M=AV:S=SD
1790 ZA=3
1800 GOTO 860
1810 PRINT"DO YOU WANT TO SEE THE INPUT DATA (Y/
N)"
1820 Q$=INKEY$:IF Q$="" THEN 1820
1830 IF Q$="Y" THEN 1840 ELSE RUN 10
1840 PRINT"OUTPUT TO PRINT ALSO"
1850 QQ$=INKEY$:IF QQ$="" THEN 1850
1860 IF QQ$="Y" THEN LP=1 ELSE LP=0
1870 GOTO 2180
1880 'SORTING ROUTINE
1890 CLS:LOCATE 9,1:PRINT"SORTING INPUT VALUES:"
;
1900 FOR I=1 TO N
1910 U(I)=X(I)
1920 NEXT I
1930 D=1
1940 D=2*D:IF D<N THEN 1940
1950 D=INT((D-1)/2)
1960 IF D=0 THEN 2050
1970 IT=N-D
1980 FOR I=1 TO IT
1990 J=I
2000 L=J+D
2010 IF U(L)<U(J) THEN TEMP=U(J):U(J)=U(L):U(L)=
TEMP:J=J-D:IF J>0 THEN 2000
2020 NEXT I
2030 GOTO 1950
2040 END
2050 'PRINT SORTED ARRAY
2060 PRINT
2070 FOR I=1 TO N
2080 PRINT U(I),
2090 NEXT I
2100 IF INT(N/2)=N/2 THEN 2160
2110 ME=U(((N-1)/2)+1)
2120 SK=(3*(AV-ME))/SD:MD=AV-(SK*SD)
2130 IF SK<0 THEN SK$="LEFT (PEAK TO THE RIGHT)"
 ELSE SK$="RIGHT (PEAK TO THE LEFT)"
2140 FOR I=1 TO 1500:NEXT I
2150 RETURN
2160 ME=(U(N/2)+U((N/2)+1))/2
2170 GOTO 2120
2180 CLS
```

Listing 8-3. Distributions. (Continued From Page 147.)

```
2190 PRINT"UNSORTED INPUT"
2200 FOR I=1 TO N
2210 PRINT X(I),
2220 NEXT I
2230 PRINT
2240 PRINT"SORTED DATA"
2250 FOR I=1 TO N
2260 PRINT U(I),
2270 NEXT I
2280 PRINT
2290 FOR I=1 TO 1000
2300 NEXT I
2310 IF LP=1 THEN 2330 ELSE 1630
2320 LPRINT STRING$(3,10)
2330 LPRINT"UNSORTED"
2340 FOR I=1 TO N
2350 LPRINT X(I),
2360 NEXT I
2370 LPRINT" ":LPRINT" "
2380 LPRINT"SORTED"
2390 FOR I=1 TO N
2400 LPRINT U(I),
2410 NEXT I
2420 LPRINT" ":LPRINT" "
2430 LPRINT N;" ITEMS ENTERED, THE SMALLEST BEIN
G;";SM;", THE LARGEST BEING";LG;".  THE FOLLOWIN
G ITEMS WERE COMPUTED:":PRINT      SUM =";SX;"
 AVERAGE";AV;"   MEDIAN";ME;"    MODE =";MD;"    S
KEW =";SK;"   STANDARD DEVIATION =";SD
2440 LPRINT" ":LPRINT"IN A POISSON DISTRIBUTION
THE STANDARD DEVIATION WOULD BE =";PA
2450 LPRINT STRING$(3,10)
2460 GOTO 1630
2470 END
2480 PRINT:PRINT"(A)nother set          (M)ain m
enu
2490 Q$=""+INKEY$:IF Q$="" THEN 2490
2500 IF Q$="A" OR Q$="a" THEN RUN 1 ELSE IF Q$="
M" OR Q$="m" THEN RUN "A:MENU"
```

or so. Use the polynomial program to evaluate these data in order to determine the utility of the approach. Explain the results.

4. Count the number of people arriving at the front door of a place of business from thirty minutes before to thirty minutes after the nominal opening or start of the work day. Determine the mean number of arrivals during each time interval. Assume the arrival times resemble those predicted by a Poisson distribution. From these data, compute the expected number of arrivals sixty minutes on either side of the nominal start time. Validate your forecast, if possible.

5. Repeat exercise 4, but use the normal distribution as the predictor format. Which approach gives better results? Why?

SUGGESTED READING

Adler, I., 1957. *Magic House of Numbers.* New York: The John Day Company, Inc.

Bruning, J. L. and B. L. Kintz, 1968. *Computational Handbook of Statistics.* Glenview, IL: Scott, Foresman Company.

Selby, S., 1973. *Standard Mathematical Tables.* Cleveland: The Chemical Rubber Co.

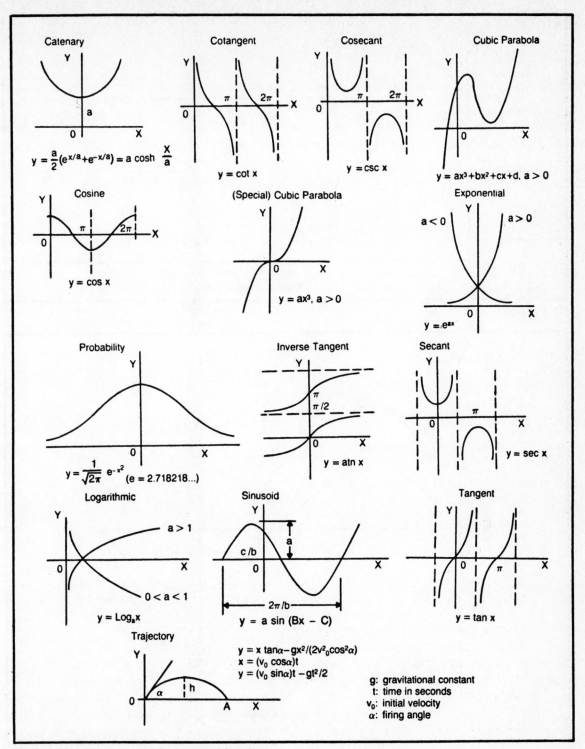

Fig. 8-5. Standard curves and trigonometric functions.

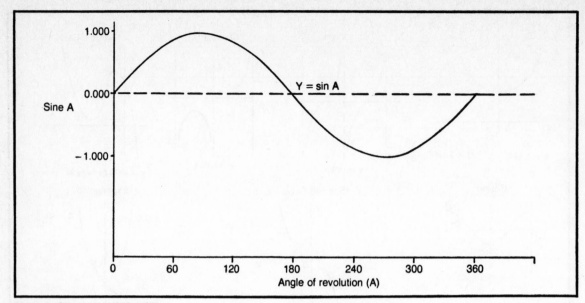

Fig. 8-6. Sinewave relationships.

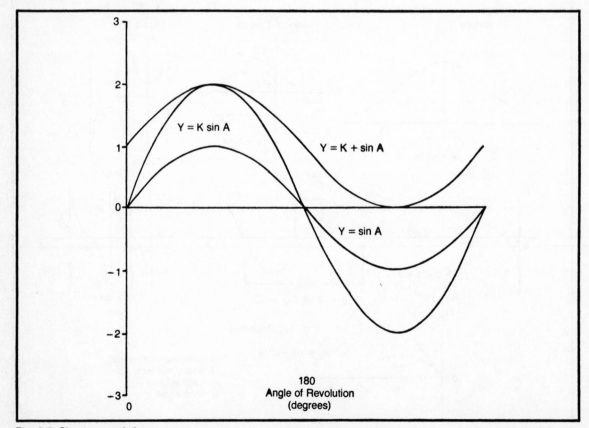

Fig. 8-7. Sinewave variations.

150

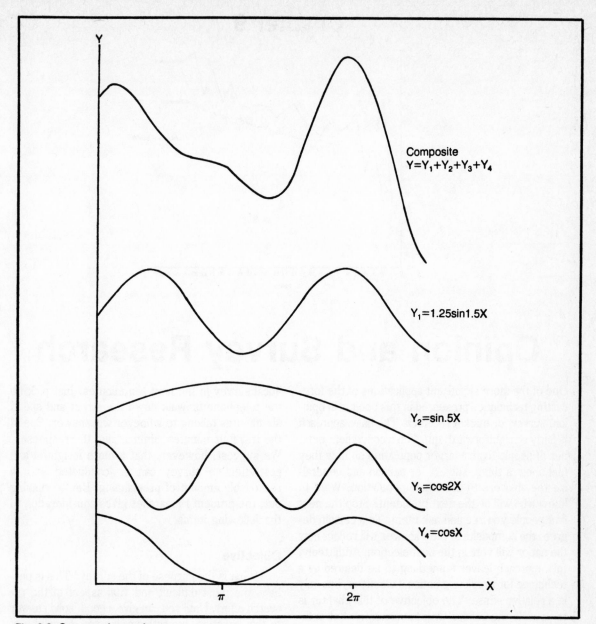

Fig. 8-8. Compound wave form.

Chapter 9

Opinion and Survey Research

One of the more significant applications of the forecasting techniques presented in this book is in opinion, survey, or market research. The basic approach is fairly straightforward: question a convenient number of people from a larger population on how they feel about a thing, subject, or person and generalize the answers to the whole population. Want to know who will be the next president? Stop the next five people you see and ask them. To a certain degree, the composite of their answer will reflect how the nation will vote in the next election. Admittedly, this approach leaves something to be desired as a technique for predicting national elections, but only in a relative sense. The objective of this chapter is to provide the reader with fundamental, but sufficient, statistical and research tools with which to conduct usable and responsible survey research. These tools include: planning, sample size, survey questionnaire, interviewing considerations and data collection, and data analysis.

SURVEY PLANNING

It is possible for you to conduct a complete political survey in the next ten minutes. Just pick up the telephone or walk down the street and spend six minutes talking to whoever will answer. Spend the last four minutes summarizing the responses. We suggest, however, that a more insightful and cost-effective survey can be conducted with a reasonable amount of preplanning. Before rushing out, the prudent researcher gives consideration to the following items.

Objective

What is the purpose of the survey? This is perhaps the most difficult and vital aspect of the research effort. Until you can give a good, solid answer to this question, everything else you do will be of little value. Identifying the objective will give a focus to the rest of your planning and make many decisions very simple. Is your objective to identify the true voter intent with regard to your client? Or, is your objective to give your client a sense of support and confidence, regardless of the real voter intent? If it is the former, select a good sample from the relevant population, and measure the proportion favoring your client. On the other hand, if the objective is the latter, select a sample from those voters known to be solidly on your side (such as known straight ticket voters, voters who have publicly supported your client, etc.), measure the proportion favoring your client, and apply this to the voting population as a whole. If you are doing a market survey, is your objective to identify consumer behavior, consumer preference for your client's product, consumer preference for the competition's product, consumer desires as opposed to consumer actions . . . ? How you answer these kinds of questions will give shape and meaning to the balance of your efforts. As concisely and concretely as possible, define your objective.

Techniques and Limitations

There are a number of techniques available to the researcher. Each one serves a useful purpose if properly applied and is assigned significant limitations. Just as a mechanic has a box filled with tools, each with a specific function, the researcher has quite an arsenal of techniques. To use one simply because you understand how to do it is shortsighted. Instead, you should use the technique best suited to the objective. Some of the techniques, with their applications and limitations, are described on the following pages.

Telephone Interviews. The telephone survey is useful for short questionnaires with fairly easy to understand questions and in surveys looking for gross statistical generalities. Interviewers must have a pleasant telephone personality and be able to read well and to record responses accurately and quickly, but otherwise they are not required to have exceptional research skills. This technique is handy for quick surveys, but can easily be criticized for excluding from your sample a portion of population either too poor or too transient to have a telephone, yet who might otherwise be suitable subjects. To overcome this limitation, the next option can be used.

Interviews In-depth. This method involves meeting the people to be surveyed face-to-face and asking them the relevant questions. The advantage of this method is that the questionnaire can go into

greater subtlety and depth, and take more time, covering a broader range of subject matter. It overcomes the criticism of exclusion in the telephone technique. On the other hand, it is a very time-consuming technique, and requires a much larger number of interviewers in order to contact the same number of subjects in the same time period as a telephone survey. The interviewers in this approach must present a clean and professional appearance as well as a pleasing personality. They must understand survey techniques well enough to deal with the unexpected quickly and without extraordinary resort to notes or other guidance. Volunteers can generally be trained quickly to do telephone work, but effective and reliable field survey work generally requires a paid staff.

Mail Surveys. This technology shifts the emphasis from interviewer skill to skill in questionnaire design. Compared to field survey work, it is a very inexpensive technique. Large portions of the population can be contacted in fairly short order and asked a broad range of questions of exceptional depth and sophistication. The primary objection to this technique is that the response to the questionnaire is likely to be only a slight fraction of the total number contacted. Professionals in mail survey work consider a five percent response to be quite good. This means that, if you have determined the proper sample size to be 1000, you need to contact at least 20,000 addresses. Using a printing and postage cost of $0.50 for each questionnaire mailed out, this implies a research cost starting at $10,000. If an interviewer can complete an average of twelve interviews a day, at $5 an hour, $10,000 would obtain 2000 in-depth interviews in a little over 166 interview days. The second criticism of this technique is one of validation. There is no satisfactory way to know that the person identified on the questionnaire actually answered the items or that the answers are truthful. The surveyor must accept on faith the accuracy and honesty of the responses. Selection of this technique should be in part a function of the degree to which accuracy and honesty in response are rewarded. A survey asking the subject's age and sex, as well as suggestions for five kinds of television programs desired, sponsored by a television station or network, is more likely to receive valid responses than one offering a prize for a paragraph on why a certain product is better than another. Using this technique, the surveyor must assume that if it is in the interests of the subjects to lie, they will.

Observation Analysis. There are a number of variations on this basic technique, but what they have in common is a time period during which the social system under investigation is observed by a data collector. Political influence analysis, for example, is conducted by observing participants in a political matrix and recording very carefully who initiates different sorts of interactions with what sort of consequences. This technique normally requires a considerable amount of time and training effort to prepare the observers for their duties. Even under fairly ideal conditions, the observations can become very subjective in nature unless strict controls are applied.

Archive Analysis. The determination of voter trends is often better computed from historical records than from interview research. This approach is often implemented as part of a larger effort in voter analysis in which current trends or preferences (obtained from interviews) are contrasted with historical trends identified from data in voting record archives.

Cost Considerations

As noted several times, each technique carries with it certain predictable costs. Before making a selection, the surveyor should first determine the degree of precision necessary and the level of confidence desired in the outcome of the research. Then, given two or more techniques which are adequate to the task (that is, they yield results within the required range), the researcher should select the technique costing the least—even though its results may not be quite as good as another. Since people come in integer units, an expensive technique that promises precision to five decimal places is no more valuable than an inexpensive technique promising precision to only one or two decimal places. In counting potential voters, for example, 233.4232934366 voters are essentially equivalent to 233.42 voters. Table 9-1 offers a nominal matrix for estimating personnel requirements and costs for a survey effort.

Table 9-1. Survey Time Scheduling.

Operation	Study Director	Research Associate	Interviewer	Clerks	Total Pers.	$ Admin. Costs
Formulation and Design:	60	60	5	30	155	100
Development of Materials:	15	15	15	30	75	200
Development of Interview:	15	15	5	45	80	450
Data Collection:	30	30	120	15	195	600
Data Coding/Compiling:	5	10	5	60	80	450
Statistical Analysis:	10	20	0	20	50	300
Report Writing:	30	45	0	60	135	200
Final Admin Work:	5	5	0	5	15	50
Total Working Days:	170	200	150	265	785	2350
Wage Factor:	5	4.5	1.5	1	n/a	n/a
Product:	850	900	225	265	n/a	n/a

Sum of Column Products = 2240 × Basic Wage (3.50) = Labor Cost = $7840.99
Total Labor Cost + Total Admin. Cost = Total Research Cost = 7840 + 2350 = 10,190

To this figure is added the administrative costs that are associated with the selected technique. For example, if the technique of choice is a mail survey, printing and postage costs are likely to be quite high. Listing 9-1 provides computer assistance in evaluating two or more alternative techniques based on the format in Table 9-1.

Sponsorship

While not strictly a part of the statistical aspect of forecasting, it is appropriate to enter a word here on the ethical responsibility to identify yourself to the subject of the interview. While it is not necessary to give your personal identity to those you interview, it is responsible to identify the organization

Listing 9-1. Survey Estimator.

```
1 '**********************************************
2 '*            Listing 9-1                   *
3 '*          Survey Estimator                *
4 '**********************************************
5 '
10 CLS:KEY OFF:PRINT "SURVEY TIME/COST ESTIMATES
":PRINT:PRINT
20 P$(1)="DIRECTOR":P$(2)="ASSISTANT":P$(3)="INT
ERVIEWER":P$(4)="CLERKS"
30 FOR I=1 TO 4
40 PRINT"WHAT IS THE WAGE FACTOR FOR THE ";P$(I)
;:INPUT W(I)
50 NEXT
60 PRINT:INPUT"WHAT IS THE BASE WAGE";BP:PRINT
70 F$(1)="FORMULATION AND DESIGN":F$(2)="DEVELOP
MENT OF MATERIALS":F$(3)="DEVELOPMENT OF INTERVI
EW":F$(4)="DATA COLLECTION":F$(5)="DATA CODING":
F$(6)="STATISTICAL ANALYSIS":F$(7)="REPORT WRITN
G":F$(8)="FINAL ADMIN WORK"
80 PRINT"PHASE"
90 FOR J=1 TO 8
100 PRINT F$(J)
110 FOR I=1 TO 4
120 PRINT"          ";P$(I);": HOW MANY WORK DAYS
TOTAL   ";
130 INPUT V
140 R(J)=R(J)+V:TD=TD+V:P(J,I)=V:P(0,I)=P(0,I)+V
150 NEXT
160 PRINT"     TOTAL MANPOWER THIS PERIOD = ";R(
J);"MAN-DAYS"
170 PRINT"     ADMIN COSTS";
180 INPUT AC(J)
190 TA=TA+AC(J)
200 PRINT
210 NEXT J
220 Z$="\              \ ###        ##.##      ##
###.##     ######.##"
230 A$="                MAN          WAGE
           ACTUAL"
240 B$="                DAYS         FACTOR      P
RODUCT        WAGES"
250 CLS:PRINT A$:PRINT B$:PRINT
260 FOR I=1 TO 4
270 PRINT USING Z$;P$(I);P(0,I);W(I);W(I)*P(0,I)
;W(I)*P(0,I)*BP:TW=TW+(W(I)*P(0,I)*BP)
280 NEXT
```

Listing 9-1. Survey Estimator. (Continued From Page 155.)

```
290 PRINT USING Z$;"TOTAL";TD;TW/(TD*BP);TW/BP;T
W
300 PRINT:PRINT"TOTAL ADMIN = ";TA
310 PRINT"TOTAL WAGES = ";TW
320 PRINT"        ---------------"
330 PRINT"TOTAL COSTS = ";TW+TA
340 LOCATE 20,1:PRINT"(C)ONTINUE    (N)EW    (P
rtSc for printout)";
350 Q$=""+INKEY$:IF Q$="" THEN 350
360 IF Q$="C" OR Q$="c" THEN 380 ELSE IF Q$<>"N"
 THEN 350
370 RUN
380 CLS
390 PRINT A$:PRINT B$:PRINT
400 FOR I=1 TO 8
410 FOR J=1 TO 4:W=W(J)*P(I,J)*BP:TT=TT+W:NEXT
420 WF=TT/(BP*R(I)):PF=WF*R(I):TC=TC+TT+AC(I)
430 PRINT USING Z$;RIGHT$(F$(I),15);R(I);WF;PF;T
T+AC(I):TT=0
440 NEXT
450 PRINT:PRINT USING Z$;"TOTAL";TD;TW/(TD*BP);T
W/BP;TC
460 TC=0
470 GOTO 340
```

for which you are working or the agency sponsoring the research. If your research is self-initiated, you may want to create a business or small corporation as a sponsor. Failure to do so is not grave, but might limit the number of people willing to respond. Many people are properly concerned about revealing personal information to strangers. If you are able to provide some credential the subject could contact or refer to later, you are likely to realize greater success. If you create your own business framework, whether a proprietorship or a corporation, it should be legitimate to the extent that should your subject contact the local state or county registry, they would have the proper documentation, and that your telephone or mailing addresses be authentic. A person who has responded to your survey and then investigates your credentials and finds them wanting may well initiate complaints against you with the police or other authorities. The business you establish need not be an expensive proposition involving rented offices and furniture. You can do a very respectable business from a room of your home. Simply represent yourself with the truth so that your subject perceives that you have a legitimate purpose

in your inquiries, and you should realize reasonable success.

Listing 9-2 is a short routine using the computer to help you chart out the project development through the different phases. It is offered more as an example of how to implement such a program than as a finished program, although it is complete within a limited scope.

THE SAMPLE

It is almost inevitable that to survey an entire population would require more time and resources than we could ever muster. If the target area for a telephone survey, for example, has a million people, and each interview takes five minutes, the survey would take one interviewer, working eight hours a day, seven days a week, better than twenty-eight and a half years to complete. To complete the survey in one week would require at least 1488 interviewers working in eight-hour shifts, 496 at a time. These computations leave no room for slippage or error. Nor do they contemplate the problems of interviewing people at 3:00 A.M.

Listing 9-2. Survey Scheduling.

```
1 '***********************************************
2 '*               Listing 9-2                  *
3 '*           Survey Scheduling                *
4 '***********************************************
5 '
10 SCREEN 0:CLS:KEY OFF
20 CLS:PRINT "SURVEY SCHEDULING":PRINT:PRINT
30 F$(1)="DESIGN     ":F$(2)="MATERIALS ":F$(3)="
INTERVIEW ":F$(4)="COLLECTION":F$(5)="CODING
":F$(6)="ANALYSIS   ":F$(7)="REPORT     ":F$(8)="F
INAL WORK"
40 INPUT"HOW MANY DAYS ARE ALLOWED FOR THE PROJE
CT";D:TD=0
50 PRINT:PRINT"WHAT IS YOUR ESTIMATE OF THE TIME
 REQUIRED FOR:?
60 FOR I=1 TO 8
70 PRINT"      ";F$(I),:INPUT V:T(I)=V:TD=TD+V
80 NEXT
90 CLS:S=TD-D:IF TD=D THEN 130
100 IF TD<D THEN 120
110 PRINT:PRINT"SORRY, THESE ESTIMATES REQUIRE";
TD-D;" MORE DAYS THAN ALLOWED":PRINT:GOTO 40
120 PRINT"CONGRATULATIONS, YOU HAVE";D-TD;"DAYS
SLACK AVAILABLE":GOTO 140
130 PRINT"THE PROGRAM CAN BE COMPLETED ON SCHEDU
LE"
140 FOR X=0 TO 620:PSET(X,40):NEXT
150 FOR X=132 TO 620 STEP 10:PSET(X,39):NEXT
160 LOCATE 7,1:PRINT"";
170 FOR I=1 TO 8:PRINT F$(I):NEXT
180 FOR Y=21 TO 170:PSET(132,Y):NEXT
190 LOCATE 3,31:PRINT"DAYS FROM START";
200 LOCATE 4,1:PRINT"PHASE";
210 J=0
220 FOR I=0 TO D STEP (D/10)
230    LOCATE 4,16+(J*7):PRINT INT(I);
240    J=J+1:IF (16+(J*7))>78 THEN 260
250 NEXT I
260 A=0
270 FOR I=1 TO 8
280 S(I)=A:C(I)=S(I)+T(I)-1
290 ZOG%=336+(I*64)+INT((95*(A/D)/2)):GOSUB 460:
PRINT "^";
300 FOR J=A TO D
310 IF J<(A+T(I)) THEN 330
320 ZOG%=336+(I*64)+INT((95*(J/D))/2):GOSUB 460:
PRINT "^ ";:A=J:GOTO 350
330 ZOG%=336+(I*64)+INT((95*(J/D))/2)+1:GOSUB 46
0:PRINT ".";
340 NEXT J
350 NEXT I
360 IF S=0 THEN 410
370 LOCATE 15,1:PRINT"SLACK";
380 ZOG%=912+INT((95*(J/D))/2):GOSUB 460:PRINT "
^ ";
390 FOR I=J+2 TO D:ZOG%=912+INT((95*(I/D))/2)+1:
```

Listing 9-2. Survey Scheduling. (Continued From Page 157.)

```
GOSUB 460:PRINT ".";:NEXT
400 LOCATE 15,64:PRINT"^   ";
410 LOCATE 24,1:PRINT"(N)EW     (M)ain menu  (Use
 PrtSc for hardcopy)";
420 Q$=""+INKEY$:IF Q$="" THEN 420
430 IF Q$="N" OR Q$="n" THEN RUN 20 ELSE IF Q$="
M" OR Q$="m" THEN RUN "A:MENU"
440 RUN
450 FOR I=1 TO 8:LPRINT F$(I),S(I),C(I),T(I):NEX
T:LPRINT""
460 ZAG%=INT(ZOG%/64):ZOG%=ZOG%-64*ZAG%+1:ZAG%=Z
AG%+1:                           LOCATE ZAG%,
ZOG%:RETURN
```

A practical alternative is to select a portion of the population and survey the sample. In doing so, we assume that if 35 percent of the sample indicate preference for a given political candidate, then 35 percent of the entire electorate will be for the same candidate. How reasonable this assumption is will be a function of several factors: homogeneity of the population, size of the sample, size of the population, the allowable degree of error, the level of confidence required, and the sampling procedure.

Homogeneity

The homogeneity of a population is the degree to which the members of the population are alike with respect to the subject of the survey. The more alike a population is on a given subject, the smaller the sample needed to achieve desirable results. For example, we could assume that attitudes toward farming would be as easily defined from a small sample in Des Moines as from a large sample in New York City.

Sample Size

In general, the larger the sample, the more reliable the findings. At the same time, the cost of the survey is most often a direct function of sample size; that is, the larger the sample, the more expensive the research. In this chapter we will present techniques to optimize sample size relative to the other parameters of the research.

Population Size

Up to a point, the size of the sample as a per-

centage of the population is critical. When the population begins to be considerable (that is, greater than one hundred thousand or a million), sample size as a percentage of the population is negligible. For example, if the population is 100, then a reliable sample size might have to be 30 to 60 percent of the total. On the other hand, the Gallup and Roper polls both do very reliable research work using a sample of less than 1900, or less than 0.00088 percent of the national population.

Allowable Error

No experiment or research effort is totally free from error. No research sponsor should expect error-free research data. It is far more responsible to specify the degree of allowable error. How much this should be is a function of the type of research undertaken. If we are examining certain phenomena in the physical sciences, we normally demand a very small degree of allowable error, perhaps less than one-tenth of one percent. On the other hand, research work in the social sciences must tolerate considerable error, perhaps as much as 5 to 10 percent, or 20 percent in some difficult situations. One equation computes the standard error of a percentage as:

$$S = \sqrt{\frac{PQ}{N}}$$

where P = percentage (45% = .45) Q = 1 − P, and N is the population.

Level of Confidence

As a particular subject of research moves away

from the mean of the population or the sample, the amount of error increases. That is, if we are studying the relationship between level of education and income, we will compute a mean educational and income level from the sample data. An individual whose education is near the educational mean will normally have an income level not too far from the income mean. We say the error, the difference between the actual data and the forecast or mean, is small. On the other hand, the difference between the income of a person at one extreme of the educational spectrum or the other and the mean income for all those at that educational level will be greater. So, we usually combine allowable error and level of confidence into one expression and say that we will accept the data as being valid if it applies to 95 percent of the population (or 99 percent, or whatever) within 1 (or 5) percent error. For example, a political survey of 100 people indicates that 57.63 percent of the sample prefer candidate Able over candidate Baker. When we report this finding to the media and our client, what we really are saying is that 95 percent of the population prefer candidate Able by 57.63 percent, plus or minus 5 percent. What the remaining 5 percent of the population choose to do is not forecast. Given these data and a population of one million voters, the outcome could range from 499,999 $((.5763 - .05) \times 950000)$ to 644,998 $(((.5763 + .05) \times 950000) + (.05 \times 1000000))$ votes for Able. In this fashion, an electorial defeat could occur despite a positive forecast, although, given these data, this is not likely. By increasing the sample size to 200, the sample error drops to 3.5 percent, thus (if the basic percentage for Able remains at 57.634) the expectation ranges from 514,249 to 630,748—a sure win!

Sampling Procedure

There are several techniques for drawing a sample from a population: simple random selection, stratified samples, and cluster samples, to mention three. Each approach has an effect on the desirable sample size.

Simple Random Selection. In this process the sample is drawn or selected from the general population at random. If you throw a dart at a page

selected at random from the telephone directory and dial the number closest to the embedded point of the dart, you are selecting the sample randomly. Each member of the population has an equal probability of selection. To implement this approach on a more rational basis than dart throwing, however, is rather tedious and generally requires identifying each memory of the population with some sort of an identification number and then generating as many random numbers as required for an adequate sample size. We then interview each member of the population whose identification number matches one on the list of random numbers. Listing 9-3 is a simple program that generates random telephone numbers that can be used as identification numbers.

Cluster Samples. This procedure simplifies the task a bit. By some definable process, we group people into manageable-size clusters and then select clusters randomly and interview everyone in that cluster.

Stratified Samples. This method is often used in an effort to ensure that the sample resembles the population in terms of various demographic characteristics: sex, race, age, occupation, and so forth. Each characteristic adds another dimension to the sample matrix. For example, with the four categories above, we might have a matrix to fill that has two sexes times three basic racial groups times eighty age categories times x number of possible occupation groups. Each cell need not be filled (we suspect there will be few 2-year-old bank directors) except to the same proportion as in the general population.

The stratified sample, properly constructed, requires the smallest sample size for a given allowable error and level of confidence. Cluster samples, on the other hand, usually require a larger sample than either the stratified or simple random sample. As a practical matter, however, the cluster sample approach is often selected as the most feasible and cost-effective approach.

Computation of Sample Size

Listing 9-4 offers an extensive routine for computing a variety of statistics related to sample size. Underlying this program is the assumption that, in

Listing 9-3. Telephone Selector.

```
1 '*********************************************
2 '*              Listing 9-3               *
3 '*           Telephone Selector           *
4 '*********************************************
5 '
10 CLS:KEY OFF:RANDOMIZE
20 PRINT"THIS ROUTINE GENERATES A RANDOM SET OF
TELEPHONE NUMBERS AT RANDOM, WITH        REPLACE
MENT.  IF A SET WITHOUT REPLACEMENT IS DESIRED,
INSERT CHECKING LOOP        BETWEEN LINES 130 AND 1
40":PRINT
30 INPUT"ENTER NUMBER OF TELEPHONE EXCHANGES TO
BE SURVEYED";TE
40 DIM E$(TE)
50 FOR I=1 TO TE
60 PRINT"ENTER THE THREE DIGIT EXCHANGE # ";I,:I
NPUT E$(I)
70 NEXT I
80 INPUT"HOW MANY NUMBERS ARE TO BE GENERATED";N
90 FOR I=1 TO N
100 A=INT(RND(100)*TE)+1:A$=E$(A)+" -"
110 FOR J=1 TO 4
120 B=INT(RND(100)*10):A$=A$+STR$(B)
130 NEXT J
140 'ENTER LOOP TO CHECK FOR DUPLICATE NUMBERS H
ERE.
150 PRINT A$,:LPRINT A$,
160 NEXT
170 PRINT"(A)nother        (M)ain menu ";
180 GOSUB 200
190 IF Q$="A" OR Q$="a" THEN RUN 10 ELSE RUN "A:
MENU"
200 Q$=""+INKEY$:IF Q$="" THEN 200
210 RETURN
```

Listing 9-4. Sample Size.

```
1 '*********************************************
2 '*              Listing 9-4               *
3 '*             Sample Size                *
4 '*********************************************
5 '
10 CLS:KEY OFF:PRINT"SAMPLE SIZE":PRINT:PRINT
20 Z(1)=3.8416:Z(2)=5.4289:Z(3)=6.6564
30 INPUT"ENTER POPULATION SIZE";PS
40 PRINT"OUTPUT TO PRINTER?   (Y/N)":PRINT
50 Q$=""+INKEY$:IF Q$="" THEN 50 ELSE IF Q$="Y"
OR Q$="y" THEN LP=1 ELSE LP=0
60 P=.5:Q=.5
70 PRINT:INPUT"WHAT IS THE ALLOWABLE PER CENT OF
 ERROR (5%=5)";E:E=E/100
80 PRINT:PRINT"","        DEGREE OF CONFIDENCE":PR
INT"","95 %","98 %","99 %":PRINT:PRINT"NUMBER",
90 FOR I=1 TO 3
100 SS(I)=INT((Z(I)*.25)/(E^2))+1:IF SS(I)>PS TH
EN SS(I)=PS
```

```
110 PRINT SS(I),
120 NEXT
130 PRINT:PRINT"PER CENT",
140 FOR I=1 TO 3:PRINT 100*(SS(I)/PS),:NEXT I:PR
INT
150 GOTO 240
160 FOR R=0 TO 14
170 FOR C=0 TO 63
180 L=PEEK(15360+(R*64)+C):IF L<32 THEN L=L+64
190 LPRINT CHR$(L);
200 NEXT C
210 LPRINT""
220 NEXT
230 LPRINT"":RETURN
240 PRINT:INPUT"DESIRED SAMPLE SIZE";DS
250 PRINT:PRINT"","      DEGREE OF CONFIDENCE"
260 PRINT"","95 %","98 %","99 %":PRINT:PRINT"% E
RROR",
270 FOR I=1 TO 3
280 B=SQR((Z(I)*.25)/DS):PRINT 100*B,
290 NEXT I
300 PRINT:IF LP=1 THEN GOSUB 160
310 PRINT B,E
320 IF B>E THEN 340
330 PRINT:PRINT"SAMPLE SIZE IS ADEQUATE":PRINT:G
OTO 380
340 PRINT:PRINT"THE SAMPLE SIZE OF";DS;"IS INADE
QUATE IN TERMS YOU'VE SPECIFIED.    TO STAY WITHI
N THE LIMITS YOU'VE CITED, THE SAMPLE SIZE MUST
BE AT LEAST ";(Z(1)*.25)/(E^2);", OTHERWISE THE
DEGREE OF CONFIDENCE WILL ONLY BE ";
350 Z=SQR((DS*(E^2))/(P*Q))
360 FX=.398942*(2.71828^-((Z^2)/2)):T=1/(1+(.231
64*Z)):QX=FX*((.319382*T)+(-.356564*(T^2))+(1.78
1478*(T^3))+(-1.821256*(T^4))+(1.330274*(T^5)))+
7.5E-08:PRINT 100*(1-(2*QX));" %"
370 PRINT:RUN 30
380 PRINT:PRINT"THIS SECTION WILL ASSIST YOU IN
THE SELECTION OF";DS;"SURVEY SUBJECTS.   YOU HAVE
  THE CHOICE OF:":PRINT"":PRINT"                 1
  ---    SAMPLE WITH REPLACEMENT":PRINT"":PRINT"
                 2   ---    SAMPLE WITHOUT REPLACEMENT"
:PRINT"":PRINT"
Sele
390 Q$=""+INKEY$:IF Q$="" THEN 390
400 PRINT:PRINT"SURVEY THE FOLLOWING MEMBERS OF
THE POPULATION:":PRINT
410 LPRINT"SURVEY THE FOLLOWING MEMBERS OF THE P
OPULATION:":LPRINT""
420 ON VAL(Q$) GOTO 430,480
430 PRINT"SAMPLING WITH REPLACEMENT":LPRINT"SAMP
LING WITH REPLACEMENT":LPRINT""
440 FOR I=1 TO DS
450 S=INT(RND(0)*PS):PRINT I;S,:LPRINT I;S,
460 NEXT
470 RUN 30
480 PRINT"SAMPLING WITHOUT REPLACEMENT":LPRINT"S
AMPLING WITHOUT REPLACEMENT":LPRINT""
```

Listing 9-4. Sample Size. (Continued From Page 161.)

```
490 DIM S(DS)
500 FOR I=1 TO DS
510 S=RND(PS)
520 FOR J=0 TO K
530 IF S(J)=S THEN 510
540 NEXT
550 S(J)=S:K=J:PRINT I;S,:LPRINT I;S,
560 NEXT I
570 RUN 30
580 FOR I=1 TO DS
590 S=INT(RND(0)*PS)
600 FOR J=0 TO K
610 IF S(J)=S THEN 590
620 NEXT
630 S(J)=S:K=J:PRINT I;S,:LPRINT I;S,
640 NEXT I
650 PRINT"(A)nother       (M)ain menu ";
660 GOSUB 680
670 IF Q$="A" OR Q$="a" THEN RUN 10 ELSE RUN "A:
MENU"
680 Q$=""+INKEY$:IF Q$="" THEN 680
690 RETURN
```

terms of the research characteristics, the population is normally distributed. If this is true, 95 percent of the population will lie within 1.9208 standard deviations from the mean, 98 percent within 2.71445 standard deviations, and 99 percent within 3.3282 standard deviations. These values are referred to in the program by the variable Z. The portion of the population to which the data are to apply (level of confidence) is P (95% = .95). The allowable error is E (1% = .01). We compute: Q = 1 − P. The minimum sample size is estimated from:

$$S = (ZPQ) / E^2$$

To compute the minimum sample size to be applicable to 95 percent (Z = 3.8416 and P = .95, Q = .05) of the population with an error of plus or minus 2 percent (E = .02), we compute:

$$
\begin{aligned}
S &= (3.8416 \times .95 \times .05)/ (.02^2) \\
&= .182476 / .0004 \\
&= 456.19
\end{aligned}
$$

Therefore, we should sample at least 457 subjects in order to reach the level of confidence stated. The balance of the equations in the program are built around this basic relationship.

Before we leave the enchanted land of samples, we offer the following footnote concerning the probability of having no repetitions in a sample (Listing 9-5). If a sample of n items is taken from a population of m objects, the probability (P) of finding an object in the sample that meets a particular criterion is P = 1 / m. The probability (Q) of finding two or more items in the sample which meet the criterion is given in:

$$Q = 1 - \left(\left(1 - \frac{1}{m}\right)\left(1 - \frac{2}{m}\right)....\left(1 - \frac{n-1}{m}\right) \right)$$

The common illustration of this routine is that of computing the probability of two or more people at a party sharing the same birthday. In this example, m is the number of days in the year and the sample size, n, is the number of people at the party. Without further illustration, we note that if n = 48, P = .96. A lot of wagers have been won on this equation and its implications.

(The normal form of the equation is for the value P, which is the complement of Q: P = 1 − Q. We offer the present form because Q is more often the value of common interest.)

Listing 9-5. Probabilities No Repetition in a Sample.

```
1 '*******************************************
2 '*              Listing 9-5                 *
3 '*   Probabilities No Repetition in a Sample *
4 '*******************************************
5 '
10 CLS:LOCATE 1,1:PRINT"     * * * PROBABILITY O
F NO REPETITIONS IN A SAMPLE * * *":FOR I=1 TO 5
00:NEXT I
20 LOCATE 3,1:PRINT" ":INPUT"ENTER THE SIZE OF T
HE ENTIRE POPULATION TO BE EVALUATED:";M
30 PRINT:INPUT"ENTER THE SAMPLE SIZE:";N
40 CLS:LOCATE 3,1:PRINT"IF THERE IS ONE ELEMENT
OF THIS POPULATION OF";M;"ITEMS THAT SATISFIES Y
OUR CRITERION, YOU HAVE A PROBABILITY OF";1/M;"O
F FINDING IT ON ANY ONE TRY."
50 P=1
60 FOR A=1 TO N-1
70 P=P*(1-(A/M))
80 IF N<50 THEN 100
90 LOCATE 11,1:PRINT"STILL WORKING, PLEASE BE PA
TIENT.";
100 NEXT A
110 LOCATE 9,1:PRINT"OUT OF A POPULATION OF";M;"
ITEMS, THE PROBABILITY THAT THERE WILL BE TWO OR
 MORE ELEMENTS THAT WILL FIT    YOUR CRITERION I
S =";1-P
120 PRINT:PRINT"(PROBABILITY OF NO REPITIONS IN
SAMPLE =";P;")"
130 PRINT"(A)nother        (M)ain menu ";
140 GOSUB 160
150 IF Q$="A" OR Q$="a" THEN RUN 10 ELSE RUN "A:
MENU"
160 Q$=""+INKEY$:IF Q$="" THEN 160
170 RETURN
```

THE SURVEY QUESTIONNAIRE

A congressional personality appeared on national television and was asked his opinion concerning an opinion survey showing a lack of support for a program with which he was associated. The Congressman's response was to the effect that, given control of the writing of the questionnaire, he could guarantee any desired outcome of a survey. An artful evasion indeed, but not without some validity.

We assume your interest in this subject is honest and straightforward. Your objective is to obtain unbiased and comprehensive information with regard to a given subject. We also assume you are primarily interested in quantitative research instead of anecdotal inquiry. Considerable valid research has been conducted using the case study method or an anecdotal approach in which essential elements of a subject are elicited in a conversational manner, but the results are generally unsuitable for statistical analysis. Microcomputers can assist in anecdotal research by keeping track of the archival data related to the study (names, dates, addresses, and phone numbers of interviewees, location of reference documents, etc.), and by performing text evaluation studies. That is, a verbatim transcript of an interview can be statistically evaluated by a microcomputer to identify particular word selections, speech patterns, and similar data. Nonetheless, this book will limit the applications to quantifiable research. This limitation will make the questionnaire preparation process a lot easier.

The first "rule" of questionnaire design, then,

is to include only those questions the answers to which can be quantified, that is, turned into some sort of a number. We can have three kinds of numbers: scalar values, dichotomous values, and demographic values.

Scalar Values. We use scalar values to measure things: attitudes, social values or rankings, income, educational levels, and so forth. Chapter 2 contains a comprehensive review of the different sorts of scales we use to measure attitudes, tell time, weigh fish, or count automobiles. It is in this process of survey design that such distinctions are critical. The questionnaire writer must pay scrupulous attention to the advantages and shortfalls of each of the types of scalar data. Of particular concern are attitudinal type questions: "On a scale from 1 to 10...." In such cases there is a strong temptation to subject the responses to rigorous statistical analysis in an effort to summarize the study by saying: "The mean response was 4.988856 or slightly below "no opinion" with a standard deviation of 1.02345." Unfortunately, ordinal scale data cannot rationally be subjected to this level of analysis. It is acceptable to determine the median response to a given item using an ordinal scale. It is also acceptable to compare median responses to the same item over a period of time. This is frequently done in national newspaper political polls attempting to determine how the citizens feel about the candidates for president or how well the incumbent president is performing. Although much is made of a percentage point shift up or down, it is really more fair simply to note that a shift has taken place.

Dichotomous Values. Questions that seek yes/no, true/false, male/female, accept/reject type answers are seeking dichotomous responses. We can use the results to divide the population into proportionate quantities: X% are for candidate Y (therefore, (100 − X)% are either neutral or against), A% are females and 100 − A% are either males or transsexuals. The standard error of the results of a survey can be computed from this kind of a proportion. The basic equation is:

$$S = \sqrt{\frac{PQ}{n}} \%$$

Notice that as the value of P moves toward either extreme, the value of the standard error gets much smaller. For example, a political poll of 1000 people reveals a 49-51% split on an issue. The standard error in this instance = +/− 1.58082%. This means the actual division of public opinion could reasonably fall anywhere between 47.41918 to 50.58082% against, and 49.41618 to 52.58082% for. On the other hand, if the same 1000 people are surveyed later and found to be split 36-64 on an issue, the standard error is computed to be 1.51789%. The actual split is estimated to be from 34.48211 to 37.51789% against, and 61.48211 to 65.51789% for.

As with ordinal data, there are strict limits on the kinds of mathematical manipulations to which you can subject dichotomous data. It is not acceptable to compute the mean, median, or standard deviation of such data. What is relevant is the proportion computed.

Demographic Values. These include a number of quantities related to the natural characteristics of the people in the survey. Age, height, weight, sex, educational level, number (population), and so forth. While sex, male or female, is a dichotomous variable, the remaining values are generally adequate for detailed statistical computations of mean, standard deviation, median, mode, distribution analysis, percentages, percentiles, etc. It is entirely acceptable to compute correlations between these types of demographic data and the dichotomous data obtained in true/false, accept/reject type of questions by using the Point-Biserial correlation tests discussed in Chapter 5.

Length of Questionnaire

The questionnaire must be long enough to obtain the essential answers concerning the main objective of the survey. It shouldn't be longer than necessary to collect relevant data. If it's too short, the survey is pointless. If it's too long, the subject will become annoyed and the quality of answers will suffer. Just how long is too long depends a lot on the setting for the interview. The longest interviews are usually most successfully completed in the subject's home with an in-person interview. They are even more successful if the interview is of interest to the subject or one in which the subject perceives some personal gain or reward for participation.

At the other extreme are surveys conducted in shopping malls or other public areas. In these settings there are frequently a large number of potential respondents, especially if the survey is a marketing survey. The trouble is that most of these people are going somewhere and have little time to answer a questionnaire. Often, it's easier to plot a course around the interviewer or simply ignore their request for time. What is the significance on the outcome of such research when a portion of the crowd can avoid the interview?

Telephone surveys are somewhere in-between the interview on the street and the interview in the home. Because the subject is at home, a longer questionnaire can be used, but the impersonality of the telephone limits that benefit and permits the subject to hang up at any time. Telephone surveys also tend to eliminate from the sample the poor and the transient. To the extent the survey can afford to let this portion of the population pass unsampled, there is little problem.

Questionnaire Completion

Unless mandated by circumstances, the interviewer should complete the survey form. This is done for several reasons. First, many of the answers may require special coding. Second, the data should be in a consistent form. Third, the interviewer will provide some measure of subjective validation. Only in the most extreme cases should the survey be mailed to the respondents. In a blind survey, wherein the respondents are chosen at random, the response is likely to be quite poor, 5-7 percent at best. On the other hand, in the worst case, 20 percent of those called in telephone surveys respond, and 80 percent in the house-to-house survey respond.

DATA ANALYSIS

Given the task of data analysis, you should select those techniques which are:

— Logically related to the desired output.

— Precise enough to satisfy program objectives.
— Simple enough to be completed with available resources.
— Short enough to be completed within the specified schedule.
— Inexpensive enough to fit within the project budget.

Analysis techniques will vary with the data to be analyzed. That is, demographic data are suitable for one set of techniques, while subjective attitude study data are suitable for another.

Demographic Analysis

A frequent component of a research report is a description of the sample in fairly straightforward, quantifiable terms such as age, sex, race, height, weight, economic status, and educational level. It is frequently useful to compare these data with the corresponding data for the general population. Normally, the more the sample demographic data resemble those of the general population the more ready we are to accept the attitudes of the sample as representative of those of the general population.

Researchers often don't know the parameters of the general population. That is, we can note in our research report that the mean age of the respondent was 42.45 years; how this compares to the population at large depends on the nature of that population. If we are referring to the national population, we are really just comparing the mean from one sample of the population to another. We really don't know exactly how many people there are in the country, nor, therefore, do we know exactly how old we all are, so we can't compute a true mean national age. Instead, we estimate it from various census activities. On the other hand, if the sample is from a small college enrollment, it may be possible to make a more precise comparison. Listing 9-6 is a general purpose routine meant to illustrate an approach to evaluating demographic data. It requires that the user have available not only the sample demographic data but also the corresponding population data, whether actual or estimated.

Evaluating Subjective Data

Due to the slippery nature of attitude scales and

Listing 9-6. Demographic Analysis.

```
1 '*********************************************
2 '*                 Listing 9-6               *
3 '*            Demographic Analysis           *
4 '*********************************************
5 '
10 CLEAR 2500
20 CLS:PRINT"DEMOGRAPHIC ANALYSIS":
30 PRINT:PRINT"ENTER VALUES IN NEAREST INTEGER V
ALUE.  FOR DICHOTOMOUS VALUES ASSIGN ONE ASPECT
'1' AND THE OTHER, '0'.  FOR MEAN VALUE, ENTER '
D'":PRINT:PRINT
40 INPUT"ENTER NUMBER OF SUBJECTS IN SAMPLE";NS
50 INPUT"NUMBER OF PEOPLE IN GENERAL POPULATION"
;NP
60 INPUT"ENTER NUMBER OF DEMOGRAPHIC CHARACTERIS
TICS";C
70 DIM QC(C),C$(C),D$(NS,C),PM$(C):CLS
80 FOR I=1 TO C:PRINT"NAME OF CHARACTERISTIC #";
I,:INPUT C$(I):INPUT"POPULATION MEAN FOR THIS VA
LUE";PM$(I):NEXT:CLS
90 FOR I=1 TO NS
100 PRINT"SUBJECT #";I
110 FOR J=1 TO C
120 PRINT"",C$(J)
130 INPUT"ENTER SPECIFIC VALUE";D$(I,J):
140 NEXT J
150 NEXT I
160 PRINT:PRINT:PRINT"(R)EVIEW ALL INPUT DATA  (
C)ORRECT SELECTED DATA  (E)ND INPUT";
170 Q$=""+INKEY$:IF Q$="" THEN 170
180 IF Q$="E" THEN 300 ELSE IF Q$="C" THEN 290
190 FOR I=1 TO NS
200 CLS:PRINT I;
210 FOR J=1 TO C
220 PRINT C$(J);"  ";D$(I,J),
230 NEXT J
240 PRINT:PRINT"ALL OK?  (Y/N)";
250 Z$=""+INKEY$:IF Z$="" THEN 250
260 IF Z$="Y" THEN 280
270 INPUT"ENTER NUMBER OF ITEM TO BE CHANGED, AN
D CORRECT VALUE";X,D$(I,X):GOTO 200
280 NEXT I
290 PRINT:INPUT"ENTER SUBJECT NUMBER, ITEM NUMBE
R, AND CORRECT VALUE";X;Y;D$(X,Y):GOTO 160
299 INPUT"File Name ";F$
300 OPEN "O",1,F$
310 PRINT#1,NS,C
320 FOR I=1 TO NS
330 FOR J=1 TO C
340 PRINT#1, D$(I,J)
350 NEXT J
360 NEXT I
370 CLOSE
380 CLS:PRINT"PRELIMINARY ASSESSMENT.  NOW COMPU
TING.":PRINT:PRINT
390 FOR I=1 TO C
```

```
400 PRINT C$(I),:LG=0
410 FOR J=1 TO NS
420 D=VAL(D$(J,I)):IF D<LG THEN 440
430 LG=D
440 NEXT J
450 FOR J=1 TO LG
460 FOR K=1 TO NS
470 D=VAL(D$(K,I))
480 IF D<>J THEN 500
490 JJ=JJ+1:LOCATE 10,1:PRINT JJ,JJ/NS;
500 NEXT K
510 NEXT J
520 JJ=0:R=R+1
525 NEXT I
530 LOCATE 16,1:PRINT"Use PrtScn to Save Screen
    (A)nother set      (M)ain menu "
540 Q$=""+INKEY$:IF Q$="" THEN 540
550 IF Q$="A" OR Q$="a" THEN RUN 10
560 IF Q$="M" OR Q$="m" THEN RUN "A:MENU"
```

the variations within these kinds of scales, it is difficult at best and often ill-advised to attempt the mathematical evaluations of such scalar data to compute means and standard deviations. What does have greater meaning and utility is to make comparisons between people with identifiable demographic differences or to make comparisons of the differences in attitudes among the same group of people over a period of time. Listing 9-7 facilitates this sort of processing. As with the program in Listing 9-6, it is more illustrative than utilitarian. It works well with the data we contrived for the purpose of demonstrating the program, but probably should be modified to suit your own program requirements better.

Listing 9-7. Attitude Analysis.

```
1 '***********************************************
2 '*                Listing 9-7                  *
3 '*             Attitude Analysis               *
4 '***********************************************
5 '
10 CLEAR 2500:KEY OFF
20 CLS:PRINT"ATTITUDE ANALYSIS":PRINT
30 INPUT"ENTER NUMBER OF SUBJECTS IN SAMPLE";NS
40 INPUT"ENTER NUMBER OF ITEMS IN SURVEY";S
50 DIM V$(NS,S):CLS
60 FOR I=1 TO NS
70 PRINT"SUBJECT #";I
80 FOR J=1 TO S
90 PRINT"ENTER RESPONSE TO ITEM #";J,:INPUT V$(I
,J)
100 NEXT J
110 NEXT I
120 PRINT:PRINT:PRINT"(R)EVIEW ALL INPUT DATA   (
C)ORRECT SELECTED DATA   (E)ND INPUT";
130 Q$=""+INKEY$:IF Q$="" THEN 130
140 IF Q$="E" THEN 260 ELSE IF Q$="C" THEN 250
150 FOR I=1 TO NS
160 CLS:PRINT I;
170 FOR J=1 TO S
180 PRINT J;V$(I,J),
```

Listing 9-7. Attitude Analysis. (Continued From Page 167.)

```
190 NEXT J
200 PRINT:PRINT"ALL OK?  (Y/N)";
210 Z$=""+INKEY$:IF Z$="" THEN 210
220 IF Z$="Y" THEN 260
230 INPUT"ENTER NUMBER OF ITEM TO BE CHANGED, AN
D CORRECT VALUE";X,V$(I,X):GOTO 160
240 NEXT I
250 PRINT:INPUT"ENTER SUBJECT NUMBER, ITEM NUMBE
R, AND CORRECT VALUE";X;Y;V$(X,Y):GOTO 120
260 OPEN "O",1,"ATTITUDE"
270 PRINT#1,NS,S
280 FOR I=1 TO NS
290 FOR J=1 TO S
300 PRINT#1,V$(I,J)
310 NEXT J
320 NEXT I
330 CLOSE #1
340 INPUT"LARGEST NUMBER OF OPTIONS";N:DIM A$(S,
N),A(S,N)
350 FOR I=1 TO S:FOR J=1 TO N:A$(I,J)=STR$(J):NE
XT J:NEXT I
360 CLS:PRINT"PRELIMINARY ASSESSMENT.  NOW COMPU
TING.":PRINT:PRINT
370 FOR I=1 TO NS
380 FOR J=1 TO S
390 V=VAL(V$(I,J)):A(J,V)=A(J,V)+1
400 NEXT J
410 NEXT I
420 CLS
430 PRINT"ITEM","OPTION","NUMBER","PER CENT"
440 FOR I=1 TO S
450 PRINT I,
460 FOR J=1 TO N
470 PRINT J,A(I,J),100*(A(I,J)/N)
480 NEXT
490 PRINT:PRINT"(C)ONTINUE   (P)RINT";
500 Q$=""+INKEY$:IF Q$="" THEN 500
510 IF Q$="C" THEN 550
520 LPRINT"ITEM # ";I
530 FOR J=1 TO N:LPRINT J,A(I,J),100*(A(I,J)/N):
NEXT J
540 LPRINT""
550 NEXT I
560 PRINT"(A)nother       (M)ain menu ";
570 GOSUB 590
580 IF Q$="A" OR Q$="a" THEN RUN 10 ELSE RUN "A:
MENU"
590 Q$=""+INKEY$:IF Q$="" THEN 590
600 RETURN
```

CASE STUDY: WHAT MIGHT HAVE BEEN

During the campaign for the 1980 primary elections in a southwestern state, one of the candidates, a popular favorite, suffered a back injury in an automobile accident. One of the consequences of the injury was that it made it impossible for the candidate to walk through each of the precincts to personally meet with residents at their homes. In past elections this technique had been perceived as vital to establishing an effective rapport with the voters. The candidate, a woman, felt it essential to meet the voters on a personal level to overcome chauvinist attitudes in several ethnic neighborhoods in which being male, in the absence of any other influence, was considered an asset. Her personality was such that personal contact with the voters was normally sufficient to offset this attitude. Although she won the election on the basis of votes registered in the polls, she lost the total vote with the addition of the absentee vote. After reviewing the election returns, she was convinced that her inability to walk through a good portion of the precincts made the difference between winning and losing the election. That is, she and her staff believed that if she had been able to walk through the precincts, enough additional votes could have been collected to offset the impact of the absentee vote. A lawsuit was initiated against the driver of the other car involved in the accident for damages and lost potential income on this basis. To support the lawsuit, we were retained by her legal counsel to perform a statistical analysis of the election results to determine if there was any quantitative basis to the action. What follows is an abridged version of the report to the attorney. Although names have been changed at the request of those involved, the numerical data is exactly as it was provided and analyzed. While we would have preferred to see the candidate win the lawsuit, we had to approach the study from a strictly objective perspective. We anticipated that the defense counsel would retain a statistician to evaluate any work we submitted and that any effort to slant the data in favor of our client would have been detected and the whole work, rightly or wrongly, discredited. Accordingly, in each test that suggested support for our client, we devised a counter-test to at least challenge the first finding.

Abstract

Election results from the 39 precincts which constitute Area H in the State Legislature are statistically reviewed and evaluated. One candidate, Mary Smith, was forced to withdraw from active compaigning after making personal appearances in 12 precincts due to injuries received in an automobile accident. Analysis reveals the vote for Smith to be significantly higher in those precincts where she made personal appearances than in those where she did not. The data suggest and support the notion that had Smith been able to appear in all of the precincts the vote in her favor would have been as much as 5000 to 7000 votes greater.

Summary

This study reviews the election results in the legislative district from the 1980 General Election. In particular, we review those results related to the race between the candidates for the House seat, Smith (D) and Jones (R). The results are especially interesting in that those voting at the polls clearly preferred Smith over Jones (21313 to 19236) by a margin of 2077 votes. When the absentee ballots are counted, however, the outcome swings to favor Jones (25807 to 24674) by 1133 votes. A change in 567 votes would have altered the outcome of this race. These data are shown in Table 9-2.

It is interesting to note that early in the campaign Smith was seriously injured in an automobile accident and, as a consequence, was unable to make personal appearances in nearly two-thirds of the precincts. It is even more interesting to note that in those precincts where Smith had made an appearance, walking door-to-door, the average vote in her favor (56.0714%) was 5.940% higher than in the precincts where she didn't walk (50.1315%). We believe the data support two hypotheses:

A — The absentee vote results reflect the overall political mood of the country at the time of the election, and the partisan attitudes of the electorate in the county without particular regard for Jones specifically.

B — A personal appearance in a given precinct by Smith was likely to result in a more favorable walk-in vote for her at the polls.

The implications of these findings are significant: it is not unreasonable to conclude that had Smith been able to appear in all of the precincts, then, providing the remaining precincts voted as the first twelve did, the result would have been a win for Smith, not Jones. Applying the percentages, 56.0714

Table 9-2. Regional Voting Results (1980 General Election).

Precinct	Number Registered Voters	Number Voting	Straight Republican Votes	Straight Democrat Votes	For Jones	For Smith	Total Votes	For Reagan	For Carter	Walked
1	114	1972	940	---	---	61	783	844	111	799	Yes
2	117	2011	1101	---	---	102	892	994	174	888	Yes
3	136	1343	811	---	---	305	457	762	431	342	No
4	215	1933	935	33	636	91	799	890	119	761	No
5	227	1693	952	76	378	201	727	928	283	637	Yes
6	228	2373	1253	269	157	657	535	1729	753	392	No
7	233	2854	1585	349	133	865	654	1519	1085	375	No
8	234	2964	1749	409	178	978	715	1693	1175	456	No
9	235	647	431	78	35	213	195	408	273	123	No
10	237	2600	1732	422	171	944	735	1679	1120	479	No
11	238	1094	632	196	60	384	231	615	434	152	No
12	239	1909	1118	279	176	615	456	1071	687	347	Yes
13	240	873	558	130	55	313	230	543	381	142	No
14	241	2886	1959	558	144	1128	751	1879	1343	472	Yes
15	242	3130	1909	342	341	730	1126	1856	1135	671	Yes
16	243	2483	1501	229	334	533	926	1459	813	624	No
17	247	1034	644	215	67	396	211	607	470	143	No
18	249	1571	755	38	372	90	598	688	136	565	No
19	250	1573	896	127	230	287	594	881	489	407	No
20	251	1801	1084	152	236	353	698	1051	566	440	Yes
21	252	70	42	7	4	15	23	38	22	16	No
22	253	132	71	23	5	49	19	68	50	16	No
23	254	2694	1590	343	157	896	626	1522	1030	446	No
24	255	1710	1111	237	91	688	400	1088	784	269	No
25	260	2166	1212	144	354	382	770	1152	493	639	No
26	263	915	452	109	65	261	163	424	310	122	No
27	264	2383	1360	326	94	806	483	1289	956	316	Yes
28	265	1400	824	165	150	410	391	801	479	288	No
29	266	1678	964	238	116	530	388	918	621	260	No
30	267	890	549	116	72	278	239	517	322	191	No
31	268	2113	1289	268	159	734	524	1258	834	389	No
32	269	2921	1873	375	285	838	964	1802	1155	622	Yes
33	270	1902	973	31	615	822	65	887	106	797	No
34	273	1572	917	112	246	295	577	872	426	446	No
35	274	4324	2556	506	309	1324	1141	2465	1618	768	Yes
36	275	1534	937	118	349	263	645	908	408	466	Yes
37	334	2673	1409	500	82	984	385	1369	1124	225	No
38	352/370	2003	1299	379	50	877	361	1238	1013	228	No
39	382	618	410			295	97	392	321	69	No
Absentee	---	n/a	9932	4278	1173	6571	3361	9932	6571	3361	n/a
Totals 39	Prec.	72442	52324	12177	8079	25807	24674	50481	30621	19149	12 Precincts

170

percent of the 40549 walk-in votes cast is 22736 votes, while Jones' share would have been 17813. Adding the absentee votes (without modification) the final tally would have been: Smith 26097, Jones 24384—Smith by a margin of 1713 votes. An even finer estimate of voter behavior will be illustrated later in this paper in which a linear regression estimate is computed based on the number of registered voters in a given precinct. In this particular estimate the outcome would have been: Smith 28842, Jones 21376—Smith by 7466 votes. These are the outcomes clearly suggested by the data. The relevant question is whether it is statistically appropriate and rationally supported to apply these pragmatic observations against the available data to come to the conclusions noted above. It is the purpose of this paper, then, to examine this question and display the results. As we believe the following tests will show, the data support the conclusions that a personal appearance by Smith in a precinct resulted in a favorable vote and, had she been able to appear in all precincts, she would have won the election by a greater margin than that by which she lost.

The Data

Table 9-2 is a simple tabulation of the election results in the area in the 1980 General Election. Column 11 indicates whether or not Smith made a personal appearance in the indicated precinct. Table 9-3 summarizes the data from Table 9-2. These constitute the entire body of data evaluated in this study. The numbers are derived directly from official election reports and records.

The Analysis

Given the data on Tables 9-2 and 9-3, the project was divided into two phases. Phase 1 consisted of discovering what the data contained. Phase 2 consisted of determining whether any one or more of the findings was, in statistical terms, significant. That is, does it mean anything?

Summary of Phase 1. Table 9-3 is the first product of this phase. It clearly shows that Smith won the majority of the walk-in votes, 21313 to 19236. Although she lost the combined absentee votes, it is interesting to note the very slight mar-

Table 9-3. Detailed Analysis of Voting Results.

	Smith			Jones			Line Total
	Straight	Split	Total	Straight	Split	Total	
Actual Vote							
Absentee	1173	2188	3361	4278	2293	6571	9932
Walk-in	6906	14407	21313	7899	11337	19236	40549
Total	8079	16595	24674	12177	13630	25807	50481
Percent of Total Vote							
Absentee	2.324%	4.334%	6.658%	8.474%	4.542%	13.017%	19.675%
Walk-in	13.680	28.539	42.220	15.647	22.458	38.105	80.325
Total	16.004	32.874	48.878	24.122	27.000	51.122	100.000
Percent of Total Personal Vote							
Absentee	4.754%	8.868%	13.622%	16.577%	8.885%	25.462%	19.675%
Walk-in	27.989	58.389	86.378	30.608	43.930	74.538	80.325
Total	32.743	67.257	100.000	47.185	52.815	100.000	100.000

gin of her loss on the split ticket absentee ballot count, 2188 to 2293. The probability that the 105 vote difference means anything other than chance variation is very slight. On the other hand, note the large difference between the absentee results on the straight ticket votes, 1173 to 4278. Since this was a general election where a first-term incumbent president was voted out of office, we believe it more likely that the straight ticket vote Jones received was much more an expression for Reagan (or against Carter) than a vote against Smith in favor of Jones. A large number of the absentee voters are governmental employees assigned out of the country. That a significant number of these voters would be following the particulars of the local aspects of the political campaign is very unlikely. Without submitting the data to rigorous test and examination (since this matter is not the issue in question), we would like the reader to share our perception that the absentee vote is really a reflection of the outcome of the national election issues and not significantly related to the campaigning efforts of either Smith or Jones. Rather, we propose that if Smith had been able to properly campaign in the area, she would have won the election on walk-in votes in spite of the absentee ballot; she would have influenced and obtained the support of at least 567 additional votes out of the 50481 cast for the local candidates.

Estimating Potential Votes. We begin with the assumption that if Smith had walked all of the 39 precincts as she did twelve, she would have re-

ceived a larger share of the vote. How much larger? The simplest estimate is obtained by applying her advantage in the twelve precincts against the total vote. 40549 votes were cast in the local race. In the twelve walked precincts Smith's percentage was 56.0714%. This equates to 22736 votes for Smith and 17813 for Jones. Even if the absentee ballots are added in, the outcome is Smith 26097 and Jones 24384. At this point a series of curve-fitting computer routines were applied to the data. This is a statistical effort to define the elements of standard curve equations that provide an estimate of the vote based on some variable. We found the highest correlation or "goodness of fit" when the actual votes were compared with the number of registered voters in a given precinct. The four major curves used in this type of analysis are: linear, exponential, logarithmic, and power.

Tables 9-4 to 9-7 summarize the results of the data being processed against various dependent and independent variables. The value R is the correlation of one variable to the other. Its range is from −1 to 1. A value at either end of the range means the equation is a good predictor. The closer the value approaches zero, the less reliably the equation will predict Y. The t-Test is an additional test of the equation and gives an indication of the reliability of the R value. Its value range is theoretically unlimited (that is, to infinity, plus or minus), and its interpretation is beyond the scope of this paper. Nonetheless, if the value is less than −1.796 or greater than

Table 9-4. Curve Fitting, Number of Registered Voters Versus Number of Votes for Smith.

Input X	Y	X	Y	X	Y	X	Y
1972	763	2011	892	1693	727	2854	654
1909	456	2886	751	3130	1126	1801	698
2383	483	2921	964	4324	1141	1534	645

Output	A	B	R	t-Test	Equations
Linear	324.087	.183934	.670688	2.85936	Y = A + BX
Exponential	437.199	2.1812E-04	.604895	2.40215	Y = EXP(LOG A + BK)
Logarithmic	−2762.12	455.844	.636209	2.60768	Y = A + B LOG X
Power	11.3396	.539572	.572739	2.20944	Y = EXP(LOG A+B LOG X)

Input

X	Y	X	Y	X	Y	X	Y
940	763	1101	892	952	727	1584	654
1118	456	1959	751	1909	1126	1084	698
1360	483	1873	964	2556	1141	937	645

Output

	A	B	R	t-Test	Equations
Linear	377.349	.274668	.654783	2.73956	Y = A + BX
Exponential	464.586	3.2738E-04	.593561	2.33229	Y = EXP(LOG A + BX)
Logarithmic	−2030.77	388.531	.608196	2.42292	Y = A + B LOG X
Power	27.0872	.459192	.546684	2.0646	Y = EXP(LOG A + B LOG X)

+1.796, the R value is considered very reliable. The portion labeled "Input" contains the values entered for processing.

Figure 9-1 illustrates the lines or curves resulting from the foregoing tables. In all cases, the independent (horizontal) variable is the number of registered voters in a precinct and the dependent variable (vertical) is the number voting. Each line or curve is labeled to show for whom they are voting. The line Y_t confirms common wisdom: the larger the precinct, the larger the number of voters going to the polls. The line Y_d shows the larger the precinct, the larger the number of people voting for Smith. It would be misleading, however, not to mention that as the precincts get larger, the vote for Smith (both actual and predicted) gets smaller when expressed as a percentage of the total vote. The foregoing is based on the data of the 12 precincts Smith walked. The dotted line (Y_{all}) is based on the data from all 39 precincts and, for the range of precinct sizes that actually exist, follows the previous example: the larger the precinct, the smaller the percentage voting for Smith. Finally, the curved line Y_p is based on the vote for Jones. Interestingly enough, the same fate awaits Jones with the larger precincts. With all curves, the S_y expression is the standard error of the (Y) estimate. While the equation computes the estimate of the Y-variable as a function of the value of the X-variable, it must be understood that the real data upon which these lines are com-

Input

X	Y	X	Y	X	Y	X	Y
1972	61	2011	102	1693	201	2854	865
1909	615	2886	1128	3130	730	1801	353
2383	806	2921	838	4324	1324	1534	263

Output

	A	B	R	t-Test	Equations
Linear	−469.868	.439337	.858182	5.28652	Y = A + BX
Exponential	55.3842	8.40416E-04	.685501	2.97738	Y = EXP(LOG A + BX)
Logarithmic	−8364.51	1156.22	.864461	5.43796	Y = A + B LOG X
Power	1.2373E-05	2.23913	.699065	3.09155	Y = EXP(LOG A + B LOG X)

Table 9-7. Curve Fitting, Number of Registered Voters Versus Number Actually Voting.

Input								
X	Y	X	Y	X	Y	X	Y	
1972	940	2011	1101	1693	952	2854	1585	
1909	1118	2886	1959	3130	1909	1801	1084	
2383	1360	2921	1873	4324	2556	1534	937	

Output	A	B	R	t-Test	Equations
Linear	− 115.198	.637582	.975191	13.9308	Y = A + BX
Exponential	499.709	4.10977E-04	.95719	10.4571	Y = EXP(LOG A + BX)
Logarithmic	− 11279.1	1653.06	.967756	12.1495	Y = A + B LOG X
Power	.296735	1.08724	.969238	12.4531	Y = EXP(LOG A + B LOGX)

puted will deviate from this prediction. The standard error indicates the limits (plus and minus) within which the bulk of the data points will appear when plotted against the estimate at any given point. Therefore, while we compute that the expected vote for Jones in a precinct with 2000 registered voters will be about 692, the standard error suggests this value could and probably will vary by as much as 156+ or− votes, or from 536 to 848 votes. Although specific data points will vary from the prediction, those points below the estimate will be balanced out by about the same number above the estimate.

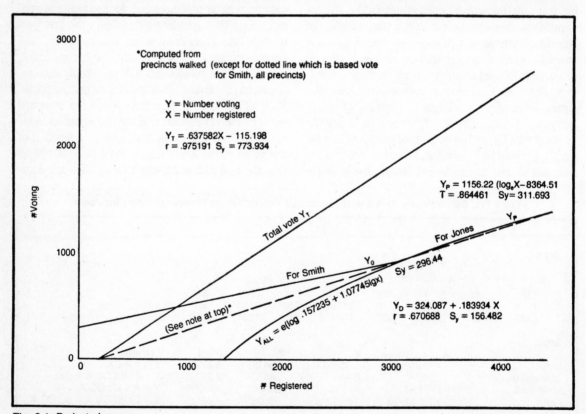

Fig. 9-1. Projected curves.

We know the real data will vary to a degree from the predictions. The standard error gives us an estimate of how great a variation is still normal.

Significance of the Data

The observations just given have been computed with a great deal of precision. They clearly show a difference in the voter preference in the precincts Smith walked as opposed to those she didn't. We apply both the simple percentage difference and the curve-fitting estimates to the different precincts and find that had the patterns noted in the 12 walked precincts been applied and effective in the non-walked precincts, Smith should have won the election handily. The pivotal question, then, is whether these observations are statistically valid. That is, to what degree are the observed differences simply the result of chance deviation and circumstance, and to what extent are the differences not explained by random voter behavior? The differences repeatedly support the notion that observed differences are significant, that is, not the result of chance or random error. There were a number of tests conducted leading to this conclusion.

The first test was a Monte Carlo experiment. There are 3,910,797,436 different and unique combinations of 12 precincts out of a total of 39. Even at the rate of one complete computation per second, it would take nearly 124 years to actually check out all three billion plus combinations. Instead, a computer simulation was developed to select 12 precincts at random, total the vote and compute the percentage voting for Smith. After 21746 trial combinations, we find the percentage of precinct combinations giving a vote for Smith better than the actual result to be about 4.244%. That is, if you picked any 12 precincts at random, there is a 95.756% chance that the vote for Smith would be less than 56%. Smith was asked to name the precincts in which she had made personal appearances. Immediately she named the 12 picked in the study, referring only to the data shown in Table 9-2, and looking only at the precinct numbers. This took about 30 seconds. The probability she chose the 12 at random, yet happened to select 12 that would lead us to the conclusions in her favor is .0424446. It is not very likely she did it at random. Rather, we conclude, the selections were based on reality and the subsequent findings are significant and valid.

Table 9-8, summarizes the data resulting from a "Differences Between Proportions" test. The question implied was: Don't these 12 particular precincts usually favor the Democratic candidate more than the other 27 precincts? The z-Score in the right-hand column is a measure of dispersion of one data set from another. Only if the score is greater than 1.6449 are the data considered to be better than 95% chance-free. Only in the 1980 general election does there appear to be a significant difference between the two sets of precincts.

Table 9-9 is the summary of a "Point-Biserial Correlation" test. This test evaluates the relationship between some more or less continuous data

Table 9-8. Comparative Statistics, 1978 to 1980.

Election Type/Year	12 Precincts Walked			Remaining Precincts			Test Results	
	Total Vote	Candidate* Vote	Percent	Total Vote	Candidate* Vote	Percent	Standard Error	Z-Score
1978 General	8337	4700	56.3746%	11379	5960	52.3772%	.0364715	1.09603
1980 Primary	2142	1425	66.5266	2493	1585	63.5780	.0412833	.714234
1980 Runoff	2543	1772	69.6815	3226	2167	67.1730	.0281058	.892525
1980 General	16586	9300	56.0714	23963	12013	50.1315	.0297854	1.994250

*Winning Candidate

Table 9-9. Point-Biserial Correlation, 1980 Election.

PCT 0	# Regist. 1	# Voting 2	Smith 3	Jones 4	Walked 5
114	1972	940	763	61	4
117	2011	1101	892	102	2
227	1693	952	727	201	5
233	2854	1585	654	865	5
239	1909	1118	456	615	3
241	2886	1959	751	1128	1
242	3130	1909	1126	730	3
251	1801	1084	698	353	5
264	2383	1360	483	806	2
269	2921	1873	964	838	1
274	4324	2556	1141	1324	4
275	1534	937	645	263	5
136	1343	811	457	305	0
215	1933	935	799	91	0
228	2373	1253	535	657	0
234	2964	1749	715	978	0
235	647	431	195	213	0
237	2600	1732	735	944	0
238	1094	632	231	384	0
240	873	558	230	313	0
243	2483	1501	926	533	0
247	1034	644	211	396	0
249	1571	755	598	90	0
250	1573	896	594	287	0
252	70	42	23	15	0
253	132	71	19	49	0
254	2694	1590	626	896	0
255	1710	1111	400	688	0
260	2166	1212	770	382	0
263	915	452	163	261	0
265	1400	824	391	410	0
266	1678	964	388	530	0
267	890	549	239	278	0
268	2113	1298	524	734	0
270	1902	973	822	65	0
273	1572	917	577	295	0
344	2673	1409	385	984	0
352	2003	1299	363	877	0
382	618	410	97	295	0

1 = .4567
Point-biserial correlation of column 2 = .455595
Point-biserial correlation of column 3 = .536778
Point-biserial correlation of column 4 = .224276

(votes for a candidate) with some dichotomous criterion (in this study, walked versus didn't walk). Note that the greatest correlation between whether or not a precinct was walked and some continuous data set was with the vote for Smith (.536778). We conclude from this there is a meaningful significance in the observed differences.

Tables 9-10 through 9-12 display the outcome of several tests in the statistical family of analysis of variance. The test assumes that the test subjects (voters) are otherwise identical in personal makeup and disposition but have been divided into two or more groups. Each group has received a different degree of treatment (being walked, personal appear-

Source	SS	DF	MS	F	P
Total	10874300.00	38			
Between	2257050.00	1	＊2257050.00	9.69	0.003800
Within	8617220.00	37	＊232878.00		

Variations noted are likely to be the result of the treatment.

Input Values

Group 1	Group 2	
940	811	
1101	935	
952	1253	
1585	1749	
1118	431	
1959	1732	
1909	632	
1084	558	
1360	1501	
1873	644	
2556	755	
937	896	
	42	
	71	
	1590	
	1111	
	1212	
	452	
	824	
	964	
	549	
	1298	
	973	
	917	
	1409	
	1299	
	410	
17374	25018	Sum
1447.83	926.593	Average

Table 9-10. Comparison Between Precincts Walked Versus Those not Walked (One-Way ANOVA).

ance of the candidate). Table 9-10 and Table 9-11 tend to confirm the observation that Smith walked significantly larger precincts. Table 9-12 shows the results of a "Two-Way Analysis of Variance Test" and actually tests two questions simultaneously: Is there a significant difference in the vote for Smith depending on whether or not she walked a precinct, and in a specific kind of precinct (walked versus appear) are there significant differences in voter preference? From the output data we conclude that the probability that walking a precinct results in a favorable vote for Smith is about .9860.

Table 9-13 gives the results from another series of statistical tests in the chi-square family. The purpose and outcome of these tests are the same as the analysis of variance. From section 1 we conclude that walking a precinct had only a slight (.770896) influence on voter turnout whereas, section 2, there is an extremely significant difference in voter preference between Smith and Jones related to whether Smith walked a given precinct.

Table 9-14 shows the impact of applying the voting estimate from Table 9-2 on each precinct. The column labeled "12-Precinct" is the estimate of the

Source	SS	DF	MS	F	P
Total	29323300.00	38			
Between	6116080.00	1	%6116080.00	9.75	0.003700
Within	23207200.00	37	%627223.00		

Variations noted are likely to be the result of the treatment.

Input values

Walked	Didn't Walk
Group 1	**Group 2**
1972	1343
2011	1933
1693	2373
2854	2964
1909	647
2886	2600
3130	1094
1801	873
2383	2483
2921	1034
4324	1571
1534	70
	132
	2694
	1710
	2166
	915
	1400
	1678
	890
	2113
	1902
	1572
	2673
	2003
	618
	1573
29418	43024 Sum
2451.5	1593.48 Average

Table 9-11. Comparison Between Precincts Walked Versus Those not Walked, Registered Voters (One-Way ANOVA).

vote from that precinct had Smith campaigned there.

Whether the reader would come to the same conclusions as we did is unknown. We believe the data support the conclusions as well as possible. Limiting the study was the fact that nearly a year had passed since the election before we were retained to do the study. While the election results were not perishable, we believed that the research could have been improved by a survey of the voters immediately after the election to see if there was any candidate recognition or attitudinal differences measurable in the precincts that we could attribute to the presence or absence of the client in the precinct during the campaign. Unfortunately, too much time had passed and other (favorable) public events involving our client had appeared in the local press. We were fearful that such study could be successfully challenged by the defense. As a consequence,

Table 9-12. Comparison of Votes Considering Votes for the Candidates and Whether Precincts Were Walked (Two-Way ANOVA).

Source	SS	DF	MS	F	P	
Total	7670000.00	77				
Column	55282.00	1	%55282.00	0.63	0.564600	Smith vs. Jones
Row	1016320.00	1	%1016320.00	11.60	0.001400	Walk vs Didn't Walk
Row X col	113806.00	1	%113806.00	1.30	0.257000	
Error	6484590.00	74	%87629.60			

Significant findings:
Row effects are significant

Input variables

```
Cell Group 1 1 :    763    892    727    654    456    751   1126
698                 483    964   1141    645
Cell Group 1 2 :     61    102    201    865    615   1128    730
353                 806    838   1324    263
Cell Group  2 1:    457    799    535    715    195    735    231
230                 926    211    598    594     23     19    626
400                 770    163    391    388    239    524    822
577                 385    363     97
Cell Group 2 2 :    305     91    657    978    213    944    384
313                 533    396     90    287     15     49    896
688                 382    261    410    530    278    734     65
295                 984    877    295
```

we had to predict an alternative history based on a "what-if" analysis.

A recent political science study project identified a number of factors associated with the win or loss of a presidential election. These factors are incorporated into the program in Listing 9-8. To get a feel for its operation and to test its validity, load and run the program using historical data for a past

Table 9-13. Chi-Square Analysis of Votes.

1.	Walked	Didn't	Total
# Registered	29418	43024	73342
# Voting	17374	25018-	42392
Total	46792	68042	114834

Chi-Square = 1.54303 with 3 Degrees of Freedom
Density Function = .229104

2.	Walked	Didn't	Total
For Smith	9300	12013	21313
For Jones	7286	11950	19236
Total	16586	23963	40549

Chi-Square = 138.459 with 3 Degrees of Freedom
Density Function = 4.03227E-30

Table 9-14. Projected Voting Results.

Item	Precinct	Registered	Smith	12-Precinct	Difference	All Precincts	Difference
1	114	1972	763	686.805	76.1951	558.058	204.942
2	117	2011	892	693.978	198.022	569.958	322.042
3	227	1693	727	635.487	91.5128	473.476	253.524
4	233	2854	654	849.035	195.035	831.117	177.117
5	239	1909	456	675.217	219.217	538.872	82.8724
6	241	2886	751	854.921	103.921	841.162	90.1623
7	242	3130	1126	899.8	226.2	918.032	207.968
8	251	1801	698	655.352	42.6479	506.098	191.902
9	264	2383	483	762.402	279.402	684.329	201.329
10	269	2921	964	861.358	102.642	852.159	111.841
11	274	4324	1141	1119.42	21.5824	1300.38	159.38
12	275	1534	645	606.242	38.7582	425.744	219.256
13	136	1343	457	571.11	114.11	368.915	88.0855
14	215	1933	799	679.631	119.369	546.176	252.824
15	228	2373	535	760.562	225.562	681.236	146.236
16	234	2964	715	869.267	154.267	865.683	150.683
17	235	647	195	443.092	248.092	167.952	27.0478
18	237	2600	735	802.315	67.3154	751.703	16.7025
19	238	1094	231	525.311	294.311	295.78	64.7797
20	240	873	230	484.661	254.661	231.939	1.93925
21	243	2483	926	780.795	145.205	715.32	210.68
22	247	1034	211	514.275	303.275	278.339	67.3391
23	249	1571	598	613.047	15.0473	436.819	161.182
24	250	1573	594	613.415	19.4152	437.418	156.582
25	252	70	23	336.962	313.962	15.2957	7.70433
26	253	132	19	348.366	329.366	30.2958	11.2958
27	254	2694	626	819.605	193.605	781.026	155.026
28	255	1710	400	638.614	238.614	478.6	78.6002
29	260	2166	770	722.488	47.512	617.43	152.57
30	263	915	163	492.387	329.387	243.984	80.9843
31	265	1400	391	581.595	190.595	385.812	5.18793
32	266	1678	388	632.728	244.728	468.958	60.9575
33	267	890	239	487.788	248.788	236.809	2.19072
34	268	2113	524	712.74	188.74	601.167	77.1671
35	270	1902	822	673.929	148.071	536.744	285.256
36	273	1572	577	613.231	36.2313	437.118	139.882
37	344	2673	385	815.743	430.743	774.467	389.467
38	352	2003	363	692.507	329.507	567.516	204.516
39	382	618	97	437.758	340.758	159.856	62.8555

Listing 9-8. Picking a Winner.

```
1 '*********************************************
2 '*              Listing 9-8               *
3 '*           Picking a Winner             *
4 '*       After Lichtman & Keilis-Borak    *
5 '*********************************************
6 '
10 CLS:KEY OFF:PRINT "PICKING WINNERS":PRINT:PRI
NT
20 PRINT"DID THE PARTY IN POWER RECEIVE AT LEAST
 51 % OF THE POPULAR VOTE IN THE PREVIOUS ELECTI
ON?  (Y/N)   ";:GOSUB 450
30 GOSUB 470
```

```
40 PRINT"IS THE INCUMBENT PRESIDENT RUNNING FOR
RE-ELECTION?   (Y/N)    ";:GOSUB 450
50 GOSUB 470
60 IF Q$="Y" THEN 80
70 GOSUB 480:GOTO 100
80 PRINT"DID HE INITIATE MAJOR CHANGES IN NATION
AL POLICY?   (Y/N)    ";:GOSUB 450
90 GOSUB 470
100 PRINT"DID THE PARTY IN POWER ACHIEVE A MAJOR
 SUCCESS IN FOREIGN OR MILITARY POLICY?   (Y/N)
 ";:GOSUB 450
110 GOSUB 470
120 PRINT"IS ITS CANDIDATE CHARISMATIC OR A NATI
ONAL HERO?   (Y/N)    ";:GOSUB 450
130 GOSUB 470
140 PRINT"WAS THE YEARLY MEAN PER CAPITA RATE OF
 GROWTH IN REAL GROSS NATIONAL PRODUCT DURING TH
E INCUMBENT ADMINISTRATION EQUAL TO OR GREATER
THAN 1 PER CENT AND EQUAL TO OR GREATER THAN THA
T OF THE PREVIOUS 8 YEARS?   (Y/N)    ";
150 GOSUB 450
160 GOSUB 470
170 PRINT"WAS THERE A SERIOUS CONTEST FOR THE NO
MINATION OF THE INCUMBENT PARTY?   (Y/N)    ";
180 GOSUB 450
190 GOSUB 500
200 PRINT"WAS THERE A MAJOR THIRD PARTY OR INDEP
ENDENT CAMPAIGN ACTIVITY DURING THE ELECTION YEA
R?   (Y/N)    ";
210 GOSUB 450
220 GOSUB 500
230 PRINT"WAS THERE AN ELECTION YEAR RECESSION O
R DEPRESSION?   (Y/N)    ";
240 GOSUB 450
250 GOSUB 500
260 PRINT"WAS THERE MAJOR SOCIAL UNREST IN THE N
ATION DURING THE INCUMBENT ADMINISTRATION?   (Y/N
)    ";
270 GOSUB 450
280 GOSUB 500
290 PRINT"WAS THE INCUMBENT ADMINISTRATION TAINT
ED BY MAJOR SCANDAL?   (Y/N)    ";
300 GOSUB 450
310 GOSUB 500
320 PRINT"DID IT SUFFER A MAJOR SETBACK IN FOREI
GN OR MILITARY POLICY?   (Y/N)    ";
330 GOSUB 450
340 GOSUB 500
350 PRINT"IS THE CHALLENGING PARTY CANDIDATE CHA
RISMATIC OR WAR HERO?   (Y/N)    ";
360 GOSUB 450
370 GOSUB 500
380 CLS
390 LOCATE 8,1:PRINT"";
400 IF S>5 THEN 440
410 IF S=5 THEN 430
420 PRINT"THE INCUMBENT IS LIKELY TO WIN":GOTO 5
10
```

Listing 9-8. Picking a Winner. (Continued From Page 181.)

```
430 PRINT"THE OUTCOME IS UNCERTAIN":GOTO 510
440 PRINT"THE CHALLENGING CANDIDATE IS LIKELY TO
 WIN":GOTO 510
450 Q$=""+INKEY$:IF Q$="" THEN 450
460 PRINT Q$:PRINT:RETURN
470 IF Q$="Y" THEN 490
480 S=S+1
490 RETURN
500 IF Q$="N" THEN 490 ELSE 480
510 PRINT"(A)nother        (M)ain menu ";
520 GOSUB 540
530 IF Q$="A" OR Q$="a" THEN RUN 10 ELSE RUN "A:
MENU"
540 Q$=""+INKEY$:IF Q$="" THEN 540
550 RETURN
```

presidential election and see how well it works. If you're satisfied with the results, try it against the upcoming presidential election in 1988.

SUGGESTED READING

Backstrom, C. H. and G. D. Hursh, 1963. *Survey Research*. Minneapolis: Northwestern University Press.

Dixon, W.J. and F.J. Massey, 1951. *Introduction to Statistical Analysis*. New York: McGraw-Hill.

Festinger, L. and D. Katz (eds.), 1953. *Research Methods in the Behavioral Sciences*. New York: Dryden Press.

Selltiz, C. et al., 1965. *Research Methods in Social Relations (Revised)*. New York: Holt, Rinehart and Winston.

Chapter 10

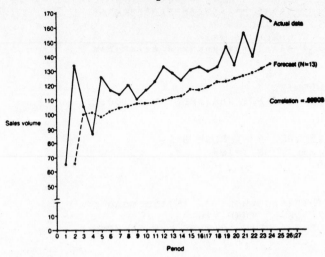

Economic Forecasting

Economic forecasting is one of the nation's favorite pastimes. Those of us longer on imagination than investment capital often "pick a stock," invest some play money, and watch our fortunes grow. The number of people who've made a fortune with "funny money" in a simulation, then have lost a fortune in real cash playing the same stock in real life, is unknown, but it must be considerable. The difficulty in accurately forecasting market behavior is illustrated in Listing 10-1. (A graph of the results is shown in Fig. 10-1).

The pattern generated is purely random, yet it suggests a convincing portrait of the stock market sales volume or prices. A number of different techniques have been applied to the analysis of stock market behavior by some very sophisticated analysts using powerful computers—all to little avail. If anyone has really found a universal stock market predictor, they're not talking. While there are analysts and counselors who have enjoyed a certain period of fame and fortune as a consequence of their forecasting, the only ones who have survived from decade to decade are those who employ well-known and more conservative approaches to the market. The lesson of their lives is to use a number of different analytical techniques, and combine that forecast with a lot of good common sense. Accordingly, this book does not support any global approach to forecasting the stock market, although it examines a few, but puts forth some of the more specialized tools for market analysis. The reader will have to supply the common sense evaluation of the analysis. In addition to the stock market, this chapter also deals with a number of business-related forecasting and estimating techniques. In all cases, the programs and equations used are believed to be correct and accurate for the purposes for which they are composed. Nonetheless, neither the author nor the publisher can assume any responsibility or liability for the consequences of investment decisions based on these routines.

STOCK MARKET ANALYSIS

Stock market analysis breaks down into two basic tasks, each of which has two subsets. The first aspect is total market forecasting. The assumption

Listing 10-1. Drunkard's Walk.

```
1 '**********************************************
2 '*                Listing 10-1                 *
3 '*                Drunkard's Walk              *
4 '**********************************************
5 '
10 SCREEN 2
20 CLS:KEY OFF:RANDOMIZE
30 LOCATE 3,1:PRINT"";:INPUT"VARIABLE";V:Y=100:C
LS
40 FOR X=1 TO 640
50 A=RND(X):IF A<.5 THEN B=-1 ELSE B=1
60 Y=Y+(B*V):IF Y>199 THEN Y=199
70 IF Y<0 THEN Y=0
80 PSET(X,200-Y)
90 NEXT X
100 LOCATE 1,1:PRINT"(A)nother        (M)ain menu";
110 Q$=""+INKEY$:IF Q$="" THEN 110
120 IF Q$="A" OR Q$="a" THEN 10 ELSE RUN "A:MENU
"
```

is that as a whole market goes, so go individual stocks. The second aspect is individual stock forecasting. In each of these approaches is the concept of long and short-term forecasting. The techniques used to do a short-term forecast are not necessarily those used for the long-term forecast, and vice-versa. From a proper historical perspective, we can see long-term growth in both market and individual stock values, yet, within that overall pattern, a more microscopic analysis reveals hectic periods of heart-stopping plunges in price and volume. A technique that reliably gives forecasts one or two hundred years in advance is useful only in corporate and estate planning. To the individual with an expected

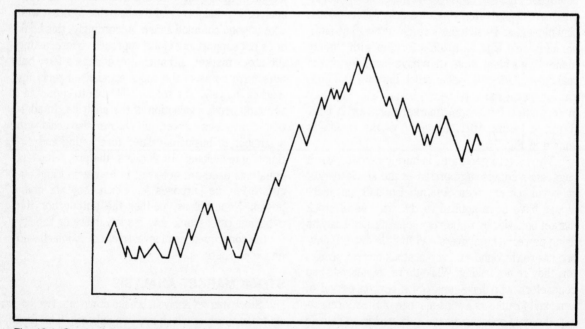

Fig. 10-1. Graph of the "Drunkard's Walk."

adult economic life of only forty years or so century-long cycles are only of nominal interest. Within the foregoing framework, then, here are some techniques that may be useful.

Long-Term Market Analysis

Figure 10-2 illustrates the composite market behavior for the last 160 years based on several governmental sources. The overall impression is one of long-term growth, which is the objective of a healthy capitalist economy. Without growth there is little incentive for investment, the basis of the market, and with too much growth per unit of time, values become unrealistic and investment risky beyond an acceptable level. Conservative economists generally agree a growth rate of 4 to 6 percent annually results in comfortable and workable market conditions. A rough evaluation of the data in Fig. 10-2 suggests a long-term growth, since 1800, of

about 46566.67 percent. Assuming there will be no further historical surprises, such as a world war or total loss of petroleum supplies, it is not unreasonable to conclude that the trend line of the overall market performance will continue the pattern established in the past few decades. The distance between this rather presumptuous observation and a wise investment strategy is incredibly long, however. The only utility of such a trend line is to suggest the direction or level the market might seek at a point in time, provided there are no other more significant market forces or predictors operating. It is a level to which the market will eventually float, but only after some rather dramatic exceptions to the trend.

Virtually every budding market analyst has approached the problem of analyzing these data for the purpose of discovering the underlying cycles that may be present in the long-term trend. They assume that all significant market purchases are based on

Fig. 10-2. Generalized market performance, 1800-1950.

rational analysis (assuming the volume of investments made by the insane and irrational are insignificant) of commonly-held information, and therefore, that the market behavior will vary in direct proportion to the natural variations in the underlying forces to which the market responds. These forces include weather patterns, population growth, technological innovations, and so forth. While it is probably true that investors tend to look at such things for guidance, it is clear that interpretations as to the significance of each of these components vary as widely as the number of analysts. As a result, one analyst will panic and sell at the same time another analyst is mortgaging his home to raise investment capital. The net effect, frequently, is a confusing pattern similar to the Drunkard's Walk in Listing 10-1. The basic principle, however, is to select a period of time, compute the basic trend line for the included data, and use this line as the level to which the market will move. The difference between the poor and the rich, in this effort, is the skill and accuracy with which one selects the period to be analyzed.

It is for such an effort the smoothing and decomposition techniques in Chapter 6 are useful. While we will avoid recommending a specific period for analysis, we think it prudent to consider data in some historical perspective. That is, it is probably counterproductive to compute a two-hundred-year trend line. First of all, there is no single source of indexed or standardized data. Second, the technologies driving the industrial component of the market no longer compete in the same relationships. For example, the demand for leather for buggy whips has given way to the demand for plastics for steering wheels. Third, political realities, both national and global, have altered economic forces. The current level of foreign aid spending creates a market influence that just didn't exist in the year 1800. Fourth, while we can compute some sort of index, as we did in Fig. 10-2, it is really more of a "guesstimate" than a precise measure. One method of index pricing is the *market basket* technique in which a specified set of commodities is periodically priced.

If the price of bread and milk doubles in ten years, the theory goes, so has everything else.

While the actual components of the basket are actually much more extensive than bread and milk, the shortcomings of the technique remain: the production factors to produce the components are not consistent, nor is the relative utility of the components to each other. When the price of a given commodity changes, does it reflect a basic change in the overall market or just in a limited aspect of it? When the price of bread goes up, is that due to an inflationary increase throughout the economy, or is it due to a crop failure? These questions are difficult enough within a fifty-year period, let alone in a period lasting a couple of centuries.

Nonetheless, there are a broad variety of statistical and mathematical techniques with which we may evaluate short- and long-term economic trends and events. Before proceeding, however, we need to examine some basic mathematics considerations relevant to economics.

BUSINESS MATHEMATICS

There is a whole branch of mathematics that frequently gets poor coverage in standard math courses in our public schools: business mathematics. The mainline courses avoid deep study of the subject as a biology teacher might avoid woodworking during the study of trees. Even in business math courses the concentration is on accounting practices and the routines below remain relatively neglected. So, this section is for those readers who went to the same school the author did or one like it. It covers the areas of interest, annuities, amortization, bond values, return on investment, selling price, goodwill, and breakeven points—all essential components in the forecasting of business trends and decision making.

Interest

At the heart of many of the routines involving time and money is the simple expression: $(1 + r)^n$. We commonly see this in the equation for compound interest: $A = P(1 + 4)^n$, where A is the future total of an account that starts with the principal amount, P, and has an interest rate of r paid to it in each of n periods. This section deals with the various forms of the expression and the wide variety of applications to which it can be put.

The first task is to compute the remaining terms of the compound interest equation. By simple division, the equation is solved to P as: $P = A/(1 + r)^n$. To solve for n is a little more tedious, but it becomes:

$$n = \frac{\text{Log } (A/P)}{\text{Log}(1 + R)}$$

The solution for r becomes:

$$r = \sqrt[n]{A/P} - 1.$$

The basic equation for simple interest is: $A = P(1 + nr)$. The solution for the various parts of this form are straightforward and avoid some of the problems of the exponential math of compound interest. The following equations summarize the procedures used to deal with interest.

Interest Equations

Compound

1. $A = P(1 + r)^r$
2. $P = A/(1 + r)^n$
3. $n = \text{Log}(A/P)/\text{Log}(1 + r)$
4. $r = \sqrt[n]{A/P} - 1$

Simple

1. $A = P(1 + nr)$
2. $P = A/(1 + nr)$
3. $n = (A/P - 1)/r$
4. $r = (A/P - 1)/n$

Annuities

An annuity is the payment of a fixed sum of money over a period of time. This can be a payment into a savings or investment account, a payment received from a bank or investment account, or a combination of both. The compound interest equations above might be taken as a special case of an annuity with one payment. If an item we want to buy costs $200.00 and we have $100.00, how long must we wait to accumulate $200.00 in a savings account paying seven percent interest? $A = 200$, $P = 100$, $r = 7/(12 \times 100) = .0058333$:

$n = \log (A/P)/\log(1 + r)$

= log(200/200)/log(1.0058333)

= .693147 / .005816

= 119.1714686 or 119 months, 5+ days

The only problem is that we don't want to wait nearly twenty years to buy the item, and the seller will not guarantee the price for more than twelve months. Since the bank won't budge on the interest rate, what amount must we deposit in order to accumulate the $200.00 within twelve months? $A = 200$, $r = .0058333$, $n = 12$:

$$P = A / (1 + r)^a$$
$$= 200 / 1.0058333^a$$
$$= 200 / 1.0722897$$
$$= 186.52$$

This is still no good: we don't have the $186.52, either. We do have, however, a steady income and can put a little into savings. The question now is how much must we put into the bank each month so that it accumulates to the needed $200.00? This is the amount of the annuity. The fund that is built is called a *sinking fund*, an amount established or accumulated for a special future purpose. The purpose is based on the basic equations:

$$A = S\left(\frac{(1 + r)^n - 1}{r}\right) \qquad S = A\left(\frac{r}{(1 + r)^n - 1}\right)$$

In these equations, A is the amount accumulated after n payments of S each have been paid into an account paying r interest. Continuing the example above, $A = 200$, $r = .0058333$, $n = 12$.

$$S = A\left(\frac{r}{(1 + r)^n - 1}\right)$$

$$= 200\left(\frac{.005833}{1.005833^n - 1}\right)$$

$$= 200 (.005833 / .0722858)$$
$$= 200 \times .0806934 = 16.13868$$

Since payments must be either $16.13 or $16.14, we should compute eleven payments and subtract this sum from $200.00 to compute the last payment: $n = 11$, $S = 16.14$, $r = .0058333$.

$$A = S\ \frac{(1 + r)^n - 1}{r}$$

$$= 16.14\ \left(\frac{1.0058333^n - 1}{.0058333}\right)$$

$$= 16.14\ (.0660674\ /\ .0058333)$$
$$= 16.14 \times 11.325912 = 182.80022$$

The last payment, then, is equal to 200.00 less 182.80 plus the interest on 182.80 for the twelfth month:

$$LP = 200 - (182.80 \times 1.005833) = 200 - 183.87$$
$$= 16.13$$

If we can afford to put away $16.14 for eleven months and make a final payment of $16.13, we can have the $200.00 item within twelve months. If we can afford to put the $100.00 we have on hand into the account at the beginning, the adjusted equation becomes:

$$S = (A - (P\ (1 + r)^n))\ \left(\frac{r}{(1 + r)^n - 1}\right)$$

$$= (200 - (100 \times 1.005833^n))\ \left(\frac{.005833}{1.005833^n - 1}\right)$$

$$= (200 - (100 \times 1.0722897))\ (.005833/.0722897)$$

$$= (200 - 107.22897) \times .0806934 = 7.49$$

For a total investment of $189.88 (100 + 12 × 7.49), or so, we can buy a $200.00 item. These computations have led us through the evaluation of the amount of an annuity. There is another side to annuities in which our concern is not with putting money into an account, but in periodic withdrawals from an account. These lead us into the present values of annuities.

We are most familiar with this type of annuity from pension programs. At a certain moment, we begin receiving a certain amount of money from an account and will receive this sum either until we die (from a perpetual account) or for a specified number of payments, such as a series of hospitalization payments received from an insurance company for a limited time. With the advent of IRA retirement accounts, more and more people will find these equations useful for computing relevant data. For example, we want to establish a retirement account that will pay us a certain amount (S) for 25 years, assuming that will be sufficient for our retired years (we also disregard inflation for the time being). We need to compute how large an account is required to support 300 (12 × 25) payments of S each, starting N months from now. The equations for the present value of an annuity are:

$$A = S\left(\frac{1 - (1 + r)^{-n}}{r}\right)\qquad S = A\left(\frac{r}{1 - (1 + r)^{-n}}\right)$$

If we want a monthly annuity of $1000, and our bank pays seven percent annual interest, the amount we need to start our retirement fund is:

$$A = S\ \left(\frac{1 - (1 + r)^{-n}}{r}\right)$$

$$= 1000\ \left(\frac{1 - 1.005833^{-n}}{.005833}\right)$$

$$= 1000\ \left(\frac{1 - .1745771}{.005833}\right) = 1000\ \left(\frac{.8253229}{.005833}\right)$$

$$= 1000 \times 141.4847349 = 141484.73$$

$141,484.73! Wow, that's a lot of cash! Or is it? The answer depends on how much time we have to accumulate it. If we're 64 and plan to retire at 65, then it is probably a tough problem. On the other hand, if we have thirty or forty years, then it probably is possible to achieve. Let's see. A = 141484.75, r = .005833, n = 420 (12 × 35). From the amount of an annuity:

$$S = A\ \left(\frac{r}{(1 + r)^n - 1}\right)$$

$$= 141484.73\ \left(\frac{.005833}{1.005833^n - 1}\right)$$

$$= 141484.73 \left(\frac{.005833}{10.50599}\right)$$

$$= 141484.73 \times .0005552355 = 78.55734$$

There it is: 420 monthly payments of $78.56 each will provide a retirement account of at least $141,484.73, from which 300 monthly annuity payments of $1000.00 can be paid.

Now, for purpose of example, let's assume that $78.56 is just too much, that all we can afford is $50.00 a month. Using the basic equation, this will yield a retirement account of $90,051.87. To determine the pension annuity available, we use these values and the second equation: A = 90051.87, n = 300, r = .005833.

$$S = A \left(\frac{r}{1 - (1 + r)^{-n}}\right)$$

$$= 90051.87 \left(\frac{.0058333}{1 - 1.0058333^{-n}}\right)$$

$$= 90051.87 \left(\frac{.0058333}{.82533853}\right)$$

$$= 90051.87 \times .0070674 = 636.43$$

It is now for you to decide whether $636.43 is sufficient for your needs and if not, whether you can find a better savings interest rate or increase the dollar amount of the investment annuity. The task of determining the interest rate necessary to yield the desired $141,484.73 is more complicated than the preceding procedures. There is no straightforward equation that says, given S, n, and A, r = ... Rather, r must be approximated by a trial and error method that, eventually, causes one of the equations to yield the desired values. The basic algorithm is:

1. Establish the values for S, A, and n.
2. Establish a trial value for r and Δ r.
3. Compute a trial value for A (AX) using one of the appropriate annuity equations.
4. If the value of AX is less than A, then go to step 5a, otherwise, go to step 5b.
5a. Add Δ r to r. Go to step 3.
5b. Subtract Δ r from r. Reduce the size of Δ

r by dividing by 2 or some similar number. If Δ r is smaller than, for example, .000001, then go to step 6, otherwise, go to step 5a.

6. The current value of r is a reasonable approximation of the true r yielding the desired values. Proceed with balance of work.

To improve the accuracy of r, simply make the Δ r limit factor in step 5b smaller. Using the algorithm above, the retirement problem is recomputed to determine the interest rate required to yield a retirement account equal to $141,484.73, S = 50, n = 420, r = .005, Δ r(Δr) = .001.

$$AX = 50 \left(\frac{2.006^n - 1}{.006}\right)$$

$$AX = 94461.35: \text{too small. Increase } r$$
$$r = r + \Delta r = .006 + .001 = .007$$

$$AX = 50 \left(\frac{1.007^n - 1}{.007}\right)$$

$$AX = 126593.53: \text{still too small. Increase } r$$
$$r = .008$$

$$AX = 50 \left(\frac{1.008^n - 1}{.008}\right)$$

$$AX = 171292.98: \text{too large. Reduce } r \text{ and } \Delta r$$
$$r = r - \Delta r + (\Delta r/2) \text{ and } \Delta r = \Delta r/2$$
$$r = .0075 \quad \Delta r = .0005$$

Continue with this process until Δr is smaller than .000001 and r has approached .007373 (8.8456 annual interest rate).

So, if we can find a bank or an investment opportunity that will guarantee us an annual interest rate of at least 8.8456 percent per year, payable monthly, then we can still achieve our objective.

The worst case would be when no such interest rate can be found. Then we need to readjust our retirement date so that we can increase the number of $50.00 payments into the account that pays at seven percent. The period of an annuity, n, can be found from:

$$n = \frac{\log (1 + (r(A/S)))}{\log (1 + r)}$$

Using A = 141484.73, S = 50, r = .0058333:

$$n = \frac{\log (1 + (.005833 \,(141484.73/50)\,))}{\log 1.0058333}$$

$$= \frac{\log 27.506458}{\log 1.0058333} = 492.158977 \text{ months}$$

This result means that a savings period of better than 492 months, or 42 years is required. Starting age thirty, retirement must be put off until age seventy-one. There is a fallacy here though. At the beginning of this example, we made the assumption that allowing for twenty-five years of retirement would be sufficient. Although we have control over a number of the variables in such a routine, life-expectancy is not an easily controlled variable. We should stay with the expectation of death at or before age 90. Accordingly, at age seventy-one, the amount required for the retirement account is not $141,484.73, but $126,648.58. By reducing the amount required, we also reduce the time necessary to accumulate it—in this case, to 474.26 months, 39 years and 6+ months. And so on. What we have established as constants are the variables S, which is equal to 50, and r, which is equal to .0058333, and the total number of periods for investment and retirement, which is equal to 720. As with interest rates, we must go through an iterative process to compute the number of periods of investment necessary to reach an amount sufficient to support the desired pension annuity. The process to do this is based on this equation:

$$Si = Sa \left(\frac{1 - (1+r)^{-n_2}}{r} \right) \left(\frac{r}{(1+r)^n - 1} \right)$$

This equation is written as part of an iterative process in which a trial value of n is varied until the value of Si that is equal to or less than the periodic investment ceiling is obtained.

A similar set of problems can be resolved with a set of equations known as *double annuities*. They are:

$$S' = S'' \left(\frac{(1 + r1)^n - 1}{1 - (1 + r2)^{-n}} \right)$$

$$S'' = S' \left(\frac{1 - (1 + r2)^{-n^2}}{(1 + r1)^n - 1} \right)$$

where S' is the payment for the investment and S'' is the annuity returned from the account.

Perpetual annuities are those that continue without a termination point, n2 = infinity. This is the same as living on the interest earned on a principal amount A. If r is the available interest, then S'' = A × r and A = S''/r. Also, S'' = S' ((1 + r1)^r - 1).

Amortization

The process of computing amortization figures is very similar to annuities, especially amortizations such as those used in computing mortgage payments, car payments, and the like. The three basic equations involved in this process are:

1. $S = \dfrac{P\, r\, (1 + r)^n}{(1 + r)^n - 1}$

2. $A = \dfrac{S(\,(1 + r)^n - 1\,)}{r\, (1 + r)^n}$

3. $n = \log (S/(S - (A \times r)\,)\,) / \log (1 + r)$

where P is the amount to be financed.

The value of the interest rate, given the values for n, A, and S, is determined through an iterative process. From these equations we can also compute the sum of payments from n × S, total interest paid from (n × S) − P, and so forth.

To demonstrate these equations, let's compute the monthly payments on a car where P = 10000, n = 36, and r = .011667 (14% annually):

$$S = \frac{P\, r\, (1 + r)^n}{(1 + r)^n - 1}$$

$$S = \frac{10000 \times .0116667 \times 1.0116667^n}{1.0116667^n - 1}$$

$$S = \frac{116.667 \times 1.518267795}{.518267795} = 341.7765$$

The car payment is $341.78. If this value is too high, it can be reduced by either extending the number of payments, n, or reducing the amount financed, P, or the interest rate, r, or a combination of these actions.

A principle of the foregoing procedure is that the interest due and payable is computed on the current unpaid balance of the principal. As the unpaid balance declines, the amount paid in interest declines. For this reason, the first few years of ownership of a car or house are the most fruitful for tax purposes since most of the payment will go against the tax-deductible interest payment. In the later years, the situation is reversed. While the payment is the same, the larger part of the payment goes against the unpaid balance and the smaller is paid on the interest due.

To compute the unpaid balance (B) after k payments, we use:

$$B = S \, \frac{1 - (1 - r)^{-x}}{r}$$

where $x = n - k$.

The kth payment at which B is a specified amount is given in:

$$K = \frac{\log S - \log (S - (B \times r))}{\log (1 + r)}$$

In addition to the procedure just described, there are at least three other ways to amortize notes or loans. Two of them, not commonly used these days, are the *add-on* and *discount* notes. The third is the popular *revolving* or *declining balance* approach.

Add-on and Discount Notes. The names of these notes refer to the point in the loan transaction when the interest fee is added to the principal. In the add-on technique, the interest is computed and added to the principal before the payment amount is computed. As a consequence, each monthly payment contains a constant amount for interest and principal. In the discount technique, the interest is computed and subtracted from the principal prior to the computation of the monthly payment. Payments, therefore, are made against the principal only; the interest having been paid in advance. The equations used in these approaches are:

Add-On Notes	Discount Notes
1. $S = \dfrac{P\,r\,n + P}{n}$	$S = \dfrac{P - P\,r}{n}$

2. $n = \dfrac{P}{S - P\,r}$ $n = \dfrac{P - P\,r}{S}$

3. $P = \dfrac{S\,n}{r\,n + 1}$ $P = \dfrac{S\,n}{1 - r}$

4. $r = \dfrac{S\,n - P}{P\,n}$ $r = 1 - \dfrac{S\,n}{P}$

5. $C = P$ $C = P - P\,r$

where S = monthly payment, P = principal, n = number of payments, r = interest rate per payment, and C = cash advanced to customer.

Declining Balance Method. This is the technique used in most revolving credit systems in which the monthly payment is a percentage of the current unpaid balance. The unpaid balance is normally the unpaid principal plus the amount of interest on this principal. If r_1 is the interest rate and r_2 is the payment percentage, the payment due (S) on a starting balance of P is:

$$S = r_2 \, (P \, (1 + r_1))$$

If n is the number of payments that have been made on a regular basis, the current unpaid balance (B) is:

$$B = P \, ((1 + r_1) - r_2)^n$$

There are a number of amortization routines available and the following is one more. It's a routine that facilitates an amortization schedule of a house loan as easily as that of a car. It makes provisions for depreciation (or appreciation) of the asset, as well as down payments. The input values include: sales price (include tax), down payment, life span of asset in years, interest rate, and number of monthly payments. The printed output of the program includes the monthly mortgage payment, the sum of the payments, total interest paid, current depreciated (appreciated) value, net equity, and unpaid balance on loan until paid off. It includes a graphic display of the unpaid balance, current value, and net equity.

The depreciation routine used is the *Variable Rate Declining Balance* method expressed in the equation:

$$V = P\left(1 - \frac{R\,k}{L}\right)$$

where V = value, P = original value, R = depreciation (appreciation) factor, L = life span of asset, and k = current age of asset (in same units as L).

If the asset depreciates, as in most automobiles, use a positive value for R. For cars, a value between .50 and 1.75 is about right. For assets which appreciate in value, use a negative value. If you think you know how much the asset should be (V) after a certain number of years (k), you can estimate R from:

$$R = L(1 - V / P)$$

We use this method for computing depreciation (appreciation) because it seems to present the most realistic curves. Straight line depreciation is the easiest to compute, but has few real-life counterparts. If the depreciation figures are to be used in an effort to evaluate tax options, it is suggested you use IRS-approved life spans for the given asset and the depreciation factors identified in official IRS documents.

Bonds

Bonds are a means by which a corporation raises capital. They are, in effect, fancy promissory notes, normally issued in multiples of $1000 each and are designed to be marketable for resale. For the life of the bond, anywhere from a few months to as long as fifty years or more, interest on the bond will be paid periodically, usually every six months. At the maturity of the bond, the face value or principal is paid. Frequently, the bond contains a provision which gives the seller the right to *call* the bond prior to the normal maturity date at some agreed upon price.

Buyers of bonds are primarily concerned with the return on investment or *yield to maturity* (YTM) of their bonds or that of bonds offered for sale. There are two ways to compute YTM. An approximation is quickly computed from:

1. $C = \dfrac{1000X}{M}$

2. $YTM = \dfrac{2 C}{P + M} + \dfrac{M^n}{P} - 1$

Where X is the total annual interest income, M is the maturity value of the bond, P is the selling price of the bond, and n is the life of the bond in years.

There is a more accurate way to compute the YTM. In the algorithm below, the iteration makes an estimate of the selling price as a function of the maturity value and the annual interest rate. The iteration continues until the estimate closely matches the actual selling price. The assumption is that the value of r used to compute the estimate is equal to the yield.

1. Set r and Δr (Δr) equal to some arbitrary value, normally .01.
2. Compute X, the estimate of price, from:

$$X = \frac{M}{(1 + r)^n} + C \, \frac{(1 + r)^n - 1}{r \, (1 + r)^n}$$

3. If X is larger than P, go to step 4b, otherwise, go to step 4a.
4a. $r = r + \Delta r$, go to step 2.
4b. $r = r - \Delta r$. $\Delta r = \Delta r/2$. If Δr is greater than .0000001, go to step 4a, otherwise, go to step 5.
5. r is approximately equal to YTM.

Additional bond-related equations include:

Present value: $A1 = M (1 + r)^n$
Present value of interest payments:

$$A2 = r M \, \frac{1 - (1 + r)^{-n}}{r}$$

Value of bond: $V = A1 + A2$

Listing 10-2 deals with bond values and equations.

GOODWILL

The procedures to compute goodwill are as varied and as many as there are accountants poring over corporate financial statements. Nonetheless, the basic function of goodwill is as a component in evaluating the worth of a company, especially when the company is being sold. The computation, regardless of the process, is an effort to estimate the difference between two otherwise equally established businesses. For example, Joe and Sam both establish a produce store on the same street with the same amount of capital investment, more or less. Several years later, Joe's store earns a gross income of $93,500 annually, while Sam's store grosses

Listing 10-2. Bond Values.

```
1 '*************************************************
2 '*                 Listing 10-2             *
3 '*                 Bond Values              *
4 '*************************************************
5 '
10 CLS:KEY OFF
20 INPUT"WHAT IS THE CURRENT PRICE OF THE BOND "
;P
30 INPUT"WHAT IS THE MATURITY VALUE OF THE BOND"
;M
40 INPUT"WHAT IS THE AMOUNT OF THE ANNUAL INTERE
ST PAYMENT";X
50 C=X/(M/1000):INPUT"FOR HOW MANY YEARS IS THE
BOND";N
60 Y=((2*C)/(P+M))+((M/P)^(1/N))-1
70 PRINT"THE APPROXIMATE YIELD TO MATURITY (YTM)
 = ";Y*100;" %"
80 PRINT:R=.01:DR=.01
90 X=(M/((1+R)^N))+(C*((((1+R)^N)-1)/(R*((1+R)^N
))))
100 IF P>X THEN 120
110 R=R+DR:GOTO 90
120 R=R-DR:DR=DR/2:IF DR>.000001 THEN 110
130 PRINT:PRINT
140 PRINT"(A)nother        (M)ain menu ";
150 Q$=""+INKEY$:IF Q$="" THEN 150
160 IF Q$="A" OR Q$="a" THEN RUN 10 ELSE RUN "A:
MENU"
```

$87,200. All other things being equal, we would say Joe enjoys $6,300 worth of goodwill. In real life, things are not quite that neat. A portion of Joe's superior profits may be due more to a superior location than his sparkling personality. In any event, one procedure for computing goodwill is found in:

$$G = \frac{E - Ar}{R}$$

where E = estimated annual future earning, A = fair market value of assets exclusive of goodwill, r = normal industry rate of return on net assets, and R = 1/number of years earnings have been in excess of the industry norm.

Use the following values for the example above: both men have about $25,000 in net assets; Joe has earned an excess above the industry norm for the last three years as has Sam for the last two; the industry return on net assets is 3.25. The goodwill for the two stores can thus be computed from:

$$\text{Joe} = \frac{93200 - (25000 \times 3.25)}{1 / 3}$$

$$= \frac{93200 - 81250}{.333333}$$

$$= \$35,850.00$$

$$\text{Sam} = \frac{87500 - (25000 \times 3.25)}{1 / 2}$$

$$= \frac{87500 - 81250}{.500}$$

$$= \$12,500.00$$

Joe's $35,850 is a composite of his personality and location, to the extent all other characteristics are normal. What part is location and what part is Joe is hard to determine. Only if Joe and Sam swap stores could we begin to sort out the answer. In any event, bankers are reluctant to loan significant sums on goodwill alone, especially in the event of the sale of a property in which the owner/manager (Joe) will not stay on to perpetuate the goodwill. It is, nonetheless, an acceptable measure of the health of a business. It is easily computed for small business with a single location and limited staff. In an event of major corporations with multinational facilities and operations, there are many other statistical tools for evaluation.

Return on Investment (ROI)

Investors use ROI to gauge how well an investment is proceeding or how likely a potential investment will prove worthwhile. It is a rate of return as a percentage of the amount invested. Corporations also use ROI as a measure of their success (or failure) in the market place. A simple approach is to compute ROI from:

$$ROI = 100 ((A/P) - 1)$$

in which A represents the proceeds from a sale and P is the cost of the asset sold.

For example, if John buys a house for $69,500 and sells it at a later date for $81,000, the ROI is 16.5468 percent. An alternative approach is to use the amount of interest equation reviewed earlier in this section: $4 = A / P - 1$, from $A = P (1 + r)^n$, where r is the ROI. Using the same data, and assuming John owned the house one year, the ROI is computed to be the same 16.5468. On the other hand, if he held the house four years, $n = 4$, the ROI is computed to be only 3.9023 percent. The first approach gives John an estimate of the growth of his investment. Conversely, with a given investment amount (P), the user can compute the maximum length of time to hold an asset and still maintain an acceptable profit margin from: $n = (\log A/P)/(\log(1 + 4))$. The second approach allows him to compare the house investment with other investment options.

In a corporate setting the variables are much more complex and ROI is more easily computed as:

$$ROI = \frac{Sales - Related\ Expenses}{[((N1 - L1) + (N2 - L2)) /2]}$$

where N and L are assets and liabilities, N1 meaning the beginning assets and L2 the end of period liabilities.

This approach is, in effect, a method to determine the ratio between net sales revenue to average net worth.

Selling Price

The following equations are useful in the computation of selling prices (s):

1. $S = C(1 + R)$ Mark up on cost

2. $S = \dfrac{C}{1 - R}$ Mark up based on price

3. $S = \dfrac{C}{1 = (R + r)}$ Mark up on price w/comm.

4. $S = \dfrac{C (1 + R)}{(1 - r)}$ Mark up on cost w/ comm.

where R is the mark up percentage, r is the salesman's commission, and C is the item cost.

For example, Harry's Furniture store has a policy of marking prices up 60% over wholesale (R = .60). At the beginning of the year, Harry decides to put his sales staff on a straight commission basis, paying 15% (r = .15). A new line of chairs has been delivered which have a $50.00 wholesale price. What price must Harry charge to maintain his normal margin? Using equation number 4:

$$S = \frac{C (1 + R)}{1 - r}$$
$$= \frac{50 \times 1.60}{.85} = 112.9411765$$

Harry will normally price the $50.00 chair (wholesale) at $112.94. So long as he keeps the actual selling price at C/(1-r), or in this case $58.82, or more, he will at least break even on the sale. In the long run he must do better than that to meet other expenses related to the operation of the store, but on individual sales he has the $54.11 margin to bargain with.

Breakeven Points

Many business ventures begin with a rosy glow of adventure and big profits. At the end of the first bill-paying session, however, the owners start looking for ways to avoid bankruptcy. In well-managed businesses, new ventures begin with estimates of sales volumes necessary to meet all expenses related to the starting up of the new venture and those related to the sale of the product. Another phase in the preliminary planning is an estimate of the market for the product. If the break-even point is determined to be 100 units and market analysis can only support optimism for the sale of 25 units, the wise (or conservative) business will terminate development of the new product. We believe this is an area where considerable fortunes are made and lost (it also forms a large part of the justification for this book!) In real life the break-even requirement is likely to be more like 3945 units while the market analysis suggests a market demand of something like 3925 or 3965. That one-half percent sampling error can make or break a struggling new company (and some long-established ones, too) and give executives a lot of gray hair.

There are two equations available for the determination of break-even points. They both require the input to be in dollars (or other monetary units). The first produces a break-even point in dollars (or other monetary units), while the second gives the point in units of the item to be sold. One is essentially equivalent to the other. The user selects the one which is more useful.

1. $B = \dfrac{\text{Total fixed costs}}{1 - \dfrac{\text{Total variable costs}}{\text{Corresponding sales volume}}}$

2. $B = \dfrac{\text{Total fixed costs}}{\text{Selling price - variable cost per unit}}$

For example, Harry has constant annual expenses totaling $75,000. These include the wages of the warehouse crew and the secretarial staff, plus rent and utilities. If he sells only those ugly $50 chairs, his break-even analysis looks like this:

$$B = \frac{\text{Total fixed costs}}{\text{Selling price - variable cost per unit}}$$

$$= \frac{75000}{112.94 - 50}$$

$$= 75000/62.94 = 1191.6111058 \text{ chairs}$$

Harry must sell at least 1192 chairs (no fractional chairs, please) to break even. If his own income is included in the $75,000, then he will survive the year; otherwise, Harry will have to sell some more chairs.

Total fixed costs consist of all the costs associated with the project that are not unit item-related; that is, plant construction and tooling costs, design costs, and other similar investments. Variable costs are unit item-related. These include the cost of materials, labor, transportation of the product, and administrative costs directly related to each item sale. Whether a cost is fixed or variable is determined by the answer to the question: does the amount vary with the number of units sold? That is, is the cost (Y) a function of the number of units sold (X) as in: $Y = A + BX$? If so, then the cost is a variable cost, not fixed.

METHODS OF STOCK MARKET ANALYSIS

As noted in the beginning of this chapter, Fig. 10-2 illustrates a generalized summary of market prices or their rough equivalent since 1800. Visual inspection suggests, and mathematical analysis confirms, that the data conform to a logarithmic trend. Based on the data in Fig. 10-2, 1900 to 1970, the equation takes on the form:

$$\text{Log } Y = 3.839093 + .341027 X$$
$$r = .924022$$
$$X = \text{year}$$

By projecting ahead, we can forecast the average industrial average to be 1000 in the year 1979, 2000 in the year 2000, 4000 in the year 2020, and so forth. But what does all this mean?

If the average stock price does continue to follow the pattern suggested by historical data, we must also note that wages and investment income, the primary means by which we purchase stocks, will rise to keep some sort of pace with the prices. If they don't, it is inevitable that prices would rise above a point where anyone could purchase the stocks. At that point the stocks become valueless! A thing is worth only what people can and will pay for them. Artwork may rise in value to a point beyond which most of us can afford. Some artwork may even become so esteemed that no meaningful value can be attributed to the object and no one, then, has the means to purchase the object. Stocks, on the other hand, however handsome their certificates may be, are not works of art to be held in awe and at a distance, but are the fundamental tools of the marketplace. A dynamic capitalist marketplace requires that the prices of stocks (partial ownership in business and the source of new capital) must remain with a certain relationship to the means to acquire these stocks. No sale of stocks yields no new capital, and therefore, no new growth. As economic growth slows, the ability of businesses to pay wages or dividends also decreases. As a consequence, there will be fewer resources available for stock purchases. Prices, therefore, should increase by some identifiable rate. Failure to maintain this relationship ultimately leads to a situation in which prices are high, relative to income, but sales volumes are very low. It seems logical, then, that wages can be expected to rise according to some exponential rate and that prices will rise ahead of wages/income for a period, until they have exceeded some market threshold, stabilize for a time, until income rises to a point where the price/income ratio is again "reasonable," then the prices will again begin to rise, and the cycle will repeat.

Left unattended, one might expect this model to develop to a point where actual prices are stated in such large terms as to be unwieldly; e.g., in the tens of thousands of dollars for an average share of stock. At that point it might be prudent to issue new currency, restating the new monetary unit as a fraction of the old. $1.00 new would buy what $1,000 old did, but the computations would be much simpler. After one year growth at 10 percent, $1,000 would grow to $1,100. After revaluation, the price would grow from $1.00 to $1.10. The rate of growth is the same, 10 percent, but the numerical expression is easier to handle, mathematically. Politically, it may be more difficult to coax the population into believing $1 now is still the same as $1,000, but that's not the concern of the forecaster.

The primary significance of this long-term analysis is to predict where income and prices will ultimately head. It is understood that there will be periods of uncertain duration where both prices and income will deviate significantly from the long-term trend. The computed trend line is, however, not preordained, but simply a function of available historical data. As each day passes, that day's data becomes a part of the database upon which such computations are based. A more accurate approach will make a provision for the inclusion of new data. Listing 10-3 is a routine to compute least squares trend lines, much like the programs in Chapter 5. The difference is that the routine begins with the accumulated historical data, then continues by a daily input of new data. At each entry point the trend line is recomputed and new forecasts made.

An alternative to this approach are the routines found in Chapter 6 for moving averages, exponential smoothing, and other time-series analysis.

Listing 10-3. Economic Curve Fitting.

```
1 '*********************************************
2 '*              Listing 10-3               *
3 '*          Economic Curve Fitting         *
4 '*********************************************
5 '
10 CLS
20 PRINT"******   ECONOMIC CURVE FITTING   *****
*"
30 PRINT:PRINT"THIS ROUTINE ACCEPTS THE DATA IN
PAIRED X,Y FORMAT AND ATTEMPTS TO  IDENTIFY THEB
EST LINEAR OR CURVE FIT.  IT ALSO PROVIDES AN ES
TIMATE OF THE COEFFICIENT OF  CORRELATION.":PRI
NT
40 PRINT:INPUT"ENTER NUMBER OF PAIRS:";N:DIM XY(
N),XX(N),YY(N):PRINT
50 FOR I=1 TO N:INPUT"ENTER X & Y VALUES:";XX(I)
,YY(I):NEXT I
```

```
60 CLS:PRINT"# ";"X ";"Y ","# ";"X ";"Y ","# ";"
X ";"Y ","# ";"X ";"Y":FOR I=1 TO N:PRINT I;XX(I
);YY(I),:NEXT I:PRINT
70 PRINT:PRINT"ARE THESE VALUES CORRECT?   (Y/N)"
80 QQ$=INKEY$:IF QQ$="" THEN 80
90 IF QQ$="Y" OR QQ$="y" THEN 110
100 INPUT"ENTER ITEM NUMBER, NEW X VALUE, NEW Y
VALUE:";I,XX(I),YY(I):GOTO 70
110 CLS:LOCATE 9,1:PRINT"PLEASE BE PATIENT, COMP
UTING"
120 FOR I=1 TO N
130 X=XX(I):Y=(YY(I)):E(1)=E(1)+(X*Y):E(2)=E(2)+
(X*LOG(Y))
140 IF XX(I)>LX THEN LX=XX(I)
150 E(3)=E(3)+(Y*LOG(X)):E(4)=E(4)+(LOG(X)*LOG(Y
))
160 IF XX(I)<SX THEN SX=XX(I)
170 F(1)=F(1)+X:F(2)=F(1):F(3)=F(3)+LOG(X):F(4)=
F(3)
180 IF YY(I)>LY THEN LY=YY(I)
190 G(1)=G(1)+Y:G(3)=G(1):G(2)=G(2)+LOG(Y):G(4)=
G(2)
200 IF YY(I)<SY THEN SY=YY(I)
210 H(1)=H(1)+X^2:H(2)=H(1):H(3)=H(3)+LOG(X)^2:H
(4)=H(3)
220 I(1)=F(1)^2:I(2)=I(1):I(3)=F(3)^2:I(4)=I(3)
230 J(1)=J(1)+Y^2:J(3)=J(1):J(2)=J(2)+LOG(Y)^2:J
(4)=J(2)
240 K(1)=G(1)^2:K(3)=K(1):K(2)=G(2)^2:K(4)=K(2)
250 LOCATE 11,1:PRINT"I =";I;
260 NEXT I
270 P=N
280 FOR M=1 TO 4
290 B(M)=(E(M)-(F(M)*G(M))/P)/(H(M)-I(M)/P)
300 A(M)=(G(M)-B(M)*F(M))/P
310 R(M)=SQR((E(M)-F(M)*G(M)/P)^2/((H(M)-I(M)/P)
*(J(M)-K(M)/P)))
320 LOCATE 12,1:PRINT"M =";M;
330 NEXT M
340 CLS:PRINT"","A","B","R":PRINT"LINEAR:",A(1),
B(1),R(1):PRINT"EXPONENTIAL:",EXP(A(2)),B(2),R(2
):PRINT"LOGARITHMIC:",A(3),B(3),R(3):PRINT"POWER
:",EXP(A(4)),B(4),R(4):A(4)=EXP(A(4)):A(2)=EXP(A
(2))
350 FOR I=1 TO 6:R(I)=ABS(R(I)):NEXT I
360 IF R(1)>R(2) THEN 400
370 IF R(2)>R(3) THEN 420
380 IF R(3)>R(4) THEN 450
390 M=4:GOTO 460
400 IF R(1)<R(3) THEN 380
410 IF R(1)>R(4) THEN 430 ELSE 390
420 IF R(2)>R(4) THEN 440 ELSE 390
430 M=1:GOTO 460
440 M=2:GOTO 460
450 M=3
460 PRINT
470 F$(1)="LINEAR":F$(2)="EXPONENTIAL":F$(3)="LO
GARITHMIC":F$(4)="POWER":E$(1)="Y = A + BX":E$(2
```

Listing 10-3. Economic Curve Fitting. (Continued From Page 198.)

```
)="Y = EXP(LOG A + BX)":E$(3)="Y = A + B LOG X":
E$(4)="Y = EXP(LOG A + B LOG X)"
480 PRINT"THE BEST CURVE FIT IS ";F$(M):PRINT"TH
E EQUATION IS: ";E$(M):PRINT"A =";A(M);"    B =";
B(M);"    R =";R(M):PRINT:PRINT"DO YOU WANT TO CO
MPUTE A TERM?  (Y/N)"
490 IF SX=>0 AND SY=>0 THEN 510
500 ZZ=1:PRINT:PRINT"(DATA INCLUDES NEGATIVE VAL
UES, ONLY THE LINEAR EQUATION ISVALID.  IF ANOTH
ER FORM IS RECOMMENDED, PROGRAM WILL DISREGARD A
ND COMPUTE LINEAR.)"
510 QZ$=INKEY$:IF QZ$="" THEN 510
520 CLS
530 IF QZ$="N" THEN 810
540 LOCATE 16,1:PRINT"ENTER '●' TO STOP:";
550 LOCATE 9,1:PRINT"WHICH VALUE (X OR Y) WILL B
E ENTERED?";:LOCATE 10,1:PRINT"
  ";
560 QX$=INKEY$:IF QX$="" THEN 560
570 IF QX$="Y" THEN 620
580 IF QX$="●" THEN 810
590 PRINT:INPUT"ENTER X-VALUE";X
600 ON M GOSUB 650,690,730,770
610 GOTO 640
620 PRINT:INPUT"ENTER Y-VALUE";Y
630 ON M GOSUB 670,710,750,790
640 CLS:LOCATE 7,1:PRINT"X =";X;"     Y =";Y:PRI
NT:GOTO 530
650 Y=A(1)+B(1)*X
660 RETURN
670 X=(Y-(A(1))/B(1)
680 RETURN
690 Y=EXP(LOG(A(2))+B(2)*X)
700 RETURN
710 X=(LOG(Y)-LOG(A(2)))/B(2)
720 RETURN
730 Y=A(3)+B(3)*LOG(X)
740 RETURN
750 X=EXP((Y-A(3))/B(3))
760 RETURN
770 Y=A(4)*(X^B(4))
780 RETURN
790 X=(Y/A(4))^(1/B(4))
800 RETURN
810 LOCATE 1,1
820 PRINT"(A)nother       (M)ain menu ";
830 Q$=""+INKEY$:IF Q$="" THEN 830
840 IF Q$="A" OR Q$="a" THEN RUN 10 ELSE RUN "A:
MENU"
```

Kondratieff Long Waves

Nicholai D. Kondratieff was a Russian economist who developed a number of economic theories regarding the behavior of capitalist economies. While his motives may have been less than friendly, his observations regarding Wall Street behavior bear some examination.

In Fig. 10-2, the upper data stream is a representation of the wholesale price index from 1800 to 1960. His analysis of such data led him to postulate a theory of long-term economic behavior in which prices fluctuate more or less according to the general wave form shown in Fig. 10-3.

This wave consists of three parts, according to Kondratieff.

A — A fairly long (25 years) period of strong growth.

B — A shorter length (8 years) plateau, marked at the start by a recessionary period.

C — A depressionary period of some 20 to 30 years.

If we superimpose the Kondratieff waves over the data from 1800 to about 1945, (Fig. 10-2) there is considerable conformity. Beyond that point, however, there is a significant deviation from the theory. Remember, also, that the illustration is drawn on a logarithmic chart in which changes in direction appear less dramatic than they really are. That is, slight deviations on a logarithmic chart are actually

major changes on a linear chart (Fig. 10-5). The reader may want to adapt this theory for current data and track the market for the next few years to see if the market returns to the form predicted by the Kondratieff wave.

The original premise remains: the trend line, based on market averages, simply points to the general market mean. Individual stock prices can and will frequently deviate from the market trend. The market value of a given stock will vary as much as a function of specific industry conditions as it will as a function of the general market trend. During a period of generally healthy market, most stocks will reflect the health and growth of the market. A few stocks, however, will wither and die as the management of the particular firms make lethal errors, or as advances in technology make the particular industry obsolete. Likewise, technological advances or shrewd new managers may bring into being other

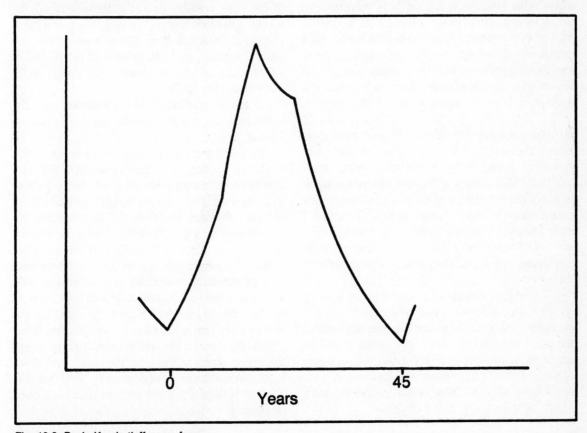

Fig. 10-3. Basic Kondratieff curve form.

businesses which bloom and experience a growth spurt at a rate far in excess of the general market trend. No simple computational procedure exists to foretell the birth of new investment opportunities. Technological forecasting (see Chapter 11) can provide indications of areas where new technology may encourage growth, but the specifics will remain generally unknown until the last moment. For these reasons, the potential investor is well-advised to retain the services of an experienced and skilled broker or investment counselor. By maintaining close watch over existing businesses, the investor may sometimes be able to spot signs of impending failure, but not always. Witness the Tylenol scare of 1982. Here was a superb product, the value of which would remain a constant asset to the business and a prudent investment for the investor. Without warning, however, the poisoning done by one deranged individual devastated the market value of the parent company. Many other businesses are similarly vulnerable to attack by insane individuals or terrorists. Where the acts of a madman can have an adverse impact on a decentralized industry across the nation, severe weather phenomena can have a similar unexpected impact on smaller businesses. Imagine what a large-scale earthquake or equivalent natural phenomenon in the Silcon Valley area of central California would do to the computer chip industry. While it would devastate the stock of the companies whose plant resources were destroyed, it would give an unnatural boost to the stock of the few companies in the industry located outside of the region. A secondary consequence is that those industries that depend upon integrated circuits (computers, microprocessors, etc.) would be unable to keep pace with their production orders and their stock value would also drop.

The market averages announced every evening on the radio, television, and newspapers are the averages of the sum of all the experiences each of the businesses in the market have experienced or are expected to experience in the near future. Some of the businesses have done well, perhaps in spite of common widsom. Some of the businesses have done worse than one would expect.

Long-term analysis and forecasting of the marketplace suggests a generally upward trend. This means that, as a society, we are continuing to develop ways to sustain and improve our quality and quantity of life. We can even compute a fairly precise estimate of the direction and magnitude of this growth. Translating this information into a viable stock investment strategy is something else. The best and most obvious strategy is given in the quotation: "Buy low, sell high." Knowing when the bottom has been reached for buying or when the ceiling has been reached for buying or when the ceiling has been reached for selling is quite another matter, and requires considerable skill in evaluating the specific markets or business. It is for this reason that we encourage the reader to use the services of a professional investment counselor, and we offer no super program with which to beat the market. The best we can do is offer routines to help those interested to track the available data. For those seriously interested in stock market tracking, we recommend *Playing the Stock & Bond Markets with Your Personal Computer,* by L. R. Schmeltz (Tab Book No. 1251). His book contains several fine programs for microcomputer application.

A routine that might aid stock market analysis, in the meantime, is given in the Market Evaluator, Listing 10-4.

A useful feature of this program is the option to change or offset the relative phasing of the data. The user can experiment with various options to evaluate leading or lagging indicators, as well as concurrent indicators. For example, we know that unemployment is a *lagging indicator,* that is, the general state of the economy will usually improve a number of weeks (around 15) before we see an improvement in employment. We use this sort of indicator to validate market trends. That is, noting an improvement in the economy, we may want to examine the unemployment rate some 12 to 20 weeks later. If the offset rate shows a similar increase, we may accept the improvement as valid. On the other hand, if the lagging indicator reveals a downward trend, we may want to conclude that the current trend is a fluke or nominal deviation.

Listing 10-4. Market Evaluator.

```
1 '***********************************************
2 '*                Listing 10-4                 *
3 '*              Market Evaluator               *
4 '***********************************************
5 '
10 CLS:CLEAR (1000):PRINT"MARKET EVALUATOR":PRIN
T:PRINT
20 PRINT"PROGRAM TO INPUT MOST RECENT DATA AND E
VALUATE MARKET TRENDS.":PRINT
30 PRINT"WILL THE LINE PRINTER BE USED?  (Y/N)
";:GOSUB 1040
40 IF Q$="Y" OR Q$="y" THEN LP=1 ELSE LP=0
50 GOSUB 1060:GOSUB 840
60 PRINT:PRINT"OPTIONS:":PRINT:PRINT
70 PRINT"1  ---   TREND LINE WITH MEAN AND STANDA
RD DEVIATION                          2   ---
  CORRELATION
                         3   ---   MOVING AVERAGE"
80 PRINT"4  --   FINISH                SELECT "
;
90 GOSUB 1040
100 IF Q$="4" THEN 1180
110 PRINT:PRINT"YOU HAVE";P;"PERIODS OF DATA, IN
CLUDING THE";X;"NEW PERIODS JUST ADDED.  ";:INPU
T"ENTER THE  NUMBER OF THE STARTING PERIOD";S1:I
NPUT"ENTER THE ENDING PERIOD";S2:M=(S2-S1)+1
120 TX=0:TY=0:X2=0:Y2=0:XY=0
130 ON VAL(Q$) GOTO 140,350,470
140 PRINT:INPUT"ENTER THE NUMBER OF THE FILE TO
BE ANALYZED";F
150 CLS:PRINT"COMPUTING TREND LINE FOR ";N$(F)
160 FOR I=S1 TO S2
170 X=I:Y=M(F,I):TX=TX+X:TY=TY+Y:X2=X2+(X^2):Y2=
Y2+(Y^2):XY=XY+(X*Y)
180 NEXT I
190 A=(XY-((TX*TY)/M))/(X2-((TX^2)/M))
200 B=(TY/M)-(A*(TX/M))
210 R=((M*XY)-(TX*TY))/SQR(((M*X2)-(TX^2))*((M*Y
2)-(TY^2)))
220 AV=TY/M:SD=SQR((Y2-((TY^2)/M))/(M-1))
230 SE=SQR(ABS(((Y2-(A*TY)-(B*XY))/(M-2))))
240 SA=SQR(ABS((X2/(M*(X2-((TX^2)/M))))))*SE
250 SB=SE/SQR(ABS((X2-((TX^2)/M))))
260 PRINT:PRINT"LINEAR TREND FOR THIS PERIOD IS:
 Y = ";
270 IF A<0 THEN 310
280 IF B<0 THEN 300
290 PRINT A;" + ";B;"X":GOTO 320
300 PRINT A;" ";B;"X":GOTO 320
310 PRINT B;"X ";A
320 PRINT:PRINT"THE CORRELATION IS ";R:PRINT"THE
 MEAN OF THE DATA IS ";AV:PRINT"THE STANDARD DEV
IATION IS ";SD
330 PRINT"","STANDARD ERRORS":PRINT"OF ESTIMATE"
,SE:PRINT"OF A",SA:PRINT"OF B",SB
340 LPRINT"":PRINT:GOTO 70
```

Listing 10-4. Market Evaluator. (Continued From Page 201.)

```
350 PRINT:INPUT"ENTER THE NUMBER OF THE FIRST FI
LE";F1:INPUT"ENTER THE NUMBER OF SECOND FILE";F2
360 CLS:PRINT"COMPUTING THE CORRELATION BETWEEN
";N$(F1);" AND ";N$(F2)
370 FOR I=S1 TO S2
380 X=M(F1,I):Y=M(F2,I)
390 TX=TX+X:TY=TY+Y:X2=X2+(X^2):Y2=Y2+(Y^2):XY=X
Y+(X*Y)
400 NEXT I
410 A1=TX/M:A2=TY/M:D1=SQR((X2-((TX^2)/M))/(M-1)
):D2=SQR((Y2-((TY^2)/M))/(M-1))
420 R=((M*XY)-(TX*TY))/SQR(((M*X2)-(TX^2))*((M*Y
2)-(TY^2)))
430 PRINT:PRINT"THE CORRELATION IS ";R:PRINT
440 PRINT"FILE","MEAN","STANDARD DEVIATION"
450 PRINT N$(F1),A1,D1:PRINT N$(F2),A2,D2
460 PRINT:GOTO 70
470 PRINT:INPUT"ENTER THE NUMBER OF THE FILE TO
BE ANALYZED";F
480 CLS:PRINT"PERIOD","DATA","MOVING AVERAGE"
490 IF LP=1 THEN LPRINT"PERIOD","DATA","MOVING A
VERAGE"
500 INPUT"ENTER PERIOD OF AVERAGE";A
510 FOR I=S1 TO S2
520 T=T+M(F,I):IF (S1-I)<(A-1) THEN 560
530 PRINT I,M(F,I),T/A
540 IF LP=1 THEN LPRINT I,M(F,I),T/A
550 T=T-M(F,I-A):GOTO 580
560 PRINT I,M(F,I),T/I
570 IF LP=1 THEN LPRINT I,M(F,I),T/I
580 NEXT I
590 IF LP=1 THEN LPRINT"PERIOD OF AVERAGE = ";A
600 GOTO 70
610 PRINT"FILE #","NAME","COMMENT"
620 FOR I=1 TO N
630 INPUT#1, N$(I),C$(I):PRINT I,N$(I),C$(I)
640 FOR J=1 TO P
650 INPUT#1, M(I,J)
660 NEXT J
670 NEXT I
680 INPUT#1, FC$:PRINT:PRINT FC$:PRINT
690 CLOSE:GOTO 710
700 INPUT "NAME OF NEW FILE";DF$
710 P=P+X
720 FOR I=1 TO N:PRINT N$(I),C$(I)
730    FOR J=1 TO P:PRINT J,M(I,J):NEXT J
740 PRINT:PRINT"ALL DATA ENTERED CORRECT?   (Y/N)
  ";:GOSUB 1040
750 IF Q$="Y" OR Q$="y" THEN 820
760 PRINT"CORRECT (N)AME   (C)OMMENT   (D)ATA    ";
:GOSUB 1040
770 IF Q$="C" OR Q$="c" THEN 790 ELSE IF Q$="D"
OR Q$="d" THEN 800 ELSE IF Q$<>"N" OR Q$<>"n" TH
EN 760
780 INPUT"ENTER CORRECT NAME";N$(I):GOTO 740
790 INPUT"ENTER CORRECT COMMENT";C$(I):GOTO 740
```

```
800 INPUT"ENTER NUMBER OF PERIOD FOR CORRECTION"
;Y
810 INPUT"ENTER CORRECT VALUE";M(I,Y):GOTO 740
820 NEXT I
830 RETURN
840 FC$=""
850 INPUT "NAME OF FILE (USE '@' FOR NEW FILE)";
DF$
860 IF DF$<>"@" THEN 900
870 INPUT"Enter Number of Files";N:DIM N$(N),C$(
N)
880 FOR I=1 TO N:PRINT"Enter name of file #";I,:
INPUT N$(I):NEXT I
890 GOTO 920
900 OPEN "I",1,DF$
910 INPUT#1, N,P
920 PRINT"THERE ARE";N;"FILES CURRENTLY ESTABLIS
HED, EACH WITH";P;"DATA ENTRIES.  HOW MANY ADDIT
IONAL PERIODS TO BE ADDED",:INPUT X
930 DIM M(N,P+X)
940 PRINT"ADD NEW DATA":PRINT
950 FOR I=1 TO N
960 PRINT N$(I)
970 PRINT"IF DATA IS UNKNOWN, ENTER 0.  IF DATA
IS ZERO, ENTER .00001"
980 FOR J=P+1 TO P+X
990 PRINT"ENTER DATA FOR PERIOD #";J,:INPUT M(I,
J)
1000 NEXT J
1010 NEXT I
1020 IF DF$="@" THEN 700
1030 GOTO 620
1040 Q$=""+INKEY$:IF Q$="" THEN 1040
1050 PRINT Q$:PRINT:RETURN
1060 FOR I=1 TO N
1070 FOR J=1 TO P
1080 IF J=1 THEN 1150
1090 IF M(I,J)<>0 THEN 1150
1100 FOR K=1 TO P
1110 IF M(I,J+K)<>0 THEN 1140
1120 NEXT K
1130 M(I,J)=.00001:GOTO 1150
1140 M(I,J)=(M(I,J+K)-M(I,J-1))/(K+1)
1150 NEXT J
1160 NEXT I
1170 RETURN
1180 OPEN "O",1,DF$
1190 PRINT#1, N
1200 PRINT#1, P
1210 FOR I=1 TO N
1220 PRINT#1, N$(I),C$(I)
1230 FOR J=1 TO P
1240 PRINT#1, M(I,J)
1250 NEXT J
1260 NEXT I
1270 PRINT#1, FC$:CLOSE
1280 PRINT:PRINT"ALL DATA SAVED."
1290 CLS:LOCATE 1,1
```

Listing 10-4. Market Evaluator. (Continued From Page 203.)

```
1300 PRINT"(A)nother          (M)ain menu ";
1310 Q$=""+INKEY$:IF Q$="" THEN 1310
1320 IF Q$="A" OR Q$="a" THEN RUN 10 ELSE RUN "A
:MENU"
```

OTHER BUSINESS AND ECONOMIC PROGRAMS

Many other tools exist to aid the small business-man in the conduct of his work. We offer a few of them here as useful applications of the microcomputer. Among them are: market sales price analysis, economic order quantity, lease/purchase evaluator, funds programming, investment amortization, and a useful spreadsheet routine.

Market Sales Price Analysis

In the Business Math section of this chapter we presented several equations to compute selling prices based on cost or selling price, with modifications for sales commissions. What the equations fail to do is help the manager select an optimum sales price relative to the relevant market. What the selling price and break-even equations do are point to minimum prices necessary to survive. We need some other basis to help select optimum price levels.

Sales volume is a function of many variables, among them: location, advertising, sales team, local demand for the product (we presume it is harder to sell air conditioning in Nome, Alaska, than in Dallas, Texas), and price. If we own the only store in town for a given product or service, our price structure is more a function of our own needs than in locations with heavy competition. Seldom, however, do businesses operate without some competition. In a competitive environment, we must consider our price structure relative to the competition. If we truly have a superior product (or a lot of nerve), we might survive and prosper by charging a superior fee. If, on the other hand, our products or services (especially services) are roughly comparable, price needs close attention. All other things being equal, we assume that if our price is zero, or close to it, demand will be very great, perhaps close to 100 percent. Our profit, however, is really a loss. (Profit = Sales Income − (Expenses + Cost of Product). (Sales Income = Number of Units Sold times Selling Price.) At the other end of the spectrum, we know that even at a price significantly above the local price norm someone will buy the item. Although the income per unit sold increases, net profit again falls into a condition of net loss. A generalized illustration of this concept is shown in Fig. 10-4.

Given the number of competitors in a market area, we can compute fair market share simply by dividing the total number of potential customers by the total number of stores selling the same product or service and superimpose this value as a horizontal line across the figure. Sales above this line signify that we are doing something right and getting more than our fair share of the market, and, hopefully, making a profit. Sales volume, under any circumstance, below the fair market share is an indication that something is wrong. If the selling price is lower than the market norm, it is quite possible that some factor other than price is the villain. If your prices are significantly above the competition, perhaps you need to become more competitive. In any event, the program developed in Listing 10-5 helps evaluate your price structure in this context. It is difficult to specify just how sales volume will vary as a function of price in a given situation. Accordingly, we assume that sales volume will follow a generalized ogive or reverse S-curve pattern like the one in Fig. 10-5. An easy way to simulate an ogive curve is to use a variation of the arctangent curve where $Y = \arctan X$. The program operates on the assumption that the curve is symmetrical about the normal price to the extent that the predicted sales volume will equal the market share, based on the specified number of competitors, when the sales price equals the market norm.

Using the market size, as well as the retail and wholesale prices, the program computes profit/loss as a function of the predicted sales volume (SV) (as

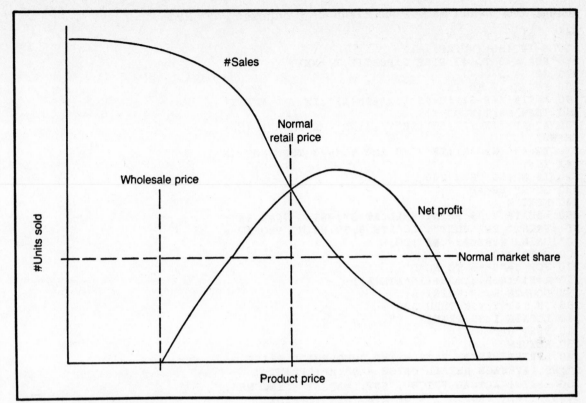

#Sales

Normal
retail price

Wholesale price

#Units sold

Net profit

Normal market share

Product price

Fig. 10-4. Market sales analysis.

Listing 10-5. Market Sales Price Evaluator.

```
1 '***********************************************
2 '*                 Listing 10-5                *
3 '*           Market Sales Price Analysis       *
4 '***********************************************
5 '
10 SCREEN 2:KEY OFF
20 CLS:F1=-.08:F2=15
30 INPUT"ENTER ESTIMATED MARKET SIZE";MS
40 INPUT"ENTER NUMBER OF COMPETITORS IN MARKET A
REA";NC
50 INPUT"ENTER THE RETAIL PRICE OF THE PRODUCT";
RP
60 INPUT"ENTER THE WHOLESALE COST OF THE PRODUCT
";WP
70 CLS:AN=(RP*MS*(1/(NC+1)))-(WP*MS*(1/(NC+1)))
80 FOR Y=0 TO 43:PSET(17,Y):NEXT Y
90 FOR X=17 TO 127:PSET(X,43):NEXT X
100 Y=43-INT(43*(1/(1+NC)))
110 FOR X=17 TO 127 STEP 3:PSET(X,Y):NEXT
120 SM=Y
130 FOR Y=0 TO 43 STEP 2:PSET(72,Y):NEXT
140 LOCATE 6,34:PRINT"RETAIL = $";USING"####.##"
```

Listing 10-5. Market Sales Price Evaluator. (Continued From Page 205.)

```
;RP;:PRINT" PER UNIT";
150 X=INT(55*(WP/RP))+17
160 FOR Y=0 TO 43 STEP 2:PSET(X,Y):NEXT
170 GOSUB 270
180 FOR X=17 TO 127
190 A=F1*(X+B-64):Y=43+(F2*ATN(A)):IF Y>0 AND Y<
=43 THEN PSET(X,43-Y)
200 AP=RP*((X-17)/55):SH=Y/43:NP=(MS*SH*AP)-(MS*
SH*WP)
210 Y2=43*(NP/AN):IF Y2>0 AND Y2<=43 THEN PSET(X
,43-Y2)
220 IF NP<LG THEN 240
230 LG=NP:SP=AP
240 NEXT X
250 LOCATE 7,39:PRINT"SELL AT $";USING"####.##";
SP;:PRINT" PER UNIT";:LOCATE 8,39:PRINT"PROFIT =
 $";USING"########.##";LG;
260 GOTO 340
270 FOR B=NC*-5 TO NC*5
280 A=F1*(8+B):Y=23+(15*ATN(A))
290 LOCATE 1,39:PRINT B;
300 IF (43-Y)<SM THEN 320
310 LOCATE 1,39:PRINT"   ",
320 NEXT B
330 RETURN
340 LPRINT"MARKET SIZE =";MS,"WHOLESALE PRICE =
$";WP,"AVERAGE RETAIL PRICE = $";RP:LPRINT""
350 LPRINT"ACTUAL PRICE","EST. MARKET","INCOME",
"COST","NET PROFIT","% OF AVE. NET":LPRINT""
360 FOR X=17 TO 127 STEP 2
370 A=F1*(X+B-64):Y=23+(F2*ATN(A))
380 AP=RP*((X-17)/55):SH=Y/43:NP=(MS*SH*AP)-(MS*
SH*WP)
390 LPRINT USING"####.##";AP,:LPRINT INT(MS*SH),
MS*SH*AP,MS*SH*WP,NP,100*(NP/AN)
400 NEXT
410 LPRINT""
420 LPRINT"BEST MARKET PRICE ESTIMATED TO BE $";
USING"####.##";SP
430 PRINT"(A)nother       (M)ain menu ";
440 Q$=""+INKEY$:IF Q$="" THEN 440
450 IF Q$="A" OR Q$="a" THEN RUN 20 ELSE RUN "A:
MENU"
460 ZAG%=INT(ZOG%/64):ZOG%=ZOG%-64*ZAG%+1:ZAG%=Z
AG%+1:                          LOCATE ZAG%,
ZOG%:RETURN
```

a function of the ogive curve) times the retail price (RP) less the wholesale price (WP): $Y = SV (RP - WP)$. It goes on to locate the maximum total profit and displays all the relevant data. Finally, it delivers a copy of the output to the printer.

Economic Order Size

Whether a retail business acquires inventory on consignment or borrowed funds, or cash payment in full, it is faced with the problem of knowing how many of an item to order at a given moment. Even

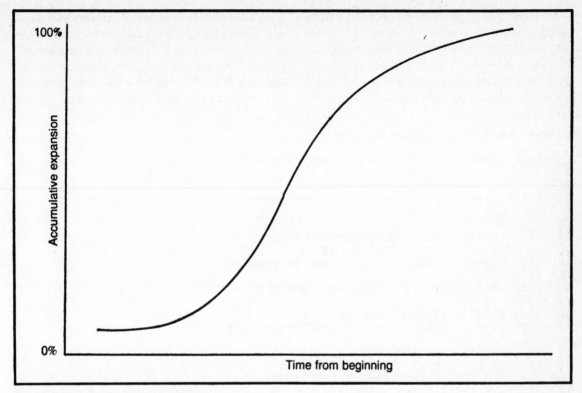

Fig. 10-5. Typical sales expansion record.

if there is no direct cost (consignment), there are associated costs in obtaining the items such as the cost of placing the order (phone bills, preparing order forms, filing, etc.) and receiving the items (stockroom labor), and the floorspace costs for storing the items until the time of sale. When the items are obtained on terms (borrowed money), there is the added cost of the money itself (interest paid). Paying cash in full ties up capital until the time of sale. In addition, that capital cost should include not only the capital itself, but the return on investment that capital could have earned if it had not been tied up in stock. The prudent businessman wants to have sufficient numbers of an item in stock so that, under normal conditions, there will be at least one available for sale when a customer wants one. On the other hand, he doesn't want to have any more on hand than are absolutely necessary, tying up capital and warehouse space. In this area, there are four questions confronting him:

1. What is the maximum inventory ($I2$) that should be maintained?
2. What is the minimum inventory ($I1$) that can be allowed?
3. At what inventory level (P) should new stock be ordered?
4. What is the optimum order size (Q)?

The answers to these questions can be computed from the following relationships:

$D = T + 1$ where T = number of days required to fill an order.

$I1 = DV$ where V is maximum normal daily sales volume.

$P = TV + I1$ this is the optimum order point.

$I2 = O + P$ where O is the standard order size.

$Q = \sqrt{\dfrac{2\,CN}{M + A}}$ where A is the annual carrying cost per unit item and is the cost to place an order.

207

Listing 10-6 implements these relationships, asking only that the user have available the five variables: T, V, O, C, and A. The program computes the remaining values, D, I1, P, I2, and ' and then recomputes I2 based on an assumption that O will be adjusted to equal '. In circumstances where the wholesaler allows odd lot orders, this is a useful option. Lines 103-107 are available in the case where the items are obtained on interest-bearing terms. Even if the items are paid for in cash, one should use lines 103-107, using for R the available return on investment rate for investment capital.

Listing 10-6. Economic Order Quantity.

```
1 '*********************************************
2 '*              Listing 10-6               *
3 '*          Economic Order Quantity        *
4 '*********************************************
5 '
10 CLS
20 INPUT"AVERAGE ANNUAL UNIT REQUIREMENTS";N
30 INPUT"MAXIMUM DAILY REQUIREMENT";U
40 INPUT"NUMBER OF DAYS FOR SUPPLIER TO FILL ORD
ER";T:D=T+1
50 I1=D*U:P=(T*U)+I1:PRINT"MINIMUM INVENTORY = "
;I1
60 INPUT"ENTER STANDARD ORDER";O
70 INPUT"COST TO PLACE ORDER";C:INPUT"UNIT COST
OF ITEM";M
80 INPUT"ANNUAL CARRYING COST PER UNIT";A
90 'SECTION FOR CREDIT EVALUATION
100 PRINT"DO YOU FINANCE PURCHASES?   (Y/N)   ";
110 Q$=""+INKEY$:IF Q$="" THEN 110
120 IF Q$="N" OR Q$="n" THEN 140
130 INPUT"ENTER ANNUAL COST OF MONEY  (5%=5)";R:
R=R/36525!:RF=(R*((1+R)^(T/2)))/(((1+R)^(T/2))-1
):GOTO 150
140 RF=1
150 A=A+(M*(1+RF))-M:I2=O+P:Q=INT(SQR((2*C*N)/((
M*R)+A))+1)
160 PRINT"MAXIMUM INVENTORY = ";I2:PRINT"ORDER P
OINT = ";P
170 PRINT"OPTIMUM ORDER SIZE = ";Q
180 OA=Q:IA=OA+P:PRINT"ADJUSTED MAXIMUM INVENTOR
Y BASED ON E.O.Q. =";IA
190 PRINT"AVERAGE INVENTORY PERIOD (ORDER TO ORD
ER) =";365.25/(N/Q);"DAYS"
200 GOTO 250
210 LPRINT"":LPRINT"ANNUAL REQUIREMENT = ";N;"UN
ITS","MAXIMUM DAILY REQUIREMENT = ";U,"DAYS TO F
ILL ORDER = ";T
220 LPRINT"COST TO PLACE AN ORDER = $";C,:LPRINT
"UNIT COST = $";M,"STANDARD ORDER = ";O;"UNITS",
230 LPRINT"MINIMUM INVENTORY = ";I1;"UNITS","MAX
IMUM INVENTORY =";I2;"UNITS","ORDER POINT =";P;"
UNITS"
240 LPRINT"OPTIMUM ORDER SIZE (E.O.Q.) = ";Q
250 PRINT"":PRINT"(A)nother        (P)rint        (
M)ain menu ";
260 Q$=""+INKEY$:IF Q$="" THEN 260
270 IF Q$="A" OR Q$="a" THEN RUN 10 ELSE IF Q$="
```

```
P" OR Q$="p" THEN 210 ELSE RUN "A:MENU"
280 ZAG%=INT(ZOG%/64):ZOG%=ZOG%-64*ZAG%+1:ZAG%=Z
AG%+1:                              LOCATE ZAG%,
ZOG%:RETURN
```

Lease-Purchase Evaluator

Businesses are often confronted with the choice of purchasing equipment or leasing it. The basic argument for leasing is that it lets the business hang on to the majority of its available capital for investment in machinery and goods that cannot be leased. For example, if a weaving machine costs $10,000, materials cost $10,000 (for a minimum run), and labor, for the minimum six-month run, costs $6,000, the cost to buy the equipment and pay for the minimum run is $26,000. If the owner has less than $26,000 available, the operation cannot even begin. If the weaving machine can be leased, however, at a cost of $300.00 a month, the cash requirement to open shop and run it for six months is $17,800. That's a 31.54 percent reduction in start-up capital required. In addition, the entire monthly payment of $300 is deductible as a business expense. If the machine were purchased, only the depreciation would be deducted. If the useful life of the machine is five years, the straight-line depreciation would be $166.67. Over the six months, the difference is $800: (300 × 6 − 166.67 × 6).

Unfortunately, as with many things in real life, things aren't always that simple. There may be investment tax credits; the lease payment might be considerably higher; there may be security deposits required; or the effective interest rate on the lease could make the long-term cost of the equipment excessive. For example, a lease for 36 months, based on 24 percent, could result in payments of $392.33, or a total cost of $14,123.83, with nothing to show for it at the end. Listing 10-7 is a routine to compute the related factors in a lease/purchase situation leading to a comparison of both options in terms of long-term costs and benefits.

Listing 10-7. Lease-Purchase Evaluator.

```
1 '*********************************************
2 '*               Listing 10-7              *
3 '*          Lease-Purchase Evaluator       *
4 '*********************************************
5 '
10 CLS:PRINT"****   COST ANALYSIS   ****":PRINT:PR
INT
20 DIM A(50)
30 A$="######.##        ######.##"
40 CLS:PRINT"****   LEASE/PURCHASE EVALUATOR   ***
*":PRINT:PRINT
50 INPUT"WHAT IS THE NAME OF THE ITEM";N$
60 PRINT"WHAT IS THE PURCHASE PRICE OF ";N$;:INP
UT PP:A(1)=PP
70 PRINT"DO YOU HAVE $";PP;"AVAILABLE IN CASH?
(Y/N)",
80 Q1$=""+INKEY$:IF Q1$="" THEN 80
90 IF Q1$="Y" OR Q1$="y" THEN 140
100 PRINT Q1$:INPUT"HOW MUCH CASH IS AVAILABLE";
CA
110 CB=PP-CA:A(3)=CB:PRINT"CAN YOU BORROW/RAISE
$";CB;"?   (Y/N)",
120 Q2$=""+INKEY$:IF Q2$="" THEN 120
130 GOTO 150
140 CA=PP
150 A(2)=CA:PRINT Q2$:INPUT"BEST ANNUAL RATE OF
```

Listing 10-7. Lease-Purchase Evaluator. (Continued From Page 209.)

```
RETURN AVAILABLE ON INVESTMENTS    (5%=5)";X:IR=X/
1200:INPUT"BEST INTEREST RATE AVAILABLE ON LOANS
    (5%=5)";Y:LR=Y/1200
160 A(4)=IR:A(5)=LR
170 IF Q2$="Y" THEN 200
180 N=LOG(PP/CA)/LOG(1+IR):A(6)=N
190 PRINT"YOU MUST INVEST THE AVAILABLE $";CA;"A
T";IR*1200;"% FOR AT LEAST";N;"MONTHS TO ACCUMUL
ATE $";PP
200 INPUT"NUMBER OF PAYMENTS AVAILABLE IN TIME -
PURCHASE";LP
210 INPUT"AMOUNT OF DOWN PAYMENT REQUIRED IN EVE
NT OF TIME-PURCHASE";DP
220 IF DP<=CA THEN 240
230 N2=LOG(DP/CA)/LOG(1+IR):A(20)=N2
240 INPUT"ESTIMATED ECONOMIC LIFE IN YEARS";EL:E
L=EL*12:A(8)=EL
250 INPUT"MONTHLY LEASE COST";ML:A(7)=ML
260 SV=.01*PP:PRINT"ESTIMATED SALVAGE VALUE (DEF
AULT =";SV;")";:INPUT SV:A(9)=SV
270 INPUT"ESTIMATED TAX BRACKET (35%=35)";TB:TB=
TB/100:A(10)=TB
280 CLS:PRINT"","","GROSS","AFTER-TAX NET"
290 CL=(EL*ML)-SV:A(11)=CL:A(12)=CL*(1-TB):PRINT
"COST OF LEASING              ";USING A$;A(11);A(
12)
300 A(13)=CL/EL:A(14)=A(12)/EL:PRINT"MONTHLY LEA
SE COST",USING A$;A(13);A(14)
310 A=PP-DP:MP=(A*LR*((1+LR)^LP))/(((1+LR)^LP)-1
):A(21)=MP:TP=DP+(MP*LP):A(22)=TP:A(23)=TP-((1-T
B)*(TP-A)):A(24)=A(23)/LP
320 PRINT"TIME PURCHASE COSTS",USING A$;A(22);A(
23)
330 PRINT"MONTHLY TIME COSTS",USING A$;A(21);A(2
4)
340 II=CA*((1+IR)^EL):A(15)=II:A(16)=II-(TB*(II-
CA)):PRINT"INVESTMENT RETURN",USING A$;A(15);A(1
6)
350 B=CA-DP:I2=B*((1+IR)^EL):A(30)=I2:A(31)=I2-(
TB*(I2-B))
360 PRINT" LESS DOWN PAYMENT",USING A$;A(30);A(3
1)
370 PRINT"   OPTION ADVANTAGES:"
380 IF CA<PP THEN 430
390 A(17)=A(15)-A(11):A(18)=A(16)-A(12):PRINT"LE
ASE VS. PURCHASE",USING A$;A(17);A(18)
400 A(25)=A(30)-A(22):A(26)=A(31)-A(23)
410 IF CA<PP THEN 430
420 PRINT"TIME PURCHASE VS. CASH",USING A$;A(25)
;A(26)
430 A(27)=A(11)-A(22):A(28)=A(12)-A(23)
440 PRINT"TIME PURCHASE VS. LEASE",USING A$;A(27
);A(28)
450 GOSUB 520
460 CLS
470 PRINT"YOU NEED $";CB;"TO COMPLETE A CASH PUR
```

CHASE"
```
480 X=LOG(PP/CA)/LOG(1+IR):PRINT"IT WILL TAKE AT
 LEAST";X;"MONTHS TO SAVE THIS AT";1200*IR;" %"
490 F=CB:AP=F/(1.005*(((1.005^LP)-1)/.005))
500 Y=(CB*LR*((1+LR)^LP))/(((1+LR)^LP)-1):PRINT"
THIS CAN BE SHORTENED TO";LP;"MONTHS THROUGH A L
OAN"
510 PRINT"WITH PAYMENTS OF $";Y;"EACH.  INSTEAD
OF A LOAN, A SINKING FUND CAN BE CREATED WITH";L
P;"PAYMENTS OF $";AP;"INTO AN ACCOUNT PAYING AT
A RATE OF 6% PER YEAR."
520 LOCATE 24,1:INPUT "Use 'PrtSc' for printout
of data.  <CR> to continue.";ZZ
530 PRINT"":PRINT"(A)nother       (M)ain menu ";
540 Q$=""+INKEY$:IF Q$="" THEN 540
550 IF Q$="A" OR Q$="a" THEN RUN 10 ELSE RUN "A:
MENU"
```

Investment Evaluator

This program, Listing 10-8, is related to the previous routine, in that it enables the comparison of two or more investment options in terms of long-term costs and benefits. With it the user can forecast likely returns on investment and associated costs.

Funds Programming

This program, Listing 10-9, is designed to aid program managers who have to manage several projects within a fixed budget. The characteristics of this kind of a problem include a matrix consisting of one or more project lines to be funded over one or more periods. (The one program/one period con-

Listing 10-8. Investment Evaluator.

```
1 '***********************************************
2 '*                 Listing 10-8               *
3 '*             Investment Evaluator           *
4 '***********************************************
5 '
10 'THIS PROGRAM ASSUMES THAT SOME ASSET WILL BE
 PURCHASED, EITHER FOR CASH, BORROWED FUNDS, OR
COMBINATION OF BOTH, THEN PUT TO SOME ECONOMIC F
UNCTION RESULTING IN MONTHLY INCOME.  THE PROGRA
M HELPS EVALUATE THE NECESSARY MATRIX OF VALUES
TO
20 'ACHIEVE SPECIFIED OBJECTIVES.
30 '
40 CLS:A$="###,###.##":KEY OFF
50 PRINT"* = Mandatory Item":PRINT"":PRINT""
60 N=0:PP=0:INPUT"PURCHASE PRICE OF ITEM";PP:P1=
PP
70 IF PP<>0 THEN 100
80 INPUT "*Monthly payment";P:INPUT "*Number of
Payments";T:INPUT "Annual Interest Rate (5%=5)";
IR:R=IR/1200:PP=P*((((1+R)^T)-1)/(R*((1+R)^T)))
90 PRINT"Purchase Price = ";PP
100 TB=0:INPUT"APPLICABLE TAX BRACKET   (5%=5)";T
B:TB=TB/100:IF TB=0 THEN N=N+1
110 IF PP=0 THEN 160
120 PRINT"WILL YOU FINANCE ANY PART OF $";PP;"
 (Y/N)";
```

211

Listing 10-8. Investment Evaluator. (Continued From Page 211.)

```
130 Q$=""+INKEY$:IF Q$="" THEN 130 ELSE IF Q$="N
" OR Q$="n" THEN 160
140 PRINT:INPUT"  *AMOUNT TO BE FINANCED";AF:INP
UT"  *INTEREST RATE (5%=5)";IR:RF=IR/1200:INPUT"
  *TERM OF NOTE (# MONTHLY PAYMENTS)";T
150 P=AF*((RF*((1+RF)^T))/(((1+RF)^T)-1)):PRINT"
    THERE WILL BE";T;"PAYMENTS OF $";USING A$;P:P
P=(PP-AF)+(T*P)-(TB*((T*P)-AF)):PRINT"   NEW PUR
CHASE PRICE = $";PP;
160 PRINT:UL=0:INPUT"USEFUL LIFE (YEARS)";UL:IF
UL=0 THEN N=N+1
170 NI=PP*(1-TB)
180 LF=0:INPUT"ANTICIPATED LEASE FEE (MONTHLY)";
LF:AI=12*LF:IF LF=0 THEN N=N+1
190 RI=0:INPUT"DESIRED RETURN ON INVESTMENT  (5%
=5)";RI:R=RI/100:IF RI=0 THEN N=N+1
200 INPUT"*SALVAGE/RESALE VALUE";SV
210 INPUT"*TOTAL OF ALL COSTS INCIDENTAL TO PURC
HASE, LEASE AND RESALE";IC:SV=SV-IC
220 IF N=1 THEN 260
230 PRINT N
240 PRINT:PRINT"SORRY....ONLY ONE UNKNOWN":PRINT
:GOTO 60
250 PRINT:PRINT"SORRY....CAN'T FIND UNKNOWN":PRI
NT:GOTO 60
260 SI=SV*(1-TB):NI=NI-SI
270 N=UL:IF PP=0 THEN 330
280 IF UL=0 THEN 340
290 IF TB=0 THEN 350
300 IF LF=0 THEN 360
310 IF RI=0 THEN 370
320 GOTO 250
330 NI=NI+(AI/((R*((1+R)^N))/(((1+R)^N)-1))):PP=
NI/(1-TB):GOTO 430
340 S=AI/NI:N=LOG(S/(S-R))/LOG(1+R):UL=N:GOTO 43
0
350 NI=NI+(AI/((R*((1+R)^N))/(((1+R)^N)-1))):TB=
(NI/PP)-1:GOTO 430
360 S=(R*((1+R)^N))/(((1+R)^N)-1):AI=S*NI:LF=AI/
12:GOTO 430
370 R=.01:DR=.1:S=AI/NI
380 SX=(R*((1+R)^N))/(((1+R)^N)-1)
390 LOCATE 15,1:PRINT"COMPUTING.... R =";R,
400 IF SX=S THEN 430
410 IF SX>S THEN 440
420 R=R+DR:GOTO 380
430 SI=SV*(1-TB):N=UL
440 R=R-DR:DR=DR/2:IF DR>.000001 THEN 420
450 CLS:LOCATE 20,1:PRINT"Original Purchase Pric
e = $";P1
460 LOCATE 1,1
470 PRINT"EFFECT. PURCHASE PRICE = $";USINGA$;PP
;:LOCATE 1,30:PRINT"NET SALVAGE       = $";USI
NGA$;SV:LOCATE 2,1:PRINT"USEFUL LIFE =";USING"##
#.##";N;:PRINT" YEARS";:LOCATE 3,1:PRINT"ANNUAL
DEPRECIATION = $";USINGA$;P1/N:LOCATE 4,1:PRINT"
TAX BRACKET =";
```

Listing 10-9. Funds Programming.

```
1 '************************************************
2 '*                 Listing 10-9                 *
3 '*               Funds Programming              *
4 '************************************************
5 '
10 CLS:CLEAR 500
20 PRINT"FUNDS PROGRAMMING":PRINT:PRINT
30 PRINT"THIS VERSION IS DESIGNED TO ALLOW THE U
SER TO PROGRAM FUNDS OVER A FIVE-PERIOD  SPAN, W
HETHER MONTHS, QUARTERS, OR YEARS.  IT WILL ACCO
MODATE UP TO 9 LINE ITEMS. AT THIS POINT,
INDICATE THE NUMBER OF LINE ITEMS DESIRED:",
40 X$=""+INKEY$:IF X$="" THEN 40 ELSE N=VAL(X$)
50 IF 0<N AND N<10 THEN 60 ELSE 10
60 A$="####.## ####.## ####.## ####.## ####.##
####.##"
70 PRINT N:PRINT:DIM LI(N,6),C(6),R(N),N$(N),CV(
5),RV(N)
80 FOR I=1 TO 5
90 PRINT"IS THERE IS CEILING LIMIT TO PERIOD #";
I;"?   (Y/N)";
100 R$=""+INKEY$:IF R$="" THEN 100
110 PRINT"  ";R$:IF R$="N" OR R$="n" THEN 130
120 INPUT"ENTER CEILING";CV(I)
130 NEXT I
140 FOR I=1 TO N
150 PRINT:PRINT"ENTER NAME OF LINE ITEM #";I;:IN
PUT Q$
160 N$(I)=LEFT$(Q$,12)
170 PRINT"IS THERE A CEILING LIMIT TO ";Q$;"?  (
Y/N)"
180 X$=""+INKEY$:IF X$="" THEN 180
190 IF X$="N" OR X$="n" THEN 210
200 INPUT"ENTER CEILING VALUE";RV(I)
210 FOR J=1 TO 5
220 A=0:PRINT"ENTER BUDGET VALUE FOR PERIOD #";J
;:INPUT A
230 IF CV(J)=0 THEN 290
240 IF (C(J)+A)<=CV(J) THEN 290
250 PRINT A;"CAUSES THE PERIOD CEILING VALUE TO
BE EXCEEDED BY";(C(J)+A)-CV(J);".  IS THIS ACCEP
TABLE?  (CEILING WILL BE ADJUSTED.)  (Y/N)"
260 X$=""+INKEY$:IF X$="" THEN 260
270 IF X$="N" THEN 220
280 CV(J)=C(J)+A
290 IF RV(I)=0 THEN 350
300 IF (R(I)+A)<=RV(I) THEN 350
310 PRINT A;"CAUSES THE CEILING VALUE TO BE EXCE
EDED BY";(R(I)+A)-RV(I);".  IS THIS ACCEPTABLE?
(CEILING WILL BE ADJUSTED.)  (Y/N)";
320 X$=""+INKEY$:IF X$="" THEN 320
330 IF X$="N" THEN 220
340 RV(I)=R(I)+A
350 LI(I,J)=A:R(I)=R(I)+A:C(J)=C(J)+A:TT=TT+A
360 NEXT J
370 NEXT I
```

Listing 10-9. Funds Programming. (Continued From Page 213.)

```
380 PRINT:INPUT"ENTER NAME OF OVERALL SYSTEM BEI
NG PROGRAMMED";S$
390 PRINT"1 - DAILY  2 - WEEKLY  3 - MONTHLY  4
- QUARTERLY  5 - YEARLY";
400 Z$=""+INKEY$:IF Z$="" THEN 400 ELSE Z=VAL(Z$
)
410 B$(1)="DAILY":B$(2)="WEEKLY":B$(3)="MONTHLY"
:B$(4)="QUARTERLY":B$(5)="YEARLY"
420 P$(1)="DAY":P$(2)="WEEK":P$(3)="MONTH":P$(4)
="QUARTER":P$(5)="YEAR"
430 CLS:LOCATE 1,34:PRINT P$(Z);:LOCATE 1,60:PRI
NT"ROW";
440 F=1:IF TT<10000 THEN 460
450 F=10^(INT(LOG(TT)/2.30259)-3)
460 IF F<>1 THEN LOCATE 1,1:PRINT"SCALE = VALUES
/";F;
470 LOCATE 2,2:PRINT"#      ITEM";:LOCATE 2,21:PR
INT"1        2        3        4        5       TOTAL"
;
480 PRINT
490 FOR I=1 TO N
500 ZOG%=128+(64*I):GOSUB 760:PRINT I;N$(I);:ZOG
%=128+(I*64)+16:GOSUB 760:PRINT USING A$;LI(I,1)
/F;LI(I,2)/F;LI(I,3)/F;LI(I,4)/F;LI(I,5)/F;R(I)/
F;
510 NEXT I
520 ZOG%=128+(64*(I+1))+2:GOSUB 760:PRINT "COLUM
N TOTAL";
530 ZOG%=128+(64*(I+1))+16:GOSUB 760:PRINT USING
 A$;C(1)/F;C(2)/F;C(3)/F;C(4)/F;C(5)/F;TT/F
540 LOCATE 15,1:PRINT"ARE THESE DATA ACCEPTABLE?
 (Y/N)";
550 Q$=""+INKEY$:IF Q$="" THEN 550
560 IF Q$="Y" OR Q$="y" THEN 730
570 LOCATE 15,1:PRINT CHR$(253);:LOCATE 15,1:PRI
NT"ENTER THE CORRECT VALUE, ROW, AND COLUMN TO BE
 ENTERED";:INPUT X,R,C
580 A=LI(R,C)
590 IF CV(C)=0 THEN 650
600 IF (C(C)+X-A)<=CV(C) THEN 650
610 LOCATE 15,1:PRINT CHR$(253);:LOCATE 15,1:PRI
NT X;"CAUSES THE PERIOD CEILING TO BE EXCEEDED.
 OK?  (Y/N)";
620 Q$=""+INKEY$:IF Q$="" THEN 620
630 IF Q$="N" THEN 570
640 CV(C)=CV(C)+X-A
650 IF RV(R)=0 THEN 710
660 IF (R(R)+X-A)<=RV(R) THEN 710
670 LOCATE 15,1:PRINT CHR$(253);:LOCATE 15,1:PRI
NT X;"CAUSES THE LINE CEILING TO BE EXCEEDED. OK
?  (Y/N)";
680 Q$=""+INKEY$:IF Q$="" THEN 680
690 IF Q$="N" OR Q$="n" THEN 570
700 RV(R)=RV(R)+X-A
710 TT=TT+X-A:C(C)=C(C)+X-A:R(R)=R(R)+X-A:LI(R,C
)=X
```

```
720 GOTO 430
730 PRINT"(A)nother        (M)ain menu ";
740 Q$=""+INKEY$:IF Q$="" THEN 740
750 IF Q$="A" OR Q$="a" THEN RUN 10 ELSE RUN "A:
MENU"
760 ZAG%=INT(ZOG%/64):ZOG%=ZOG%-64*ZAG%+1:ZAG%=Z
AG%+1:LOCATE ZAG%,ZOG%:RETURN
```

dition is essentially a trivial problem, but the routine could accommodate it if necessary.) The program allows the user to specify the various initial matrix values and then permits modifications and adjustments to meet changing circumstances.

Poor Man's Spreadsheet

An outgrowth of the previous program, this routine (Listing 10-10) provides an inexpensive, but useful, version of a number of ledger sheet computational routines. The basic design, as shown in Fig. 10-6, is simple. The user defines the name and number of rows (R) and columns (C) that will constitute the worksheet. Then the matrix values can be entered in several different modes. In the first mode, the user specifies the table total (T) from which the computer calculates ($N = R \times C$) cell values as an equal fraction of the total ($M = T/N$). In the second mode, the user specifies either the column or row totals for each row or column, then the computer enters the appropriate fractional values. In the third mode, the user may specify each of the cell values individually. The computer then computes row, column, and table totals. At this point the user can vary cell values by any one of the three modes just used to establish the initial array. Having selected the mode, the user then selects the manner of adjustment. This can be either an addition process or a multiplication process. In the addition process the adjustment factor can be either positive or negative (creating a subtraction process). In the multiplication process an input number greater than one results in a multiplication of the specified cells. If the input factor is less than one, a division process is created. This process can be repeated as necessary until the desired relationships are achieved.

Listing 10-10. Poor Man's Spreadsheet.

```
1 '************************************************
2 '*              Listing 10-10              *
3 '*          Poor Man's Spreadsheet          *
4 '************************************************
5 '
10 CLEAR 500:A$="\              \    ":B$="######.##
  ":C$=B$
20 CLS:PRINT"SPREADSHEET FORECASTING":PRINT:PRIN
T:PRINT"(NOTE: THE PROGRAM AUTOMATICIALLY CREATE
S ROW AND COLUMN TOTALS)":INPUT"NUMBER OF COLUMN
S DESIRED";C:INPUT"NUMBER OF ROWS DESIRED";R
30 PRINT:INPUT"ENTER GENERIC NAME OF COLUMNS";CN
$:INPUT"ENTER GENERIC NAME OF ROWS";RN$
40 DIM M(R,C),C$(C),R$(R):NC=R*C:C$(0)="TOTAL":R
$(0)="TOTAL"
50 PRINT:FOR I=1 TO C:PRINT"NAME OF COLUMN HEADI
NG #";I,:INPUT V$:C$(I)=LEFT$(V$,6):NEXT
60 PRINT:FOR I=1 TO R:PRINT"NAME OF ROW LABEL #"
;I,:INPUT V$:R$(I)=LEFT$(V$,6):NEXT
70 F=-1:CLS:PRINT"COLUMN HEADINGS":PRINT:FOR I=1
 TO C:PRINT I;C$(I),:NEXT:PRINT:PRINT"ARE THESE
OK?   (Y/N)";:GOSUB 920
80 IF Q$="Y" OR Q$="y" THEN 100
```

Listing 10-10. Poor Man's Spreadsheet. (Continued From Page 215.)

```
90 GOSUB 960:GOTO 70
100 F=1:CLS:PRINT"ROW LABELS":PRINT:FOR I=1 TO R
:PRINT I;R$(I),:NEXT:PRINT:PRINT"ARE THESE OK?
(Y/N)";:GOSUB 920
110 IF Q$="Y" OR Q$="y" THEN 130
120 GOSUB 960:GOTO 100
130 CLS:PRINT "OPTIONS":PRINT:PRINT:PRINT"TO CRE
ATE THE INITIAL TABLE, YOU HAVE FOUR OPTIONS:":P
RINT:PRINT:PRINT"     1   --    TABLE SUM


      2   --    COLUMN SUMS"
140 PRINT"     3   --    ROW SUMS

                                              4
    --   EACH CELL FILLED INDIVIDUALLY":PRINT:PRI
NT:PRINT"SELECT OPTION":GOSUB 920
150 ON VAL(Q$) GOTO 160,190,230,250
160 CLS:PRINT CHR$(212);"TOTAL SUM FILL PROCESS"
:PRINT:PRINT:INPUT"ENTER THE SUM OF ALL VALUES O
F THE TABLE.";TS:CV=TS/NC:PRINT:PRINT"THANK YOU.
    THIS WILL CAUSE THE VALUE";CV;"TO BE ENTERED
THROUGHOUT THE MATRIX.    NOW LOADING...":PRINT
170 FOR I=1 TO R:FOR J=1 TO C:M(I,J)=CV:NEXT J:N
EXT I
180 GOTO 270
190 CLS:PRINT "COLUMN SUM FILL PROCESS":PRINT:PR
INT
200 FOR I=1 TO C:PRINT"ENTER THE SUM OF THE";R;"
CELLS IN COLUMN";I,:INPUT X:M(0,I)=X:FOR J=1 TO
R:M(0,0)=M(0,0)+X/R:M(J,I)=X/R:NEXT J:NEXT I:PRI
NT
210 PRINT"THE TABLE TOTAL IS";M(0,0)
220 GOTO 270
230 CLS:PRINT "ROW SUM FILL PROCESS":PRINT:PRINT
240 FOR I=1 TO R:PRINT"ENTER THE SUM OF THE";C;"
CELLS IN ROW";I,:INPUT X:M(I,0)=X:FOR J=1 TO C:M
(I,J)=X/C:M(0,0)=M(0,0)+(X/R):NEXT J:NEXT I:PRIN
T:GOTO 210
250 CLS:PRINT "INDIVIDUAL CELL FILL PROCESS":PRI
NT:PRINT
260 FOR I=1 TO R:FOR J=1 TO C:PRINT"ENTER VALUE
FOR ROW #";I;", COLUMN #";J,:INPUT X:M(I,J)=X:M(
I,0)=M(I,0)+X:M(0,J)=M(0,J)+X:M(0,0)=M(0,0)+X:NE
XT J:NEXT I:GOTO 210
270 GOSUB 590:PRINT:PRINT"THE TABLE IS FILLED WI
TH THE INITIAL DATA SET."
280 PRINT"YOU NOW HAVE THESE OPTIONS:":PRINT:PRI
NT"(C)HANGE   (V)IEW   (P)RINT   (T)ABLE PRINT   (N)
EW":PRINT:PRINT"SELECT",:GOSUB 920
290 IF Q$="C" OR Q$="c" THEN 310 ELSE IF Q$="v"
OR Q$="v" THEN 690 ELSE IF Q$="P" OR Q$="p" THEN
  700 ELSE IF Q$="T" Q$="i" THEN 980 ELSE IF Q$<>
"N" OR Q$<>"n" GOSUB 920
300 GOTO 1200
310 CLS:PRINT"CHANGE OPTIONS":PRINT:PRINT"YOU MA
Y CHANGE THE TABLE VALUES BY AN ABSOLUTE OR PROP
ORTIONATE VALUE.  AS WITH ";
```

```
320 PRINT"THE INITIAL DATA ENTRY, CHANGES MAY BE
 MADE FOR THE TABLE, COLUMN, OR ROW.  FROMTHE TA
 BLE BELOW, SELECT YOUR OPTION: "
330 PRINT:PRINT"","ABSOLUTE","PROPORTIONATE":PRI
 NT"TABLE","  1","  5":PRINT"COLUMN","  2","  6":
 PRINT"ROW","  3","  7":PRINT"CELL","  4","  8":G
 OSUB 920
340 IF Q$>"4" THEN 550
350 PRINT:INPUT"ENTER THE DESIRED ABSOLUTE VALUE
 ";V
360 PRINT"(A)DD                (M)ULTIPLY",:GOSUB 94
 0
370 IF Z$="A" THEN 380 ELSE 390
380 ON VAL(Q$) GOTO 400,420,460,500
390 ON VAL(Q$) GOTO 410,440,480,500
400 FOR I=1 TO R:FOR J=1 TO C:M(I,J)=M(I,J)+(V/N
 C):NEXT:NEXT:GOTO 580
410 FOR I=1 TO R:FOR J=1 TO C:M(I,J)=M(I,J)*V:NE
 XT:NEXT:GOTO 580
420 INPUT"ENTER COLUMN NUMBER";C1
430 FOR I=1 TO R:M(I,C1)=M(I,C1)+(V/R):NEXT:GOTO
 580
440 INPUT"ENTER COLUMN NUMBER";C1
450 FOR I=1 TO R:M(I,C1)=M(I,C1)*V:NEXT:GOTO 580
460 INPUT"ROW NUMBER";R1
470 FOR I=1 TO C:M(R1,I)=M(R1,I)+V:NEXT:GOTO 580
480 INPUT"ENTER ROW NUMBER";R1
490 FOR I=1 TO C:M(R1,I)=M(R1,I)*V:NEXT:GOTO 580
500 INPUT"ENTER CELL ROW/COLUMN COORDINATES, AND
 VALUE";X,Y,V
510 ON VAL(Z$) GOTO 520,530
520 M(X,Y)=M(X,Y)+V:GOTO 580
530 M(X,Y)=M(X,Y)*V:GOTO 580
540 GOTO 580
550 PRINT:INPUT"ENTER DESIRED PERCENTAGE CHANGE
 (5%=5)";V:V=V/100
560 ON VAL(Q$)-4 GOTO 410,440,480,570
570 INPUT"ENTER CELL ROW, COLUMN NUMBER";X,Y:GOT
 O 530
580 '
590 M(0,0)=0:FOR I=0 TO C:M(0,I)=0:NEXT I:FOR I=
 0 TO R:M(I,0)=0:NEXT:FOR I=0 TO R:FOR J=0 TO C:M
 (0,0)=M(0,0)+M(I,J):M(0,J)=M(0,J)+M(I,J):M(I,0)=
 M(I,0)+M(I,J):NEXT J:NEXT I
600 LG=M(1,1):SM=M(1,1)
610 FOR I=1 TO R:FOR J=1 TO C
620 IF M(I,J)<=LG THEN 640
630 LG=M(I,J)
640 IF SM<=M(I,J) THEN 660
650 SM=M(I,J)
660 NEXT J:NEXT I
670 F=INT(LOG(LG)/LOG(10))-1:IF F=-1 THEN F=0
680 GOTO 280
690 PRINT:INPUT"ENTER FIRST ROW AND FIRST COLUMN
 TO BE DISPLAYED";R1,C1
700 CLS:ZOG%=8+((C/2)*8):GOSUB 1230:PRINT CN$:PR
 INT USING A$;RN$;
710 FOR I=C1 TO C1+5
```

Listing 10-10. Poor Man's Spreadsheet. (Continued From Page 217.)

```
720 IF I>C THEN 740
730 PRINT C$(I),
740 NEXT
750 PRINT"TOTAL   "
760 FOR I=R1 TO R1+10
770 IF I>R THEN 850
780 PRINT R$(I),
790 FOR J=C1 TO C1+5
800 IF J>C THEN 820
810 PRINT M(I,J)/(10^F),
820 NEXT J
830 PRINT M(I,0)
840 NEXT I
850 PRINT"TOTAL      ",
860 FOR I=C1 TO C1+5
870 IF I>C THEN 900
880 PRINT M(0,I)/(10^F),
890 NEXT
900 PRINT M(0,0)/(10^F)
910 LOCATE 16,1:PRINT"(C)HANGE  (V)IEW  (P)RINT
 (N)EW  (T)ABLE PRINT   SELECT";:GOSUB 920:GOTO
 290
920 Q$=""+INKEY$:IF Q$="" THEN 920
930 RETURN
940 Z$=""+INKEY$:IF Z$="" THEN 940
950 RETURN
960 PRINT:INPUT"ENTER NUMBER AND CORRECTED NAME"
;N,X$:IF F=1 THEN R$(N)=X$ ELSE C$(N)=X$
970 RETURN
980 LPRINT"","","",C$(0):LPRINT USING A$;R$(0);:
A=1:B=14
990 FOR I=A TO B
1000 IF I>C THEN 1030
1010 LPRINT USING A$;C$(I);
1020 NEXT
1030 LPRINT"TOTAL"
1040 FOR I=1 TO R
1050 IF I>R THEN 1130
1060 LPRINT USING A$;R$(I);
1070 FOR J=A TO B
1080 IF J>C THEN 1100
1090 LPRINT USING B$;M(I,J)/(10^F);
1100 NEXT J
1110 LPRINT USING C$;M(I,0)/(10^F)
1120 NEXT I
1130 LPRINT"TOTAL    ";
1140 A=1:B=C
1150 FOR I=A TO B:LPRINT USING B$;M(0,I);:NEXT
1160 LPRINT USING C$;M(0,0)/(10^F);
1170 A=B+1:IF A>C THEN 1200
1180 B=A+13:IF B>C THEN B=C
1190 LPRINT"":GOTO 980
1200 PRINT"(A)nother      (M)ain menu ";
1210 Q$=""+INKEY$:IF Q$="" THEN 1210
1220 IF Q$="A" OR Q$="a" THEN RUN 10 ELSE RUN "A
:MENU"
```

```
1230 ZAG%=INT(ZOG%/64):ZOG%=ZOG%-64*ZAG%+1:ZAG%=
ZAG%+1:                              LOCATE ZAG%
,ZOG%:RETURN
```

EXERCISES

1. Figure 10-7 shows the difference between the appreciated balance of two investments, one appreciating at 10 percent per year and the other at 5 percent.

   Assume that the upper curve represents the asking price of a home and the lower line represents the median family income in a given community. The dashed line is approximately twice the value of the lower, 5 percent, line. Whether the bottom line is 5 percent or 7.5, whether the top line is 8, 10, or 15 percent, is really immaterial. The point of this figure is that median family income normally increases at one rate and the median price for a home in the same community rises at another rate. For the purposes of granting loans, a rule of thumb often used is that families can afford a home the price of which is no more than twice the annual family income. Notice, however, that at about the 13th year the median price rises to a level greater than twice the median family income. The significance of this is that more than half the population can no longer afford to buy a home. During the 10- to 15-year period ending sometime in 1980, real estate sales people were touting the purchase of homes as an obviously wise investment. The median price of homes was exceeding the annual inflation rate by almost a factor of two to one. "How could one lose?" they would ask. Some even went so far as to suggest that this incredible rate differential would go on forever. One look at Fig. 10-7, however, tells the real story. No matter what the rates are, so long as the appreciation rate for the median sales price of used or new homes is greater than the rate of increase of median family incomes, there is an inevitable point at which the sales price becomes excessive and unrealistic. Until the income level of the majority of potential home-owners increases to the point at which median income is realistically related to sales price, sales will slump and/or prices will level off.

   Figure 10-8 gives what we believe is the more realistic price curve as a function of median family income. This exercise has three parts:

   A. Gather used-home prices for your community for the last 25 years or so, as well as the local median family income. Plot these data more or less as shown in Fig. 10-8.

   B. From these data, test the hypothesis illustrated in Fig. 10-8. If the hypothesis is not sustained, go on to the next exercise. Otherwise, go on to the next step.

   C. Compute the interval between the beginning and the end of a rising price cycle. Compute the mean length of the price plateau period. We suspect the ratio of the rising time to plateau time to be roughly 10 to 1. That is, prices will rise steadily for about ten years, and then level off for a year or so until income rises to meet the minimum levels for significant major purchases. Develop the data and the procedure to sustain or revise this hypothesis.

2. Collect stock market data for a month. Use the drunkard's walk, decomposition, and regression techniques to forecast the subsequent 30-day activity record. Which technique gives the most satisfying results? Why?

219

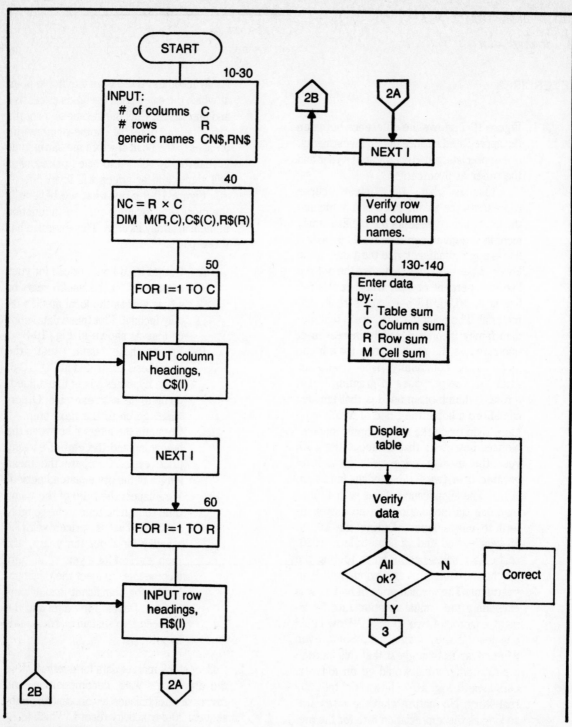

Fig. 10-6. Flowchart of Listing 10-10.

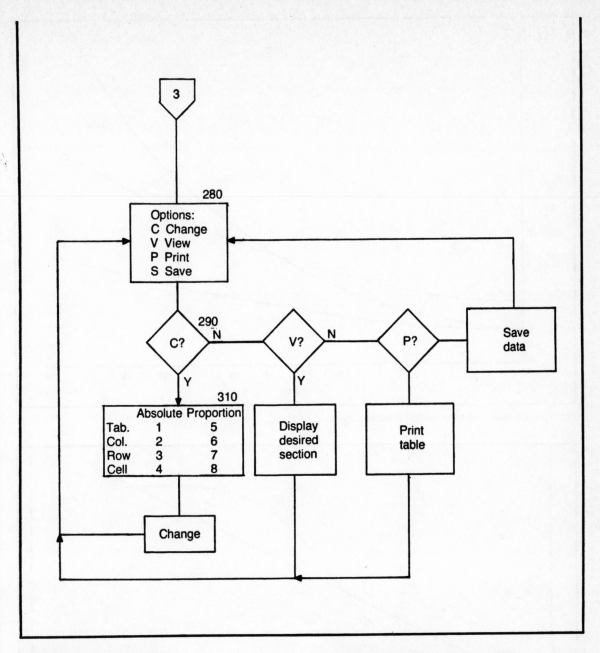

SUGGESTED READING

Edwards, R.D. and J. Magee, 1976. *Technical Analysis of Stock Trends*. Springfield, MA: John Magee & Associates.

Hardy, C. C., 1978, *Investors Guide to Technical Analysis*. New York: McGraw-Hill.

Hefert, E. A., 1978. *Techniques of Financial Analysis*. Homewood, IL: Dow Jones-Irwin.

Malinvaud, E., 1966. *Statistical Methods of Econometrics*. Amsterdam: North Holland Publishing Co.

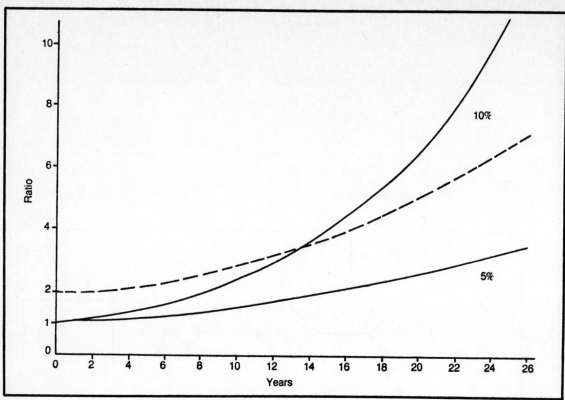

Fig. 10-7. Comparative accumulated interest curves.

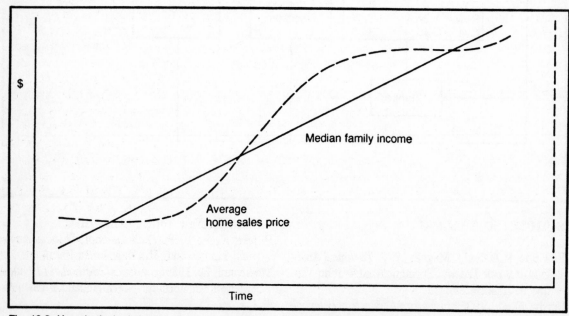

Fig. 10-8. Hypothetical relationship between median income and sales prices of homes.

Chapter 11

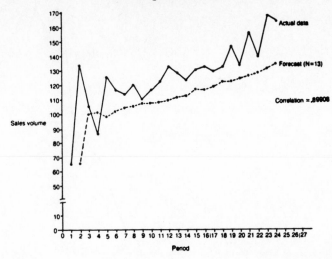

Technological Forecasting

Although Leonardo da Vinci did a remarkable job of forecasting a wide variety of technological innovations (among them, the helicopter and submarine), technological forecasting (or TF) was not developed as a coherent art or craft until the 1960s. The reasons for the disinterest in TF until then, and the reasons for the dramatic change in corporate attitudes, are many. Perhaps one of the more significant factors is the rate of growth in technological capability.

In da Vinci's time decades might pass between technological innovations that would advance a capability one order of magnitude. For example, in 1400 AD a pump drains a field at the rate of ten gallons an hour, and it might be another century until a better pump is developed that can remove one hundred gallons per hour. Today, on the other hand, technological developments are advancing faster than we can design and market the finished product. Airplanes, for example, are often technologically obsolete before they take their maiden flight for certification. In computer science the growth rate is chilling (see Fig. 11-1). In 1944, the processing speed of the Harvard Mark I computer was .403 operations per second. By 1946, the Eniac computer could rush along at 44.65 operations per second—an improvement of some 10979.40 percent. By 1964, the CDC 6600 operated at a rate of 4,091,293 operations per second—an improvement of over one billion percent from 1944!

While not all aspects of the twentieth century are rushing along at that rate, and while there are upper limits to many technological systems, the fact remains that the rate of technological advance in general is increasing to the point where we have to pay close attention to developments to ensure, from a corporate viewpoint, that we are not overrun by the competition, and, from a social viewpoint, that technology does not devastate our lives but is exploited effectively to improve the quality of life. This chapter reviews some of the major technological forecasting techniques, identifies those suitable for application on or to microcomputers, and provides programs and algorithms useful in forecasting technology.

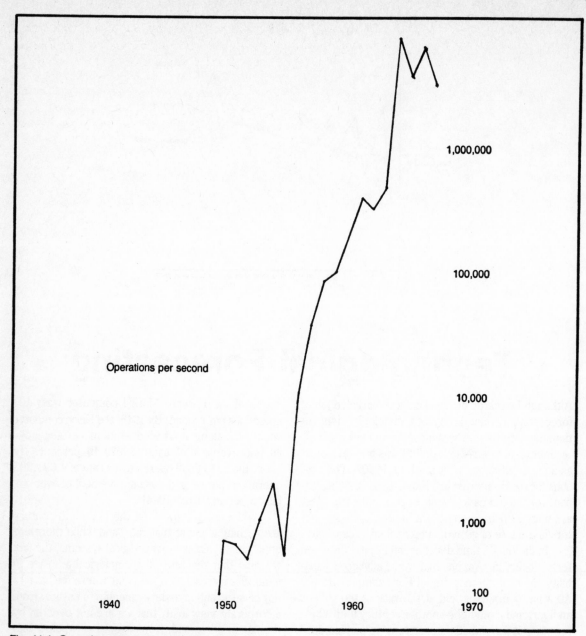

1,000,000

100,000

Operations per second

10,000

1,000

100

1940   1950   1960   1970

Fig. 11-1. Operating speeds of computers, 1940-1970.

TECHNOLOGICAL FORECASTING TECHNIQUES

Emerging from the scientific and management literature of the last 15 to 20 years are a number of forecasting techniques, each with some advantage and utility. Among them are: intuitive forecasting, goal-oriented forecasting, dynamic modeling, and trend extrapolation methods.

Intuitive Forecasting

This is an approach based on informed or expert option. One of the more notable examples of this technique is called the Delphi Technique. An approach developed by the RAND Corporation, the Delphi technique exploits informed or expert opinion concerning future events or developments. The technique relies on three characteristics: anonymity, statistical analysis, and feedback of reasoning. In brief, a panel of experts is given a list of anticipated events or future technologies and asked to make an estimate of when each item will actually occur. The responses are then evaluated statistically, and the results are returned to the panel members for comment. If a member's own estimate is significantly different from the concensus, the member is asked to either defend the exceptional position or conform to the group standard. The comment, statistical analysis, and feedback process is repeated two to four times. In the end the forecasting team creates a chart somewhat similar to the one in Fig. 11-2.

In reality, in order to preserve the advantage of anonymity, the panel never meets in conference but is addressed as individuals, none of whom know who the other members are. The reasoning for this feature is that good (perhaps more accurate) response may come from those on the panel with only very modest credentials. It is felt that if these people were to know that some distinguished and recog-

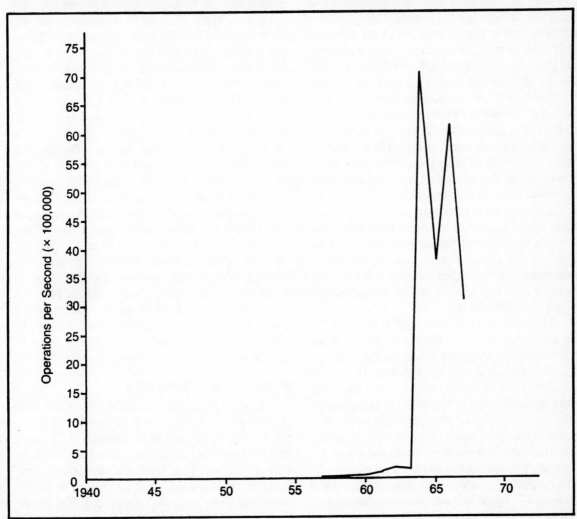

Fig. 11-2. Scaled version of the graph shown in Fig. 11-1.

nized world authority was on the panel and that that person was taking issue with the lesser figure's estimate, the first person might back off and concede the position more because of reputation than because of fact or reason. Conversely, the technique forces the responsible world expert to rely upon reason and fact in defense of his position rather than depending on reputation to support his credibility. Those using this technique hope that the interaction of experts will elicit meaningful estimates of future events or technologies.

The technique is not without some difficulties. This approach is time-consuming for all involved. The staff must prepare and cull out hundreds of items prior to beginning the test and then spend considerable time in the computation of the statistics after each round. The technique rests on the assumption that the experts will spend a responsible amount of time considering each of the options presented them. An adequate response may take days, if not weeks, for each expert to consider and prepare. The greater the stature of the expert, the more difficult it is to spare the kind of time required, not to mention the difficulty keeping the panel members motivated during each subsequent round. Having evaluated a subject two or three times, and having settled on a firm estimate, it is most demanding to expect the expert to review the material the fourth or fifth time with the same enthusiasm as the first time. As a consequence, more recent Delphi experiments have modified the approach by shortening the list of topics and by limiting the reappraisals to only two or three iterations.

A difficult aspect of the Delphi technique is the framing of the items to be evaluated. One approach is to brainstorm a number of technologies that appear to have some chance of coming into being sometime in the future—no matter how distant. Another approach might be to present the panel members with a scenario or protocol within which they generate the list of topics or future developments. For example, each member could be asked to: "Identify ten sources of electrical energy not currently available, five modes of transportation not yet developed." These lists are then consolidated into a master list, eliminating redundant items.

Regardless of the technique selected, each item must be clearly stated and not ambiguous; that is, each item must be limited to one topic, one distinct technology, or one event. Further, as a technical consideration, the number of panelists must be large enough to produce meaningful statistics. It is most often pointless, for example, to compute standard deviations on a sample consisting of fewer than 15 to 20 items (read panelists). Fifty to several hundred panelists are even better if you can round them up. We know of one study that involved several thousand panelists. However, don't abandon an experiment with the Delphi process if you can only collect a dozen, or two, panelists, or if your list only has several items. Previous chapters have referred to the principle of central tendency in research statistics. Even the opinion of one panelist will ordinarily fall somewhere in the range of the median or concensus view. Two or three such opinions will definitely begin to highlight the concensus.

In any event, it is beyond the scope of this book to really aid you in the selection of panelists or the selection of the survey items, although the microcomputer can be used to keep track of the panel participants in a mailing list, or the survey items in a word-processing system. Rather, the program found in Listing 11-1 computes the statistical data required to summarize the responses of the panelists. It also identifies those panelists who, because of significant departure from the norm, will be required to explain or defend their positions, or to conform to the majority view. Listing 11-1 depends on Listing 11-2, which is a short program that allows you to save your data concerning the events. This data is reloaded and used by the program in Listing 11-1.

Goal-Oriented Forecasting

This technique is based on the assumption that technology develops to satisfy the needs of society: "Necessity is the mother of invention." To forecast the future technology, one makes the best possible projection of social needs and extrapolates from these technologies that must be created to satisfy those social needs. In the very early 1960s, President Kennedy announced the objective of putting a

Listing 11-1. Delphi Analysis.

```
1 '*********************************************
2 '*              Listing 11-1                 *
3 '*              Delphi Analysis              *
4 '*********************************************
5 '
10 CLS:KEY OFF
20 CLEAR 1000:PRINT"Delphi Analysis:":PRINT:PRIN
T
30 PRINT"Have panelist names been filed?   (Y/N)"
;:GOSUB 690
40 IF Q$="Y" OR Q$="y" THEN 60
50 RUN "A:C11P2"
60 OPEN "I",1,"DELPHI.DAT"
70 INPUT N,M:DIM T(3,N,M),N$(M),MN(M,3),SD(M,3),
SX(M,3),X2(M,3)
80 FOR I=1 TO M:INPUT #1,N$(I):NEXT I
90 CLOSE
100 T$(1)="Earliest":T$(2)="Probable":T$(3)="Lat
est"
110 PRINT"Use (T)oday's date (";DATE$;") or use
(A)nother date as the base? "
120 GOSUB 690
130 IF Q$="T" OR "t" THEN GOTO 150
140 INPUT "Enter desired base date (MM/DD/YYYY)"
;DD$:GOTO 160
150 DD$=DATE$
160 GOSUB 710:BY=JD
170 FOR I=1 TO N
180    PRINT"Panelist # ";I
190   FOR J=1 TO M
200     PRINT"Event:    ";N$(J)
210      FOR K=1 TO 3
220        PRINT T$(K);" date (MM/DD/YYYY)",:INPUT
 DD$:GOSUB 710:T(K,I,J)=JD-BY
230      NEXT K
240    NEXT J
250 NEXT I
260 PRINT""
270 PRINT"All times correct?   (Y/N)";"gosub 6001
0
280 IF Q$="Y" OR Q$="y" THEN 310
290 INPUT "Enter panelist number, event number,
phase ('Earliest =1, Latest =3, Most Probalbe =2
), and correct date";I,J,K,DD$:GOSUB 710
300 T(K,I,J)=JD-BY:GOTO 270
310 PRINT"":PRINT"Processing Data":PRINT""
320 FOR I=1 TO N
330    FOR J=1 TO M
340      FOR K=1 TO 3
350        X=T(K,I,J):SX(J,K)=SX(J,K)+X:X2(J,K)=X
2(J,K)+(X^2)
360      NEXT K
370    NEXT J
380 NEXT I
390 FOR I=1 TO M
```

Listing 11-1. Delphi Analysis. (Continued From Page 227.)

```
400   FOR J=1 TO 3
410       MN(I,J)=BY+(SX(I,J)/N):SD(I,J)=SQR((X2(I
,J)-((SX(I,J)^2)/N))/(N-1))
420   NEXT J
430 NEXT I
440 CLS
450 PRINT"#     Name
   Mean            SD"
460  B$="###   \
\"
470  C$="                                        \
                \ \ \ #######.###"
480 FOR I=1 TO M
490   PRINT USING B$;I;N$(I)
500   FOR J=1 TO 3
510     GOSUB 770
520     PRINT USING C$;DT$;"+/-";SD(I,J);" days"
530   NEXT J
540 PRINT""
550 NEXT I
560 PRINT""
570 PRINT"The following individuals have forecas
t event dates significantly different fromthe me
an.  They should either change their forecast or
 explain the deviation:":PRINT""
580 FOR I=1 TO M
590   FOR J=1 TO N
600     FOR K=1 TO 3
610       IF T(K,J,I) >(MN(I,K)-(2*SD(I,K))) AND
T(K,J,I)<(MN(I,K)+(2*SD(I,K))) THEN 630
620         PRINT"Panelist #";J,N$(I),T$(K)
630     NEXT K
640   NEXT J
650 NEXT I
660 PRINT"(A)nother       (M)ain menu ";
670 GOSUB 690
680 IF Q$="A" OR Q$="a" THEN RUN 20 ELSE RUN A:M
ENU"
690 Q$=""+INKEY$:IF Q$="" THEN 690
700 RETURN
710 DY=VAL(MID$(DD$,4,2)):MO=VAL(LEFT$(DD$,2)):Y
R=VAL(RIGHT$(DD$,4))
720 IF MO>2 THEN X=0 ELSE X=1
730 C=INT((YR-X)/100)
740 N=DY+INT(367*(((MO-2)/12)+X))+INT(INT(365.25
*(YR-X))-(.75*C))
750 JD=N-(365.25+INT(INT(365.25*(YR-1))-(.75*C))
)
760 RETURN
770 N=MN(I,J)
780 I=INT(N):F=N-I
790 IF I>2299160! THEN 810
800 A=I:GOTO 820
810 A=INT((I-1867216.25#)/36524.25):B=I+A+1-INT(
A/4)
820 C=B+1524
```

```
830 D=INT((C-122.1)/365.25)
840 E=INT(365.25*D)
850 G=INT((C-E)/30.6001)
860 DY=INT(C+F-E-INT(30.6001*G))
870 IF G<13.5 THEN MO=G-1 ELSE MO=G-13
880 IF MO>2.5 THEN YR=D-4716 ELSE YR=D-4715
890 DT$=STR$(MO)+" /"+STR$(DY)+" /"+STR$(YR)
900 RETURN
```

man on the moon by the end of the decade. At the time of the announcement, the technologies required to achieve that goal did not exist. As the American people embraced the concept and accepted it as a political and social objective, it was possible to forecast a number of technologies that would emerge in subsequent years. Many such forecasts were valid and those who attended to them became quite wealthy. Except for recommending a Delphi approach for forecasting what social needs might exist at some point in the future, this book will pursue goal-oriented forecasting no further, however.

Dynamic Modeling Method

The user of this technique specifies the subject or limits of the study and begins seeking some starting point estimates or limits that can be quantified. Using these values, the data are allowed to run to a logical conclusion, which becomes the forecast. A simple example might be a model designed to forecast the supply of petroleum through the next ten to twenty years. The forecaster carefully attempts to construct a model of the region under study that includes all factors affecting the demand and production of oil during the period in question. Certainly, population studies are important, as are forecasts of the future of various oil-consuming equipment and industries. These, and other identifiable variables, are built into the model. When all factors have been entered, the computer follows the limits prescribed and generates a forecast.

Listing 11-2. Delphi Support.

```
1 '*****************************************
2 '*              Listing 11-2             *
3 '*             Delphi Support            *
4 '*****************************************
5 '
10 CLS:KEY OFF
20 CLS:CLEAR 1000:PRINT "DELPHI SUPPORT":PRINT:P
RINT
30 INPUT"ENTER NUMBER OF PANELISTS";N
40 INPUT"ENTER NUMBER OF EVENTS";M
50 DIM N$(M):PRINT
60 FOR I=1 TO M
70 PRINT"ENTER NAME OF EVENT # ";I,:INPUT N$(I)
80 NEXT I
90 FOR I=1 TO M:PRINT I;N$(M),:NEXT
100 PRINT:PRINT"ALL ENTRIES CORRECT?  (Y/N)   ";
110 Q$=""+INKEY$:IF Q$="" THEN 110
120 IF Q$="Y" THEN 140
130 PRINT:INPUT"ENTER ITEM NUMBER AND CORRECT NA
ME";X,N$(X):CLS:GOTO 90
140 PRINT:PRINT"LOADING DATA"
150 OPEN "O",1,"A:DELPHI.DAT"
160 PRINT#1,N,M
170 FOR I=1 TO M:PRINT#1,N$(M):NEXT
180 CLOSE
190 RUN "A:C11P1"
```

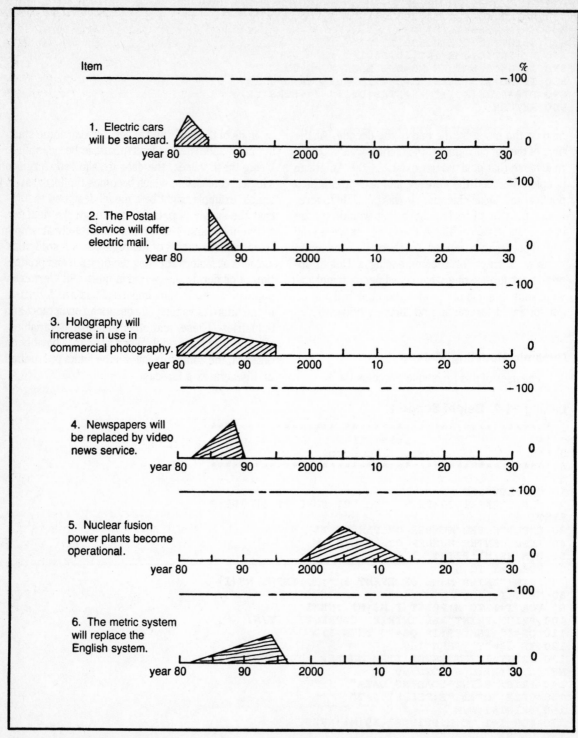

Fig. 11-3. Delphi summary page.

Often, however, many of the forecasts upon which the model is built are far from precise and unique values. Rather, the forecasts fall within some specified range of values. Seldom can we certify that the population of a region will be exactly X people, but we must say the population will range between this value and that. The model and subsequent forecast often become complicated, especially if there are a large number of input variables, each of which has a range of possible values. In such an instance, the user of this technique can elect to use one of the three options. The first makes the computer generate a forecast based on all possible combinations of all the input variables. Even with the most sophisticated computers a serious task of any significant scope would take an extraordinary length of time to complete. An alternative is to use an expert to interact with the computer in selecting several sets of parameters that intuitively seem correct or more appropriate. A third approach is to assign probabilities to the probabilities and use only the more probable. For example, while the regional population may be estimated to vary from 1,000,000 to 3,000,000, the extremes will only be realized under very improbable circumstances, and the most probable population projection is for the population to range from 1,760,340 to 1,890,000. Instead of sending the computer through the entire two million person range, we limit it to the range of the 130 thousand or so it is most likely to have to handle.

Trend Extrapolation

This technique exploits the mathematical trend line and regression analysis tools.

Trend Line Analysis

To make an estimate of the future, the trend line analyst simply looks at the historical data, computes a best-fit trend, and projects it some distance into the future. If the population growth rate is 5 percent a year and the population of the United States in a given year is 200 million, we can project that ten years later the population will be about 325,778,925 people. Chapter 13 deals in greater detail with population estimates.

EXERCISES

1. Run a Delphi exercise in your class to make an estimate of ten technological advances likely to occur.
2. The S or ogive-curve is frequently the best description of the accumulative expansion of an innovation in a given technological or economic environment. Research the sources of sales information concerning microcomputers. Collect total sales volume (number of units) sold each year from 1965 to the present. Develop a routine to fit an S-curve to these data. On the basis of your work, forecast the approximate date microcomputer sales will reach a natural plateau. What is the annual sales volume at this point?

SUGGESTED READING

Blohm, H., and K., Steinbuch, eds., 1973. *Technological Forecasting in Practice*. London: Saxon House.

Bright, J. R., 1980. *Practical Technological Forecasting*. Austin, TX: Technologies Futures, Inc.

Cetron, M. J., ed., 1971: *Industrial Applications of Technology Forecasting*. New York: John Wiley and Sons.

Martino, J. P., 1972. *Technological Forecasting for Decision Making*. New York: American Elsevier Publishing Company.

Chapter 12

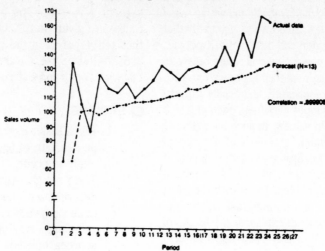

Astronomical Applications

The stars appear at both ends of the forecasting spectrum. At one extreme, the positions of the stars have been thought to hold the fates of all living creatures. It is believed that Adolph Hitler made major decisions concerning the conduct of the German offensives during World War II based on astrological advice. But, despite the bizarre extents to which advocates of astrology may have taken their beliefs, we owe a great debt to generations of mystics for their preoccupation with the positions of the planets and the stars. From them we have remarkably long and accurate records from which we can reconstruct any number of useful and helpful pieces of astronomical information.

Today's star-gazers may have more practical applications in mind, but the task of forecasting astronomical phenomena remains a dark and tedious science. Our national and global economies rise and fall, based in part on the ability of astronomers and astrophysicists to accurately control the orbits of earth resources satellites. That task requires skill in determining the positions of not only the space-craft itself, but also of the stars and the planets for reference points. In the quest for knowledge and scientific advancement, we must also be able to chart the courses, which will enable us to safely land equipment and eventually people on these planets.

While this chapter cannot offer detailed solutions to all astronomical problems, it can offer a starting point. In this chapter we will sort out some of the problems in telling time and the seasons, both through ancient techniques devised by those who built Stonehenge and through systems used by NASA to compute courses to the planets. Since weather forecasting is a science the complexity of which normally exceeds the capabilities of the microcomputer, we feel unable to adequately devote a chapter to the subject. Nonetheless, since weather is a function of the natural universe and greatly influenced by astronomical phenomena, the chapter does include weather-related forecasting routines. The bibliography recommends advanced reading for those whose interest in weather forecasting remains unabated.

CALENDARS AND TELLING TIME

Ancient man must have noticed at least two natural phenomena: the cycle of day and night, and the passage of the seasons from summer to winter to summer again.

Somewhere in these beginnings there must have been a useful purpose in learning how to count. While the concept of zero or nullity is a relatively recent Arab invention, man has been counting beans, eggs, days, months, and years for as long as we have any recorded history. Indeed, many of the original artifacts we have as evidence of man's emergence are inventory or shipping records containing numbers. The length of the year in days must have been one of man's original constants. As we became more aware of the function of smaller fractions of time as useful tools in estimating things, like the distance we have sailed in open seas, the more important became the task of dividing the day into meaningful portions such as hours, minutes, and seconds. With the coming of the second, the wiser among us became aware that the year was not precisely 365 days, but a touch longer. So long as the best clocks were only accurate to the nearest hour or so, and navigation was still mainly coastal, people were satisfied with exactly 24 hours in a day, minutes and seconds being one-sixtieth of the larger value. Since then we become a bit more precise. A second, now, is roughly the interval of time it takes for 9,192,631,770 cycles of the radiation corresponding to the transition of the caesium-133 atom. Try counting to over nine billion between the tick and the tock of the clock—that's a second! Sixty of those make a minute, sixty of which make an hour, twenty-four of which, more or less, make a day. Beyond a day the relationships cease to exist. It's true that years (a set of days) and centuries are computed in the course of astronomical work, but years are not precise functions of days. Some years contain more days than others, and the number of days in a given year work out to a very odd number. Depending on the type of year one is referring to, a year contains either 365.2564 or 365.24215 days, each of which actually consists of 23 hours, 56 minutes and 4.09 seconds—at last count. Why the difference? Well, it takes one tropical year for the earth to complete its 360 degree course around the sun, and that is equal to 365.24215 days or so. However, if you were to gaze out at a particular star at midnight on the first of January one year, you would have to wait until about 12.20.52 AM a year later to see the same star in the same position. This illustrates differences between the tropical and sidereal time.

Stonehenge

Sometime during the second millenia B.C. a group of ambitious stonecutters cut and dragged massive 30-ton sandstone blocks from up to 135 miles away to the Salisbury Plain and there constructed that circular monument to man's obsession with solar and lunar phenomena: Stonehenge. While many of the larger stones in the center of the arrangement are now lying in disarray, it is possible to confirm that many of them were used to foretell the positions of the sun and the moon at significant moments, such as the summer solstice, the vernal equinox, and so forth. Surrounding the central ring of stones is an equally interesting, if less obvious, set of holes. Numbering 56, they are called the Aubrey holes. It wasn't until 1963 that British astronomer Gerald Hawkins used a computer to support a hypothesis that the holes can be, and probably were, used to determine the position of the moon and sun, as well as the likelihood of lunar and solar eclipses. For the purposes of this kind of solar astronomy, it is acceptable and perhaps easier to accept the original convention that the sun moves about the earth in an orbit as the planets revolve about the sun. Figure 12-1 is a rough representation of such an orbit, as well as the actual orbit of the moon. Notice that the orbit of the moon is inclined somewhat in relationship to the "orbit" of the sun. The two points where the orbit of the moon crosses that of the sun are the *nodes* of the moon's orbit. These points, relative to an observer on earth, are not stationary, but revolve slowly in a clockwise direction. If a full moon occurs when the moon is at one of the nodes, there will be a lunar eclipse. If the moon is new and at one of the nodes, there will be a solar eclipse.

Using four stones, the ancient Britons could predict a number of phenomena. One stone is marked

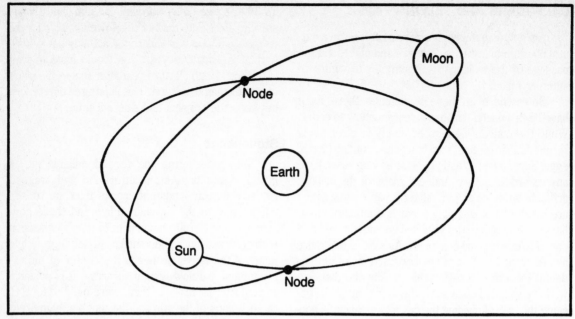

Fig. 12-1. Conceptutal notion of lunar and solar nodes.

to represent the moon and another, the sun, and the remaining two are marked and placed to represent the two nodes, one opposite the other. By observing the following rules the priests could make their forecasts:

1. Move the moon's marker one hole counterclockwise twice a day, at morning and evening.
2. Move the sun's marker one hole counterclockwise every 6.5 days.
3. Move the node markers one hole clockwise three times a year.

When the moon's marker falls into a hole occupied by one of the node markers, there is a possibility of an eclipse, depending on the position of the sun. If the sun is very close to being on the opposite side of the ring, the moon will be full and a lunar eclipse is likely. If both the moon and sun markers are close to each other, a solar eclipse is possible, but dependent on the time of day and the actual relative positions.

Out of all these combinations of orbits and cycles comes another interesting feature, the *saros*.

It happens that if we know the date and time of an eclipse, we can very quickly predict the date and time of the last and the next eclipse of the same type simply by adding or subtracting 6585 days and approximately seven hours to the date and time of the known eclipse. This period is also equal to exactly 223 full moons. This is the saros.

We leave it to your imagination to figure out how people who left behind no trace of a written language or artifacts of civilization other than Stonehenge itself could make the necessary longterm observations and computations in order to develop the 56-hole arrangement. The truth may be that they moved the stones and dug the holes according to some much simpler protocol, but as an idiot-savant reaches astounding conclusions, inadvertently constructing their clever machine.

Modern Calendars

During the reign of Julius Caesar a calendar routine was established, the features of which persist to a large degree to this date. A fundamental characteristic of the Julian calendar was the concept of the 365.25-day solar year contrasted with the 365-day

234

civil year. The compensation used, until the 1500s, was to simply increase the length of a month one day once every four years. Because of the slight, but eventually significant disparity between the 365.24215-day year and the 365.25-day year, the calendar drifted so that the seasons were no longer in step with the calendar. Upon the recommendation of his learned staff, Pope Gregory instituted a minor, but profoundly effective, change in the rule. Leap years would continue to be implemented once every four years except for century years—those ending in 00 (1900, 2000, 21000)—unless the century year was also evenly divisable by 400 (such as 2000). This modification keeps the years even with the seasons for a significantly long period. The calendar scheme we now use in the western world is the Gregorian calendar.

A vestige of the older calendar is the sequential numbering of the days from January 1 each year. Thus, the Julian date refers not to the older protocol, but simply the place a date has in the year. In most years, May 29 is the 149th day of the civil year (150th in Leap Years).

It is frequently useful or even necessary to be able to compute the number of days between two dates and to determine the day of the week given a date. In astronomy it is essential to be able to compute the number of days between a benchmark date, called the *epoch*, and any other date.

If we specify a date of Y = year, M = month (January = 1), and D = day of month, the first step is to convert this to a standardized day number form. This is done with the following algorithm:

1. If M is larger than 2, make $X = 0$; otherwise make $X = 1$.

2. Let C = the integer part of $\dfrac{Y - X}{100}$.

3. Let $N = D$ plus the integer part of $365 \times \dfrac{M - 2}{12} + X$ plus the integer part of the

   $365.25 \times (Y - X - .75 \times C)$.

4. The day of the week (Sunday = 0) = the integer part of $7 \times (N/7 - $ integer part of $N/7)$.

5. The Julian date is computed from $N - 336$ plus the integer part of the integer part of $365.25 \times (Y - 1)$ less $.75 \times C$.

By computing the basic N for two dates, the number of days between those dates can be computed by simple subtraction. Steps 4 and 5 in the algorithm yield the day of the week of a given date and the Julian date of the date. A number of computer programs supporting accounting activities, banking transactions, or any other time-based event often use Julian dates as part of the file identifiers.

Listing 12-1 implements these basic rules. It also allows the user to input the time of day and expresses the day of the week by its name.

It is also possible to reverse the process and convert the base day number back into a recognizable date. The process to accomplish this is:

1. Let N = the notional Julian date $N = 2445210.45$.
2. Let I be the integer and F $I = 2445210$ the fractional part of N $F = .45$.
3. If I is greater than 2299160, then do step 3A, otherwise, do step 3B.

3A. A = integer part
   $(I-1867216.25)/36524.25$ $A = 15$
   $B = I + A + 1 - $ integer
   part $(A/4)$ $B = 2445223$.

3B. $A = 1$

4. $C = B + 1524$ $C = 2446747$.

5. D = integer part
   $(C - 122.1)/365.25$ $D = 6698$.

6. E = integer part
   $365.25 \times D$ $E = 2446444$.

7. G = integer part $(C - E)/30.6001$ $G = 9$.

8. Compute the day of the month from $D = C + F - E - $ integer part 30.6001.
   $\times G$ $D = 28$.

9. If G is less than 13.5 then $M = G - 1$ else $M = G - 13$. This is the month number $M = 8$.

10. If M is greater than 2.5,

then $Y = D - 4716$ else $Y = D - 4715$. This is the year. $Y = 1982$.

Listing 12-1. Basic Calendar.

```
1 '***********************************************
2 '*                Listing 12-1                 *
3 '*              Basic Calendar                 *
4 '***********************************************
5 '
10 CLS:KEY OFF
20 PRINT"CALENDAR":PRINT:PRINT
30 DW$(0)="SUNDAY":DW$(1)="MONDAY":DW$(2)="TUESD
AY":DW$(3)="WEDNESDAY":DW$(4)="THURSDAY":DW$(5)=
"FRIDAY":DW$(6)="SATURDAY"
40 DIM M$(12):MM$="JANFEBMARAPRMAYJUNJULAUGSEPOC
TNOVDEC":FOR I=1 TO 12:M$(I)=MID$(MM$,((I-1)*3)+
1,3):NEXT I
50 DIM MD(12):D$="312831303130313130313031":FOR
I=1 TO 12:MD(I)=VAL(MID$(D$,((I-1)*2)+1,2)):NEXT
60 PRINT"A   --   JULIAN DATE, GIVEN DAY, MONTH,
 AND YEAR                      B   --
   DAY, MONTH, AND YEAR, GIVEN JULIAN DATE":PRINT
:PRINT"ENTER CHOICE  ";
70 Q$=""+INKEY$:IF Q$="" THEN 70 ELSE IF Q$="B"
OR Q$="b" THEN 310
80 PRINT:INPUT"ENTER DATE DESIRED   (DD,MM,YYYY)"
;D,M,Y
90 GOSUB 130
100 PRINT:PRINT"THE JULIAN DATE OF ";M$(M);D;","
;Y;", IS ";
110 PRINT N;".   THE DAY IS ";DW$(DW):PRINT"AND I
S DAY #";JD;"OF THE YEAR."
120 GOTO 450
130 IF M>2 THEN X=0 ELSE X=1
140 'COMPUTE CENTURY
150 C=INT((Y-X)/100)
160 'CHECK FOR LEAP YEAR
170 IF (Y/4)<>INT(Y/4) THEN 210
180 IF (Y/100)<>INT(Y/100) THEN 200
190 IF (Y/400)<>INT(Y/400) THEN 210
200 LY=1:GOTO 220
210 LY=0
220 IF FL=0 THEN 250
230 RETURN
240 'COMPUTE JULIAN NUMBER
250 N=D+INT(367*(((M-2)/12)+X))+INT(INT(365.25*(
Y-X))-(.75*C))
260 'COMPUTE DAY OF WEEK
270 DW=INT(7*((N/7)-INT(N/7)))
280 'COMPUTE ANNUAL JULIAN DATE
290 JD=N-(336+INT(INT(365.25*(Y-1))-(.75*C)))
300 RETURN
310 PRINT:FL=1:INPUT"ENTER JULIAN DATE (LONG FOR
M:   1/1/1900 = 693932)";N
320 Y=1950
330 A=N-712193!:M=1:D=1
```

```
340 GOSUB 170:IF LY=1 THEN 390
350 IF A<=365 THEN 400
360 A=A-365:Y=Y+1
370 GOSUB 170:IF LY=0 THEN 350
380 A=A-1:GOTO 340
390 IF A>366 THEN 360
400 MD(2)=MD(2)+LY
410 IF A<=MD(M) THEN 430
420 A=A-MD(M):M=M+1:GOTO 410
430 D=A:FL=0:GOSUB 130
440 GOTO 100
450 PRINT:PRINT"(A)nother          (M)ain menu ";
460 GOSUB 480
470 IF Q$="A" OR Q$="a" THEN RUN 10 ELSE RUN "A:
MENU"
480 Q$=""+INKEY$:IF Q$="" THEN 480
490 RETURN
```

Thus the day number 2445210.45 converts to August 28, 1982. The fractional portion, .45, converts to 10.48 AM.

A routine to implement this conversion is found in Listing 12-2.

These routines are simple and straightforward tools that can be used in a number of different routines. Listing 12-3 can be used in a number of different routines. It is a full-blown calendar routine. It calls out the days by their names as it does the months. In addition, it permits the computation of a date by either the Julian (old style) or Gregorian protocols, and gives the phase of the moon. It computes the number of days between two dates and

Listing 12-2. Julian to Calendar Date.

```
1 '***********************************************
2 '*                 Listing 12-2                *
3 '*            Julian to Calendar Date          *
4 '***********************************************
5 '
10 CLS
20 INPUT"ENTER JULIAN DATE";N
30 I=INT(N):F=N-I
40 IF I>2299160! THEN 60
50 A=I:GOTO 70
60 A=INT((I-1867216.25#)/36524.25):B=I+A+1-INT(A
/4)
70 C=B+1524
80 D=INT((C-122.1)/365.25)
90 E=INT(365.25*D)
100 G=INT((C-E)/30.6001)
110 DM=C+F-E-INT(30.6001*G)
120 IF G<13.5 THEN M=G-1 ELSE M=G-13
130 IF M>2.5 THEN Y=D-4716 ELSE Y=D-4715
140 LOCATE 3,1:PRINT"JULIAN DATE";N;"IS EQUIVALE
NT TO";M;"/";INT(DM);"/";Y
150 LOCATE 5,1:PRINT"(A)nother          (M)ain menu
";
160 GOSUB 180
170 IF Q$="A" OR Q$="a" THEN RUN 10 ELSE RUN "A:
menu"
180 Q$=""+INKEY$:IF Q$="" THEN 180
190 RETURN
```

Listing 12-3. Super Calendar.

```
1 '***********************************************
2 '*              Listing 12-3                   *
3 '*             Super Calendar                  *
4 '***********************************************
5 '
10 CLS:KEY OFF:D$(0)="SUNDAY":D$(1)="MONDAY":D$(
2)="TUESDAY":D$(3)="WEDNESDAY":D$(4)="THURSDAY":
D$(5)="FRIDAY":D$(6)="SATURDAY"
20 DIM M$(12),ML(12):M$(1)="JANUARY":ML(1)=31:M$
(2)="FEBRUARY":M$(3)="MARCH":ML(3)=31:M$(4)="APR
IL":ML(4)=30:M$(5)="MAY":ML(5)=31:M$(6)="JUNE":M
L(6)=30:M$(7)="JULY":ML(7)=31:M$(8)="AUGUST":ML(
8)=31:M$(9)="SEPTEMBER":ML(9)=30
30 M$(10)="OCTOBER":ML(10)=31:M$(11)="NOVEMBER":
ML(11)=30:M$(12)="DECEMBER":ML(12)=31:CLS:FL=0:P
RINT "****  CALENDAR  ****":PRINT:PRINT
40 PRINT"1  --  ADVANCED CALENDER          2  --
   CALENDAR OF MONTH                       3  --
# DAYS BETWEEN TWO DATES  4  --  DATE, GIVEN # D
AYS BETWEEN            5  --  OPEN CONDITIONS
           6  --  END":PRINT:PRINT"ENTER CHOICE";
50 Q$=""+INKEY$:IF Q$="" THEN 50 ELSE ON VAL(Q$)
 GOTO 60,430,610,640,920,1290
60 CLS:PRINT"           ********  ADVANCED CALEND
AR  ********":PRINT:PRINT:PRINT"THIS ROUTINE COM
PUTES THE NUMBER OF DAYS SINCE 1 FEB 0 AD IN";
70 PRINT"EITHER THE JULIAN OR GREGORIAN CALENDAR
 SYSTEMS.  IT ALSO COMPUTES THE JULIAN DATE OF T
HE DAY OF THE CURRENT YEAR,",
80 PRINT"THE DAY OF THE WEEK, AND THE PHASE OF T
HE MOON FOR THAT DATE.":PRINT:PRINT:INPUT"ENTER
YEAR, MONTH, DATE (YYYY,MM,DD)";Y,M,D:PRINT
90 PRINT"GREGORIAN CALENDAR (NEW) -- 1
                                       JULIAN
CALENDAR (OLD)     -- 0",
100 S$=""+INKEY$:IF S$="" THEN 100 ELSE S=VAL(S$
)
110 PRINT S:PRINT:IF S>1 THEN 90 ELSE GOSUB 130
120 GOSUB 240:INPUT"'ENTER' TO RETURN TO MAIN PR
OGRAM";ZZ:RUN
130 IF M>2 THEN X=0 ELSE X=1
140 IF S=0 THEN C=2 ELSE C=INT((Y-X)/100)
150 IF (Y/4)<>INT(Y/4) THEN 190
160 IF (Y/100)<>INT(Y/100) THEN 180
170 IF (Y/400)<>INT(Y/400) THEN 190
180 LY=1:GOTO 200
190 LY=0
200 N=D+INT(367*(((M-2)/12)+X))+INT(INT(365.25*(
Y-X))-(.75*C))
210 P=N/29.53059:P=P-INT(P):DW=INT(7*((N/7)-INT(
N/7)))
220 JD=N-(336+INT(INT(365.25*(Y-1))-(.75*C)))
230 IF LY=1 THEN ML(2)=29 ELSE ML(2)=28:RETURN
240 CLS:ZOG%=(F2*448):GOSUB 1340:PRINT "";:PRINT
 M$(M),D,Y:PRINT"DAY NUMBER (SINCE 1 FEB 0 AD) =
";N
250 IF LY=0 THEN 270
```

```
260 CLS:PRINT Y;"IS A LEAP YEAR"
270 PRINT"JULIAN DATE WITHIN YEAR          =";JD
280 PRINT"DAY OF WEEK :                    ";D$(D
W)
290 PRINT"PHASE OF MOON                    =";P
300 PRINT"(0 = 1ST QTR   .25 = FULL    .50 = 3RD
QTR   .75 = NEW MOON)"
310 RETURN
320 'PRINT ROUTINE
330 PRINT:PRINT"DO YOU WANT TO SEE A PRINTOUT?
(Y/N)";
340 Q$=""+INKEY$:IF Q$="" THEN 340 ELSE IF Q$="N
" THEN 420
350 PRINT Q$:LPRINT"","",D;M;Y,"",:IF FL=1 THEN
LPRINT DD;MM;YY ELSE LPRINT""
360 LPRINT""
370 LPRINT"DAY NUMBER (SINCE 1 JAN 4713 BC)   =";
N,"",:IF FL=1 THEN LPRINT N1 ELSE LPRINT""
380 LPRINT"JULIAN DATE WITHIN YEAR          =";
JD,"",:IF FL=1 THEN LPRINT J1 ELSE LPRINT""
390 LPRINT"DAY OF WEEK :                    "
;D$(DW),"",:IF FL=1 THEN LPRINT D$(D1) ELSE LPRI
NT""
400 LPRINT"PHASE OF MOON                    =";
P,:IF FL=1 THEN LPRINT P1 ELSE LPRINT""
410 LPRINT"":IF FL=1 THEN LPRINT"DIFFERENCE BETW
EEN THESE TWO DATES IS";ABS(N1-N);"DAYS."
420 LPRINT STRING$(2,10):FL=0:RUN 10
430 'CALENDAR OF MONTH
440 CLS:PRINT CHR$(212);"**  CALENDAR OF MONTH
**":PRINT:PRINT:INPUT"ENTER YEAR AND MONTH (JANU
ARY = 1)";Y,M:D=1:S=1:GOSUB 130
450 DW=DW-1
460 IF DW<7 THEN 470 ELSE DW=0
470 IF M<>2 THEN 490
480 IF LY=1 THEN ML(2)=29 ELSE ML(2)=28
490 L=INT((LEN(M$(M))+6)/2):CLS:ZOG%=32-L:GOSUB
1340:PRINT M$(M);Y;
500 FOR I=0 TO 6:ZOG%=130+(I*9):GOSUB 1340:PRINT
 LEFT$(D$(I),3);:NEXT I
510 WK=1:DT=1:DX=DW
520 ZOG%=130+(DW*9)+(64*WK):GOSUB 1340:PRINT DT;
:DW=DW+1
530 IF DW<7 THEN 550
540 DW=0:WK=WK+1
550 DT=DT+1:IF DT<=ML(M) THEN 520
560 LOCATE 12,1:PRINT"HARDCOPY DESIRED?   (Y/N)";
570 Q$=""+INKEY$:IF Q$="" THEN 570
580 IF Q$="Y" THEN 600
590 RUN 10
600 FOR I=0 TO 10:FOR J=0 TO 63:LPRINT CHR$(PEEK
(15360+(64*I)+J));:NEXT J:LPRINT"":NEXT I:RUN 10
610 '# DAYS BETWEEN TWO DATES
620 CLS:PRINT CHR$(212);"**  # DAYS BETWEEN TWO
DATES  **":PRINT:PRINT:S=1:INPUT"ENTER FIRST DAT
E (YYYY,MM,DD)";Y,M,D:GOSUB 130:CLS:GOSUB 240:FL
=1:N1=N:INPUT"ENTER SECOND DATE (YYYY,MM,DD)";Y,
M,D:GOSUB 130:F2=1:GOSUB 240
```

Listing 12-3. Super Calendar. (Continued From Page 239.)

```
630 PRINT"THE DIFFERENCE BETWEEN THE TWO DATES I
S";ABS(N1-N);"DAYS":GOTO 120
640 CLS:PRINT CHR$(212);"**   DATE, GIVEN # DAYS
BETWEEN   **":PRINT:PRINT:S=1
650 PRINT"A  --   DATE PRIOR TO SPECIFIED START
B  --   DATE SUBSEQUENT TO SPECIFIED START":PRINT
:PRINT"ENTER CHOICE";
660 Q$=""+INKEY$:IF Q$="" THEN 660
670 PRINT:INPUT"START DATE (YYYY,MM,DD)";Y,M,D:G
OSUB 130:CLS:GOSUB 240:N1=N:PRINT:PRINT:INPUT"NU
MBER OF DAYS DIFFERENCE";ND
680 IF Q$="A" THEN 700
690 NX=N1+ND:GOTO 710
700 NX=N1-ND
710 Q=INT((ND-(INT(ND/365.25)*365.25))/30.4375):
IF NX<N1 THEN 740
720 Y=Y+INT(ND/365.25):M=M+Q:IF M<13 THEN 760
730 M=1:Y=Y+1:GOTO 760
740 Y=Y-INT(ND/365.25):M=M-Q:IF M>0 THEN 760
750 M=12:Y=Y-1
760 GOSUB 130:LOCATE 1,51:PRINT ABS(N1-N);
770 IF N<NX THEN 850
780 IF N=NX THEN 910
790 D=D-1
800 IF D>0 THEN 760
810 M=M-1
820 IF M=0 THEN 840
830 D=ML(M):GOTO 760
840 M=12:Y=Y-1:GOTO 830
850 D=D+1
860 IF D>ML(M) THEN 880
870 GOTO 760
880 M=M+1:D=1
890 IF M<13 THEN 760
900 M=1:Y=Y+1:GOTO 760
910 F2=1:GOSUB 240:LOCATE 16,1:PRINT"'ENTER' TO
CONTINUE";:INPUT ZZ:RUN
920 CLS:S=1:PRINT CHR$(212);"** OPEN CONDITIONS
 **":PRINT:PRINT
930 PRINT"THIS ROUTINE ALLOWS YOU TO SPECIFY THR
EE OF THE FOUR VALUES BELOW.  USE '0' FOR THE UN
KNOWN.  THE PROGRAM FINDS THE ANSWER.":PRINT
940 PRINT"   YEAR (ANY POSITIVE VALUE)
                                          MON
TH (1-12)
                            DATE (1-31)"
950 PRINT"   DAY (1-7)  (Sunday = 1)"
960 LOCATE 16,1:PRINT"USE '0' FOR UNKNOWN VALUE"
;:LOCATE 12,1:PRINT"ENTER YEAR":INPUT XY:IF XY>0
 THEN 980
970 LOCATE 12,1:PRINT"SEARCH BEGINS IN WHAT YEAR
":INPUT FY:LOCATE 12,1:PRINT"SEARCH ENDS IN WHAT
 YEAR   ":INPUT YL:Y=FY-1:LOCATE 12,1:PRINT"
                   ";
980 LOCATE 7,41:PRINT XY;:LOCATE 12,1:PRINT"ENTE
R MONTH":INPUT XM:LOCATE 8,41:PRINT M$(XM);:LOCA
```

```
TE 12,1:PRINT"ENTER DATE ":INPUT XD:LOCATE 9,41:
PRINT XD;:LOCATE 12,1:PRINT"ENTER DAY OF WEEK":I
NPUT XW:XW=XW-1:IF XW=>0 THEN LOCATE 10,41:PRINT
 D$(XW)
990 PRINT:PRINT:IF XY=0 THEN 1060
1000 IF XM=0 THEN 1070
1010 IF XD=0 THEN 1080
1020 IF XW=-1 THEN 1090
1030 PRINT"NO UNKNOWNS?   (Y/N)";
1040 Q$=""+INKEY$:IF Q$="" THEN 1040 ELSE IF Q$=
"Y" THEN 920
1050 RUN
1060 M=XM:D=XD:GOTO 1100
1070 Y=XY:D=XD:GOTO 1140
1080 Y=XY:M=XM:GOTO 1190
1090 Y=XY:M=XM:D=XD:GOTO 1240
1100 Y=Y+1:GOSUB 140
1110 IF Y>YL THEN 1270
1120 IF DW<>XW THEN 1100
1130 GOSUB 1280:GOTO 1100
1140 M=1
1150 GOSUB 140
1160 IF DW<>XW THEN 1180
1170 GOSUB 1280
1180 M=M+1:IF M=13 THEN 1270 ELSE 1150
1190 D=1
1200 GOSUB 140
1210 IF DW<>XW THEN 1230
1220 GOSUB 1280
1230 D=D+1:IF D>ML(M) THEN 1270 ELSE 1200
1240 CLS:GOSUB 130
1250 GOSUB 240
1260 PRINT:GOTO 120
1270 PRINT:PRINT"THAT CONCLUDES THE SURVEY OF AV
AILABLE DATA":PRINT:GOTO 120
1280 LOCATE 22,1:PRINT Y,M$(M),D,D$(DW):LPRINT Y
,M$(M),D,D$(DW):RETURN
1290 PRINT"(A)nother        (M)ain menu ";
1300 GOSUB 1320
1310 IF Q$="A" OR Q$="a" THEN RUN 10 ELSE RUN "A
:MENU"
1320 Q$=""+INKEY$:IF Q$="" THEN 1320
1330 RETURN
1340 ZAG%=INT(ZOG%/64):ZOG%=ZOG%-64*ZAG%+1:ZAG%=
ZAG%+1:                         LOCATE ZAG%
,ZOG%:RETURN
```

prints out actual calendar pages. Finally, given any three of the four calendar features (day, day of week, month, or year), it computes all those dates (between a specified starting and stopping date) that satisfy the three criteria. For example, if we need to compute on what years Friday the 13th occurs in October, between 1969 and 1990, the program computes that these conditions exist in 1972, 1978, and 1989.

Easter

Unlike many holidays and religious periods which have standard dates or easily computed periods (Christmas = December 25, Thanksgiving = fourth Thursday in November, etc.), Easter is a movable date defined as the first Sunday March 21. The routine given in Listing 12-4 relies heavily on modular math. That is, $2000_{mod19} = 19 \times (2000/19 - $ integer part of $(2000/19)) = 5$. The algorithm for computing the date of Easter, given the year Y, is:

1. $A = Y_{mod19}$
2. $B = $ integer part Y/100 $C = Y_{mod100}$
3. $D = $ integer part B/4 $E = B_{mod4}$

4. $F = $ integer part $\dfrac{B + 8}{25}$

5. $G = $ integer part $\dfrac{B - F + 1}{3}$

6. $H = (19A + B - D - G + 15)_{mod30}$

7. $I = $ integer part C/4 $K = C_{mod4}$
8. $L = (32 + 2E + 2I - H - K)_{mod7}$

9. $M = $ integer part $\dfrac{A + 11H + 22L}{451}$

10. $N = $ integer part $\dfrac{H + L - 7M + 114}{31}$

$$P = (H + L - 7M + 114)_{mod31}$$

11. The day of the month on which Easter falls is $= P + 1$
12. The month of Easter is $= N$ (January = 1)

COMPUTING PLANETARY POSITIONS

On January 1, 1980 the nine planets of the solar system were positioned as shown in Fig. 12-2. This chart is useful if one is interested in planetary positions for the first of January, 1980. A difference of only a day, one way or the other, makes the chart totally inadequate and inaccurate. Books are available (see the bibliography under "Astronomy") that give planetary positions, but only for a sampling of days. For example, one resource consulted in this work lists the positions of the planets in increments of 40 days. The routines that follow facilitate the computation of planetary positions for any given day in any specified year.

Listing 12-4. The Date of Easter.

```
1 '*********************************************
2 '*              Listing 12-4               *
3 '*           The Date of Easter            *
4 '*********************************************
5 '
10 CLS:KEY OFF
20 M$(2)="FEBRUARY":M$(3)="MARCH":M$(4)="APRIL":
M$(5)="MAY"
30 DEF FNM(X,Y)=Y*(X/Y-INT(X/Y))
40 INPUT"ENTER YEAR (YYYY)";Y
50 A=FNM(Y,19)
60 B=INT(Y/100):C=FNM(Y,100)
70 D=INT(B/4):E=FNM(B,4)
80 F=INT((B+8)/25):G=INT((B-F+1)/3)
90 H=FNM((19*A)+B-D-G+15,30)
100 I=INT(C/4):K=FNM(C,4)
110 L=FNM(32+(2*E)+(2*I)-H-K,7)
120 M=INT((A+(11*H)+(22*L))/451)
130 Z=H+L-(7*M)+114:N=INT(Z/31):P=FNM((H+L-(7*M)
+114),31)
140 PRINT:PRINT"EASTER SUNDAY";Y;"FALLS ON";INT(
P+1)+1;M$(N):PRINT
150 PRINT"(A)nother      (M)ain menu ";
160 GOSUB 180
170 IF Q$="A" OR Q$="a" THEN RUN 10 ELSE RUN "A:
MENU"
180 Q$=""+INKEY$:IF Q$="" THEN 180
190 RETURN
```

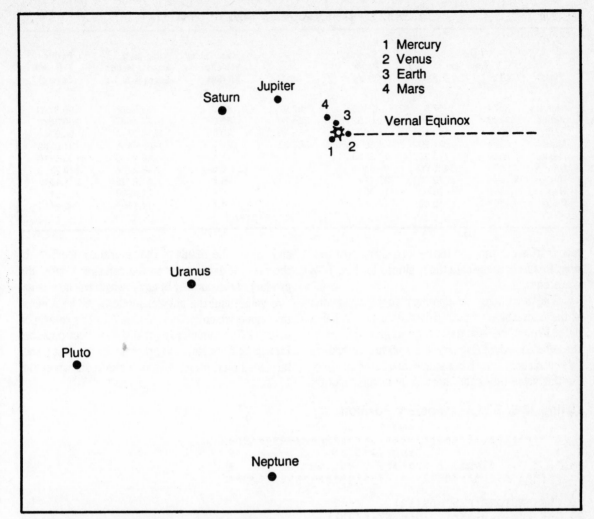

Fig. 12-2. Planetary relationships, January 1, 1980.

The primary concern of the users of these routines will be the precision of the forecast. Precision in astronomical forecasting carries a heavy price in complexity of programs and the consumption of memory. If the purpose of the effort is simply to determine the position of the planets relative to signs of the zodiac for astrological reference, the first program to follow should be sufficient. On the other hand, those using this volume to develop programs to accurately position and aim powerful telescopes will have to use the second routine as a starting point or foundation program for a yet more precise and complicated program.

The first program is based on several assumptions known to be false from the outset. Among these are the assumptions that the orbits of the planets are circular, that the center of the orbit is at the center of the sun, that the mean distances and mean angular motions of the planets are constant, and that the planes of all the orbits are coincidental; that is, they are all in one plane. We accept these assumptions to the extent the results are sufficiently accurate for our purposes due to the ease and speed of computation.

Table 12-1 gives the fairly precise locations of the planets as of January 1, 1980, plus the mean dis-

Table 12-1. Planetary Positions, January 1, 1980.

Planet	Distance From Sun AU's	10⁶Km	Sidereal Period Years	Days	Mean Orbital Velocity Km/Sec	Mean Daily Angular Motion Seconds of Arc	Position 1-1-1980 Degrees
Mercury	.3871	57.91	.24085	87.97	47.9	14731.9608	196.5770
Venus	.7233	108.21	.61521	224.70	35.0	5767.4497	356.3670
Earth	1.000	149.60	1.000039	365.26	29.8	3548.0544	99.3364
Mars	1.5237	227.90	1.88089	686.98	24.1	1886.4435	131.0189
Jupiter	5.2037	778.30	11.8653		13.1	298.9930	150.6210
Saturn	9.5803	1428.00	29.6501		9.6	119.7180	170.7233
Uranus	19.1410	2872.00	83.7445		6.8	41.9780	231.4843
Neptune	30.1982	4498.00	165.9510		5.4	21.4930	259.9150
Pluto	39.4387	5910.00	247.6870		4.7	14.1160	198.4410

tances from the sun, and the mean daily angular motion. It is from these data the positions for Fig. 12-2 were computed.

The first stage in computing planetary positions is the conversion of the desired date into a Julian date. From the Julian date, the number of days to the reference date (January 1, 1980) are computed by subtraction. It is then a simple matter of multiplying this value times the mean daily angular motion

and adding the result to the reference position. In the case of dates prior to the reference date, the product of the number of days (which will be a negative value) and the angular motion, will be a negative value which, when "added" to the reference point, will automatically yield the correct position. Listing 12-5 contains the program for the first planetary position routine. A sample run is shown in Fig. 12-3.

Listing 12-5. Simple Planetary Position.

```
1 '**********************************************
2 '*                 Listing 12-5               *
3 '*          Simple Planetary Position         *
4 '**********************************************
5 '
10 CLS:RESTORE:DIM MO$(12)
20 DEF FNM(A,B)=B*((A/B)-INT(A/B)))
30 RD=1.745329277777778D-02
40 GOSUB 180
50 FOR I=1 TO 9:READ Z$(I),D(I),M(I),P(I):NEXT
60 D1=ND:T=D1/36525!:D2=D1/10000:PM=N/29.53059:P
M=360*(PM-INT(PM))
70 SR=180+((JD+103.62893#)*.985626):IF SR>360 TH
EN SR=SR-360
80 MR=SR+PM:IF MR>360 THEN MR=MR-360
90 PRINT"R.A. OF SUN = ";SR:PRINT"R.A. OF MOON =
";MR
100 PRINT:PRINT"PLANET","POSITION  (DEGREES FROM
 VERNAL EQUINOX)"
110 FOR I=1 TO 9
120 P1(I)=ABS(P(I)+((D1*M(I))/3600))
130 IF P1(I)<=360 THEN 150
140 P1(I)=P1(I)-360:GOTO 130
150 PRINT USING"\                \       ###.######"
;Z$(I);P1(I)
```

```
160 NEXT
170 PRINT:GOTO 480
180 DW$(0)="SUNDAY":DW$(1)="MONDAY":DW$(2)="TUES
DAY":DW$(3)="WEDNESDAY":DW$(4)="THURSDAY":DW$(5)
="FRIDAY":DW$(6)="SATURDAY"
190 J$="JANFEBMARAPRMAYJUNJULAUGSEPOCTNOVDEC":FO
R I=1 TO 12:MO$(I)=MID$(J$,(3*(I-1))+1,3):NEXT
200 INPUT"ENTER DATE DESIRED   (DD,MM,YYYY)";D,M,
Y:M0=M:D0=D:GOSUB 280
210 INPUT"ENTER GREENWICH TIME DESIRED   (24-HOUR
 CLOCK: HHMM)";T
220 TH=INT(T/100):DM=((T/100)-TH)/.6:T=((12+TH+D
M)/24)-.5:ND=N+T-2444239!
230 PRINT"JULIAN DATE =";N:PRINT"ADJUSTED FOR TI
ME =";N+T:PRINT"DAY OF WEEK = ";DW$(DW):PRINT"JU
LIAN DATE WITHIN YEAR =";JD:PRINT"NUMBER OF DAYS
 SINCE EPOCH (NOON, 31 DEC 1979) = ";ND
240 IF LY=0 THEN 260
250 PRINT Y;"IS A LEAP YEAR"
260 PRINT:RETURN
270 D1=N-2415020!+T:T=D1/36525!:D2=D1/10000
280 IF M>2 THEN X=0 ELSE X=1
290 C=INT((Y-X)/100)
300 IF (Y/4)<>INT(Y/4) THEN 340
310 IF (Y/100)<>INT(Y/100) THEN 330
320 IF (Y/400)<>INT(Y/400) THEN 340
330 LY=1:GOTO 350
340 LY=0
350 N=D+INT(367*(((M-2)/12)+X))+INT(INT(365.25*(
Y-X))-(.75*C))+1721088.5#
360 W=N-1721088.5#:DW=INT(7*((W/7)-INT(W/7)))
370 JD=N-(336+INT(INT(365.25*(Y-1))-(.75*C)))-17
21088.5#
380 RETURN
390 DATA MERCURY,.3871,14732.42,196.577
400 DATA VENUS,.7233,5767.668,356.367
410 DATA EARTH,1,3548.192,99.3364
420 DATA MARS,1.5237,1886.4435,131.0189
430 DATA JUPITER,5.2037,298.993,150.621
440 DATA SATURN,9.5803,119.718,170.7233
450 DATA URANUS,19.141,41.978,231.4843
460 DATA NEPTUNE,30.1982,21.493,259.915
470 DATA PLUTO,39.4387,14.116,198.441
480 PRINT
490 PRINT"(A)nother        (M)ain menu ";
500 GOSUB 520
510 IF Q$="A" OR Q$="a" THEN RUN 10 ELSE RUN "A:
MENU"
520 Q$=""+INKEY$:IF Q$="" THEN 520
530 RETURN
```

The algorithm usd in this program is very simple and straightforward:

1. Compute the number of days from January 1, 1980 (N).
2. For each planet, multiply this value times the mean daily angular motion, M_x, and add the product to the planet's longitude as of 1/1/1980, L_x: $L_x' = L_x + (N * M_x)$.

Due to the elipitcal nature of each planet's orbits, however, this routine produces incorrect

```
ENTER DATE DESIRED  (DD,MM,YYYY)? 1,9,01982
ENTER GREENWICH TIME DESIRED  (24-HOUR CLOCK: HHMM)? 1200
JULIAN DATE = 2445213.5
ADJUSTED FOR TIME = 2445214
DAY OF WEEK = WEDNESDAY
JULIAN DATE WITHIN YEAR = 244
NUMBER OF DAYS SINCE EPOCH (NOON, 31 DEC 1979) = 975
R.A. OF SUN =  162.6321263220745
R.A. OF MOON =  65.73370904723675
PLANET          POSITION  (DEGREES FROM VERNAL EQUINOX)
MERCURY          226.607417
VENUS            118.443750
EARTH            340.305067
MARS             281.930681
JUPITER          231.593271
SATURN           203.146925
URANUS           242.853342
NEPTUNE          265.736021
PLUTO            202.264033
```

Fig. 12-3. Results of Listing 12-5.

results. Whether the results are acceptable or not is a function of the use to which they are put. They are adequate to obtain a general notion of the direction of a planet relative to the sun and, deduced from that, relative to the position of the earth.

For those in need of greater precision, there are several routines that yield the accuracy desired but require considerably more computation. The following several algorithms provide fairly accurate locational data for the sun, moon, and the nine planets of the solar system.

Orbits

As noted above, celestial orbits are eliptical in shape, instead of circular. The basic form is shown in Fig. 12-4. The sun is colocated with one of the two *foci* (F, F'). The point along the major axis, $\overline{AB}$, at which the plane comes closest to the sun is called the *perihelion* and the farthest point is called the *aphelion*. One-half of the distance from A to B is called the *semi-major* axis and is frequently used in orbital computations.

To the ancient astronomers, and to casual present day observers, the sun appears to revolve around the earth instead of the other way around. The following routine leads to the computation of the sun's location along an imaginary orbit around the earth against a background of stars and constellations. This value is called the *right ascension* of the sun and is illustrated in Fig. 12-5. A detailed diagram of celestial relationships is shown in Fig. 12-6.

The algorithm to compute the sun's position on a given date is:

1. Compute the number of days, D, from the beginning of 1980: January 0.0, 1980.
2. Calculate N = 360 × D. This is equal to:

$$\frac{}{365.2422}$$

   N = .985648 × D.
3. Add or subtract multiples of 360 until 0 < = N < = 360.
4. Calculate M = N − 3.762863. If the result is less than zero, add 360.

246

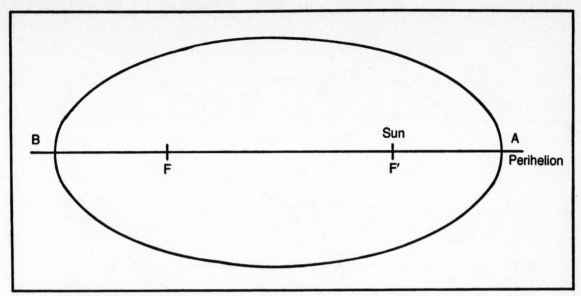

Fig. 12-4. Standard elliptical orbit.

5. Calculate $E = \dfrac{360}{\pi} e \sin M$. This is equal to: $E = 1.91574 \sin M$.

6. Calculate $L = N + E + 278.83354$. If the result is greater than 360, subtract 360. This is the sun's geocentric (earth-centered) ecliptic longitude.

7. Calculate $T = N - \dfrac{2415020}{36525}$

8. Calculate $OE = 23°27'08.26'' - 46.845''T - .0059''T^2 + .00181''T^3$.

9. Calculate $RA = \tan^{-1}\left[\dfrac{\sin L \cos OE}{\cos L}\right]$. This is the right ascension of the sun.

10. Calculate $DE = \sin^{-1}[\sin OE \sin L]$. This is the declination of the sun (see Figs. 12-4 and 12-5).

11. During the computation of RA, the use of the arc tangent function can introduce an ambiguity of a multiple of 180°. It is sometimes necessary to add or subtract 180° to bring RA into the correct quadrant. Use this subalgorithm for this:

    a. $X = \cos L$
    b. $Y = \sin L \cos OE$

	Y positive	Y negative
X positive	$0 <= RA <= 90$	$270 <= RA <= 360$
X negative	$90 <= RA < 180$	$180 <= RA <= 270$

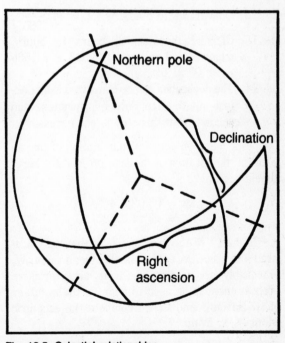

Fig. 12-5. Celestial relationships.

247

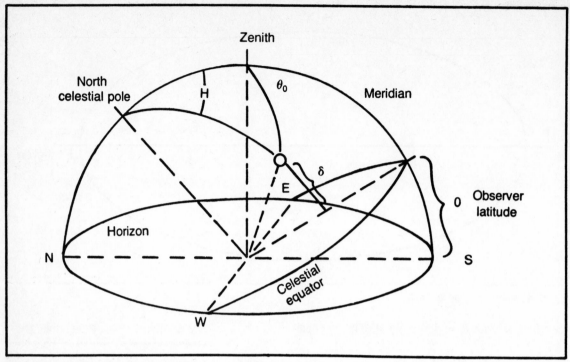

Fig. 12-6. Detailed celestial relationships.

12. Convert RA to hours by $RA = 24 \frac{RA}{360}$.

13. Convert the decimal hours to hours, minutes, and seconds. $(32.34° = 2.156h = 2h\ 09'21.6')$.

14. The declination can be converted from decimal degrees to degrees, minutes, and seconds, but this step is not necessary.

As a check on your implementation of this algorithm, the location of the sun, on July 27, 1980, should be:

$$RA = 08h\ 25'\ 44''$$
$$DE = 19°\ 13'\ 53''$$

In step 4 of the previous algorithm we calculated the value M, which is the mean anomaly, reasonably accurately. There is an alternative process that can be used to improve the accuracy of M. Having found M, we compute the eccentric anomaly, E, from:

$$E = e \sin E = M/57.29577$$

where E is expressed in radians, and e is the eccentricity, .016718.

This relationship requires an iterative solution to fine E.

1. $E = M$.
2. $X = E - .016718 \sin E - M$.
3. If $X = .0000001$, go to step 6.

4. $E = E - \dfrac{X}{1 - .016718 \cos E}$.

5. Go to step 2.
6. Go to the computation of the *true anomaly*.

The true anomaly is found from:

$$V = 2 \tan^{-1} \frac{(1.01686 \tan E)}{2}$$

L, then is computed from:

$$L = (57.29577\ V + 282.596403$$

The processing then continues from the second half of step 6 in the main algorithm. Using this procedure should lead to a revised location where:

$$RA = 08h\ 23'\ 46''$$
$$DE = 19°\ 20'\ 38''$$

The distance to the sun and its angular diameter, using the data just computed, is found from:

$$R = \frac{-9.55792 \times 10^8}{(1 + 2.7828 \cos V)}$$

$$TH = .533128 \quad \frac{(1 + 2.7828 \cos V)}{-6.39905}$$

R will be the distance of the sun from the earth in kilometers. TH is the apparent angular diameter of the sun. Solving from the data for July 27, 1980:

$$R = 1.519196 \times 10^8 \text{ kilometers}$$

$$TH = 0°\ 31'\ 30''\ (.525°)$$

Sunrise and Sunset. Closely related to computing the location of the sun at a given instant is the task of determining the time of sunrise and sunset. The algorithm for this process is:

1. Input the month and day of the year, MO and DY.
2. Input the latitude and longitude of the observer, LA and LO.
3. Determine TD: TD = (LO − INT(L))/15.
4. If daylight savings time is in effect, DL = 1, else DL = 0.
5. Let J = the Julian date within the year.
6. $X = \frac{J}{7}$ and PL = .120831 $(\pi/26)$
7. Calculate:
   a. D = .456−22.915*cos(2*PL*X)−43* cos (2*PL*X)−.156*cos (3*PL*X) + 3.82sin (PL*X)+.06*sin (2*PL*X)− .082*sin (3*PL*X)

(This is approximately equal to the declination of the sun).

   b. E = .008 + .51*cos(PL*X)−3.197 *cos (2*PL*X)−.106*cos (3*PL*X)−.15*

cos(4*PL*X) − 7.317*sin(PL*X) − 9.47 1* sin(2*PL*X) − .391*sin(3*PL*) − .242* sin(4*PL*X)

[This is the "equation of time" (see below)].

   c. Convert LA, D to radians. (Divide by 57.29577.)
   d. If the absolute value of (sinD/cos LA) is less than 1, go to sub-step f.
   e. There is no sunrise or sunset, observer is in polar region. Go to step 1.
   f. Y = (sin D/cos LA)
   g. Z1 = 90 − (tan⁻¹(Y/ $\sqrt{(1-Y^2)}$)) *57.29577
   h. Z2 = 360 − Z1

8. The azimuth of sunrise is Z1. The azimuth of sunset is Z2.
9. Convert Z1 to radians: Z = Z1/57.29577.
10. Compute ST − sin Z/cos D.
11. If the absolute value of ST is equal to or greater than 1, then T = 6 and TT = 6; go to step 15.
12. CT = $\sqrt{1 - ST^2}$.
13. T = $\dfrac{57.29577}{15*\text{arc tan (ST/CT)}}$.
14. TT = T.
15. If D is greater than zero, go to step 17.
16. TT = 12, T = T + TD − E/60 − .04.
17. Compute time of sunrise:
    a. T1 = INT(T) = The hour of sunrise
    b. T2 = T−T1
    c. T2 = INT(T2*600 + 5)/10) = minutes after the hour
18. Compute the time of sunset:
    a. T = 12 − TT and T = TD − E/60 + .04
    b. T1 = INT(T) = The hour of sunset
    c. T2 = T − T1
    d. T2 = INT((T2*600 + 5)/10) − minutes.

Equation of Time. In step 7b above we computed the value E and called it the equation of time. The rate at which the sun moves through the sky is not as nearly constant as we would think, due to the elliptic nature of the earth's orbit and the inclination of the earth on its axis. The equation of time is the difference between the time computed from the average rate of the sun's motion and the time determined from the sun's actual position. The value E is added to the time estimate (mean sun time) to arrive at the real sun time. Listing 12-7 includes the algorithms to compute the equation of time and the times of sunrise and sunset.

Planetary Positions. Listing 12-6 is a major routine to compute the positions of the planets in both heliocentric (sun-centered) and geocentric modes with a fair degree of precision. Figure 12-7 shows a flowchart of the program, and Fig. 12-8 shows the references and variables for the program. Figure 12-9 shows a sample run through the program. Routines to obtain a degree of precision significantly greater than given here quickly become quite extensive and tedious both for the programmer and the computer. The routines given here should be sufficient for most purposes.

Listing 12-6. Complex Planetary Positions.

```
1 '*********************************************
2 '*              Listing 12-6                 *
3 '*        Complex Planetary Positions        *
4 '*********************************************
5 '
10 CLS:KEY OFF
20 RD=1.745329277777778D-02:EE=RD*23.441884#:M$=
"\        \        ###.######      ###.######      ##
#.######"
30 DEF FNA(X)=ATN(X/SQR(-X*X+1)):DEF FNM(A,B)=B*
(A/B-INT(A/B))
40 GOSUB 1020
50 PRINT"LOADING DATA FOR:":PRINT
60 RESTORE:FOR I=1 TO 9:READ Z$(I),P(I),LE(I),LP
(I),EC(I),RA(I),OI(I),LO(I),AD(I),AB(I):LOCATE 1
2,25:PRINT Z$(I);"   ";:NEXT
70 GOSUB 1390:CLS:GOSUB 1460
80 A$="####.####  \          \":D$="DEGREES"
90 FOR I=1 TO 9
100 ZOG%=(30-(LEN(Z$(I))/2)):GOSUB 1530:PRINT "
  ";Z$(I);"      ";:Q=I
110 NP=.985695*ND/P(I):NP=FNM(NP,360):M=NP+LE(I)
-LP(I):M=FNM(M,360):LOCATE 3,38:PRINT USING A$;M
;D$;:M=M*RD
120 HL=NP+(114.5915573#*EC(I)*SIN(M))+LE(I):IF H
L<0 THEN HL=HL+360 ELSE IF HL>360 THEN HL=HL-360
 ELSE HL=HL
130 LOCATE 4,38:PRINT USING A$;HL;D$;
140 V(I)=(HL-LP(I))*RD:GOTO 150
150 LOCATE 5,38:PRINT USING A$;V(I)/RD;D$;
160 L(I)=(V(I)/RD)+LP(I):L(I)=FNM(L(I),360):R(I)
=(RA(I)*(1-(EC(I)^2)))/(1+(EC(I)*COS(V(I))))
170 LOCATE 6,38:PRINT USING A$;L(I);D$;:LOCATE 7
,38:PRINT USING A$;R(I);"AU'S";
180 X=SIN((L(I)-LO(I))*RD)*SIN(OI(I)*RD):PS(I)=F
NA(X)/RD
190 LOCATE 8,38:PRINT USING A$;PS(I);D$;
200 A=(L(Q)-LO(Q))*RD:Y=SIN(A)*COS(OI(Q)*RD):X=C
OS(A)
210 A=ATN(Y/X)/RD:GOSUB 760
220 L1=A+LO(Q):R1=R(Q)*COS(PS(Q)*RD):Z=(L(3)-L1)
```

```
*RD:ZZ=(L1-L(3))*RD
230 IF I<3 THEN 260
240 IF I=3 THEN 370
250 A=((ATN((R(3)*SIN(ZZ))/(R1-(R(3)*COS(ZZ)))))
/RD)+L1:L2=A:GOTO 280
260 A=ATN((R1*SIN(Z))/(R(3)-(R1*COS(Z))))/RD
270 L2=180+L(3)+A
280 L2=FNM(L2,360)
290 B=ATN((R1*TAN(PS(Q)*RD)*SIN((L2-L1)*RD))/(R(
3)*SIN((L1-L(3))*RD))):GOSUB 960:AS(Q)=L2:DE(Q)=
TH
300 LOCATE 9,38:PRINT USING A$;AS(Q);"HOURS";:LO
CATE 10,38:PRINT USING A$;DE(Q);D$;
310 RH(Q)=SQR(ABS((R(3)^2)+(R(Q)^2)-(2*R(3)*R(Q)
*COS((L(Q)-L(3))*RD)))))
320 LOCATE 11,38:PRINT USING A$;RH(Q);"AU'S";
330 TT(Q)=8.316*RH(Q):TH(Q)=AD(Q)/RH(Q):LOCATE 1
2,38:PRINT USING A$;TT(Q);"MINUTES";:LOCATE 13,3
8:PRINT USING A$;TH(Q);"";
340 F(Q)=.5*(1+COS((L(Q)-L(3))*RD)):LOCATE 14,38
:PRINT USING A$;F(Q);"";
350 Z=(R(Q)*RH(Q))/(AB(Q)*SQR(F(Q))):LZ=LOG(Z)/L
OG(10)
360 M(Q)=(5*LZ)-26.7:LOCATE 15,38:PRINT USING A$
;M(Q);"";
370 LOCATE 16,11:PRINT"(P)RINT    ANY OTHER KEY T
O CONTINUE";
380 Q$=""+INKEY$:IF Q$="" THEN 380
390 IF Q$<>"P" OR Q$="p" THEN 410
400 GOSUB 1360
410 LOCATE 16,11:PRINT"
             ";
420 NEXT I
430 CLS:PRINT "                            GEOCEN
TRIC POSITIONS":PRINT"       RT ASCEN.  DECL.
 DISTANCE  TIME  DIAM.  BRIGHT. PHASE":PRINT"PLA
NET  (HOURS)   (DEG.)    AU'S   MIN.   ARCSEC
":PRINT
440 M$="\      \ ###.#### ###.#### ###.#### ###.#
### ###.#### ##.# #.##"
450 FOR Q=1 TO 9
460 IF Q=3 THEN 480
470    PRINT USING M$;Z$(Q);AS(Q);DE(Q);RH(Q);TT(
Q);TH(Q);M(Q);F(Q)
480 NEXT Q
490 N=.9856473*ND:N=FNM(N,360)
500 M=N-3.76286:IF M<0 THEN M=M+360
510 M=M*RD:E=M
520 EX=E-(.016718*SIN(E))-M
530 IF ABS(EX)<.000001 THEN 550
540 E=E-(EX/(1-(.016718*COS(E)))):GOTO 520
550 V1=1.01686*TAN(E/2):V=2*ATN(V1)
560 L0=(V/RD)+282.596403#:L0=FNM(L0,360)
570 PRINT:L2=L0:B=0:GOSUB 960
580 R=1.495985E+08/1.496E+08:T=8.316*R:TA=.53312
8/R
590 PRINT USING M$;"SUN";L2;TH;R;T;TA;0;0
600 N=(360/365.2422)*ND:N=FNM(N,360)
```

Listing 12-6. Complex Planetary Positions. (Continued From Page 251.)

```
610 M=(N-284.40761#):IF M<0 THEN M=M+360:M=M*RD
620 E=6.291076591#*SIN(M)
630 L2=N+E+64.975464#:IF L2>360 THEN L2=L2-360
640 L1=(13.176396#*D)+64.975464#:L1=FNM(L1,360)
650 MM=L1-(.111404*D)-349.383063#:MM=FNM(MM,360)
660 N=151.950429#-(.052953*D):N=FNM(N,360)
670 EV=1.2739*SIN(((2*(L1-L2))-MM)*RD):AE=.1858*
SIN(M):A3=.37*(M):M1=(MM*RD)+EV-AE-A3:EC=6.2886*
SIN(M1):A4=.214*SIN(2*M1):LL=(L1*RD)+EV+EC-AE+A4
:V=.6583*SIN(2*(LL-L2)*RD):LT=LL+V
680 N1=(N*RD)-(.16*SIN(M)):Y=SIN(LT-N1)*.99597
690 X=COS(LT-N1):A=(ATN(Y/X))/RD:GOSUB 760
700 L2=A+(N1/RD):X=SIN(LT-N1)*.0896834:B=FNA(X)
710 GOSUB 960
720 D=LT-(L2*RD):PH=.5*(1-COS(D)):R=.996986/(1+(
.0549*COS((MM*RD)+EC))):R=(R*384401!)/1.496E+08:
T=8.316*R:TA=.5181001/R:BR=0:D=(LT-(L2*RD)):PH=.
5*(1+COS(D))
730 PRINT USING M$;"MOON";L2,TH;R;T;TA;BR;PH:A=0
:B=8
740 GOSUB 1360
750 GOTO 1500
760 IF Y=>0 AND X=>0 THEN 830
770 IF Y<0 AND X=>0 THEN 870
780 IF Y=>0 AND X<0 THEN 910
790 IF 180<=A AND A<=270 THEN 950
800 IF A<180 THEN A=A+180
810 IF A>270 THEN A=A-180
820 GOTO 790
830 IF 0<=A AND A<=90 THEN 950
840 IF A<0 THEN A=A+180
850 IF A>90 THEN A=A-180
860 GOTO 830
870 IF 270<=A AND A<=360 THEN 950
880 IF A<270 THEN A=A+180
890 IF 360<A THEN A=A-180
900 GOTO 870
910 IF 90<=A AND A<=180 THEN 950
920 IF A<90 THEN A=A+180
930 IF 180<A THEN A=A-180
940 GOTO 910
950 RETURN
960 L=L2*RD
970 X=(SIN(B)*COS(EE))+(COS(B)*SIN(EE)*SIN(L)):T
H=FNA(X)/RD
980 Y=(SIN(L)*COS(EE))-(TAN(B)*SIN(EE)):X=COS(L)
990 A=ATN(Y/X)/RD:GOSUB 760
1000 L2=A/15:RETURN
1010 END
1020 DW$(0)="SUNDAY":DW$(1)="MONDAY":DW$(2)="TUE
SDAY":DW$(3)="WEDNESDAY":DW$(4)="THURSDAY":DW$(5
)="FRIDAY":DW$(6)="SATURDAY"
1030 J$="JANFEBMARAPRMAYJUNJULAUGSEPOCTNOVDEC":D
IM MO$(12):FOR I=1 TO 12:MO$(I)=MID$(J$,(3*(I-1)
)+1,3):NEXT
1040 INPUT"ENTER DATE DESIRED  (DD,MM,YYYY)";D,M
```

```
,Y:M0=M:D0=D:GOSUB 1160
1050 INPUT"ENTER GREENWICH TIME DESIRED  (24-HOU
R CLOCK: HHMM)";T
1060 TH=INT(T/100):DM=((T/100)-TH)/.6:T=((12+TH+
DM)/24)-.5:ND=N+T-2444239!
1070 PRINT"JULIAN DATE =";N:PRINT"ADJUSTED FOR T
IME =";N+T:PRINT"DAY OF WEEK = ";DW$(DW):PRINT"J
ULIAN DATE WITHIN YEAR =";JD:PRINT"NUMBER OF DAY
S SINCE EPOCH (NOON, 31 DEC 1979) = ";ND
1080 IF LY=0 THEN 1100
1090 PRINT Y;"IS A LEAP YEAR"
1100 LPRINT DW$(DW);",";D0;MO$(M);",";Y,T*2400;"
HOURS"
1110 '
1120 LPRINT"JULIAN DATE = ";JD,"DAYS SINCE 0.0 J
AN 1980 = ";ND
1130 LPRINT""
1140 PRINT:RETURN
1150 '
1160 IF M>2 THEN X=0 ELSE X=1
1170 C=INT((Y-X)/100)
1180 IF (Y/4)<>INT(Y/4) THEN 1220
1190 IF (Y/100)<>INT(Y/100) THEN 1210
1200 IF (Y/400)<>INT(Y/400) THEN 1220
1210 LY=1:GOTO 1230
1220 LY=0
1230 N=D+INT(367*(((M-2)/12)+X))+INT(INT(365.25*
(Y-X))-(.75*C))+1721088.5#
1240 W=N-1721088.5#:DW=INT(7*((W/7)-INT(W/7)))
1250 JD=N-(336+INT(INT(365.25*(Y-1))-(.75*C)))-1
721088.5#
1260 RETURN
1270 DATA "MERCURY",.24085,231.2973,77.1442128,.
2056306,.3870986,7.0043579,48.0941733,6.74,1.918
E-06
1280 DATA VENUS,.61521,355.73352,131.2895792,.00
67826,.7233316,3.394435,76.4997524,16.92,1.721E-
06
1290 DATA EARTH,1.00004,98.83354,102.596403,.016
718,1,0,0,0,0
1300 DATA MARS,1.88089,126.30783,335.6908166,.09
33865,1.5236883,1.8498011,49.4032001,9.36,4.539E
-06
1310 DATA JUPITER,11.86224,146.966365,14.0095493
,.0484658,5.202561,1.3041819,100.2520175,196.74,
1.994E-04
1320 DATA SATURN,29.45771,165.322242,92.6653974,
.0556155,9.554747,2.4893741,113.4888341,165.6,1.
74E-04
1330 DATA URANUS,84.01247,228.0708551,172.736328
8,.0463232,19.21814,.7729895,73.8768642,65.8,7.7
68E-05
1340 DATA NEPTUNE,164.79558,260.3578998,47.86721
48,.0090021,30.10957,1.7716017,131.5606494,62.2,
7.597E-05
1350 DATA PLUTO,250.9,209.439,222.972,.25387,39.
78459,17.137,109.941,8.2,4.073E-06
1360 LOCATE 20,1:PRINT"Use PrtSc for hard copy o
```

Listing 12-6. Complex Planetary Positions. (Continued From Page 253.)

```
f data.   <CR> to return to output"
1370 INPUT ZZ
1380 RETURN
1390 NE=.9856473*ND/1.00004:NE=FNM(NE,360):ME=NE
-3.763857
1400 ME=FNM(ME,360)*RD
1410 LE=NE+(1.915742*SIN(ME))+98.83354:LE=FNM(LE
,360)
1420 V(3)=(LE-102.596403#)*RD
1430 L(3)=(V(3)/RD)+102.596403#:L(3)=FNM(L(3),36
0)
1440 R(3)=(1-(EC(3)^2))/(1+(EC(3)*COS(V(3)))):PS
(3)=0
1450 RETURN
1460 LOCATE 3,1:PRINT"MEAN ANOMOLY = ";:LOCATE 4
,1:PRINT"HELIOCENTRIC LONGITUDE = ";:LOCATE 5,1:
PRINT"TRUE ANOMOLY = ";:LOCATE 6,1:PRINT"CORRECT
ED HELIOCENTRIC LONGITUDE = ";:LOCATE 7,1:PRINT"
RADIUS VECTOR = ";:LOCATE 8,1:PRINT"HELIOCENTRIC
 LATITUDE = "
1470 LOCATE 9,1:PRINT"RIGHT ASCENSION = ";:LOCAT
E 10,1:PRINT"DECLINATION = ";
1480 LOCATE 11,1:PRINT"DISTANCE FROM EARTH = ";:
LOCATE 12,1:PRINT"TIME (LIGHT SPEED) = ";:LOCATE
 13,1:PRINT"APPARENT DIAMETER = ";:LOCATE 14,1:P
RINT"PHASE = ";:LOCATE 15,1:PRINT"BRIGHTNESS = "
;
1490 RETURN
1500 PRINT"(A)nother        (M)ain menu ";
1510 Q$=""+INKEY$:IF Q$="" THEN 1510
1520 IF Q$="A" OR Q$="a" THEN RUN 10 ELSE RUN "A
:MENU"
1530 ZAG%=INT(ZOG%/64):ZOG%=ZOG%-64*ZAG%+1:ZAG%=
ZAG%+1:                          LOCATE ZAG%
,ZOG%:RETURN
```

Listing 12-7. Sunrise/Sunset.

```
1 '********************************************
2 '*              Listing 12-7                *
3 '*              Sunrise/Sunset              *
4 '********************************************
5 '
10 CLS:KEY OFF:DIM N(12):PL=3.141593/26:RD=57.29
577:A$="####.## \          \"
20 FOR I=1 TO 12:READ N(I):NEXT
30 LINE INPUT"NAME OF LOCATION?   ";N$
40 PRINT"LATITUDE OF ";N$;"  (DD,MM)";:INPUT D,M
:LA=D+M/60
50 PRINT"LONGITUDE OF ";N$;"  (DDD,MM)";:INPUT D,
M:LO=D+M/60
60 LO=75+((INT(LO/15)-5)*15)
70 PRINT"IS DAYLIGHT SAVINGS TIME IN EFFECT?   (Y
/N)"
80 Q$=""+INKEY$:IF Q$="" THEN 80 ELSE IF Q$="Y"
```

```
OR Q$="y" THEN DL=1 ELSE DL=0
90 TD=(D+M/60-LO)/15:INPUT"ENTER MONTH AND DAY (
JAN=1)";M,DA
100 X=(N(M)+DA)/7:D=.456-22.915*COS(PL*X)-.43*CO
S(2*PL*X)-.156*COS(3*PL*X)+3.83*SIN(PL*X)+.06*SI
N(2*PL*X)-.082*SIN(3*PL*X):PRINT
110 PRINT"DECLINATION OF SUN = ";USING A$;D;"DEG
REES"
120 E=8.000001E-03+.51*COS(PL*X)-3.197*COS(2*PL*
X)-.106*COS(3*PL*X)-.15*COS(4*PL*X)-7.317*SIN(PL
*X)-9.471*SIN(2*PL*X)-.391*SIN(3*PL*X)-.242*SIN(
4*PL*X)
130 PRINT"EQUATION OF TIME =    ";USING A$;E;"MIN
UTES"
140 CL=COS(LA/RD):SD=SIN(D/RD):CD=COS(D/RD):Y=SD
/CL:IF ABS(Y)=>1 THEN PRINT"NO SUNRISE OR SUNSET
":PRINT:GOTO 230
150 Z=90-RD*ATN(Y/SQR(1-Y*Y)):PRINT"AZIMUTH OF S
UNRISE = ";USING A$;Z;"DEGREES"
160 PRINT"AZIMUTH OF SUNSET =    ";USING A$;360-Z;
"DEGREES"
170 ST=SIN(Z/RD)/CD:IF ABS(ST)=>1 THEN T=6:TT=6:
GOTO 190
180 CT=SQR(1-ST*ST):T=RD/15*ATN(ST/CT):TT=T
190 IF D<0 THEN T=12-T:TT=T:T=T+TD-E/60-.04
200 GOSUB 260
210 PRINT"TIME OF SUNRISE =     ";T1$;":";T2$;"
 ";T$;"AM S.T.":T=12-TT:T=T+TD-E/60+.04:GOSUB 26
0
220 PRINT"TIME OF SUNSET =      ";T1$;":";T2$;"
 ";T$;"PM S.T.":PRINT:PRINT
230 GOTO 290
240 RUN
250 END
260 T1=INT(T):T2=T-T1:T1$=STR$(T1+DL):T2=INT((T2
*600+5)/10):T2$=STR$(T2):T2$=RIGHT$(T2$,LEN(T2$)
-1):IF INT(T2)<10 THEN T2$="0"+T2$
270 RETURN
280 DATA 0,31,59,90,120,151,181,212,243,273,304,
334
290 PRINT"(A)nother        (M)ain menu ";
300 GOSUB 320
310 IF Q$="A" OR Q$="a" THEN RUN 10 ELSE RUN "A:
MENU"
320 Q$=""+INKEY$:IF Q$="" THEN 320
330 RETURN
```

Figure 12-10 shows a sample run through Listing 12-7, the Sunrise/Sunset program.

Table 12-2 contains the essential elements for
computing the planetary positions, based on the epoch of January 0.0, 1980. These data are included
in the data section of the program at line 280.

The algorithm for determining planetary positions, in general, is:

1. Compute the number of days since epoch,
   D.
2. Compute the mean anomaly, M from:

$$M = .985648 \left(\frac{D}{T_p} \right) + LE - LP$$

where T_p is the orbital period of the planet
in tropical years; LE is the longitude at ep-

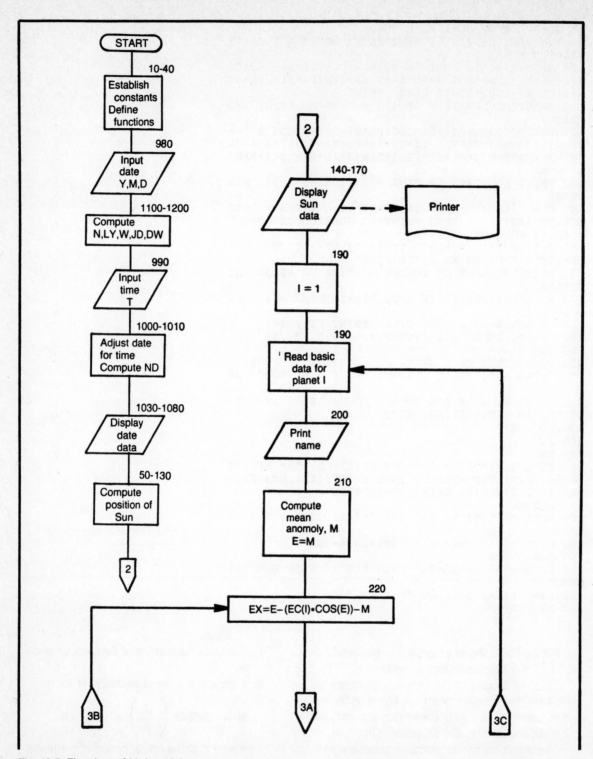

Fig. 12-7. Flowchart of Listing 12-6.

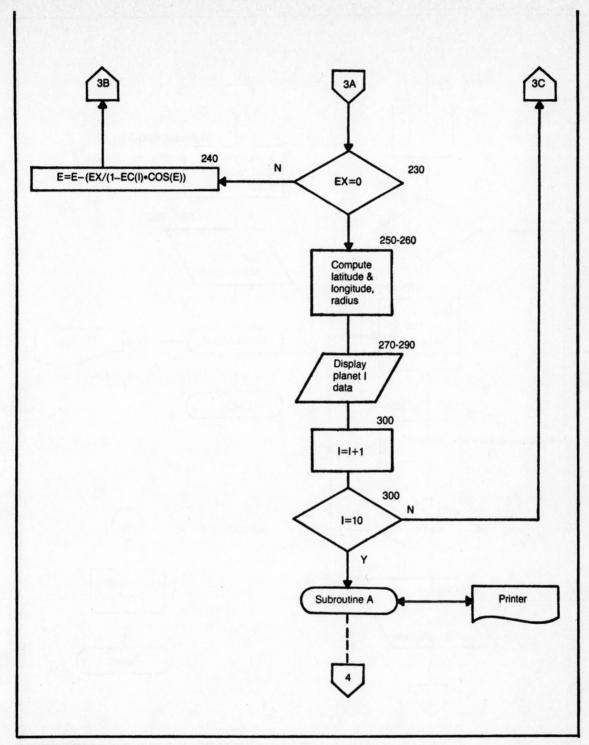

Fig. 12-7. Continued.

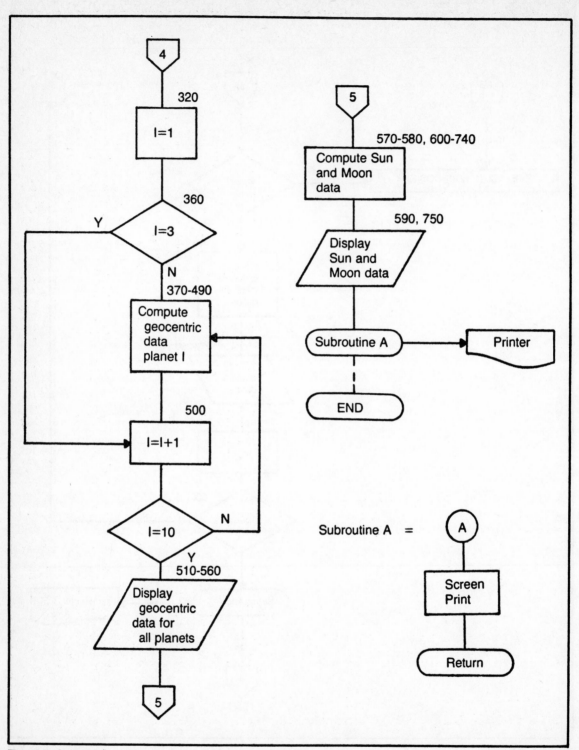

Fig. 12-7. Continued.

```
LINE     REFERENCES
00100  00120
00130  00110
00220  00240
00250  00230
00500  00360
00560  00540
00620  00630
00640  00620
00780  00390 00710 00930
00820  00780
00830  00790
00840  00800
00850  00810 00820 00830 00870 00880
00880  00860
00890  00850
00900  00440 00570 00730
00960  00040
01040  01020
01100  00980
01150  01130
01160  01120 01140
01170  01150
01310  00330 00760
VARIABLE REFERENCES
A      00010 00030 00030 00030 00030 00070 00150 00380 00380 1. Angular diameter of Sun.
       00380 00390 00400 00410 00420 00710 00720 00720 00850 2. Intermediate variable (380)
       00850 00860 00870 00870 00880 00880 00910 00930 00940
A3     00690 00690                                           Correction factor #3 (moon)
A4     00690 00690                                           Correction factor #4 (moon)
AB     00190 00480                                           Apparent brightness, planet
AD     00190 00460                                           Apparent diameter, planet
AE     00690 00690 00690                                     Annual equation, moon
AS     00440 00550                                           Right Ascension, planet
B      00030 00030 00030 00030 00440 00570 00720 00910 00910 Latitude
       00920
BR     00740 00750                                           Brightness, moon
C      00810 00820 00830 00840 00850 00860 01110 01170 01190 Intermediate variable
D      00600 00600 00660 00670 00680 00740 00740 00740 00740 Intermediate variable
       00980 00980 01170
DE     00090 00440 00550 00610                               Intermediate variable
DM     01000 01000                                           Minutes
DW     01010 01040 01180                                     Day of Week
DW$    00960 00960 00960 00960 00960 00960 00960 01010 01040 Name of the Day
```

Fig. 12-8. References and variables for Listing 12-6.

Variable	References	Description
E	00090 00090 00100 00120 00120 00130 00210 00220 00220 00240 00240 00250 00580 00610 00620 00620 00630 00630 00640 00740	True anomoly
EC	00070 00100 00120 00130 00150 00190 00220 00240 00250 00260 00260 00690 00740	Eccentricity of orbit
EE	00020 00690 00690 00910 00910 00920 00920	Intermediate variable
V	00690 00690 00690	Correction for evection
EX	00100 00110 00120 00220 00230 00240	Trial value for anomaly
F	00150 00150 00120 00470 00480 00550	Intermediate value
H	00010	Intermediate value
I	00190 00190 00190 00190 00190 00200 00220 00240 00250 00250 00260 00260 00260 00260 00280 00290 00260 00270 00270 00280 00280 00300 00320 00320 00320 00320 00350 00360 00370 00380 00380 00400 00400 00440 00440 00440 00450 00450 00450 00460 00460 00460 00460 00470 00470 00480 00480 00490 00530 00540 00550 00550 00550 00550 00550 00970 00970 00970 00970 01310 01330 01380 01320 01330 01360	Loop counter,intermediate value
J	01320 01330 01360 00970 00970 00970	Loop counter
J$	01010 01060 01190	Month string
JD	00260 00260 00260	Julian Date
L	00260 00260 00270 00280 00320 00380 00400 00420 00440 00450 00450 00470 00470 00910 00920 00900 00920	Intermediate variable
LO	00140 00140 00140 00140 00570 00660 00670 00400 00400 00440 00440 00660 00660	Intermediate variable
L1	00690	Intermediate variable
L2	00420 00420 00420 00430 00430 00440 00440 00570 00590 00650 00650 00660 00690 00720 00740 00750 00900 00940 00970	Intermdediate variable
L3	00040 01050	Intermediate variable
L4	00040 01050	Intermediate variable
LE	00070 00080 00190 00210	Solar longitute at epoch
LL	00690 00690 00690 00690	Intermediate variable
LO	00190 00280 00380 00400	Longitude, ascending node, planet
LP	00070 00080 00140 00190 00210 00260	Solar longitude at perigee
LT	00690 00700 00710 00720 00740	Intermediate variable
LY	01020 01150 01160	Leap Year flag
LZ	00480 00490	Log of Z to base e, line 480
M	00010 00030 00080 00080 00080 00090 00090 00100 00210 00210 00210 00220 00490 00550 00610 00620 00650 00660 00670 00680 00690 00690 00700	Mean anomoly

Variable	Line references	Definition
M$	00810 00820 00830 00840 00850 00980 01040 01100 01170	String definition
MO	00020 00320 00520 00550 00590 00750 00930	Month
M1	00690 00690 00690 00690 00690 00690 00740	Intermediate variable
MM	00970 01040	Moon's corrected anomoly
MO$	00670 00670 00670 00670 00740 00970 01040	Name of month
N	00060 00060 00060 00060 00080 00600 00600 00600 00610 00680 00680 00700 01000 01010 01010 01170 01180 01190	Number of degrees since epoch
N$	00070 00070	String
N1	00700 00700 00710 00720 00720	Intermediate variable
ND	00060 00190 00210 00210 00280 00600 01000 01010 01060	Number of days since epoch
OI	00190 00280 00280 00380	Orbital inclination, planet
P.	00190 00210 00210	Intermediate variable
PH	00740 00740 00740 00750	Phase of moon
PS	00280 00290 00320 00320 00480 00580 00580	Heliocentric latitude
R	00070 00150 00190 00260 00270 00320 00400 00410 00440 00440 00450 00450 00480 00580 00580 00580 00590 00740 00740 00740 00740 00750	Radius
RO	00150 00160	Radius
R1	00400 00410 00410 00440	Intermediate variable
RD	00020 00020 00090 00140 00210 00260 00280 00280 00380 00380 00380 00400 00410 00440 00440 00440 00450 00470 00610 00650 00690 00690 00690 00700 00710 00720 00740 00740 00900 00900 00910 00930	Radian conversion factor
RH	00450 00460 00460 00480 00550 00550 00990 01000 01000 01000	Planetary radius
T	00510 00590 00740 00740 00750 00750 01000 01000 01010 01040 01090 01090	Time
TA	00580 00590 00590 00550 00750 00910 01000	Time required for light travel
TH	00150 00170 00170 00440 00460 00590 00750 01000	Time, hours
TT	00460 00550 00150 00250 00260 00640 00650 00690	Apparent diameter
V	00130 00140 00140 00250 00260 00640 00690	Intermediate variable
V1	00130 00130 00130 00030 00280 00280 00280 00380	Intermediate variable
W	01180 01180 01180 00620 00630 00710 00710 00720 00780	Intermediate variable
X	00030 00030 00030 00390 00620 00700 00710 00780 00800 00910 00920 00930 00930 00980 01110 01120 01130 01140 01170	Intermediate variable
Y	00010 00380 00920 00930 01040 01140 01170 01190	Intermediate variable

Fig. 12-8. Continued.

```
Z       00400 00410 00410 00480 00780 00780 00790 01330 Intermediate variable
        01340 01340 01340 01350
Z$      00190 00200 00320 00370 00550                    String
END OF LIST - RESTART?


SATURDAY, 22 NOV. 1988                    1200 HOURS
JULIAN DATE = 327                DAYS SINCE 0.0 JAN 1980 =  327


                            MERCURY

MEAN ANOMOLY =                                    52.4229  DEGREES
HELIOCENTRIC LONGITUDE =                         148.2420  DEGREES
TRUE ANOMOLY =                                    71.0978  DEGREES
CORRECTED HELIOCENTRIC LONGITUDE =              148.2420  DEGREES
RADIUS VECTOR =                                   0.3476  AU'S
HELIOCENTRIC LATITUDE =                           6.8942  DEGREES
RIGHT ASCENSION =                                14.5840  HOURS
DECLINATION =                                   -12.7648  DEGREES
DISTANCE FROM EARTH =                             1.0377  AU'S
TIME (LIGHT SPEED) =                              8.6294  MINUTES
APPARENT DIAMETER =                               6.4952
PHASE =                                           0.5141
BRIGHTNESS =                                      0.3937
                (P)RINT      ANY OTHER KEY TO CONTINUE

                              GEOCENTRIC POSITIONS
            RT ASCEN.   DECL.     DISTANCE   TIME   DIAM.   BRIGHT.   PHASE
PLANET      (HOURS)     (DEG.)    AU'S       MIN.   ARCSEC

MERCURY     14.5840    -12.7648   1.0377     8.6294    6.4952    0.4     0.51
VENUS       13.7450     -8.8623   1.3202    10.9791   12.8159    3.0     0.41
MARS        18.0257    -24.5013   2.1757    18.0929    4.3021    4.3     0.19
JUPITER     12.3123     -0.7672   5.9429    49.4215   33.1048    0.7     0.28
SATURN      12.5051     -0.8834  10.0927    83.9308   16.4079    3.6     0.23
URANUS      15.6258    -19.1922  19.7775   164.4700    3.3270   14.3     0.00
NEPTUNE     17.3584    -21.8301  31.2527   259.8970    1.9902   12.4     0.04
PLUTO       13.9989      5.5284  30.8067   256.1890    0.2662   17.7     0.09
SUN         15.8443    -20.1211   1.0000     8.3159    0.5331    0.0     0.00
MOON         6.0871     19.0825   0.0027     0.0225  191.3040    0.0     0.54


SATURDAY, 22 NOV. 1980                    1200 HOURS
JULIAN DATE =  327              DAYS SINCE 0.0 JAN 1980 =  327
```

Fig. 12-9. Results of Listing 12-6.

och; and LP is the longitude at perihelion.

3. Then compute V = M + 114.49155 EC_p sin M (degrees) solved iteratively). V is the "true anomaly." EC_p is the eccentricity of the planet's orbit.

4. Compute L_p = V + LP. This is the heliocentric longitude.

5. Compute the distance of the planet from the sun, the *radius vector*:

$$R_p = \frac{R(1 - EC_p^2)}{1 + EC_p \cos V}$$

where R is the semimajor axis.

6. The heliocentric latitude of the planet is

```
NAME OF LOCATION? WASHINGTON D.C.
LATITUDE OF WASHINGTON D.C.  (DD,MM)? 38,54
LONGITUDE OF WASHINGTON D.C. (DDD,MM)? 77,01
TIME ZONE (E, C, M, P)   E
IS DAYLIGHT SAVINGS TIME IN EFFECT?  (Y/N)
ENTER MONTH (JAN =1) AND DAY? 9,1
DECLINATION OF SUN =   8.21 DEGREES
EQUATION OF TIME =     0.03 MINUTES
AZIMUTH OF SUNRISE =  79.42 DEGREES
AZIMUTH OF SUNSET = 280.58 DEGREES
TIME OF SUNRISE =       6:33  AM S.T.
TIME SUNSET =           7:37  PM S.T.
ANOTHER DATE?  (Y/N)
```

Fig. 12-10. Results of Listing 12-7.

found from:

$$PS = \arcsin (\sin L_p - LO_p) \sin OI_p$$

where LO_p is the longitude of the ascending node and OI_p is the orbital inclination.

These six steps have led to the computation of a planet's celestial latitude and longitude relative to the sun. Often, however, it is very useful to compute these positions relative to the Earth to make the task of locating the planet easier for observers and astronomers. To do this the following steps are given:

1. Compute:
   a. $A = L_p - LO_p$
   b. $Y = \sin A \cos OI_p$
   c. $X = \cos A$
   d. $A = \tan^{-1} (Y/X)$ (Be sure to resolve the arc tan ambiguity.)
   e. $L1 = A + LO_p$
   f. $R1 = R_p \cos PS_p$
   g. $Z = L_3 - L1$
   h. $A = \tan^{-1} ((R1 \sin Z)/(R_3 - R1 \cos Z))$
   i. $L2 = 180 + L_3 + A$ (Adjust to keep within 360°.)
   j. $B = \tan^{-1} (R1 \tan PS_p \sin (L2 - L1))/(R_3 \sin (L1 - L_3))$
   k. $L = L2$ converted to radians.
   l. $X = (\sin B \cos EE) + (\cos B \sin EE \sin L)$
   m. $TH = \tan^{-1}X$
   n. $Y = (\sin L \cos EE) - (\tan B \sin EE)$
   o. $X = \cos L$
   p. $AS_p = \dfrac{\tan^{-1}(Y/X)}{15}$

2. AS_p is the right ascension.
3. TH is the declination.

ASTROLOGICAL SIGNS

For those interested in astrology, the sign of the zodiac in which you will find the sun, your sun sign, is given is the equation:

$$Z = INT(JD - 79)/30.4375) + 1$$

Table 12-2. Planetary Ephemeral Data, January 1, 1980.

Planet	Period, T (tropical years)	Longitude at epoch (degrees)	Longitude perihel. (degrees)	Eccent. of orbit	Semi-major axis (AUs)	Inclinat. of orbit	Longitude of ascen. node	Angular size at 1 AU	Brightness factor A
Mercury	.24085	231.2973	77.14421	.2056306	.387099	7.004358	48.09417	6.74	1.918×10^{-6}
Venus	.61521	355.7335	131.28958	.0067826	.723332	3.394435	76.49975	16.92	1.721×10^{-5}
Earth	1.00004	98.8335	102.59640	.0167180	1.000000	---	---	---	---
Mars	1.88089	126.3078	335.69082	.0933865	1.523688	1.849801	49.40320	9.36	4.539×10^{-6}
Jupiter	11.86224	146.9664	14.00955	.0484658	5.202561	1.304182	100.25202	196.74	1.994×10^{-4}
Saturn	29.45771	165.3222	92.66540	.0556153	9.554747	2.489374	113.48883	165.60	1.740×10^{-4}
Uranus	84.01247	228.0709	172.73633	.0453232	19.218140	.772990	73.87686	65.80	7.768×10^{-5}
Neptune	164.79558	260.3579	47.86721	.0090021	30.109570	1.771602	131.56065	62.20	7.597×10^{-5}
Pluto	250.90000	209.4390	222.97200	.0253870	39.784590	17.137000	109.94100	8.20	4.073×10^{-6}

If $z < 0$, then $z = 13 - z$

where z = zodiac number and $z = 1$ = Aries.

Alternatively, the sign of the zodiac for the sun and any of the planets can be found by dividing the right ascension in the geocentric mode by 2 and adding 1 to the integer value. That is:

$$z = INT(RA/2) + 1$$

WEATHER AND THE COMPUTER

While picnics can be very important events in our lives, our interest in weather has a practical foundation that justifies our interest far beyond pleasant outings. A little precaution can save us millions of dollars in crop and property damages. By knowing when bad weather is going to strike, we can adjust our plans and prevent loss. What is bad weather? During the few days before and after planting a crop rain is a "bad" thing. The farmer doesn't want to plow in a field of mud, nor does he want to see the fresh seed wash down to the river. After the planting, a little rain, just enough to nurture the crop, is acceptable. Even when the crop has rooted and sprung from the soil, a heavy rain can still destroy many crops, either from the physical beating of the plants or from subsequent rotting of the plant sitting in saturated soil. On the other hand, we certainly can't do without rain somewhere in the world. While we can irrigate deserts and bring forth crops, that irrigation water was at some point rain. In a general sense, what we want is some rain, not too much, at the right time.

In a similar fashion, we have an ambivalent attitude toward wind. A little wind at the right time can be put to good service. We used to use it to drive cargo ships from continent to continent. We use it today to generate electricity in remote locations. We use it to pump subsurface water to irrigate our crops. Too much wind, on the other hand, can literally blow away everything we own, starting with the crops in the field. Combine a severe wind with a severe rain (or the frozen form, snow) and we have a disaster of great dimension. While foreknowledge of a storm does nothing to help us prevent the storm, we can take defensive measures. We can put off planting the crop; we can board up the windows on the beach house; we can place sand bags along the river banks, and so forth. But, what does this have to do with microcomputers?

Modern meteorologists use computers in two main ways: forecasting and display. Every evening we are treated to grand demonstrations of the power of the computer as the television weather reporters dazzle us with computer-generated maps of the nation, the state, or the local area. They superimpose radar returns from thunderstorms. They animate the short-range weather pattern so we can see the course of the weather through the day. The graphic displays of the map sections are well within the reach of the microcomputer and are available in a number of commercial packages and published map routines. The remaining functions require access to the basic data and radar systems. Unfortunately, for our purposes, long-range forecasting requires access to vast amounts of current and accurate weather conditions throughout the world. Without special knowledge of the forecasting equations involved and access to the current weather database, weather forecasting on the modern scale is generally not within the range of the microcomputer owner. In this book we offer several routines to be used to help predict tides, and to compare current weather with historic weather, but with one modest exception, we make no real attempt to turn your micro into a home version of the National Weather Service.

Timing the Tides

Tides, the movement of large masses of water, are the result of the gravitational forces exerted by the sun and moon, and are influenced by the rotation of the earth on its axis. Normally where there is a very large lake, sea, or ocean, there will be four tides every day, two high tides and two low tides. Between the two high (and the two low) tide peaks there is normally an interval of 12 hours 25 minutes, although this can vary from 6 hours to over 24 hours, depending on local bottom and shore conditions.

The height or magnitude of the tides is a function of the relative position of the sun and the moon, and the shape of the particular coast. Coastlines that are generally smooth with open expanses of sandy

264

beaches and shallow bottoms that extend far out into the sea will generally experience undramatic tides of little consequence. The Mediterranean has regions where the tides are measured in inches. At the other extreme, harbors located at the upper regions of long, narrow channels leading to the sea may experience dramatic tidal actions. The Bay of Fundy is said to have normal tides on the order of 53 feet. Where the channel to the sea is intersected by one or more other channels to the same or other large bodies of water, the tidal action and timing can get quite complicated. The program that follows, Listing 12-8, offers a routine to predict the times of low and high tides based on recent tidal time data. It assumes that the period between tides is a linear constant and simply computes a linear line of regression based on the known times of high and low tides. Due to inherent inaccuracies of this approach, it is best used with fairly current data and is not to be projected too far in the future—at least not until it can be further validated by the user. The program, based on the normal tidal conditions in the Washington, D.C. area, which consist of two high and low tides, separated by about 13 hours 7 minutes, can easily be adapted for conditions throughout the world. In regions where there are more or less than

Listing 12-8. Tidal Timer 1.

```
1 '***********************************************
2 '*                Listing 12-8                 *
3 '*                Tidal Timer 1                *
4 '***********************************************
5 '
10 CLS:PRINT"TIDE TIMER":PRINT:PRINT
20 INPUT"FOR HOW MANY DAYS DO YOU HAVE DATA";D:D
IM DN(D),TT(D,2)
30 PRINT:PRINT
40 FOR I=1 TO D
50 INPUT"ENTER DAY NUMBER";DN(I)
60 INPUT"TIME OF FIRST HIGH TIDE";T:GOSUB 290
70 TT(I,1)=T:INPUT"TIME OF SECOND HIGH TIDE";T:G
OSUB 290
80 TT(I,2)=T
90 PRINT
100 NEXT I
110 FOR I=1 TO 2
120 TX=0:TY=0:X2=0:Y2=0:XY=0
130 FOR J=1 TO D
140 X=DN(J):Y=TT(J,I)
150 TX=TX+X:TY=TY+Y:X2=X2+(X^2):Y2=Y2+(Y^2):XY=X
Y+(X*Y)
160 NEXT J
170 B(I)=(XY-(D*((TX/D)*(TY/D))))/(X2-(D*((TX/D)
^2)))
180 A(I)=(TY/D)-(B(I)*(TX/D))
190 R(I)=((D*XY)-(TX*TY))/SQR(((D*X2)-(TX^2))*((
D*Y2)-(TY^2)))
200 NEXT I
210 T=(A(2)+B(2))-(A(1)+B(1)):T1=T/100:GOSUB 300
:PRINT"MEAN TIME BETWEEN TIDES = ";H;"HOURS";M;"
MINUTES.
                STANDARD ERROR = +/- ";:T=SQR((X
2-((XY^2)/Y2))/(D-2)):GOSUB 300:PRINT H;":";M
220 PRINT:PRINT"TIDE","ALPHA","BETA","CORRELATIO
N"
230 PRINT"HIGH # 1",A(1),B(1),R(1):PRINT"HIGH #
```

Listing 12-8. Tidal Timer 1. (Continued From Page 265.)

```
2",A(2),B(2),R(2)
240 PRINT"(A)nother          (M)ain menu ";
250 GOSUB 270
260 IF Q$="A" OR Q$="a" THEN RUN 10 ELSE RUN "A:
MENU"
270 Q$=""+INKEY$:IF Q$="" THEN 270
280 RETURN
290 H=INT(T):M=(T-H)/.6:T=INT(H)+M:RETURN
300 H=INT(T/100):M=INT(60*((T/100)-H)):IF H>23 T
HEN H=H-24
310 RETURN
```

two high tides daily, the program can be adjusted in lines 20, 70-110, 140, 230, 290 by simply changing 4 to the actual number of daily tides. In line 210, we compute and display the mean period between tides, and the standard error of this value.

Theoretically, though unlikely, the actual time of a tide could deviate from the forecast by as much as the number of days ahead of actual data multiplied by the standard error. That is, if the standard error is 8.5 minutes, a forecast for a high tide 20

days ahead could be off by as much as 2 hours 49.6 minutes, plus or minus. The standard error can be reduced by increasing the number of days of data used. The program in Listing 12-9 is used to compute tidal times from known periods.

As noted before, the height of the tides is a function of changing factors (the position of the sun and the moon) and the geological structure of the local region. While we can compute a nominal tidal magnitude from the relative positions of the sun and the

Listing 12-9. Tidal Timer 2.

```
1 '********************************************
2 '*                  Listing 12-9             *
3 '*                  Tidal Timer 2            *
4 '********************************************
5 '
10 CLS:PRINT"TIDE TIMER":PRINT:PRINT
20 INPUT"ENTER ALPHA AND BETA COEFFICIENTS";A,B
30 INPUT"ENTER MEAN TIME BETWEEN TIDES";T:GOSUB
120
40 T2=T:T1=(A+B)/100
50 T$(1)="FIRST HIGH TIDE":T$(2)="SECOND HIGH TI
DE"
60 PRINT:PRINT:INPUT"ENTER DAY NUMBER DESIRED";N
70 FOR I=1 TO 2
80 T=A(I)+(B(I)*N):GOSUB 130
90 PRINT T$(I);" WILL OCCUR AT ",H;M
100 NEXT I
110 PRINT:GOTO 150
120 H=INT(T):M=(H-INT(H))/.6:T=INT(H)+M:RETURN
130 H=INT(T/100):M=INT(60*((T/100)-H)):IF H>23 T
HEN H=H-24
140 RETURN
150 PRINT:PRINT"(A)nother          (M)ain menu ";
160 GOSUB 180
170 IF Q$="A" OR Q$="a" THEN RUN 10 ELSE RUN "A:
MENU"
180 Q$=""+INKEY$:IF Q$="" THEN 180
190 RETURN
```

moon, there is no routine available from which we can accurately forecast tidal magnitude without having available a good model of the local geological structure. The deviations between the hypothetical (sun/moon) and actual tidal magnitudes are often so great that we make no effort here to develop such a routine. It might be interesting, however, for the reader to develop such a program to track the actual times and heights of tides in a region. The graph of regional tidal actions are often quite elegant.

Annual Temperatures

Listing 12-10 is a brief routine used to compare current temperatures with historic records for a given locality. The user enters in the mean, high, and low temperatures for each month of the year, as well as the temperature for a given recent day. The computer then displays the annual record in graphic form and highlights the current temperature against these curves so the user can get an impression of whether the current weather is warmer or colder than the established norms.

The Great Seattle Weather Machine

There are nearly as many ways to forecast the weather as there are television studios broadcasting evening weather forecasts. While many of them depend upon the National Weather Service for their background information and long-range forecasts, a handful of independent forecasters use a curious batch of homemade or secret techniques. The routines the publishers of the *Old Farmer's Almanac* use are said to be nearly as old as the country itself, yet they are rather reliable, as long-range (more than five days in the future) forecasts go. One routine, developed in a university setting and relied upon by millions of viewers of one of the major morning news broadcasts, is based in part on an observation that the major weather patterns of the United States move from west to east in six-day intervals. That is, occasional disruptions notwithstanding, a weather pattern occurring in Seattle on Sunday is likely to drift eastward and hit the Atlantic coast sometime on Friday or Saturday. The leading exponents of this technique are quick to add that they temper their forecasts in consideration of sunspot cycles, volcanic eruptions, and other such phenomena. The short program in Listing 12-11 incorporates the six-day concept. The user specifies his location and the weather in Seattle for any given day. The computer then computes the angular distance between the two locations and from that the time required for the weather to drift eastward at the rate of about 7.6 degrees a day. It adds this time to the starting date and displays the forecast.

Listing 12-10. Annual Temperatures.

```
1 '*********************************************
2 '*              Listing 12-10               *
3 '*           Annual Temperatures            *
4 '*********************************************
5 '
10 CLS:KEY OFF:DIM M$(12),M(12),MX(12),MN(12)
20 FOR I=1 TO 12
30   READ M$(I):PRINT:PRINT"ENTER MEAN TEMPERATU
RE FOR ";M$(I),:INPUT M(I)
40   INPUT"MAXIMUM TEMPERATURE";MX(I):INPUT"MINI
MUM TEMPERTURE";MN(I)
50 NEXT I
60 CLS:SM=M(1):LG=M(1)
70 PRINT"MONTH","MEAN","MAXIMUM","MINIMUM"
80 FOR I=1 TO 12:PRINT I;M$(I),M(I),MX(I),MN(I):
NEXT
90 FOR I=1 TO 12
100 TN=TN+MN(I):TX=TX+MX(I):TM=TM+M(I)
110 IF SM<MN(I) THEN 130
```

Listing 12-10. Annual Temperatures. (Continued From Page 267.)

```
120 SM=MN(I)
130 IF MX(I)<LG THEN 150
140 LG=MX(I)
150 NEXT
160 PRINT:PRINT"MEAN",TM/12,TX/12,TN/12:R=LG-SM:
L=SM:H=LG:M=H-(R/2)
170 INPUT "<CR> to continue";ZZ
180 GOTO 260
190 DATA JAN,FEB,MAR,APR,MAY,JUN,JUL,AUG,SEP,OCT
,NOV,DEC
200 PRINT:PRINT"(A)nother        (M)ain menu ";
210 GOSUB 230
220 IF Q$="A" OR Q$="a" THEN RUN 10 ELSE RUN "A:
MENU"
230 Q$=""+INKEY$:IF Q$="" THEN 230
240 RETURN
250 ZAG%=INT(ZOG%/64):ZOG%=ZOG%-64*ZAG%+1:ZAG%=Z
AG%+1:LOCATE ZAG%,ZOG%:RETURN
260 '
270 GOSUB 430:SCREEN SC
280 CLS
290 FOR I=1 TO 12:LOCATE I,1:PRINT 130-(I*10);:L
OCATE 13+I,1:PRINT-1*(I*10);:NEXT I
300 LINE (20,YY/2)-(XX,YY/2):LOCATE 13,1:PRINT"O
 F";
310 FOR I=1 TO 12
320    X=I*((XX-20)/12)
330    IF MX(I)>120 THEN MX(I)=120
340    IF MN(I)<-120 THEN MN(I)=-120
350    Y=(YY/2)-((M(I)/120)*(YY/2))
360    YX=(YY/2)-((MX(I)/120)*(YY/2))
370    YN=(YY/2)-((MN(I)/120)*(YY/2))
380    PSET(X,Y):PSET(X,YX):PSET(X,YN)
390 NEXT I
400 LOCATE 25,20:INPUT"<CR> to continue";ZZ
410 LOCATE 25,1:INPUT"Use PrtScrn to save Graph,
 <CR> to Continue";XX
420 GOTO 200
430 CLS
440 PRINT"1  --  320 X 200    2  --  640 X 200
  3  --  640 X 400 "
450 PRINT:PRINT"Indicate screen dimensions ";
460 Q$=""+INKEY$:IF Q$="" THEN 460
470 IF Q$<"1" OR Q$>"3" THEN 460
480 ON VAL(Q$) GOTO 490, 500, 510
490 XX=320:YY=200:SC=1:XL=39:ZY=8:ZX=4:RETURN
500 XX=640:YY=200:XL=39:SC=2:ZY=8:ZX=8:RETURN
510 XX=640:YY=400:SC=100:XL=79:ZY=16:ZX=8:RETURN
```

EXERCISES

1. Modify the program in Listing 12-6 to identify dates of lunar and solar eclipses.
2. We have been taught that the number of sunspots in a year vary from high to low over what appears to be an eleven-year cycle. Numerical analysis of the number of sunspots occurring annually, however, has led scientists to conclude that the cyclic nature of sunspots is best represented by a

Listing 12-11. Seattle Weather Machine.

```
1 '************************************************
2 '*              Listing 12-11                   *
3 '*         Seattle Weather Machine              *
4 '************************************************
5 '
10 CLS:KEY OFF:PRINT"SEATTLE WEATHER MACHINE":PR
INT:PRINT
20 INPUT"ENTER YOUR LONGITUDE";LO:LP=122.5
30 ND=(LP-LO)/7.583333
40 INPUT"WHAT IS THE WEATHER IN SEATTLE TODAY";W
$
50 INPUT"WHAT IS TODAY'S DATE, MONTH   (DD,MM)";D
,M
60 M$="JANFEBMARAPRMAYJUNJULAUGSEPOCTNOVDEC"
70 D$="31283130313031313031313031"
80 MO$=MID$(M$,((M-1)*3)+1,3)
90 DV=VAL(MID$(D$,((M-1)*2)+1,2))
100 WD=D+ND:IF WD<=DV THEN 120
110 M=M+1:D=D-DV:GOTO 80
120 PRINT"ON";WD;MO$;" THERE WILL BE ";W$;" IN Y
OUR LOCATION"
130 PRINT"(A)nother       (M)ain menu ";
140 GOSUB 160
150 IF Q$="A" OR Q$="a" THEN RUN 10 ELSE RUN "A:
MENU"
160 Q$=""+INKEY$:IF Q$="" THEN 160
170 RETURN
```

composite wave of six cycles with the respective periods of 5.5, 8.1, 9.7, 11.2, 100, and 180 years. Write a program which incorporates this information and generates a forecast of the sunspot sequence.

3. Use a microcomputer to attempt to determine the total length, if there is one, of the entire cycle of these six sub-cycles. If there is such a complete period, attempt to locate the current date along that scale. (Detailed sunspot data may be obtained from the World Data Center in Boulder, Colorado.) If there does not seem to be an overall cycle, develop a program to overlay actual recent data over an extended version of the model to determine a pragmatic best fit.

4. Chapter 7 in the Herman-Goldberg book listed below contains an extensive table of correlations between sunspot activity and a number of terrestrial atmospheric and meteorological phenomena. Obtain a copy of the table and devise experiments to validate one or more of the correlations as they pertain to your location.

SUGGESTED READING

Abell, G., 1963. *Exploration of the Universe*. New York: Holt, Rinehart, and Winston.

Duffett-Smith, P., 1981. *Practical Astronomy with Your Calculator*. Cambridge, England: Cambridge University Press.

Herman, J. R. and R. A. Goldberg, 1978. *Sun, Weather, and Climate*. Washington, DC: NASA.

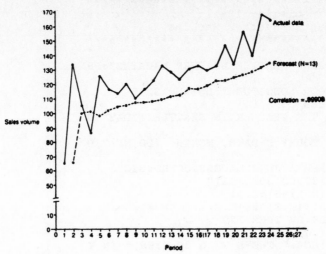

## Chapter 13

Population Estimates

Making population estimates is one of the more practical aspects of forecasting. It is essential to know what the population of a school, city, state, nation, or the world is going to be at some point in the future for one level of planning or another. Prudent resource management requires that we make strategic purchases of goods and materials at optimum times with regard not only to price, but to the expected degree of demand. Demand, we believe, is partially a function of population.

A second aspect to population estimation is found in a variety of natural or environmental sciences, such as biology or animal management. In these areas the task is as much to determine what the current population is, from a sample, as it is to forecast what it will be at some time in the future.

The tools we have available include nearly all the basic techniques that have been presented so far in this book. Successful population estimates have been made using curve fitting techniques, modeling and simulations, numerical analysis, and probabilistic approaches. In the final analysis, the technique of choice will be that which consistently provides the most reliable forecast. Nonetheless, each of the techniques, given a particular forecasting task, have their own advantages or benefits, as well as liabilities. In this chapter we shall examine some of the more common techniques, highlighting their contributions and limitations.

FORECASTING SOCIAL POPULATIONS

The very nature of living populations, their reproductive and changing aspects, suggest a series of applicable techniques. As with modeling techniques, the approaches all begin with a determination of the current or baseline population. Second, we must know the rate at which the population reproduces and increases as well as the rate at which the same population decreases through deaths of its members. Listing 13-1 is a short routine based on the population factors of the birth and death rates.

This routine has only limited utility. Of all of the procedures, it is the simplest to compute and manage. The user can alter the birth and death rates so that over a certain time span, the forecast based on a population of some years ago matches current

Listing 13-1. Population Estimator.

```
1  '************************************************
2  '*              Listing 13-1              *
3  '*           Population Estimator          *
4  '************************************************
5  '
10 CLS:DEFDBL B,D,E,N,P
20 INPUT"ENTER CURRENT POPULATION";P:P1=P
30 INPUT"POPULATION YEAR";Y
40 INPUT"NUMBER OF LIVE BIRTHS PER 1000 POPULATI
ON";B:B=B/1000
50 INPUT"NUMBER DEATHS PER 1000 POPULATION";D:D=
D/1000
60 INPUT"TARGET YEAR";TY
70 PRINT"YEAR","# BIRTHS","# DEATHS","POPULATION
"
80 FOR I=1 TO (TY-Y)
90 NB=B*P:ND=D*P:P=P+NB-ND
100 PRINT Y+I,INT(NB)+1,INT(ND)+1,INT(P)+1
110 NEXT I
120 EI=((P/P1)^(1/(TY-Y)))-1
130 PRINT:PRINT"EFFECTIVE ANNUAL POPULATION CHAN
GE = ";100*EI;" %"
140 PRINT:PRINT"DO YOU WANT TO COMPUTE ANY OTHER
 POPULATION YEAR FROM THIS VALUE?  (Y/N)   ";
150 GOSUB 240
160 PRINT Q$:IF Q$="N" THEN 210
170 PRINT:INPUT"ENTER DESIRED YEAR";DY
180 EP=P1*((1+EI)^(DY-Y))
190 PRINT"ESTIMATED POPULATION IN";DY;"IS";INT(E
P)+1
200 GOTO 140
210 PRINT"(A)nother        (M)ain menu ";
220 GOSUB 240
230 IF Q$="A" OR Q$="a" THEN RUN 10 ELSE RUN "A:
MENU"
240 Q$=""+INKEY$:IF Q$="" THEN 240
250 RETURN
```

reality, although this is a little risky. Nonetheless, once the effective rate of population increase (EI) is computed, it is a fairly simple matter to project future populations from:

$$P' = P (1 + EI)^n$$

References in the media to population growth rates are the same as EI. Forecasts using this measure are best limited to short-range forecasting.

There is an immediate and major defect in the foregoing technique: it disregards the migration of people in and out of an area. For this reason, it is a technique better suited for an isolated island or similar population center. Since, in normal situations, migration consists of both immigration into a country or region, and emigration out of an area, the rate we are concerned with is the *net immigration*. This value is computed for a given period simply by subtracting the number of those leaving from the number of those entering. This value will be negative when those leaving outnumber those entering. For a country on the scale of the United States, net immigration is a significant factor in population forecasts. Listing 13-2 expands on the first program and makes provisions for net immigration.

This second program has broader utility and application, but it is still inadequate for major forecasting work. Among other things, the birthrate as a

Listing 13-2. Population Estimator II.

```
1 '***********************************************
2 '*                 Listing 13-2              *
3 '*            Populations Estimator II       *
4 '***********************************************
5 '
10 CLS:KEY OFF:DEFDBL B,D,E,N,P
20 INPUT"ENTER CURRENT POPULATION";P:P1=P
30 INPUT"POPULATION YEAR";Y
40 INPUT"NUMBER OF LIVE BIRTHS PER 1000 POPULATI
ON";B:B=B/1000
50 INPUT"NET IMMIGRATION PER 1000 POPULATION";N:
N=N/1000
60 INPUT"NUMBER DEATHS PER 1000 POPULATION";D:D=
D/1000
70 INPUT"TARGET YEAR";TY
80 PRINT"YEAR","# BIRTHS","# DEATHS","POPULATION
"
90 FOR I=1 TO (TY-Y)
100 NB=B*P:NI=N*P:ND=D*P:P=P+NB+NI-ND
110 PRINT Y+I,INT(NB)+1,INT(ND)+1,INT(P)+1
120 NEXT I
130 EI=((P/P1)^(1/(TY-Y)))-1
140 PRINT:PRINT"EFFECTIVE ANNUAL POPULATION CHAN
GE = ";100*EI;" %"
150 PRINT:PRINT"DO YOU WANT TO COMPUTE ANY OTHER
 POPULATION YEAR FROM THIS VALUE?  (Y/N)   ";
160 Q$=""+INKEY$:IF Q$="" THEN 160
170 IF Q$="N" OR Q$="n" THEN 220
180 PRINT:INPUT"ENTER DESIRED YEAR";DY
190 EP=P1*((1+EI)^(DY-Y))
200 PRINT"ESTIMATED POPULATION IN";DY;"IS";INT(E
P)+1
210 GOTO 150
220 PRINT"(A)nother          (M)ain menu ";
230 GOSUB 250
240 IF Q$="A" OR Q$="a" THEN RUN 10 ELSE RUN "A:
MENU"
250 Q$=""+INKEY$:IF Q$="" THEN 250
260 RETURN
```

function of the total population is often too crude a measure, especially for forecasts over an extended period of time. A modification often made is to determine the birthrate as a function of the number of those females in the population normally considered to be in the primary age range for conception and delivery. Among humans in this country the practice is to consider the birthrate as a function of the number of females between 15 and 44 years of age. While there are births recorded involving women younger than 15 and older than 44, their numbers have been statistically insignificant. With the current increase in the numbers of women giv-ing birth later in life than the previous limit of 44, and a possible decline in the number of adolescent mothers, these limits may have to be adjusted upward from, say, 15 to 16 or 17, and from 44 to 45 or 50, or at least expanded to include the range 15 to 46 or 47 years. It is just this sort of change in social behavior that will always make the process of population forecasting tedious and long-range population estimates speculative at best. In any event, Listing 13-3 includes provisions for this component of population forecasting. In addition to knowing the baseline female population between 15 and 44, we must also know the population of the females 14

Listing 13-3. Population Forecaster III.

```
1 '***********************************************
2 '*                   Listing 13-3              *
3 '*            Population Forecaster III         *
4 '***********************************************
5 '
10 CLS:DEFDBL B,D,E,N,P
20 INPUT"ENTER CURRENT POPULATION";P:P1=P
30 INPUT"POPULATION YEAR";Y
40 INPUT"TOTAL NUMBER OF FEMALES";TF
50 INPUT"NUMBER FEMALES, AGE 0 TO 14";F1:F2=F1/P
60 INPUT"NUMBER FEMALES, AGE 15-44";F:F3=F/P
70 INPUT"NUMBER OF LIVE BIRTHS PER 1000 FEMALES
AGE 15-44";B:B=B/1000
80 INPUT"NET IMMIGRATION PER 1000 POPULATION";N:
N=N/1000
90 INPUT"NUMBER DEATHS PER 1000 POPULATION";D:D=
D/1000
100 INPUT"TARGET YEAR";TY
110 PRINT"YEAR","# BIRTHS","# DEATHS","POPULATIO
N"
120 FOR I=1 TO (TY-Y)
130 NB=B*F:NI=N*P:ND=D*P:P=P+NB+NI-ND
140 A1=(1/30)*F:A2=D*F:A3=(1/15)*F1:A5=D*F1:A6=N
B/2:A7=NI*F3:A8=NI*F2
150 F=F-A1-A2+A3+A7:F1=F1-A3-A5+A6+A8
160 PRINT Y+I,INT(NB)+1,INT(ND)+1,INT(P)+1
170 NEXT I
180 EI=((P/P1)^(1/(TY-Y)))-1
190 PRINT:PRINT"EFFECTIVE ANNUAL POPULATION CHAN
GE = ";100*EI;" %"
200 PRINT:PRINT"DO YOU WANT TO COMPUTE ANY OTHER
 POPULATION YEAR FROM THIS VALUE?   (Y/N)   ";
210 Q$=""+INKEY$:IF Q$="" THEN 210
220 PRINT Q$:IF Q$="N" OR Q$="n" THEN 270
230 PRINT:INPUT"ENTER DESIRED YEAR";DY
240 EP=P1*((1+EI)^(DY-Y))
250 PRINT"ESTIMATED POPULATION IN";DY;"IS";INT(E
P)+1
260 GOTO 200
270 PRINT"(A)nother        (M)ain menu ";
280 GOSUB 300
290 IF Q$="A" OR Q$="a" THEN RUN 10 ELSE RUN "A:
MENU"
300 Q$=""+INKEY$:IF Q$="" THEN 300
310 RETURN
```

years and younger. Each year a portion of the younger set will become 15, and a portion of the child-bearing group will become 45 and theoretically cease child-bearing. In studies involving other than human populations, the basic technique is essentially the same, only the year brackets will change according to the particular animal involved. Population studies aimed at determining the total animal population of an area, such as a national forest, require combining the separate population for each species.

The analyst can expand the population program to include an input of the current or baseline population for each age group in the population, as well as the birth and death rates. It is also useful to include data on race and sex as well. Each level of detail, of course, increases the workload and computer memory requirements, as well as increasing the accuracy of the forecast.

There is an alternative theory that suggests that it is as simple and as meaningful to apply numerical techniques to the task, especially in studies of large populations. These include curve fitting techniques, multivariate correlations, and polynomial evaluations.

Curve Fitting Techniques

Using the technique of least squares analysis and curve fitting, the period is represented by the X variable and the population of record the Y variable. We can use either the actual year (e.g., 1978) or apply an arbitrary measure (e.g., 1978 = 1, 1979 = 2, 1980 = 3, etc.). The only restriction on using the arbitrary measure is that the intervals must be properly labeled in proportion to the interval. That is, if 1960 = 1, and 1970 = 2, then 1985 must be 3.5, not 4. Further, it is possible and advisable to truncate the population data to a more manageable form. For example, the U.S. population in 1950 was estimated to be 151,325,798 (U.S. Census Bureau). Algebraically, it doesn't matter if that number is expressed in the full form, as above, or as: 151.325798, or 15.1325798, or whatever multiple. As a practical matter, it is often easier for the computer to munch away at the truncated numbers than the expanded form. Having made the forecast, the only consideration is to remember to expand the forecast results. That is, if we truncate the input by dividing by one million, then we must multiply the output by the same amount to obtain the actual forecast. Listing 13-4 provides a routine to accept period population data and to perform least squares curve fitting analysis. The user of this routine may input the total population estimates for several known periods or may do several subsets of these data if available. That is, the first run may consist of com-

Listing 13-4. Population Estimate from Sample.

```
1 '*********************************************
2 '*              Listing 13-4                 *
3 '*      Population Estimate from Sample       *
4 '*********************************************
5 '
10 CLS:KEY OFF:A(1)=1.96:A(2)=2.33:A(3)=2.58:A(4
)=3.3
20 INPUT"ENTER NUMBER OF ORGANISMS MARKED AND RE
LEASED IN THE GENERAL POPULATION";A
30 PRINT:INPUT"ENTER NUMBER OF ORGANISMS COLLECT
ED IN SUBSEQUENT ACTIVITY";B
40 PRINT:INPUT"ENTER NUMBER OF ORGANISMS IN SECO
ND COLLECTION THAT ARE MARKED";M
50 PRINT:PRINT"1 -- 95 %    2 -- 98 %    3 -- 99 %
    4 -- 99.9 %":PRINT
60 PRINT"CONFIDENCE LEVEL DESIRED    ";
70 Q$=""+INKEY$:IF Q$="" THEN 70
80 PRINT Q$:Z=A(VAL(Q$)):P=M/B:Q=(B-M)/B
90 P1=A/(P-(Z*SQR((P*Q)/B))):P2=A/(P+(Z*SQR((P*Q
)/B)))
100 PRINT:PRINT"THE TOTAL POPULATION IS ESTIMATE
D TO BE ABOUT ";INT((A*B)/M)+1;
110 PRINT", RANGING FROM ";INT(P2)+1;"TO ";INT(P
1)+1
120 PRINT:PRINT:PRINT"(A)nother          (M)ain menu
";
130 GOSUB 150
140 IF Q$="A" OR Q$="a" THEN RUN 10 ELSE RUN "A:
MENU"
150 Q$=""+INKEY$:IF Q$="" THEN 150
160 RETURN
```

puting a curve for the male component, while the second consists of the curve for the female component. The total forecast, then, is the sum of the two subsets.

ESTIMATING ANIMAL POPULATIONS

Listing 13-5 is a short routine useful in estimating wild animal populations. The basic approach is to collect a sample (A) of creatures under study and mark them in some fashion, such as with a dye mark, ear tags, or some other nondestructive device. The animals are then released and allowed to mingle for a reasonable period of time: sufficient to become ran-

domly redistributed among their own species.

After this period of time, another sample (B) of animals is collected with no special effort to select the marked animals. The animals are counted. Those with the marking from the first sample are also noted (M). The general estimate of the actual local population is found from:

$$P = INT \left(\frac{A \times B}{M}\right) + 1$$

The program includes a subroutine to compute the probable limits on either side of this estimate as a function of a normally distributed population.

Listing 13-5. Population Curve-Fitting.

```
1 '*************************************************
2 '*                Listing 13-5                   *
3 '*           Population Curve-Fitting            *
4 '*************************************************
5 '
10 CLS:KEY OFF:CLEAR 250:DEFDBL A-H,N-Z
20 PRINT:PRINT"THIS ROUTINE ACCEPTS POPULATION D
ATA IN PAIRED X,Y FORMAT AND ATTEMPTS TO        I
DENTIFY THE BEST LINEAR OR CURVE FIT.  IT ALSO P
ROVIDES AN ESTIMATE OF THE      COEFFICIENT OF CO
RRELATION.":PRINT
30 PRINT"YOU MAY USE ANY INTERVAL (YEARS, DECADE
S, CENTURIES, ETC.), BUT THE INTERVAL    MUST BE
 CONSTANT, WITH NO GAPS IN THE DATA.  DO NOTUSE
THE YEAR, BUT, INSTEAD,   NUMBER EACH INTERVAL FR
OM 1 TO N.":PRINT
40 PRINT:INPUT"ENTER NUMBER OF PAIRS:";P:DIM XY(
30),XX(P),YY(P):PRINT
50 FOR I=1 TO P:PRINT"ENTER POPULATION FOR PERIO
D # ";I,:INPUT YY(I):XX(I)=I:NEXT I
60 A$=" ####  ####.###      "
70 CLS:PRINT"PERIOD   POPUL.     PERIOD    POPUL.
   PERIOD    POPUL."
80 FOR I=1 TO P
90 PRINT USING A$;I;YY(I);
100 IF (I/3)<>INT(I/3) THEN 120
110 PRINT
120 NEXT
130 PRINT:PRINT"ARE THESE VALUES CORRECT?   (Y/N)
"
140 QQ$=INKEY$:IF QQ$="" THEN 140
150 IF QQ$="Y" OR QQ$="y" THEN 170
160 INPUT"ENTER PERIOD AND CORRECT POPULATION";I
,YY(I):GOTO 70
170 CLS:LOCATE 9,1:PRINT"PLEASE BE PATIENT, COMP
UTING"
180 FOR I=1 TO P
190 GOTO 210
```

Listing 13-5. Population Curve-Fitting. (Continued From Page 275.)

```
200 ON ERROR GOTO 1090
210 X=XX(I):Y=(YY(I)):E(1)=E(1)+(X*Y):E(2)=E(2)+
(X*LOG(Y))
220 IF XX(I)>LX THEN LX=XX(I)
230 E(3)=E(3)+(Y*LOG(X)):E(4)=E(4)+(LOG(X)*LOG(Y
))
240 IF XX(I)<SX THEN SX=XX(I)
250 F(1)=F(1)+X:F(3)=F(3)+LOG(X)
260 IF YY(I)>LY THEN LY=YY(I)
270 G(1)=G(1)+Y:G(2)=G(2)+LOG(Y)
280 IF YY(I)<SY THEN SY=YY(I)
290 H(1)=H(1)+X^2:H(3)=H(3)+LOG(X)^2
300 I(1)=F(1)^2:I(3)=F(3)^2
310 J(1)=J(1)+Y^2:J(2)=J(2)+LOG(Y)^2
320 K(1)=G(1)^2:K(2)=G(2)^2
330 LOCATE 11,1:PRINT"I =";I;
340 NEXT I
350 F(2)=F(1):F(4)=F(3):G(3)=G(1):G(4)=G(2):H(2)
=H(1):H(4)=H(3):I(2)=I(1):I(4)=I(3):J(3)=J(1):J(
4)=J(2):K(3)=K(1):K(4)=K(2)
360 FOR M=1 TO 4
370 B(M)=(E(M)-(F(M)*G(M))/P)/(H(M)-I(M)/P)
380 A(M)=(G(M)-B(M)*F(M))/P
390 R(M)=SQR((E(M)-F(M)*G(M)/P)^2/((H(M)-I(M)/P)
*(J(M)-K(M)/P)))
400 LOCATE 12,1:PRINT"M =";M;
410 NEXT M
420 B$="\            \  ####.####    ####.####
   ##.######"
430 CLS:PRINT"","A","B","R":PRINT USING B$;"LINE
AR:";A(1);B(1);R(1):PRINT USING B$;"EXPONENTIAL:
";EXP(A(2));B(2);R(2):PRINT USING B$;"LOGARITHMI
C:";A(3);B(3);R(3):PRINT USING B$;"POWER:";EXP(A
(4));B(4);R(4):A(4)=EXP(A(4)):A(2)=EXP(A(2))
440 FOR I=1 TO 6:R(I)=ABS(R(I)):NEXT I
450 IF R(1)>R(2) THEN 490
460 IF R(2)>R(3) THEN 510
470 IF R(3)>R(4) THEN 540
480 M=4:GOTO 550
490 IF R(1)<R(3) THEN 470
500 IF R(1)>R(4) THEN 520 ELSE 480
510 IF R(2)>R(4) THEN 530 ELSE 480
520 M=1:GOTO 550
530 M=2:GOTO 550
540 M=3
550 PRINT
560 F$(1)="LINEAR":F$(2)="EXPONENTIAL":F$(3)="LO
GARITHMIC":F$(4)="POWER":F$(5)="PARABOLIC":E$(1)
="Y = A + BX":E$(2)="Y = EXP(LOG A + BX)":E$(3)=
"Y = A + B LOG X":E$(4)="Y = EXP(LOG A + B LOG X
)":E$(5)="Y = A0 + A1 X + A2 X^2"
570 C$="#####.######"
580 PRINT"THE BEST CURVE FIT IS ";F$(M):PRINT"TH
E EQUATION IS: ";E$(M):PRINT"A =";USING C$;A(M);
:PRINT"    B =";USING C$;B(M);:PRINT"    R =";USIN
G C$;R(M):PRINT:PRINT"DO YOU WANT TO COMPUTE A T
```

```
ERM?   (Y/N)"
590 IF SX=>0 AND SY=>0 THEN 610
600 ZZ=1:PRINT:PRINT"(DATA INCLUDES NEGATIVE VAL
UES, ONLY THE LINEAR EQUATION IS VALID.  IF ANOT
HER  FORM IS RECOMMENDED, PROGRAM WILL DISREGARD
 AND COMPUTE    LINEAR.)"
610 QZ$=INKEY$:IF QZ$="" THEN 610
620 CLS
630 IF QZ$="N" OR QZ$="n" THEN 920
640 LOCATE 16,1:PRINT"ENTER '●' TO STOP:";
650 LOCATE 9,1:PRINT"WHICH VALUE (X OR Y) WILL B
E ENTERED?";:LOCATE 10,1:PRINT"
  ";
660 QX$=INKEY$:IF QX$="" THEN 660
670 IF QX$="Y" THEN 720
680 IF QX$="●" THEN 920
690 PRINT:INPUT"ENTER X-VALUE";X
700 ON M GOSUB 750,800,840,880
710 GOTO 740
720 PRINT:INPUT"ENTER Y-VALUE";Y
730 ON M GOSUB 770,820,860,900
740 CLS:LOCATE 7,1:PRINT"X =";X;"      Y =";Y:PRI
NT:GOTO 630
750 Y=A(1)+B(1)*X
760 RETURN
770 X=(Y-(A(1)))/B(1)
780 RETURN
790 RETURN
800 Y=EXP(LOG(A(2))+B(2)*X)
810 RETURN
820 X=(LOG(Y)-LOG(A(2)))/B(2)
830 RETURN
840 Y=A(3)+B(3)*LOG(X)
850 RETURN
860 X=EXP((Y-A(3))/B(3)
870 RETURN
880 Y=A(4)*(X^B(4))
890 RETURN
900 X=(Y/A(4))^(1/B(4))
910 RETURN
920 GOSUB 1060
930 LPRINT"":LPRINT""
940 LPRINT" ":LPRINT"TABLE OF INPUT/OUTPUT VALUE
S":LPRINT" "
950 LPRINT"INPUT":LPRINT"X","Y","X","Y","X","Y",
"X","Y"
960 FOR I=1 TO P:LPRINT XX(I),YY(I),:NEXT I
970 IF RR=2 THEN 1040
980 LPRINT" ":LPRINT"OUTPUT":LPRINT" ","A","B","
R","t-TEST","EQUATIONS"
990 LPRINT"LINEAR",A(1),B(1),R(1),TT(1),E$(1)
1000 LPRINT"EXPONENTIAL",A(2),B(2),R(2),TT(2),E$
(2)
1010 LPRINT"LOGARITHMIC",A(3),B(3),R(3),TT(3),E$
(3)
1020 LPRINT"POWER",A(4),B(4),R(4),TT(4),E$(4)
1030 LPRINT STRING$(5,10):CLS:RUN 10
1040 LPRINT STRING$(3,10)
```

Listing 13-5. Population Curve-Fitting. (Continued From Page 277.)

```
1050 GOTO 1110
1060 FX=(LX-SX)/126:FY=(LY-SY)/46
1070 ZX=127*(ABS(SX)/(LX-SX)):ZY=47-(47*(ABS(SY)
/(LY-SY)))
1080 GOTO 1110
1090 RESUME NEXT
1100 'USE THIS SECTION TO RUN GRAPHIC DISPLAYS O
F DATA.  SEE 'GRAPHICS.BAS'      PROGRAM.
1110 PRINT"(A)nother       (M)ain menu ";
1120 GOSUB 1140
1130 IF Q$="A" OR Q$="a" THEN RUN 10 ELSE RUN "A
:MENU"
1140 Q$=""+INKEY$:IF Q$="" THEN 1140
1150 RETURN
```

EXERCISES:

1. From county records, obtain the population of your county for the last hundred years. From county health authorities obtain a reliable estimate of the birth and mortality rates for your county. From these data, compute the best estimate of the county population for the next hundred years.

2. Having conducted the research in exercise 1, contact the local branch of the Chamber of Commerce and make an appointment to discuss your findings with a business analyst. Compare your projections with the Chamber's projections. How close are they? At what point, if at all, do they diverge? Why? Are these factors you can include in your program? How do the revised projections compare?

3. Develop a routine to compute world population data for the next fifty years.

4. Develop a study which implements the major features of the Population Estimator II.

SUGGESTED READING

Makridakis, S. and S.C. Wheelwright, 1978. *Forecasting Methods & Applications.* New York: John Wiley & Sons.

Chapter 14

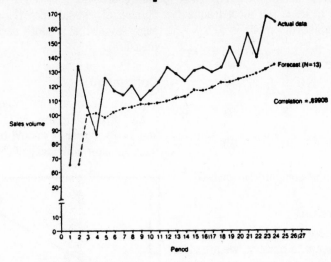

Educational Testing

It is the premise of this chapter that there is a place and a legitimate need for responsible educational testing. Opponents of testing argue that tests discriminate. By this they would imply that discrimination is inherently wrong. We would argue that only discrimination based on irrelevant factors is unfair and wrong. Tests, by their very nature, discriminate: that is, they identify differences in one or more characteristics in people.

The purpose of this chapter, however, is not to resolve social issues, but to provide the reader with sufficient information to use in microcomputer applications in testing or at least to make use of the microcomputer in a rational evaluation of testing programs. All modern testing is, or should be, precise and scientific. As with all other activities involving humans, the number of variables, and the indeterminate nature of many of them, are such that precision becomes a relative term. The primary objective of such testing, then, is that these tests be reliable and valid. In the pages that follow we shall attempt to provide routines with which one may measure the reliability and validity of tests.

STATISTICAL BASICS

Before proceeding further, you should become familiar with the material in Chapters 2 and 5. Among the principles presented, the key points applicable to educational testing include, but are not limited to, the concept of central tendency, measures of dispersion, and the various measures of correlation.

Central Tendency

A normal, fundamental aspect of data related to a specific characteristic is a concentration of points at or near the center of the data. For example, an easily identified characteristic of people is height. If we measure the height of a group of people chosen at random and chart the data, we will see a grouping of the data about the mean of the collection. Some people will be rather short or rather tall, but most will be of normal height. We measure central tendency by one of three characteristics: mean, mode, or median. The mean is simply the sum of each of the data points divided by the number of items. The median is the center value in an ordered list of the data. That is, if we list the data points in order of their magnitude, the median is the middle point in that list. The mode is the most frequent score. In the following list, the mode is 62:

Item #	Value	Item #	Value
1	58	6	62
2	61	7	62
3	61	8	63
4	62	9	63
5	62	10	65

The median is also 62. The computed mean is 61.7.

Measures of Dispersion

While our first concern is to determine the point about which the data seem to revolve, we are also interested in the degree to which the data deviate from the center point. The primary measures of dispersion are the range and standard deviation of the data. The range is simply the numerical distance between the smallest and the largest values in the data. In tests in which the score is a percentage, the largest score is, of course, 100. The smallest possible is zero. Regardless of the center of the data, whether 35, 50, or 60 percent, we are interested in knowing how far on either side of that point the data fall. However the test is scored, the range is useful as a first estimate of the utility of a test. If the range is small relative to the potential, there is a question of whether the test is really doing a good job of discriminating. Assume that we have a school program in which students are to be placed in one of five courses of instruction in French, depending on their starting French language facility. If all the scores on the screening test fall between 78 and 79 percent, the test has no use as a discriminator. Instead, we need another test in which, even if the mean is still 78.5, the range is at least from 76 to 81, and preferably larger. Up to a point, the wider the range, the more sure we are the test is a reliable tool. We can use the standard deviation to gauge whether the range is excessive. From the computation of the standard deviation, as well as the skew and kurtosis, we can infer the degree to which the data reflect random distribution. That is, if the range

of the data is from zero to 100 percent and each possible score was achieved by more or less the same number of test subjects, the distribution is flat and suggests the test is poorly correlated to the criterion measure.

Correlation

Test items may be either positively or negatively correlated to the test criterion (see Figs. 14-1 and 14-2), but they should be correlated in some way. An alternative way of illustrating this require-

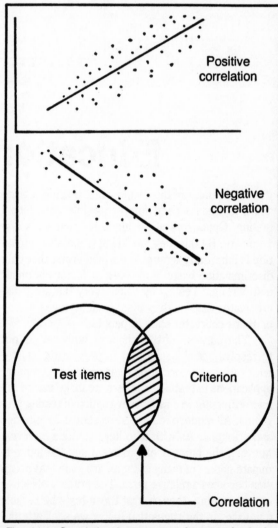

Fig. 14-1. Correlation between test items and criterion measures.

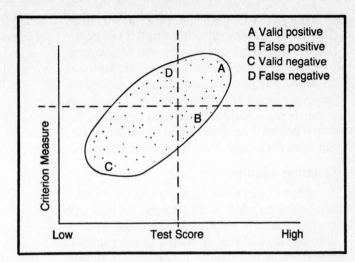

Fig. 14-2. Test scores correlated to criterion measures.

ment is shown in Fig. 14-3. Chapter 5 provides a detailed analysis and description of correlation computation techniques.

VALIDITY

A test is considered to be valid if it measures what it is designed to measure. There are three aspects to this concept of validity: content, criterion, and construct validity.

Content Validity

We are often concerned that a test adequately

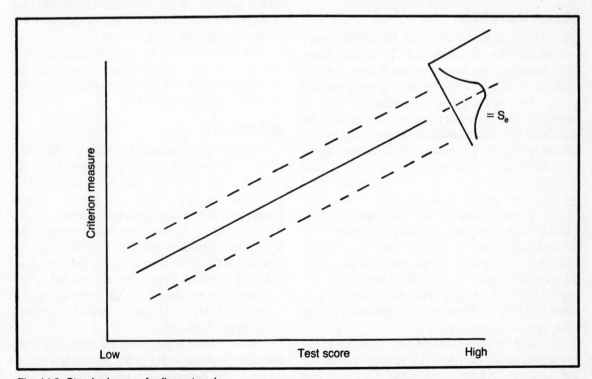

Fig. 14-3. Standard error of a linear trend.

covers the total content of the course of instruction. That is, if the course involves a matrix of instruction involving economic, political, and demographic comparisons of three countries, a content valid test should have at least nine items to cover each of the topics presented. Whether they are distinct items or one or more of them covers two or more of the matrix options is immaterial. What is relevant is that the items adequately cover the material presented.

Criterion Validity

A test is, in a sense, a sampling of the information held in the minds of the subjects. We trust that a properly constructed French examination is somehow logically and reliably related to the students' fluency in the language. If, for example, a student may readily receive a perfect score on a final French examination in a course in conversational French, yet cannot carry on a conversation in French, the examination lacks criterion validity. Therefore, an aspect of criterion validity is the predictive power of the examination. Does one who does well on the test do well in the related field?

Construct Validity

This is an aspect of testing about which many of the emotional issues revolve. This aspect raises the question of the degree to which there is a casual relationship between the test or test items and the underlying theory or the attribute it seeks to measure. One portion of a screening examination for applicants for employment as firemen may include some mathematics questions involving trigonometry. While such items may be shown to be somehow correlated with mental acuity and mental acuity is somehow related with success in combating fires, they may well be successfully challenged as irrelevant items lacking construct validity in the entry level screening process. On the other hand, a portion of the test which includes a measure of the amount of dead weight that the subject can lift and carry or the speed he or she can move over a specified distance may well be directly correlated (construct valid) to the tasks to be performed.

Figure 14-2 illustrates the general notion of the relationships between test scores and their validity as related to the criterion measures of the test. The sectors of the score results within the scattergram of the data are described as:

A — Valid Positives: test scores that correctly identify those who should be selected.

B — False Positives: test scores of those who passed the test but shouldn't have been selected.

C — Valid Negatives: test scores that properly identify those not capable of the task.

D — False Negatives: test scores of those who failed, but should have been selected.

In the development of any test, our objective is to maximize sectors A and C. To the extent that we are able to do this, we are more sure that a failing grade or score will be properly given to a person who actually fails to meet the basic criterion, and a passing grade is given to a capable respondent. As a rule of thumb, the better the correlation, either positive or negative, the better we have achieved the objective of minimizing sectors B and D, and maximizing sectors A and C.

To the extent that we have properly stated the criterion measure, the correlation between the test score and the criterion measure is equivalent to the validity coefficient of the test.

RELIABILITY

Another way of viewing reliability is in the sense of the consistency of results. Regardless of the validity of a test, a reliable test should be consistent each time it is given. If our test tends to identify people with high mathematics skills in one instance, it should do so in all instances. Alternatively, if the test, administered on Monday, indicates a person is skilled in a subject, it should make the same forecast in a retest on Friday. We are not concerned with what we are measuring but with how well it is measured. Figure 14-3 illustrates a key concern in the area of reliability.

The objective in improving reliability is to minimize the degree of error in the distribution of test scores when charted against the criterion measure.

There are several techniques used to compute the reliability of a test. These include retesting using the same test, testing with parallel tests, using the subdivided test, and using the Kuder-Richardson estimates.

Retesting Using the Same Test

The basic approach is to administer the same test to the same subjects. The scores obtained on one test are correlated (as shown in Chapter 5) with the scores on the retest. There are two methods of using this technique. The first is to retest immediately after the first test. The second is to retest after some interval, using the same test on the same subjects. The greater the correlation the more reliable the test. The correlation, R, is often referred to as the *Coefficient of Reliability*.

Parallel Tests

On the chance or suspicion that test scores obtained using the previous technique are a function of the subject's memory, test administrators will often attempt to administer *parallel* tests, tests that are as identical to each other as possible. One method to do this is to create a large pool of test items from the material being taught or otherwise tested and then randomly selecting items for the two tests. As with the single test, the parallel tests may be administered either in close proximity in time or with an interval. The coefficient of reliability is calculated as before by computing Pearson's *rho* correlation between the two sets of test scores.

Subdivided Tests

Subdivided tests contain pairs of items attempting to measure the same thing with the same degree of difficulty. In this sense, the test is much like the parallel test approach, only the two tests are administered simultaneously. The computation of the coefficient of reliability, known as the Spearman-Brown prophecy formula, is a two-step process. The first step is to compute a *rho* coefficient (r) between the two halves of the test as above. The second step is to compute the coefficient of reliability (R) from:

$$R = \frac{2r}{1+r}$$

If the correlation between the two halves of a test is .55, then the reliability of the test is presumed to be:

$$R = \frac{2 \times .55}{1 + .55} = \frac{1.100}{1.55} = .709677$$

The shortcomings of this technique are three. First, there is no chance to test variations in the individual over time. A student may do well one day and not so well the next, or vice-versa. What we really want out of a testing situation is not how excellently or how horribly someone can do under extreme conditions, but what we can normally expect of that person over a period of time. Second, unless great care is exercised, the test items may not be as distinctly random or independent as they should be, but dependent to the extent that if the student gets one correct, the paired item will also normally be answered correctly. The third defect is that the technique is of little value in timed tests where the objective is to answer correctly as many items as possible in a limited span of time, without expecting that all items will be answered or even attempted. In selecting items to answer, the subject might not choose to answer the second of paired items. Those purchasing tests from commercial publishers should be sure the reliability measures quoted are based on either extensive use of the instrument or on parallel test measurements.

Kuder-Richardson Estimates

Leaders and innovators in testing and statistical measurements, the Kuder-Richardson team gave their names to a number of equations for test-related statistical measures. One of these, "Formula 20," is a fairly precise equation requiring the user to compute the standard deviation, s, of the test scores, the percentage of students passing a given item, P, and the percentage failing each item, Q: (Q = 1 − P). From these the coefficient of reliability is computed as:

$$R = \left(\frac{N}{N-1}\right)\left(\frac{s^2 - \sum pq}{s^2}\right)$$

The second equation, "Formula 21," simplifies

the process somewhat and requires only the computation of the standard deviation and the mean test score, M, for the group being tested. While the results are a bit more conservative than those obtained using Formula 20, the computation is simpler. With a microcomputer, the slight increase in complexity required when using the first equation should be no problem, but we offer the second form for those whose tasks are not as demanding. The equation is:

$$R = \left(\frac{N}{N-1}\right)\left[1 - \frac{M\left(1 - \frac{M}{N}\right)}{s^2}\right]$$

Interpretation of the Coefficient of Reliability. We would like to have some method of translating the coefficients just computed into some more meaningful form. In Fig. 14-3 we noted the range of test scores around a trend line. This range is known as the standard error of measurement, s'. If we have computed the standard deviation of the test scores and have computed the coefficient of reliability, we can compute the standard error of measurement from:

$$s' = s\sqrt{1 - R}$$

Given a set of test scores from which we have computed the standard deviation to be 12 points and reliability to be .7096774, the standard error is:

$$s' = 12\sqrt{1 - .7096774} = 12\sqrt{.2903226} = 6.4658$$

Normally, better than 68 percent of the students' scores will be within 6.47 points, plus or minus, of the true score.

Effect of Length of a Test on Reliability

Common sense suggests that a test of ten items is more reliable than a test with two items. We have an equation available that gives us an estimate of how well lengthening a test improves its reliability. To use it, we must have first computed the basic coefficient of reliability of the original test and know the number of items on that test, N_1, and the number of items proposed on the second test, N_2. From these we can compute the new reliability coefficient, R':

1. $N = N_2/N_1$.

2. $R' = \dfrac{NR}{1 + (N - 1)R}$.

Suppose, using the previous example (R = .7096774), there were 40 items on the first test and the proposition is to triple the length to 120 items. What is the effect on the reliability of the second test?

1. $N = 120 / 40 = 3$.

2. $R' = \dfrac{3 \times .7096774}{1 + (3 - 1) \times .7096774} = .8799999$.

By tripling the length, we have increased the reliability 24 percent. Even if the standard deviation remains at 12, the standard error of measurement is only plus or minus 4.156, a reduction in error by 35.7091 percent.

Reliability of Difference in Scores

Assume we have tested a group of students in a given subject using two different tests, a pretest and a final exam. The final exam scores suggest the majority of the class have improved their knowledge of the subject matter. The question we have is: how reliable are the differences noted in the scores? To answer this we need three values: R', the reliability of the first test; R'', the reliability of the second test; and r, the correlation between the two tests. The reliability of the difference score is computed from:

$$R = \frac{\dfrac{R' + R''}{2} - r}{1 - r}$$

Using the data from the examples above, assume the pretest has a correlation with the final exam of .7856663. The reliability of the differences noted is:

$$R = \frac{\dfrac{.7096774 + .879999}{2} - .7856663}{1 - .7856663}$$

$$= .04280966$$

The correlation is not good: this highlights a curious aspect of this kind of correlation. The closer the correlation of the two scores approaches the average of the two separate correlations, the closer the reliability of the differences approaches zero. To improve the reliability of the difference scores, it is useful to reduce the correlation between the two screening measures and increase the reliability of the separate measures.

Listing 14-1 offers a program to handle each of the reliability measures just reviewed. You may elect to retain the entire program, or to extract from it just those sections desired.

Student Record Book

An informal measure of the reliability of a test is the degree to which it correlates with the student's other grades in the subject being tested. Listings 14-2 and 14-3 constitute a routine for establishing and maintaining student scores and grades over an entire school year. Not a mere elec-

tronic record book, it computes the relevant statistics for each of the students and each of the tests recorded. The user may specify whether the output is given as the actual score, the percentage (if the score is not already in percentage form), percentiles, or a letter grade (A to E) based on a normal curve.

For each student the program computes the current grade or score average and the trend of the grades to date. With the alpha and beta coefficients final grades can be estimated, thus giving the teacher advance warning of students in need of special assistance.

Listing 14-2 is a data management program used once for each class to establish the basic data file. Listing 14-3 is the main program used to maintain the record through the year.

Listing 14-1. Test Reliability Conference.

```
1 '*********************************************
2 '*               Listing 14-1                *
3 '*        Test Reliability Coefficients      *
4 '*********************************************
5 '
10 CLS:KEY OFF:PRINT"RELIABILITY COEFFICIENTS":P
RINT:PRINT
20 PRINT"1   ---   RESTESTING/PARALLEL TESTING":PR
INT"2   ---   SUBDIVIDED TESTS":PRINT"3   ---   KUDE
R-RICHARDSON ESTIMATES":PRINT"4   ---   STANDARD E
RROR OF MEASUREMENT":PRINT"5   ---   LENGTH OF TES
T":PRINT"6   ---   RELIABILITY OF DIFFERENCE SCORE
S":PRINT:PRINT"
SEL
30 Q$=""+INKEY$:IF Q$="" THEN 30 ELSE ON VAL(Q$)
 GOTO 40,160,280,570,680,760
40 CLS:PRINT"RETESTING/PARALLEL TESTING RELIABIL
ITY":PRINT:PRINT
50 INPUT"NUMBER OF STUDENTS";N
60 PRINT
70 FOR I=1 TO N
80 PRINT"STUDENT #";I;", ENTER SCORE TEST 1 AND
TEST 2";:INPUT X,Y
90 GOSUB 840
100 NEXT
110 PRINT
120 GOSUB 850
130 S1=SQR((X2-((TX^2)/N))/(N-1)):S2=SQR((Y2-((T
Y^2)/N))/(N-1))
140 M1=TX/N:M2=TY/N
150 PRINT:PRINT"THE COEFFICIENT OF RELIABILITY I
S = ";R:PRINT:PRINT"","TEST # 1","TEST # 2":PRIN
T"MEAN SCORE",M1,M2:PRINT"STAN. DEV.",S1,S2:F=1:
GOTO 610
```

Listing 14-1. Test Reliability Conference. (Continued From Page 285.)

```
160 CLS:PRINT"SUBDIVIDED TESTS":PRINT:PRINT
170 INPUT"NUMBER OF ITEMS ON TEST";N
180 IF (N/2)=INT(N/2) THEN 200
190 PRINT"SORRY, THERE MUST BE AN EVEN NUMBER OF
 ITEMS.":GOTO 170
200 P=N/2
210 FOR I=1 TO P
220 PRINT"ENTER THE NUMBER CORRECT RESPONSES, IT
EM # ";I,:INPUT X
230 INPUT"     ENTER THE NUMBER CORRECT RESPONSE
S FOR THE PAIRED ITEM";Y
240 GOSUB 840
250 NEXT I
260 GOSUB 850
270 F=2:R=(2*R)/(1+R):GOTO 130
280 CLS:PRINT"KUDER-RICHARDSON ESTIMATES":PRINT:
PRINT
290 INPUT"ENTER NUMBER OF STUDENTS";M
300 INPUT"ENTER NUMBER OF TEST ITEMS";N
310 DIM G(M),T(N)
320 FOR I=1 TO M
330 PRINT:PRINT"STUDENT # ";I
340 FOR J=1 TO N
350 PRINT"TEST ITEM #";J;", (C)ORRECT   (I)NCORRE
CT ";
360 Q$=""+INKEY$:IF Q$="" THEN 360
370 PRINT Q$:IF Q$="I" THEN 390
380 T(J)=T(J)+1:G(M)=G(M)+1
390 NEXT J
400 NEXT I
410 FOR I=1 TO M
420 TX=TX+G(I):X2=X2+(G(I)^2)
430 NEXT
440 S2=(X2-((TX^2)/N))/(N-1):M=TX/N:S=SQR(S2)
450 FOR I=1 TO N
460 P=T(I)/N:Q=1-P
470 SP=SP+(P*Q)
480 NEXT I
490 R1=(N/(N-1))*((S2-SP)/S2)
500 M=TX/N
510 R2=(N/(N-1))*(1-((M*(1-(M/N)))/S2))
520 PRINT:PRINT"MEAN GRADE = ";M
530 PRINT"STANDARD DEVIATION = ";SQR(S2)
540 PRINT"","FORM. 20","FORM. 21"
550 PRINT"COEF. OF REL.",R1,R2
560 F=3:GOTO 610
570 CLS:PRINT"STANDARD ERROR OF MEASUREMENT":PRI
NT:PRINT
580 INPUT"ENTER STANDARD DEVIATION";S
590 INPUT"ENTER COEFFICIENT OF RELIABILITY";R
600 GOTO 640
610 IF F=3 THEN 640
620 S=S1:GOTO 640
630 S=S2:F=0:GOTO 640
640 SY=S*SQR(1-R)
650 PRINT"STANDARD ERROR OF MEASUREMENT = ";SY
```

```
660 IF F=1 OR F=2 THEN 630
670 GOTO 860
680 CLS:PRINT"LENGTH OF TEST":PRINT:PRINT
690 INPUT"ENTER LENGTH OF CURRENT TEST";M
700 INPUT "RELIABILITY OF CURRENT TEST";R1
710 INPUT"ENTER PROPOSED LENGTH OF NEW TEST";N
720 N=N/M
730 R2=(N*R1)/(1+((N-1)*R1))
740 PRINT:PRINT"RELIABILITY OF NEW TEST SHOULD B
E = ";R2
750 GOTO 860
760 CLS:PRINT"RELIABILITY OF DIFFERENCE SCORES":
PRINT:PRINT
770 INPUT"ENTER RELIABILITY OF FIRST TEST";R1
780 INPUT "RELIABILITY OF SECOND TEST";R2
790 INPUT"ENTER CORRELATION BETWEEN TWO TESTS";R
800 PRINT
810 RD=(((R1+R2)/2)-R)/(1-R)
820 PRINT"RELIABILITY OF DIFFERENCE SCORE = ";RD
830 GOTO 860
840 TX=TX+X:TY=TY+Y:X2=X2+(X^2):Y2=Y2+(Y^2):XY=(
X*Y):RETURN
850 R=((N*XY)-(TX*TY))/SQR(((N*X2)-(TX^2))*((N*Y
2)-(TY^2))):RETURN
860 LOCATE 24,1:PRINT"(A)nother          (M)ain menu
";
870 GOSUB 890
880 IF Q$="A" OR Q$="a" THEN RUN 10 ELSE RUN "A:
MENU"
890 Q$=""+INKEY$:IF Q$="" THEN 890
900 RETURN
```

Listing 14-2. Student Record Book Set-up.

```
1 '*********************************************
2 '*                Listing 14-2                *
3 '*          Student Record Book Setup         *
4 '*********************************************
5 '
10 CLS:KEY OFF:CLEAR 1500
20 INPUT"NUMBER OF STUDENTS";N:DIM N$(N),S(N,1)
30 FOR I=1 TO N
40 PRINT"NAME OF STUDENT # ";I,:INPUT N$(I)
50 INPUT"FIRST TEST SCORE ";S(I,1)
60 NEXT
70 FOR I=1 TO N
80    IF S(I,1) < LG THEN 100
90    LG=S(I,1)
100 NEXT I
110 MX(1)=LG
120 PRINT:PRINT"ALL INPUTS CORRECT?  (Y/N)";
130 Q$=""+INKEY$:IF Q$="" THEN 130 ELSE IF Q$="Y
" THEN 160
140 PRINT:INPUT"ENTER STUDENT NUMBER AND CORRECT
 NAME";X,N$(X)
150 GOTO 120
160 PRINT:INPUT"CLASS FILE NUMBER";F:T=1
```

Listing 14-2. Student Record Book Set-Up. (Continued From Page 287.)

```
170 F$="class"+STR$(F)+".dat"
180 OPEN F$:PRINT#1,N,T,MX(1)
190 PRINT#1, MX(1)
200 NEXT I
210 FOR I=1 TO N
220   PRINT#1, N$(I)
230   PRINT#1, S(I,1)
240 NEXT I
250 CLOSE
260 PRINT"(A)nother      (M)ain menu ";
270 GOSUB 290
280 IF Q$="A" OR Q$="a" THEN RUN 10 ELSE RUN "A:
MENU"
290 Q$=""+INKEY$:IF Q$="" THEN 290
300 RETURN
```

Listing 14-3. Student Record Book.

```
1 '***********************************************
2 '*                    Listing 14-3             *
3 '*               Student Record Book           *
4 '***********************************************
5 '
10 CLS:CLEAR 1500
20 INPUT"CLASS FILE NAME";F$
30 OPEN "I",1,F$:INPUT#1, N,T
40 DIM N$(N),S(N,T+1),RT(N),CT(T+1),SD(N),SE(N),
A(N),B(N),ES(T+1),L(T+1),H(T+1),MX(T+1),TX(T+1),
TY(T+1),X2(T+1),Y2(T+1),XY(T+1),P(N)
50 FOR I=1 TO T
60 INPUT#1, MX(I)
70 NEXT I
80 FOR I=1 TO N
90 INPUT#1, N$(I):PRINT N$(I);
100 FOR J=1 TO T
110 INPUT#1, S(I,J):PRINT S(I,J),
120 NEXT J
130 NEXT I
140 CLOSE
150 PRINT:PRINT"MAXIMUM POSSIBLE SCORE FOR TEST
";T+1,:INPUT MX(T+1)
160 FOR I=1 TO N
170 PRINT"ENTER CURRENT TEST SCORE FOR ";N$(I),:
INPUT S(I,T+1)
180 NEXT
190 PRINT:PRINT"ALL DATA CORRECT?   (Y/N)";
200 Q$=""+INKEY$:IF Q$="" THEN 200
210 IF Q$="Y" THEN 240
220 INPUT"ENTER STUDENT NUMBER AND CORRECT SCORE
";X,S(X,T+1)
230 GOTO 190
240 T=T+1:CLS:LOCATE 1,1:PRINT"COMPUTING ";T;" T
EST SCORE RESULTS":B$=" #### "
250 LPRINT"#  NAME","TEST SCORES";STRING$((T*6)-
11," ");"SUM  MEAN     S.D.     S.E.     ALPHA
   BETA"
```

```
260 A$="####  ###.##  ##.###  ###.###  ####.###
 ####.###":B$=" ### "
270 FOR I=1 TO N
280 LPRINT I;N$(I),:PRINT N$(I);
290 TX=0:TY=0:X2=0:Y2=0:XY=0
300 FOR J=1 TO T
310 X=J:Y=S(I,J):RT(I)=RT(I)+Y:TT=TT+Y:LPRINT US
ING B$;Y;:PRINT Y;:TX=TX+X:TY=TY+Y:X2=X2+(X^2):Y
2=Y2+(Y^2):XY=XY+(X*Y)
320 NEXT
330 SD(I)=SQR((Y2-((TY^2)/T))/(T-1)):SE(I)=SD(I)
/SQR(T)
340 B(I)=(XY-(TX*(TY/T)))/(X2-(T*((TX/T)^2))):A(
I)=(TY/T)-(B(I)*(TX/T))
350 LPRINT USING A$;RT(I);RT(I)/T;SD(I);SE(I);A(
I);B(I)
360 PRINT RT(I);RT(I)/T;SD(I);SE(I);A(I);B(I)
370 NEXT I
380 C$="##.# "
390 LPRINT"TOTAL",
400 FOR I=1 TO T
410 FOR J=1 TO N
420 X=J:Y=S(J,I):CT(I)=CT(I)+Y:TX(I)=TX(I)+X:TY(
I)=TY(I)+Y:XY(I)=XY(I)+(X*Y):X2(I)=X2(I)+(X^2):Y
2(I)=Y2(I)+(Y^2)
430 NEXT J
440 LPRINT USING B$;CT(I);
450 NEXT I
460 LPRINT TT,TT/T:LPRINT"MEAN",
470 FOR J=1 TO T
480 LPRINT USING C$;CT(J)/N;
490 NEXT J
500 LPRINT TT/N,(TT/N)/T:LPRINT"S. D.",
510 FOR I=1 TO T
520 SD(I)=SQR((Y2(I)-((TY(I)^2)/N))/(N-1)):LPRIN
T USING C$;SD(I);
530 NEXT I
540 LPRINT"":LPRINT"S. E.",
550 FOR I=1 TO T
560 S=SD(I)/SQR(N):LPRINT USING C$;S;
570 NEXT I
580 LPRINT"":LPRINT"COEF. OF REL.",
590 FOR I=1 TO 7
600 LPRINT USING" #.###";(N/(N-1))*(1-((CT(I)/N)
*(1-((CT(I)/N)/N))/SD(I));
610 NEXT I
620 DIM SM(T),LG(T)
630 LPRINT"":LPRINT"LOW SCORE",
640 FOR I=1 TO T
650 SM(I)=1E+30:LG(I)=1E-30
660 FOR J=1 TO N
670 IF SM(I)<S(J,I) THEN 690
680 SM(I)=S(J,I)
690 IF S(J,I)<LG(I) THEN 710
700 LG(I)=S(J,I)
710 NEXT J
720 LPRINT USING B$;SM(I);
730 NEXT I
```

Listing 14-3. Student Record Book. (Continued From Page 289.)

```
740 LPRINT"":LPRINT"HIGH SCORE",
750 FOR I=1 TO T
760 LPRINT USING B$;LG(I);
770 NEXT I
780 LPRINT"":LPRINT"MAX. POSS.",
790 FOR I=1 TO T
800 LPRINT USING B$;MX(I);
810 NEXT I
820 OPEN "O",1,F$
830 PRINT#1, N,T
840 FOR I=1 TO T
850 PRINT#1, MX(I)
860 NEXT I
870 FOR I=1 TO N
880 PRINT#1, N$(I)
890 FOR J=1 TO T
900 PRINT#1, S(I,J)
910 NEXT J
920 NEXT I
930 CLOSE
940 FOR I=1 TO N
950 FOR J=1 TO N
960 IF J=I THEN 990
970 IF S(I,T)<S(J,T) THEN 990
980 TS=TS+1
990 NEXT J
1000 P(I)=100*(TS/N):TS=0
1010 NEXT I
1020 CLS:PRINT"# NAME","SCORE","PER CENT","% - T
ILE LETTER"
1030 LPRINT"":LPRINT"#","NAME","SCORE","PERCENTA
GE","PERCENTILE","LETTER"
1040 FOR I=1 TO N
1050 C=INT((S(I,T)-(CT(T)/N))/SD(T))+3:IF C<0 TH
EN C=0
1060 IF C>4 THEN C=4
1070 PRINT I;N$(I),S(I,T),S(I,T)/MX(T),P(I);CHR$
(69-C)
1080 LPRINT I,N$(I),S(I,T),INT(10000*(S(I,T)/MX(
T)))/100,P(I),CHR$(69-C)
1090 NEXT I
1100 PRINT"(A)nother        (M)ain menu ";
1110 GOSUB 1130
1120 IF Q$="A" OR Q$="a" THEN RUN 10 ELSE RUN "A
:MENU"
1130 Q$=""+INKEY$:IF Q$="" THEN 1130
1140 RETURN
```

OTHER TESTS AND TESTING TECHNIQUES

There have been numerous tests and testing techniques developed to investigate an equally broad range of human behavior and education. What follows are some of these which may be usefully exploited with a microcomputer.

Guttmann Scalar Analysis

The long history of research into the measurement of attitudes has long been clouded by the problem of being sure that the attitude statement to which the subjects are to respond belongs to the same scale. For example, one statement reads, in effect, that wars are not cost-effective even for the winners, while another statement says that wars to defend oneself are legitimate while other forms of military action are not. It has been pointed out that subjective responses to these two items are not suitable for comparison because they are really measures of two different scales. In the early 1950's a technique was developed to determine the degree to which a set of statements fall upon the same scale. The theory is that if the statements are perfectly ordered and unidimensional, responses by a set of subjects can be arranged in this pattern:

Agree with Item Number

Subject	1	2	3	4	5	6	7	8	9	Score
1							X	X	X	3
2						X	X	X	X	4
3					X	X	X	X	X	5
4				X	X	X	X	X	X	6
5			X	X	X	X	X	X	X	7
6		X	X	X	X	X	X	X	X	8
7	X	X	X	X	X	X	X	X	X	9

The utility of this approach is that by scoring an attitude survey with the items so arranged, it is assumed that if the subject agrees with item number 3, the same subject will also agree with items 4 through 9. In the beginning of the analysis, we understand that the items and the respondents are not so neatly arranged. Instead, the initial distribution may appear as:

Agree With Item Number

Subject	1	2	3	4	5	6	7	8	9	Score
1		X	X	X			X	X	X	6
2	X	X	X	X	X	X	X	X	X	9
3		X		X			X		X	4
4	X	X	X				X	X	X	7
5		X		X			X	X	X	5
6		X					X		X	3
7	X	X	X			X	X	X	X	8
Total	3	7	4	6	1	2	7	5	7	

The procedure at this point is to reorder the matrix so that either the column totals or the row totals form a numerical sequence. Ordering the row scores gives us:

Agree With Item Number

Subject	1	2	3	4	5	6	7	8	9	Score
6		X					X		X	3
3		X		X			X		X	4
5		X		X			X	X	X	5
1		X	X	X			X	X	X	6
4	X	X	X				X	X	X	7
7	X	X	X			X	X	X	X	8
2	X	X	X	X	X	X	X	X	X	9
Total	3	7	4	6	1	2	7	5	7	

Reordering the columns in a similar fashion gives us:

Subject	5	6	1	3	8	4	2	7	9	Score
6							X	X	X	3
3						X	X	X	X	4
					.....					
2	X	X	X	X	X	X	X	X	X	9

(The same as the first)

We can use this technique to simplify the construction of both surveys and tests. Assume that we have a test containing 40 items, which we administer to ten students. By using an "asterisk" to indicate an item answered incorrectly, we table the responses by the procedures noted above. The final table looks like this:

Item Numbers

Student	1	5	10	15	20	25	30	35	40
1					** ** ***	**** *** *			
2				* ** ** ** **	**** ***** *****				
3			* **** ** ***	**** *** ***					
4	**** *** *** *** * ** **** **								
5	**** ** **** ** *** ***** ***								
6	** **** * **** **** *** ** **** *								
7	******* *** ******** *** ******* *								
8	***** ****** **** **** ** ******* *** *								
9	**** *** ****** ***** * ** ** *********								
10	**** **** ***** ** * *** *** ** **** *** *								

291

Judging from the table, items numbered 21 through 40 do not appear to add anything to the discrimination process. That is, if we review the responses to each of the items numbered greater than 20, we cannot identify which student made the particular set of responses. On the other hand, by reviewing the responses to items 1 through 20 (as renumbered in the rearranging process) we can identify the particular student. Additionally, by noting which item number a student first makes a mistake on, one can immediately compute a fair estimate of the total number missed. For example, if a student first misses item number 15, then we assume the remaining 25 items will also be incorrectly answered, yielding a score of 37.5 (15/40 = .375). Armed with these data, we have a rational basis for deleting from the test items 21 through 40, using only the first 20. The program in Listing 14-4 takes the drudgery out of reordering the tables of test data into the format shown above. It is up to the user to determine which of the items appear to be superfluous.

Forecasting From Entry Indicators

Educational resources are limited. Whether there is a shortage of classroom space during periods of increased student population (from previous "baby booms") or a shortage of teachers (especially technically trained teachers who have been lured into industry), there never seems to be a flush period where anyone desiring to learn something can be sure of finding a seat in a class where the subject is taught by the most qualified teacher.

It is prudent, then, to make an attempt to forecast the likely academic performance of an applicant before admission so that those enrolled in a course of study are those most likely to make the most effective use of the resources available. When the target program is an extension of previous training or experiences, the screening process is simplified. For example, the study of mathematics covers a number of years. Entry into an advanced algebra course can be controlled simply by examining one's grades in previous algebra course(s).

Listing 14-4. Guttmann Scalar Analysis.

```
1 '*********************************************
2 '*              Listing 14-4              *
3 '*        Guttmann Scalar Analysis        *
4 '*********************************************
5 '
10 CLS:KEY OFF:SCREEN 0:INPUT"ENTER NUMBER OF TE
ST ITEMS";TI
20 INPUT"ENTER NUMBER OF STUDENTS";NS
30 DIM A(NS,TI),RT(NS),CT(TI),TR(NS),TC(TI)
40 CLS:LOCATE 16,1:PRINT"1 = CORRECT       0 = WR
ONG"
50 FOR I=1 TO NS
60 TR(I)=I
70 FOR J=1 TO TI
80 TC(J)=J
90 LOCATE 9,1:PRINT"STUDENT #";I;", ITEM #";J;
100 R$=""+INKEY$:IF R$="" THEN 100
110 R=VAL(R$)
120 A(I,J)=R:RT(I)=RT(I)+R:CT(J)=CT(J)+R
130 NEXT J
140 NEXT I
150 CLS
160 GOSUB 180
170 GOTO 270
180 CLS
190 FOR I=1 TO NS
200 FOR J=1 TO TI
210 IF A(I,J)=1 THEN LOCATE J,I:PRINT CHR$(219);
```

```
220 NEXT J
230 NEXT I
240 GOSUB 730
250 GOSUB 620
260 RETURN
270 M=NS
280 M=M/2
290 IF INT(M)=0 THEN 430
300 K=NS-M:J=1
310 I=J
320 L=I+M
330 IF RT(I)<=RT(L) THEN 410
340 T=RT(I):RT(I)=RT(L):RT(L)=T
350 T=TR(I):TR(I)=TR(L):TR(L)=T
360 FOR Z=1 TO TI
370 T=A(I,Z):A(I,Z)=A(L,Z):A(L,Z)=T
380 NEXT Z
390 I=I-M
400 IF I<1 THEN 410 ELSE 320
410 J=J+1
420 IF J>K THEN 280 ELSE 310
430 GOSUB 180
440 M=TI
450 M=M/2
460 IF INT(M)=0 THEN 600
470 K=TI-M:J=1
480 I=J
490 L=I+M
500 IF CT(I)<=CT(L) THEN 580
510 T=CT(I):CT(I)=CT(L):CT(L)=T
520 T=TC(I):TC(I)=TC(L):TC(L)=T
530 FOR Z=1 TO NS
540 T=A(Z,I):A(Z,I)=A(Z,L):A(Z,L)=T
550 NEXT Z
560 I=I-M
570 IF I<1 THEN 580 ELSE 490
580 J=J+1
590 IF J>K THEN 450 ELSE 480
600 GOSUB 180
610 GOTO 810
620 C=0
630 FOR I=1 TO NS
640 FOR J=1 TO TI
650 IF (I+J)>(NS+TI)/2 THEN 670
660 IF A(I,J)=0 THEN C=C+1
670 NEXT J
680 NEXT I
690 LOCATE 16,21:PRINT"C =";C;
700 LPRINT"C =";C
710 LPRINT"":FOR I=1 TO TI:LPRINT TC(I);:NEXT:LP
RINT"":FOR I=1 TO TI:LPRINT CT(I);:NEXT I:LPRINT
 STRING$(2,10)
720 RETURN
730 FOR I=1 TO NS
740 LPRINT I;TR(I),
750 FOR J=1 TO TI
760 IF A(I,J)=1 THEN LPRINT"*"; ELSE LPRINT" ";
770 NEXT J
```

Listing 14-4. Guttmann Scalar Analysis. (Continued From Page 293.)

```
780 LPRINT"";RT(I)
790 NEXT I
800 RETURN
810 LOCATE 16,1:PRINT"(R)OW,  (C)OLUMN OR (E)ND?
                   ";
820 Q$=""+INKEY$:IF Q$="" THEN 820
830 IF Q$="R" OR Q$="r" THEN 1010
840 IF Q$="E" OR Q$="e" THEN RUN "A:MENU"
850 Q$=""
860 LOCATE 16,1:PRINT"ENTER COLUMN NUMBER 1 AND
COLUMN NUMBER 2";:INPUT M,N
870 T=CT(M):CT(M)=CT(N):CT(N)=T
880 T=TC(M):TC(M)=TC(N):TC(N)=T
890 FOR Z=1 TO NS
900 T=A(Z,M):A(Z,M)=A(Z,N):A(Z,N)=T
910 NEXT Z
920 CLS
930 FOR I=1 TO NS
940 FOR J=1 TO TI
950 IF A(I,J)=1 THEN LOCATE J,I:PRINT CHR$(219);
960 NEXT J
970 NEXT I
980 GOSUB 730
990 GOSUB 620
1000 GOTO 810
1010 LOCATE 16,1:PRINT"   ENTER ROW 1 AND ROW 2
NUMBERS";:INPUT M,N
1020 T=RT(M):RT(M)=RT(N):RT(N)=T
1030 T=TR(M):TR(M)=TR(N):TR(N)=T
1040 FOR Z=1 TO TI
1050 T=A(M,Z):A(M,Z)=A(N,Z):A(N,Z)=T
1060 NEXT Z
1070 GOTO 920
```

Problems arise when there is no precursor course or obvious indicators. One such example is in the area of language training. Numerous tests exist which identify persons on the basis of something called verbal skills, but this indicator score is only slightly correlated to proficiency in learning a number of modern languages. Even the experience of having learned one language in a high school setting is no guarantee of success in a more intense and extensive program.

The author was, for several years, professionally involved in a major program to provide practical language training for a large organization requiring a number of people trained in a number of foreign languages. Over the years a number of screening tools had been used, and discarded, to select from employees, those to attend an intensive language program in which a full two to four-year college-level language program is compressed into four to ten months. Classic indicators of success were of little use. Several screening devices had been developed, but even these only had a correlation with the terminal criterion (success in the program) of about .45 to .55. The significance of these correlations is that a large number of students were selected who were, in the final analysis, ill-suited to the program. We were interested in identifying some other factors which might shed some light on the screening problem and improve the selection process. Failing that, could we identify students who were more inclined to experience difficulty in training? We hypothesized that if we could identify these problem-prone students in advance, we could extend an early helping hand through our counselling staff. A major deviation from previous studies, which involved a number of tests of verbal skills and other measures of intellectual functioning, was the desire to use readily noted and obvious characteristics (age, sex, height, weight, etc.) as the independent variables. What we wanted was a screening tool we could implement as the students arrived for training. In addition to the basic demographic characteristics, we also had available the employee's job grade rating (1-9), educational level, the grade-point average from previous training, as well as the scores from the basic employment screening tests and the language aptitude test. The basic plan of the study consisted of six phases:

Phase 1. Design and develop study plan and materials. Select test variables.

Phase 2. Distribute data collection forms to the counselling staff. Brief staff on program technique and objectives.

Phase 3. Collect and tabulate data for three-month period.

Phase 4. Perform statistical analysis of data, correlating the relationships between the test variables and the periodic test grades the students receive at well-defined intervals. Identify, if possible, useful indicator variables. Brief counselling staff on outcome of studies and those students who seem to be high-risk.

Phase 5. Maintain records on academic performance of subjects through completion of course.

Phase 6. Perform final statistical analysis and prepare report.

Phase 1: The product of this phase was the program plan identified just above. In addition, we developed the data collection forms and selected the characteristics to be measured. We finally settled on eight independent variables: employment grade, age, height, weight, educational level, grade-point average, language aptitude score, and employment screening score. The dependent variable was to be the grades obtained by each student after six to nine weeks of training and after the completion of the program. Tables 14-1 through 14-3 summarize these variables.

Phases 2 and 3. These phases were conducted as planned without exceptional incident.

Phase 4. For the analysis, we were fortunate to have access to the institution's main computer system through which we could access a remote system upon which was a powerful set of statistical programs designed to evaluate large numbers of multivariate statistical problems. Table 14-4 summarizes the simple correlations between each of the independent variables and the dependent variable.

The program used to evaluate these data was one of a large set of biomedical statistical programs resident on a large mainframe computer system. We hypothesized that the magnitude of the dependent variable, the grade on the first (and, presumably, subsequent tests), was a function of the multivariate form:

$$Y = A_0 + A_1X_1 + A_2X_2 + A_3X_3 + \ldots + A_nX_n$$

We knew from experience that the best (highest

Table 14-1. Summary of Student Characteristics, Males.

	Grade	Age	Height	Weight	Ed Level	GPA	Job Score	Apt. Score	Test Score
Number	106	106	106	106	69	65	45	57	95
Mean	3.981	25.189	70.802	168.594	13.812	2.945	347.556	31.719	86.453
Stan. Dev.	1.648	4.957	2.579	26.980	1.365	.576	26.804	7.223	7.269
Variance	2.717	24.568	6.650	727.940	1.863	.331	718.473	52.167	52.837
Coef. of Var.	41.401	19.678	3.642	16.003	9.883	19.546	7.712	22.771	8.408
Stan. Skew	− .229	.894	.328	.515	.411	− .215	−1.427	.606	−1.060
Stan. Excess	− .529	.451	− .467	− .156	− .738	− .494	2.374	− .042	1.361
Smallest Entry	1	18	66	133	12	1.7	250	21	59
Largest Entry	8	42	77	245	17	4.0	380	51	99

(Male Students)

Table 14-2. Summary of Student Characteristics, Females.

	Grade	Age	Height	Weight	Ed Level	GPA	Job Score	Apt. Score	Test Score
Number	31	31	31	31	31	31	21	30	27
Mean	1.452	20.516	64.968	129.452	13.194	3.275	281.000	33.167	82.926
Stan. Dev.	.874	2.662	2.236	12.152	1.712	.456	37.677	7.979	9.189
Variance	.764	7.008	4.999	147.667	2.930	.208	1419.530	63.672	84.439
Coeff. of Var.	60.205	12.977	3.441	9.387	12.975	13.924	13.408	24.059	11.081
Stan. Skew	1.598	.802	− .117	.092	1.010	− .529	− .218	1.059	−1.229
Stan. Excess	.982	− .567	− .339	− .666	− .663	.334	− .840	1.006	.809
Smallest Entry	1	18	60	107	12	2.0	205	20	57
Largest Entry	4	26	69	157	17	4.0	346	55	94

(Female Students)

correlation) form of the equation is not necessarily derived from using all the independent variables. Instead, it was likely that the best predictor of the grade might be computed by using only some of the independent variables. But, which ones? The fundamental task of the program we used was to sort through the available data and compute the correlation between the dependent and a given set of independent variables. Having computed the various correlations, the task falls back on us to select the combination that provides us with the best predictor tool. The secondary function of the program was to specify the coefficients to use in the regression equation. The coefficients, A_1, A_2, A_3, etc., are computed for each of the independent variables. To these is added the residual or constant A_0. The result, for a given individual, is the predicted six-week grade. The implication of these data is that, for a new female student, for example, the predicted six-week grade (Y), would be:

$$Y = 178.02117 + 1.75139 \times \text{Age} + .09345 \times \text{Job Score}$$
$$- .03996 \times \text{Weight} - .41554 \times \text{Aptitude Score}$$
$$- .87122 \times \text{Educational Level} - 1.89512 \times \text{Height}$$
$$- 2.559 \times \text{GPA}$$

Thus, age (maturity?) and something in the basic employment screening tests were positively related to success in the program, while a higher rating in any of the other areas tended to predict failure.

The correlation between the predicted scores and the actual test scores was: $r = .57137$, superior to the correlation between the aptitude test and the grades. The equation above suggests that age is the fundamental determinant of success in the program. Was this a function of maturity, or were there unmeasured variables closely related to age that were

Table 14-3. Summary of Student Characteristics, All.

	Grade	Age	Height	Weight	Ed Level	GPA	Job Score	Apt. Score	Test Score
Number	137	137	137	137	99	102	66	87	122
Mean	3.409	24.131	69.482	159.737	13.596	3.048	326.379	32.218	85.672
Stan. Dev.	1.843	4.943	3.498	29.409	1.497	.558	43.618	7.524	7.872
Variance	3.395	24.435	12.235	864.880	2.241	.312	1902.510	56.608	61.975
Coef. of Var.	54.053	20.485	5.034	18.411	11.010	18.310	13.364	23.352	9.189
Stan. Skew	.040	1.000	− .232	.552	.564	− .406	− .917	.812	−1.209
Stan. Excess	−1.101	.750	− .208	− .200	− .858	− .295	− .030	.572	1.639
Smallest Entry	1	18	60	107	12	1.7	205	20	57
Largest Entry	8	42	77	245	17	4.0	380	55	99

(All Students)

Table 14-4. Correlations Between Characteristics.

	Grade	Age	Height	Weight	Ed Level	GPA	Job Score	Aptitude	Test Score
Grade	1.0000	.82436	.42700	.50335	.29047	−.17263	.65758	−.01235	.11713
Age		1.00000	.25512	.38580	.58706	−.19561	.46259	.11025	.07440
Height			1.00000	.72337	.07756	−.23437	.47622	−.16012	.08234
Weight				1.00000	.14018	−.28537	.41309	−.18328	.04066
Ed. Level					1.00000	−.10110	.27349	.30966	.26751
GPA						1.00000	−.04231	.24628	−.10835
Job Score							1.00000	.15661	.37971
Aptitude Score								1.00000	−.05177
First Test									1.00000

really operative? It didn't really matter. The objective was to identify the relationships, which we did. Our primary task was to see how the different variables interacted to produce a predictor tool. The limitation of this routine was that it simply rank-ordered the independent variables. The processing began with the factor that seemed to have the most significant relationship to the dependent variable, and then added in, one at a time, each of the remaining variables until the least significant factor was added. At the time of the study we were told that a more sophisticated routine, one that would evaluate each combination, was not available on the immediate system, and, in any event, would be a very difficult problem to handle.

We are very happy to note, however, that the microcomputer industry has made life a bit easier. Very recently, we recomputed the related data from this study on the author's microcomputer system using the Multiple Linear Regression program found in Listing 5-5. Not only did it perform the computations that, ten years ago, were beyond reach, but it completed the task in less than two hours, most of which was consumed by printing the results.

EXERCISES

1. Write the following as a mathematical formula:
   The standard error of the estimate equals the square root of the sum of the squared deviations of the predicted scores from the observed scores divided by one less than the number of observations.

2. State the following equation in words:

$$r = \frac{XY}{(N-1)s_x s_y}$$

3. Describe how you would develop a test to predict later high school dropouts from a population of junior high school students.

SUGGESTED READING

American Psychological Association, 1966. *Standards for Educational and Psychological Tests and Manuals.* Washington, D.C.: American Psychological Association.

Guilford, J.P., 1965. *Fundamental Statistics in Psychology and Education.* New York: McGraw-Hill.

Thorndike, R.L. and E. Hagen, 1969. *Measurement and Evaluation in Psychology and Education.* New York: John Wiley & Sons.

Chapter 15

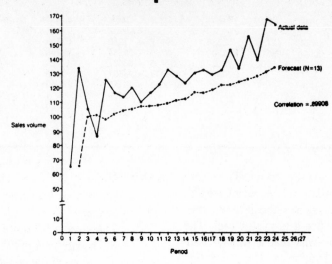

Forecasting Random Events

By definition, we ought not be able to forecast random events. After all, if we can predict an outcome of a random event, it doesn't seem to be very random does it? The truth of the matter is that while we really can't predict the exact outcome of a given random event, we can develop some generalized notions about a set of otherwise random data.

For example, dice are frequently used to determine the outcome of various games. We use dice to play craps and to determine the moves to be made in a variety of board games. Some of the more recent fantasy games employ many-sided dice having anything from 4 to 24 sides. Given the identity of a die (number of sides) we can compute probable outcomes. In craps, for instance, we use two six-sided dice. The sides are numbered consecutively from one to six. By throwing the two die concurrently, the possible sum of any two faces ranges from two to twelve. While the probability of any one side appearing is $\frac{1}{6} = .166667$, there is a range of probabilities from .027778 (for 2 and 12) to .166667 (for 7) for the combined scores. We cannot predetermine the outcome of a particular throw of the dice, but we can determine the likely average outcome of a number of throws. From this knowledge we can develop a betting strategy designed to minimize losses and maximize winnings.

This chapter examines several common activities with randomly determined outcomes and offers some solutions to minimize the uncertainty involved. The computing power of today's microcomputers makes short work of problems that have puzzled analysts of random events for centuries. It provides a way to pragmatically identify the underlying and true game-odds of a number of activities. It certainly is a lot easier than flipping coins thousands of times. The routines involved are only suggested solutions. This is an area where the reader can derive great enjoyment in developing alternative approaches to these problems.

THE UNIVERSAL GAME MACHINE

Winning, in its larger sense, is a national, if not global, preoccupation. We demonstrate this by noting that given a choice, most people elect to win than lose, to realize a profit from their investments of time, money, and energy. The competition is so intense, however, that the rate of return on "sure things" is usually only a nominal five to ten percent. Conservative investors are not ordinarily satisfied with just even odds; they seek opportunities where the chance of failure is virtually nonexistent. A project that offers only a five percent return on investment may go wanting for funding. Yet, a few people make a respectable living at the gaming tables in Nevada and New Jersey. In addition to the owners of the casinos, successful gamblers are making investment decisions and winning in situations where the normal rate of return is certainly no greater than five percent and the odds of winning big are nil.

The key, of course, is not really the number of times one wins in a game where the odds are unfavorable (which is more often than not the case) but the strategy of betting one uses. To stay in a game, one must continue to bet, even though he or she frequently loses. The net profit of the professional gambler is derived by placing a significantly more sizeable wager at the appropriate moment: i.e., just before a winning play. Success depends on the limited ability to foretell the future and a workable betting strategy. These factors require an understanding of the probabilities involved and the experimental development of a betting strategy suited to the game. Until the last couple of centuries, mankind had to rely upon intuition or hunch, as well as a profound superstition, to shape their fortunes. With the development of probability theory and statistics, however, we have acquired the tools needed to handle the difficult odds situation in a rational manner. From an experimental standpoint, however, data generation and collection was a very tedious process. It was one thing to predict the outcome of a series of dice throws theoretically but quite something else to confirm the theory in a scientifically acceptable and consistent manner—especially if confirmation requires several tens of thousands of repetitions. Reference works, except those written very recently, refer to authoritative works in which conclusions are reached on the basis of three or four thousand trials. Flipping coins to a more satis-

factory level of fifty or one hundred repetitions is very hard work, to say the least.

With the advent of the modern computer we gained the means to examine these realms electronically. The solution of such problems, however, remained either in the domain of the private corporations that could afford a computing system or was considered too trivial by those controlling publicly-owned computing resources. With microcomputers all this has changed. Indeed, the basis for this section of the book began in 1976 with original work done by the author on hand-held programmable calculators. The project had two objectives: to develop a sense of the underlying probability of winning at games—a "win" is the function of one or more conditional events (such as craps or blackjack, etc.)—and to study the phenomenon of extended runs of wins or losses. It was for the latter the Universal Game Machine (UGM) was invented.

We believed that underlying all standard games of chance was some "true" underlying probability of winning, regardless of the complexity of the rules. If we adequately defined the rules of the game, we would eventually be able to compute its true odds. Of greater interest at that moment, however, was the phenomenon of runs.

The professional gambler frequently laughs at the novice who insists on playing good money after bad on the presumption that some "law of averages" will intervene and permit a winning combination. The wiser gambler knows, of course, that the outcome of the toss of the dice has absolutely no bearing on the outcome of the next or any other toss of the dice—the probability of any given combination remains constant.

At the same time common sense intrudes to the extent of noting that in games where the odds are fairly even, such as coin tossing, one wins fairly frequently and the number of times one loses more than two or three times in a row is really quite rare. On the other hand, in games where the odds of winning are quite slim (lotteries, drawings, etc.), one loses with a great consistency—winning more than one raffle in a row is quite extraordinary. We took this line of reasoning one step further and hypothesized that the number of times we could reasonably expect to win or lose in a row was a function of the probability of winning one trial: as the probability of losing increased, we should expect the number of times we would lose in a row to increase by some rational function. The basic hypothesis is illustrated in Fig. 15-1.

The next step was to develop a process by which the actual values of the chart could be computed. The UGM serves this purpose quite well. Rather than simulating the rules of actual games, the UGM assumes there is a game in which the probability of winning is a known value, P, where $0 = <$ $= P < = 1$. For each trial the UGM generates a random number, X, in the same range. If X is found to be greater than P, we assume that a loss has occurred. On the other hand, if X is less than P, we assume there has been a "win." For the purpose of our study, statistics were maintained on the number of trials, the number of wins and losses, the record lengths of win and loss runs, and so forth. The basic UGM is specified in Listing 15-1. You may wish to alter it to include provisions for record-keeping based on the results of different betting strategies.

Table 15-1 summarizes the outcome of several runs of the program.

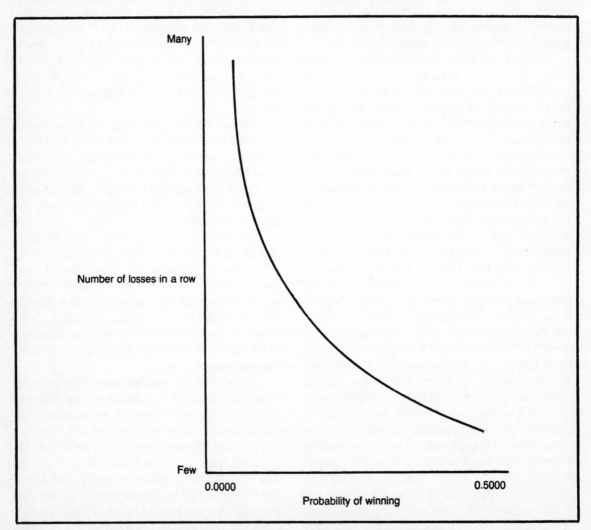

Fig. 15-1. Hypothetical number of losses in a row as a function of the probability of winning.

Listing 15-1. Universal Game Machine.

```
1 '***********************************************
2 '*                 Listing 15-1               *
3 '*          Universal Game Machine            *
4 '***********************************************
5 '
10 CLS:KEY OFF:RANDOMIZE:WIDTH LPRINT 180
20 CLS:LPRINT"PROBABILITY   # TRIALS      # WINS
 RATIO   LONGEST SET   AVERAGE   S.E.      # LOSSE
S   RATIO   LONGEST SET   AVERAGE       S.E.":LPRI
NT""
30 FOR P=.05 TO .5001001 STEP .05
40 LOCATE 1,17:PRINT"PROBABILITY OF WINNING = ";
P;
50 LOCATE 4,9:PRINT"CURRENT","TOTAL","% OF # TRI
ALS":LOCATE 5,1:PRINT"WINS";:LOCATE 6,1:PRINT"LO
SSES",
60 FOR N=1 TO 100
70 LOCATE 2,17:PRINT"NUMBER OF TRIALS PLAYED = "
;N;
80 X=RND(N)
90 IF X<P THEN 160
100 TL=TL+1:CL=CL+1
110 IF CL<>1 THEN 220
120 W2=W2+CW^2
130 IF CW<=LW THEN 150
140 LW=CW
150 NW=NW+1:CW=0:GOTO 220
160 TW=TW+1:CW=CW+1
170 IF CW<>1 THEN 220
180 L2=L2+CL^2
190 IF CL<=LL THEN 210
200 LL=CL
210 NL=NL+1:CL=0
220 LOCATE 5,9:PRINT CW,TW,TW/N;
230 LOCATE 6,9:PRINT CL,TL,TL/N;
240 NEXT N
250 SW=SQR((W2-((TW/NW)^2))/(NW-1)):SL=SQR((L2-(
(TL/NL)^2))/(NL-1))
260 LPRINT USING" #.######     #######      ####
##   #.####   ######    ##.#### ###.### #####
#   #.####   ######      ###.###   ###.###";
P;N-1;TW;TW/(N-1);LW;TW/NW;SW/SQR(NW);TL;TL/(N-1
);LL;TL/NL;SL/SQR(NL)
270 LW=0:LL=0:TW=0:TL=0:NW=0:NL=0
280 NEXT P
290 PRINT"(A)nother         (M)ain menu ";
300 GOSUB 320
310 IF Q$="A" OR Q$="a" THEN RUN 10 ELSE RUN "A:
MENU"
320 Q$=""+INKEY$:IF Q$="" THEN 320
330 RETURN
```

Figure 15-2 illustrates the plot of the number of record loss runs as a function of the probability of winning.

For us, the outcome of this experiment was very interesting and gratifying. (It's always gratifying to have one's suspicions proven. . .) From the

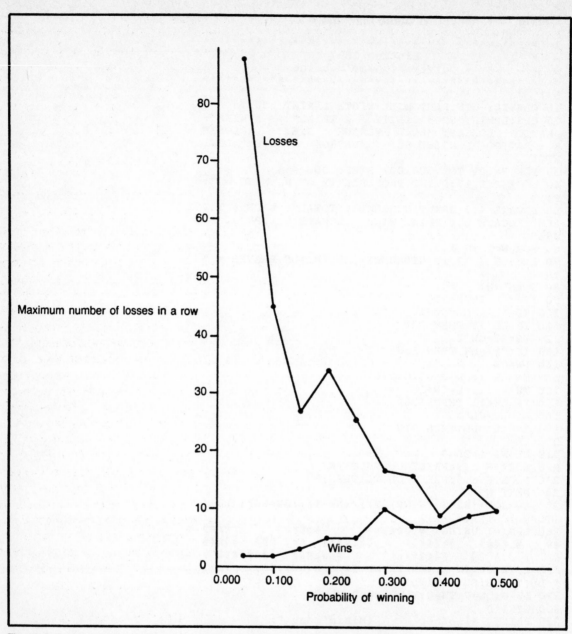

Fig. 15-2. Actual number of losses in a row as a function of the probability of winning.

data it is clear that we can compute all we need to know about a game and our chance of making a net profit from it by simply knowing what the underlying game probability is and how much we have to bet. We can also judge whether or not we should even try the game to begin with. In a simple appli-

cation of the information, if we know that a losing streak of ten times in a row is not exceptional, we should be prepared to lose at least ten times, yet have sufficient funds left with which to make a bet large enough to recoup our losses to that point plus make a little profit. Examination of these data and

Table 15-1. Result of Universal Game Machine Run.

Probability	#Trials	#Wins	Ratio	Longest Set	Average	S.E.	#Losses	Ratio	Longest Set	Average	S.E
0.050000	1000	45	0.0450	2	1.0000	0.152	955	0.9550	88	21.705	4.364
0.100000	1000	97	0.0970	2	1.0899	0.142	903	0.9030	45	10.146	2.578
0.150000	1000	145	0.1450	3	1.1694	0.152	855	0.8550	27	6.895	2.027
0.200000	1000	213	0.2130	5	1.2604	0.155	787	0.7870	34	4.657	1.578
0.250000	1000	225	0.2250	5	1.3554	0.197	775	0.7750	25	4.669	1.679
0.300000	1000	323	0.3230	10	1.5236	0.199	677	0.6770	17	3.193	1.347
0.350000	1000	360	0.3600	7	1.5385	0.214	640	0.6400	16	2.735	1.242
0.400000	1000	401	0.4010	7	1.6849	0.247	599	0.5990	9	2.506	1.232
0.450000	1000	431	0.4310	9	1.7737	0.280	569	0.5690	14	2.351	1.231
0.500000	1000	512	0.5120	10	2.1513	0.333	488	0.4880	10	2.050	1.262

the data obtained from previous runs of this routine have led us to the following set of relationships:

1. P = probability of winning
2. Q = $1 - P$
3. L_q = Q/P Average number of losses in a row
4. $P(L_q)$ = Q^{L_q} Probability of L_q losses in series
5. L_y = $80.4848 \times 2.71828^{-4.379 \times P}$ Most likely number of losses in a row given P, the probability of winning.

The relationship noted in equation 5 was empirically derived from the experimental data obtained in 1976. On the basis of the data in Table 15-1, similar equations can be developed (using the curve fitting routine from Chapter 6) that can be used to predict the longest normal run of losses using the game odds as the base. While it is always possible that a player could encounter a run of bad luck longer than that computed, it would be very unlikely. Based on the most recent run of ten thousand trials for each increment of P, from .05 to .50 in steps of .05, the longest normal run of losses can be computed.

BETTING STRATEGIES

There are about as many betting strategies as there are people who have spent two minutes in a casino or a hot poker game. To date, no one has announced a sure-fire scheme—and we are not about to do so here—but if wagering is your hobby, there are some useful lessons to be learned from the UGM and from something called a *Markov Process*.

The simplest betting strategy is to make the same wager, trial after trial. If you have a good enough bankroll and if the odds are ever so slightly in your favor, you will eventually end up a winner if you stay with it long enough. On the other hand, if the odds are not in your favor, as in most games in a casino, you will, in the long run, always lose. From a special subset of the Markov Process, Markov Chains, we can derive a set of equations that tell us just about how long it will take to reach some specified profit or to lose all of a bankroll. In *Probability: An Introductory Course* by Norman R. Draper and Willard E. Lawrence, there is a comprehensive discussion of the Markov Process and an explanation of the development of the equations given below. We will leave the history of the equations to the truly curious. A Markov Chain is, in this perspective, a random walk wherein a gambler moves from a condition of a certain degree of wealth (bankroll) in a series of steps indicating wins or losses. Whether a given step will be a win or loss is unknown, but the "randomness" of the outcome is known to be influenced by the basic game odds. Such an analysis produces the following equations:

1. P = Probability of winning at each step or trial
2. Q = $1 - P$
3. J = Starting investment of bankroll
4. V = Objective or goal
5. L = $((Q/P)^J - (Q/P)^V)/(1 - (Q/P)^V)$ Probability of a total loss
6. E = $V - J - (V \times L) = V(1 - L) - J$ Expected loss or gain

303

7. T — E/(P − Q) Mean time (in number of plays) to reach a loss or the objective.

Where P = Q(P = .5), the equations become a little simpler. Rules 1-4 remain the same. The others become:

5. L = (V − J)/V.
6. E = 0
7. T = J(v − J)

Listing 15-2 is a short routine based on the foregoing equations from the Markov Process.

Another approach to betting is a routine called the Martingale system. Simply put, one begins with a unit wager. This can be one dollar, five, ten, or twenty. It doesn't matter; the first wager, whatever the amount, is the unit bet. If the first trial or game is lost, the second bet is twice the first. If the second trial or game is lost, the third bet is twice the second, and so on until either the bankroll is exhausted or a win condition is satisfied. At the point where a win is experienced, the subsequent bet is returned to one unit: the same as the first bet. Theoretically, it doesn't matter how bad the game odds are, the player will always end up winning using the Martingale system—*theoretically*, that is. In practice there are a couple of facts of life that diminish the utility of the Martingale system. The first is that one could lose a lot of money before winning anything. In fact, it was this aspect of the system that drove the creation of the UGM and the study to determine the length of normal loss strings. The size of a bet after N loses is equal to 2^{N-1}. After five losses the bet will be 16 times the first. After ten losses the bet will be 512 times the first. As you can see from Table 15-1, even with even odds a string of ten losses in a row is not unusual. In the range of odds where most casino games are found (P = .45), loss strings of 14 or 15 are common. Bets in this range would easily be 16384 to 32768 times the first bet. Assuming a $1.00 initial bet, after 15 losses the bet would be 32768, and the accumulated losses up to that point would be 32767. The second reality is that virtually every casino that has the resources to handle 32768 dollar bets also has bet limits, usually of about five hundred or a thousand dollars. And the final fact of life is that the profit gained by using the Martingale system is exactly equal to the number of times the player wins. That is, if the unit bet is a dollar in a game where the probability of winning is .45, and a thousand games are played, the bettor will have a net profit of $450.00.

An alternative approach to the Martingale system is to use a multiple other than two. You could also use 1.5, 3.76, .98, or any other value desired. If we call the multiple A, the following is true:

Bet after N losses = A^{N-1}
Sum of all such bets up to the Nth trial =

$$\frac{A^N - 1}{A - 1}$$

In the sense of a footnote, there is also a Reverse Martingale system wherein the bet is doubled every time there is a win and reduced to unity when there is a loss. Unless the game odds are strongly in your favor, you would be further ahead just giving the money to charity and taking the tax deduction.

Listing 15-2. Markov Odds.

```
1 '**********************************************
2 '*                Listing 15-2              *
3 '*                Markov Odds               *
4 '**********************************************
5 '
10 CLS:PRINT"WELCOME TO THE GAMBLERS' ADVISOR.":
PRINT:PRINT:PRINT"THIS PROGRAM WILL NOT IMPROVE
YOUR GAMING SKILLS.  INSTEAD, IT  WILL SIMPLY AD
VISE YOU WHAT THE REALISTIC ODDS ARE OF WINNING
   (IF AT ALL) AND WHERE SOME OF   THE PITFALLS M
IGHT BE."
```

```
20 PRINT""
30 PRINT"TO FACILITATE THIS VENTURE, I NEED TO K
NOW THE PROBABILITY OF   WINNING IN THE  GAME YO
U HAVE CHOSEN.   IF YOU KNOW WHAT THIS VALUE IS,
 SIMPLY ENTER IT BELOW.  IF YOU DON'T, PLEASE DU
MP THIS PROGRAM AND RUN A SIMULATION TO DETERMIN
E";
40 PRINT"THE TRUE GAME ODDS.   WHEN YOU HAVE IT,
 ENTER BELOW."
50 PRINT:INPUT"PROBABILITY OF WINNING THE GAME A
T ANY RANDOM POINT";P:Q=1-P:IF P=.5 THEN 70
60 PL=100/LOG(Q/P)
70 INPUT"WHAT IS THE AMOUNT OF YOUR BANKROLL";BR
:J=BR
80 INPUT"WHAT IS YOUR GOAL, HOW MUCH DO YOU WANT
 TO LEAVE WITH";G:V=G
90 IF P=>.5 THEN 120
100 IF V<PL THEN 120
110 V=V/10:J=J/10:GOTO 100
120 CLS:PRINT"FIRST, THE SIMPLE COMPUTATIONS....
":PRINT:PRINT"          ASSUMING YOU BET A CONSTANT
 WAGER EACH PLAY...":PRINT
130 IF P=.5 THEN 160
140 L=(((Q/P)^J)-((Q/P)^V))/(1-((Q/P)^V))
150 E=(V*(1-L))-J:T=E/(P-Q):GOTO 170
160 L=(V-J)/V:E=0:T=J*(V-J)
170 PRINT"THE PROBABILITY OF A TOTAL LOSS (WIN)
= ";L
180 PRINT"THE EXPECTED LOSS (GAIN) = $ ";E
190 PRINT"MEAN NUMBER OF PLAYS TO LOSS (WIN)";T
200 AL=E/T
210 PRINT"AVERAGE LOSS (GAIN) PER PLAY = $ ";AL
220 W=INT(P*100):NG=G/W
230 PRINT:PRINT"LET'S ASSUME YOU PLAY THIS GAME
100 TIMES.  WE PREDICT YOU WILL WIN";W;"TIMES, O
N THE AVERAGE.  THIS MEANS EACH WIN MUST NET YOU
 AT LEAST $";NG;".   ";
240 IF NG<AL THEN 260
250 PRINT"YOU WILL HAVE TO ADOPT A BETTING STRAT
EGY A BIT MORE SOPHISTICATED THAN A        CONSTA
NT BET IF YOU HOPE TO REALIZE YOUR GOAL OF $";G:
PRINT
260 PRINT"Congratulations !!":PRINT""
270 PRINT"(A)nother       (M)ain menu ";
280 GOSUB 300
290 IF Q$="A" OR Q$="a" THEN RUN 10 ELSE RUN "A:
MENU"
300 Q$=""+INKEY$:IF Q$="" THEN 300
310 RETURN
```

SODA POP SIMULATION

A prominent manufacturer of a popular carbonated beverage has run a contest in which the bottle cap plays a pivotal role. Under the plastic seal on each cap is either one of the twenty-six letters of the alphabet, or a cash value of $.25, $.50, or $1.00. The letters are used to spell out designated words. Twenty-two letters appear in a normal and random distribution. Four of the letters, key to winning the major prizes, a shirt, chair, or cash of either $100 or $2000, are distributed in much smaller quantities. The promotional material provides the odds of winning the various prizes:

Prize	Probability Of Winning	Number in 2,000,000	Accumulative Total
$.25	.0400000	80,000	80,000
$.50	.0020000	4,000	84,000
$1.00	.0010000	2,000	86,000
Shirt	.0001000	200	86,200
Chair	.0000100	20	86,220
$100	.0000050	10	86,230
$2000	.0000005	1	86,231

The random function on a computer such as the TRS-80 works only within the integer range of the Z-80; that is, only between 0 and 32767. That fact creates a little problem. The direct way to begin a simulation of this game would be to generate a random number in the range 1 to 2,000,000 (as in RND(2000000)), but, as we have just noted, the normal limit is 32767. To circumvent this, we use the expression: X = INT (RND(0)*2000000), trusting that the random number generator will give us a reasonably even distribution of values between 0 and 1,999,999, two million numbers in all. Having generated a number, X, the next step is to determine whether or not it signifies a win, and if so, what kind.

By examining the right-hand column, "Accumulative Total," we can see that out of two million caps, there will be only 86,231 winning caps. Therefore, we will say that if X is greater than 86,231, then there is no win of any kind. All we do is buy another bottle (debiting our bank balance) and try again. On the other hand, if X is less than 86232, check to determine where in the range it falls and what kind of prize it wins. Using the table of odds, we will say that if X is less than 80001, the prize is $.25. If X is in the range 80001 to 84000, then the prize is $.50, and so on. A flowchart of this process is given in Fig. 15-3.

From this flowchart the program in Listing 15-3 was developed.

Listing 15-3. Soda Pop Simulation.

```
1 '*********************************************
2 '*              Listing 15-3               *
3 '*           Soda Pop Simulation           *
4 '*********************************************
5 '
10 CLS:KEY OFF:LPRINT"BALANCE","WON","SHIRTS","C
HAIRS","RATIO: WON TO INVESTMENT"
20 RANDOMIZE:DEFDBL X:CLS
30 FOR P=1 TO 650
40 B=B-.35:X=0
50 X=INT(RND(0)*2000000!)
60 IF X>80000! THEN 80
70 B=B+.25:W=W+.25:GOTO 200
80 IF X>84000! THEN 100
90 B=B+.5:W=W+.5:GOTO 200
100 IF X>86000! THEN 120
110 B=B+1:W=W+1:GOTO 200
120 IF X>86200! THEN 140
130 T=T+1:GOTO 200
140 IF X>86220! THEN 160
150 C=C+1:GOTO 200
160 IF X>86230! THEN 180
170 B=B+100:W=W+100:GOTO 200
180 IF X<>86231! THEN 200
190 B=B+2000:W=W+2000:GOTO 200
200 LOCATE 1,16:PRINT P;:LOCATE 1,31:PRINT X,:LO
CATE 3,1:PRINT"BANK = $ ";B;
210 LOCATE 3,31:PRINT W,W/(P*.41825);
220 LOCATE 4,1:PRINT T;"T-SHIRTS",,T/P;
```

```
230 LOCATE 5,1:PRINT C;"DIRECTORS' CHAIRS",C/P;
240 NEXT
250 LPRINT B,W,T,C,W/271.8625
260 PRINT"(A)nother      (M)ain menu ";
270 GOSUB 290
280 IF Q$="A" OR Q$="a" THEN RUN 10 ELSE RUN "A:
MENU"
290 Q$=""+INKEY$:IF Q$="" THEN 290
300 RETURN
```

One of the rules of the game is that to win you have to spell a word or a phrase from the collected letters. The program makes no provision for this aspect on the basis that better than 95.69% of all the caps will have the letters necessary to spell the bal-ance of the words, and by the time a winning letter comes up, sufficient numbers of letters will have been collected to complete the phrase. From a strictly logical point of view this is not necessarily true, but this theory is adequate to demonstrate the

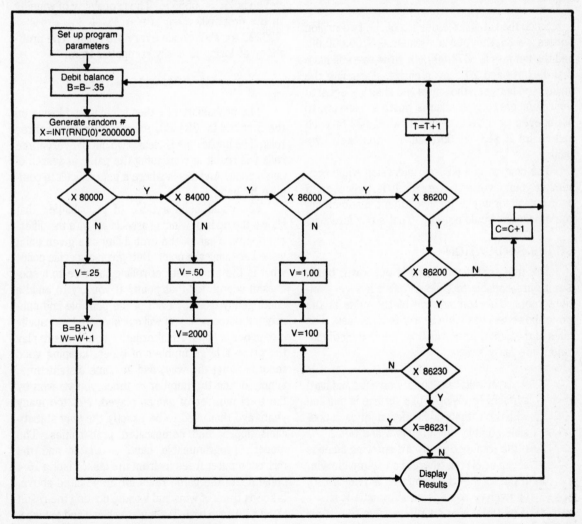

Fig. 15-3. Flowchart of soda pop simulation.

essential aspects of the game and the probability of winning.

Assuming one buys two million bottles, there should be approximately 86,231 winning caps. Based on the odds provided, one would end up with:

Prize	Number	Value
$.25	80,000	$20,000.00
$.50	4,000	2,000.00
$1.00	2,000	2,000.00
$100.00	10	1,000.00
$2000.00	1	2,000.00
Total Cash		$27,000.00

Since the retail price of each of the two million bottles is $.35, the total investment is $700,000.00, and the net loss is $673,000.00. Now, we still have 200 T-shirts and 20 canvas chairs. Assuming the value ratio between the shirts and chairs is equal to their numbers (e.g., a chair is worth ten shirts), to break even we have to sell shirts at $1,682.50 each and chairs at $16,825.00 each: not too likely, we think.

The contest is a pleasant diversion while consuming your favorite beverage. It is, however, a poor reason for any major investment in something you otherwise would not buy. That's our forecast.

CRAPS SIMULATION

The true age of this game is unknown, but it is not unreasonable to believe that it has very ancient roots. The computation of the odds in the game, however, has been a very tedious task. The rules of the game, from which we begin the computation, are fairly simple:

1. A player rolls two fair dice on a flat and hard surface. In casinos, this surface is marked with the various odds offered for each possible combination of points and bets.
2. If the total of the upward showing faces is seven or eleven, there is an automatic win.
3. If the total of the two faces is two, three, or twelve, there is an automatic loss.
4. If the total is some other value (i.e., four to six, or eight to ten), that value becomes

the "point" and the player continues to roll the dice.
5. The player continues to roll the dice until
   a. the point value appears again

   or

   b. the player rolls a seven combination.
6. If the player rolls the "point," there is a win.
7. If the player rolls a seven there is a loss.

The computation of the odds for the first three steps is pretty straightforward. The probability of a seven is $6/36$ = .166667. The probability of an eleven is $2/36$ = .055556. The probability of winning on the first roll, then, is P = $6/36$ + $2/36$ = $8/36$ = .222222 (or about once every 4.5 rolls). The probability of losing is easily computed from:

$$Q = 1/36 + 2/36 + 1/36 = .111111$$

The probability of either winning and losing on the first roll is .333333, exactly once every three rolls. The implication is clear: two out of every three rolls will result in continuing the game in search of one's point. And this is where it gets difficult to compute by hand.

You could build a table of probabilities that shows the odds of winning associated with the different points. That is, the probability of a given point value becoming the point. But, given a specific point, what is the probability of rolling the dice to a successful search for that point? If you try to build a contingency tree for each of the possible and subsequent outcomes, you will quickly note how rapidly it gets out of hand. An alternative solution is to play the game a large number of times, keeping good records along the way, and at some distant time, simply divide the number of times you've won by the total number of games played. Not too many years ago that used to be exactly the way statisticians approached complicated probabilities. The modern programmable hand calculator and the microcomputer frees us from the task. Listing 15-4 implements the game rules for craps cited above. It keeps track of wins and losses, posting the result along with each trial. Try it yourself and find out what your chances are.

Listing 15-4. Craps Simulator.

```
1 '*********************************************
2 '*              Listing 15-4                 *
3 '*            Craps Simulator                *
4 '*********************************************
5 '
10 CLS:RANDOMIZE:WIDTH LPRINT 120
20 CLS:KEY OFF:LOCATE 1,26:PRINT"CRAPS SIMULATOR
"
30 INPUT "Enter number of games";NG
40 FOR I=1 TO NG
50 LOCATE 4,1:PRINT"# GAMES","DIE #1","DIE #2","
TOTAL"
60 LOCATE 7,1:PRINT"# WINS","# LOSSES","WIN/LOSS
 RATIO"
70 LOCATE 10,13:PRINT"    1          2          3
      4         6";
80 LOCATE 11,1:PRINT"DIE # 1";:LOCATE 12,1:PRINT
"DIE # 2";
90 D1=INT(RND(TD)*6)+1:D2=INT(RND(TD)*6)+1:TD=D1
+D2
100 G=G+1
110 D(1,D1)=D(1,D1)+1:D(2,D2)=D(2,D2)+1
120 LOCATE 5,3:PRINT G,D1,D2,TD
130 ZOG%=645+(9*D1):GOSUB 360:PRINT D(1,D1);:ZOG
%=709+(9*D2):GOSUB 360:PRINT D(2,D2);
140 IF TD=7 THEN 260
150 IF TD=11 THEN 260
160 IF TD<4 THEN 270
170 IF TD=12 THEN 270
180 P=TD
190 D1=INT(RND(TD)*6)+1:D2=INT(RND(TD)*6)+1:TD=D
1+D2
200 D(1,D1)=D(1,D1)+1:D(2,D2)=D(2,D2)+1
210 LOCATE 5,3:PRINT G,D1,D2,TD
220 ZOG%=645+(9*D1):GOSUB 360:PRINT D(1,D1);:ZOG
%=709+(9*D2):GOSUB 360:PRINT D(2,D2);
230 IF TD=7 THEN 270
240 IF TD=P THEN 260
250 GOTO 190
260 W=W+1:WL=W/G:GOTO 280
270 L=L+1:WL=W/G
280 LOCATE 8,3:PRINT W,L,WL
290 NEXT I
300 LOCATE 16,1
310 PRINT"(A)nother      (S)ummary      (M)ain me
nu ";
320 GOSUB 340
330 IF Q$="A" OR Q$="a" THEN RUN 10 ELSE IF Q$="
S" OR Q$="s" THEN GOTO 370 ELSE   RUN "A:MENU"
340 Q$=""+INKEY$:IF Q$="" THEN 340
350 RETURN
360 ZAG%=INT(ZOG%/64):ZOG%=ZOG%-64*ZAG%+1:ZAG%=Z
AG%+1:LOCATE ZAG%,ZOG%:RETURN
370 LPRINT "Number of Games Played: ";NG
380 LPRINT "# Wins = ";W,"# Losses = ";L,"Ratio
= ";WL
```

Listing 15-4. Craps Simulator. (Continued From Page 309.)

```
390 LPRINT""
400 LPRINT"",1,2,3,4,5,6
410 LPRINT"Die 1",:FOR I=1 TO 6:LPRINT D(1,I),:N
EXT
420 LPRINT""
430 LPRINT"Die 2",:FOR I=1 TO 6:LPRINT D(2,I),:N
EXT
440 LPRINT""
450 GOTO 300
```

CARD GAMES

Not too long after ancient man made his first pair of dice out of pebbles, just as soon as a reliable paper technology was developed, card games came along to help fill out a television and radio-free evening. Today's card decks used for bridge, poker, blackjack, canasta, and a number of similar games consist of 52 cards each, and contain four suits (hearts, diamonds, clubs, and spades) with thirteen cards in each suit, ranging from the ace to the king. In virtually all of these games, the first step is to shuffle the cards so the location of any given card is randomly determined. Listing 15-5 is a short routine used to shuffle one deck of cards into a random sequence. Each card is conceived to be numbered from 1 to 52. The shuffling routine creates a matrix

Listing 15-5. Basic Card Dealing.

```
1 '***********************************************
2 '*                 Listing 15-5                 *
3 '*              Basic Card Dealing              *
4 '***********************************************
5 '
10 CLS
20 RANDOMIZE
30 DIM A(52)
40 PRINT"Printout Desired?  (Y/N) ";:GOSUB 240
50 IF Q$="Y" OR Q$="y" THEN LP=1 ELSE LP=0
60 CLS
70 FOR I=1 TO 52
80 A(I)=I
90 NEXT
100 FOR I=1 TO 52
110 X=INT(RND(1)*52)+1
120 Y=INT(RND(1)*52)+1
130 H=A(X)
140 A(X)=A(Y)
150 A(Y)=H
160 NEXT
170 FOR I=1 TO 52
180 PRINT I;A(I),
190 IF LP=1 THEN LPRINT I;A(I),
200 NEXT
210 PRINT:PRINT:PRINT"(A)nother        (M)ain menu
";
220 GOSUB 240
230 IF Q$="A" OR Q$="a" THEN RUN 60 ELSE RUN "A:
MENU"
240 Q$=""+INKEY$:IF Q$="" THEN 240
250 RETURN
```

in which these 52 numbers appear randomly.

    To determine the suit to which a card belongs, take the integer value of the card number, divide it by thirteen (and a nudge), and add one:

$$\text{Suit} = \text{integer part } (C / 13.01) + 1$$

Using this approach, card number 25 is found to be in the second suit:

$$\text{Suit} = \text{INT} (25/ 13.01) + 1 = \text{INT} (1.92160) + 1 = 2$$

    The determination of the value of the card is done in a similar fashion, using a modulus form:

$$\text{Value} = \text{INT}((13*((C/13.01) - \text{INT}(C/13.01)))) + 1$$

$$= \text{INT}((13*((25/13.01) - \text{INT}(25/13.01)))) + 1$$
$$= \text{INT}(13*(1.922 - 1)) + 1$$
$$= \text{INT}(11.98078) + 1 + 12 \text{ (Queen)}$$

With the foundation of a procedure to shuffle the cards and an algorithm to identify the suit and value of each card, we can implement any number of routines on the microcomputer to check out card games and their outcomes. Listing 15-6 offers a short program to shuffle any number of decks of cards for subsequent dealing to a user-specified number of players. The reader can use this routine as the first step in the development of a card game evaluation program.

Listing 15-6. Card Dealer.

```
1 '*********************************************
2 '*              Listing 15-6                 *
3 '*              Card Dealer                  *
4 '*********************************************
5 '
10 CLS:KEY OFF:RANDOMIZE:PRINT"HOW MANY DECKS?
(1 TO 9)";
20 D$=""+INKEY$:IF D$="" THEN 20
30 D=VAL(D$):IF D<D1ORD>9 THEN 20
40 NC=52*D:DIM A(NC),PC(8,12)
50 FOR A=1 TO NC
60 A(A)=A:LOCATE 16,51:PRINT A;
70 NEXT
80 FOR B=1 TO NC
90 X=INT(RND(B)*NC)+1:Y=INT(RND(B)*NC)+1
100 H=A(X):A(X)=A(Y):A(Y)=H
110 LOCATE 16,51:PRINT B;
120 NEXT
130 S$(1)="SPADES":S$(2)="HEARTS":S$(3)="DIAMOND
S":S$(4)="CLUBS"
140 CC$="A23456789TJQK"
150 PRINT
160 FOR I=1 TO NC
170 X=A(I):V=1+INT((13*((X/13.01)-INT(X/13.01)))
)
180 C$=MID$(CC$,V,1)
190 V=1+INT((4*((X/4.01)-INT(X/4.01))))
200 PRINT I;" ";C$;" OF "S$(V)
210 NEXT
220 PRINT"(A)nother      (M)ain menu ";
230 GOSUB 250
240 IF Q$="A" OR Q$="a" THEN RUN 10 ELSE RUN "A:
MENU"
250 Q$=""+INKEY$:IF Q$="" THEN 250
260 RETURN
```

Listing 15-7, built upon the routine in Listing 15-6, facilitates the playing of a game of blackjack or "21." This game comes close to a game of skill that casinos offer their customers. A number of routines have been developed and successfully applied to "beat the odds" and win significant sums. Unfortunately, many of the better systems depend on the version of the game in which only one deck of cards is used. The more decks used, the more difficult it is to compute appropriate strategies. The reason for this is that with one deck it is feasible to keep track of the number of cards of each point value, especially the 10s and face cards, which can quickly change a potential win to a loss. Knowing the number of 10s that have been played (since there are only four), it is easy to compute the probability that the next card will be a 10. Likewise, we can compute the probability of a face card (also carrying a value of ten). As the number of decks increases, however, the task of tracking the played cards quickly becomes too difficult to be a practical approach.

The most effective and recent algorithm for managing to win in multiple-deck versions of the game concentrates on evaluating the cards that can be seen face up on the playing surface, rather than trying to keep mental count of cards, many of which cannot be seen.

Listing 15-7. Blackjack Dealer.

```
1  '****************************************
2  '*              Listing 15-7           *
3  '*            Blackjack Dealer          *
4  '****************************************
5  '
10 CLS:G=1:DIM C$(13):GOTO 970
20 'CARD DEALING SUBROUTINE
30 C=C+1:CD=CD+1:X=A(C):X=X-(INT(X/52)*52):V=1+I
NT((13*((X/13.1)-INT(X/13.1)))):LOCATE 16,45:PRI
NT"CARD #";CD;"OF";NC;
40 M$="A23456789TJQK"
50 IF CD>SP THEN 150
60 IF V>1 THEN 120
70 IF I<=P THEN 90
80 C$="A":IF S(I)<=10 THEN S(I)=S(I)+11 ELSE S(I
)=S(I)+1:GOTO 180
90 PC(I,N)=1:C$="A":ZOG%=76+(I*64)+(3*N):GOSUB 1
190:PRINT C$;:LOCATE 12,1:PRINT"HOW MANY POINTS
SHALL THIS ACE BE WORTH, (O)NE  OR  (E)LEVEN";
100 Z$=""+INKEY$:IF Z$="" THEN 100 ELSE IF Z$="O
" THEN V=1 ELSE V=11
110 S(I)=S(I)+V:LOCATE 12,1:PRINT CHR$(255);:V=1
:GOTO 180
120 IF V<10 THEN 140
130 S(I)=S(I)+10:GOTO 180
140 S(I)=S(I)+V:GOTO 180
150 LOCATE 1,1:PRINT"SHUFFLING
          ";
160 GOSUB 200
170 CD=0:C=0:GOTO 20
180 'CARD NAMER
190 C$=MID$(M$,V,1):PC(I,N)=V:RETURN
200 'SHUFFLING SUBROUTINE
210 FOR A=1 TO NC:A(A)=A:LOCATE 16,51:PRINT A;:N
EXT
220 FOR B=1 TO NC:X=INT(RND(B)*NC)+1:Y=INT(RND(B
)*NC)+1:H=A(X):A(X)=A(Y):A(Y)=H:LOCATE 16,51:PRI
```

```
NT B;:NEXT:RETURN
230 'INITIAL TABLE SET-UP
240 CLS:PRINT"DEALING....GAME #";G;
250 FOR I=1 TO P
260 IF I<>YP THEN 280
270 ZOG%=64+(I*64):GOSUB 1190:PRINT "   YOU":GOT
O 290
280 ZOG%=64+(I*64):GOSUB 1190:PRINT "     ";I
290 NEXT
300 PRINT" DEALER"
310 FOR N=1 TO 2
320 FOR I=1 TO P
330 GOSUB 20:ZOG%=71+(I*64):GOSUB 1190:PRINT S(I
);:ZOG%=76+(I*64)+(3*N):GOSUB 1190:PRINT C$;:IF
N=1 THEN 390
340 BJ(I)=0:IF S(I)<>11 THEN 360
350 IF PC(1,1)=1 OR PC(1,2)=1 THEN 370 ELSE 380
360 IF S(I)<>21 THEN 380
370 BJ(I)=1:ZOG%=110+(I*64):GOSUB 1190:PRINT "BL
ACKJACK";:S(I)=21:ZOG%=71+(I*64):GOSUB 1190:PRIN
T S(I);
380 BE(I)=1
390 NEXT I
400 GOSUB 20:ZOG%=71+(I*64):GOSUB 1190:PRINT S(I
);:IF N=2 THEN 430
410 X$=C$
420 ZOG%=76+(I*64)+3:GOSUB 1190:PRINT CHR$(219);
:GOTO 440
430 ZOG%=76+(I*64)+6:GOSUB 1190:PRINT C$;
440 NEXT N
450 FOR I=1 TO P
460 IF S(I)>21 THEN 610
470 N=2:NC(I)=2
480 N=N+1:LOCATE 1,1:PRINT"PLAYER #";I;", YOUR T
URN";
490 LOCATE 15,1:PRINT"(S)TAND        (H)IT";
500 A$=""+INKEY$:IF A$="" THEN 500
510 IF A$="S" OR A$="s" THEN 610
520 IF A$="H" OR A$="h" THEN 540
530 NC(I)=3:GOSUB 20:ZOG%=76+(I*64)+(3*N):GOSUB
1190:PRINT C$;:ZOG%=71+(I*64):GOSUB 1190:PRINT S
(I);:DF(I)=1:GOTO 600
540 NC(I)=NC(I)+1:GOSUB 20
550 ZOG%=76+(I*64)+(3*N):GOSUB 1190:PRINT C$;:ZO
G%=71+(I*64):GOSUB 1190:PRINT S(I);:IF S(I)<22 T
HEN 480 ELSE 600
560 ZOG%=76+(I*64)+6:GOSUB 1190:PRINT "  ";
570 X$=MID$(M$,PC(I,2),1)
580 ZOG%=105+(I*64):GOSUB 1190:PRINT X$;
590 BE(I)=2
600 IF S(I)>21 THEN ZOG%=110+(I*64):GOSUB 1190:P
RINT "BUST";
610 IF NC(I)>2 THEN 650
620 IF PC(I,1)<>1 OR PC(I,2)<>1 THEN 650
630 S(I)=S(I)+10
640 ZOG%=71+(I*64):GOSUB 1190:PRINT S(I);
650 NEXT I
660 N=3
```

Listing 15-7. Blackjack Dealer. (Continued From Page 313.)

```
670 'DEALER'S PLAY RULES
680 POKE 15360+(I*64),128:LOCATE 1,1:PRINT"DEALE
R IS PLAYING......";
690 GOTO 710
700 ZOG%=76+(I*64)+3:GOSUB 1190:PRINT X$;
710 IF S(I)<22 THEN 730
720 GOTO 850
730 IF PC(I,1)=1 THEN 760
740 IF PC(I,2)=1 THEN 770
750 GOTO 800
760 IF PC(I,2)>10 THEN 790
770 IF PC(I,1)>10 THEN 790
780 N=N+1:GOTO 800
790 BJ(I)=1
800 IF S(I)>17 THEN 850
810 IF S(I)<17 THEN 830
820 IF PC(I,1)<>1 AND PC(I,2)<>1 THEN 850
830 GOSUB 20
840 ZOG%=76+(I*64)+(3*N):GOSUB 1190:PRINT C$;:ZO
G%=71+(I*64):GOSUB 1190:PRINT S(I);:GOTO 710
850 ZOG%=76+(I*64)+(3*N):GOSUB 1190:PRINT C$;:ZO
G%=71+(I*64):GOSUB 1190:PRINT S(I);
860 D=P+1
870 PRINT:PRINT"ANOTHER GAME   (Y/N)";
880 Q$=""+INKEY$:IF Q$="" THEN 880
890 IF Q$="N" THEN 1090
900 PRINT:PRINT"SAME PLAYERS AND RULES?   (Y/N)";
910 Q$=""+INKEY$:IF Q$="" THEN 910
920 IF Q$="N" THEN 960
930 FOR I=1 TO P+1:BJ(I)=0:S(I)=0:NEXT
940 G=G+1
950 GOTO 230
960 RUN 10
970 'BASIC GAME DATA
980 PRINT"BLACKJACK TRAINER":PRINT:PRINT
990 RANDOMIZE:PRINT"HOW MANY DECKS?   (1 TO 9)";
1000 D$=""+INKEY$:IF D$="" THEN 1000
1010 D=VAL(D$):IF D<1 OR D>9 THEN 1000
1020 NC=52*D:DIM A(NC),PC(8,12)
1030 PRINT D:PRINT"NUMBER OF PLAYERS?   (1 TO 7)"
;
1040 P$=""+INKEY$:IF P$="" THEN 1040
1050 P=VAL(P$):IF P<1 OR P>7 THEN 1040
1060 PRINT P:PRINT"YOUR POSITION AT TABLE?   (1 T
O 7)";
1070 YP$=""+INKEY$:IF YP$="" THEN 1070
1080 YP=VAL(YP$):IF YP<1 OR YP>7 THEN 1070
1090 SP=NC/2:PRINT YP:INPUT"RE-SHUFFLE AFTER HOW
MANY CARDS";SP
1100 IF SP>NC THEN 1090
1110 PRINT"RE-SHUFFLE WILL OCCUR WHEN";SP;"CARDS
HAVE BEEN DEALT":PRINT"SHUFFLING";D;"DECK(S), W
ITH A TOTAL OF";NC;"CARDS..."
1120 GOSUB 200
1130 GOTO 230
1140 PRINT"(A)nother        (M)ain menu ";
```

```
1150 GOSUB 1170
1160 IF Q$="A" OR Q$="a" THEN RUN 10 ELSE RUN "A
:MENU"
1170 Q$=""+INKEY$:IF Q$="" THEN 1170
1180 RETURN
1190 ZAG%=INT(ZOG%/64):ZOG%=ZOG%-64*ZAG%+1:ZAG%=
ZAG%+1:                              LOCATE ZAG%
,ZOG%:RETURN
```

MONOPOLY® SIMULATOR

A product of the Parker Brothers Company, Monopoly has long fascinated young and old alike. The program in Listing 15-8 lets the user simulate the play of a game with from one to five players. The program does not attempt to actually play the game, trading properties, paying penalties, and so forth, but is designed to determine which if any properties or locations seem to be visited by players more often than others. Knowing which ones are the more popular can help you shape a winning strategy.

Since the game uses two dice, the most common value expected is seven. We might assume that over an extended play of the game those properties whose sequential numbers are multiples of seven would be more popular than the others. We've not run the program extensively enough to reach any definitive conclusions, but maybe a reader will pick up the challenge and probe this mystery.

RANDOM NUMBER GENERATION

Central to all of the foregoing programs in this chapter, and to many simulations, is the concept of a random number. We use random numbers to simulate the action of a game such as Monopoly, just as we use random numbers to help us know where in a neighborhood to conduct a survey. Random numbers are the key to modern cipher systems used to encrypt confidential commercial and classified military communications. This last concept leads us to the first characterization of random numbers.

We frequently refer to random numbers when we really are talking about *pseudo-random* numbers. Pseudo-random numbers, when viewed on a list, appear to have occurred in a random fashion. The truth is that the numbers actually appear in a very rational order. Usually, these numbers are generated by an algorithm, often keyed by the user with a *seed number*. One such algorithm is expressed in the

Listing 15-8. Monopoly Simulator.

```
1 '***********************************************
2 '*              Listing 15-8                   *
3 '*           Monopoly Simulator                *
4 '***********************************************
5 '
10 CLS:RANDOMIZE
20 PRINT"MONOPOLY SIMULATOR":PRINT:PRINT
30 INPUT"ENTER NUMBER OF PLAYERS (1-5)";P
40 INPUT"ENTER NUMBER OF TURNS IN GAME";T
50 DIM A(5,T),L$(40),T(5)
60 FOR I=1 TO 40:READ L$(I):NEXT
70 FOR I=1 TO P:A(I,J)=40:NEXT
80 CLS:PRINT"PLAYER","CURRENT POSITION";
90 FOR I=1 TO P:ZOG%=64+(I*64):GOSUB 490:PRINT I
;:NEXT
100 LOCATE 16,1:PRINT"TURN #";
110 FOR I=1 TO T
120 LOCATE 16,11:PRINT I;
```

Listing 15-8. Monopoly Simulator. (Continued From Page 315.)

```
130 FOR J=1 TO P
140 D1=INT(RND(J)*6):D2=INT(RND(I)*6):TD=D1+D2
150 PP=A(J,I-1)+TD:IF PP>40 THEN PP=PP-40
160 IF PP=30 THEN PP=10
170 A(J,I)=PP:ZOG%=80+(64*J):GOSUB 490:PRINT L$(
PP)+"              ",
180 NEXT J
190 NEXT I
200 GOTO 440
210 DATA MEDITERRANEAN AVENUE,COMMUNITY CHEST,BA
LTIC AVENUE,INCOME TAX,READING RAILROAD,ORIENTAL
 AVENUE,CHANCE,VERMONT AVENUE,CONNECTICUT AVENUE
,JAIL,ST. CHARLES PLACE,ELECTRIC COMPANY,STATES
AVENUE,VIRGINIA AVENUE,PENNSYLVANIA RAILROAD
220 DATA ST. JAMES PLACE,COMMUNITY CHEST,TENNESS
EE AVENUE,NEW YORK AVENUE,FREE PARKING,KENTUCKY
AVENUE,CHANCE,INDIANA AVENUE,ILLINOIS AVENUE,B &
 O RAILROAD,ATLANTIC AVENUE,VENTNOR AVENUE,WATER
 WORKS,MARVIN GARDENS,GO TO JAIL,PACIFIC AVENUE
230 DATA NORTH CAROLINA,COMMUNITY CHEST,PENNSYLV
ANIA AVENUE,SHORT LINE,CHANCE,PARK PLACE,LUXURY
TAX,BOARDWALK,GO
240 LPRINT"POSITION OF PLAYERS AFTER";I-1;"TURNS
":LPRINT""
250 FOR J=1 TO P:LPRINT"Player #";1,PP$(A(J,I-1)
):NEXT J
260 LPRINT""
270 NEXT
280 LPRINT"":ST=P*(I-1)
290 LPRINT"","","","PLAYER"
300 LPRINT"POSITION","    1","    2","    3","
  4","    5","TOTAL","PER CENT"
310 FOR M=1 TO 40
320 LPRINT LEFT$(L$(M),8),
330 FOR J=1 TO P:T(J)=0:NEXT:TT=0
340 FOR J=1 TO I
350 FOR K=1 TO P
360 IF A(K,J)<>M THEN 380
370 T(K)=T(K)+1:TT=TT+1:CT(K)=CT(K)+1
380 NEXT K
390 NEXT J
400 LPRINT T(1),T(2),T(3),T(4),T(5),TT,100*(TT/S
T)
410 NEXT
420 LPRINT"TOTAL",CT(1),CT(2),CT(3),CT(4),CT(5),
ST
430 LPRINT""
440 PRINT"(A)nother       (M)ain menu ";
450 GOSUB 470
460 IF Q$="A" OR Q$="a" THEN RUN 10 ELSE RUN "A:
MENU"
470 Q$=""+INKEY$:IF Q$="" THEN 470
480 RETURN
490 ZAG%=INT(ZOG%/64):ZOG%=ZOG%-64*ZAG%+1:ZAG%=Z
AG%+1:                         LOCATE ZAG%,
ZOG%:RETURN
```

equation:

$$R_{T+1} = (\pi + SN_T)^S - \text{integer part } (\pi + SN_T)^S$$

$$SN_{T+1} = R_{T+1}$$

So long as we use the same value for the first value of SN, we will always generate the same series of pseudo-random numbers. This is useful in simulations in which you want to repeat identical conditions for two or more test subjects, or in encrypted communications systems.

The other aspect of random numbers is the true (or apparently true) random number; that sequence of numbers that appear at random and cannot be forced into a repetition. We use these numbers in simulations where repeating the sequence would be meaningless. For example, we need a truly random sequence of numbers to effectively analyze the craps dice game and similar functions. In these applications we depend on the numbers being uniformly distributed throughout the allowable range. For example, in evaluating a dice routine, we want to be sure each of the faces appear in approximately equal frequencies. A bias for one number or another is most undesirable.

In queuing simulations, on the other hand, we want both the element of random events (customer arrival times), and a nonuniform distribution. Humans seldom behave uniformly. Rather, they tend to arrive at retail establishments not at discrete and even intervals, but in clumps and clusters as a function of some other factor. For example, the workload in fast food restaurants clusters around traditional meal hours. The bulk of the people arrive at peak periods. After each peak the number present gradually tapers off. The standard form of this distribution is known as the Poisson Distribution, and is given by the following equation:

$$Y = \frac{\lambda^x e^{-\lambda}}{x!}$$

where λ is the mean of the distribution and $e = 2.71828$.

The variance is equal to the mean and consequently, the standard deviation (although not commonly used in this distribution) is the square root of the variance (mean). As the mean grows larger, the distribution approaches the form of the normal distribution, which is the most common distribution. Applications of it are found throughout the whole of mathematics and industry and examples of it are shown in various other sections of this book.

It is useful to be able to compute random numbers that occur in nonuniform distributions. For example, in simulating the arrival of customers in a bank, we much prefer to use a Poisson Distribution over a uniform distribution. In other simulations, we prefer the normal distribution of random numbers over anything else.

Listing 15-9 contains the routines necessary to generate a pseudo-random series of integers in several useful distributions. The "uniform" distribution results in a set of "random" numbers more or less evenly distributed between the upper and lower limits of the set. The "normal" distribution gives a random sequence of numbers which cluster around the user-provided mean and standard deviation, and the tabulated product resembles a normal distribution. The Poisson Distribution generates a series of integers which follow the Poisson form. The exponential distribution is a set of random numbers which fall within the limits of an exponential curve.

These routines are useful in simulations requiring random event generators, and are especially useful in programs where distributions other than a uniform distribution, like that given from most internal computer RND generators, are required.

EXERCISES:

1. Table 15-1 summarizes the results of one run of the Universal Game Machine for the odds of winning from 0.05 to 0.50 in increments of 0.05. At each level, there were 1000 iterations. Repeat the experiment, but use smaller and larger numbers of iterations. What effect does this have on the number of losses in a row at p = 0.05? At p = 0.45?

2. From the data obtained in exercise 1, use a curve-fitting routine to compute the coefficients of the exponential form: $Y = A \cdot 2.71828^{Bp}$.

Listing 15-9. Random Distributions.

```
1 '****************************************************
2 '*                 Listing 15-9                     *
3 '*             Random Distributions                 *
4 '****************************************************
5 '
10 CLS:RANDOMIZE
20 PRINT"RANDOM NUMBER GENERATION":PRINT:PRINT
30 PRINT"1  --  UNIFORM I               2 --
NORMAL CURVE                              3  --
POISSON CURVE             4  --  EXPONENTIAL DIST
RIBUTION":PRINT:PRINT"SELECT    ";
40 Q$=""+INKEY$:IF Q$="" THEN 40 ELSE C=VAL(Q$)
50 PRINT C:PRINT:INPUT"NUMBER OF ITERATIONS DESI
RED";N
60 DIM NU(N),C(128)
70 ON C GOTO 80,90,100,110
80 INPUT"UPPER LIMIT OF RANGE DESIRED  (0 TO ?)"
;M:GOTO 120
90 INPUT"MEAN OF NORMAL DISTRIBUTION";X:INPUT"ST
ANDARD DEVIATION";S:GOTO 120
100 INPUT"MEAN OF POISSON DISTRIBUTION";L:GOTO 1
20
110 INPUT"THETA VALUE OF EXPONENTIAL DISTRIBUTIO
N";T
120 FOR I=1 TO N
130 R=0
140 ON C GOSUB 210,220,240,270
150 SR=SR+R:R2=R2+(R^2)
160 PRINT R,:NU(I)=R:K=INT(R+.5):IF K<0 OR K>128
 THEN K=128
170 C(K)=C(K)+1
180 NEXT I
190 SD=SQR((R2-((SR^2)/N))/(N-1)):MR=SR/N
200 ON C GOTO 280,310,290,300,310
210 R=INT(RND(I)*M)+1:RETURN
220 A=2*RND(I)-1:B=A^2+(2*RND(I)-1)^2:IF B>=1 TH
EN 220
230 R=X+(A*SQR((-2*LOG(B))/B))*S:RETURN
240 A=EXP(-L):B=1
250 B=B*RND(I):IF (B-A)<0 THEN RETURN
260 R=R+1:GOTO 250
270 R=T*LOG(RND(I)):RETURN
280 PRINT:PRINT"MEAN OF UNIFORM DISTRIBUTION ( 0
 TO";M;"):";M/2:PRINT"THEORETICAL
                ";MR:PRINT"ACTUAL (STANDARD DEVIAT
ION =              ";SD;")":GOTO 310
290 PRINT:PRINT"MEAN REQUESTED = ";X:PRINT"MEAN
OBTAINED = ";MR,"(DIFF. = ";MR-X;")":PRINT"STAND
ARD DEVIATION REQUESTED = ";S:PRINT"STANDARD DEV
IATION OBTAINED = ";SD;"         (DIFF. = ";SD-S;")
":GOTO 310
300 PRINT:PRINT"MEAN REQUESTED = ";L:PRINT"MEAN
OBTAINED = ";MR,"(DIFF. = ";MR-L;")"
310 LOCATE 25,1:PRINT"(P)RINTOUT      (N)EW     (E)
ND   (G)RAPHIC DISPLAY   ";
320 Q$=INKEY$:IF Q$="" THEN 320
```

```
330 PRINT Q$:IF Q$="P" OR Q$="p" THEN 510 ELSE I
F Q$="G" OR Q$="g" THEN 350 ELSEIF Q$="E" OR Q$=
"e" THEN RUN "A:MENU" ELSE IF Q$<>"N" THEN 310
340 RUN
350 CLS:SCREEN 2:LINE(1,180)-(320,180)
360 FOR I=1 TO N
370 IF NU(I)<LG THEN 390
380 LG=NU(I)
390 NEXT
400 LOCATE 25,36:PRINT LG;:LOCATE 25,1:PRINT 0;
410 FOR I=1 TO N
420 X=INT(320*(NU(I)/LG)):Y=179
430 IF POINT(X,Y) THEN 450
440 PSET(X,Y):GOTO 460
450 Y=Y-1:GOTO 430
460 NEXT
470 'RESUME NEXT
480 LOCATE 1,1:PRINT"(C)ONTINUE";
490 Q$=""+INKEY$:IF Q$="" THEN 490
500 GOTO 310
510 ON C GOTO 520,530,540,550
520 LPRINT"UNIFORM DISTRIBUTION I":LPRINT N;"NUM
BERS BETWEEN 0 AND";M:GOTO 560
530 LPRINT"NORMAL DISTRIBUTION":LPRINT N;"NUMBER
S ABOUT A MEAN OF";MR;"WITH A STANDARD DEVIATION
 OF ";SD:GOTO 560
540 LPRINT"POISSON DISTRIBUTION":LPRINT N;"NUMBE
RS ABOUT A LAMDA MEAN OF"L:GOTO 560
550 LPRINT"EXPONENTIAL DISTRIBUTION":LPRINT N;"N
UMBERS BASED ON A THETA VALUE OF";T
560 LPRINT""
570 FOR I=1 TO N:LPRINT I;NU(I),:NEXT
```

3. Identify a commercial or governmentally-sponsored game such as the soda pop simulation, or a state-operated lottery, preferably a recently started game. Write a program to simulate the play of the game. Contrast your findings with the advertised outcome.

SUGGESTED READING

McFadden, J.A., 1971. *Physical Concepts of Probability.* New York: Van Nostrand Reinhold Company.

Draper, N.R. and W.E. Lawrence, 1970. *Probability: An Introductory Course.*

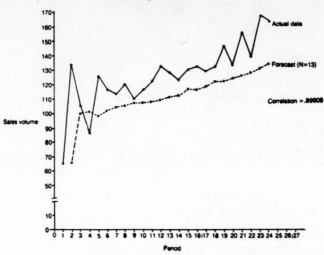

## Chapter 16

Miscellaneous Forecasting

In the course of our daily work and in researching materials for this book, we were able to organize the materials into the chapters you have read. There were, however, some materials that we desired to include in the book for which there was no obvious placement, other than in a chapter for miscellaneous routines. What follows are some of those routines.

FORECASTING PROJECT COMPLETION DATES USING PERT

Program evaluation and review technique (PERT) is a system designed to display and monitor the step-by-step progress of projects. While the comprehensive explanation of PERT is beyond the scope of this book, it is possible to use the microcomputer to aid in the evaluation of a project by someone who does understand PERT and uses the program outlined below.

There have been a number of approaches developed to illustrate a project in a PERT format over the last twenty to thirty years—each approach suiting the particular purposes of the designer. Figure 16-1 illustrates one of these approaches.

Note that from the starting point, normally at the top or the left of the chart, the project growth is shown with related activities connected by a line. Along each path is a symbol indicating the duration of the first task. This value, D_i, is normally the mean time to complete such tasks. Where appropriate, we may compute and use the standard deviations of these durations and use them to compute the total time variations in our estimates. At each event point, the symbols used may vary in shape, but will convey at least three items of information: the event number, the earliest possible time the event can begin, and the last allowable time for completion. Within this context, three rules apply:

1. The first event in a project begins at time zero, $E_1 = 0$.
2. Each event is assumed to begin as soon as possible; that is, as soon as all preceding events are completed.

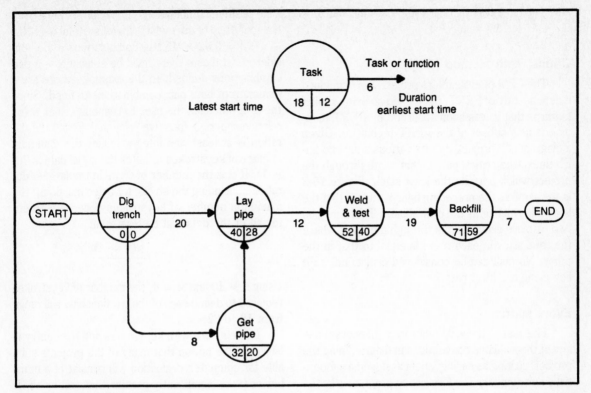

Fig. 16-1. Basic PERT event chart.

3. The "early finish" time (EF) of an event is the sum of its "early start" (ES) time and the duration of the event: $EF_i = ES_i = D_i$.

Projects normally carry a specified completion date or time, T_s. Therefore, the latest allowable finish time for the very last event within the project is equal to the completion time; $LF_j = T_s$. The latest allowable start time for an event, LS_i, is the latest allowable finish time less the duration of the task: $LS_k = LF_k - D_k$. Finally, the latest allowable finishing time for any arbitrary event is the latest allowable starting time of the succeeding event: $LF_j = LS_{j+1}$. If two or more events follow and are dependent upon event j, LF_j is equal to the earliest of the LS_1 values of the succeeding events.

With few exceptions, T_s must always be equal to or greater than E_t, the time required to complete each of the sequential tasks of the projects. For example, if it takes at least 18 hours for a fast drying concrete used in a highway to set up to a degree at which a vehicle can be supported, and a path of concrete can be poured at the rate of 50 linear feet an hour (at a given width and depth), and the contract calls for the pouring of ten miles of highway, then the project completion date must be 44 days and 18 hours beyond the exact starting date and time of the project. (More precisely, the time is 44 days and 18 hours, less 10/speed limit, assuming a car were to start down the highway at such a time that it would reach the end at exactly 44 days and 18 hours.) It would be foolish for a small contractor, owning only enough equipment to handle one section of roadway at a time, to accept the contract if it called for completion time anything less than the 44.75 days. On the other hand, if the contract calls for completion within 60 days, a bid is clearly in order. The difference between the scheduled completion date and the minimum possible time, E_t, is called *slack*. In a similar fashion, the difference between the earliest and latest start or finish times for any given event is the slack for that interval, $S_i = LS_i - ES_i$ or $LF_i = EF_i$.

Critical Path Method (CPM)

The CPM of evaluating a project was developed independently of PERT, but it used so many similar features that it was soon absorbed by PERT technicians as a subset of the PERT technique. Given a diagram of a project with its various start and finish times, the critical path is that route through the project which permits the least slack. Figure 16-2 is the same as the preceding figure, except that the heavy line highlights the critical path. There may be two or more critical paths through a project where the total slack in each route is equal to that in the other. No task can be considered critical unless it lies along a critical path.

Event Matrix

The user of these routines may, of course, use any of the available conventions in diagramming the project, so long as each event is assigned a sequential event number. The forecasting program asks the user to specify whether there is a relationship between each of the event pairs and, if so, the duration of the task to completion of the sequence. For N events, there is a maximum of $(N(N - 1))/2$ possible positive combinations. For example, in a project consisting of ten events, there is a total of $(10(10 - 1))/2 = 90/2 = 45$ pair combinations to be considered. Of these, there must be at least $N - 1$ pair combinations defined. In the example, there are a minimum of nine pair combinations defined. Since the program asks the user to respond either N (no relationship) or Y (positive relationship) and the duration is at least one integer value, the minimum number of keystrokes to enter the initial data is $2(N - 1)$. If M is the number of digits in the largest durations, including the stroke for a decimal point, the maximum number of keystrokes necessary to enter all of the data will be less than:

$$(M + 1)\frac{N(N - 1)}{2}$$

Using $N = 10$ and $M = 4$, the number of keystrokes required to define each of the relationships will range from 18 to 225.

Our concern with keystrokes and data entry is based on the notion that many of the projects suitable for computer evaluation will consist of a number of tasks significantly greater than ten or so. If the number of related events is small, relative to the total possible, it may be better for the user to define which pairs are related by typing in the matrix coordinates and entering the duration directly, in-

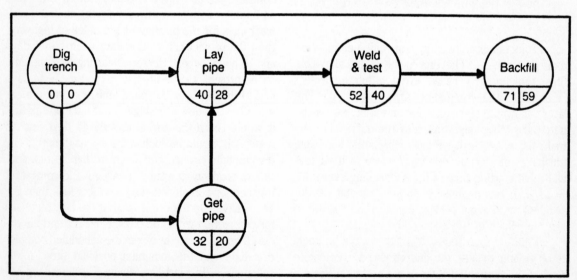

Fig. 16-2. PERT chart with critical path (heavy line).

stead of answering Y/N to each of the possible combinations. The program asks the user to enter the total number of related events, K, and the length of the largest duration and computes whether it would be advantageous to use this entry scheme in lieu of examining the whole matrix.

Once the duration data are entered, the computer takes over the task of evaluating the earliest and latest start and finishing values for each task, identifying critical jobs in the process. Given a starting date and a decision as to whether or not work continues during weekends, the program gives an estimate of the completion date: Completion = Start + E_t + Days Not Worked (weekends, etc.), and the total number of days involved. To be prudent, a bid on a project should not be made unless this completion date (or the total number of days) is earlier than (or less than) that called for in the contract. The difference between the completion date and the contract date is the amount of *free slack* in the project. It gives an indication of the total amount of time, the project may vary from the schedule without management actions required to complete the project on time.

The critical path is not computed, although the critical tasks are identified as part of the output. You can easily identify the critical path by connecting critical jobs with a heavy line or with color. (A routine to identify the critical path can be developed as a special case of a program to solve the traditional "Traveling Salesman" problem wherein the task is to specify the shortest route the salesman can take to reach a list of cities.) Listing 16-1 implements the foregoing discussion on PERT.

Listing 16-1. Forecasting with PERT.

```
1  '*******************************************
2  '*              Listing 16-1               *
3  '*          Forecasting with PERT          *
4  '*******************************************
5  '
10 CLS:KEY OFF:CLEAR 2000:PRINT"PERT EVALUATOR":
PRINT:PRINT
20 INPUT"WHAT IS THE NAME OF THE PROJECT";N$
30 PRINT:PRINT"HOW MANY EVENTS ARE REQUIRED TO C
OMPLETE ";N$;:INPUT N
40 PC=(N*(N-1))/2:DIM E$(N),E(N,N),D(N),ES(N),EF
(N),LS(N),LF(N),S(N)
50 PRINT:PRINT"THERE IS A TOTAL OF";PC;"POSSIBLE
 COMBINATIONS OF EVENTS.  ";:INPUT"HOW MANY EVEN
T CONNECTIONS ARE THERE";K
60 PRINT:Z$="N":IF PC<(2*K) THEN 100
70 PRINT:PRINT"YOU WILL SAVE TIME BY DEFINING AC
TUAL RELATIONSHIPS.  IS THIS   OPTION DESIRED?
(Y/N)";
80 Z$=""+INKEY$:IF Z$="" THEN 80
90 PRINT:PRINT
100 FOR I=1 TO N
110 PRINT"NAME OF EVENT #"I,:INPUT E$(I)
120 NEXT I
130 IF Z$="N" OR Z$="n" THEN 150
140 GOSUB 530:GOTO 230
150 FOR I=1 TO N-1
160 FOR J=I+1 TO N
170 PRINT:PRINT"IS EVENT #";I;", ";E$(I);", CONN
ECTED TO EVENT #";J;", ";E$(J);"?   (Y/N)";
180 Q$=""+INKEY$:IF Q$="" THEN 180
190 PRINT Q$:IF Q$="Y" OR Q$="y" THEN E(I,J)=1 E
LSE E(I,J)=-1
```

Listing 16-1. Forecasting with PERT. (Continued From Page 323.)

```
200 NEXT J
210 NEXT I
220 ES(1)=0
230 FOR I=1 TO N
240 PRINT"WHAT IS THE MEAN TIME TO COMPLETE ";E$
(I);:INPUT MT:D(I)=MT:TD=TD+D(I)
250 EX=0:IF I=1 THEN 310
260 FOR J=1 TO I-1
270 IF E(I,J)=-1 THEN 300
280 IF EF(J)<EX THEN 300
290 EX=EF(J)
300 NEXT J
310 ES(I)=EX:EF(I)=ES(I)+D(I)
320 NEXT I
330 PRINT:INPUT"HOW MANY DAYS ARE ALLOWED TO COM
PETE THE PROJECT";TS
340 LF(N)=TS:LS(N)=TS-D(N)
350 FOR I=N-1 TO 1 STEP -1
360 EX=N:LG=LS(N):IF I=N THEN 420
370 FOR J=I+1 TO N
380 IF E(I,J)=-1 THEN 410
390 IF LG<LS(J) THEN 410
400 EX=J:LG=LS(J)
410 NEXT J
420 LF(I)=LS(EX):LS(I)=LF(I)-D(I):S(I)=LS(I)-ES(
I):TT=TT+S(I)
430 NEXT I
440 LPRINT"":LPRINT"PROJECT: ";N$:LPRINT""
450 LPRINT"
 Earliest          Latest"
460 LPRINT"Event Name           Duration    Sta
rt      Finish     Start      Finish     Slack"
470 B$="\                        \ #####    #####
    #####   #####   #####   #####"
480 FOR I=1 TO N
490 LPRINT USING B$;E$(I);D(I);ES(I);EF(I);LS(I)
;LF(I);S(I);
500 NEXT I
510 LPRINT"":LPRINT"TOTAL SLACK = ";TS-TD
520 GOTO 640
530 FOR I=1 TO K
540 INPUT"ENTER FIRST EVENT NUMBER";E1
550 INPUT"ENTER SECOND EVENT NUMBER";E2
560 PRINT:E(E1,E2)=1
570 NEXT
580 FOR I=1 TO N-1
590 FOR J=I TO N+1
600 IF E(I,J)=1 THEN 620
610 E(I,J)=-1
620 NEXT
630 NEXT I
640 PRINT"(A)nother       (M)ain menu ";
650 GOSUB 670
660 IF Q$="A" OR Q$="a" THEN RUN 10 ELSE RUN "A:
MENU"
670 Q$=""+INKEY$:IF Q$="" THEN 670
680 RETURN
```

Influence of Statistical Variation

So far, we have assumed that each task in a project will take a certain length of time to complete. We have called this the duration of the task. In reality, this value is the mean time computed or deduced from prior experience in similar situations. This implies, however, some variation in the actual timing of the project. Computed from a simple mean duration, we may make an estimate of a completion date that is a day or two within the contract date, and yet, because of the implicit variation, we may not be able to complete the project on schedule. Expanding the preceding program to include consideration of these potential variations reduces the risk of such an error. In a project involving an automated production line, the variations may not be very significant (depending on the mechanical reliability of the line), whereas projects involving creativity and human-intensive effort may call for considerably wider tolerances.

FORECASTING DELIVERY DATES

There are a number of businesses which involve the sale of products by telephone. As part of the transaction, the seller (in theory) informs the buyer when to expect receipt of the product. Federal law requires shipment of such items within a certain period of time unless the seller specifically cites a longer period. When asked when to expect an item, the seller will frequently just add three to six weeks to the current date. Program Listing 16-2 is a simple routine that a more conscientious business can use to generate a rational and reasonable delivery date. We base the program on the assumed transaction flow in Fig. 16-3.

Order Received. The time to deliver a product begins with the completion of the sale or the receipt of the order. Ordinarily, the buyer understands that the product cannot be shipped until sometime after the order is placed. In systems which use a recording device to take orders, an additional delay may be encountered.

Processing. Most businesses will require the generation of several documents to properly record the sale, arrange for payment, and affect the shipping of the package. The time before delivery is not

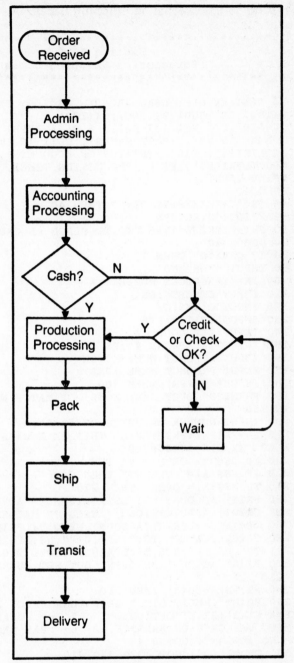

Fig. 16-3. Shipping date flowchart.

necessarily the sum of these actions, but simply the sum of those actions that must be performed sequentially and that lead to the creation of an instruction to prepare the product for shipment.

Listing 16-2. Forecasting Shipping Dates.

```
1 '**********************************************
2 '*              Listing 16-2                  *
3 '*         Forecasting Shipping Dates         *
4 '**********************************************
5 '
10 CLS:KEY OFF:CLEAR 250:DIM P$(100),SA$(1000),P
R(100),CL(1000),PT(100),PK(100)
20 'IN THIS SECTION BUILD A DATA INPUT ROUTINE T
O LOAD IN P$() (PART NAMES), CL() (CUSTOMER CRED
IT LIMITS), SA$() (STATUS OF ACCOUNTS), PR() (PR
ODUCT PRICES), PT() (PRODUCTION TIME), PK() (SHI
PPING TIME)
30 GOTO 60
40 Q$=""+INKEY$:IF Q$="" THEN 40
50 PRINT Q$:RETURN
60 PRINT:PRINT"TYPE '@' TO PLACE AN ORDER",
70 GOSUB 40
80 IF Q$<>"@" THEN 70
90 INPUT"NAME";N$
100 INPUT"ACCOUNT NUMBER";A
110 INPUT"STREET";S$
120 INPUT"CITY";C$
130 INPUT"STATE";ST$
140 INPUT"ZIP CODE";Z$
150 INPUT"TELEPHONE #";T$
160 INPUT"PRODUCT NUMBER";PN
170 INPUT"PRODUCT NAME";PN$
180 IF PN$=P$(PN) THEN 200
190 PRINT"PRODUCT NAME DOES NOT MATCH NUMBER":GO
TO 160
200 INPUT"NUMBER OF UNITS DESIRED";N
210 BD=PR(PN):PRINT"WILL THIS BE A CASH/C.O.D. S
ALE?  (Y/N)",:GOSUB 40
220 IF Q$="Y" OR Q$="y" THEN 330
230 IF AS$(A)="CURRENT" THEN 280
240 IF AS$(A)="OPEN" THEN 270
250 PRINT"ACCOUNT NOT ESTABLISHED.  ADVISE CUSTO
MER CREDIT APPLICATION    WILL BE MAILED."
260 LPRINT"":LPRINT"ACCOUNT MEMO:":LPRINT"MAIL C
REDIT APPLICATION TO:":LPRINT"",N$:LPRINT"",S$:L
PRINT"",C$;" ";ST$,Z$:LPRINT"":GOTO 210
270 PRINT"ACCOUNT IS OPEN, BUT NOT CURRENT":GOTO
 210
280 PR(PN)<=CL(A) THEN 310
290 PRINT"CREDIT LIMIT LESS THAN PRICE BY $";PR(
PN)-CL(A):PRINT"OPTIONS:       1 --    CHARGE TO LI
MIT, PAY CASH ON BALANCE, 2   --   PAY CASH, 3  --
   NO ACTION",:GOSUB 40
300 ON VAL(Q$) GOTO 320,330,310
310 RUN 60
320 BD=PR(PN)-CL(A):CL(A)=0:GOTO 330
330 PRINT"THE BALANCE DUE IS $";BD:PRINT"","1  -
- CASH (CERTIFIED CHECK), 2 -- CHECK, 3 --
C.O.D.",:GOSUB 40
340 ON VAL(Q$) GOTO 350,360,370
350 CT=7:PRINT P$(PN);" WILL BE SHIPPED UPON REC
```

```
IEPT OF FUNDS.":GOTO 370
360 CT=21:PRINT"PLEASE ALLOW 14 DAYS FOR CHECK P
ROCESSING AND CLEARANCE.":GOTO 370
370 SD=PT(PN)+CT+PK(PN)
380 PRINT PN$;" WILL BE SHIPPED IN ABOUT";SD;"DA
YS.  ALLOW 7-10 DAYS FOR POSTAL HANDLING":
390 LPRINT"":LPRINT"TRANSACTION MEMO"
400 LPRINT"SHIP";N;P$(PN);", PART NUMBER";PN;"TO
:":LPRINT""
410 LPRINT N$:LPRINT S$:LPRINT C$;" ";ST$,Z$:LPR
INT""
420 PRINT"(A)nother       (M)ain menu ";
430 GOSUB 440:GOTO 460
440 Q$=""+INKEY$:IF Q$="" THEN 440
450 RETURN
460 IF Q$="A" OR Q$="a" THEN RUN 10 ELSE RUN "A:
MENU"
```

Production. This phase begins when the actual fabrication of the product is triggered by receipt of an actual purchase order. The actual start of production may be held up pending approval from the accounting and credit division. If the production activity is physically removed from the shipping center, there may be additional packing and shipping process time involved, as well. On the other hand, if shipments are made from existing stock, production time should not be entered into the computation of delivery date.

Packaging. The time required to pack a product for shipment is included in the processing time only if packing takes place upon or after receipt of a shipping order. If packages are prewrapped, the only time involved in this step is that required to generate and apply a shipping label.

Accounting/Credit Approval. Upon receipt of cash or payment by an approved credit card, a COD agreement shipment of the product should begin promptly. Credit approval is an option, depending on whether or not the business accepts other forms of payment (personal checks) and delays shipment pending bank payment of the check, or otherwise delays shipment pending a credit evaluation and approval.

Shipping Authorization. Some businesses, especially those using the step just above, inject an authorization phase into the shipping process.

Providing the customer with an accurate estimated delivery date is frequently a courtesy extended by the seller in the interests of good customer relations. So long as the estimated delivery date is beyond the actual and normal delivery dates, however, no law exists requiring it be any more accurate.

ESTIMATING VACATION COSTS

Every now and then the urge hits us to take some time off from work and take a vacation. The essential factors that influence the cost of the vacation include: how far you are going, how many people will be traveling, how many days will the vacation last, and what will the costs for fuel, repairs, lodging and food be.

The program in Listing 16-3 helps the would-be traveller forecast the costs likely to result from a specified trip.

EXERCISES

1. The PERT program in Listing 16-1 is a simple program based on the assumption that only one person will be available to perform the tasks of a given project. Write the program to allow for concurrent processing. That is, let the program account for subtasks which can be performed together, and not necessarily consecutively.
2. Modify the Delivery Date routine in Listing 16-2 so that the various outputs are directed to the appropriate devices. That is, enable the program to write shipping labels, invoices, credit memos, and so forth.

Listing 16-3. Trip Costs.

```
1 '*********************************************
2 '*              Listing 16-3               *
3 '*              Trip Costs                 *
4 '*********************************************
5 '
10 CLS:KEY OFF:PRINT"VACATION COST PLANNING":PRI
NT:PRINT
20 INPUT"WHAT IS THE NAME OF YOUR DESTINATION";D
$
30 PRINT"HOW MANY MILES FROM YOUR HOME IS ";D$::
INPUT MD
40 INPUT"WHAT IS YOUR AVERAGE HIGHWAY DRIVING SP
EED";AS
50 INPUT"HOW MANY HOURS DO YOU DRIVE IN ONE DAY"
;HD
60 INPUT"HOW MANY PEOPLE WILL BE TRAVELING";NT
70 DT=(2*MD)/(HD*AS):PRINT"IT WILL TAKE APPROXIM
ATELY";DT;"DAYS TO TRAVEL TO ";D$;" AND RETURN":
INPUT"HOW MANY DAYS DO YOU PLAN TO STAY THERE";D
S
80 TD=DT+DS:INPUT"WHAT IS THE AVERAGE MOTEL COST
 YOU NORMALLY PAY";AM
90 IF (DT-1)<=0 THEN 110
100 NM=DT-1:PRINT"YOUR TRAVEL TIME INCLUDES AT L
EAST";INT(NM)+1;"OVERNIGHT STOPS.   WILL YOU STAY
 IN MOTELS BOTH NIGHTS?  (Y/N)   "
110 Q$=""+INKEY$:IF Q$="" THEN 110 ELSE IF Q$="Y
" OR Q$="y" THEN 130
120 INPUT"NUMBER OF NIGHTS IN MOTELS DURING TRIP
";NM
130 PRINT"HOW MANY NIGHTS WILL YOU SPEND IN A MO
TEL AT ";D$,:INPUT X:NM=NM+X
140 C$="$$#####.##"
150 MC=NM*AM:PRINT"MOTEL COST = $ ";USING C$;MC:
INPUT"WHAT DO YOU ESTIMATE TO BE THE AVERAGE COS
T PER PERSON FOR FOOD";FC:TF=FC*NT*TD:PRINT"FOOD
 COST = $ ";USING C$;TF
160 INPUT"WHAT WHAT IS THE MINIMUM NUMBER OF MIL
ES PER GALLON YOUR CAR GETS";MM
170 INPUT"WHAT IS THE BEST MILEAGE YOU CAN HOPE
FOR";XM
180 INPUT"WHAT IS THE CHEAPEST PER GALLON PRICE
FOR GAS";CP
190 INPUT"WHAT IS THE WORST PRICE FOR GAS";WP
200 G1=CP*((2*MD)/XM):G2=WP*((2*MD)/MM)
210 PRINT"YOUR FUEL COST WILL BE SOMEWHERE BETWE
EN $";G1;"AND $";G2
220 PRINT:PRINT"THE TOTAL COST OF YOUR TRIP WILL
 BE FROM $";G1+TF+MC;"TO $";G2+TF+MC
230 PRINT"(A)nother        (M)ain menu ";
240 GOSUB 250:GOTO 270
250 Q$=""+INKEY$:IF Q$="" THEN 250
260 RETURN
270 IF Q$="A" OR Q$="a" THEN RUN 10 ELSE RUN "A:
MENU"
```

3. The program in Listing 16-3 is for a vacation using an automobile. Modify the program for travel by land, sea, or air modes.

SUGGESTED READING

Martino, R. L., 1964. *Project Management and Control, Volume I: Finding the Critical Path*. New York: American Management Association.

Stires, D. M. and R. P. Wenig, 1965. *Concept-Principles-Application: PERT/COST for the New DOD and NASA Requirements*. Boston: Industrial Education Institute.

Chapter 17

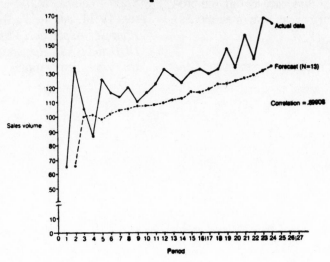

Data Displays

The finest piece of forecasting is of little use if the results cannot be communicated to the user of the information. Whether the user is the forecaster, a supervisor, a work associate, or a paying customer, the relevant data must be displayed in a clear and persuasive manner. Ideally, from an appropriate display of the data, the user should be able to come to the same conclusions that the forecaster has reached.

Data may be displayed in one of two formats: tabular and graphic. In tabular presentations, the data are placed into some sort of arrangement or table in their numeric form. In graphic representation, the data are converted into lines, curves, symbols, or divided into pie charts and so forth. Which form to be used is a function of the objective to be served by the display. The main function of tabular formats is to provide a source of precise and actual data for reference purposes and for the construction of special-purpose tables and charts or graphics. On the other hand, graphic displays are generally used to convey a sense of relationships, relative quantities, or trends. There are some standard con-

siderations in the development of both tables and graphics.

TABLE CONSTRUCTION

There are both general- and special-purpose tables. In general-purpose tables, the data should be precisely stated. That is, to the extent that it is practical, the data should not be rounded off or converted to percentages. The data should be presented in such a way as to facilitate its use as a research device. In special-purpose tables, the data may be manipulated and modified (converted to percentages or rounded off) so that specific relationships are highlighted.

In the construction of tables, certain conventions are generally observed. Among these are inclusion of the title and source, the arrangement of data, the use of rows and columns, the presentation of totals and means, and the units of measurement.

Title. All tables should have a title or caption. The title should be as brief as possible, yet clearly tell what the table contains. It must indicate the nature of the data being displayed. If the data are time-dependent (e.g., 1980 Election Results), the title should include the time domain involved. If the data are from a particular geographic region, the title should include that as well; for example, 1980 New York City Mayoral Election Results.

Source. Except for originally generated data, the table should include a note concerning the source of the data. This serves to give the table authenticity, permits the reader to independently verify the data, and serves as a guide to additional data. In researching data, be careful to observe whether the actual data are copyrighted. Weather reports, for example, are frequently copyrighted by the newspaper in which they are published; yet the actual data are not copyrighted.

Arrangement of Data. There are a number of ways data may be displayed in a table. We may arrange data in alphabetic order, numerical order, chronological order, according to geographic location, or some other convention. Again, the selection of the particular arrangement is a function of the purpose of the table.

Rows and Columns. Where there are two or more rows or columns, they should be identified by labels, numbers, or letters. Both columns and rows should have captions or labels identifying the nature of the data in the respective row or column.

Totals and Means. Column totals are normally shown at the bottom of the respective columns, while row totals are normally shown at the far right. If appropriate, the total may be divided by the number of items to compute and display the means. In those tables designed to contrast individual values with the table column or row totals, the total may be placed at the top of the column or, in an ordered listing, at the point where the total relates to the components.

Units of Measurement. It is essential to include on the table the units in which the data will appear. The scale of the units should be appropriate to the display, using conventional units of measurement.

GRAPHICS CONSTRUCTION

To the extent they are appropriate, the rules given, particularly those concerning the title, source, and units of measurement, also apply to graphics. In addition, line or bar graphs (charts using X and Y axis formats) must indicate the relevant zero point. For example, in a chart showing the price of gold over the last one hundred years, the horizontal axis may begin with the first year of the data set without showing the year 0, but the vertical scale, the price of gold, must show the zero point. In those cases in which the actual data tend to cluster about a fairly high point above zero, it is allowable to break the vertical axis to indicate the truncation of the chart.

The second consideration in this type of chart is whether to use linear or logarithmic scale intervals. When the data range across several orders of magnitude (powers of ten) it may be convenient, if not absolutely necessary, to use a logarithmic scale. Logarithmic scales are also useful in displaying data that vary exponentially because lines that are normally curved on a linear scale tend to become straight lines on a logarithmic scale. The use of this phenomenon requires a sense of responsibility on the part of the graphic designer, however—misuse of either the linear or the logarithmic scale can distort the true meaning or significance of the data.

Pie Chart

Another form frequently used is a pie chart or area chart in which the components of the total sum are illustrated as section of a geometric shape. The program in Listing 17-1 is a simple routine to build a pie chart from a set of data.

Listing 17-2 is the routine used in many of the programs in this text to display numerical data in ''line chart'' form. Since there are a number of different screen formats, it contains a module used to query the user for screen parameters. For your own use, simply enter the values that describe your system and delete the irrelevent sections of the program.

The program reviews the input data to determine the largest and smallest values, then computes the location of the zero X and Y axis lines, and scales of all the data points to fit within the limits of the screen. The quickest way to save an image of the screen on paper is, of course, the print screen func-

Listing 17-1. Pie Chart.

```
1  '**********************************************
2  '*              Listing 17-1                  *
3  '*               Pie Chart                    *
4  '**********************************************
5  '
10 CLS
20 GOSUB 500
30 PRINT"PIE CHART GENERATOR":PRINT:PRINT
40 INPUT"HOW MANY COMPONENTS ARE THERE TO THE CH
ART (N <= 26)";N:IF N<27 THEN 60
50 PRINT"SORRY, N MUST BE <= 27":PRINT:GOTO 40
60 DIM P(N)
70 FOR I=1 TO N
80 PRINT"ENTER THE AMOUNT OF PORTION #";I,:INPUT
 P(I):T=T+P(I)
90 NEXT
100 CLS:PRINT"THANK YOU":PRINT
110 FOR I=1 TO N:PRINT I;P(I),:NEXT:PRINT
120 PRINT"TOTAL = ";T,"",
130 PRINT"ARE THESE ALL CORRECT?  (Y/N)";
140 Q$=""+INKEY$:IF Q$="" THEN 140
150 IF Q$="Y" OR Q$="y" THEN 170
160 PRINT:PRINT:INPUT"ENTER ITEM NUMBER AND CORR
ECT VALUE";X,Y:T=T-P(X):P(X)=Y:T=T+Y:GOTO 100
170 CLS:KEY OFF:SCREEN SC
180 RD=2*3.141593
190 CX=XX/2:CY=YY/2:R=.9*CY
200 P1=0:P2=(P(1)/T)*RD
210 CIRCLE (CX,CY),R,1,-.00001,-P2
220 X=CX+((R/2)*COS(P2/2)):Y=CY-((R/2)*SIN(P2/2)
)
230 LOCATE Y/YC,X/XC:PRINT"A";
240 P1=P2
250 FOR I=2 TO N
260    P2=P1+(P(I)/T)*RD
270    IF P2>RD THEN P2=RD
280    TH=P1+((P2-P1)/2)
290    CIRCLE (CX,CY),R,1,-P1,-P2:P1=P2
300    X=CX+((R/2)*COS(TH)):Y=CY-((R/2)*SIN(TH))
310    LOCATE INT(Y/YC),INT(X/XC):PRINT CHR$(I+64
);
320    P1=P2
330 NEXT
340 LOCATE 1,1:PRINT"(P)RINT DATA    (N)EW DATA
 (M)AIN MENU";
350 Q$=""+INKEY$:IF Q$="" THEN 350
360 PRINT Q$;:IF Q$="P" OR Q$="p" THEN 380 ELSE
IF Q$="M" OR Q$="m" THEN RUN "A:MENU"
370 RUN
380 FOR R=3 TO 44
390 FOR C=0 TO 127
400 IF POINT(C,R) THEN LPRINT"*"; ELSE LPRINT" "
;
410 NEXT C
420 LPRINT""
430 NEXT R
```

```
440 LPRINT"SEGMENT","VALUE","FRACTION OF WHOLE"
450 FOR I=1 TO N
460 LPRINT CHR$(I+64),P(I),P(I)/T
470 NEXT
480 LPRINT""
490 GOTO 590
500 CLS
510 PRINT"1  --  320 X 200    2  --  640 X 200
   3  --  640 X 400 "
520 PRINT:PRINT"Indicate screen dimensions ";
530 Q$=""+INKEY$:IF Q$="" THEN 530
540 IF Q$<"1" OR Q$>"3" THEN 530
550 ON VAL(Q$) GOTO 560, 570, 580
560 XX=320:YY=200:SC=1:XL=39:ZY=8:ZX=4:XC=8:YC=8
:YX=8:RETURN
570 XX=640:YY=200:XL=39:SC=2:ZY=8:ZX=8:XC=8:YC=8
:RETURN
580 XX=640:YY=400:SC=100:XL=79:ZY=16:ZX=8:XC=8:Y
C=16:RETURN
590 PRINT"(A)nother          (M)ain menu ";
600 Q$=""+INKEY$:IF Q$="" THEN 600
610 IF Q$="A" OR Q$="a" THEN RUN 10 ELSE RUN "A:
MENU"
620 ZAG%=INT(ZOG%/64):ZOG%=ZOG%-64*ZAG%+1:ZAG%=Z
AG%+1:                            LOCATE ZAG%,
ZOG%:RETURN
```

Listing 17-2. Data Display Subprogram.

```
1 '********************************************
2 '*                Listing 17-2              *
3 '*          Data Display Subprogram         *
4 '********************************************
5 '
10 'DATA DISPLAY
20 'DETERMINE LARGEST AND SMALLEST VALUES
30 FOR I=1 TO N
40   IF X(I)=>SX THEN 60
50   SX=X(I):GOTO 80
60   IF X(I)<=LX THEN 80
70   LX=X(I)
80   IF Y(I)=>SY THEN 100
90   SY=Y(I):GOTO 120
100  IF Y(I)<=LY THEN 120
110  LY=Y(I)
120 NEXT I
130 GOSUB 400:SCREEN SC
140 CLS
150 D=INT(LOG(LX)/2.302585)+1        ' DETERMINE LE
NGTH OF NUMBER
160 XA=INT(.1328*XX):YA=INT(.7875*YY):XB=XX-XA
       ' SET LEFT AND BOTTOM BOUNDARIES
170 RX=LX-SX:RY=LY-SY                  ' COMPUTE RANGE
180 LINE(XA,1)-(XA,YA):LINE(XA,YA)-(XX,YA)        '
 DRAW BOUNDARY
190 ' COMPUTE AND DRAW INTERVAL MARKERS
200 FOR I=1 TO 9:LINE(XA-2,(I*(YA/10))-1)-(XA,(I
```

Listing 17-2. Data Display Subprogram. (Continued From Page 333.)

```
*(YA/10))-1):NEXT
210 FOR I=1 TO 9:LINE(XA+(I*((XX-XA)/10)-1),YA+2
)-(XA+(I*((XX-XA)/10)-1),YA):NEXT
220 ' COMPUTE AND DRAW ZERO AXIS LINES
230 IF LX=<0 THEN X0=XX ELSE X0=XX-(INT((XX-XA)*
(LX/RX)))
240 IF LY=<0 THEN Y0=1 ELSE Y0=INT(YA*(LY/RY))
250 X1=X0:X2=X1:Y1=1:Y2=YA:LINE (X1,Y1)-(X2,Y2)
260 X1=XA:X2=XX:Y1=Y0:Y2=Y1:LINE (X1,Y1)-(X2,Y2)
270 ' PRINT SCALE VALUES
280 LOCATE 1,(XA/8)-4:PRINT LY;:LOCATE 20,(XA/8)
-4:PRINT SY;:LOCATE 21,(XA/8)-1:PRINT SX;:LOCATE
 21,(XX/8)-(D+2):PRINT INT(LX);:LOCATE (Y0/ZY)+1
,(XA/8)-3):PRINT 0;:LOCATE (YA/ZY)+1,X0/8:PRINT
0;
290 ' DISPLAY LOCATION OF ACTUAL DATA ON SCALE
300 FOR I=1 TO P:X1=XA+INT(XB*((XX(I)-SX)/RX))+1
:Y1=INT(YA-(YA*((YY(I)-SY)/RY))):PSET(X1,Y1):NEX
T I
310 'PLOT PROJECTED DATA
320 IF SX=>0 AND SY=>0 THEN 330
330 FOR I=1 TO LX
340    X1=XA+INT(XB*((I-SX)/RX))+1
350    X=I:ON M GOSUB ' enter source of actual da
ta here
360    Y1=INT(YA-(YA*((Y-SY)/RY)))
370    PSET(X1,Y1)
380 NEXT I
390 LOCATE 24,1:INPUT"Use PrtScrn to save Graph,
<CR> to Continue";XX:RETURN
400 CLS
410 PRINT"1  --  320 X 200    2  --  640 X 200
  3  --  640 X 400 "
420 PRINT:PRINT"Indicate screen dimensions ";
430 Q$=""+INKEY$:IF Q$="" THEN 430
440 IF Q$<"1" OR Q$>"3" THEN 430
450 ON VAL(Q$) GOTO 460, 470, 480
460 XX=320:YY=200:SC=1:XL=39:ZY=8:ZX=4:RETURN
470 XX=640:YY=200:XL=39:SC=2:ZY=8:ZX=8:RETURN
480 XX=640:YY=400:SC=100:XL=79:ZY=16:ZX=8:RETURN
```

tion. For a more elegant printed copy, you will need to write a subroutine that either replicates the screen graphics procedure for the printer, or scans a portion of the screen. In the original version of this program for the first edition, the program scanned each of the 6144 pixels on the TRS-80 monitor and printed an asterisk wherever it found an "on" pixel. At medium-high resolution (620 × 200), this would require checking the status of up to 128,000 pixels— quite a time-consuming process—and was not considered very practical. If quality printed graphic representations are required, it is probably better and easier to write a specific routine for your system and your printer/plotter configuration than it would be to try to make the screen output the printer source.

EXERCISES

1. Review a copy of the *Statistical Abstract of the United States*. (If it is not in your library, it is for sale through the Government Printing Office, Washington, D.C.) Note

the number of tables and charts that conform to the rules in this chapter. Note the number that don't. What reason would the chart designer have for deviating from the basic guides?

2. In the same book, note the tables on population estimates. One principle in table construction is that the intervals remain constant. What advantage or purpose does the table designer achieve by using several different intervals?

3. Using the data in the population forecasts of the *Abstract*, write a table showing the population forecast for the year 2000 in age group intervals of exactly five years each.

SUGGESTED READING

Enrick, N. L., 1972. *Effective Graphic Communication*. Princeton, NJ: Auerbach.

Hall, A. S., 1958. *The Construction of Graphs and Charts*. London: Pitman.

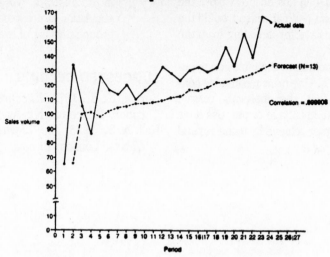

Decision-Making
Based on Forecasts

We've come full circle. We began this book on the premises that forecasting is as much an art as a science and that the reader was equipped with a microcomputer and ambition. We shared some of our philosophy concerning prognostication, and then led the reader through the underlying fundamentals of computer database management and the essential mathematical procedures and relationships. Then, we wandered our way through eight chapters of specialized forecasting techniques. Now, several hundred pages and ninety programs later, we've come to mankind's greatest question: What's it all about? Having developed the means to do forecasting, what do we do with the skill?

The first answer is that we share our forecasts with others. A lot of people make a nice living collecting data, chomping it up in a forecasting routine, and then selling the results to their customers. Many of these are doing market research or political surveys. The costs of running a political campaign being what they are, an interesting activity for many of you would be to approach a local politician and of-

fer your research skills for the next campaign. Design a survey and collect the data. Process it and deliver the product to the client. You might want to offer your first effort gratis or for expenses. If you find the experience rewarding and successful, go ahead, do it again. The better and more confident you become, the more you should charge. But that's not decision-making. The decision-making is done by your client.

Your client should know that all forecasts are characterized by two realities:

—No forecast is a mandate for the future.
—All forecasts contain a margin of error.

Because of these realities, good forecasts should make note of the margin of error to be expected and include encouragement to accept that margin as a reality. If the client is unable to accept the margin of error, the alternative is to make a decision based on some other criterion. Sometimes this is smart and necessary, sometimes it isn't. The political candidate whose conscientious researcher has, over the period of the campaign, selected reliable samples, performed an appropriate set of analysis routines, and come to the conclusion that the candidate will not pull in twenty percent of the vote, should be listened to. On the other hand, we can push the stock market data for a whole year through our computer and conclude that the market will hit a daily average of 1100 for the next week. Nonetheless, a seasoned market analysis, while agreeing with our mathematics, may conclude that the market will plunge to 800 or below next week. Such decisions are often based on a multitude of factors which affect the stock market that are very difficult to process in a computer. Even sophisticated stock market simulation routines frequently fail to include all the relevant factors.

Well, what good are they, then? Forecasts provide data or estimates of data where the data are not otherwise available. They help us interpolate between the known and unknown. If we have some other, firm basis for "knowing" what the future will be, forecasting is an inappropriate use of time. If, for example, we are present when the Federal Reserve Board decides to drop (or raise) the interest rate five percent, we don't need a forecast based on open market data to know what the market will do after the Board decision is announced. Few of us, however, are blessed with such access.

This book was not written to provide answers to those whose personal or professional background and experiences better equip them to gauge future events than someone simply manipulating available data. Instead, it was written to aid the individual who has come to the point where intuition and professional judgment are leading to unsatisfactory conclusions—except for the conclusion that some other approach, such as microcomputer forecasting, might provide better answers.

The balance of this chapter attempts to provide some techniques one can use to evaluate forecast data and use the microcomputer to reach rational decisions. We concern ourselves, first, with the measurement of error, and then turn our attention to four approaches to decision-making.

MEASUREMENT OF ERROR

Standard error is a useful technique in estimating the extent to which reality might deviate from our prediction. For example, during the 1982 elections, one of the national television broadcasting networks announced that their prediction indicated that 34 of the Democratic candidates for Congress would win seats in the House. In the same breath, they admitted that there was a standard estimate of error of plus or minus 9. As of the writing of this chapter, the actual result was 26 seats won by Democrats, an error of 8, reasonably well within the computed standard error. Also keep in mind that the standard error, like the standard deviation, is not the whole spectrum but merely a fraction of it. The example above means that there is slightly better than a 68 percent chance that the outcome would be a certain value, plus or minus 9. It also means there is a 98 percent chance the outcome will be the mean value, plus or minus 18!

Some of the primary estimates of error include those for the sum, mean median, standard deviation, and coefficient of correlation.

Standard Error of a Sum

The standard error for a sum is particularly useful for large sets of numbers that have been added by hand. If n quantities are selected at random from an infinite population and added up, we can compute the sum and the standard deviation. From these statistics we can conclude that the sum (T) of any n items from the same data base will be equal to the computed sum plus or minus the standard error. The equation to compute this value is:

$$s = \sigma/\sqrt{n}$$

Standard Error of a Mean

In addition to computing a sum and the standard deviation of a set of numbers, we can also compute the mean of the set from $M = T/n$. The standard error of this mean can be computed from:

$$s = \sigma/\sqrt{n}$$

Standard Error of a Median

We first encountered the median of a distribution in Chapter 2. In normal distributions, the mean and median are expected to be the same value. However, as the distribution becomes more and more skewed to one direction or another, the mean value will shift significantly away from the median. Nonetheless, the computation of the standard error of a median is quite simple: compute the standard error of the mean as shown above, and then multiply that value by 1.2533:

$$1.2533 \; (\sigma/\sqrt{n})$$

Standard Error of a Standard Deviation

More often than not, our statistical work involves sampling from a large population. We know that if we could interview or examine every member of a population we could, among other things, compute the standard deviation of a characteristic of that population. If we use, instead, a sampling from that population, we can compute the standard deviation of the sample, and can estimate the true population standard deviation from:

$$s = \sigma/\sqrt{2n}$$

It is not necessary to compute the standard error for every value we use in our work. We should compute it, however, for those concluding values upon which our decision-maker will relay for final judgment. In all fairness, that person must know the chances for failure as well as for success.

DECISION-MAKING TECHNIQUES

Deciding what to do with forecast data can often be as tedious and time-consuming as the forecasting process itself. If the data are fairly straightforward and *univariate* (having only one independent variable), the process is not so difficult. If the forecast is univariate and suggests that the price of a stock or a commodity will be such and such at a given point in time, the user has to decide on the reliability of the forecast, and then decide whether the reliability is sufficient to act on the information.

Multivariate data, on the other hand, don't always resolve themselves so neatly. We offer here two routines to use with multivariate forecast data. The first is known as the Multivariate Evaluator and is based on a standard industrial procedure for the evaluation of several options against a number of criteria by several decision-makers. The second is simply called the Decision-Maker and is designed for use by one person and attempts to facilitate a rational decision-making process, eliminating as much personal bias as possible.

Multivariate Evaluator

This approach is most easily described by an example. Four neighbors, John, Sam, Joe, and Pete, decide to pool their money and purchase a car or van to share. After some research, each of the men nominates one or two vehicles for consideration. These include a Ford, A Chevrolet, a Chrysler, a Mercury, and a Lincoln. After some discussion, the five men decide on four characteristics of the cars to use for evaluation. These include price, economy of operation, styling, and maximum speed performance. As a final measure, the decision is made that the car will be used for five functions: shopping, hunting, camping, transportation to work, and recreational travel other than for hunting or camping.

The cars all range from around $11,000. The cash contribution from each man is:

John	$1,000
Sam	2,000
Joe	3,000
Pete	5,000

The men will decide to allocate votes among themselves according to the actual cash contribution.

On this basis, the men polled themselves on the relative importance of the different functions the vehicle is expected to perform. They used a rating scheme in which the most valuable function is rated an "8" and the least is rated "1." The votes for each of the functions are shown in Table 18-1.

The first step in the multivariate analysis process is to convert the voting strengths into

Table 18-1. Initial Votes for Missions.

Owner	Votes	Missions				
		Shopping	Hunting	Camping	Work	Travel
John	1	5	8	3	1	2
Sam	2	8	3	5	2	1
Joe	3	5	3	2	8	1
Pete	5	3	1	2	5	8

weighted factors so that the total of the factors is 1.00. The easiest way to do this is to total the votes and then compute each man's vote as a percentage of the total. In a similar fashion, each of the ratings in the table matrix is converted into a percentage of the row totals. The final step in this first stage is to multiply the voter's vote weight times the matrix percentage value. Table 18-2 gives the results of this operation. The column totals under each function give an estimate of the relative importance the owners attach to the function.

The second stage is to evaluate the alternatives against the stated criteria. This step is not nearly as subjective as the first. In this example, the comparisons can be readily made from published price and performance data. Table 18-3 shows the actual results of the first step in this stage. The only subjective factors are the weights assigned, by the owners, to the criterion factors. The remaining matrix values were computed from published data. Table 18-4 illustrates the results of the matrix multiplications of the weights converted to percen-

tages. An adjustment is made so that the column totals for the alternatives total unity.

The data shown in Table 18-5 were computed by multiplying the column totals from Table 18-3 times the column totals in Table 18-4. A comparison of the row total leads us to a conclusion on the most desirable option. In this example, the Mercury ended up with a desirability factor of .258, higher than any of the others. If everything has been entered properly and the raters have been fair and objective, the Mercury should be the most satisfying purchase.

Although not included in this analysis, it is quite possible to include another evaluation routine in which the owners/raters allocate the criterion weights in the same fashion they determine the function weights.

Listing 18-1 implements the procedures just described. The particular layout of the data was selected solely for the purposes of illustrating the routine. There is no reason to limit your version of the program to this 4 × 5 matrix.

Table 18-2. Votes for Missions Computed for Weighting.

```
                    *            SUB-FUNCTIONS
NAME     WEIGHT     *  SHOPPI  HUNTIN  CAMPIN  WORK    TRAVEL
*********************************************************************
JOHN     0.0909     *  0.0239  0.0383  0.0144  0.0048  0.0096
SAM      0.1818     *  0.0766  0.0287  0.0478  0.0191  0.0096
JOE      0.2727     *  0.0718  0.0431  0.0287  0.1148  0.0144
PETE     0.4545     *  0.0718  0.0239  0.0478  0.1196  0.1914
*********************************************************************
TOTAL    1.0000     *  0.2440  0.1340  0.1388  0.2584  0.2249
```

Table 18-3. Votes for Criteria and Alternatives.

			Alternatives			
Criterion	Weight	Ford	Chevrolet	Chrysler	Mercury	Lincoln
Speed	2	2	3	1	8	5
Style	4	1	2	3	5	8
Economy	6	8	5	3	2	1
Price	8	5	8	3	1	2

Table 18-4. Votes for Criteria and Alternatives Computed for Weighting.

		*		ALTERNATIVES		
CRIT.	WEIGHT	* FORD	CHEVRO	CHRYSL	MERCUR	LINCOL
SPEED	0.1000	* 0.0105	0.0158	0.0053	0.0421	0.0263
STYLE	0.2000	* 0.0053	0.0105	0.0158	0.0263	0.0421
ECONOM	0.3000	* 0.0421	0.0263	0.0158	0.0105	0.0053
PRICE	0.4000	* 0.0263	0.0421	0.0158	0.0053	0.0105
TOTAL	1.0000	* 0.0842	0.0947	0.0526	0.0842	0.0842
ADJUST	1.0000	0.2105	0.2368	0.1316	0.2105	0.2105

Table 18-5. Final Analysis Results.

		*		MISSIONS				
ALTER.	WEIGHT	* SHOPPI	HUNTIN	CAMPIN	WORK	TRAVEL	SUM
FORD	0.2105	* 0.0514	0.0578	0.0321	0.0514	0.0514	0.244
CHEVRO	0.2368	* 0.0282	0.0317	0.0176	0.0282	0.0282	0.134
CHRYSL	0.1316	* 0.0292	0.0329	0.0183	0.0292	0.0292	0.139
MECUR	0.2105	* 0.0544	0.0612	0.0340	0.0544	0.0544	0.258
LINCOL	0.2105	* 0.0473	0.0533	0.0296	0.0473	0.0473	0.225
TOTAL	1.0000	* 0.2105	0.2368	0.1316	0.2105	0.2105	

Decision-Maker

If you've ever been confronted with several options from which you have to make a choice and have been more or less overwhelmed by the alternatives and the related factors, Listing 18-2 is for you. It won't make decisions for you, but it will provide a logical structure in which to evaluate each option, then let you know what the score is. The basic form of the program works like this. It begins by assuming that whatever your options are, you are applying some set of criteria against them. The first step of the program asks you to state what these criteria are. The next assumption is that among these criteria some are more important to you than others; therefore, the second step presents each of the criteria to you, paired with each of the other criteria.

Listing 18-1. Multivariate Evaluator.

```
1 '**********************************************
2 '*                Listing 18-1                *
3 '*           Multivariate Evaluator           *
4 '**********************************************
5 '
10 CLEAR 400
20 GOSUB 850
30 SCREEN SC
40 KEY OFF
50 PRINT"MULTIVARIATE EVALUATOR":PRINT:PRINT
60 FOR I=1 TO 4
70 PRINT"NAME OF DECISION-MAKER #";I,:INPUT N$:D
$(I)=LEFT$(N$,6)
80 PRINT"VOTING STRENGTH OF ";D$(I),:INPUT V(I):
SV=SV+V(I)
90 NEXT
100 FOR I=1 TO 4:WV(I)=V(I)/SV:NEXT
110 FOR I=1 TO 5
120 PRINT"NAME OF MISSION #";I,:INPUT N$:M$(I)=L
EFT$(N$,6)
130 NEXT
140 FOR I=1 TO 4
150 PRINT"WHAT IS ";D$(I);"'S VOTE FOR:"
160 FOR J=1 TO 5
170 PRINT"     ";M$(J),:INPUT MV(I,J):TV=TV+MV(I
,J)
180 NEXT J
190 FOR J=1 TO 5:WM(I,J)=MV(I,J)/TV:NEXT:TV=0
200 NEXT I
210 CLS:PRINT"                              SUB-F
UNCTIONS"
220 FOR I=1 TO 4:FOR J=1 TO 5:M(I,J)=WV(I)*WM(I,
J):CT(J)=CT(J)+M(I,J):NEXT J:NEXT I
230 B$="\    \  \    \    \     \    \        \\
  \\    \  \      \"
240 PRINT USING B$;"NAME";"WEIGHT";M$(1);M$(2);M
$(3);M$(4);M$(5)
250 GOSUB 840
260 A$="\     \  #.####    #.####  #.####  #.####
  #.####  #.####"
270 FOR I=1 TO 4
280 LOCATE 4+I,1:PRINT USING A$;D$(I);WV(I);M(I,
1);M(I,2);M(I,3);M(I,4);M(I,5)
290 NEXT
300 LOCATE 5+I,1:PRINT USING A$;"TOTAL";1;CT(1);
CT(2);CT(3);CT(4);CT(5)
310 GOSUB 830
320 GOSUB 820
330 FOR I=1 TO 5
340 PRINT"NAME OF ALTERNATIVE #";I,:INPUT N$:A$(
I)=LEFT$(N$,6)
350 NEXT
360 FOR I=1 TO 4
370 PRINT"NAME OF CRITERION #";I,:INPUT N$:C$(I)
=LEFT$(N$,6)
380 PRINT"CRITERION WEIGHT OF ";C$(I),:INPUT CW(
```

341

Listing 18-1. Multivariate Evaluator. (Continued From Page 341.)

```
I):TC=TC+CW(I)
390 NEXT
400 FOR I=1 TO 4:WC(I)=CW(I)/TC:NEXT
410 FOR I=1 TO 4
420 PRINT"CONSIDERING ";C$(I);", WHAT IS THE VAL
UE OF:"
430 FOR J=1 TO 5
440 PRINT"      ";A$(J),:INPUT CV(I,J):VC=VC+CV(I
,J)
450 NEXT J
460 FOR J=1 TO 5:AM(I,J)=CV(I,J)/VC:NEXT J
470 NEXT I
480 CLS:PRINT"                          ALTE
RNATIVES"
490 FOR I=1 TO 5:FOR J=1 TO 5:AM(I,J)=AM(I,J)*WC
(I):CC(J)=CC(J)+AM(I,J):NEXT J:NEXT I
500 PRINT USING B$;"CRIT.";"WEIGHT";A$(1);A$(2);
A$(3);A$(4);A$(5)
510 GOSUB 840
520 FOR I=1 TO 4
530 LOCATE 4+I,1:PRINT USING A$;C$(I);WC(I);AM(I
,1);AM(I,2);AM(I,3);AM(I,4);AM(I,5)
540 NEXT
550 LOCATE 10,1:PRINT"";USING A$;"TOTAL";1;CC(1)
;CC(2);CC(3);CC(4);CC(5)
560 FOR I=1 TO 5:XX=XX+CC(I):NEXT
570 FOR I=1 TO 5:CC(I)=CC(I)/XX:NEXT
580 LOCATE 11,1:PRINT"";USING A$;"ADJUST.";1;CC(
1);CC(2);CC(3);CC(4);CC(5)
590 GOSUB 830
600 GOSUB 820
610 FOR I=1 TO 5
620 FOR J=1 TO 5
630 M(I,J)=CT(I)*CC(J):TR(I)=TR(I)+M(I,J):TC(J)=
TC(J)+M(I,J)
640 NEXT J
650 NEXT I
660 CLS:PRINT"                          MISSI
ONS"
670 PRINT USING B$;"ALTER.";"WEIGHT";M$(1);M$(2)
;M$(3);M$(4);M$(5);:PRINT"SUM"
680 GOSUB 840
690 FOR I=1 TO 5
700 LOCATE 4+I,1:PRINT USING A$;A$(I);CC(I);M(I,
1);M(I,2);M(I,3);M(I,4);M(I,5);:PRINT USING"   #
.###";TR(I);
710 NEXT
720 LOCATE 10,1:PRINT"";USING A$;"TOTAL";1;TC(1)
;TC(2);TC(3);TC(4);TC(5);
730 GOSUB 830
740 GOSUB 820
750 FOR I=1 TO 5
760 IF TR(I)<LG THEN 780
770 LG=TR(I):L=I
780 NEXT I
790 PRINT"":PRINT"BEST OPTION APPEARS TO BE ";A$
```

```
(L):PRINT""
800 GOTO 940
810 END
820 LOCATE 22,1:INPUT "Use PrtSc to save these d
ata.  <CR> to continue ";ZZ:RETURN
830 LINE (1,YY*.4681)-(XX,YY*.4681):LINE (XX*.2,
1)-(XX*.2,YY*.5532):RETURN
840 LINE (1,YY*.1277)-(XX,YY*.1277):RETURN
850 CLS
860 PRINT"1  --   320 X 200    2  --   640 X 200
   3  --   640 X 400 "
870 PRINT:PRINT"Indicate screen dimensions ";
880 Q$=""+INKEY$:IF Q$="" THEN 880
890 IF Q$<"1" OR Q$>"3" THEN 880
900 ON VAL(Q$) GOTO 910, 920, 930
910 XX=320:YY=200:SC=1:XL=39:ZY=8:ZX=4:RETURN
920 XX=640:YY=200:XL=39:SC=2:ZY=8:ZX=8:RETURN
930 XX=640:YY=400:SC=100:XL=79:ZY=16:ZX=8:RETURN
940 PRINT"(A)nother        (M)ain menu ";
950 Q$=""+INKEY$:IF Q$="" THEN 950
960 IF Q$="A" OR Q$="a" THEN RUN 10 ELSE RUN "A:
MENU"
```

Listing 18-2. Decision-Maker.

```
1 '*********************************************
2 '*                Listing 18-2               *
3 '*               Decision-Maker              *
4 '*********************************************
5 '
10 CLS:PRINT "****  DECISION-MAKER  ****":PRINT:
PRINT
20 PRINT"THIS ROUTINE ENABLES THE USER TO ENTER
A SET OF CRITERIA AGAINST WHICH A SET OF OPTIONS
 OR ALTERNATIVES MAY BE EVALUATED.  AT THIS POIN
T, PREPARE A LIST OF THE AVAILABLE ALTERNATIVES,
 A ";
30 PRINT"LIST OF THE CRITERIA THAT APPLY, AND TH
E RELATED DATA."
40 PRINT:PRINT"WHEN READY, TOUCH ANY KEY.";
50 Q$=""+INKEY$:IF Q$="" THEN 50
60 CLS:CLEAR 1000
70 INPUT"HOW MANY OPTIONS ARE THERE TO BE EVALUA
TED";V:DIM V$(V),Q(V),QQ(V):PRINT:FOR I=1 TO V:P
RINT"NAME OF OPTION #";I,:INPUT V$(I):NEXT
80 PRINT:INPUT"HOW MANY CRITERIA ARE THERE";F:A=
(F*(F-1))/2:DIM F$(F),C(F,F),S(F):PRINT:FOR I=1
TO F:PRINT"ENTER CRITERION NAME #";I,:INPUT F$(I
):NEXT
90 FOR I=1 TO F:S(I)=1:NEXT
100 FOR I=1 TO F-1
110 FOR J=I+1 TO F
120 CLS:LOCATE 7,1:PRINT"";:PRINT I,F$(I):PRINT
J,F$(J):PRINT:PRINT"ENTER NUMBER OF MORE IMPORTA
NT CRITERION:";
130 N$=""+INKEY$:IF N$="" THEN 130 ELSE N=VAL(N$
)
140 IF N<>I AND N<>J THEN 130
```

343

Listing 18-2. Decision-Maker. (Continued From Page 343.)

```
150 C(I,J)=N:S(N)=S(N)+1
160 NEXT J
170 NEXT I
180 CLS:PRINT"LIST OF PRIORITIES":PRINT:PRINT"CR
ITERIA","","SCORE","WEIGHT":PRINT""
190 FOR I=F+1 TO 0 STEP -1:FOR J=1 TO F
200 IF S(J)<>I THEN 220
210 PRINT F$(J),"",I,I/(F+1):S(J)=I/(F+1)
220 NEXT:NEXT
230 PRINT:PRINT"ARE THESE CRITERIA IN PROPER PRI
ORITY ORDER? (Y/N)";
240 Q$=""+INKEY$:IF Q$="" THEN 240 ELSE IF Q$="N
" THEN 90
250 FOR I=1 TO V-1:FOR J=I+1 TO V:FOR K=1 TO F
260 CLS:LOCATE 7,1:PRINT"";:PRINT F$(K):PRINT:PR
INT:PRINT"A",V$(I):PRINT"B",V$(J):PRINT:PRINT"EN
TER THE LETTER OF THE OPTION WHICH IS SUPERIOR O
N THIS SCALE",
270 Q$=""+INKEY$:IF Q$="" THEN 270
280 IF Q$<>"A" AND Q$<>"B" THEN 270
290 IF Q$="A" THEN N=I ELSE N=J
300 Q(N)=Q(N)+S(K):IF Q(N)>LG THEN LG=Q(N)
310 NEXT:NEXT:NEXT
320 CLS:PRINT"TABLE OF RESULTS":PRINT"OPTION",""
,"SCORE":PRINT
330 FOR I=LG TO 0 STEP -(1/F):FOR J=1 TO V
340 IF Q(J)<1 THEN 360
350 PRINT V$(J),"",Q(J):Q(J)=-1
360 NEXT:NEXT
370 PRINT:PRINT"ARE THESE RESULTS ACCEPTABLE? (Y
/N)";
380 Q$=""+INKEY$:IF Q$="" THEN 380 ELSE IF Q$="Y
" THEN 410
390 PRINT:PRINT"A -- CRITERIA  B -- OPTIONS":PRI
NT:PRINT"ENTER LETTER OF ELEMENT TO BE ADJUSTED"
;
400 Q$=""+INKEY$:IF Q$="" THEN 400 ELSE IF Q$="A
" OR Q$="a" THEN 90 ELSE 250
410 PRINT"":PRINT"":PRINT"REMEMBER! THE VALUE OF
 THE RANKING OF THE OPTIONS IS A FUNCTION OF:
420 PRINT"      A.   THE COMPREHENSIVENESS OF THE
LIST OF OPTIONS.  BE SURE ALL RELEVENT      OPTION
S ARE CONSIDERED, EVEN THE DISAGREEABLE ONES."
430 PRINT"      B.   THE COMPREHENSIVENESS OF THE
LIST OF CRITERIA."
440 PRINT"      C. THE CANDOR WITH WHICH YOU RESP
OND TO EACH OF THE SUBJECTIVE COMPARISONS."
450 PRINT"      D.   THE ACCURACY OF THE OBJECTIVE
 DATA.  IF YOU ARE DISPLEASED WITH THESE  RESULT
S, IT IS LIKELY THERE IS A PROBLEM WITH ONE OF T
HE ITEMS ABOVE."
460 PRINT"":PRINT""
470 PRINT"(A)nother      (M)ain menu ";
480 Q$=""+INKEY$:IF Q$="" THEN 480
490 IF Q$="A" OR Q$="a" THEN RUN 10 ELSE RUN "A:
MENU"
```

```
Criteria                  Score    Weight

X-factor                    7       .875
Cultural opportunities      6       .75
Communications              4       .5
Climate                     3       .375
Cost of living              3       .375
Recreational facilities     3       .375
Tax rate                    2       .25

Table of results
option                    Score

New York                  6.625
San Francisco             5.875
Chicago                   4.375
Washington                4.125
```

Remember!   The value of the ranking of the options is a function of:
    A. The comprehensiveness of the list of options. Be sure all relevant options are considered, even disagreeable ones.
    B. The comprehensiveness of list of criteria.
    C. The candor with which you respond to each of the subjective comparisons.
    D. The accuracy of the objective data.
If you are displeased with these results, it is likely there is a problem with one of the four items above.

Fig. 18-1. Results of Listing 18-2.

For each pair you are asked to identify which criterion of the pair you consider to be more significant. Once you've completed this phase, the program asks you to identify each of the options available.

The program now shows you three items at a time: a criterion measure and a pair of options. You are asked to choose which of the options is superior to the other in terms of the criterion shown. To the extent that the criterion is a quantifiable variable, this choice should be fairly easy. This process continues until all combinations of the options have been evaluated in terms of each of the criteria. At each step of this process the winning option is scored according to the relative weight of the criterion.

The last phase of the evaluation displays the options in order of their scores, the preferred choice first. If you don't like the result, you can always go back and start over.

The printed output of the program, Fig. 18-1, is based on a run where the objective was to pick a city to live in. The user had been able to narrow the choice of cities down to four. He knew that he could evaluate each of the options on at least six measures: tax rate, climate, cost of living, cultural opportunities (museums, operas, etc.), recreational facilities, and communications. On the first run of the program, the user felt a little dissatisfied with some of the combinations and factors. This was quickly solved by adding a seventh criterion, the "x-factor." Without further definition or any quantification, this allowed the user to score a subjective attitude toward the option pair. It was a way of saying, "all other things being equal, this is *my* vote . . . ."

Appendix A: Menus

There are over one hundred programs or spreadsheets in this text, and better than ninety of the programs are in BASIC. For ease of entry onto your disks, or for reading the TAB version of the software, we assign each program an abbreviated file label. For example, program number three in Chapter Five is found in file C5P3.

To retrieve the files quickly you must know the file label or have some means of identifying the program you want. The two programs that follow do just that. The first program, "Master Menu" (MENU.BAS on the software, Listing A-1), asks for the desired chapter and program number, then runs the specified program. To do this you must know the chapter and program number, or you must look up the program in the book. The second program, Listing A-2, "Expanded Menu" (EXMENU.BAS on the software), lists all the chapter titles, from which you can select the appropriate chapter. The program then shows you the program contents of the chapter, from which you select the desired program. The program loads the selected file for you.

For those who do not have the TAB software but are preparing a collection of programs from the text, we recommend the first and shorter program,

unless you use these programs frequently enough to warrant the effort involved in entering the expanded version. If you have the TAB software, then, by all means, use the EXMENU version.

From a programmer's point of view, these programs offer two variations on one approach to menu-making, useful for any programming effort. The programs simply obtain the name of the file to be run from the user, then call that file for operation. A second approach would have been to write (or copy) all the programs into one massively long file. Then, the menu operation would have been to select the desired chapter and program. The program would have been invoked by using an ON . . . GOTO command.

We elected not to do it this way for several reasons. First, the longer a program written in interpreted BASIC becomes, the slower will be the whole program operation . Secondly, we haven't counted, but suspect that it would push or exceed the 65,529 line number limit in BASIC. Third, even if we could squeeze it in, editing or modifying the program would be a very difficult proposition. By writing in shorter modules, using, editing, and modifying become much simpler.

Listing A-1. Master Menu.

Title: menu

```
1 '
2 '          Appendix A
3 '          Master Menu
4 '
5 '
10 CLS:KEY OFF
20 PRINT"                              Master Me
nu":PRINT:PRINT
30 INPUT "Enter Chapter Number ";C$
40 INPUT "Enter Program Number ";P$
50 PG$="A:C"+C$+"P"+P$
60 RUN PG$
70 END
```

Listing A-2. Expanded Menu.

Title: exmenu

```
1 '
2 '          Appendix A
3 '          Expanded Menu
4 '
5 '
10 CLS:KEY OFF
20 ON ERROR GOTO 800
30 PRINT"                              Expanded Me
nu":PRINT:PRINT
40 DIM C$(18),P$(18,12),NP(18),D$(18)
50 RESTORE
60 FOR I=1 TO 18
70    READ C$(I),NP(I)
80    IF NP(I)=0 THEN 130
90    FOR J=1 TO NP(I)
100     READ P$(I,J)
110    NEXT J
120    READ D$(I)
130 NEXT I
140 GOTO 510
150 DATA Forecasting Philosophies,1,Double-Preci
sion Demonstrator,outlines the rational foundati
ons for statistical analysis of data and the
   requirements for effective and useful forecast
ing.
160 DATA Underlying Mathematical Principles,6,Ro
utine to Tally Raw Data,Data Distribution Analys
is,"Simple Baye's Theorem","Complex Baye's Theor
em",Combinations and Permutations,Combinations a
nd Permutations Modified
170 DATA "explores the statistics of combination
s, permutations, and probabilities, and il
lustrates their role in the forecasting process.
"
180 DATA Data Base Management,4,Data File (Const
```

ruct),Data File (Extract),Delimited Data File Bu
ild,Delimited File Extract
190 DATA "describes the structure and function o
f modern microcomputer data basefiles. Provid
es routines to build and use data files."
200 DATA Technique Selections,0
210 DATA Correlation and Regression Analysis,10,
Linear Trend,Linear Curve Fitting,Least Squares
Parabolic Fit,N-th Order Regression,Multiple Lin
ear Regressions,Miscellaneous Correlations,Kenda
ll's Coefficient of Concordance
220 DATA Chi-Square Correlations,Combined Analys
is of Variance,Rows and Columns
230 DATA "provides the resources for curve-fitti
ng, correlation analysis of various sets of dat
a, and associated data analysis routines."
240 DATA Time-Series Analysis,6,Moving Averages,
Composite Moving Averages,Time-Series Smoothing,
Ratio-to-Moving Averages,Autoregression,S-Curve
of Adoption
250 DATA "provides for the analysis of data as a
 function of time.
260 DATA Modeling and Simulations,4,Swamp Simula
tion,Island,Queuing,Economic Model
270 DATA illustrates the uses of the microcomput
er to experiment with complex business or other
systems in dynamic operation.
280 DATA Numerical Analysis,4,N-th Order Polynom
ial,Modification to N-th Order Polynomial,Poisso
n Distributions,Distributions
290 DATA offers some techniques useful in the nu
merical analysis of data sets with applications
to forecasting.
300 DATA Opinion and Survey Research,7,Survey Sc
heduling I,Survey Scheduling II,Telephone Select
or,Sample Size,Probability No Repetitions in a S
ample,Demographic Analysis,Attitude Analysis
310 DATA "offers some practical routines useful
in designing and conducting a public opinion
survey program for political or market applica
tions."
320 DATA Economic Forecasting,10,Drunkard's Walk
,Bond Values,Economic Curve Fitting,Market Evalu
ator,Market Sales Price Analysis,Economic Order
Quantity,Lease-Purchase Evaluator,Investment Eva
luator,Funds Programming,Poor Man's Spreadsheet
330 DATA "covers a broad range of topics dealing
 with econmics and finance. Offers routin
es to monitor or evaluate various financial prog
rams or investments."
340 DATA Technological Forecasting,2,Delphi Supp
ort,Delphi Analysis
350 DATA supports the use of the 'Delphi Techniq
ue' in forecasting technological advance
s.
360 DATA Astronomical Applications,11,Basic Cale
ndar,Julian to Calendar Date,Super Calendar,The

Date of Easter,Simple Planetary Positions,Comple
x Planetary Positions,Sunrise-Sunset,Tidal Timer
 I,Tidal Timer II,Annual Temperatures
370 DATA Seattle Weather Machine
380 DATA "enables the user to compute planetary
positions,calendar dates in the far past or futu
re, and other astronomical data."
390 DATA Population Estimates,5,Population Estim
ator I,Population Estimator II, Population Estim
ator III,Population Estimate from Sample,Populat
ion Curve Fitting
400 DATA "helps in the analysis of population st
atistics, and to estimate future popula
tions."
410 DATA Educational Testing,4,Test Reliability
Coefficients,Student Record Book--Setup,Student
Record Book,Guttmann Scalar Analysis
420 DATA provides statistical support to the edu
cator.
430 DATA Forecasting Random Events,9,Universal G
ame Machine,Markov Odds,Soda Pop Simulation,Crap
s Simulator,Basic Card Dealing,Card Dealer,Black
jack Trainer,Monopoly Simulator,Random Number Ge
nerator
440 DATA helps predict the unpredictable. Even
random events demonstrate useful charact
eristics for the forecaster and game player.
450 DATA Miscellaneous Forecasting,3,Forecasting
 with PERT,Forecasting Shipping Dates,Trip Costs
460 DATA a final assembly of forecasting routine
s.
470 DATA Data Displays,2,Pie Chart,Line Chart
480 DATA offers a brief discussion of the techni
ques used to display statistical data.
490 DATA Decision-Making Based on Forecasts,2,Mu
ltivariate Evaluator,Decision-Maker
500 DATA "provides practical techniques for usin
g the microcomputer in decision-making."
510 'menu program
520 CLS
530 PRINT"   Forecasting on
 Your Microcomputer":PRINT
540 FOR I=1 TO 18
550   PRINT I,C$(I)
560 NEXT I
570 PRINT:PRINT I,"End Program"
580 LOCATE 24,1:INPUT "Enter Chapter Number";CN$
:C=VAL(CN$)
590 IF C<1 OR C>19 THEN 580
600 IF C=I THEN 790
610 CLS
620 LOCATE 1,1:PRINT"Chapter";C:LOCATE 2,1:PRINT
 C$(C)
630 IF NP(C)=0 THEN 770
640 PRINT:PRINT"Program #","Title"
650 FOR I=1 TO NP(C)
660   LOCATE 4+I,1:PRINT I,P$(C,I)
670 NEXT I

```
680 PRINT:PRINT I,"Return to Chapter Menu"
690 PRINT"":PRINT"This chapter...."
700 PRINT D$(C)
710 LOCATE 24,1:INPUT"Enter number of desired pr
ogram:  ";PN$
720 IF VAL(PN$)<1 OR VAL(PN$)>(NP(C)+1) THEN 710
730 IF VAL(PN$)=I THEN 510
740 LOCATE 25,1:PRINT"Loading Program #";C;"-";V
AL(PN$),P$(C,VAL(PN$))
750 PG$="A:C"+CN$+"P"+PN$
760 RUN PG$
770 CLS
780 PRINT"Chapter";C;C$(C):PRINT:INPUT"There are
 no programs for this chapter.  <CR> to continue
.";ZZ:GOTO 510
790 END
800 IF ERR=53 THEN 820
810 PRINT"Try Again.....":RUN 30
820 PRINT"Selected file not on disk.  <CR> to co
ntinue.":PRINT:PRINT:INPUT ZZ:RUN 10
```

Appendix B:
Guide To The Software

The programs listed in this text are recorded on the TAB software disk in standard IBM PC disk format (originally from an AT&T 6300 using MS-DOS 2.11). We recommend you make a back up copy of the disk before any other transaction. Use the back up copy for day-to-day use.

Two-Disk Operation: For operation of the BASIC programs (identified with .BAS) on a system with one or two floppy disks, place the back up copy of the program disk into the drive you normally use when running BASIC programs, and issue the command: **BASIC A:MENU [or BASIC A:EXMENU]** (see Appendix A). This program is useful for calling up any program.

If you prefer (or must) to use drive B, or some other drive designation, place the disk into the desired drive and invoke BASIC without the MENU [or EXMENU] selection. **LOAD "B:MENU"** (or whatever the correct drive designation is), then edit line 50 to correct the drive designation. Then save the program using: **SAVE "B:MENU"**. Also, load and edit line 730 of EXMENU in the same way. From then on the programs should run without prob-

lem. The menu programs simply need to know where to look for the program files.

One Floppy Disk and a Hard Drive: The programs may be run from drive A without further modification or manipulation. While in drive C and in the directory containing BASIC, simply type: **BASIC A:MENU [or A:EXMENU]**. Alternatively, the files may be installed on drive C. We recommend the creation of a separate directory for the programs.

To install: (< > means carriage return)

> MKDR TAB < >
> CD\TAB < >
> COPY A:*.* C:

Then, either **COPY BASIC.COM** or **GWBASIC.COM** over to the TAB directory, or:

> CD \ < >
> COPY A:??MENU.BAS.C:

Enter BASIC and edit lines 50 and 730 respectively, in MENU and EXMENU, as:

50 PG$ = "C:\TAB\C"+C$+"P"+
    P$ (in MENU)
730 PG$ = "C:\TAB\C"+C$"P"+
    PN$ (in EXMENU)

To run, type **BASIC MENU [or EXMENU] < >**

The first edition of this text and software was written for the Tandy Corporation line of TRS-80 computers (primarily the Model III), with the EXATRON Stringy Floppy (ESF) as the high speed data storage medium. After translating the programs (using *CONV3TOPC* by Education Micro Systems Inc.) to the IBM PC format, each of them were executed to validate a successful transfer, and to fine-tune them to make better use of the additional commands in GW-BASIC. In this process, we hopefully identified and eliminated all of the ESF references and command instructions (identified by the use of @ with a command, as in @CLEAR. Although not likely, it is possible we left a stray ESF command in a software backwater not often visited by the programs. If you encounter one, it can be deleted or changed to the appropriate GWBASIC expression. The @CLEAR command is the only one whose function is obscure [the same function as CLOSE in a disk system]; the others reflect standard disk I/O command protocol. **@OPEN n** is the same as **OPEN "O",n, [filename]**.

Accompanying the BASIC programs are a number of translations of these programs into files readable by several spreadsheet and database management systems. These listings are found in Appendix C.

Appendix C:
Spreadsheet Listings

SYMPHONY/1-2-3 and dBase III PLUS Files: Program files for use with *Symphony* use the extension .WRK; *1-2-3* uses .WKS. *dBase III PLUS* files use the .DBF extension. *1-2-3* files can be imported into *dBase III PLUS* using the APPEND FROM <filename> [TYPE <file type] command. For example: APPEND FROM LOTUS123.WR1 TYPE WKS. Likewise, *Symphony* programs are imported using the same WKS file type: e.g., AP-PEND FROM SYMPFILE.WRK TYPE WKS. Chapter 3 includes routines to create and read file formats readable by all three of these software packages.

The listings that follow were created with *Symphony* (version 1.0), and have been translated into DIF file formats (on the floppy disk containing the software) for systems unable to read the *Symphony* product.

Listing C-2-1. Spreadsheet Version.

```
A1: 'LISTING 2-1  Spreadsheet Version
A3: '
D3: 'Range
E3: 'Frequency
A4: 'Sum:
B4: @SUM(B15..B17)
D4: (F2) 0
E4: 0
A5: 'Average:
B5: (F4) @AVG(B15..B17)
D5: (F2) +B10/9
E5: 0
A6: 'Number:
```

Listing C-2-1. Spreadsheet Version. (Continued From Page 353.)

```
B6: @COUNT(B15..B17)
D6: (F2) +D5+$D$5
E6: 1
A7: 'Variance:
B7: (F4) @VAR(B15..B17)
D7: (F2) +D6+$D$5
E7: 1
A8: 'Standard Deviation:
B8: (F4) @STD(B15..B17)
D8: (F2) +D7+$D$5
E8: 0
A9: 'Smallest Entry:
B9: @MIN(B15..B17)
D9: (F2) +D8+$D$5
E9: 0
A10: 'Largest Entry:
B10: @MAX(B15..B17)
D10: (F2) +D9+$D$5
E10: 0
A11: 'Range:
B11: +B10-B9
D11: (F2) +D10+$D$5
E11: 0
D12: (F2) +D11+$D$5
E12: 0
A13: ^Item #
B13: '
D13: (F2) +D12+$D$5
E13: 1
B14: '
E14: 0
A15: 1
B15: 691
A16: 2
B16: 345
A17: 3
B17: 455
A19: 'Instructions: Count number of data items, n, and <I>nsert n-3
A20: '                rows between rows 15 and 16.  Enter data.
```

Listing C-2-4. Spreadsheet Version.

```
A1: 'LISTING 2-4  Spreadsheet Version
A2: '
A3: 'Simple Bayes' Theorem
E3: 'Probability
E4: 'p(A)
F4: (F5) +C6
A5: 'Name of Event:
C5: 'Poison
E5: 'p(A')
F5: (F5) 1-F4
A6: 'Probability =
C6: 0.333
E6: 'p(B|A)
F6: (F5) +H12
E7: 'p(B|A')
```

```
F7: (F5) +H13
A8: 'Name of
E8: 'p(A|B)
F8: (F5) (+F4*F6)/((F4*F6)+(F5*F7))
A9: 'Related Event:
C9: 'Stomach Ache
A10: 'Probability =
C10: 0.667
A11: '
A12: 'Probability of
C12: +C9
E12: 'given
F12: +C5
G12: ^=
H12: 0.8
A13: 'Probability of
C13: +C9
E13: 'given no
F13: +C5
G13: ^=
H13: 0.05
A15: 'Probability of
C15: +C5
E15: 'given
F15: +C9
H15: +F8
A18: 'Complex Bayes' Theorem
A20: 'Name of Event:
C20: 'A
D20: 'Winter
F20: 'Probability
E21: "p(Bx)
F21: "p(A|Bx)
G21: 'p(Bx|A)
H21: 'p(Bx)p(A|Bx)
A22: 'Ass. Event
C22: 'B1
D22: 'Wind
E22: 0.333
F22: 0.75
G22: (E22*F22)/$H$25
H22: +E22*F22
A23: 'Ass. Event
C23: 'B2
D23: 'Rain
E23: 0.15
F23: 0.05
G23: (E23*F23)/$H$25
H23: +E23*F23
A24: 'Ass. Event
C24: 'B3
D24: 'Snow
E24: 0.25
F24: 0.9
G24: (E24*F24)/$H$25
H24: +E24*F24
A25: 'sum
E25: '
```

Listing C-2-4. Spreadsheet Version. (Continued From Page 354.)

```
F25: '
H25: @SUM(H22..H24)
```

Listing C-5-1. Spreadsheet Version.

```
A1:  'LISTING 5-1  Spreadsheet Version
A3:  '
B3:  "X
C3:  "Y
D3:  "X^2
E3:  "Y^2
F3:  "X*Y
G3:  ^Y'
H3:  ^Dev.
B4:  92
C4:  86
D4:  +B4^2
E4:  +C4^2
F4:  +B4*C4
G4:  (F3) +$B$19+($B$18*B4)
H4:  (F3) +G4-C4
B5:  50
C5:  76
D5:  +B5^2
E5:  +C5^2
F5:  +B5*C5
G5:  (F3) +$B$19+($B$18*B5)
H5:  (F3) +G5-C5
B6:  20
C6:  68
D6:  +B6^2
E6:  +C6^2
F6:  +B6*C6
G6:  (F3) +$B$19+($B$18*B6)
H6:  (F3) +G6-C6
B7:  '
B8:  "X
C8:  "Y
D8:  "X^2
E8:  "Y^2
F8:  "X*Y
G8:  "N
A9:  'Sum
B9:  (F3) @SUM(B4..B6)
C9:  (F3) @SUM(C4..C6)
D9:  (F3) @SUM(D4..D6)
E9:  (F3) @SUM(E4..E6)
F9:  (F3) @SUM(F4..F6)
G9:  (F3) @COUNT(B4..B6)
H9:  (F3) @SUM(H4..H6)
A10: 'Min
B10: (F3) @MIN(B4..B6)
C10: (F3) @MIN(C4..C6)
A11: 'Max
B11: (F3) @MAX(B4..B6)
C11: (F3) @MAX(C4..C6)
E11: 'To use: <I>nsert between row 2 and
```

```
A12:  'Mean
B12:  (F3) +B9/$G$9
C12:  (F3) +C9/$G$9
D12:  (F3) '
E12:  (F3) 'row 3 the number of data points,
F12:  (F3) 'number of data points,
A13:  'Var.
B13:  (F3) @VAR(B4..B6)
C13:  (F3) @VAR(C4..C6)
E13:  'less 3, in the matrix.  Then, <C>opy
A14:  'S.D.
B14:  (F3) @STD(B4..B6)
C14:  (F3) @STD(C4..C6)
E14:  (F3) 'the formulae in D2...H2 to D3...Hn.
A15:  'S.E.
B15:  (F3) +B14/@SQRT(G9)
C15:  (F3) +C14/@SQRT(G9)
A16:  'r =
B16:  (F3) ((G9*F9)-(B9*C9))/@SQRT(((G9*D9)-(B9^2))*((G9*E9)-(C9^2)))
C16:  (F3) '
E16:  (F3) 'Enter correct data in cells B2...Cn.
A17:  'R.E.
B17:  (F3) +C14*@SQRT(1-(B16^2))
C17:  (F3) '
A18:  'B =
B18:  (F3) (F9-(G9*B12*C12))/(D9-(G9*(B12^2)))
A19:  'A =
B19:  (F3) +C12-(B18*B12)
A21:  'X =
B21:  4
C21:  'Section for trial estimates of Y' based on a given X
A22:  'Y' =
B22:  +B19+(B21*B18)
B23:  '
A24:  'Y =
B24:  68
C24:  'Section for trial estimates of X' based on a given Y.
A25:  'X' =
B25:  (B24-B19)/B18
```

Listing C-5-2. Spreadsheet Version.

```
A1:  'LISTING 5-2  Spreadsheet Version
A2:  '
A3:  '
B3:  "F1&F2
C3:  "G1&G3
E3:  ^E1
F3:  ^E2
G3:  ^E3
H3:  "E4
I3:  "F3&F4
J3:  "G2&G4
K3:  "H1&H2
L3:  "H3&H4
M3:  "J1&J3
N3:  "J2&J4
```

Listing C-5-2. Spreadsheet Version. (Continued From Page 357.)

```
A4:  ^#
B4:  "X
C4:  "Y
D4:  "Y'
E4:  "X * Y
F4:  "X*Log Y
G4:  "Y*Log X
H4:  'LogX*LogY
I4:  "Log X
J4:  "Log Y
K4:  "X^2
L4:  "(Log X)^2
M4:  "Y^2
N4:  "Log Y^2
A5:  1
B5:  1
C5:  5
E5:  (F3) +B5*C5
F5:  (F3) +B5*J5
G5:  (F3) +C5*I5
H5:  (F3) +I5*J5
I5:  (F3) @LN(B5)
J5:  (F3) @LN(C5)
K5:  (F3) +B5^2
L5:  (F3) @LN(B5)^2
M5:  (F3) +C5^2
N5:  (F3) +J5^2
A6:  +A5+1
B6:  2
C6:  8
E6:  (F3) +B6*C6
F6:  (F3) +B6*J6
G6:  (F3) +C6*I6
H6:  (F3) +I6*J6
I6:  (F3) @LN(B6)
J6:  (F3) @LN(C6)
K6:  (F3) +B6^2
L6:  (F3) @LN(B6)^2
M6:  (F3) +C6^2
N6:  (F3) +J6^2
A7:  +A6+1
B7:  3
C7:  15
E7:  (F3) +B7*C7
F7:  (F3) +B7*J7
G7:  (F3) +C7*I7
H7:  (F3) +I7*J7
I7:  (F3) @LN(B7)
J7:  (F3) @LN(C7)
K7:  (F3) +B7^2
L7:  (F3) @LN(B7)^2
M7:  (F3) +C7^2
N7:  (F3) +J7^2
A9:  "Sigma
B9:  @SUM(B5..B7)
C9:  @SUM(C5..C7)
```

```
E9:  (F3) @SUM(E5..E7)
F9:  (F3) @SUM(F5..F7)
G9:  (F3) @SUM(G5..G7)
H9:  (F3) @SUM(H5..H7)
I9:  (F3) @SUM(I5..I7)
J9:  (F3) @SUM(J5..J7)
K9:  (F3) @SUM(K5..K7)
L9:  (F3) @SUM(L5..L7)
M9:  (F3) @SUM(M5..M7)
N9:  (F3) @SUM(N5..N7)
B11: '
B12: "X
C12: "Y
D12: (F3) "N =
E12: (F3) +A7
A13: 'Sum
B13: (F3) @SUM(B5..B7)
C13: (F3) @SUM(C5..C7)
E13: (F3) "A
F13: (F3) "B
G13: (F3) "r
H13: (F3) "t
A14: 'Min
B14: (F3) @MIN(B5..B7)
C14: (F3) @MIN(C5..C7)
D14: (F0) 1
E14: (F3) (G27-F14*F27)/$E$12
F14: (F3) (E27-(F27*G27))/(H27-(E$12*(F27^2)))
G14: (F3) +I14/@SQRT(J14)
H14: (G14*@SQRT($E$12-2))/@SQRT(1-(G14^2))
I14: (H) ($E$12*E27)-(F27*G27)
J14: (H) (($E$12*H27)-(F27^2))*(($E$12*J27)-(G27^2))
A15: 'Max
B15: (F3) @MAX(B5..B7)
C15: (F3) @MAX(C5..C7)
D15: (F0) 2
E15: (F3) (G28-F15*F28)/$E$12
F15: (F3) (E28-(F28*G28))/(H28-(E$12*(F28^2)))
G15: (F3) +I15/@SQRT(J15)
H15: (G15*@SQRT($E$12-2))/@SQRT(1-(G15^2))
I15: (H) ($E$12*E28)-(F28*G28)
J15: (H) (($E$12*H28)-(F28^2))*(($E$12*J28)-(G28^2))
A16: 'Mean
B16: (F3) +B13/A7
C16: (F3) +C13/A7
D16: (F0) 3
E16: (F3) (G29-F16*F29)/$E$12
F16: (F3) (E29-(F29*G29))/(H29-(E$12*(F29^2)))
G16: (F3) +I16/@SQRT(J16)
H16: (G16*@SQRT($E$12-2))/@SQRT(1-(G16^2))
I16: (H) ($E$12*E29)-(F29*G29)
J16: (H) (($E$12*H29)-(F29^2))*(($E$12*J29)-(G29^2))
A17: 'Var.
B17: (F3) @VAR(B5..B7)
C17: (F3) @VAR(C5..C7)
D17: (F0) 4
E17: (F3) (G30-F17*F30)/$E$12
F17: (F3) (E30-(F30*G30))/(H30-(E$12*(F30^2)))
```

Listing C-5-2. Spreadsheet Version. (Continued From Page 359.)

```
G17: (F3) +I17/@SQRT(J17)
H17: (G17*@SQRT($E$12-2))/@SQRT(1-(G17^2))
I17: (H) ($E$12*E30)-(F30*G30)
J17: (H) (($E$12*H30)-(F30^2))*(($E$12*J30)-(G30^2))
A18: 'S.D.
B18: (F3) @STD(B5..B7)
C18: (F3) @STD(C5..C7)
A19: '
B19: (F3) '
C19: (F3) '
D19: (F0) @IF(G14>=G19,D14,@IF(D15>=G19,D15,@IF(G16>=G19,D16,D17)))
F19: (F3) 'Best r =
G19: (F3) @MAX(G14..G17)
A20: '
B20: (F3) '
C20: (F3) '
A21: 'Equation of
A22: 'Best Fit:
C22: @IF(G14=G19,A27,@IF(G15=G19,A28,@IF(G14=G19,A29,A30)))
E26: (F3) "E
F26: (F3) "F
G26: (F3) "G
H26: (F3) "H
I26: (F3) "I
J26: (F3) "J
K26: (F3) "K
A27: 'Linear        Y = A + B X
E27: (F3) +E9
F27: (F3) +B9
G27: (F3) +C9
H27: (F3) +K9
I27: (F3) +B9^2
J27: (F3) +M9
K27: (F3) +C9^2
L27: (F0) 1
A28: 'Exponential   Y = EXP(Log A + B X)
E28: (F3) +F9
F28: (F3) +F27
G28: (F3) +J9
H28: (F3) +H27
I28: (F3) +I27
J28: (F3) +N9
K28: (F3) +J9^2
L28: (F0) 2
A29: 'Logarithmic   Y = A + B Log X
E29: (F3) +G9
F29: (F3) +I9
G29: (F3) +G27
H29: (F3) +L9
I29: (F3) +I9^2
J29: (F3) +M9
K29: (F3) +K27
L29: (F0) 3
A30: 'Power         Y = EXP(Log A + B Log X)
E30: (F3) +H9
F30: (F3) +F29
```

```
G30:  (F3)  +J9
H30:  (F3)  +H29
I30:  (F3)  +I29
J30:  (F3)  +N9
K30:  (F3)  +K28
L30:  (F0)  4
A32:  (F3)  'To use: <I>nsert between row 2 and
A33:  (F3)  'row 3 the number of data points,
B33:  (F3)  'n number of data points,
A34:  (F3)  'less 3, in the matrix.  Then, <C>opy
A35:  (F3)  'the formulae in E6...N6 to E7...Hn+1.
A37:  (F3)  'Enter correct data in cells B5...Cn+2.
```

Listing C-5-5. Spreadsheet Version.

```
A1:  'Listing 5-5  Spreadsheet Version
A2:  '
B3:  '1. Count the number of data points.
B4:  '2. <I>nsert the number lines for each data point less two
B5:  '   between lines 13 and 14
B6:  '3. <C>opy the formulae from B13...N13 to B14...Nn-1.
B7:  '4. Enter data, results are computed automatically.
D9:  'Multiple Regression of Y on X and Z (Least Squares Estimates)
A10: '
H10: '
J10: '
N10: '
A11: 'Data
M11: ^(Yr-Ym)*
N11: ^(Y-Ym)*
A12: 'Point
B12: "Y
C12: "X
D12: "Z
E12: "Xv=X-Xm
F12: "Zv=Z-Zm
G12: "Y*Xv
H12: "Y*Zv
I12: "Xv^2
J12: "Zv^2
K12: ^X*Z
L12: ^Yr
M12: ^(Yr-Ym)
N12: ^(Y-Ym)
A13: '
G13: '
I13: '
A15: 1
B15: (F3) 1800
C15: (F3) 1
D15: (F3) 7.2
E15: (F3) +C15-$C$23
F15: (F3) +D15-$D$23
G15: (F3) +B15*E15
H15: (F3) +B15*F15
I15: (F3) +E15^2
J15: (F3) +F15^2
K15: (F3) +E15*F15
```

Listing C-5-5. Spreadsheet Version. (Continued From Page 361.)

```
L15: (F3)  ($J$31+($J$30*C15)+($J$29*D15))
M15: (F3)  ($B$23-L15)^2
N15: (F3)  ($B$23-B15)^2
A16: 2
B16: 1900
C16: 2
D16: 8
E16: (F3)  +C16-$C$23
F16: (F3)  +D16-$D$23
G16: (F3)  +B16*E16
H16: (F3)  +B16*F16
I16: (F3)  +E16^2
J16: (F3)  +F16^2
K16: (F3)  +E16*F16
L16: (F3)  ($J$31+($J$30*C16)+($J$29*D16))
M16: (F3)  ($B$23-L16)^2
N16: (F3)  ($B$23-B16)^2
A17: 3
B17: (F3)  2000
C17: (F3)  4
D17: (F3)  8.6
E17: (F3)  +C17-$C$23
F17: (F3)  +D17-$D$23
G17: (F3)  +B17*E17
H17: (F3)  +B17*F17
I17: (F3)  +E17^2
J17: (F3)  +F17^2
K17: (F3)  +E17*F17
L17: (F3)  ($J$31+($J$30*C17)+($J$29*D17))
M17: (F3)  ($B$23-L17)^2
N17: (F3)  ($B$23-B17)^2
A18: '
H18: (F3)  '
J18: (F3)  '
N18: (F3)  '
A19: 'Total
B19: (F3)  @SUM(B15..B17)
C19: (F3)  @SUM(C15..C17)
D19: (F3)  @SUM(D15..D17)
E19: (F3)  @SUM(E15..E17)
F19: (F3)  @SUM(F15..F17)
G19: (F3)  @SUM(G15..G17)
H19: (F3)  @SUM(H15..H17)
I19: (F3)  @SUM(I15..I17)
J19: (F3)  @SUM(J15..J17)
K19: (F3)  @SUM(K15..K17)
L19: (F3)  @SUM(L15..L17)
M19: (F3)  @SUM(M15..M17)
N19: (F3)  @SUM(N15..N17)
A20: '
H20: (F3)  '
J20: (F3)  '
N20: (F3)  '
E21: (F3)  ':
A22: 'Means
B22: (F3)  "Ym
```

```
C22: (F3) "Xm
D22: (F3) "Zm
E22: (F3) ':
F22: (F3) 'Final Equation
H22: (F3) "Y =
I22: (F3) +J31
J22: (F3) '      +
K22: (F3) +J30
L22: (F3) 'X      +
M22: (F3) +J29
N22: (F3) 'Z
B23: (F3) @AVG(B15..B17)
C23: (F3) @AVG(C15..C17)
D23: (F3) @AVG(D15..D17)
E23: (F3) ':
E24: (F3) ':
H24: (F3) 'Coefficient of Determination    =
L24: (F3) +M19/N19
M24: (F3) 'r^2
E25: (F3) ':
H25: (F3) 'Sample Correlation Coefficient =
L25: (F3) @SQRT(L24)
M25: (F3) 'r
A26: '
H26: (F3) '
J26: (F3) '
N26: (F3) '
A28: 'Equations
C28: (F3) +G19
E28: (F3) +I19
F28: (F3) 'b+
G28: (F3) +K19
H28: (F3) 'c
C29: (F3) +H19
E29: (F3) +K19
F29: (F3) 'b+
G29: (F3) +J19
H29: (F3) 'c
I29: (F3) "c =
J29: (F3) +C34/G34
I30: (F3) "b =
J30: (F3) (C28-(J29*G28))/E28
C31: (F3) +G19
E31: (F3) +I19
F31: (F3) 'b+
G31: (F3) +K19
H31: (F3) 'c
I31: (F3) "a =
J31: (F3) (B23+(J30*C23*(-1))+(J29*D23*(-1)))
A32: 'Solution
C32: (F3) (C29*(E28/E29))
E32: (F3) (E29*(E28/E29))
F32: (F3) 'b+
G32: (F3) +G29*E28/E29
H32: (F3) 'c
C33: (F3) '
G33: (F3) '
H33: (F3) '
```

Listing C-5-5. Spreadsheet Version. (Continued From Page 363.)

```
C34: (F3) +C28-C32
E34: (F3) +E28-E32
F34: (F3) 'b+
G34: (F3) +G28-G32
H34: (F3) 'c
A35: '
C35: (F3) '
L35: (F3) '
A37: 'ANOVA TABLE
C37: (F3) 'SOURCE
D37: (F3) ^SS
E37: (F3) "D.F.
F37: (F3) 'MEAN SQUARE
C38: (F3) '
G38: (F3) '
H38: (F3) '
C39: (F3) 'REGR
D39: (F3) +M19
E39: (F3) 2
F39: (F3) +D39/E39
H39: (F3) "F =
I39: (F3) +F39/F40
C40: (F3) 'ERROR
D40: (F3) +N19-M19
E40: (F3) +A17
F40: (F3) +D40/E40
C41: (F3) '
H41: (F3) '
C42: (F3) 'TOTAL
D42: (F3) +M19
```

Listing C-5-6. Spreadsheet Version.

```
A1: 'Listing 5-6  Spreadsheet Version
A3: '1.  Count the number of data points, N.
A4: '2.  <I>nsert the number of lines for each data point less two (N-2)
A5: '      between the existing data lines.
A6: '3.  <C>opy the formulae from first data line to new data lines.
A7: '4.  Enter data.
C9: '
D9: 'Point-Biserial Correlation
A11: 'Item #
B11: 'Dichot.
C11: 'Contin.
D11: ^X^2
E11: ^N(0)
F11: ^N(1)
G11: ^S(0)
H11: ^S(1)
A12: 1
B12: 1
C12: 3.45
D12: +C12^2
E12: @IF(B12=0,1,0)
F12: @IF(B12=1,1,0)
G12: @IF(B12=0,C12,0)
H12: @IF(B12=1,C12,0)
```

```
A13: +A12+1
B13: 1
C13: 5.6
D13: +C13^2
E13: @IF(B13=0,1,0)
F13: @IF(B13=1,1,0)
G13: @IF(B13=0,C13,0)
H13: @IF(B13=1,C13,0)
A14: +A13+1
B14: 0
C14: 78.5
D14: +C14^2
E14: @IF(B14=0,1,0)
F14: @IF(B14=1,1,0)
G14: @IF(B14=0,C14,0)
H14: @IF(B14=1,C14,0)
A16: 'Sum
C16: @SUM(C12..C14)
D16: @SUM(D12..D14)
E16: @SUM(E12..E14)
F16: @SUM(F12..F14)
G16: @SUM(G12..G14)
H16: @SUM(H12..H14)
A17: '
A18: 'S =
B18: @SQRT((D16-((C16^2)/A14))/(A14-1))
C18: '= Standard Deviation
A19: 'Y0 =
B19: +G16/E16
C19: '= Mean of Y0
A20: 'Y1 =
B20: +H16/F16
C20: '= Mean of Y1
A21: 'P =
B21: +E16/A14
A22: 'Q =
B22: 1-B21
A23: 'RB =
B23: ((B20-B19)/B18)*@SQRT(B21*B22)
C23: '= Point-Biserial Correlation
B26: 'Spearman's Rank Correlation
B28: ^Rank
C28: ^Rank
A29: 'Item #
B29: ^Var. 1
C29: ^Var. 2
D29: 'R1 - R2
E29: ^DI
A30: 1
B30: 23
C30: 29
D30: +B30-C30
E30: +D30^2
A31: +A30+1
B31: 32
C31: 41
D31: +B31-C31
E31: +D31^2
```

Listing C-5-6. Spreadsheet Version. (Continued From Page 365.)

```
A32: +A31+1
B32: 45
C32: 54
D32: +B32-C32
E32: +D32^2
A34: 'Sum
B34: @SUM(B30..B32)
C34: @SUM(C30..C32)
D34: @SUM(D30..D32)
E34: @SUM(E30..E32)
A36: 'RS =
B36: 1-((6*E34)/(A32*((A32^2)-1)))
C36: '= Spearman's Rho
A37: 'Z =
B37: +B36*@SQRT(A32-1)
C37: '= Z-score
A38: 'R =
B38: 2*@SIN(0.5235991*B36)
C38: '=Pearson's Rho Correlation
C41: 'Partial Correlations
A43: 'R(1) =
B43: 0.34
D43: 'PR(1) =
E43: (B43-(B44*B45))/(@SQRT(1-(B44^2))*@SQRT(1-(B45^2)))
A44: 'R(2) =
B44: 0.87
D44: 'PR(2) =
E44: (B44-(B43*B45))/(@SQRT(1-(B43^2))*@SQRT(1-(B45^2)))
A45: 'R(3) =
B45: 0.65
D45: 'PR(3) =
E45: (B45-(B43*B44))/(@SQRT(1-(B43^2))*@SQRT(1-(B44^2)))
D46: 'PR(4) =
E46: (((B43^2)+(B44^2))-(2*B43*B44*B45))/(1-(B45^2))
```

Listing C-5-7. Spreadsheet Version.

```
A1: 'Listing 5-7  Spreadsheet version
C3: 'Kendall's Coefficient of Concordance
D5: 'Scores by Judge #
F5: "K
A6: 'Subjects
B6: 1
C6: +B6+1
D6: +C6+1
E6: +D6+1
F6: +E6+1
G6: ^Row Sum
H6: ^RS^2
A8: 1
B8: 9
C8: 9
D8: 8
E8: 9
F8: 9
G8: @SUM(B8..F8)
H8: +G8^2
```

```
A9:  +A8+1
B9:  8
C9:  8
D9:  7
E9:  8
F9:  8
G9:  @SUM(B9..F9)
H9:  +G9^2
A10: +A9+1
B10: 5
C10: 6
D10: 7
E10: 8
F10: 9
G10: @SUM(B10..F10)
H10: +G10^2
A11: +A10+1
B11: 9
C11: 8
D11: 7
E11: 6
F11: 5
G11: @SUM(B11..F11)
H11: +G11^2
A12: +A11+1
B12: 6
C12: 7
D12: 6
E12: 7
F12: 6
G12: @SUM(B12..F12)
H12: +G12^2
A13: +A12+1
B13: 5
C13: 5
D13: 6
E13: 5
F13: 5
G13: @SUM(B13..F13)
H13: +G13^2
G14: '
A15: 'Score
B15: @SUM(B8..B13)
C15: @SUM(C8..C13)
D15: @SUM(D8..D13)
E15: @SUM(E8..E13)
F15: @SUM(F8..F13)
G15: @SUM(G8..G13)
H15: @SUM(H8..H13)
A16: 'Av. Score
B16: (F1) +B15/A13
C16: (F1) +C15/B13
D16: (F1) +D15/C13
E16: (F1) +E15/D13
F16: (F1) +F15/E13
H16: (F1) "SN
A18: 'W =
B18: ((12*H15)/((F6^2)*(A13*((A13^2)-1)))))-((3*(A13+1))/(A13-1))
```

Listing C-5-7. Spreadsheet Version. (Continued From Page 366.)

```
C18: 'Kendall's Coefficient of Concordance
A19: 'Chi^2 =
B19: +F6*(A13)*B18
C19: 'with
D19: +A13-1
E19: 'degrees of freedom
```

Listing C-5-8. Spreadsheet Version.

```
A1: 'Listing 5-8  Spreadsheet version
A3: 'Item #
B3: 'Expected
C3: 'Observed
D3: "E^2
E3: "O^2
F3: "O-E
G3: "NI
A4: 1
B4: 34
C4: 34
D4: +B4^2
E4: +C4^2
F4: (((C4-B4)^2)/B4)
G4: +B4+C4
H4: +D4/G4
I4: +E4/G4
A5: +A4+1
B5: 45
C5: 45
D5: +B5^2
E5: +C5^2
F5: (((C5-B5)^2)/B5)
G5: +B5+C5
H5: +D5/G5
I5: +E5/G5
A6: +A5+1
B6: 67
C6: 56
D6: +B6^2
E6: +C6^2
F6: (((C6-B6)^2)/B6)
G6: +B6+C6
H6: +D6/G6
I6: +E6/G6
A7: +A6+1
B7: 23
C7: 45
D7: +B7^2
E7: +C7^2
F7: (((C7-B7)^2)/B7)
G7: +B7+C7
H7: +D7/G7
I7: +E7/G7
A8: +A7+1
B8: 43
C8: 67
D8: +B8^2
```

```
E8:  +C8^2
F8:  (((C8-B8)^2)/B8)
G8:  +B8+C8
H8:  +D8/G8
I8:  +E8/G8
A9:  +A8+1
B9:  67
C9:  87
D9:  +B9^2
E9:  +C9^2
F9:  (((C9-B9)^2)/B9)
G9:  +B9+C9
H9:  +D9/G9
I9:  +E9/G9
A10: +A9+1
B10: 78
C10: 89
D10: +B10^2
E10: +C10^2
F10: (((C10-B10)^2)/B10)
G10: +B10+C10
H10: +D10/G10
I10: +E10/G10
G11: '
H11: '
I11: '
A12: 'Sum
B12: @SUM(B4..B10)
C12: @SUM(C4..C10)
D12: @SUM(D4..D10)
E12: @SUM(E4..E10)
F12: @SUM(F4..F10)
G12: +B12+C12
H12: +D12/G12
I12: +E12/G12
G13: "N
H13: "SA
I13: "SB
A14: 'X2 =
B14: ((A10*E12)/C12)-C12
C14: 'Expected Values Equal
A15: 'X2 =
B15: +F12
C15: 'Expected Values Unequal
A16: 'X2 =
B16: ((G12/B12)*H12)+((G12/C12)*I12)-G12
C16: '2 x K Contingency Table
F16: @IF(B16<0,-1*@SQRT(@ABS(B16/(G12+B16))),@SQRT(B16/(G12+B16)))
G16: '= Pearson's Coefficient
A20: '2 x 2 Table with Yates' Correction
B22: '          Set
A23: 'Group
B23: ^A
C23: ^B
D23: "Sum
A24: 1
B24: 23
C24: 34
```

Listing C-5-8. Spreadsheet Version. (Continued From Page 369.)

```
D24: +B24+C24
A25: 2
B25: 44
C25: 45
D25: +B25+C25
A26: 'Sum
B26: +B24+B25
C26: +C24+C25
D26: +D24+D25
A28: 'N =
B28: (D26*((@ABS((B24*C25)-(C24*B25))-((B24+C24+B25+C25)/2))^2))
A29: 'D =
B29: ((B24+C24)*(B24+B25)*(B25+C25)*(C24+C25))
A30: 'X2 =
B30: +B28/B29
```

Listing C-7-3. Spreadsheet Version.

```
A1: 'Listing 7-3  Spreadsheet version
A3: '                   Queuing
C3: '
D3: 'Variable
E3: ^With Balk
A5: '* Ave. # Customers/Hour:
B5: 3
D5: 'L
A6: 'Interval Between Customers:
B6: 60/B5
C6: 'minutes
A7: '*  Ave. Minutes/Customer:
B7: 5
D7: 'S
A8: '*  Number of Servers:
B8: 3
D8: 'K
A9: 'Max. Cust./Hour/Server:
B9: +B8*(60/B7)
C9: '
D9: 'M
A10: 'Utilization Factor
B10: +B5/B9
D10: 'U
A11: 'Maximum Slack Time
B11: (B8*60)-(B5*B7)
C11: 'minutes
D11: 'ST
B12: 1-B10
D12: 'PW
A13: '*  Trial # Customers:
B13: 1
D13: 'N
A14: 'Probability N Customers:
B14: +B12*(B10^B13)
D14: 'PN
A15: 'Mean # Customers in System:
B15: +B5/(B9-B5)
D15: 'EN
```

```
E15: (B10/(1-B10))-((B23+1)*(B10^(B23+1))/(1-(B10^(B23+1))))
B16: (B5^2)/(B9*(B9-B5))
C16: '
D16: 'EL
B17: +B5/(B9*(B9-B5))
D17: 'EW
B18: 1/(B9-B5)
D18: 'ET
A19: 'Mean Waiting Time:
B19: 60*B16
C19: 'minutes
E19: (+E15-1+((1-B10)/(1-(B10^(B23+1)))))*60
A20: 'Mean Time in Que:
B20: 60*B17
C20: 'minutes
E20: 60*(E19-(1/B9))
A21: 'Mean Total Time in System:
B21: 60*B18
C21: 'minutes
E21: 60*((1/(B9*(1-B10)))-((B23*(B10^B23))/(B9*(1-(B10^B23)))))
A23: '*   Balk Point
B23: 3
C23: '
D23: 'Q
```

Listing C-10-6. Spreadsheet Version.

```
A1: 'Listing 10-6  Spreadsheet version
A2: '
A3: '*  Average Annual Requirements:
B3: 3653
C3: 'N
A4: '*  Maximum Daily Requirement:
B4: 30
C4: 'U
A5: '*  Number Days to Fill Order:
B5: 3
C5: 'T
B6: +B5+1
C6: 'D
A7: 'Minimum Inventory:
B7: +B6*B4
C7: 'I1
A8: 'Order Point:
B8: +B7+(B5*B4)
C8: 'P
A9: '*  Standard Order Size:
B9: 5
C9: 'O
A10: '*  Cost to Place Order:
B10: (C2) 100
C10: 'C
A11: '*  Unit Cost of Item:
B11: (C2) 4
C11: 'M
A12: '*  Annual Carrying Cost of Item:
B12: (C2) 8
C12: 'A
A13: '*  Annual Cost of Money (5%=.05):
```

Listing C-10-6. Spreadsheet Version. (Continued From Page 371.)

```
B13: (%2) 0.05
C13: 'R
A14: 'Daily Cost of Money:
B14: (%2) +B13/365.25
C14: 'R'
B15: (B14*((1+B14)^(B5/2)))/(((1+B14)^(B5/2))-1)
C15: 'RF
B16: +B12+(B11*(1+B15))-B11
C16: 'A'
A17: 'Maximum Inventory:
B17: +B8+B9
C17: 'I2
A18: 'Optimum Order Size:
B18: @INT(@SQRT((2*B10*B3)/((B11*B14)+B12)))
C18: 'Q
A19: 'Adjusted Maximum Inventory:
B19: +B18+B8
C19: 'IA
A20: 'Ave. Number of Days Between Orders:
B20: 365.25/(B3/B18)
```

Listing C-10-7. Spreadsheet Version.

```
B1: 'Listing 10-7  Spreadsheet version
B2: '
A3: +C4
B3: 'Item Name:
C3: 'Car
D3: 'N$
A4: +C4
B4: '*  Purchase Price:
C4: (C2) 16000
D4: 'PP
A5: +C7
B5: '*  Available Cash:
C5: (C2) 6000
D5: 'CA
B6: '*  Credit Line:
C6: (C2) 5000
B7: 'Required to Borrow:
C7: (C2) +C5-C6
D7: 'CB
B8: ^Investments
A9: +C22
B9: '*  Annual Interest Rate (5%=.05):
C9: (%2) 0.09
D9: 'X
A10: +C21
B10: 'Periodic Interest Rate:
C10: (%2) +C9/12
D10: 'IR
A11: +C23
B11: ^Loans
A12: +C24
B12: '*  Annual Interest Rate (5%=.05):
C12: (%2) 0.18
D12: 'Y
```

```
A13: +C25
B13: 'Periodic Interest Rate:
C13: (%2) +C12/12
D13: 'LR
A14: +C25*(1-C24)
B14: 'Time Required to Raise Price (Invest):
C14: (F2) @LOG(C4/C5)/@LOG(1+C10)
D14: 'N
A15: +C25/C21
B15: 'Time Required to Raise Shortfall (Invest):
C15: (F2) @LOG((C5+C7)/C5)/@LOG(1+C10)
A16: +A14/C21
B16: '*  Number of Payments Available on Time:
C16: 60
D16: 'LP
A17: +C29
B17: '*  Downpayment Required (5%=.05):
C17: (%2) 0.05
D17: 'DP
A18: +A17-(C24*(A17-C5))
B18: 'Downpayment:
C18: (C2) +C17*C4
A19: +A17-A13
C19: @IF(C18<=C5,0,@LOG(C18/C5)/(1+C10))
D19: 'N2
A20: +A18-A14
B20: '*  Estimated Economic Life (Years):
C20: 5
D20: 'EL
C21: 12*C20
D21: 'EL'
A22: +C19
B22: '*  Monthly Lease Cost:
C22: (C2) 350
D22: 'ML
A23: +C27
B23: '*  Salvage Value:
C23: (C2) 500
D23: 'SV
A24: +C28
B24: '*  Tax Bracket (5%=.05):
C24: (%2) 0.35
D24: 'TB
A25: +C28-((1-C24)*(C28-C26))
C25: (C2) (C21*C22)-C23
D25: 'CL
A26: +A25/C16
C26: (C2) +C4-C18
D26: 'A
A27: +A32-A24
C27: (C2) (C26*C13*((1+C13)^C16))/(((1+C13)^C16)-1)
D27: 'MP
A28: +A33-A25
C28: (C2) +C18+(C27*C16)
D28: 'TP
A29: +A13-A24
C29: (C2) +C5*((1+C10)^C21)
```

Listing C-10-7. Spreadsheet Version. (Continued From Page 373.)

```
D29: 'II
A30: +A14-A25
C30: (C2) +C5-C18
D30: 'B
C31: (C2) +C30*((1+C10)^C21)
D31: 'I2
A32: +C31
A33: +A32-(C24*(A32-C30))
B34: "Summary
B35: '
C35: (C2) ^Gross
D35: ^After-Tax
B36: 'Cost of Leasing:
C36: (C2) +A13
D36: (C2) +A14
B37: 'Monthly Lease Cost:
C37: (C2) +A15
D37: (C2) +A16
B38: 'Time Purchase Costs:
C38: (C2) +A24
D38: (C2) +A25
B39: 'Monthly Time Costs:
C39: (C2) +A23
D39: (C2) +A26
B40: 'Investment Return:
C40: (C2) +A17
D40: (C2) +A18
B41: '   Less Downpayment:
C41: (C2) +A32
D41: (C2) +A33
B43: 'Lease vs. Purchase
C43: (C2) +A19
D43: (C2) +A20
B44: 'Time Purchase vs. Cash Purchase:
C44: (C2) +A27
D44: (C2) +A28
B45: 'Time Purchase vs. Lease:
C45: (C2) +A29
D45: (C2) +A30
```

Listings C-12-1, 12-2, 12-4. Spreadsheet Versions.

```
A1: 'Listings 12-1, 12-2, 12-4  Spreadsheet versions
A2: '
A3: '            Month
C3: '# Days
G3: 'SUNMONTUEWEDTHUFRISAT
A4: 1
B4: @MID(G$4,((A4-1)*3),3)
C4: @MID(G$5,((A4-1)*2),2)
G4: 'JANFEBMARAPRMAYJUNJULAUGSEPOCTNOVDEC
A5: +A4+1
B5: @MID(G$4,((A5-1)*3),3)
C5: @MID(G$5,((A5-1)*2),2)
D5: 'except Leap Year
G5: '312831303130313130313031
A6: +A5+1
```

```
B6:  @MID(G$4,((A6-1)*3),3)
C6:  @MID(G$5,((A6-1)*2),2)
A7:  +A6+1
B7:  @MID(G$4,((A7-1)*3),3)
C7:  @MID(G$5,((A7-1)*2),2)
A8:  +A7+1
B8:  @MID(G$4,((A8-1)*3),3)
C8:  @MID(G$5,((A8-1)*2),2)
A9:  +A8+1
B9:  @MID(G$4,((A9-1)*3),3)
C9:  @MID(G$5,((A9-1)*2),2)
A10: +A9+1
B10: @MID(G$4,((A10-1)*3),3)
C10: @MID(G$5,((A10-1)*2),2)
A11: +A10+1
B11: @MID(G$4,((A11-1)*3),3)
C11: @MID(G$5,((A11-1)*2),2)
A12: +A11+1
B12: @MID(G$4,((A12-1)*3),3)
C12: @MID(G$5,((A12-1)*2),2)
A13: +A12+1
B13: @MID(G$4,((A13-1)*3),3)
C13: @MID(G$5,((A13-1)*2),2)
A14: +A13+1
B14: @MID(G$4,((A14-1)*3),3)
C14: @MID(G$5,((A14-1)*2),2)
A15: +A14+1
B15: @MID(G$4,((A15-1)*3),3)
C15: @MID(G$5,((A15-1)*2),2)
A17: '*  Day:
B17: 29
C17: 'D
E17: '
F17: '
A18: '*  Month:
B18: 5
C18: 'M
E18: 'Day of Week:
F18: @INT(7*((C22/7)-@INT(C22/7)))
A19: '*  Year:
B19: 1987
C19: 'Y
E19: 'Day:
F19: @MID(G$3,((F18-1)*3),3)
A21: 'Leap Year
B21: @IF(B19/4<>@INT(B19/4),0,@IF(B19/100<>@INT(B19/100),1,@IF(B19/400<>@IN
     T(B19/400),0,1)))
C21: '(1 = Yes)
E21: @IF(B18>2,B19,B19-1)
F21: 'Y'
G21: @INT(E21*365.25)
H21: 'C
A22: 'Julian Date Number
C22: +E24+G21+G22+B17+1720994.5
E22: @IF(B18>2,B18,B18+12)
F22: 'M'
G22: @INT(30.6001*(E22+1))
H22: 'D
```

```
E23:  @INT(E21/100)
F23:  'A
E24:  2-E23+@INT(E23/4)
F24:  'B
A27:  'Listing 12-2  Spreadsheet version
A29:  '*  Julian Date:
C29:  2446944.5
F29:  +C29+0.5
G29:  'JD
H29:  +F33+1524
I29:  'C
F30:  @INT(F29)
G30:  'I
H30:  @INT((H29-122.1)/365.25)
I30:  'D
A31:  'Day:
C31:  @INT(+H29-H31+F31-@INT(30.6001*H32))
E31:  'DM
F31:  +F29-F30
G31:  'F
H31:  @INT(365.25*H30)
I31:  'E
A32:  'Month:
C32:  @IF(H32<13.5,H32-1,H32-13)
E32:  'M
F32:  @IF(F30>2299160,@INT((F30-1867216.25)/36524.25),F30)
G32:  'A
H32:  @INT((H29-H31)/30.6001)
I32:  'G
A33:  'Year:
C33:  @IF(C32>2.5,H30-4716,H30-4715)
E33:  'Y
F33:  @IF(F29>2299160,F30+1+F32-@INT(F32/4),0)
G33:  'B
A36:  'Listing 12-4  Spreadsheet version
A38:  'Year:
B38:  +C33
G38:  'Integer
H38:  'Fraction
C39:  +B38
D19
E39:  (F2) +C39/D39
F39:  "-
G39:  @INT(E39)
H39:  @INT((E39-G39)*D39)
I39:  'a
A40:  'Easter
C40:  +B38
D40:  100
E40:  (F2) +C40/D40
F40:  "b
G40:  @INT(E40)
H40:  @INT((E40-G40)*D40)
I40:  'c
A41:  '     Month:
B41:  @MID(G4,(G48-1)*3,3)
```

```
C41: +G40
D41: 4
E41: (F2) +C41/D41
F41: "d
G41: @INT(E41)
H41: @INT((E41-G41)*D41)
I41: 'e
A42: '       Day:
B42: +H48+1
C42: (G40+8)
D42: 25
E42: (F2) +C42/D42
F42: "f
G42: @INT(E42)
H42: @INT((E42-G42)*D42)
I42: '-
C43: (+G40-G42+1)
D43: 3
E43: (F2) +C43/D43
F43: "g
G43: @INT(E43)
H43: @INT((E43-G43)*D43)
I43: '-
C44: ((19*H39)+G40-G41-G43+15)
D44: 30
E44: (F2) +C44/D44
F44: "-
G44: @INT(E44)
H44: @INT((E44-G44)*D44)
I44: 'h
C45: +H40
D45: 4
E45: (F2) +C45/D45
F45: "i
G45: @INT(E45)
H45: @INT((E45-G45)*D45)
I45: 'k
C46: (32+(2*H41)+(2*G45)-H44-H45)
D46: 7
E46: (F2) +C46/D46
F46: "-
G46: @INT(E46)
H46: @INT((E46-G46)*D46)
I46: 'l
C47: (H39+(11*H44)+(22*H46))
D47: 451
E47: (F2) +C47/D47
F47: "m
G47: @INT(E47)
H47: @INT((E47-G47)*D47)
I47: '-
C48: (H44+H46-(7*G47)+114)
D48: 31
E48: (F2) +C48/D48
F48: "n
G48: @INT(E48)
H48: @INT((E48-G48)*D48)
I48: 'p
```

Glossary

absolute—Independent, not relative.

accuracy—The most common criterion for measuring the relative strength of alternative forecasting methods.

acre—A unit of area measure equal to 4,840 square yards.

adaptive response rate—The rate at which a forecasting technique responds to change in pattern.

algorithm—A standardized procedure for solving a given problem.

altitude (of a celestial object)—The spherical coordinate of the object measured in the plane of the circle passing through the object and crossing the horizon at right angles.

amortization—To pay off an expenditure or debt by prorating the cost plus interest over a fixed period.

annular eclipse—An eclipse of the sun in which the moon is surrounded by a ring of light.

anomalistic year—The time taken by the earth to travel in its orbit from the point where it is closest to the sun, perihelion, to the next such point. This is computed to be 365.25964 mean solar days, or 365 days, 6 hours, 13 minutes, and about 53 seconds. This value is about 25 minutes, 7 seconds greater than the tropical year.

aphelion—The point in the orbit of an object around the sun at which it is the farthest from the sun.

apogee—The point in the orbit of an object about the earth at which it is the farthest from the earth.

apparent solar noon—The moment when the center of the sun crosses the meridian of a location.

array—A display of data in rows and columns, as in tables or determinants.

assets—Things of value that may be used to pay off debts. For corporations, these may include cash, securities, buildings, machinery, land, inventory, etc.

astronomical unit (AU)—The mean distance from the center of the earth to the center of the sun. Taken to be about 92,897,000 miles.

autocorrelation—The correlation between items on one list lagged in time or sequence.

balance sheet—A report of the financial condition of a company as of a given date, usually the end of the firm's accounting year. Interim reports are often issued on a quarterly basis.

biannual—Twice a year.

biennial—Once every two years.

bimodal—A distribution of data with two distinct peaks.

bond—A legal document or expression of the fact money has been loaned to a corporation or governmental unit.

The bond states that the issuer will pay interest at a specified rate until the debt is repaid at face value some time in the future.

book value—The net value of a corporation to common share-holders. Usually expressed on a per-share basis obtained by dividing the corporation's net worth by the number of common shares outstanding.

Boolean algebra—A mathematical interpretation of the rules of logic developed by Boole in the mid-1880's.

Boolean connectors—An expression of relationships in a database. They are often found in a search of a database for two or more pieces of information that satisfy the stated Boolean criteria.

break-even point—The price at which an investment instrument, if sold, would fully reimburse all costs connected with its acquisition and subsequent sale.

broker—Firm or individual holding a seat on the exchange of interest employed by an investor to execute securities transactions.

business cycle—Period of business profitability followed by periods of business lassitude or failure.

buy order—An order placed by an investor directing a broker to purchase a specified number of shares of stock, options, bonds, etc. Limits or conditions specifying price, time, or numerous factors may be imposed if desired.

calculus—A field of mathematics, developed independently in the 1700's by Leibniz and Newton, that deals with rates of changes, the lengths of curves, the area under curves, and the areas and volumes of various objects.

calendar—The division of time into arbitrary sections as years, months, days, generally based on the earth's revolution about the sun. The tropical year consists of 365.2422 days (each day consisting of 23 hours, 56 minutes, and 4.09 seconds).

call—The date before maturity on which all or part of a bond issue may be redeemded by the issuing company. Definite conditions are imposed for a bond to be called.

capital—Money or property needed by a person or corporation to carry out normal business activities.

catenary—The curve described by a rope or heavy cable hanging freely between two points of suspension.

causal model—Statistical or forecasting models in which there is presumed causal relationships between the input variables and the output.

central limit theorem—A theorem of statistics that states that the sampling distribution of means approaches a normal distribution when the sample size becomes sufficiently large; i.e., when $s > 30$.

classic decomposition—An approach used in forecasting which assumes a time-series data set consists of cyclic, seasonal, trend, and random error components. As each component is eliminated from the data, the remainder is assumed to contain the remaining components.

commission—The fee paid to a broker for executing a securities transaction, usually a percentage of the dollar amount involved and often subject to a minimum fee established by the brokerage firm.

commodity—Anything bought or sold. Investment usage refers to futures contacts bought or sold for delivery of specific quantities of corn, wheat, metals, or approximately 30 other tangible goods.

common stock—An ownership interest purchased in a corporation, entitling the holder to a share in any profits realized and to some influence in the management of the company.

computation—The process of determining a quantified result from numerical data using the mathematical tools of addition, multiplication, subtraction, division, and algebraic techniques.

computer—A mechanical or electronic device employed in the process of computation. Modern computers go beyond simple numerical manipulation and exploit the data switching and comparison capability to implement word processing, data handling and graphics tasks.

curve fitting—An approach in forecasting to fit the data to some form of standard or definable curve.

cyclic stocks—Stocks of corporations whose earnings are sensitive to business cycles and, most often, accentuate the peaks and valleys of the cycle. Prices of these stocks fluctuate widely over a complete business cycle.

data—The plural of the Latin word datum, which means "that which is given." In a larger sense, data can include anything used in the process of a logical effort. In the sense often used in this book, data refer to those numerical values used in the different programs.

declination (of a celestial object)—The angular altitude of an object above the celestial horizon.

degrees of freedom—The number of variables in a data set less an adjustment for different statistical tests. In computing the mean of a set of n items, there are n − 1 degrees of freedom.

delphi method—A forecasting technique using the professional opinions of a panel of experts.

dependent variable—A quantity which is the function of one or more independent variables.

depreciation—An amount charged against earnings to write off the cost, less salvage, of an asset over its estimated useful life.

dividend—A portion of corporate profits received by shareholders. It may be paid in cash or shares.

diversification—Investing funds in several different industry groups in an attempt to hold securities that do not fluctuate in a similar fashion.

dollar cost averaging—A method of investing in which a set amount is invested in a selected stock at regular intervals. It is presumed that this amount of money will buy more shares when prices are low and fewer shares during periods of high prices. When averaging is used over a long enough period of time, the cost per share should be less than in strategies in which larger blocks of stock are purchased aperiodically.

economic indicator—An economic component which demonstrates an apparent correlation between itself and the national economy in general.

equity—The ownership interest of all classes of stockholders of a corporation. Also, the difference between the value of securities and the debit balance of a margin account.

exchange—An auction market for stocks, bonds, and other securities.

exponential data distribution—A pattern which exhibits the characteristics of an exponential curve.

file—A collection of data arranged in some pattern or order.

forecasting—The scientific art of predicting future conditions.

gain—An increase in the value of an investment relative to the purchase price.

gross national product (GNP)—The total amount of goods and services for a given economy over a period of time, normally a year.

growth stocks—Ideally, the stock of a corporation that gets bigger and better each year, causing the price of its stock to move up. In practice, the criteria used for defining a growth stock vary with an investor's ultimate objectives and perception of what is significant growth.

heteroscedasticity—A condition which exists when errors do not demonstrate constant variance across the whole range of the data values in a set.

heuristic—A system using trial and error to achieve an objective.

historic data—Data gleaned from a specific time period in the past. Generally they are used in an attempt to identify trend sequences likely to be repeated for some time in the future.

homoscedasticity—A condition that exists when errors demonstrate a constant variance across the whole data set.

income stock—A stock that yields generous current returns, often purchased by investors who have an immediate need for income combined with the assurance of capital preservation.

independent variable—Something whose value is determined outside of the system being examined.

index—An indicator constructed in such a fashion as to reflect the market performance of a specific group of securities or identify general market trends.

indicators—An index or economic group whose changes in basic trend or direction tend to signal changes in the economy as a whole. As their names imply, leading indicators reflect future market trends, lagging indicators trail behind and confirm market trends.

investment—Any financial instrument purchased in the anticipation of selling the same instrument at a later time for a significantly higher price.

Julian date—Normally, the day number of a date in a year with January 1 being Julian date 1, February 1 being Julian date 32, and so on. Alternatively, the Julian date is the number of days a given date is from a zero reference date far in the past.

Kuder-Richardson equations—A set of equations developed by the Kuder-Richardson team to aid in the validation and measurement of reliability of test instruments.

leverage—The degree to which a corporation or an individual uses borrowed funds as opposed to equity. If the anticipated return is significantly greater than the cost of borrowing money, leverage can increase gains. Maximum leverage, and risk, is obtained with the smallest use of equity. Margin buying, options, warrants, and rights are all ways for an individual investor to obtain leverage.

liabilities—Monies or debt obligations for which an individual or corporation is responsible. Usually defined in terms of current liabilities (due in less than one year) and long-term debt. Liabilities may include money owed to suppliers, debt retirement, taxes due, dividends payable, and so forth.

liquidity—The ability to convert to cash or its equivalent any investment instrument. Stocks and bonds are regarded as having good liquidity because disposing of them in the open market is readily accomplished. Some other forms of investment holdings may show significantly less liquidity. Real estate or collectibles, for instance, may take a long time to convert to cash.

margin—Buying on margin is using your securities as a collateral for a loan from your broker and is a way to increase an investor's leverage. Margin accounts are subject to strict limit for minimum equity as established by the Federal Reserve Board.

market—A broad term to encompass securities exchanges, although usually the "market" implies the New York Stock Exchange or the American Stock Exchange.

market value—The total amount investors would be willing to pay for all the common shares of a corporation.

mean—Normally taken as the arithmetic average of a set of data.

median—The middle number in a data set.

microcomputer—A colloquial term referring to a family of "small" computing systems distinguished, normally, by the amount of memory available in the basic system, generally 4 to 64 thousand bytes, with from one to four disk drives using floppy disk storage media. The precise boundary between micro- and mini-computing systems is not formally defined.

mode—The most frequently appearing number in a set of data.

model—A symbolic representation of an aspect of reality.

moving average—An average which moves with the unit of time considered. Primarily used as trend indicators, moving averages tend to smooth out short-term fluctuations and react slowly, particularly to swift market changes.

mutual fund—A form of investment company that sells shares for the purpose of providing investor diversification, professional management and maximum liquidity of funds. All funds received for shares are comingled and invested in securities (or other forms of investment, depending on the purpose of the fund). The price of each share reflects the net value of its holdings at the time of purchase or redemption.

n—The number of observations or the size of a sample.
N—The number of periods used in a moving average or the total size of a population.

net income—The amount remaining when all the expenses of doing business are subtracted from the total sales or revenue of a corporation.

net worth—A figure derived by subtracting all liabilities from the total assets.

noise—The random component of a set of data.

over-the-counter—Transactions in securities which do not take place on an exchange. There is no centralized place for trading, virtually any type of security may be listed, and brokers may act as principles or agents in the transaction.

par value—A dollar amount assigned to each share of stock or bond by a corporation. It is common practice to exclude assigning par value to common stock, but preferred stock and bonds usually carry a par value.

polynomial—An algebraic expression that carries two or more terms.

preferred stock—A security between common stocks and bonds which has fixed dividends and preference on all corporate income available after payment of bond interest and amortization.

price to earnings ratio (P/E)—A figure derived by dividing the price of a share of stock by the company's twelve month earnings per share.

quote—A term used to denote current price level, market volume, and other relevant data related to a security.

redemption price—The price at which a bond was redeemed before maturity by the issuing company, the price a corporation must pay to call in certain types of preferred stocks, or the amount received on liquidating mutual funds shares.

regression—A line or equation that expresses the average relationship between a dependent variable and one or more independent variables.

residual—The degree of error or deviation between a forecast and reality.

retained earnings—The amount of corporate earnings retained and reinvested in the business rather than being paid out as dividends to shareholders.

round lot—A standard unit of trading securities, usually one hundred shares of stock and $1000 par value for bonds.

sample—A limited number (relative to the total population) of observations or data values from the population.

S-curve—The normal curve of product innovation, dissemination and life.

Securities and Exchange Commission (SEC)—The agency responsible for administering federal laws regarding securities.

simulation—A model constructed to closely approximate the action of a large system with many interacting parts. Stock market simulations allow an investor to try different courses of action without actually risking capital.

standard deviation—The square root of the variance of a set of data. It is a statistical measure of dispersion of the data from the mean.

standard error—The distribution of statistical measures about a predicted value.

tender—An offer made by a corporation to buy back its own shares. Also, an offer by one corporation, interested in acquiring control, to buy the shares of another. Usually, tender offers are made at a price above that of the going market.

time-series—A set of data in which the independent variable is time.

trend—The general direction or movement of statistical data related to the stock market, populations, business activity, and other data that may change in magnitude as a function of time or changes in other independent variables.

undervalued stock—Shares of a corporation which are selling below book value, provided the company reports good profitability and growth.

variance—The amount of variation from the mean within a set of data.

volatility—The extent to which the price of stock rises or falls in comparison to others in its industry group or designated market index.

volume—The number of shares of stock, bonds, or options that changed hands during a particular period. It is usually stated in terms of daily volume.

warrants—An option to buy a specific number of shares of a security at a set price for a designated period of time.

weighting—A mathematical process in which statistical ratios are combined or in which sets of numbers are given coefficients establishing their relative importance.

x-axis—The first axis in the Cartesian system of coordinates.

y-axis—The second axis in the Cartesian system of coordinates.

year—The longest standard unit of time, measured by the earth's rotation about the sun. Between vernal equinoxes there are 365 days, 5 hours, and 48 minutes.

yield—The amount in dividends or interest paid by a company, expressed as a percentage of the current stock or bond price. Yield is one component of total return, capital gain being the other.

z-axis—The third axis in the Cartesian system of coordinates.

z-score—A statistical measure of a distribution computed by dividing the value of a given score less the mean, by the standard deviation.

zenith—The point on the celestial sphere directly above the observer.

Index

Forecasting on Your Microcomputer—2nd Edition

If you are intrigued with the possibilities of the programs included in *Forecasting on Your Microcomputer—2nd Edition* (TAB Book No. 2907), you should definitely consider having the ready-to-run disk containing the functions. This software is guaranteed free of manufacturer's defects. (If you have any problems, return the disk within 30 days, and we'll send you a new one.) Not only will you save the time and effort of typing the programs, the disk eliminates the possibility of errors that can prevent the programs from functioning. Interested?

Available on DS/DD disk for IBM PC and compatibles with 256 K, DOS 2.0, and BASICA or GW-BASIC, at $24.95 for each disk plus $1.00 each shipping and handling.